HIGH TIDE AT GETTYSBURG

HIGH TIDE AT GETTYSBURG

The Campaign in Pennsylvania

by GLENN TUCKER

BARNES
&NOBLE
BOOKS
NEW YORK

This edition published by special arrangement with Konecky & Konecky.

ISBN: 0-7607-5505-1

Manufactured in the United States of America

Foreword

ALL OF MY ADULT LIFE I have wanted to write a book about Gettysburg—since the time when, as a young captain in World War I, I studied the contour map of the Gettysburg terrain almost nightly in problems involving minor tactics.

While in Washington newspaper work I made frequent visits to Gettysburg as a hobby and on bonus occasions covered news stories on the field. Thereafter I had a recurring interest in this exciting battle, the most gripping three days of American history. What person who reads history has not?

In 1930 the Reverend Dr. William E. Barton, of Oak Park, Illinois, a great Lincoln scholar, in inscribing to me his *Life of Abraham Lincoln,* wrote: "Dear Mr. Tucker—I have told the story of Lincoln's speech at Gettysburg in a book to appear in February. Now you please tell the story of the battle." I made a resolution and a beginning. Less interesting writing work intruded, but the ambition lingered.

Then D. Laurance Chambers, chairman of the board of The Bobbs-Merrill Company, one who is rich with the experience of fifty-five years in book publishing, and has contributed immeasurably to the present generation's reading of American history, suggested out of a clear sky about three years ago that I write this book. His gently phrased but unsparing criticism had guided me through other efforts. Though he is now retired from active publishing work, I am indebted to him for proposing the book, patiently reading it in manuscript, and making numerous recommendations, usually involving less content and more clarity.

My original draft greatly exceeded book length. Necessity arose to eliminate incidents and personality sketches and condense preliminary details—treasured episodes to me which the reader will not miss.

To say that the literature on this battle is extensive is an inordinate understatement. Perhaps more has been written about Gettysburg than Waterloo or any other battle. Many studies concentrate on certain limited aspects; relatively few take up the whole battle with approximately equal attention to both sides. To cover all sources carefully would require decades, possibly a lifetime, and the story would not then be complete. Many stirring incidents were unrecorded; many others cannot be included in a book of normal length.

Still, I felt there was occasion for this and for other studies that may be undertaken, because of the tremendous impact of this battle on our present-day life and customs. Gettysburg is much more deeply imbedded in American institutions than is implied by the mere preservation of the union of thirty-three states, now grown to forty-nine.

The weakening of the doctrine of States' rights on the battlefield reduced the restraints on a fuller expression of the opposing concept. Centralized government then strengthened has asserted its supremacy more strongly with the years. A government which in 1861 was ordinarily remote now touches the life of the citizen many times daily.

The war, fought for national solidarity, became a fierce, relentless war of subjugation. Never did a nation struggle against stupendous odds with greater devotion to its cause than did the new Confederacy. Because it was burdened with the repelling incubus of slavery, it had to fight unaided.

The South came near to victory—how near may be judged by these pages. After a series of triumphs, Lee's army reached the field of greatest opportunity at Gettysburg. Had Lee destroyed Meade's forces there and captured Washington, Baltimore, or other seaboard cities, of what possible consequence would have been the loss of Vicksburg or the threat of other Northern armies? This was indeed the moment when the Confederate cause was at high tide.

Gettysburg is a fascinating battle from the standpoint of maneuver. Fortunes rose and waned; victory seemed to flutter back and forth between the two armies. A frequent explanation is that destiny shaped the result. If God had grown weary of Napoleon at Waterloo, did He in like manner at Gettysburg withdraw His hand from the cause He had seemed to prosper?

More clearly than by destiny or chance, it seems to this writer that the result was governed at various stages by the steadfastness and initiative of a particular group or officer. Character played a more decisive role than caprice. Leadership, often of smaller units, was the vital quality in the outcome of this battle. Decisions by brigadier generals and colonels were of paramount significance.

In reading about the battle I have felt often that these commanders of divisions, brigades, and regiments appeared only as names in the books, not as persons at the head of their troops. Because I have always wanted to know more about them, I have given, where space and the sequence of the story permit, personality sketches of those who had forward positions in the fighting, from Meade and Lee down to the grown-up Senate page boy, Colonel Henry A. Morrow, and tough old Central American filibusterer, Colonel Birkett D. Fry, who headed the Confederate advance as the battle opened.

The task of dealing dispassionately with General James Longstreet is quite obviously difficult for the historian. This book does not follow him beyond the battle, though in order to understand his personality as fully as possible, I made two visits to Gainesville, Georgia, to talk with any who might remember him from personal contact or observation. These—boys who had picked his muscadine grapes—recalled him both as a compassionate old soldier, gentle to the lads who came to his vineyards, and also as a man apart in the community, almost a pariah, unyielding, stern, aloof.

Sitting erect in his saddle, a black patch over his blind eye, his right arm grown almost useless from the wound he had taken in the Wilderness, he rode alone through the streets, where he had the tolerance but never the friendship of his home people. He was looked on as a religious and political apostate, and was, in turn, bitter and defiant against his detractors to the very end.

The attitude was different among the old soldiers, who respected or admired him. The survivors of the war invariably tipped their hats to the white-haired, white-whiskered veteran about whose character so much of the battle of Gettysburg and destiny of the Southern republic had turned.

Perhaps it is too often forgotten that the conflicts of Longstreet's later years have no place in a strict appraisal of his work at Gettysburg. I have tried to deal with him impartially, and to set forth objectively the sequence of the events he influenced.

The intimate accounts of the men and lower-grade officers, and the regimental and brigade histories, etc., have been carefully considered along with the more studied reports of the generals. The action exceeds in importance the explanation. An attempt has been

made to clear up some misunderstandings. The splendid role of Pettigrew's and Trimble's men on the third day has often been obscured.
Actually some of Pettigrew's men made the deepest penetration of the
Federal position. None could have struck harder than the North Carolina, Tennessee, Alabama, and Mississippi units that accompanied
Pettigrew, yet they are usually neglected in accounts of what history
has come to know as Pickett's charge.

While I do not presume to disclose many new facts at this late date,
those presented probably have not been assembled before in the same
volume. From them I have made my own, at times perhaps uncon-
ventional, evaluations. I have attempted to show dispassionately how
the battle was won and lost, and why the Gettysburg campaign remains such an appealing study to large numbers even after the passing
of nearly a century.

GLENN TUCKER

Contents

Maps

HIGH TIDE AT GETTYSBURG

Theater of Lee's Gettysburg Campaign

CHAPTER ONE

Substitutes for Genius

1. Summertime in Southern Hearts

Judge James F. Crocker, of Isle of Wight County, Virginia, reflecting on the Confederate War a quarter of a century after Lee's surrender at Appomattox, declared that the phase of his personal history which he recalled with the greatest satisfaction and delight was the ardor and unquestioning devotion with which he took up arms for the independence of the South.

This was no mere matter of pride, he explained, nor passionate excitement nor ebullition, but a sheer joy of conviction "akin to what we feel for our religion and our God in our most devout moments."[1] Twelve years before his enlistment, young Crocker had journeyed to the drowsy little town of Gettysburg, Pennsylvania, in the beautifully rolling country of the Catoctin and South Mountain foothills, to attend the small school then known as Pennsylvania College. He had applied himself, led his class, and been valedictorian at the commencement exercises in 1850. Then he had returned to his Virginia home to practice law, serve in the House of Delegates, and, when Virginia reasserted her state sovereignty, step forward with "the glow that burned in every true heart of the South."[2]

More than two years afterward, in mid-1863, the ardor of his enlistment had not abated, but had been warmed by the high fervor of apparent triumph, as had that of most of his comrades of the Virginia regiments. It remained a glorious exaltation, a cause far greater than himself. A member of Armistead's brigade of Pickett's division, Long-

3

street's corps, he had been reunited with Lee's army after the march
back from Suffolk, where the spring calm and ample rations drawn
from the fertile valleys of the Roanoke and Chowan rivers had given
rest and robustness to Longstreet's men. And now he was moving out
on a campaign which virtually every soldier in the Army of Northern
Virginia believed would determine the destiny of the Southern republic. By one of those caprices of chance which often stand out boldly in
the unfolding record of events, this destiny was to be decided while he
was battling in front of a low stone fence near a little clump of trees he
had often looked out on from his remote and secluded college halls.

The Confederate march began on June 3, 1863. As the freshness
of early summer touched the tent-covered hills along the Rappahannock, and tinted the fields of wheat with the amber promise of the
approaching harvest, General Lee put his magnificent army into motion for the invasion of the North.

It was summer, too, in the heart of the Confederacy. The superiority of Southern arms appeared to have been fully established on many
fields. Lee had just won at Chancellorsville, in early May, another and
perhaps the greatest of his splendid triumphs. He had enmeshed Hooker
in the thickets along the Rapidan River, by skillful maneuvers had
nullified his vast numerical superiority, and for a time had threatened
him with destruction or capture.

Hooker had scarcely regained the north bank of the river before
Lee began his preparations to move to Northern soil. The death of
Jackson necessitated a reorganization. Rarely had the loss of one
man compelled such extensive readjustments. The infantry of the
Army of Northern Virginia had been divided into two corps, commanded by Lieutenant Generals Longstreet and Jackson. In the interests of greater flexibility, and because there was no other Jackson,
Lee now adopted a three-corps arrangement, and shifted and added
to his units so that each corps had three divisions of approximately
equal strength.

2. Old Peter Has Lee's Confidence

Longstreet, taciturn, thorough, and blunt almost to arrogance, retained
the command of the First Corps. Between him and Lee there appeared
to be an extraordinary affection, baffling at times in the light of Longstreet's stubborn self-assertion. But almost from the day he assumed
command of the army in front of Richmond, Lee had pitched his headquarters tent near that of the great hulk of vibrant manhood to whom

the other officers applied the West Point nickname of "Old Peter." Anyone supposing that Lee rode and tented with Longstreet because he believed "Old Peter" needed prodding where Jackson required neither spur nor restraint, found this reasoning unsupported after Jackson's passing. Manifestly Jackson's untried successors as corps commanders would need even closer scrutiny, for a period at least. But Lee continued to move with Old Peter—Peter the deliberate, the hard hitter, and on occasion in the Richmond gossip, "Peter the Slow."[3]

There had been little companionship between the cultured, stimulating General Lee, accustomed to the society of the leading intellects in both South and North, and the peculiar, uncommunicative genius, Jackson, who had proved as much of an enigma to the army as he had as "Tom Fool" Jackson to the Virginia Military Institute cadets.[4]

Close as the professional ties may have been between Lee and Jackson, the commander-in-chief's association with Longstreet was of a more personal and also of a somewhat challenging nature. Longstreet was not a fluent conversationalist nor an engaging speaker. He was more dogged than dynamic. But there was something so robust, dominating and unyielding about him—in character as well as physique—that he enjoyed a store of affection from his troops ample enough for them to pass it on to their sons, grandsons and great-grandsons in the South, despite the fact that Longstreet's personality and generalship were to be subjected to the hammerings of unsympathetic historians over the greater part of three generations.

Brigadier General G. Moxley Sorrel, the Savannah bank clerk who rose to be Longstreet's chief of staff and by almost a consensus to be regarded as the best staff officer in the army, gives a picture of Longstreet as he appeared when he first became conspicuous, at Blackburn's Ford in the first Manassas campaign. He was then "a most striking figure, about forty years of age, a soldier every inch, and very handsome, tall and well proportioned, strong and active, a superb horseman, and with . . . expression and features fairly matched." His eyes were "glint steel-blue, deep and piercing." He wore a full, brown beard and his head was "well shaped and poised."[5]

Major General Fitzhugh Lee saw him likewise for the first time at Blackburn's Ford and his initial impression was of Longstreet's insensibility to danger. "I recollect well my thinking, there is a man that cannot be stampeded."[6] Fitz Lee then gave a view of him at the time the curtain descended: ". . . the night before the surrender at

Appomattox Court House, . . . there was still the bull dog tenacity, the old genuine sang froid about him which made all feel he could be depended on to hold fast to his position as long as there was ground to stand on." These were the solid characteristics that "gained for him the sobriquet of 'General Lee's old war-horse.' "[7]

The Indiana-born author, George Cary Eggleston, who as a Confederate soldier had opportunities to observe General Lee closely at different occasions, felt that common impressions about high-ranking Confederate officers were at times woefully inaccurate. Jackson, he pointed out, though he was a military genius second only to Lee, had a reputation as a superb marcher who was always on time. Yet he quoted Lee as saying that "Jackson was by no means as rapid a marcher as Longstreet," and that "he had an unfortunate habit of *never being on time.*"[8] But Longstreet's main trait was his care for his soldiers, extending to a parsimonious husbanding of them out of a concern that they were not expendable. This more than any other quality won and held their affection. At Fredericksburg he said, "if we only save the finger of a man, that's enough."[9] Sorrel noticed that he never failed to encourage and praise good work. "There was no illiberality about him, and the officers knew it and tried for his notice."[10] An example was the report of Colonel John R. Cooke at Sharpsburg, when Longstreet dispatched Sorrel to commend the colonel and tell him to hold firm. Cooke sent back thanks, and: "But say, by God almighty, he needn't doubt me. We'll stay here, by Jesus Christ, if we must all go to hell together."[11]

Stonewall Jackson's chaplain and biographer, Robert Lewis Dabney, specified three varieties of courage: that of the man insensible to danger; that of one who conquers his fears with pride, and that of one who keenly appreciates danger but rises above it out of a high sense of duty.[12] It is clear that Longstreet's bravery was of the rare, first sort. Someone has called him "Bull" Longstreet and the name is apt. It implies his power in combat and his blind charging when tormented by the red flag of verbal attack. This insensibility to danger shone clearly at Monterey and when he was shot down while carrying the flag at Chapultepec. He was fearless.

Longstreet had experienced a spiritual regeneration in the early days of the war, caused by the loss in a single week of three of his children from scarlet fever.[13] The change in him was pronounced when he returned from the funeral to the army at Centerville. Along with Earl Van Dorn, Gustavus W. Smith and Burnett Rhett, he had been one of the gay coterie of officers who drank and stayed up most of the night playing poker.[14] But after his family tragedy Longstreet quit his cards, drank so sparingly as to be almost abstemious, became a devout member of the Episcopal Church, and grew reserved in his attitude and conduct.[15]

Longstreet's poker playing helps to explain his military thinking. He was rated a good player—"very skillful," according to Sorrel. A good poker player is rarely a gambler at heart. Not addicted to playing against odds, he is, instead, a student of averages who calculates his chances carefully. He is not emotional and regards that trait in others a weakness. He does not try to force the cards when they are running against him.

Longstreet liked to win. He was not a man to gamble much in battle. He would rather wait for a situation like the one at Fredericksburg, where he could sit behind his defenses and let Burnside shatter the Federal army against his well-protected ranks. If the odds were not in his favor, he would wait for a fresh deal. Eventually he would hold the aces.

What Longstreet possessed, the faculty of stirring his soldiers to unusual responsiveness, he had no doubt acquired from his remarkable uncle, Augustus Baldwin Longstreet, one of the outstanding writers and educators of the pre-war South. James Longstreet as a youth, after the death of his father when he was twelve years old, lived for a time with this uncle, then president of Emory University, which he built up from an obscure neighborhood school to an institution of standing. Known widely for his extraordinary ability to inspire young people to their supreme effort, he was the undoubted source of the same power in Longstreet the general.

Longstreet radiated ideas. Sometimes they were bold notions dealing with the grand strategy of the war, in which he, with an ambition commendable in a new nation that had appalling casualty lists and was always requiring fresh army leaders, would play a heroic role. At times they were minor tactical recommendations. Often they had to be discarded. But Longstreet did not take unsolved problems to his chief. The trait must have proved a relief to Lee in an army where subordinates, due to his own able leadership and Jackson's, had often been more disposed to await instructions than generate suggestions.

Lee possessed a staff grievously small even by nineteenth-century standards. In 1863 it was composed of officers of relatively modest rank, whose main functions were reconnaissance, the writing and transmittal of orders, and the preparation of reports. It had no plans board, no intelligence branch, no propaganda corps—none of the numerous other requirements of a modern high command. To European observers it appeared puny.

Lee did not resort to the custom frequent in the Northern army of holding councils of war. Very apparently Longstreet's concepts, at times presumptuously advanced and irritatingly adhered to, served to test and sharpen his own conclusions. Lee's keen perceptive powers would not allow him to fall into a failing fairly common among lesser commanders, of desiring the attendance of sycophants.[16] He could have freed himself at any moment from Longstreet's presence, and that he did not do so is testament of his respect and fondness.

So Old Peter retained command of the First Corps of the Army of Northern Virginia. There was never a doubt about it in the mind of either Lee or President Jefferson Davis. He was the general on whom the fortunes of the Confederacy would depend should Lee be incapacitated in battle. Much of the striking power of the army was in Longstreet's three divisions, commanded by Lafayette McLaws, George E. Pickett and John B. Hood.

3. The Dragoon Rides in a Buggy

The dead hand of Jackson influenced the appointment of the commander of the Second Corps, composed of Jackson's old foot cavalry. But the Richard S. Ewell who became a lieutenant general and the army's third-ranking officer, was not the hard-riding, hard-swearing, quick-tempered old trooper Jackson had known in the Shenandoah Valley. Marriage and the wound he received at the Second Manassas had bridled and subdued his fierce spirit, while conversion to the life of a devout Christian had softened his temper and curbed his profane tongue.

Richard Taylor, son of President Zachary Taylor, who commanded one of his brigades in Jackson's Valley campaign, has given a description of Ewell's peculiarities, which were excessive. "He fancied he had some mysterious internal malady, and would eat nothing but frumentary, a preparation of wheat; and his plaintive way of talking of his disease, as if he were someone else, was droll in the extreme."[17] Ewell, however, suspected not his own, but Jackson's rationality. He overheard Stonewall remark that he never seasoned his food with pepper because it weakened his left leg. That was enough for Ewell to judge him crazy, although, of course, a sheer genius.

Ewell was so nervous and fidgety he could not sleep regularly. He had "bright, prominent eyes, a bomb-shaped, bald head, and a nose like that of Francis of Valois" which "gave him a striking resemblance to a woodcock." This his subordinate found to be emphasized by "his bird-like habit of putting his head to one side to utter his quaint speeches."[18] Sorrel found him "a perfect horseman" and "without a superior as a cavalry captain." Ewell talked much about a horse named "Tangent" he had owned in Texas. The name was apparently well chosen, for the horse went off in all directions and never won a race. Ewell always lost money backing him, but his confidence never weakened. His boasts about "Tangent" gave the officers secret amusement.

In excitement Ewell tended to lisp. This became so pronounced at times as to be an affliction. Sorrel said he called him "Mather Torrel."

Perhaps the summit of Ewell's genius may be found in his instructions to Brigadier General L. O'Brien Branch to travel lightly when he advanced from Gordonsville to the Valley. They ended with the injunction: "The road to glory cannot be followed with much baggage."[19] The words were Ewell's closest approach to the Napoleonic. In the Valley fighting he could be seen at times, when Jackson was not at hand, stealing forward to the skirmish line and dodging about so as not to be detected by "Old Jackson." In all of the Valley campaign there was only one note that might have sounded caution about entrusting a corps to Ewell's leadership: he always wanted the confirmation of another officer's judgment before putting his own ideas into operation.[20] That did not promise the resolution called for from the leader of a corps, who would often be on independent missions.

One moment of initiative the army told of with relish—the night at Fairfax Court House when Ewell was still a colonel. The Federal cavalry stormed into town and drove back the Confederate horse. An apparent stranger rushed from a house to rally the men. The Richmond *Whig* told the story.[21] Though unarmed and directly from his bed, he stood in the middle of the street, "defied the Yankees, and rained down upon them a torrent of imprecations such as were never heard before." His fury was more effective than bullets. When the atmosphere cleared someone thought to look at the man who could master the enemy with the violence of his oaths, and discovered it was Richard S. Ewell. And they noticed he had rallied the defenders and routed the Yankees while wearing merely his nightshirt.

Sometimes even the champion, knocked senseless to the canvas, is never the same fighter again. That appears to have been the case with

Ewell. After he lost his leg at Groveton, he was no longer, even in spirit, the tough old hussar who liked to crash pell mell into the timber and plunge through water, but a sedate, bald-headed old man who campaigned in a buggy. The junior officers were the first to detect the change.[22] Ewell reached camp from his long convalescence on May 20, 1863, accompanied by his new wife, the widow Lizinka Campbell Brown. Even after the marriage the lovesick general, a trifle muddled, continued to introduce his wife as "Mrs. Brown."[23] Ewell had courted her in his early life but she had jilted him and he had remained a bachelor.

The impact of the new situation appears to have been overwhelming. Observed the clear-speaking Lieutenant Randolph H. McKim, a staff officer of the Stonewall Brigade: "From a military point of view, the addition of the wife did not compensate for the loss of the leg. We were of the opinion that Ewell was not the same soldier he had been when he was a whole man—and a single man."[24]

Mrs. Ewell, who had nursed the general back to health after his wound, was definitely the dominant force in the family, even to the supervision of the headquarters couriers. The result was much talk about petticoat control over the army.

Longstreet worked well with Ewell and rated him "a safe, reliable corps commander, always zealously seeking to do his duty." But he, too, found that Ewell "lost much of his efficiency with his leg at the Second Manassas."[25] In Longstreet's eyes, Ewell's tremendous handicap was Jubal Early, "who, as a division commander, was a marplot and a disturber."[26] Early, of course, disliked Longstreet as cordially.

Jackson was quoted as saying on his deathbed that Ewell should succeed him as a protection to his men.[27] His statement apparently impressed Lee, for the commanding general, who had seen little of Ewell, could not have known at firsthand much about his capabilities, or his lack of them.

But the new Richard S. Ewell filled the boots and saddle that had once been Stonewall's and commanded three hard-fighting, veteran divisions, led by Jubal A. Early, Robert Emmett Rodes and Edward Johnson, all major generals and all, like the corps commander, Virginians.

4. The Punctilious Mr. Hill

Lee created a Third Corps by taking one division away from what had been Jackson's corps and one from Longstreet. Jackson's lost A. P.

Hill's division and Longstreet lost that of Richard H. Anderson of South Carolina. A third division was built up and assigned to Major General Henry Heth, a Virginian who had been a rifle expert in the old Federal army. These three divisions comprised the Third Corps. Command was given to Ambrose Powell Hill, called A. P. Hill in the army records and Powell Hill by his friends. Hill's old division was then assigned to the newly commissioned major general, the twenty-nine-year-old North Carolinian W. Dorsey Pender.

Hill is a nebulous, inconsistent figure, the most difficult to characterize of Lee's generals. He had not been distinguished in the old army, from which he had resigned prior to secession. The West Point accolade, the most persuasive recommendation to President Davis, gave him the command of a regiment at the start. He performed well but not conspicuously under Johnston in northern Virginia, and had little opportunity to distinguish himself at the First Manassas. At Williamsburg he appeared strong as a brigadier and soon thereafter was a major general.

A comparison might be made between Powell Hill and Timothy Pickering, in that it was said of Pickering, when he was elevated in the President's Cabinet, that Washington had "spoiled a good Postmaster General in order to make a bad Secretary of State."[28] Hill had developed into an able combat leader with a division but never rose to any heights with a corps. The son of a Culpeper County, Virginia, merchant, Hill had stretched his stay at West Point to five years, owing to frail health. He had commanded his division at times under both Longstreet and Jackson and had been placed under arrest for petty rebelliousness by both generals. Perhaps the fact that he was not of the landed aristocracy of the South made him more than ordinarily punctilious about matters of right and honor. The "social noodles of Richmond"[29] were surprised when Powell Hill became a lieutenant general. Somewhere along the line he had come by money, and he complained that the Federal general Ambrose E. Burnside, a West Point classmate, owed him a personal debt of $8,000, which he had never made an effort to repay.[30] There was a suggestion of swagger in the fact that he put on a flaming red shirt when he went into battle, at a time when officers were learning that they and their cause had better protection from sharpshooters if they wore a private's blouse.

The controversy with Longstreet arose when Hill was the object of a puff story in a Richmond newspaper, the *Examiner,* written by Editor John M. Daniel, who had served in his command on the Peninsula, and who gained reflected glory out of exalting Hill.[31] Hill made no effort to set the facts in their proper light, although he was erroneously credited with the genius that hurled back the invaders and with commanding Longstreet's division as well as his own, when the opposite was the case. Hill had not inserted the stories, and Lee had ignored them, but Longstreet fretted about them and sent Major Sorrel with a correction to be inserted in an opposing paper.[32] This so incensed Hill that he wrote to Lee asking to be transferred out of Longstreet's command. He then went on a sort of sit-down strike, refusing to hold conversation with Major Sorrel or to pay any further attention to Longstreet's communications.

Finally Longstreet, who had handled the matter smoothly and without passion, sent Sorrel with notice to Hill that he was under arrest. The situation degenerated to apprehension of a duel between Hill and Longstreet, which according to Sorrel was averted only by Lee's intercession.[33] The commanding general a short time later transferred Hill's division to Jackson, then on his way to confront the Federal general John Pope. The disagreeable affair could not have left a comradely feeling for Powell Hill with Longstreet or his subordinates.[34]

Again, Hill's controversy with Jackson revealed his sulky nature. Jackson, apparently on one of his bad mornings, became irritated when Hill was half an hour late in marching his division and Jackson directed that he turn the command over to his subordinate, General Branch. This Hill, with flashing anger, deeply resented. He unbuckled his sword and handed it to Jackson with the remark that his own services apparently were not needed, and, according to one version, with the scathing addition that Jackson wasn't "fit to be a general."[35] The pressure from the martinet Jackson had finally made him explode, but it was childish in a major general nearly forty years old. Jackson "stopped him with stern abruptness," in the words of observer Kyd Douglas,[36] and placed him under arrest, but released him temporarily for the battle of Sharpsburg.

Back in Virginia after the Maryland campaign, Hill demanded a hearing on Jackson's charges. Now he exchanged bitter recriminations with Jackson just as he had done with Longstreet. His fuming was a trifle ludicrous. Lee in the end managed to pigeonhole the compendious record but never was able to allay the bad feeling.

Lee meantime wrote to President Davis that Hill "fights his troops well and takes good care of them."[37] There was much high spirit and bursts of hotheadedness were not infrequent in the Southern army, but

Lee recognized that docile men did not make the good officers. Personalities were clashing and Hill was forgiven. He was intrepid and seemed to have quick perceptions. His expression was "grave but gentle" and "his manner so courteous as almost to lack decision," but those who knew him still found firmness in his mouth and chin and his "bright, flashing eyes."[38]

Longstreet in later years of reflection thought there was "a good deal of 'curled darling' about Hill."[39] Though gallant, he was uncertain. He could perform what Longstreet called prodigies, but at other times he would fall below expectations. Old Pete judged that Hill's capacity was about equal to the command of a division. Ewell was "greatly Hill's superior in every respect"[40] as a corps commander.

At the time of the reorganization Longstreet recommended Major General Lafayette McLaws, a Georgian who commanded the first division of the First Corps.[41] There was nothing Jacksonian about McLaws but Sorrel thought he "could always be counted on,"[42] was exceedingly careful and fond of detail, and kept his command in excellent condition. He was as hard a fighter as Powell Hill and had carried one of the heavy loads at Chancellorsville, as he had earlier at Fredericksburg.

5. Another Hill Is Absent

Lee completed his reorganization plans May 20 and President Davis approved them. They left the high command topheavy with Virginians.

Of the fifteen ranking positions in the army, Virginia officers held ten: Lee, Ewell, A. P. Hill, Jeb Stuart, Early, Edward Johnson, Pickett, Rodes, Heth and the chief of artillery, William N. Pendleton. There were forty-three Virginia infantry regiments, thirty-seven Georgia, twenty-nine North Carolina, and smaller numbers from the other Confederate states and Maryland. North Carolina, with many regiments well recruited, probably supplied as many soldiers as any other state, yet was represented by a single new division commander, the youthful Dorsey Pender. Georgia had Longstreet and McLaws, Texas John B. Hood[43] and South Carolina Richard H. Anderson.

Davis and the War Department had insisted that in so far as was practical the brigades should be organized out of regiments from the same state, which was undoubtedly one of the reasons for the superb fighting power of the Southern army. But if the army was to be organized thus, then leadership might have been distributed more generously among the states. No possible affront to Lee as a general was involved in this system, as none had been to Washington by the prudent continental policy of sharing the general officers among the different colonies. The Confederacy was a new nation in which fragmentation was always a danger. Davis leaned heavily on the archaic system of giving top consideration to seniority, even seniority in the old Federal service.

No army ever had more latent talent than the Army of Northern Virginia. Its main strength, aside from its commanding general and the fighting quality of its foot soldiers, was in its brigadiers. Some of them were to show later that they could accomplish as much with meager resources as their superiors had with much greater advantages in and before the Gettysburg campaign. But if it was too early in the war to detect the high capacity of these brigadier generals, there were still other possibilities. At Gettysburg some of the North Carolinians clearly believed they did not have close at hand anyone of high rank to whom they might confide their wishes, and who would protect the record of their performance.[44] They felt forced to rely on correspondence with their Governor, Zebulon Vance.

One of the best fighting records in the army—perhaps the best after Jackson's—was that of the North Carolinian Daniel Harvey Hill, Jackson's brother-in-law. He had won the first brush of the war at Bethel and had been one of the main strengths on the Peninsula and at Sharpsburg. Governor Vance had him back in North Carolina in the spring of 1863 and presumably the Governor would not again surrender him to the Army of Northern Virginia. But no individual in the South was more imbued with the spirit of Confederate victory than Vance. Most of North Carolina's young manhood was with Lee. An explanation of the need undoubtedly would have taken Harvey Hill back to Virginia to command the Third Corps, and possibly to change the fate of the Confederacy at a critical moment at Gettysburg.[45] A void in the army as it moved north was the absence of the other Hill.

CHAPTER TWO

The Gray Host Unleashed

1. "...No Beggars, No Complaints"

As the war for Southern independence moved into its third year, the Confederate capital was buoyant with verve and confidence but was beginning to show ragged at the elbows. Inflation was daily gaining ground: gold in mid-March was worth five dollars in Confederate paper. Much of the financial difficulty was attributed to "the stupidity of our Dutch Secretary of the Treasury, Mr. Memminger."[1]

In the sure light of hindsight, the complaint recorded was that he lacked prescience: obviously he should have bought up cotton when it was selling at seven cents a pound. Profits that would have been realizable by early 1863 would have "defrayed the greater portion of the cost of the war," besides "affording immense diplomatic advantages." The presumption was that the cotton could have been slipped past the lurking Federal blockaders.

Money in early 1863 was merely sliding on to the first gentle slopes of the toboggan ride on which it would plunge later in the year. "There are some pale faces seen in the streets from deficiency of food; but no beggars, no complaints. We are all in rags, especially our underclothes."[2] The South was long on cotton at the gins, short on garments in the homes.

On April 2 Richmond women rioted for food. They met on Capitol Square, two or three hundred at the beginning. Soon there were a thousand women and boys milling about the streets. They marched in Ninth, Main and Clay streets, ransacking the stores and emptying them of merchandise. They seized all the drays and carts in the streets and loaded them with food, mainly flour and meal. They stripped the shoe stores, which had stocks on hand though General Lee had been writing that many of his men were barefoot.

The mob grew as pillaging continued. A boy was seen rushing from a store with his hat full of money.[3] Brigadier General Josiah Gorgas, Confederate chief of ordnance, noted in his diary that "the pretense was bread, but their motive really was license."[4] He pointed out that laborers were earning $2.50 to $3.00 a day and women and children from $1.50 to $2.50, and that they would not starve even with "flour at thirty dollars." These were the statistics, but the women no doubt were hungry. They had been whipped into riotous indignation by charges of rampant profiteering. Most merchants, however innocent, were grouped as "extortionists," but War Clerk Jones put the blame for the mob scenes on "foreigners and Marylanders."[5] Many thought the looting was incited by Northern agents.

President Davis was a distressful figure, with frail constitution and recurring illness. Momentarily he was disturbed by the theft of his favorite mount on the night before the riot. He was feeble, nervous, and easily agitated; one eye was blind and the sight of the other was seriously weakened. "But he works on and no visitors are admitted."[6] He was occasionally forced to remain away from his office for ten days at a time.

Like the President, the Secretary of War was emaciated and unhealthy. James Alexander Seddon, a former Virginia Congressman, was so sallow that many thought he would break down quickly. But he went about his work briskly, to the surprise of the War Department, where he was declared to "resemble an exhumed corpse after a month's interment."[7]

By mid-April garden planting was in progress. The city brightened with the knowledge that in a month the Alabama wheat would be harvested. Of the happy events the most inspiring was the passage and return through Richmond of two divisions of Longstreet's corps, on the trip to the south side of the James River to be boarded out in fresh country. Hood's division, containing the tough, rollicking Texas brigade, had been the center of attention when it marched along Main Street during a heavy snow. The Texans, unfamiliar with snow of such depth, fought snowball battles, to the delight of the city crowds. That night they slept in the snow without tents. "Can such soldiers be vanquished?"[8] asked the busy War Department scribe.

Finally on May 8 Longstreet's troops were a heartening sight as they marched north to rejoin Lee—"perhaps 15,000 of the best fighting men of the South."[9] This time the attention of Richmond was fastened on the Virginia regiments. "General Pickett himself, with his long, black ringlets, accompanied his division, his troops looking like fighting veterans. . . ."

2. Lee Makes the Decision

Against a background of hunger, sacrifice and assiduous effort, Lee planned his invasion of the Northern states. The gloom of the early spring had been largely dispelled and the army had slowly recovered from the anguish that attended Stonewall Jackson's passing. Lee was in Richmond May 15 for conferences, appearing a little pale after the exactions of Chancellorsville. The city buzzed with gossip: First, Pickett would be sent to Mississippi[10] to help Pemberton: then all was to be changed and he would go with Lee to raid the North, capture Philadelphia, march on to New York.

Lee's eagerness to invade the North sprang from the simple reasoning that since he had gained no major advantages from defeating four Federal armies in succession in Virginia, he would have to alter his strategy. The sands of the Confederacy were running out in triumphs. McClellan, Pope, Burnside and Hooker had been hurled back bloody and staggering. The victories had been impressive but in the end almost futile. After each stunning defeat the Army of the Potomac and its appendages had been able to re-form behind its entrenchments north of the Rappahannock or in the Washington defenses. It had bandaged its wounds, filled in the gaps with recruits, and resumed its merciless pressure against the diminishing resources of the South.

The apparent remedy was for Lee to advance boldly northward and draw the Army of the Potomac away from the Washington forts and the Virginia tidewater where it had been so easily provisioned by the Federal fleet. Then he might overwhelm it and operate against its communications. He could follow his victory with a series of hammer-like blows that would possibly open the way to seizure of Washington or other Northern cities.

Colonel Armistead L. Long, Lee's military secretary, said Lee went so far, in considering the place where the Federal army might be defeated remote from its capital city, as to mention Gettysburg and York, Pennsylvania, as suitable points for a battle.[11] Later, in reviewing his thinking, Lee told General Heth: "An invasion of the enemy's country breaks up all his preconceived plans, relieves our country of his presence, and we subsist while there on his resources. The question of food for this army gives me more trouble than everything else combined. . . ."[12]

Of equal urgency was the way in which Confederate territory was being sliced off by Federal armies in the West. The head and shoulders of the Confederacy along the Atlantic seaboard were safe enough at the moment, but the vitals were being hacked at and lacerated up and down the Mississippi. Chattanooga was menaced. Assistance was imperatively demanded by the Western armies. President Davis was gravely concerned over the Federal drive deep into his home state of Mississippi and talked about little else.[13] The Confederacy occupied the interior lines and might shift troops more readily than the Federals. But they were long, long lines, connected by slow, overtaxed transportation systems.

Lee's army was woefully inferior in numbers to what Hooker might momentarily throw against it. Certainly Lee could not at this stage detach any worth-while force for the journey to faraway Mississippi. Too much time would be required to draw the force back if some supreme emergency arose in Virginia.

Nevertheless, the plan of sending troops to Mississippi was under contemplation at the time Longstreet passed through Richmond. He found Secretary of War Seddon engaged in seeking to create a succoring force for Pemberton, around whom Grant was then tightening the noose at Vicksburg. No doubt the plan was an example of what military men have liked to call the "crude strategical conceptions of the Confederate President,"[14] but in any event Seddon said Longstreet's corps might be required to make the journey if the succoring army was to be strong enough to be effective. He asked Longstreet's opinion. The Georgian, thus invited, advanced the more realistic counterproposal—a plan which worked admirably during the Chickamauga campaign a few months later—of transferring two of his divisions to reinforce General Braxton Bragg, who was being pressed back step by step by the Federal general Rosecrans. Bragg was at Tullahoma, about midway between Murfreesboro and Chattanooga. The army forming under General Joseph E. Johnston at Jackson, Mississippi, for the relief of Pemberton, would move simultaneously to join Bragg. This grand combined force could brush Rosecrans aside, march through Tennessee and Kentucky and threaten the invasion of Ohio. The plan, in Longstreet's opinion, would compel the Washington government to recall Grant from Vicksburg.[15]

Seddon hummed over it for a time but expressed opposition because it involved the detachment of such a large force from Lee's army, though his own strategy would have required the same or a larger detachment of troops to be sent about twice the distance. But Longstreet had the bit in his teeth and was unwilling to be hauled up so briskly. Although he had not been the author of the proposal to transfer his divisions to the relief of the Western armies, his own adaptation of the idea grew on him as he rode back to army headquarters at Hamilton's Crossing on the Rappahannock. He immediately sought out Lee and outlined to him "with the freedom justified by our close personal and official relations"[16] his proposition to take two of his divisions to help Bragg drive Rosecrans into the Ohio River. By that time the plan had become the most certain method of freeing the Deep South from invading armies and winning the war.

Lee analyzed Longstreet's proposal carefully. Doubtless it had already passed through his alert mind along with other projects he had been contemplating since the victory at Chancellorsville. But Lee was understandably opposed to a prolonged division of his army. He was thinking in aggressive terms, but of an invasion of Maryland and Pennsylvania rather than of Tennessee and Kentucky. He tested the Pennsylvania plan with Longstreet, who opposed it as being too hazardous. It would take the army into states thoroughly Federal in sentiment, and so would call for much greater preparation than a movement into states like Tennessee and Kentucky, where a friendly population would more gladly assist with food and provisions. It is difficult to read any inordinate lust for personal glory in Longstreet's advocacy of the Kentucky movement. Certainly the chances for distinction would seem greater under Lee in Pennsylvania than under the somewhat phlegmatic Bragg in the Western theater. Either plan might well prove successful if properly carried out. As is generally true, execution was the question.

But the invasion of Pennsylvania appeared to Lee and eventually to Davis to offer greater promise than an advance toward Ohio. The war might be lost in the West but it had to be won in the East. What benefit could the North gain from Grant's siege of Vicksburg or Rosecrans' capture of Chattanooga if Lee could deliver a crushing defeat to the Army of the Potomac in Pennsylvania? The tail might wiggle but the snake would be dead. Success of the Confederacy in the West

would only prolong the defensive; a march into Pennsylvania offered
the opportunity to win the war with a single stroke. Of the South's
many requirements, food remained the number-one priority. The South
needed wheat and the season of the Pennsylvania harvest was approaching. Said Brigadier General John B. Gordon: "The hungry hosts of
Israel did not look across Jordan to the vine-clad hills of Canaan with
more longing eyes than did Lee's braves contemplate the yellow grain-
fields of Pennsylvania beyond the Potomac."[17]

Also, an invasion threatening Philadelphia and New York might
create a panic in the financial centers, put gold at a high premium and
cause the great business interests of the North to demand peace. That,
at least, was the hope of many, the expectation of some. Jubal Early
held that a victory north of the Potomac would do "more to produce a
financial crisis in the North and secure our independence than a succession of victories on the soil of Virginia."[18]

Greater reliance was placed in the old trust that the Confederacy
would be recognized ultimately by friendly European powers. Some
additional stimulus to bring recognition was now imperiously required.
The demand for cotton in England had not been a sufficient cause to
give the Confederacy relief. The cotton statesmen at the beginning of
the war had calculated that England would be depleted of stocks by
the summer of 1862,[19] and hence would be compelled to liberate Southern ports from the Federal blockade.

But cotton had not proved to be that kind of king. Another year
was almost past and England did not appear perturbed. Bales were
piled high on Nassau docks. Recognition by Great Britain or France,
or both, might come with Southern victory—victory that would be clear
and compelling. The ghastly incubus of slavery was a check on the
conscience of the scrupulous British queen. She was not persuaded
there was need for haste. It was apparent that recognition of Southern
independence would come only as a *fait accompli*. It would spring not
from British economic conditions but from Southern triumph on the
field of battle.

3. Lee Looks Across the River

Lieutenant Randolph H. McKim, who had been sojourning in Staunton, received a letter from Brigadier General George H. Steuart, a
fellow Marylander whom he served as a staff officer, directing him to
"come to Fredericksburg immediately by the shortest route."[20] Complying, he arrived at Lee's headquarters at 1:45 P.M. May 28, and

although only a first lieutenant, paid his respects to the commanding
general. Lee, even amid preparations for a momentous and complicated movement, had time for the military and social amenities. He
and young McKim were distantly akin, both being descended from the
Virginia landowner Robert Carter, commonly called "King" Carter, a
colonial governor, legislator and patron of William and Mary College.
Lee, when he was building Fort Sellars in Baltimore Harbor, had been
a guest at the McKim house, "Belvidere." The lieutenant was not
overwhelmed by the commanding general's presence, although he
explained that "the simple courtesy and genial hospitality of General
Lee would have put me at ease, if I had been a stranger."[21] A gracious
host, General Lee conversed during the meal about the young man's
family, then looked across the shallow Rappahannock at the point
where it deepened into tidewater, and fixed his attention on the scattered tents of the Federal infantrymen on the hills. "I wish I could get
at those people over there," he said ruefully.[22]

The words summed up the purpose for the march northward—to
find a place where he could come to grips again with the Federal army.
In Longstreet's conversations with Lee about the invasion, he had
urged—and later claimed he had exacted from the commanding general
a promise—that although the army would move north on an offensive
campaign, when it fought it would stand on the defensive. Lee did not
so understand it nor did he feel committed: he intended to give battle
when conditions were inviting.

Lee issued his marching orders. McLaws would break camp first, to
be followed a day later by Rodes and then by Early and Edward Johnson. In the predawn blackness of the third of June he commenced
the unobtrusive movement, westward and northward, of his three great
corps, each with its three divisions—Old Peter Longstreet, ruffled,
tough and innately pugnacious; maimed Richard Ewell, the buggy-
riding dragoon; and sickly, headstrong Powell Hill.

Anxious for new adventures, the army was at its peak in zest and
confidence. Colonel Risden T. Bennett of the 14th North Carolina
looked on it and judged it "as tough and efficient as any army of the
same number ever marshaled on this planet."[23] Randolph McKim
was impressed with its devoutness. When he could look back after
four years of soldiering and forty-five years in the ministry, he declared
that "in my whole experience I have never found men so open to the
frank discussion of the subject of personal religion."[24]

The British lieutenant colonel, Arthur J. L. Fremantle, was "tre-

mendously impressed with the *élan*," as well as with the manner in
which "they wore their tooth brushes like roses in their button-holes."[25]
General Harry Heth summed it up: ". . . there was not an officer or
soldier in the Army of Northern Virginia, from General Lee to the
drummer boy, who did not believe . . . that it was able to drive the
Federal army into the Atlantic Ocean."[26]

The press was confident. "It is said," chirped the Richmond *Whig,*
"that an artificial leg ordered some months ago awaits General Ewell's
arrival in the city of Philadelphia."[27]

Over the hills moved the long lines of gray and drab-brown soldiers,
the dust from their feet rolling off toward the more distant haze of
the Blue Ridge, and behind lumbered the guns and caissons and the
forty-two miles of wagon trains. The Southern host was at last unleashed for its march through the North, few indeed believing they
would halt before they planted their cannon on the banks of the
Schuylkill, perhaps even of the Hudson.

4. "Without Offending . . . a High Civilization"

Twice the army was delayed by business in Virginia. Hooker, growing
curious, threw his cavalry with infantry supports across the Rappahannock River and fought at Fleetwood with Jeb Stuart on June 8. The
Northern horse under Pleasanton showed a new audacity and forced
Lee to call up infantry from Culpeper, which disclosed to Hooker that
the Southern army was moving westward.

The second pause came after Ewell had pressed across the Blue
Ridge and reached Winchester, where the Federal commander, Major
General Robert H. Milroy, inadvertently remained in his path. Edward
Johnson skillfully closed the gap behind the Federals at Stephenson's
Depot and captured 2,300 of Milroy's army, though the general per-
sonally wiggled through the cordon and escaped.

As Lee marched, the stifling heat of the Virginia summer demanded
its toll as surely as ever had Northern bullets. On June 15, one of the
hottest days of the summer, five hundred of Hood's soldiers fell out
exhausted and a number died by the roadside. Some attributed the
deaths to drinking cold water and wading creeks and rivers without
the men taking off their shoes.[28] That night the division "slept gloriously" on a cushion of blue grass and clover. It reached Upperville on
June 17. The country was "perfectly charming." "I cannot see why
any Virginian ever leaves Virginia," a Texan reflected.[29] On June 18
they waded the yellow, swollen Shenandoah River, the water coming

up to their armpits. They crossed in column, the four men of each rank holding hands as a life line against the current and slippery boulders.

They camped a mile west of the river, where a driving rainstorm soaked their uniforms again and drenched the blankets and cartridge boxes they had held so carefully above their heads as they crossed the river. The discomfort was duplicated on the following day. Word that the Federal cavalry was in their rear caused Longstreet to order Hood's and McLaws' divisions to recross the Shenandoah and march through Snicker's Gap to the eastern side of the mountains, there to maintain a screen shielding the northern movement of the balance of Lee's army, aiding Stuart's cavalry.

Rain continued in torrents. Each morning the Texans awoke cold, wet and stiff. The mails did not come up as expected, although there were rumors that stacks of letters from home had accumulated at the Texas depot in Richmond.[30] On the night of June 19 the command "experienced the hardest storm of rain and wind I ever saw,"[31] a superlative statement for a Texan accustomed to northers blowing across the plains.

And so the gray host pressed on, like a great tide inundating the roadways, advancing and receding, marching and countermarching, but relentless in its progress northward. When finally released from Fredericksburg, Hill's corps made a rapid passage to the Shenandoah Valley. The South Carolinians of McGowan's brigade, among them cotton and rice men from lowlands and swamps, were delighted with the rolling cattle and grain farms of northern Virginia and even more elated by the friendliness of the people. Spencer Glasgow Welch, surgeon of the 13th South Carolina, noted that "the ladies waved their handkerchiefs from every little farm house."[32] Bands played sprightly music as the Palmetto boys made their Sunday march through Front Royal. "The people were in ecstacies." Surgeon Welch attributed the excellent health of his men to the abundance of meat, bread and milk. "I have never before seen them get along half so well on a march," he observed. "Not a man has given out since the rain."

Major General Isaac Ridgeway Trimble wrote Lee on June 18, stating that he was again fit for service. He was one of the elders of the army, reaching toward sixty years. A Virginian whose family had moved to Kentucky, he had been appointed to West Point from that border state, had served in the artillery ten years after his graduation in 1822, and had resigned to build and operate railroads, live in Baltimore, and become in most respects a Marylander. But when Maryland

remained with the Union he had gone to Virginia and by persistence
had won the command of a brigade in Joseph E. Johnston's and later
Stonewall Jackson's army. Scoffed at as "Old Trimble," he finally
found opportunity calling to him at Cross Keys, where he became the
deciding factor in Ewell's victory over Frémont. The success added
glory to the closing phases of Jackson's Valley campaign.

Trimble had been wounded by an explosive bullet at Groveton, of a
type later outlawed as inhumane in warfare. Although his leg was
injured, he recovered partially, returned to duty and before Sharpsburg
told Jackson, "By God, I intend to be a major general or a corpse!"[33]
Jackson looked dour and unimpressed, though he must have seen
Trimble's fire, for a little later he recommended the Marylander for
promotion, explaining that it was largely because of Trimble's distinguished service at Manassas Junction in the campaign against Pope.
Undoubtedly the elevation had been well earned by fighting and night
marching that would have done credit to a man half Trimble's age.

Trimble had been recuperating from trouble with his old wound
and from erysipelas at Shocco Springs, North Carolina.[34] None knew
better than he did the Maryland and southern Pennsylvania country
over which he had supervised much railroad construction. Lee told
him to come on and suggested that he raise a division of Maryland
troops—there being no vacancy for a major general. Otherwise he could
have command of the troops left behind in the Shenandoah Valley.

Trimble reached Berryville just as Lee was completing a lunch of
mutton. Lee told him to eat also and then come to the headquarters
tent. There the commanding general explained that the army had been
compelled to push on without him and added, "But you must go with
us and help to conquer Pennsylvania." Before Trimble could reply,
Lee continued with enthusiasm:

"We have again outmaneuvered the enemy, who even now does not
know where we are or what our designs are. Our whole army will be
in Pennsylvania day after tomorrow, leaving the enemy far behind and
obliged to follow us by forced marches. I hope with these advantages
to accomplish some signal result and to end the war, if Providence
favors us."[35]

Lee then alluded to a decision that was to make his Gettysburg campaign outstanding for its humaneness. He told Trimble he had received
letters from many prominent men in the South pointing to the ravages
committed by Northern armies and urging a campaign of retaliation
against Northern property.

"What do you think should be our treatment of the people in Pennsylvania?" he asked Trimble.

"General," said Trimble, "I have never thought that a wanton destruction of property of noncombatants in an enemy's country advanced any cause. Our aims are higher than to make war on defenseless citizens or women and children."

Trimble observed that when Lee replied it was "with that solemnity and grandeur so characteristic of the man." He told Trimble:

"These are my own views. I cannot hope that heaven will prosper our cause when we are violating its laws. I shall, therefore, carry on the war in Pennsylvania without offending the sanction of a high civilization and of Christianity."

In Trimble's description of the meeting, he said he was never so much impressed with the exalted moral worth and true greatness of Lee than when he perceived the "serene earnestness" of his words and saw "the noble expression of magnanimity and justice which beamed from his countenance."[36]

5. *Lee Gives Davis His Peace and War Views*

Lee was indeed subjected to strong pressure to carry ruthless warfare into the North. But he had his own positive views on the philosophy of warfare, quite as much as on the strategy of a campaign or the tactics on the field of action. He had, on June 10, just after the battle of Fleetwood, written a letter to President Davis which disclosed the breadth of his generalship. The purport was to admonish Southern firebrands gently and to substitute a policy of restraint for one of vehemence. Lee obviously recalled the inflammatory statements of the Richmond press when nine months earlier he had set out on his Maryland campaign. "The fate of Carthage must be that of Washington" breathed the fiery Richmond *Whig*.

Now, in June 1863, the South appeared to hold the position of near victor. The odds against her in a long and bitterly contested war remained stupendous. But a quick peace might be attainable after another successful battle. Lee could appreciate the value of what has since become known as psychological warfare. He wanted to reflect a soft rather than vengeful attitude. Peace should be made attractive, not humiliating. He asked that the government and press "abstain from measures or expressions that tend to discourage any [Northern] party whose purpose is peace." He pointed out that Southern journalists and others had in the past responded to Northern peace advocates in a manner to weaken them and to encourage those who wanted to pursue the war to the bitter end.[37] Manifestly his thinking was that a campaign for "unconditional surrender" might be showy for history but costly in battle casualties. It could have no other result than to make the enemy more resolute. Lee felt that peace should be held out as an inviting lure and not a bitter dreg that had to be swallowed at the point of a pistol:

> Should the belief that peace will bring back the Union become general, the war would no longer be supported, and that, after all, is what we are interested in bringing about. When peace is proposed to us, it will be time enough to discuss its terms, and it is not a part of prudence to spurn the proposition in advance, merely because those who wish to make it believe, or affect to believe, that it will result in bringing us back into the Union. . . .[38]

Lee's desire to encourage the Northern peace party by restraint came at a time when the peace advocates appeared to be gaining ground. The Richmond press gave play to all stories of Northern discord. It carried on June 11 an account of the great peace rally held in New York under the aegis of Horatio Seymour and Fernando Wood, attended by thirty thousand. The meeting adopted resolutions denouncing the war and calling for immediate peace, and declaring the Federal government had no constitutional power to coerce a state. The Southern capital was stirred by the news.

It was by all odds the hour to strike. The peace hope was high in the South. President Davis entrusted a carefully prepared letter to Vice President Alexander Hamilton Stephens, who had been a friend and close political ally of Lincoln in the Thirtieth Congress.[39] The diminutive but resolute Georgian would carry it toward Norfolk, where he would be prepared at the proper moment to ask for passage into the Federal lines, and proceed to Fortress Monroe and Washington if possible. This letter was the peace offer. It would be laid on the White House table when Lee had shattered the Northern army somewhere beyond the Potomac.

CHAPTER THREE

The Army Crosses

1. The Horses Are Hid in the Houses

Jenkins was over the river with his 2,000 troopers, riding beyond the Mason-Dixon line on June 15, the day that Rodes, opposite Williamsport, threw over Ramseur, Iverson and Doles—three brigades and three batteries. They were followed shortly by Daniel and O'Neal and four days later, when Longstreet was approaching, by Ewell in person with the rest of the corps.

The 14th North Carolina infantry waded the Potomac to spearhead the invasion. The "Rough and Ready Guards" of Asheville encountered at once the divided sentiments of Maryland. A beautiful young lady seized the reins of Colonel Risden T. Bennett's horse and tried to tell about the "oppression" the citizens had been suffering under Northern rule.[1] Equally emphatic was an old Dutch woman who brandished a paddling stick and shouted: "You eats up everything. The Union soldiers fetch in something and you scoundrels waste it." She threatened to hit the officers until one, pretending severity, told her to be quiet or he would "pull every hair out of her head."[2] Understanding direct action, she desisted. As the balance of Ramseur's brigade came up, the advance guard of Lee's army marched to Hagerstown.

Wild excitement already prevailed in Pennsylvania. Highways leading north were choked with caravans of wagons and carts, former slaves fleeing in fear of impressed servitude, men and women carrying on their shoulders their most valued household effects, great droves of cattle and horses being driven to security north of the Susquehanna

27

River. Dashing through Chambersburg went forty wagons of McReynold's train, a portion of Milroy's scattered command from Winchester, the teamsters lashing at the mules and glancing back over their shoulders, fearful that the Southern cavalry was close behind.[3]

Both North and South appeared amused over the stark terror of the civilians in the face of what from the very outset promised to be a merciful invasion. A published letter from Baltimore described how "in many instances the refugees saw no rebels and were pursued only by their fears."[4] They crowded the Baltimore & Ohio railroad station and slept on the benches. Continually they asked the station master if he had any reports of depredations.[5]

The mountainous section of Pennsylvania offered many hiding places, and numerous citizens took to the hills. The mails were suspended. Stores and schools were closed.[6] Work was stopped. Citizens who in the past had been critical of the Northern army's movements were suspected as spies. Homes were deserted. It was something of a relief to the distressed territory when Ewell finally arrived to restore order, even that of an unwelcomed invader.[7]

Six cavalrymen rode into Chambersburg on the night of June 15, the advance element of Lee's army, followed shortly by two hundred others and later in the night by Jenkins and the balance of the brigade.[8] They camped on the ground of Alexander K. McClure (later editor of the Philadelphia *Times*), where Mrs. McClure cooked up a propitiatory supper for the officers.[9] Jenkins' main purpose was to collect provisions for the infantry, which he did with an efficiency that appalled the Pennsylvania Dutch farmers. He paid for everything in Confederate script, and was diligent to prevent looting. When he saw a soldier in Chambersburg stealing some women's apparel, he jerked the man back into the store, brandished his sword, and declared that he had a mind to cut off the miscreant's head.

"Sell my men all the goods they want," he told the merchant, "but if anyone attempts to take anything without paying for it, report to me at my headquarters. We are not thieves."[10]

When the Richmond *Examiner* learned that Jenkins was paying Confederate money at Chambersburg, it could scarcely credit the information. On June 22 its readers were told:

This sounds strange. If our army has invaded the enemy's soil merely to respect private property, and pay out their money to the Yankees, they had better never have gone. We had hoped that if our army had ever have put its foot on Northern soil, it would have been to bring the horrors of war to the homes of the Yankees—burn, destroy, devastate, and make them feel the ravages of war—in a word, treat them as enemies who have never spared us.

Some of the farmers hid their horses in their own homes, but Artilleryman Stiles bore witness that however ingenious the tricks, the sharp Confederate commissary and impressment squads became even more adept in searching. He and others saw that the great Percherons, Conestogas and other draught breeds common on the Pennsylvania farms were of little value to the Southern army. They consumed twice the feed "our compact, hard-muscled little horses required" yet could perform only half the service and stand about half the hardship. "It was pitiful later," he said, "to see these great brutes suffer when compelled to dash off at full gallop with a gun, after pasturing on dry broom sedge and eating a quarter of feed of weevil-eaten corn."[11]

Lee kept close check on the cost of commodities. He wrote Davis on June 23, as he was about to cross the Potomac, that he was purchasing flour in Maryland at $6.50 a barrel, beef at $5.00 a hundred gross, and salt at 75 cents a bushel. "We use Confederate money for all payments," he said.[12] Its value was of course dependent on the outcome of the campaign. The invasion was already boosting the purchasing power of Confederate script in the South. At a Richmond auction on July 2, lawns which only a week before sold at from $2.50 to $2.75 a yard went for 75 cents. The Examiner reported that other staple dry goods showed a decline because of ample stocks and "an increased confidence in Confederate money."[13]

The Examiner on June 16 had attributed the depreciation of the currency to a wait-and-see attitude about the invasion, with investments going into real estate or gold. "If our champion rises victor from the death struggle of this month, Confederate notes will recover their value as suddenly as they did after the second battle of Manassas last year," the paper explained.

The route of the Confederate army could be marked through the towns by the old boots, shoes and hats thrown into the gutters as better ones were purchased.[14] Two of the main requirements of the quartermasters were onions and sauerkraut, both antiscorbutics, and they were in more than ample supply in this Dutch country.

Jenkins' cavalry brigade, after delivering provisions to Lee, returned to Chambersburg on June 23. On the following morning the citizens heard the distant strains of "The Bonnie Blue Flag" and a little later witnessed the approach of Rodes's division, the first Confederate infantry to march north of the Mason-Dixon line. The soldiers, mostly North Carolinians, passed directly through the town and north on the Harrisburg road, then halted at Shirk's Hill, where Jenkins already was in position. All day long the march of Rodes's strung-out division continued, first the infantry and the rolling guns and caissons, then immense wagon trains, and finally great droves of cattle that had been rounded up by Jenkins from the lush Pennsylvania farms. The alert Chambersburg citizens kept count; that day 10,300 men marched through the town.[15]

Half an hour after the head of Rodes's division passed the square a two-horse carriage stopped in front of the Franklin Hotel, followed by a group of horsemen. A "thin, sallow-faced man, with strongly marked Southern features"[16] emerged slowly, assisted by some of his escort. The crowd that had gathered saw that he had a wooden leg and walked with a crutch. He entered the hotel aided by the other officers, took over the large front parlor, ran up the Confederate flag and established the headquarters of the Second Corps of Lee's army.

Richard S. Ewell's first order prohibited the sale of intoxicants and required all who possessed whisky to report it so that a guard might be placed over the stock. Said the observant Jacob Hoke: "If there were any cases of drunkenness among the soldiers, I did not see [them]."[17] Ewell did convene a court-martial which cashiered one lieutenant for drunkenness on duty. He issued a series of requisitions to which the community responded with varying degrees of reluctance, but some of Ewell's officers who had been merchants made an inventory of what the town possessed and commandeered what they wanted. The presses were set to rolling and a great deal of army printing work was completed, including many thousands of parole papers, few of which were ever used since they were for the parole of the Army of the Potomac.

One of the Confederate officers engaged in procuring supplies was identified by Hoke as Major Todd, brother of President Lincoln's wife. Hoke was a careful reporter but this statement has not been verified. Mrs. Lincoln had one full brother and three half brothers in the Confederate army. Three served in the west and the fourth is not known to have accompanied Lee into Pennsylvania, though the possibility cannot be eliminated. Dr. George Todd, Mrs. Lincoln's full brother, was a medical officer who ordinarily had charge of a Confederate hospital at Rickersville, South Carolina, four miles from Charleston. All of her half brothers were killed in the Confederate service: Samuel Todd at Shiloh, Alexander Todd at Baton Rouge, and David Todd, mortally wounded at Vicksburg.[18]

2. *Lee Has His Letter Repeated*

Before crossing into Maryland Lee was confronted with one of the misunderstandings that contributed heavily to his drama of shattered hopes. His cavalry was severed from the main army. When Longstreet left Stuart in Virginia, the cavalry commander had a loose authority directly from Lee allowing his discretionary action, which by his interpretation authorized him to ride around the rear of the Federal army and join Ewell on the Susquehanna.

The story of the missing cavalry began on June 21, when Lee was camped in tents in a stubble field near Millwood. Strong wind and rain lashed at the canvas. Lee adhered in spite of the weather to his custom of tenting, although a large white house where he was well acquainted was close at hand—a house built in the Revolutionary War by British prisoners whom General Daniel Morgan had sent to Winchester.[19] While the storm blew, Lee learned that Stuart, watching the Blue Ridge passes to prevent penetration of the Valley by Federal cavalry, had been engaged in a whirl of cavalry clashes and was being pressed severely by the aggressive Federal horse, emboldened by the showing they had made at Fleetwood. Sharp encounters—little Fleetwoods—had been fought at Aldie, Middleburg, and Upperville. Being typical cavalry affrays, none was decisive.

The New York *World* took a realistic view of these cavalry clashes, which at times have been given places of undue importance in the history of the Gettysburg campaign. The *World* quoted reports that the cavalry was "fighting like fiends," then noted that the battles lasted only about twenty minutes and that the Federal loss would be about ten killed and a hundred wounded. Take four New York fire companies in a "muss," the *World* contended, give them no arms except fists, wrenches and the megaphones of the foremen, and "we will engage that the number killed and wounded will equal that of Pleasanton and Stuart's cavalry 'fighting like fiends.' "[20] Somewhere, the *World* felt, something must be wrong with the accounts. The battles were, indeed, inconclusive and neither hastened nor impeded Lee's movement northward.

When Lee, as a precaution, ordered Longstreet to recross the Shenandoah River, move along the east side of the Blue Ridge, and remain in supporting distance of Stuart until Hill's corps had cleared the Valley behind him, Longstreet was thereby put in command east of the mountains, and consequently of Stuart's movements.

On the next day, at Berryville, Lee instructed his aide, Colonel Charles Marshall, to write a series of orders; these were destined to have vital bearing on the campaign. The army was beginning to clear the Valley. Hill had crossed the Shenandoah at Front Royal and was approaching Berryville. Lee decided to cross the Potomac with Hill the next day, so as to close on Ewell, who was still waiting around Chambersburg. Marshall wrote the first of the orders, a letter to Ewell which suggested that his best course toward the Susquehanna River was on a front reaching from Emmitsburg through Chambersburg to McConnellsburg. Especially, he emphasized, success in gathering supplies would control whether or not the balance of the army could follow. Then came the heart of the order: "If Harrisburg comes within your means, capture it."[21]

Before Colonel Marshall wrote his next letter, Lee told him of a conversation he had held with Jeb Stuart at headquarters near Paris a day or so earlier. Lee had advised Stuart that cavalry details should be left in Snicker's and Ashby's gaps—the two passes of the Blue Ridge by which the Federals might menace the army's rear—and the remainder of the cavalry should go with the main army directly into Pennsylvania. Stuart, according to Lee, countered with the suggestion that he should move close to Hooker and impede his crossing of the Potomac, then, when Hooker crossed, "rejoin the army in good time."[22] Stuart "ardently favored" this plan.[23] Longstreet had agreed to it and Lee then consented, at least tacitly, but insisted that when Stuart learned of Hooker's actual crossing, he himself must cross immediately and take his proper position on the right flank of the army.

On later reflection Lee was disturbed about the arrangements with Stuart, who had been persuasive in his presentation. He told Marshall he wanted to make certain that Stuart and the cavalry should join the main army immediately after Hooker crossed. That was the paramount consideration. Perhaps, he said, Stuart could cross east of the Blue Ridge, thus avoiding the long march through Snicker's or Ashby's Gap, but he foresaw that circumstances might work against such a route and he wanted to be sure that Stuart understood the urgency of rejoining the main army with speed.[24] He therefore directed Marshall to write Stuart a letter containing more explicit directions.

Marshall wrote the letter, showed it to Lee and sent it by messenger.

It expressed concern that Hooker might cross undetected. The heart of the letter said: "If you find he is moving northward, and that two brigades can guard the Blue Ridge and take care of your rear, you can move with the other three into Maryland, and take position on General Ewell's right, place yourself in communication with him, guard his flank, keep him informed of the enemy's movements, and collect all the supplies you can for the use of the army."[25] It went on to explain that one of Ewell's columns was probably moving by Emmitsburg and the other by Chambersburg and that there were no Federals west of Frederick.

The letter did not specify routes nor annul any oral orders Stuart had received, but it pointed up the main task of the cavalry: to patrol Ewell's right flank. Marshall forwarded the letter through Longstreet, who sent it on and then wrote Lee, explaining that he had suggested at the same time that Stuart "pass to the enemy's rear, if he thinks he can get through."[26] Here again everything was reverting to the understanding reached at the conferences among Lee, Longstreet and Stuart, during which Stuart's route into Pennsylvania was left strictly to the cavalryman's own judgment.

What Lee said in his letter to Longstreet, with which he conveyed his written instructions to Stuart, probably never will be known, for the text is missing. This lost letter may have supplied additional incentive to Stuart in a correspondence marked by much vagueness.

Longstreet referred to it in writing to Stuart: "He [Lee] speaks of your leaving via Hopewell Gap and passing by the rear of the enemy. If you can get through by that route, I think you will be less likely to indicate what our plans are than if you should cross by passing in our rear."[27] Passing in the rear would be through Snicker's or Ashby's Gap and crossing above Harpers Ferry. Hopewell is a gap in the Bull Run Mountains which would lead to a crossing of the Potomac between Washington and Harpers Ferry, east of the Blue Ridge.

Later in the afternoon of June 22 Lee again wrote Ewell, telling him that he had directed Stuart, in case the enemy had left his front, to move three brigades across the Potomac and place them on Ewell's right. Imboden had been directed to cross with his brigade and place himself on Ewell's left.

Recognizing that now more than ever before he needed full information, Lee was still dissatisfied with the situation and directed Colonel Marshall to repeat his last letter to Stuart. Marshall demurred; Stuart had been instructed orally and then had received a "very full and explicit" explanation in the letter already written.[28] But Lee insisted that, to guard against error, the instructions should be repeated. Marshall therefore wrote again, using different wording. The heart of this letter, written on the afternoon of June 23, was:

If General Hooker's army remains inactive, you can leave two brigades to watch him, and withdraw with the three others, but should he not appear to be moving northward, I think you had better withdraw this side of the mountains tomorrow night, cross at Shepherdstown next day, and move to Frederickstown.

You will, however, be able to judge whether you can pass around their army without hindrance, doing them all the damage you can, and cross the river east of the mountains. In either case, after crossing the river, you must move on and feel the right of Ewell's troops, collecting information, provisions, etc.[29]

It is not clear from Marshall's comments whether or not Lee read this letter, as he had the first, before it was dispatched. Marshall stated that Lee read the first, but made no reference to submitting the second for approval. But again, Marshall, the composer of it, left conditions as they had been when the earlier letter was sent, or as they had been at the time of the conferences among Lee, Stuart and Longstreet.

Colonel Charles Marshall usually wrote Lee's orders. His legal training might have tended to make his sentences guarded and involved, and ambiguities did creep in. Marshall was of a family that had produced both good soldiers and good lawyers. His grandfather, Thomas Marshall, had commanded one of the Virginia infantry regiments in the Revolutionary War, and his distinguished uncle, John Marshall, had been Chief Justice. Charles Marshall, after graduation from the University of Virginia, had been a professor at Indiana University, in Bloomington, Indiana. He had left teaching to study law, had established his practice in Baltimore, and had returned to Virginia after that state seceded. Bad health kept him out of the early engagements but in March 1862 he joined Lee as an aide, beginning an association that was to endure until the final hours at Appomattox.

Marshall's letter to Stuart was not a model of conciseness or clarity. Had Lee been disturbed before, he had no reason to feel assured after it was sent. The specific instructions it contained were those to be followed if Hooker's army *remained inactive,* which it was not likely to do: Stuart was to leave two brigades on watch, retire with three others west of the mountains, and cross at Shepherdstown.

The orders to be followed in case Hooker moved northward were stated merely by implication, and they left matters to Stuart's judgment. Virtually all that had happened since Lee's conference with Stuart and Longstreet had pointed to the likelihood that the cavalry commander would ride around Hooker's rear unless restrained by a firm negative, which had not been forthcoming. Blackford noted that Stuart had presented two plans to Lee—one for the cavalry to follow the army down the Valley, and the other for it to ride around Hooker's rear. Stuart himself eagerly favored the second, which would allow him to get between the enemy and Washington, "cutting his communications, breaking up the railroads, doing all the damage possible."[30] Both letters written by Marshall for Lee, as well as Longstreet's suggestions, appeared to court a ride around Hooker if Stuart felt it compatible with the rest of his instructions. Nothing in either of the letters covered what should be done if he judged he could get around Hooker and then found himself blocked.

3. *The Wanderers Reach the Maryland Shore*

Lee's last letter reached Stuart's camp near Middleburg by courier before midnight on June 23, the day it was written, but Stuart was asleep. He was rolled in oilcloth and blankets beneath a tree while the rain fell in torrents—a "pitiless rain," Adjutant McClellan called it—unwilling to go into a near-by house while his men were exposed. He had ordered McClellan to sleep on the front porch, where he might light a candle if dispatches came.

McClellan risked Stuart's displeasure by breaking the confidential seal of Lee's letter, then woke Stuart, who reproved him "mildly" for the technical violation of orders. They managed to keep a light burning under the dripping tree long enough for Stuart to read the message. The words that leaped out boldly were: "You will . . . be able to judge whether you can pass around their army without hindrance . . . and cross the river east of the mountains."[31]

Clearly this was assent and assent was all that Stuart required. As McClellan put it: "The whole tenor of the letter gave evidence that the commanding general approved of the proposed movement, and thought that it might be productive of the best results." He nevertheless left the responsibility of the decision with Stuart.

Stuart went back to sleep and McClellan prepared the orders for the movement east of the mountains, then slept himself, and woke Stuart again at daybreak.

The restriction imposed on Stuart was that he be able to ride around
Hooker's army "without hindrance," a condition about which he could
not be certain until he explored the possibility. Major John Mosby
advised him that the Federal army was scattered but immobile, with
gaps between the different corps ample to let the Southern cavalry
pass. Complying with Lee's stipulation that two brigades be left to
protect the rear, Stuart detached those of Robertson and William E.
(Grumble) Jones, a force of three thousand men, with Robertson in
command. This force dallied behind in Virginia and did not reach Lee's
army until the closing phases of the Gettysburg campaign.

After waiting another day for Longstreet to follow Hill, Stuart assembled at Salem his remaining three brigades—those of Munford, Cham-
bliss and Hampton—and on June 25, just after midnight, set out on
his adventure, carrying three days' rations for the men and a day's
forage for the horses. "No one could ride along the lines of this
splendid body of men," said Blackford, "and not be struck with the
spirit which animated them."[32]

Passing through the Bull Run Mountains at Glascock's Gap, Stuart
was moving toward Haymarket when the big Second Corps of the
Army of the Potomac loomed immediately in his path, marching from
Thoroughfare Gap to Gum Springs. Manifestly the thought of turning
back never entered seriously into his calculations. He paid the Federals
the courtesy of a few rounds from his artillery, then detoured to the
south, using up his forage, so that he was compelled to wait half a day
while his horses grazed. On June 26 he crossed the Occoquan at Wolf
Run Shoals and passed through Fairfax Court House, thus making a
wide circuit to the east and entering into the environs of Washington.

Instead of riding around Hooker, he was in the rear of the Federals
as they moved north on a broad front. Danger was ever present. Each
stop showed the recent presence of Federal infantry. He entered
Dranesville a few hours after the Federal Sixth Corps had left, then
came up to the Potomac at Great Falls, the spectacular cataract about
twelve miles above Washington. Rowser's Ford, a short distance
upstream, was deep and difficult and would have been judged impass-
able for artillery by a less enterprising general. But he took all the
ammunition from the caissons and distributed it among the men, who
kept it above water as they rode through the flooded stream. The cannon and wagons disappeared from sight entirely as they were drawn
through the current by the mules. It required four hours to make the

crossing in the darkness, but at three o'clock on the morning of June 28 they "stood wet and dripping on the Maryland shore."[33]

Two mountain ranges divided Stuart from Lee's infantry. The Army of Northern Virginia was moving into the Free States in two separate invasions.

4. Lee Recommends an "Army in Effigy"

On June 25, when Lee was on the Potomac opposite Williamsport, he wrote a letter to President Davis that was destined to have profound bearing on the outcome of the campaign. He acknowledged the President's answer to his "psychological warfare" letter and emphasized again his belief that nothing should be done to discourage the peace feeling in the North.

He then called attention to a proposal he had made on earlier occasions, that the Confederate government organize an "army in effigy"[34] under General Beauregard, and concentrate it at Culpeper, where it would not only defend Richmond but also impose a threat against Washington. He suggested the concentration of such brigades from North and South Carolina as Generals D. H. Hill and Arnold Elzey, commanding those two departments, could spare. He particularly wanted Beauregard, even if that general should be lent only temporarily by South Carolina. Beauregard had commanded high respect in the North ever since the first battle at Manassas and, Lee felt, his presence at Culpeper would have a cautioning effect on Washington, highly beneficial during the invasion of Pennsylvania.[35]

The road from Culpeper to Washington could not be left wide open to one of Beauregard's reputed resourcefulness. Part of the Army of the Potomac, surely a minimum of one corps, would have to be added to the normal Washington garrison. In the Confederate Department of North Carolina on June 30, 1863, were the brigades of Cooke, Colquitt, Ransom, Clingman, Martin and Micah Jenkins, together with a body of troops under Major General W. H. C. Whiting at Cape Fear and scatterings of unattached infantry and three unattached cavalry regiments.[36] From what might have been spared from these brigades and brought up from South Carolina, a presentable Fourth Corps could be created. Corse's brigade and the 44th North Carolina regiment of Pettigrew's brigade were in or near Richmond and available as impressive additions. But Lee wanted Corse and Micah Jenkins to join him in Pennsylvania. Both brigades belonged to Pickett's division.

Lee dispatched his recommendations, then continued his march with hope and apparently some confidence that a distraction by Beauregard at Culpeper would slow the Federal pursuit and give him time for leisurely operations.

Lee was exposed to some warnings from subordinates as he rode northward. Hood was uncertain. Colonel Eppa Hunton of the 8th Virginia was far from sanguine.

Dick Garnett, who commanded the first of Pickett's three brigades, was ill, and suffering also from a foot injury. He had to be carried in an ambulance, so Hunton led the brigade. As he was riding up the Shenandoah Valley a party of horsemen came up from the rear and General Lee fell in beside him. They talked for half an hour as they rode. Hunton boldly advanced objections to the movement into Pennsylvania. His main fear was that if the army encountered disaster, Lee would have great difficulty in getting it back to Virginia.

Lee explained the necessity. He said provisions of every variety were nearly exhausted and that the army had to go to Pennsylvania for supplies. He did not know in 1863 just how tight the Confederacy would be able to draw in its belt before the end of the trail at Appomattox. Lee radiated confidence. He forecast that the invasion would be a great success. If so, he said, it would mean an end to the war and everyone could then rest. Hunton found the commander's ardor contagious. "I threw away my doubts and became as enthusiastic as he was."[37]

On June 24, while Ewell waited in Chambersburg, A. P. Hill's corps crossed the Potomac at Williamsport and Longstreet crossed at Shepherdstown. Both concentrated that night in Hagerstown.

As Longstreet's men marched through Martinsburg, Virginia, they were greeted by a native daughter, Belle Boyd, who was home briefly between spells in Northern prisons. This "most sensational of Southern spies," called also "the Secesh Cleopatra," who had won Stonewall Jackson's unstinted praise by her daring exploits,[38] was an admiring, blue-eyed girl, twenty years old, when the soldiers of her beloved Confederacy passed by. An unappreciative New Orleans artilleryman complained that as usual she wanted buttons, but "we cut and ran."[39] He thought she had "no soul above buttons." Jackson, Turner Ashby and many others would have disputed that if they could.

For all of the brigades the invasion was proving fascinating and eventful. Perrin's South Carolinians, unaccustomed to such profligate abundance, found the country glorious, despite the continued rainfall.

"In every direction yellow fields of grain extended themselves; in every farm were droves of the largest, fattest cattle; gardens thronged with inviting vegetables; orchards gave promise of a bounteous fruit yield."[40] Nor were the residents disagreeable: "The citizens were amazed at our moderation. Many of them bade us help ourselves to poultry, milk, vegetables, fruit, honey, bread, whatever we wanted to eat, provided we spared more valuable property."[41]

Physician Welch was still impressed with both the beauties of the land and the health of the troops: "Such wheat I never dreamed of, and so much of it! . . . The free Negroes are all gone, as well as thousands of white people. My servant, Wilson, says 'he don't like Pennsylvania at all,' because he 'sees no black folks.' "[42]

Fitzgerald Ross, British magazine writer, trudged along with the Southern infantry and left one of the best descriptions of Lee's army as it moved northward. The hotels were so jammed at Martinsburg that he stayed at the home of Colonel Charles J. Faulkner, Ewell's chief of staff, a Virginia Congressman whom President Buchanan had appointed Minister to France. The town was filled with cavalry and infantry hurrying to the front. "The men's shoes are good, and so are their clothes, though they look very coarse."[43] Ross noticed that many of the blankets were made from carpets of bright colors. Southern families in 1863 were living on bare floors. Invariably the soldier had cut a hole in the center through which he could put his head in cold or rainy weather. With the gay carpet tones, "the effect is marvelously picturesque."[44] That was especially the case when the men were squatting in groups about a fire, cooking their meals.

The roads were loaded far beyond capacity, with men and trains going forward, droves of cattle and sheep "the spoils of Pennsylvania," being sent to the rear. The army was already living off the bounty of the enemy. Ross compared some of the Confederate wagons to Noah's ark—they were "of extraordinary size, being drawn by six or eight horses." Perhaps the thing that most impressed the British observer was the army's temperance. He offered a drink to a soldier, who refused and said he would not drink again until the end of the war. "Teetotallers will rejoice to hear," said Ross, "that none of the Confederate soldiers ever touch spirits, and they get on very well without."[45] The statement was extravagant, of course, and Ross no doubt would have corrected it with longer observation, for the army had plenty of drinkers. But it was correct in substance to say that Lee's was not a drinking army.

CHAPTER FOUR

Feasting on Northern Plenty

1. The Texans Have Food by the Acre

Benjamin Russell Hanby, of Westerville, Ohio, a sophomore in Otterbein College, read a story in the Cincinnati *Gazette* in 1856 about a beautiful mulatto slave girl who had been torn away from her Negro lover in Kentucky and sold to a planter who had taken her to Georgia. Although he had never written a song before, that night he composed "My Darling Nellie Gray," which the *Gazette* published. Soon it was being hummed and whistled on nearly every street corner of the country.

The era was one of Negro tunes and minstrel shows. Daniel Decatur Emmett, a more experienced song writer of Mt. Vernon, Ohio, whose compositions already included "Old Dan Tucker" and "Jordan Is a Hard Road to Travel," in 1859 composed a song for the Bryant Minstrels, of 470 Broadway, New York, entitling it, "I Wish I was in Dixie Land." The Bryant Brothers used it without creating much commotion and in 1860 it was copyrighted by another firm farther up Broadway.[1]

In the spring of 1861 Mrs. John Wood was playing *Pocahontas,* by John Brougham, in the Varieties Theater in New Orleans. Any slight inconsistency with the Pocahontas title did not prevent Carlo Patti, the orchestra leader, from introducing in the last scene a march of the Zouaves, for which many tunes had been tried out in the rehearsals. Then Patti ran across the Emmett minstrel air of "Dixie" and adapted it for the jaunty Zouaves.

In New Orleans Miss Susan Denin led the singing as the brightly

40

garbed Zouaves marched. The audience went wild with excitement. It was a season of high emotions, with states seceding and war imminent. Encore after encore was demanded. On the next day "Dixie" rang out in the parlors and music rooms of stately homes, in water-front saloons, in army barracks and on every New Orleans street.

The Washington Artillery, oldest military organization of Louisiana, was preparing to depart for Virginia. When it took the cars for the front, to become a celebrated unit of Longstreet's corps, it carried with its baggage and caissons something of greater worth even than its ammunition—the refrain that would inspire Lee's army, sweep through the Confederacy as a martial air comparable to the "Marseillaise," and in time come to be surrounded with all the romance and nostalgia of the old South, to which it would give its name.[2] Back in Ohio the innocent Emmett, who was merely trying to entertain, was abused and threatened and some suggested that he would look good on a gallows.

Next most popular among the Southern soldiers was the plaintive refrain about the slave girl snatched from the old Kentucky shore. And now as Longstreet's troops approached the Potomac and the guns of the Washington Artillery rolled out of the Virginia mountains and the soldiers looked across to the green Maryland hills, the bands struck up "Dixie" and "Nellie Gray." Regiment after regiment took up the chorus as the men moved down the bank to ford the swollen river. John Hood had never before witnessed such enthusiasm in the Southern army as when his troops touched Maryland, or when, a little later, "amid extravagant cheers," and with bands blaring "Dixie," they passed the Mason-Dixon line.[3]

Drink followed song. Hood, shortly after the men waded the Potomac, issued a ration of whisky from captured supplies. Colonel William C. Oates, commanding the 15th Alabama Infantry of Law's brigade, said the result was "quite a number of drunken officers and men.[4] Although there were ample rations in camp, the men preferred to forage off the country and care had to be taken to enforce Lee's orders. Adjutant Wadell encountered some of the Alabamians committing "depredations" on Dutch farmers. These were venial offenses— pilfering food and using fence rails for fuel—but he reprimanded them and ordered them back to camp. Some were milking cows and catching the milk in canteens, which required accurate aim and showed they were in no manner inebriated.[5]

Oates and Wadell ate with a family where one of the young women, while expressing her loyalty to the Union, thought that the best way to stop the war would be for the armies to hang both President Lincoln and President Davis. According to the Alabama colonel, the people were "remarkably ignorant" of the causes of the war and thought it a quarrel between "two ambitious men."[6]

Private West, fresh from Texas, summed up the march, his first: "We have crossed and recrossed streams, waist deep, with water cold and chilling. We have passed four or five nights and days without changing clothes, which were soaking wet the entire time. . . . A soldier's motto is to sleep at all hazards whenever he has a chance." The country was the most beautiful he had ever beheld. The barns were "positively more tastily built than two-thirds of the houses in Waco." The cherries were delicious. He wrote to his wife, "I enclose two varieties of cherry seed and will endeavor to bring some if I ever get back." That question of returning to Texas was on his mind. As he passed a woman who was inducing some small girls to sing the "Red, White and Blue," she remarked, "Thank God, you will never come back alive." The private had a quick response: "No, we intend to go to Cincinnati by way of New York." Still, thoughts of the future could not be shaken off: "My impression is that we will have a desperate battle in a few days." Then reassuringly: "I would not have missed this campaign for $500."[7]

West was elated with "breakfast in Virginia, whisky in Maryland and supper in Pennsylvania." It was, he said, "a brilliant and eventful day."

Robertson's brigade of Texas and Arkansas troops found the whisky ration ample because many nondrinkers passed their doles to the imbibers. In the 3rd Arkansas those who walked tortuously were doused in the cold streams.[8] By June 27 the Texas brigade was camped in a beautiful grove of great trees near Chambersburg. When the men went out to buy fresh supplies, much was given to them and they returned loaded with delicacies. At the mess call "every square foot of an acre . . . was covered with choice food."[9] The Texans remembered the menu. They had turkeys, chickens, ducks, geese, corned beef, hams, sides of bacon, cheeses, loaves of bread, crocks of apple butter, jelly, jam, pickles, preserves, bowls of yellow butter and demijohns of buttermilk. They feasted until three o'clock in the afternoon. When the march call sounded they "moved lazily and plethorically"[10] into line.

Pennsylvania was fairly stripped of cherries. Even Sorrel, Longstreet's chief of staff, was tempted. From the saddle he pulled the fruit down, "branch after branch," and remembered the pleasure of it through later decades.[11] He remembered also the bolt of velveteen he procured in Chambersburg. Well he might, for the suit he made from it was what he wore for the remainder of the war.[12] Like other Confederates, Sorrel was quite surprised that so many Pennsylvania citizens could speak no English. To him they were "a hard-working, thrifty class, with, it seems, no thought but for their big horses and barns, huge road-wagons like ships at sea, and the weekly baking, and apple butter. This last appeared to be their staple food."[13]

Randolph A. Shotwell of the 8th Virginia mimicked what he termed the propitiating "Deutchers," saying they talked about "Dose nice Rebel gentlemens from de Souf."[14]

Marching toward the Potomac, Kershaw's South Carolinians heard reports that Washington had been thrown into confusion by the invasion and that "Lincoln was the only one who seemingly had not lost his head."[15] Reaching the Pennsylvania line, they were met by a delegation of "rigorously righteous old Quakers," who stood in the roadway and commanded, as though speaking the word of God, "So far thou can go, but no farther." The Confederates moved on; obviously they doubted the authority of the Quakers, but they were certain of Lee's orders. The Quakers went home, "perfectly satisfied," according to Dickert, with their passive resistance.[16] To a woman who displayed a large flag across her bosom, a Texan cautioned: "Take care, Madam, for Hood's boys are great at storming the breastworks when the Yankee colors is on them."

The British correspondent Ross noticed that groups of curious civilians gathered about the wells where Confederate soldiers drank. The conversation was friendly. At one halt a man who "seemed half crazy" was preaching in "very abusive style." He "used Bible language, but words of wrath."[17] The soldiers laughed and joshed at him in good humor. At Greencastle Ross fell in with a train and tramped through the dark beside the wagons. "Innumerable fires" burned along the side of the road, each surrounded by soldiers, "a strange and picturesque sight."[18] Great swarms of men were scattered over the countryside. They bivouacked in the fields, slept in hay in the barns, often marched through the night. Ross got milk for breakfast from a farmer's wife. He found that the population was called Dutch, "though neither they nor their ancestors ever had anything to do with Holland." When he asked a farmwife and her daughters what part of Germany they were from, they replied merely, "Pennsylvania Dutch." He found the mother's accent decidedly Swabian.[19]

2. Pickett Salutes the Little Flag Waver

Pickett's progress was marked by letters to his sweetheart. Because the ardors of middle age are warmer, or less easily dissembled, the commanding general of Longstreet's second division wrote passionate missives at every halt, blatantly indiscreet—at least by modern army standards—in their coverage of army movements. The indiscretion was the more pronounced because the young lady to whom he was affianced was attending a girls' school at Lynchburg, and at such a college conversation is free and letters home frequent.

En route to Pennsylvania, it was: "Each day, my darling, takes me farther and farther away from you, from all I love and hold dear. . . . Today, under orders from Marse Robert, we cross the Potomac." Then, as he reflected on the coming battle: "Oh, the desolate homes, the widows, the orphans, and the heart-broken mothers, that this campaign will make!"[20]

Possibly it was because of his sentimentality that when his men entered Greencastle the band played "Her Bright Smile Haunts Me Still."[21] In any event, from this town he indited a prose poem to his fair lady which suggests he was not much of a killer at heart, although destined to have one of the bloodiest assignments in history. "I want to lie down in the grass, away off in the woods somewhere or in some lone valley on the hillside far from all human sound, and rest my soul and put my heart to sleep and get back something—I know not what—but something I had that is gone from me—something subtle and unexplainable—something I never knew I possessed till I had lost it—till it was gone—gone."[22] What Stonewall Jackson would have thought of such feverish ebullience may readily be judged, although that hardheaded realist was not without sentiment.

Pickett had a chance for a bit of knight-errantry at Greencastle, where a young girl rushed out on a porch and waved the United States flag while the band was playing "Dixie." She fastened the flag around her waist like an apron. Holding each side, she waved it defiantly and shouted, "Traitors—traitors—traitors. Come and take this flag, the man of you who dares." Pickett, fearful that some of the soldiers "might forget their manhood," took his hat off, bowed to the girl, saluted the flag, and had the men present arms. "They were all Virginians," he wrote. "Almost every man lifted his cap and cheered the little maiden." The result was that she stopped calling them traitors, let her flag fall and, according to Pickett, finally said, "Oh, I wish I had a rebel flag. I'd wave that, too."[23] But she was last seen clutching the Union flag to her bosom.

In Chambersburg Pickett found groups of "uncheerful Boers of Deutschland descent" talking, "more sylvan shadows than smiles wreathing their faces."[24] The general had silenced the bands for this march-through but young ladies on a veranda requested music. So the bands resumed and they serenaded with the old songs, among them "Home, Sweet Home," "Annie Laurie," "Nellie Gray," "Hazel Del," "The Old Oaken Bucket," "Swanee River," "The Old Arm Chair," "The Lone Rock by the Sea," and finally, "Auld Lang Syne." There could have been few dry eyes in the town, with a battle looming. Pickett marched out on the Cashtown road four miles and camped. From there he wrote that Lee's order was a sermon on the text of "Vengeance is Mine, saith the Lord." He thought "the mourner's bench was not overcrowded with seekers for conversion" and said the soldiers were thinking of "their own despoiled homes, looted of everything, and were not wildly enthusiastic as they obediently acquiesced to our beloved Commander's order."[25]

Pickett's letters from Pennsylvania to his fiancée, LaSalle Corbell, suggested one thing very definitely: that it was not because he lacked power of expression that he was last in his class at West Point.

Another view of the Southern army's advance was provided by Thomas McCammon, a Hagerstown blacksmith, "a good man" to the Federals, who rode through Armistead's brigade on July 28 to give Federal officers a fuller picture of the invasion.[26] Jenkins' cavalry had arrived on June 15, begun the herding of cattle for the infantry, and sent back large quantities of beef. Ewell had come on June 20 and on the day following, Sunday June 21, had attended services at the Catholic Church with Rodes and two other generals. Confederate soldiers had continued through the town every day that week, and finally Lee and Longstreet had made their headquarters on the James H. Groves place just north of town. The leading Confederate sympathizer of Hagerstown, James D. Roman, a lawyer, had announced on June 27 that the entire Confederate army, 100,000 strong, was in Maryland or Pennsylvania, with the exception of the cavalry.

William H. Protzman had checked the infantry as it passed and "could not make the total over 80,000." Union men assembled each night to compare figures. Their count of the artillery showed 275 guns.

Many regiments were woefully reduced, having only 175 men, while two had only 150. The largest Protzman counted was a Maryland regiment of about 700, apparently in Steuart's brigade. He estimated the average regiment at 400 men. The army had good and ample transportation, many of the wagons having been captured from the Federals, and well-cared-for horses. Officers and men, who appeared in good condition, said they were going to Philadelphia. They carried their paper money in flour barrels and used it freely. The blacksmith reported that they paid five dollars for two horseshoes, the ordinary charge being fifty cents in United States money.

Pleased with the invasion was an old Dutchman with whom a member of the Washington Artillery ate and spent the night. The German couple were paid $100 a year for tending a large farm. The artillery-man gave them two silver half dollars, which Hans looked at with delight. "Johanna," he said, "put dis silber mit der du-bit piece dat you got last Christmas. Py jimminy, dis war is big luck for some peebles."[27]

Gordon told a story of a Pennsylvanian who found his stall empty and would not be solaced with Confederate money. "I've been married, sir, t'ree times," he said, "and I vood not geef dot mare for all dose voomans."[28]

A sincere admirer of women, Gordon was not impressed by the words, but because of the man's acute anguish he had the mare returned.

While Ewell's corps tarried in Chambersburg, its assistant quarter-master, Captain Sandy Garber, learned how poignantly the memory of Jackson lingered with his old foot cavalry. Garber came into camp late and did not know the countersign. At the outpost he was halted by a diligent sentry. Groping about for something that might serve the purpose, he drew from his blouse an old pass which had been signed by Stonewall. The sentry lighted a match and read the pass carefully. His eyes lingered fondly over the signature. He handed it back, looked up at the stars and said sadly, "Captain, you can go to Heaven on that pass, but you can't get by this post."[29]

Jackson was remembered also in unexpected quarters. Seeing an elderly woman on a porch, Major Stiles requested water for his horse. She gave permission and invited him to rest, and consented to mail a letter for him to a sister living in New Haven, Connecticut. She asked if he had ever seen Stonewall Jackson and when he answered yes, she said she expected to see Jackson soon. It startled Stiles, but she explained, "If any one ever left this earth who went straight to Heaven, it was he."[30] Born in Virginia, she had been taken to Pennsylvania when a girl, but home was still across the river.

When Correspondent Ross reached Chambersburg, McLaws' division was marching through "in high spirits." That day he heard the Rebel yell, a "very peculiar sound," which could be heard a mile off. "They learned it from the Indians I believe."[31] He noticed that most of the Confederate bands were composed of Germans, and explained that the Southerners are "extremely fond of music" but had never taken the trouble to learn to play, as this had always been done for them by slaves.

3. Lee Touches the Map at Gettysburg

While waiting near Hagerstown on June 26, Lee held another meeting with Old Trimble, who suggested that a brigade be sent to capture Baltimore and stir Maryland into action. The state had responded indifferently to Lee on his first invasion, but Trimble was hopeful Maryland could be shaken out of her lethargy by vigorous measures. Lee thought well of the plan and wrote to A. P. Hill, whose corps was then closest at hand, asking if he could spare a brigade for a descent on Baltimore. It would have been a bold move to sever Washington from the North, but the detachment of a brigade for operations that far from the main army would have been hazardous indeed, as Lee must have recognized. In any event, when Hill said it would weaken his corps too severely, Lee did not pursue the matter.

That afternoon he called Trimble to his tent again,[32] unfolded a map of Pennsylvania, and began to inquire about the topography of the country east of the South Mountain range, the continuation of the Blue Ridge north of the Potomac. He was interested in Adams County and the terrain around Gettysburg.

"As a civil engineer," he said to Trimble, "you may know more about it than any of us." Trimble described the area and explained that every square mile contained good battle positions or ground for maneuvering.

"Our army is in good spirits," Lee continued, "not overfatigued, and can be concentrated at any one point in twenty-four hours or less. I have not yet heard that the enemy have crossed the Potomac and am waiting to hear from General Stuart. When they hear where we are, they will make forced marches to interpose their forces between us and Baltimore and Philadelphia. They will come up, probably through Frederick, broken down with hunger and hard marching, strung out on a long line, and much demoralized when they come into Pennsylvania. I shall throw an overwhelming force on their advance, crush it, follow up the success, drive one corps back on another, and by successive repulses and surprises before they can concentrate create a panic and virtually destroy the army."

Trimble said he recalled and recorded the words "nearly verbatim." They give the clearest view available of what was in Lee's mind when the campaign began to take focus. Lee then asked Trimble's opinion and Trimble said the plan should prove successful.

"I never knew the men in finer spirits," he added.

"That is, I hear, the general impression," Lee responded. As he brought the interview to a close, he put his hand to the map and touched Gettysburg.

"Hereabout we shall probably meet the enemy and fight a great battle, and if God gives us the victory, the war will be over and we shall achieve the recognition of our independence." Then he instructed Trimble: "General Ewell's forces are by this time in Harrisburg; if not, go and join him and help him take the place."

The astute Jacob Hoke busily conversed with the Confederates and kept a record of everything that happened in Chambersburg. While Washington groped to know whether the blow would fall against Harrisburg and Philadelphia, or whether Lee would turn back toward the capital and Baltimore, Hoke thought of a ready means of answering the question, to his own satisfaction at least.

Chambersburg was at an important crossroads. As the Southern troops passed through, some of them turned—at the diamond, or public square—onto the road from Pittsburgh to Baltimore which ran toward Cashtown and Gettysburg; others continued straight ahead, toward Harrisburg, thus giving no clew to the real direction of the army. But Hoke decided that he would watch the direction Lee himself selected, and thus would know the Southern commander's true aims.

At length, there was a break in the long line of infantry and General A. P. Hill stopped in front of a grocery store. Townsmen crowded about and someone asked when Lee would come.

"I expect him at any minute," Hill replied. He glanced down the main street and added, "There he comes now."[33]

The crowd stirred and all heads turned instantly. Riding along the shaded street beneath the arching trees, mounted on a tall, gray, slim-ankled horse and followed by a small staff, came the awesome figure of Southern victory.

Lee paused at the grocery store to converse privately with Hill. They talked briefly, then Lee remounted, took up the reins, and moved to the divergence of the highways. A tingle must have passed through Hoke as he witnessed this drama of his own deduction.

The cavalryman's pressure of the left rein fell gently across the horse's neck. The ears of the spirited steed pointed upward, and Lee turned sharply to the right. It must be Baltimore and Washington and battle with the Army of the Potomac.[34]

The deduction was judged valid enough for Hoke and other Union sympathizers in Chambersburg to rush off a messenger to Governor Curtin in Harrisburg, who relayed it to Halleck in Washington. It was the first information reaching the War Department that Lee might be turning toward the South Mountain passes.

Lee stopped on the Cashtown Pike on the eastern outskirts of Chambersburg and set up his headquarters at Shetter's Woods, a place where Fourth of July picnics were held. Farmers who at first had fled now crowded into Chambersburg for a closer look at the Confederates. The town was packed with Northern civilians and Southern soldiers. The headquarters grove was soon as busy as any Pennsylvania public square on Saturday morning. One of Lee's early acts was to issue an order for flour to be distributed to the needy of the town.[35]

Lee was joined on June 27 by Longstreet, who set up his headquarters near by. Sorrel saw the many visitors who went to Lee's headquarters, usually with trumped-up complaints, and judged that they merely wanted to see the two celebrated soldiers.[36]

At Chambersburg Hood paid his respects to Lee, whom he found in "the same buoyant spirits which pervaded his magnificent army." Lee greeted him and exclaimed, "Ah, General, the enemy is a long time finding us. If he does not succeed soon, we must go in search of him."[37] There was no hint of defensive tactics here.

In Maryland and Pennsylvania Lee apparently made the mistake of eating an abundance of fresh fruit. The entire army indulged in the cherries. On his earlier invasion of Maryland a lad named Leighton Parks had met him and now Parks returned with a quantity of raspberries for the general. Fresh raw fruit undoubtedly was the cause of Lee's partial indisposition on the second day of the battle of Gettysburg.

4. The General Has a Well-Worn Coat

Most of those who encountered Lee at this period commented on his handsome strength. Age had given serenity to what had always been a reserved bearing. He was then in his fifty-seventh year. His hair, black at the outbreak of the war, was grizzled after little more than two years of conflict. In place of the black mustache he wore a full gray beard. The alertness of his posture and graveness of his countenance were softened by gentle brown eyes. "Sad eyes!" wrote Sorrel.[38] "The saddest it seems to me of all men's—beaming the highest intelligence and with unvarying kindliness. . . ."

George Cary Eggleston felt that the war years altered Lee's appearance so sharply that a picture of the middle-aged man of the spring of 1861 would scarcely have been recognized as that of the general with furrowed face and whitened hair and beard. But the furrows added intensity to his commanding appearance. He was a large man with a big head and a countenance which told instantly of his high character and "perfect balance of faculties, mental, moral and physical."[39] A Northerner who saw him commented on his large neck. "Yes" was the ready reply of a Confederate soldier. "It takes a damn big neck to hold his head."[40]

Although Eggleston spoke of Lee's grace of movement, the quality that he found most emphasized was Lee's "robustness," a term applicable both physically and mentally. "If his shapely person suggested a remarkable capacity for endurance, his manner, his countenance and his voice quite as strongly hinted at [his] great soul."[41]

Sorrel was impressed with "the perfect poise of head and shoulders," and said, "his white teeth and winning smile were irresistible." True to the pattern of the southern planter, he liked the company of ladies and "had a good memory for pretty girls."[42] The sophisticated Mrs. Chesnut said she "blushed like a schoolgirl" when Lee smiled at her in recognition as they were leaving church.[43]

Lee possessed a trait of continuous activity suggesting strong extroversion. When not otherwise engaged he took rambles of inspection about post or camp. Eggleston saw him in South Carolina in the winter of 1861-1862 when he was on detached service strengthening the coastal defenses. He would wander unescorted through the stables and gun park almost every afternoon. As he wore no insignia of rank, he excited curiosity. "I say, sergeant," exclaimed a teamster, "who is that darned old fool? He's always pokin' round my horses just as if he meant to steal one of 'em."[44]

Eggleston became an established author after the war and eventually a trenchant editorial writer of the rejuvenated New York *World,* where one of Joseph Pulitzer's main requirements was terseness. During the war he was attentive to Lee's concise language. A competent judge, he found the words chosen happily. "A single sentence from his lips left nothing more to be said." Many of Lee's remarks were recorded by his auditors in the stilted rhetoric of the day and must lack the crispness of their original form, but they still suggest that he usually thought and spoke with compactness.

Lieutenant Colonel Fremantle, introduced to Lee by Longstreet, judged him "the handsomest man of his age I ever saw." Lee was "tall, broadshouldered, very well made, well set up, a thorough soldier in appearance."[45] During this campaign he wore a long gray jacket that showed age, and hence seemed in keeping with an army dressed largely in homespun. His hat on this campaign was a high black felt. His blue trousers were tucked into Wellington boots. These were high leather boots covering the knee in front but cut low behind. The only evidence of rank were the three stars on his collar. Despite his worn coat Fremantle found his appearance "smart and clean." He never carried firearms but always had his binoculars handy, carried in a strap around his neck in battle.

Other qualities which impressed this British observer were the courteous dignity of his manner and his complete freedom from small vices. "His bitterest enemies never accused him of any of the greater ones." Fremantle also was impressed by the fact that Lee was a campaigner and camper in the fullest sense. The general had not slept in a house since assuming command of the Army of Northern Virginia more than a year before.

At Chambersburg British correspondent Ross called at headquarters. After Lee's council with Longstreet and A. P. Hill, Ross was presented to him, and Lee invited him to a modest dinner. "The general has little of the glorious pomp and circumstance of war about his person," the writer said. At the headquarters were tents, baggage wagons, ambulances, and a private carriage, or ambulance, for the personal service of the commanding general. It had been captured from the Federal general John Pope, but Lee preferred his mount, Traveler, and never used it.

5. "Washington . . . There Was None Like Him"

Perhaps none had a closer grasp of Lee's character and habits than his military secretary, Colonel Long, who was by his side at Gettysburg. Lee, he said, was not only abstemious but was "pained" by intemperance in subordinates. "I cannot consent to place in the control of others one who cannot control himself."[46] Lee, according to Long, never used tobacco in his life. On rare occasions he took a glass of wine but not whisky or brandy.

Lee had a nice conception of the limits of the military authority. Benjamin Harvey Hill, who served as chairman of the Judiciary Committee of the Confederate Senate, declared the commanding general had contempt for "military statesmen and political generals," and never expressed his views to the Congress, the President or even friends, on public questions not strictly military.

Hill once met him on a Richmond street.[47] "General," he said, "I wish you would give me your opinion as to the propriety of changing the seat of government, and going further South."

"That is a political question, Mr. Hill, and you politicians must determine it," Lee replied. "I shall endeavor to take care of the army and you must make the laws and control the government."

"Ah, General," Hill continued, "you will have to change that rule, and form and express political opinions; for, if we establish our independence, the people will make you Mr. Davis' successor."

"Never, sir," Lee asserted firmly. "That I will never permit. Whatever talents I may possess, and they are but limited, are military talents. My education and training are military. I think the military and civil talents are distinct, if not different, and full duty in either sphere is about as much as one man can qualify himself to perform. I shall not do the people the injustice to accept high civil office, with whose questions it has not been my business to become familiar."

Hill was insistent. "Well, General," he countered; "history does not sustain your view. Caesar and Frederick of Prussia and Bonaparte were all great statesmen as well as great generals."

"And all great tyrants," Lee replied quickly. "I speak of the proper rule in republics, where, I think, we should have neither military statesmen nor political generals."

"But Washington was both, and yet not a tyrant."

At that General Lee's face took on a beautiful smile and he spoke with finality: "Washington was an exception to all rule, and there was none like him."[48]

Hood, who had a strong affection for his chief, found greatness in Lee's willingness to perform humble tasks. Hood had served under Lee in the 2nd Cavalry in Texas. Upon reaching Richmond after the outbreak of war he naturally reported to his old superior. Lee had an office on the fourth floor of the Mechanics Institute. Gathered around him was every cobbler in Richmond. Lee was showing them how to make cartridge boxes, haversacks, bayonets and scabbards, of which the Confederacy was destitute. "He was studiously employing his great mind to this apparently trivial but most important work."[49]

This care about details had to be sacrificed at times in the interest of allowing others to discharge their responsibilities but it was deep in Lee's character. One of his near relatives emphasized the quality, describing it as a "beautiful neatness and love of order."[50] Mrs. Lee told how he returned from the Mexican war "with every article of clothing he had taken with him, and a bottle of brandy which he had taken in case of sickness, *unopened*."[51] Some have questioned Lee's scholarship, saying he was not a careful student of military history like Jackson, or even a habitual reader. But his attentiveness to details and mental orderliness implies capacity as a student, and such Lee showed not only at West Point, where he was second in his class, but also in the school of Benjamin Hallowell at Alexandria, Virginia, where he studied mathematics in the winter of 1824-1825. Hallowell said Lee was never behind in his studies and observed all the rules perfectly, but his specialty was finishing with a neatness and completeness everything he undertook. In making complicated diagrams for a course in conic sections, he used a slate for his drawings which obviously had no permanency. But according to the school principal he drew each one of them "with as much accuracy and finish, lettering and all, as if it were to be engraved and printed."[52]

Nevertheless, he shunned army paper work and simplified it as much as possible. "I never presented a paper . . . unless it was of decided importance," said his chief of staff, Colonel Charles Marshall.[53] One of his rules was that petitioners for clemency should not be admitted. He asked to be spared the anguish of meeting relatives of condemned men whose cases had been decided by court-martial. He favored conciliation in personal grievances. When he received a written complaint from an officer, he usually passed it over to Marshall with the instructions, " 'Suage him, Colonel, 'suage him."[54]

A revealing incident is cited by Marshall. A caller having a complaint against the Confederate government gained access to the headquarters tent and punished Lee with a long rant. When he finally departed Lee came out "flushed in anger" and delivered a severe rebuke. "Why did you permit that man to come to my tent and make me show my anger?"[55] If necessary, he could be patient during the strain of unnecessary talk. Marshall said he had never heard Lee speak of

President Davis in any except terms of kindly respect, but he did comment once, after being closeted with Davis for several hours, that "he had lost a good deal of time in fruitless talk."[56]

The soldiers knew how compassionate he could be in a reprimand. After Chancellorsville he stopped in front of a Mississippi boy who had been wounded in the hand. The lad said, "By God, General, the Yankees have done me up, but we have given them hell."

"Well, you are a brave soldier but you must not swear," Lee replied. Then he jumped from his horse, took out a white linen handkerchief, bandaged the wound, made a sling from another silk handkerchief, and sent the lad to the hospital to get a better dressing.[57]

A Missive Among the Roses

1. *"Extra Billy" Parades into York*

In response to Lee's orders, Ewell began a wide movement toward Harrisburg, intending to employ Early and Rodes as his attacking force and use Johnson in reserve to maintain contact with the balance of the army. Rodes moved through Greencastle and Chambersburg to Carlisle. Early marched by Waynesboro and halted on June 25 on the Chambersburg-Gettysburg pike at Greenwood. At daybreak June 26 he moved toward Gettysburg.

Early was accompanied by a battalion of cavalry under Colonel Elijah V. White, a scant complement for work of the magnitude cut out for him. As the eastern wing of Lee's army, he was, in fact, serving the role of Stuart's absent squadrons. Preceded by the meager cavalry detail, he took three of his brigades over the wet dirt roads through Hilltown to Mummasburg, while he detached Gordon's brigade to march on the macadam through Cashtown to Gettysburg.

En route he had the pleasure of burning the Caledonia Iron Works owned by the vociferous anti-Southern Congressman, Thaddeus Stevens. John Sweeney, the manager, argued that the only persons Early would hurt were poor people who would be thrown out of employment and said the industry was unprofitable.

"That's not the way Yankees do business," Early answered sourly as he ordered up the torches.[1]

On learning that Gettysburg was occupied by a Federal force of unknown strength, he directed Gordon to amuse it in front while he

55

endeavored to gain its rear. But before reaching Gettysburg he learned that White's cavalry had already encountered the Federals, who proved to be the 26th Pennsylvania Militia, containing a company of Gettysburg townsmen. They had formed an irresolute line on the heights west of Gettysburg but fled across the fields toward Mummasburg when the Southern troopers, followed by Gordon's infantry, appeared. Hays sent two regiments to help White pursue them and 175 were captured and paroled.[2]

Early and Gordon entered Gettysburg in a downpour on the evening of June 26. The town was placid and unresisting and had little the Confederates might want. Early seized 2,000 rations found on some railroad cars, issued them to Gordon's brigade, and then burned the cars.[3] He requisitioned clothing, provisions and $10,000 in currency. Mayor Kendlehart representing the town authorities answered that it was impossible to comply because the quantities requested were far beyond what Gettysburg possessed.

Early had to move to York at daybreak the next morning and did not have time to investigate the town's resources, which he judged to be limited. It seemed a trivial matter, but had he done so the conditions of the campaign probably would have been greatly altered. He sent back word to Hill's men, who were soon on the road from Chambersburg to Cashtown, that the town had been touched lightly and possessed a supply of shoes.

White's cavalry destroyed the railroad bridges toward Hanover Junction while the infantry was again put on the road eastward. Gordon still moved on the macadam, the other brigades in the mud. Ahead was York, once the capital of the American continental government,[4] but in 1863 only the trade center of one of the richest farming communities of the Northern states.

On the following morning, with the division near the town, it was Smith's turn to head the column.

Brigadier General William ("Extra Billy") Smith, commanding the third brigade of Jubal Early's division, was a Virginian who symbolically tied the secession era to the days of Monroe and Andrew Jackson. He had served as Governor of Virginia during the War with Mexico, and now, just prior to Lee's march to Pennsylvania, he had been elected to the same office for the term beginning January 1, 1864. None in the South surpassed him as a politician of personal magnetism and instinctive leadership. His generalship, however, was proving deficient, and Early judged it advisable at times to keep his brigade in the close proximity of that of Gordon so that the Georgian could exercise what amounted to a joint command. Smith had not had a happy introduction to the military, for at the beginning of his career he had read law in the Baltimore office of William Henry Winder, the Maryland attorney who commanded the American army at the battle of Bladensburg, where his ludicrous tactics exposed Washington to capture by the British invading army in the War of 1812.

The name "Extra Billy," by which Smith was known to both North and South, had been the inspiration of Senator Benjamin W. Leigh of Virginia. As a mail contractor in Jackson's administration, Smith had once handled a daily postal service between Washington, D.C., and Milledgeville, Georgia, and had extended it to numerous spur routes, for which he received extra payments. When Postmaster General William T. Barry came under political attack for increasing payments to contractors, Smith's "extras" were disclosed. Hence the sobriquet. He served a number of terms in the Federal Congress prior to the war.

Major Robert Stiles, of the Confederate artillery, who was riding with Extra Billy across southern Pennsylvania, had been reared from early boyhood in New York City, and had been graduated from Yale in 1859, but having been Georgia-born, he had elected to fight for the South. He had first seen Smith when he had sat in the House galleries to hear the prolonged speakership debate of 1859-1860, in which the Virginian had been active. Now he was about to witness the high point of the old politician's career, his entry of York, Pennsylvania, amid antics that delighted both friend and enemy.

York, in the path of the invasion, had built no defenses, although redoubts were being thrown up at Philadelphia and even New York was sending valuables to Poughkeepsie for storage. As Early's division approached, the mayor came out to surrender,[5] followed by a deputation of citizens with notice that the populace would not resist. Stiles, being certain that "there would be a breeze blowing at the head of the column,"[6] as he put it, rode up to where he could observe Extra Billy.

Smith was instructing his son and aide, Fred, to hurry up the music. "Go back and look up those tooting fellows and tell them to come up here and march into town tooting 'Yankee Doodle' in their best style."[7]

Quickly the band appeared, the June sun glinting off their polished brass, but the refrain they were playing was "Dixie." As they reached the head of the column, however, they struck up the Northern song as a compliment to the good citizens of the old continental capital. Smith might have been leading any Virginia torchlight political procession.

His hat off, he rode into town bowing to crowds, first on one side then the other, saluting especially every pretty girl "with that manly, hearty smile which no man or woman ever doubted or resisted."[8] Stiles noticed that the attitude of the York residents changed from astonishment to pleasure, until finally, when the head of the column reached the town square, they broke out into a hearty cheer for Extra Billy. Most of the citizens were on the street. Bells were ringing and the crowds were going to church. Now they congregated at the square. The pack became so dense that the gray column which the Northern army often had been unable to slow in battle, was surrounded and finally halted by the crowd of curious, milling, peacefully disposed citizens. Smith cleared enough room for his men to stack arms. He did not dismount, but from his saddle he launched into "a rattling, humorous speech," which both the Pennsylvanians and his own brigade applauded.[9]

"My friends," he said, "how do you like this way of coming back into the Union? I hope you like it; I have been in favor of it for a good while. . . . We are not burning your houses or butchering your children. On the contrary, we are behaving ourselves like Christian gentlemen, which we are."

He rambled on, explaining the reason for the invasion. "We needed a summer outing and thought we would take it in the North, instead of patronizing the Virginia springs, as we generally do. We regret to say our trunks haven't gotten up yet; we were in such a hurry to see you that we could not wait for them." Then he gave a brief picture of his brigade. "They are such a hospitable, wholehearted, fascinating lot of gentlemen. . . ." He invited the Yorkers to remain. "You are quite welcome to stay here and make yourselves at home, so long as you behave yourselves pleasantly and agreeably as you are doing now."

The speech might have continued during the sermon hours but Stiles heard a commotion back in the crowd, then a stream of oaths emitted in the "piping, querulous treble" that belonged to the irascible commander of Ewell's first division. Jubal Early, riding with Gordon's brigade, had found the street obstructed by Extra Billy's rally. Early had difficulty in elbowing his way through.

Smith, amid his exhortations, was not aware of his superior's approach until Early caught his blouse, jerked him around rudely and half-screamed, "General Smith, what in the devil are you about, stopping the head of this column in this cursed town!"

"Having a little fun, General," Smith replied good-naturedly, "which is good for all of us."[10]

Stiles observed that "even Jube did not dare curse the old general in an offensive way." Smith ordered his troops to fall in and he then marched to Laucks Mills, near the railroad two miles north of York. There he was joined by Hays's brigade and the road was cleared for the passage of Gordon toward the Susquehanna River.

2. Prompted by a Potential Catherine

General Gordon had breakfasted with a Pennsylvanian whose peculiar dining room was built directly over a spring, so that half of the room was floored with smooth limestone while the other half was a bubbling fountain of clear, fresh water. After the dusty marches, the cool room plus a meal of hot biscuits and milk and cream fresh from the rippling water were novelties the Georgian remembered into late life.[11]

Gordon entered York while the bells were still pealing and the sidewalks were filled with churchgoers. Amid the finery he felt apologetic about the slovenly appearance of his marching column, begrimed from the fine white dust of the macadamized pike. The grotesque nature of his column was accentuated by the barefoot men riding double on huge shaggy horses.

Hoke's brigade followed those of Smith and Gordon and entered York to the cadence of church bells. Colonel Hamilton C. Jones of the 57th North Carolina had been impressed with the calmness of the country through which they had marched and attributed it as much to the phlegmatic disposition of the population as to the restraint of the troops. Barns were filled and the fields were dotted with cattle; the quartermaster provided for the army's food "in an orderly way." There was virtually no straggling. He found that in York the crowds gazed at the Confederate troops "with something like stupefaction. . . ."[12] They gave up thought of church, the ladies went home and the men hobnobbed with the Confederates with little evidence of bitterness." Civilians and officers "drank together and discussed the war."[13] The ardent Union men expressed their sentiments freely but Colonel Jones thought a majority "were bitterly hostile to Mr. Lincoln's administration and condemned the war."[14] Hoke's brigade was quartered in York in a large building erected as a hospital.

Gordon halted his troops on the main street and rode forward, reassuring a group of ladies by saying that "York could have the head of any soldier who destroyed private property or insulted a woman."[15]

As he rode a girl about twelve years old rushed up to his horse and handed him a bunch of roses. He noticed a note in the center of the bouquet and found it was written in a delicate, feminine hand. It gave the number and description of Federal forces at Wrightsville, the Susquehanna River town twenty miles ahead that was his immediate objective.

"I carefully read and reread this strange note," he said. "It bore no signature and contained no assurance of sympathy for the Southern cause, but it was so terse and explicit in its terms as to compel my confidence."[16]

Gordon marched rapidly through the hot June day to gain the Susquehanna River bridge that was the key to Ewell's plan for the capture of Harrisburg. Early planned to cross with his full division, capture Lancaster, sever the main railroad connecting Philadelphia with the west, then move up the Susquehanna and approach Harrisburg from the rear while Rodes, moving from Carlisle, would invest it in front. If Harrisburg fell, Early would mount his division on Pennsylvania horses and raid westward, destroying railroads and canals.[17]

Wrightsville, a small town sleeping on the river opposite the larger community of Columbia, had not changed greatly since Revolutionary War days, when the Continental Congress had fled through it seeking a place to hold sessions during the British occupation of Philadelphia. But while Wrightsville slept, greatness had hovered over it, then passed it by. After the British burned Washington in 1814 sentiment developed in Congress for a removal of the seat of government farther west.[18] Wrightsville was mentioned and soon appeared to be highly favored. But opinion congealed to retain Washington as the capital city and Wrightsville was forgotten. Now the town on the Susquehanna was to have the simple distinction of marking the northeastern march of the Confederate army.

The note the little girl had handed Gordon suggested that he halt when he arrived at the ridge overlooking Wrightsville and examine the position of the Federal troops. From the ridge Gordon looked out over the beautiful Pennsylvania country, green and golden with corn and wheat. Immediately below him, in full view, nestled the town on one of the most beautiful of American rivers. Beyond it was the low, wide bridge he was to capture. It was a mile and a quarter long, a wooden superstructure set on stone pillars.

On its single span was a railroad, a roadway for vehicles and a towpath for the canal which here crossed the Susquehanna. In front of it was the blue line of soldiers precisely as they had been described by the missive among the roses. Their front ran along a lower ridge between Gordon and the river, and to the right was the gorge, just as described, which permitted an approach around the left flank of the Federal defending force.

Finding the note completely accurate, Gordon did not fear to follow its suggestion and move down the gorge toward the rear of the Federals, hoping to surround and capture them. The general was amazed at the military perspicacity of his correspondent, whose handwriting was clearly that of a woman, and "whose evident genius for war . . . might have made her a captain equal to Catherine."[19] Who was she? Gordon never knew.

Confronting Gordon were sensitive Pennsylvania militiamen who had no intention of being trapped. Already combustibles had been placed on the bridge preparatory to the flight of its guards. On the bursting of the third Confederate shell the militia retired hurriedly across the span, lighting the fire at the center as they passed.[20] The flames had made good headway before Gordon and his men reached the structure. The general tried to push on but was beaten back by the flames. The soldiers fought the fire as best they could while Gordon called on Wrightsville citizens for buckets. Blandly the townspeople reported that none could be found.

Flames ate at the wooden structure in both directions. At the southern bank a Wrightsville lumber yard caught fire and from it the flames soon leaped to the town. Now the buckets, pails, tubs and cans which Gordon had called for in vain suddenly appeared in abundance, and soldiers and citizens together labored to save the houses. A bucket brigade reached up from the river, and through the afternoon and night they worked until, late at night, the flames were extinguished.

The fire was arrested just before it reached the home of a kindly lady, Mrs. L. L. Rewalt, who insisted on entertaining Gordon and his officers at breakfast. Gordon found her gracious and self-possessed and wondered about her sympathies. It developed that she was staunchly Unionist and had a husband serving in the Federal army. But the Confederate general and his officers felt great respect for her, willing as she was to recognize a kindly deed from an enemy.[21]

While in York Early requisitioned 2,000 pairs of shoes, 1,000 hats, 1,000 pairs of socks, three days' rations and $100,000 in money. He received the hats and socks, about 1,200 pairs of shoes and 1,500 pairs of boots, but only $28,600.[22] The mayor seemed unable to raise more

and Early felt he had made an honest effort. Early rode to Wrightsville to inspect the ruined bridge—and his thwarted hopes—then ordered
Gordon to return on the next day to York.

3. Serenades and a New Banner

Rodes reached Carlisle on June 27 and remained three days. The rest
was luxurious but temptation was present. The town was loaded with
United States government whisky. Private Joe Duncan, in his foraging,
kicked a haystack and uncovered a full barrel.[23] He took a pail of
whisky back to the North Carolina boys. Plenty of ice was found in
icehouses for those who wanted it. More whisky was discovered. "Mint
juleps in tin cans were plentiful." That night the gay party decided to
serenade the officers. Accompanied by the bands of the 14th and 23rd
North Carolina regiments, they visited the quarters, sang, and called
for speeches.[24] The officers declined in good humor.

In the plain words of Captain Vines E. Turner of the 23rd North
Carolina, "Many of our jaded, weary boys" drank too much.[25] For a
time open hostilities appeared likely with some members of a Georgia
regiment, camped on the campus of Dickinson College, who were likewise "drowning their weariness."[26] Brigadier General Alfred Iverson,
the Georgian commanding a North Carolina brigade, had been stationed
in Carlisle as a lieutenant and now met old friends. One of Ramseur's
men ascribed the loss of Gettysburg two days later to the liquor found
in Carlisle and did not hesitate to name Iverson as showing the effects
on the battlefield.[27]

At Carlisle the mail came up from Richmond and Brigadier General Dod Ramseur got a backlog of letters. His practice when he received no letters was to make "spirit visits" to his fiancée, Miss Ellen
Richmond of Milton, North Carolina, whom he addressed as "My
Heart's Precious Darling." He wrote her ardent, graceful letters, and—
unlike Pickett—was discreet about military matters.

"Our advance has been wonderfully rapid and gloriously successful,"
he had said from Greencastle. "Our troops are in the finest spirits and
when we meet the enemy's horde we will give a good account of
ourselves."

He answered at once the letters reaching him at Carlisle: "Are you
surprised to find that we are so far advanced into the Enemy's territory? We are; or rather we are surprised that we have met with so
feeble resistance so far." He mentioned that the Federal barracks had
been well stocked. "This morning I breakfasted on salmon left in ice."

Saying it would not be prudent to detail the army's plans, he commented, "Let this suffice, they are bold and well conceived."[28]

The troops that were shooting off and receiving sparks from the North Carolinians were Doles's Georgia brigade which had forded the Potomac at sunset on the first day of the crossing and bivouacked on the edge of Williamsport. Here the men were given time to rest feet that were bruised and swollen by the rapid marching. On June 19 they broke camp, halted again for two days beyond Hagerstown and on June 22 entered Pennsylvania. They marched through Chambersburg on June 24 with bands blaring "Dixie" and arms at the right shoulder shift, exchanging banter with civilians they described as "gloomy-faced." "Here's your played-out rebellion,"[29] some of them shouted to an assembled group. When finally bivouacked on the Dickinson College campus in Carlisle, twenty miles from Harrisburg, they were "elated with the hope that we would have that city before the setting of another sun."[30]

At Carlisle the 32nd North Carolina regiment was signally honored. The official flag of the Confederate States, red with its cross of blue, which was to become so familiar to the South, was first unfurled by this regiment. The design of the flag had been adopted shortly before by the Confederate Congress[31] and was the last of the several flags flown by the Southern armies. Richmond ladies immediately made a banner of the new design and sent it to General Lee for his approval and for presentation to the regiment he judged most worthy to carry it. Lee did not make that decision but in honor of the departed Jackson sent it to Ewell, commanding Jackson's corps. Ewell passed it on to "his favorite division commander,"[32] Robert Rodes, who in turn sent it to the officer described as "his most favored brigadier," General Junius Daniel. Daniel's brigade had just come up from North Carolina and had not served under Rodes earlier. Its selection could be explained only as a compromise or on personal grounds. Neither Rodes nor Daniel survived the war to explain. Daniel designated the 32nd North Carolina as entitled to the honor.

On June 29 all of the Confederate troops in Carlisle, the major part of Rodes's division, were paraded on the spacious grounds of the United States army barracks which later became the Carlisle Indian School. Ewell and many of his officers had been stationed here before the war. "Oh! it was a grand occasion," said Private Henry A. London, of Company I of the favored regiment. He found it in "striking contrast with the sad scenes witnessed by the same soldiers, two days thereafter,

on the blood-stained heights at Gettysburg." The proud flag of the
Confederacy, crimson as the blood shed so freely beneath it, was
hoisted on the flagpole above the barracks, to meet the Northern breeze.
"And thus it was," recorded the historian of the 32nd, "that North
Carolinians can boast that it was the flag of one of their regiments that
defiantly waved on the enemy's soil at a point farther north than any
other Confederate flag during the whole war." Carlisle is farther north
than Wrightsville.

Ewell's remaining division, that of Major General Edward Johnson,
patrolled the left as the corps spread fanlike over this southern Pennsylvania section. The division crossed the Potomac at Shepherdstown,
Steuart's brigade making the passage in midafternoon of June 18.
Steuart rode with his aide and fellow Baltimorian, Lieutenant Randolph H. McKim. As their horses' feet touched Maryland sod, the
fervid and emotional Steuart sprang from the saddle, dropped to his
hands and knees and kissed the beloved soil of his own state. "We loved
Maryland," explained McKim, who followed Steuart's action. "We
felt that she was in bondage against her will, and we burned with desire
to have a part in liberating her."[33]

Steuart commanded one Maryland, two North Carolina and three
Virginia regiments, along with a battery and glamorous Major Harry
Gilmore's cavalry detachment. The Marylanders received a tremendous ovation from the ladies as they passed through Hagerstown, to
camp at midafternoon near the Pennsylvania line. On the next day they
marched through Greencastle, Upton and Mercersburg, then Cove Gap
and up over the Tuscarora Mountain to McConnellsburg. Ewell's left
wing was thus roughly one hundred miles from his right, on the Susquehanna at Wrightsville. Johnson's other brigades marched to Greenwood, a good concentration point for Rodes and Early.

Johnson's men responded with pleasant laughter to ladies who sat
at the upstairs windows and waved Union flags. When the men received
more scornful looks, they asked the names of the maidens and said
they wanted to make vinegar by writing them on pieces of paper and
putting them in bottles of water. A red-haired girl who became insult-
ing was mildly called "Brick-top" and told to put on men's clothing
and join the army.[34] To a group who scoffed at the frayed garments
of some of Johnson's soldiers, a southern Irishman shouted, "Bejabbers,
we always put on our dirty clothes when we go hog killing."[35]

McKim rode with Gilmore, one of the several giants among Steuart's
officers, and as powerful with his profanity as with his muscles. The

devout McKim, who aspired to the ministry, was amused to hear Gilmore tell a Pennsylvania farmer, amid bursts of oaths, that the Confederates were certain of victory because the army from Lee down was "composed of Christian gentlemen." Apparently observing the questioning glint in the sharp farmer's eye, Gilmore explained that he was the exception.[36]

From McConnellsburg, which was soon occupied by Imboden's cavalry coming up from Hancock, Steuart marched toward Harrisburg, by way of Green Village and Shippensburg, and camped at Big Spring. The rapid nature of his movement may be seen from the note in McKim's diary, that he slept only twelve hours in five days. At Springfield, near Big Spring, he bought seven copies of the New Testament for use among the troops. "The surprise of the storekeeper when an officer of the terrible Rebel army desired to purchase copies of the New Testament may be imagined," he wrote that night.[37] Through June 28 Steuart's men pressed toward Harrisburg, many of them marching barefoot. The shoes with which even the better-clad men had left the Rappahannock were beginning to give way and replacements had been scant.

The loose, almost trusting nature of the Confederates can be understood from the ease with which an adventurous correspondent of the New York *Herald* walked through Lee's army and casually interviewed privates and generals. Wanting to see the Confederates firsthand, he rode west from Gettysburg to find them. Soon he came to a tall, "well looking personage, very dignified and gentlemanly in manner" with a full beard and a major general's uniform. It was Early en route to York. He wore "a capacious brown hat, looped up on the right side, resting easily on his head." The journalist caught Early at a favorable moment, one of the rare times when the general was not doubled up with arthritis.

The newsman told Early that he wanted a pass to go home to the Cumberland valley. The general answered in "a sharp and decisive manner but still without being tinged with anything like discourtesy."

"I have no time to attend to you just now," Early said, "but if it is proper for you to go, there will be no obstructions offered to your departure."

The New Yorker mingled with the soldiers and noticed that private property was respected rigidly by both soldiers and officers. Those staying in the hotels paid with Confederate script. Behind Early's lines he met three Irishmen from New Orleans with a canteen of whisky.

They had been in all of Stonewall Jackson's campaigns, declared they
had never been whipped, and said the Yankees couldn't raise enough
men to do it.

"By my sowl," one was quoted, "we'll fight till the last man ov us
is kilt, and thin, be jabers, the women will take a hand in it. You may
fight us for all eternity, and then we won't be whipped afther all!"

He found that Early's men had no love for the general and the Irish
stragglers said they knew several men who would shoot him "just as
quick as they would a 'damned Yankee.'" But they all appeared to
be fond of Ewell.

He drove past the smoldering ruins of the Stevens iron works and
ran into A. P. Hill's corps, which had advanced fifteen miles on that
day and was bivouacked along the roadside from Greenwood to
Fayetteville. Foragers were coming in loaded with chickens, butter,
eggs, and all kinds of vegetables. "I passed through the entire corps
of A. P. Hill without difficulty or having any questions asked me. I
pushed boldly ahead, as if I had a perfect right to do so," he said. Was
Lee's army naïve? Or was it so self-confident as to be indifferent about
espionage?

Finally he came to Stouffertown, where he heard that Lee was
camped in a near-by woods. When he asked where Lee might be found,
one soldier pointed to "a tall, fine looking officer, sitting in front of a
spacious tent, with one leg crossed over the other." Lee's head was
depressed and his eyes were resting "evidently vacantly" on the ground.
"He appeared to be in deep thought, and seemingly did not notice what
was occurring around him." Undoubtedly he was still pondering over
what to do without Stuart.

The correspondent came at last to the Texans in Longstreet's corps.
One was demonstrating his dexterity with a lasso by throwing it over
the head of a mounted officer. As the Texans marched, a "Union dog"
came out and barked at the column and the cowhand roped him neatly.
Almost every regiment had either a fife and drum corps or a brass
band and all were playing "Dixie," the "Bonnie Blue Flag," or "Massa's
in the Cold, Cold Ground." The correspondent was able to get through
and file his story, which must have given the North a clear impression
of the carefree spirit of the Southern host.[38]

Hooker and Meade Pursue

1. Hooker Would Trust the Yeomanry

To "Old Joe Hooker," butt of the chant the Confederates sang around the Chancellorsville wilderness, fell the task of replying to Lee's maneuver, either by following him into the Shenandoah, moving hot on his flank and crowding and harassing him into engagements that would halt his progress, or devising better measures to thwart his invasion plans.

Hooker, as much of an enigma to the Army of the Potomac as to history, was unhurried about any sort of response. After he learned at the battle of Fleetwood that Lee was moving his infantry, he devoted three days to reflecting and writing letters. Although the Federal cavalry was alert and combative, he was informed by a friendly Negro, not by his scouts, that on June 12 Ewell had passed through Sperryville on the eastern slope of the Blue Ridge.

That night Hooker decided to break up his Falmouth encampment on the familiar heights above the Rappahannock, which the Federal army had come to regard almost as home. Scarcely were his leading units on the march before he was rudely awakened by the disaster to Milroy at Winchester.

Hooker's correspondence with Lincoln after June 5, the day on which he reported that Lee was north of the Rappahannock, was anything but satisfactory and consisted largely of Lincoln's denial of his recommendations. On that date Hooker suggested that in case Lee went north, he might go south. He would cross the Rappahannock and attack Hill's force left to defend the old lines. This provoked from Lincoln the homely warning not to be entangled with the river, "like an ox jumped half over the fence and liable to be torn by dogs front and rear, without a fair chance to gore one way or kick the other."[1]

He wrote to Lincoln again on June 10 that if Lee's infantry were moving north, there could be nothing to interpose "any serious obstacle to my rapid advance on Richmond."[2] This plan became known as "swapping Queens," Washington for Richmond. Lincoln replied four hours later that he would not go south of the Rappahannock if Lee were north of it.

The President disclosed a heavy memory of McClellan's operations when he patiently explained:

If you had Richmond invested today, you would not be able to take it in twenty days; meanwhile your communications, and with them your army, would be ruined. I think Lee's army, and not Richmond, is your sure objective point. If he comes toward the Upper Potomac, follow on his flank and on his inside track, shortening your lines while he lengthens his. Fight him, too, when opportunity offers. If he stays where he is, fret him and fret him.[3]

Disgust over the management of the Army of the Potomac was being expressed sharply in a quarter sensitive for President Lincoln. The Chicago *Tribune,* which had been as responsible as any one factor for his elevation to the Presidency, denounced the miserably lax conditions at the front, and the article, timed just before the invasion, was republished in Richmond on June 12. "Higher and higher mounts the summer sun," the Tribune began; "week succeeds week in the rapidly advancing season; time glides rapidly yet stealthily along, and still the great Army of the Potomac rests as quietly and with as much ease on the north bank of the Rappahannock as though it had no great mission to perform." Great pains, the correspondent said, were being taken to fit up Hooker's headquarters "and thus everything conspires to indicate another long reign of inactivity."

Continued lethargy for the army was suggested also by "the prodigality with which leaves of absence are bestowed" on both officers and men. Even the corps commanders were taking vacations. Stoneman was away for honors after his cavalry raid; Howard was "leaving his 'flying Dutchmen' to look after themselves"; Sickles "goes off in a day or two to aid in a little political pipe laying in New York." Others were departing whose presence perhaps would be required if any army movement were meditated.

The *Tribune* summed it up: "Under the leadership of 'fighting Joe Hooker' the glorious Army of the Potomac is becoming more slow in its movements, more unwieldy, less confident in itself, more of a football to the enemy, and less an honor to the country than any army we have yet raised."

On June 15, the day Hill broke camp around Fredericksburg and Ewell crossed the Potomac, the Southern army extended ninety-five air miles from the heights above the Rappahannock to the Maryland shore at Williamsport. Lincoln, observing its length and agitated by the catastrophe at Winchester, told Hooker, "the animal must be pretty slim somewhere in the middle," and wondered if he could not cut it.[4]

Lincoln did not altogether despair of Hooker despite the Chancellorsville fiasco. Hooker, to avoid the unpleasantness of contact with those who distrusted him, had come to ignore Stanton and Halleck as much as possible and corresponded over their heads directly with Lincoln. Lincoln was obviously willing to have Hooker engage the army again, while Stanton and Halleck were emphatically opposed.[5] Sometimes Stanton's fixed notions and schemes stood the Federal government in good stead. He felt strongly that Hooker should be ousted before he had further opportunity to abuse the army and perhaps wreck the Northern cause.[6] The plain fact was, to Stanton, that Hooker had been a bombastic failure.

After Hooker had left the Rappahannock, the Richmond *Examiner* sent a correspondent to Stafford Heights to study the Federal army by what it had left behind.[7] The heights above the Rappahannock were a desolation, stripped of trees and fuel, littered with "innumerable dead horses and men" and camp debris. Huge piles of manure extended in ridges half a mile long where the artillery and cavalry horses had been stabled and cattle penned. Barrels of flour, meats, bags of salt and coffee, boxes of lemons and oranges, and crates of cheese had been burst open and scattered over the countryside in the hasty withdrawal. Much of this food was in good condition, the cases being intact, while fancy articles and luxuries could be found among abandoned suttlers' supplies.

The Richmond scribe had a pleasant time scanning the reading material. He discovered in the officers' quarters occasional copies of the *Atlantic* and *Harper's* but found that "their literature for the most part is of the lowest and most depraved character." More specifically, "the works of licentious French authors, and the blood and thunder productions of Ned Buntline and Sylvanus Cobb, Jr., were strewed about as thick as autumnal leaves in Vallambrose." This literature, he told Southern readers, showed "the most dissolute and abandoned" characteristics of the Army of the Potomac. He threw in the statement that "throughout the winter the camps swarmed with women from the North." The encampments themselves stirred his admiration. They exhibited a "high degree of cleanliness, convenience, and in some instances even elegance."

Firm was the insistence in the North that Hooker should resign. It was not difficult for artful and able operators like Stanton and Halleck, who, distrusting each other in most things, could move in close harmony on matters of mutual interest, to bring that about. Halleck's dislike of Hooker dated back to their California days; Stanton's was based on discernment. The method of obtaining his resignation would have to be by fretting and fretting him, as Lincoln had recommended that Hooker fret Lee.

As the Federal army moved north, Hooker's messages were filled with considerable nonsense. Writing on June 24 that Ewell "is over the river, and is now up the country, I suppose," he hearkened back to the days of King Henry and said that "the yeomanry of that district should be able to check any extended advance of that column, and protect themselves from their aggression."[8] The yeomanry was indeed aroused. Home guards were assembling throughout Pennsylvania, New Jersey and New York—callow youths and portly men to whom a day's marching would be as devastating as a round of Southern bullets.

Hooker's task at the outset was relatively simple—to swing on the inside arc and keep his army interposed between Lee and Washington. Held beneath the restraining hand of Stanton and Lincoln's injunction to guard the capital, he had little discretion and commanded his army merely in semblance. From Falmouth he had moved his headquarters to Dumfries, then Fairfax Court House, while the corps were pushing north by well-planned marches. Hancock's Second Corps was the last to leave the old Falmouth lines, on June 15, the day Ewell's first brigades crossed the Potomac.

Upon withdrawing from Falmouth Hooker divided his army into two wings. The left wing, consisting of the First, Third, and Eleventh corps, he put under Major General John Reynolds, commander of the First Corps. Hooker retained personal command of the left wing, consisting of the Second, Fifth, Sixth, and Twelfth corps.

Brigadier General Gouverneur K. Warren made an investigation at Hooker's request and on June 24 wrote a memorandum recommending an immediate crossing of the Potomac in the neighborhood of Harpers Ferry. While Hooker was preparing to comply, he sent his chief of staff, Major General Daniel Butterfield, to Washington to request that all the troops which could be spared from the Washington and Baltimore garrisons be sent to the main army. The request was altogether reasonable in view of the certainty that the army must soon fight a major battle, but Halleck saw in it an opportunity for fretting tactics.

When Butterfield called at the War Department, Halleck could give him no encouragement. Then he went to the White House. Lincoln was disturbed by the failure of his request and summoned Halleck, who came and reported that there were no troops in Washington that might be spared to reinforce Hooker. "You hear Halleck's answer" was Lincoln's summation of the matter.

The Washington garrison was commanded by Major General Samuel P. Heintzelman, who had been the object of Hooker's barbs and could not be expected to go out of his way to co-operate. He denied Hooker the use of 2,000 men at Poolesville, where he claimed they were needed. Butterfield went on to Baltimore, where he met the department commander, Major General Robert C. Schenck. The department embraced the Federal garrison of approximately 10,000 men at Harpers Ferry, to which Major General William H. French was assigned as commander on June 26. Schenck was more accommodating than the military authorities in the capital and sent Hooker the brigade of Brigadier General Harry H. Lockwood, composed of New York and Maryland troops.

Harpers Ferry was indeed of little value, having been bypassed by Lee. It had proved no more than a trap for about 10,000 men under Colonel Dixon S. Miles when Lee invaded Maryland in 1862. Hooker meantime told General French to issue three days' rations and stand ready to co-operate with the Army of the Potomac. He ordered Slocum with the Twelfth Corps to move to the mouth of the Monocacy River and be prepared to pick up French, enter the Cumberland Valley in Lee's rear, and operate against the Southern army's communications with Virginia. On Saturday June 27 he inquired of the War Department if there was any reason why Maryland Heights, which overlooked Harpers Ferry and was the key to that position, might not be abandoned. Halleck replied promptly that the heights had always been thought an important point, fortified at much expense, and he would not approve abandonment except as an absolute necessity. Clearly he would yield nothing.

That brought another telegram from Hooker, who said he had found 10,000 men at Harpers Ferry in condition to take the field but "of no earthly account" in a garrison. Somewhere else they might be of some service, but "now, they are but bait for the rebels, should they return."[9]

As the day wore on Halleck's rebuff must have rankled. Finally, just after noon, before Hooker had received an answer, he dashed off another telegram pointing out that his original instructions required him to cover Harpers Ferry and Washington, but that he had in his front an enemy of more than his own numbers. That was a miscalculation, but made in good faith no doubt; the size of Lee's army was being exaggerated by civilians who were sending in reports. He told Halleck he could not comply with the conditions imposed on him with the means at his disposal and therefore requested to be relieved of the command.

At eight o'clock that evening Halleck sent another telegram: since Hooker had been appointed by the President, the request that he be relieved would have to be referred to the executive for action.

2. *The War Department Messenger Startles Meade*

James A. Hardie, assistant adjutant general of the Federal army, left Washington by special train on the night of June 27 for army headquarters in Frederick. Butterfield rode with him, returning from his largely unsuccessful quest for reinforcements. They chatted pleasantly, but Hardie did not disclose that he carried orders relieving Butterfield's chief from the command of the army.[10] Sickles also was on the train, returning to the Third Corps after a jaunt to the capital. At the Frederick station Hardie took a carriage alone.[11] It was two o'clock on the morning of Sunday June 28 when he reached the tent of General Meade, whom he awoke from a heavy sleep. Meade thought he was being put under arrest, and wondered about his misdeeds.

Meade's reaction to his promotion must have been one of inner exultation, yet he kept it carefully concealed and protested to Hardie, probably with sincerity, that the order was unfair to Reynolds. The two attitudes were not inconsistent, for Meade admired and respected his senior major general and had served under him long enough to appreciate his merits. Meade did not know then that he had been recommended for the top by Reynolds himself, who had been summoned to the White House by the President after the battle of Chancellorsville, where they talked late into the night of June 2.[12] Lincoln had felt him out about assuming the command if another change were necessary, and Reynolds had stipulated that he would accept only if allowed untrammeled authority to direct the army's movements, i.e., if he were free of orders from Halleck. Reynolds had mentioned Meade at that conference and said he would support him to the best of his ability.[13]

McClellan, who was one of the few earlier army commanders competent to reach solid judgments, rated Meade "an excellent officer; cool, brave and intelligent" and said he was "an honest man."[14] Lincoln's determination to go along with Hooker during the early part of the Gettysburg campaign cannot be explained by any chagrin that he had already made so many unsatisfactory changes in the last year and hated to face another.[15] But the resignation had altered the situation. For reasons never fully explained—though no doubt because he was not prepared to accept the condition imposed by Reynolds and supersede Halleck—Lincoln passed over Reynolds and selected Meade.

Meade and Hardie went together to the headquarters tent, which they reached at dawn. Butterfield, who had by this time arrived, was with Hooker when Meade conveyed the news, and Hooker suavely prevented any embarrassment by his courtesy and expressions of gratitude that Meade,[16] whose division had been in his corps at Sharpsburg, had been the choice.

Meade was deferential and polite in return, explained that the appointment came as a surprise to him and added the peculiar remark—to cover his own conscience?—that it was against his personal inclinations though as a soldier he was subject to orders. The meeting lasted half an hour. The only moment of tension came at Meade's indiscreet remark that the army, as located for him on the map by Hooker, was too widely scattered. Both Hooker and Butterfield immediately challenged him and Meade desisted, but his point was well taken; the army had been advancing on an unusually wide front, as Stuart had learned when he attempted to ride around it.

Hooker thought that since Lee had not taken pontoons with him into Pennsylvania, he could not be thinking seriously of crossing the Susquehanna River and capturing Harrisburg, but was planning instead to move down the south bank of the Susquehanna and isolate Baltimore and Washington from the northern and western states. This deduction did not take into consideration that the Susquehanna was wide and shallow near Harrisburg and that Lee always had with him his "Confederate pontoons," which meant wading.

Hooker was in jauntier spirits at this closing scene than when, less than two months before, he and Meade had faced each other after the battle of Chancellorsville. Despondently Hooker had told Meade then, as Meade described the interview to his wife, that "he was ready to turn over to me the Army of the Potomac; that he had enough of it, and almost wished he had never been born."[17]

3. *"I Ventured to Tell the President . . . Stories"*

Meade is a rather pathetic figure in American history, his career being marked more by somber frustration than gaiety and triumph. In his tendency to self-pity, the cards usually seemed stacked against him. Six weeks before achieving the top command he was writing his wife that "a poor devil like myself, with little merit and no friends, has to stand aside and see others go ahead. . . ."[18] Only three days before his elevation he told her again, in analyzing his prospects, that he had no chance because he was without friends while others had influential politicians working in their interests. Then came the customary self-depreciating note: "Besides, I have not the vanity to think my capacity so pre-eminent. . . ."

Analyzing a man on the basis of his private letters to his wife is like prying into the dressing room before the curtain is lifted. Meade's published letters suggest, however, that he was a bit of a dissembler. He was trying to ingratiate himself into the good opinion of the White House and working anxiously for promotion, and at the same time proclaiming so insistently that he did not want the high command that that has become the common impression. Mr. and Mrs. Lincoln had attended the military reviews on the Rappahannock in early April prior to the opening of the spring campaign. On April 9 Meade recorded how he had been endeavoring to make himself "agreeable to Mrs. Lincoln, who seems an amiable sort of personage. In view also of the vacant brigadier-ship in the regular army, I have ventured to tell the President one or two stories, and I think I have made decided progress in his affections. . . ."[19]

Mrs. Lincoln sent him a bouquet. "My vanity insinuated," he wrote, "that my *fine appearance* had taken Mrs. Lincoln's eye and that my fortune was made." But he soon learned from the orderly that all of the principal generals had been similarly remembered after the reviews.[20]

The letters, like Pickett's to his sweetheart, are filled with indiscreet disclosures of military matters. Jackson would have been delighted to intercept Meade's letter of April 18, saying that the Federal army would lose nearly 25,000 men in the next twenty days, and that "I see no indication of their being replaced. Over eight thousand go out of my corps alone."[21] It would have suggested that the Southerners should wait before undertaking any contemplated movement, or else should be on the lookout for Federal activity before the enlistments expired. There was also a vein of cynicism in the correspondence, as, for example, on April 17 from Falmouth: "I see some of the papers are disposed to criticise and find fault with du Pont, but I have just read a vigorous defense of him in the New York *Tribune,* so he is all right. . . ."[22]

Meade's caution and ultra-conservatism appear to have been a reaction from his father's business enterprise, which involved taking long chances. The family was of Irish descent. Robert Meade, the general's great-grandfather, immigrated to Philadelphia before 1732 and set himself up as a commission merchant in the Barbados trade. One of a small group of Catholics in the Quaker city, he was a leading factor in building the first Catholic chapel. His son, the general's grandfather, was "Honest George" Meade, a devout Catholic and an organizer, just before the Revolutionary War, of the Friendly Sons of St. Patrick.

The general's father, Richard Worsham Meade, was a big earner and a big loser.[23] He first entered his father's countinghouse, visited Europe before he was seventeen, and journeyed as a supercargo to the West Indies, where by the time he was twenty-five he had acquired wealth. Eventually, after "Honest George" had gone bankrupt in 1801, Richard settled in Cadiz, Spain, where he lived for seventeen years. During the Peninsular War he helped provision Wellington's army and sold merchandise and supplies to Spain in the uncertain Napoleonic days of shifting sovereigns. Bills accumulated. An assignee for a bankrupt British firm, he became the object of lawsuits by creditors, and although he appears to have been guilty of no moral turpitude, was arrested and held for two years in the Santa Catalina prison in Cadiz, being released finally through the intercession of the United States minister. During this imprisonment his son, George Gordon Meade, the eighth of ten children, was born, on the last day of 1815.

The Meade family thereafter tried futilely to collect the money owed them by Spain. In 1817 the father sent the family back to Philadelphia while he remained in Madrid to prosecute his claim. When the United States purchased Florida in 1819 it assumed the debts owed by Spain

to American citizens. So the elder Meade returned to the United States
and joined that group eternally present in Washington, of petitioners
for redress or payment of moneys due or alleged to be due. After he
died in 1828, his widow took permanent residence in the capital to work
for the appropriation that would re-establish the family. But the
Meades, rebuffed at the Spanish court, were to learn to put their trust
no more in republics than in princes. President Jackson at that time
was making a cipher out of the national debt, and the Meade item went
unrecognized. Where the earlier Meades had lived in affluence, George
was reared frugally. Enough money was raked together to place him
at the age of eight in a Washington school conducted by Salmon P.
Chase. Meade's reticence in maturity was shown by a letter to his wife
in 1862. General McDowell had invited him to meet some cabinet
members, including Secretary of the Treasury Chase. "I did not recall
to Mr. Chase's recollection that I was a ci-devant pupil of his, not knowing how such reminiscences might be taken. . . ."[24] West Point provided an economical education; in manhood he was to confess, "I like
fighting as little as any man."[25] President Jackson had appointed him
to fill a vacancy from Pennsylvania. He was slender and frail and
fourth from the youngest in a class of ninety-four, but at graduation he
stood nineteenth among the fifty-six commissioned.

At no point in these early years were there signs of warmth in Meade's
character; yet he was capable of the deepest affection, as was shown
clearly after his marriage in 1840 to Margaretta Sergeant. Her father,
John Sergeant, a leader of the Philadelphia bar, had been a representative in Congress and candidate for Vice President on the Henry Clay
National Republican ticket in 1832.

Their companionship and devotion form a bright spot in Meade's
rather somber personality. During his absences he wrote her daily letters expressing his intimate impressions, his hopes and confidences,
words that suggest a deep spiritual faith as well as a sense of personal
frustration, and small pleasantries that show a side the army never
perceived of the irascible, high-tempered general. Even during active
campaigning, Meade found time to write frequently—if not daily—and
without haste or brevity. His marriage brought him into contact with
Henry A. Wise, congressman for many terms and Governor of Virginia
before the war, who married another of Sergeant's daughters. A close
and lasting friendship sprang up between the brothers-in-law, which
endured after Wise's wife died and he married again and after the two
became generals in opposing armies.

Meade owed his army career to Wise's intercession. He had resigned a year after his graduation from West Point, to become a civil engineer and railroad builder, but found the going rough. Through the influence of his brother-in-law he was enabled to re-enter the service in 1842 as a second lieutenant of topographical engineers.[26] After his return from the Mexican War, Wise helped him to gain a transfer to the Army Engineer Corps. He was assigned to the Great Lakes area with headquarters in Detroit, where he was stationed, a captain, at the outbreak of the war.

Meade was intensely Unionist, was unalterably opposed to slavery, and looked on the war as one of subjugation, a term he used in letters to his wife. He told her the task was to overpower the South completely; "to do this we must have immense armies to outnumber them everywhere."[27] His irritability was well known to an army in which he had served successively as brigade, division, and corps commander. When he was aroused, according to Brigadier General Joseph W. Keifer, he "showed a fierce temper, yet was, in general, just."[28] He let his responsibilities weigh heavily and always seemed careworn. The worry trait was emphasized by bagginess under his eyes and a tendency to frown. His nearsightedness may have contributed to his nervousness and impatience. But above all else he was solid and reliable and these were the qualities most needed after the erratic Hooker.

Meade was confronted with difficult and shifty leadership in the War Department. Stanton, at heart a tyrant, was driving, ruthless, quarrelsome, but altogether patriotic; he was boisterous at his desk, contemptuous of opposition, unconcerned about niceties. He was amenable only to Lincoln, whose capacity he had eventually come to acknowledge. The conditions under which Lincoln and in turn Meade had to work were suggested by McClellan, who declared it "eminently characteristic" of Stanton to "say one thing to a man's face and just the reverse behind his back."[29]

How Stanton and Halleck pulled in harness is told, probably without much reportorial overstatement, by McClellan:

Speaking of Halleck, a day or two before he arrived in Washington Stanton came to caution me against trusting Halleck, who was, he said, probably the greatest scoundrel and most barefaced villain in America; he said that he was totally destitute of principle, and that in the Almaden Quicksilver case he had convicted Halleck of perjury in open court.[30] When Halleck arrived he came to caution me against Stanton,

repeating almost precisely the same words that Stanton had
employed. . . .

Of all the men whom I have encountered in high position Halleck
was the most hopelessly stupid. It was more difficult to get an idea
through his head than can be conceived by any one who never made
the attempt. I do not think he ever had a correct military idea from
beginning to end.[31]

4. *The Riffraff Follows the Army*

Conditions behind the Federal army at the time Meade took command
were nothing short of frightful. Whitelaw Reid, one of the best of the
Northern correspondents, had come from Washington to Frederick.
His dispatch of June 29, the day after Meade took command, said the
town was pandemonium, full of stragglers, with the liquor shops doing
a land-office business; "just under my window scores of drunken soldiers are making the night hideous."[32] Meade had ordered the army
to move north at four o'clock that morning and after it was on the
roads he established his headquarters at Taneytown.

What Reid saw was the backwash. All over Frederick soldiers were
trying to steal horses, sneak into unwatched private residences, or "are
filling the air with the blasphemy of their drunken brawls." The loose
nature of Hooker's generalship had invited rowdy elements to express
themselves.

Reid gives a picture of Meade's headquarters near Taneytown, the
Maryland hamlet named after Chief Justice Roger B. Taney, who lived
near by. The town, like its distinguished resident, was "somewhat
fallen into the sere and yellow leaf,"[33] blighted by the sudden descent
of war. The vast trains of the Army of the Potomac blocked the streets;
quartermasters were hurriedly searching for provisions, already grown
scant; along the roads and across the rolling hills "far as the eye could
reach, rose the glitter from the swaying points of bayonets." This
mighty armed host was composed of the Second and Third corps of
the Federal army, veterans as sturdy as ever marched on the continent,
and worthy of better army commanders than Pope, Burnside and
Hooker. The Second was Couch's old corps, from which Couch had
resigned despairingly, having too weak a stomach for any more of
Hooker.

Here at Taneytown was the nerve center of the army that must
determine whether the United States would be one nation or two. Here
were the hard-fighting men, quite a different crowd from the drunks

and tramps Reid had passed on the road from Frederick. Half a mile east of Taneytown he reached a large camp which he compared to that of a battalion of cavalry. Couriers were coming and departing, engineers were scanning maps, baggage train was packed for moving at an instant's notice, horses remained saddled. Reid turned into the field, found a plain little tent, walked in, and saw the serious, thin-faced general seated on a campstool, bending over a map, a pen in his hand— Meade, the new commander of the army, a man to "impress you as a thoughtful student more than a dashing soldier."[34]

He considered Meade neither ungainly nor graceful. Although he was two years short of fifty his beard was grizzled and his hair, slightly curly, receded on a retreating forehead and gave an impression of baldness. Reid had overheard Lincoln say after the battle of Chancellorsville, "I tell you, I think a great deal of that fine fellow Meade,"[35] and now the fine fellow was issuing orders in the headquarters tent.

Perhaps Meade's first caller after his elevation was Reynolds, who said the command had "fallen where it belongs."[36] Next came Howard, the Eleventh Corps commander, nineteen years Meade's junior at West Point. He had traveled with Meade on the Great Lakes before the war and had served alongside him, but thought he looked different now. "He was excited," Howard recorded. "His coat was off. . . . As I entered his tent, he extended his hand and said, 'How are you, Howard?' He demurred at my congratulation. He looked tall and spare, weary, and a little flushed. . . ."[37]

Meade took over the Harpers Ferry garrison, with authority to shift it as he saw fit, but he did not pursue the plan of moving it and the Twelfth Corps into the Cumberland Valley to sever Lee's communications. Slocum brought up the Twelfth Corps to the main army while French was ordered to march the Harpers Ferry garrison to Frederick to protect the rear. These matters and a few promotions were Meade's first business, together with a long conference with trusted John Reynolds, whom he confirmed in command of the left wing. He also retained Butterfield as his chief of staff, recognizing the disadvantages of a change when a battle was momentarily expected. Like most new commanders, he wanted to hold a grand review. He quickly abandoned all thought of it when events showed that any day might bring a battle.[38]

Concentration

1. *A Grimy Spy Finds Longstreet*

Late on the night of June 28 at Longstreet's headquarters Colonel Sorrel was awakened by the provost guard, who had captured a suspicious character trying to make his way into camp. He was ragged and dirty—Sorrel's word was "filthy"—and he appeared to be suffering from exposure.[1] But Sorrel recognized him readily behind the grime and mud; he was Harrison, a shadowy character who flitted into and out of the story of the Confederacy and was last heard of after the war living in want in Baltimore. And not in many places, if any, did he leave any record of a home or first name.

Harrison had been sent by Secretary of War Seddon to Longstreet when he was besieging Suffolk; Sorrel had put him on the payroll at $150 a month, payable in United States currency. Sorrel watched him closely, aware that through the history of warfare, spies not uncommonly give as much information as they receive and thrive on more than one payroll. Eventually he concluded that of Harrison's leading passions, his love of greenbacks was equaled only by his hatred of Yankees. He was a man of medium height, stooped and bearded although only thirty, with unobtrusive manner and soft hazel eyes, and possessed such an ability to get around unnoticed that Sorrel soon found he could cover Washington and even comb through Secretary Stanton's office in the War Department.[2] Checking on him, Sorrel found that he did come from Mississippi and was fond of danger. The information he brought proved accurate and no one could discover that he ever sold anything to the Federals. Thus a happy relationship was established between the spy—more gently termed a scout at Longstreet's headquarters—and the First Corps commander.

Before Longstreet left Culpeper for Pennsylvania he had summoned Harrison, loaded him with gold, and told him to go to the Federal camp and to Washington and bring back all the information he could garner. Asked where he could be found for a report, the general, always guarded, replied, "With the army. I shall be sure to be with it." Any man with gumption, he added, ought to be able to locate the headquarters of the First Corps of the Army of Northern Virginia.[3]

Harrison vanished, reappeared chatting in the Washington saloons, joined the Army of the Potomac as it entered Maryland, talked with the soldiers, traveled over the roads by night. When Longstreet learned later that Harrison drank and gambled, habits he judged incompatible with good intelligence work, he had Sorrel quit honoring his vouchers and turn him back to the War Department; but at the moment Harrison's methods were yielding beneficial results. When he appeared at Chambersburg he was loaded, not with liquor but with facts. He had procured a horse in Frederick and ridden the fifty miles through the rainy darkness.

Sorrel got a summary of what Harrison had and took him at once to Longstreet, whom he awoke. When Longstreet heard the report, he was "immediately on fire."[4] He had Major John W. Fairfax of his staff conduct the scout to General Lee. Lee questioned Harrison and listened with "great composure and minuteness."[5]

Harrison's first piece of news was that the entire Federal army was north of the Potomac, with headquarters at Frederick. To that moment Lee had not known of the crossing and judged it had not taken place because of his confidence in Stuart, who was expected to report any such move with all possible speed. Harrison stated also that Hooker had been relieved and Meade placed in command of the Federal army, which was all-important news to Lee, who respected Meade's ability whereas he had had little esteem for Hooker. Two corps were at Frederick and a third was near by.

Lee was disturbed and uncertain, but manifestly impressed. He had no corroborating intelligence from Stuart and did not know how much reliance he could place on Harrison. But he made quick decisions and almost at once he decided to accept the report and act on it. The word of a lone scout, about whom nobody knew a great deal, had to be relied

on in place of information that should have been forthcoming from a
cavalry division that was missing when most needed.[6]

Harrison brought another report which seemed vital. Federal troops,
he said, were close to South Mountain. Colonel Marshall had been directed by Lee earlier that night to order Longstreet to move on the
morning of the twenty-ninth to support Ewell in the attack on Harrisburg. Hill had been directed to cross the Susquehanna below Harrisburg, seize the railroad, and co-operate. Now Marshall was again
summoned. With Lee sat a man in civilian dress who, Lee told him, was
Longstreet's scout, who had brought them the first information about
the enemy's movements north of the Potomac.[7]

According to Marshall, Lee inferred from Harrison's report that the
main body of the Federals was turning west from Frederick to Middletown, which lay in the valley between the Catoctin and South Mountain ranges. Lee thought the enemy's purpose was to cross South
Mountain and enter the Cumberland Valley, thus severing the communications between the Confederate army and Virginia. After Harrison
had been dismissed, Lee pointed out that while his communications
were by no means complete, they nevertheless were all he required as
long as the Federals did not occupy the Cumberland Valley. What he
needed chiefly was a line to replenish his ammunition. If the Federals
occupied the valley, munitions convoys would be out of the question.
Therefore, Lee explained, he would move his army east of the South
Mountain range and threaten Baltimore and Washington, which would
hold the Federal army east of South Mountain so as to protect those
cities.[8]

Lee's decision was made within an hour or so after he heard Harri-
sons' report. Marshall was asked to countermand the marching orders
of Ewell and Hill and to tell Longstreet to follow Hill eastward across
South Mountain.

An element of irony here was that the Federal army was not moving
toward the Cumberland Valley. Buford's cavalry was en route to Middletown that day and this apparently is what attracted the scout Harrison and bothered Lee. The three corps that had been there, the First,
the Third, and the Eleventh, moved from Middletown to Frederick on
June 28.[9] But, as has been noted, Meade had abandoned Hooker's
plan of operating against Lee's communications. Halleck, the fretful
guardian of Washington, felt that the Federal army was too far west
already. He wanted it kept in a direct line between Lee and the capital.
In response to his suggestion, Meade was inclining the army to the east

to guard Baltimore and Washington, and not to the west to menace Lee's life line with Virginia.

Longstreet rose early and went directly to Lee's headquarters. General Lee already had issued his orders. The army would concentrate at Cashtown, where the Chambersburg-Baltimore turnpike debouched from South Mountain, or at Gettysburg, the first main road center east of the mountain.

Because the army was scattered over five southern Pennsylvania counties, most of June 29 had to be devoted to dispatching messengers and receiving the responses of the corps commanders. Dr. J. S. D. Cullen, medical director of Longstreet's corps, saw the excitement at headquarters "among couriers, quartermasters, commissaires, etc., all betokening some early movement." That afternoon Lee talked with a group in front of headquarters, Dr. Cullen among them. "Tomorrow, gentlemen," he said, "we will not move to Harrisburg as we expected, but will go over to Gettysburg and see what General Meade is after."[10]

2. Wagons, Bacon, Oats and Trouble

On the morning of June 28, when General Meade was beginning the first day of his new command, while the 32nd North Carolina Infantry was running up the official flag of the Confederacy in Carlisle and Extra Billy Smith was haranguing the York churchgoers, Jeb Stuart's wet and bedraggled troopers lay along the canal towpath near the Great Falls of the Potomac, resting and sleeping while their horses grazed on the fresh Maryland pastures.[11] The artillery horses were in the worst condition after their night's work of drawing the guns through the river. Whatever the urgency, the horses must be fed and rested or the world-famous Confederate cavalry would be rendered impotent.

When the animals had knocked the sharp edge from their hunger, Stuart ordered his men to start the search for the will-o-the-wisp right flank of Lee's army. Shortly before noon they reached the village of Rockville, nine miles from the District of Columbia line, astride the main highway linking Washington and Meade's army at Frederick. People were just leaving church. Girls attending a large female academy gathered in front of the school to watch the celebrated Confederate horsemen, who had appeared in a great gray cloud out of nowhere, riding unchallenged almost on the outskirts of fort-rimmed Washington. They greeted the gray-clad soldiers with outbursts of applause, partly no doubt because of the novelty of the spectacle and partly through sympathy with the Southern cause. Lieutenant Colonel Blackford judged it was a show of sympathy when the men stopped and the girls rushed up and cut souvenir buttons from their uniforms.[12]

Stuart was scarcely in the town when he saw a long creeping train of 150 Federal wagons winding in on the main road from Washington. Here was a luscious prize for the grasping. Hampton and a detail charged into the head of the train, surprised the unsuspecting wagoneers, and captured the guard and more than half the wagons. They were brand-new, were drawn by splendid mule teams, with fresh harness and gleaming trappings, and were loaded with provisions for Meade's army. These included hams, bacon, sugar, bread and crackers, and a goodly quantity of whisky in bottles, along with the main load of feed for stock.

While the head of the convoy was being attacked the teamsters in the rear turned around, lashed their mules, and sped back toward Washington. Hampton's men were quick to pursue. At a sharp turn a wagon overturned and something between twelve and twenty-four piled up behind it, an easy prey for the pursuers. On rushed the others, followed by Confederates, until Blackford of Stuart's staff found himself on a hill looking down on the city of Washington. There he had recall sounded and turned back. This was too big a morsel to be gobbled by a single squadron.[13]

When the total was counted Stuart found that he had captured 125 wagons, 900 mules and 400 men. Twenty-five wagons had escaped into Washington, where the teamsters spread the tidings of the Confederate Cavalry. Stuart toyed with the idea of a quick dash into Washington—how the enemy would talk about the boldness of such a stroke! —but he was already straining his orders to the limit, and such a gamble was not to be considered, although the thought of it was judged worthy of a place in his report.

As he rode out of Rockville the long train of wagons followed. Usually his failure to reach Ewell on time has been attributed to the necessity of adjusting his march to the pace of this creeping convoy. But the capture undoubtedly saved his command and was worth all the time expended. The main load was oats intended for Meade's horses.[14] The worn mounts of the Confederate cavalry, and especially the artillery horses, seemed to take on new life from one feeding after days of nothing but hasty pasturage.[15] For the time being Stuart's worry about feed could be dismissed.

Stuart's close approach threw terror into Washington. It became "a city beseiged, as after Bull Run," wrote Reid, the Cinncinnati *Gazette* correspondent. "All night long, troops were marching; orderlies with clanking sabres clattering along the streets; trains of wagons grinding over the bouldering avenues. . . . The quartermaster's department was like a bee-hive; everything was motion and hurry."[16] Stuart might have made a *coup de main* on the White House, but he could not have held the Federal capital more than half an hour.

A clear view of the enlistment difficulties in the Northern army was provided by an incident reported by Reid in Washington on the very day Stuart threatened the city. The term of enlistment of a New England regiment of more than 900 men had just expired. They marched sprucely down the street with "brilliant uniforms and unstained arms; faultless appearing officers and gorgeous drum major; clanging band; banners waving and bayonets gleaming in the morning sunlight." These men were marching home at a moment when a battle was about to decide the fate of the nation, although implored to stay two weeks, or even a week longer. "Would that Stuart could capture the train that bears them!" Reid wrote.[17]

Baltimore likewise was thrown into a near panic. Alarm bells were rung, home guards assembled.

Soon more apprehension was felt in Washington and the North. From Frederick, Meade, on his first day as commander, had sent in a list of promotions, and his recommendations had been approved by telegraph. Then the wire went dead and all communication between the army and the capital was severed. Rumors spread and Stanton feared Meade's army had encountered disaster. Halleck telegraphed Couch in Harrisburg that he had no contact with the army; Secretary of State Seward notified New York that the government was in extreme peril. Stuart had merely cut the telegraph lines as well as the railroad, and demonstrated again that fear feeds on the unknown.

Moving north to Cooksville, from which he drove a minor Federal force on the morning of the twenty-ninth, Stuart struck the Baltimore & Ohio Railroad at Hood's Mill, about midway between Baltimore and Harpers Ferry. He demolished it even though he had to work slowly with ill-suited tools, burned the bridge at Sykesville, and disrupted the flow of supplies to Meade's army; the trains which came up while the troopers hacked at the rails were able to stop at a safe distance and back away.

Meanwhile, Stuart was running short on time and information. He combed the surrounding country for intelligence from friendly Marylanders and read the newspapers eagerly. One account, "with great particularity," said that Early had reached Wrightsville; consequently, he continued his northward movement and entered Westminster, on the Baltimore-Gettysburg pike, in the late afternoon. There the Confederates were startled by a sudden gallant charge of a Federal squadron which dashed impetuously against their vastly superior force. The attackers proved to be the 1st Delaware Cavalry, who were dispersed toward Baltimore, where they carried new alarms.

Stuart's captured wagon train now became an impediment, as his sleepless and haggard men rode gropingly[18] forward. The oats that had saved the horses were exhausted. Fortunately they found at Westminster ample forage for one feeding.

At Westminster Stuart was twenty-four miles from Gettysburg, which he could readily have reached on the morning of June 30, perhaps to have formed a juncture with Johnston Pettigrew's North Carolina brigade, moving toward Gettysburg from the opposite direction.[19] But as Blackford pointed out, he knew nothing on June 29—nor did anyone else at that time—of the concentration that would occur two days later at Gettysburg. If Stuart could but have obtained an inkling of Lee's orders for concentration at Cashtown or Gettysburg, to which the other Confederate commands were responding at that very moment, his course would have been clear. As it was he guessed wrong and moved north to Hanover, instead of northwest to Gettysburg.

3. A Five Mile Gap Rules a Nation's Fate

Jeb Stuart selected the route by Hanover, still moving north, in order to avoid the Federal cavalry commanded by Judson Kilpatrick, which he heard was in the vicinity of Littlestown, fourteen miles from Westminster. But Kilpatrick outguessed him and instead of waiting at Littlestown, moved to Hanover, where Stuart ran head on into him. From the hills south of the town Stuart saw the blue column of horsemen and while he would have preferred not to fight, he had no alternative.

Before noon on June 30 the 2nd North Carolina entered Hanover, charged the Federal troopers, and drove them beyond the town limits. [20] Kilpatrick, coming up with Farnsworth's brigade, in turn struck the North Carolinians and hurled them back in confusion. Stuart and Blackford were approaching and witnessed the clash. They tried to rally the regiment but it had been scattered and had no formation.

Stuart's command had been strung out along the roadway, with Hampton two miles in the rear behind the wagon train. Fitzhugh Lee's brigade came up first and launched itself against Kilpatrick's rear at the moment when Custer was coming to the aid of Farnsworth. Thereafter the battle was a desultory charge and countercharge, then long-range firing.[21] The opposing commanders appeared to have the same desire. Kilpatrick wanted to prevent Stuart from taking the Gettysburg road, and Stuart in turn wanted to move away from the Gettysburg road and take the York road north and east, continuing his search for Early. To protect his wagons Stuart could not unite his entire command for a mass attack, nor could Kilpatrick make headway against the guns that protected the Confederate position south of the town. After fighting for four hours, both let the engagement lull, and when darkness came, both drew off. Stuart made a detour around Hanover and rode through the night toward York with his 125 wagons and the 400 prisoners he had captured since paroling the 400 teamsters he had taken at Rockville.

The engagement at Hanover, while minor, is of interest to those who believe that either destiny or chance control great events. While Stuart was trying to free himself and find the right flank of Lee's army, Early's division was passing across his front on the roads leading from York to Gettysburg and from York to Heidlersburg. Gordon's brigade and White's cavalry battalion were on the York-Gettysburg pike, which at Abbottstown is six miles north of Hanover and at the crossing of the Yellow Springs road five miles from New Oxford. As the Confederate infantry passed along the road they heard the firing five and six miles to the south, but did not suspect it was Stuart. Here Lee's staff had been at fault. After having written Stuart orders—lacking in sharpness—telling him to get in touch with Ewell's right, Colonel Marshall did not emphasize to Early the need of keeping a sharp lookout for the cavalry. In complete ignorance that he might be approaching, Early moved across Stuart's front.[22]

Possibly the fate of the Confederacy rested on a gap of five or six miles.

At York Stuart found that time had run out. Early had gone. The York residents who had fraternized with Extra Billy Smith were chary with their information about the direction Early had taken. Stuart was still gambling on the whereabouts of Lee's army. He guessed Carlisle, and again guessed wrong. On the verge of exhaustion he moved northwest through the night, his mounts jaded and mules famished and some of his men asleep in their saddles.

As he started toward Carlisle Stuart sent two staff officers, Major Andrew W. Venable and Captain Henry Lee, to look for army headquarters somewhere to the west, the direction in which Early had vanished.[23] When he approached Carlisle on the evening of July 1, he found it occupied not by Lee, but by Major General William F. ("Baldy") Smith with Federal militia forces. He had ridden 125 miles since the previous morning and was not in good spirits. When his demand for surrender was rejected, he dropped some shells into the Carlisle barracks and set them on fire. At last, after a long, difficult and almost futile ride—which had given the enemy only minor inconveniences and had severely impeded the movements of his own army—Stuart learned, from one of Lee's messengers instead of his own, the whereabouts of the Confederate army. In place of bringing intelligence, it was he who received it.

Colonel Marshall later tried to have Stuart court-martialed; he even declared, at a small dinner party, that Stuart should have been shot. He did not recognize that the lack of positive statement in his own composition of orders was perhaps more responsible for the absence of the cavalry than any other factor.[24]

4. The Wagons Roll Toward Gettysburg

Through June 27 to the night of June 28, while Lee waited in Messersmith's woods, his distress over his missing cavalry became obvious to almost the entire army. "He repeatedly observed," said Chief of Staff Marshall, "that the enemy's army must still be in Virginia as he had heard nothing from Stuart."[25] The distraught general asked virtually all comers if they had heard anything of Stuart. Marshall and others had been struck by the unusual lethargy of the army, slowed near to paralysis by lack of information. It could easily have been in Gettysburg on the morning of July 1, occupying the heights south of the town, had it known the locations of the Federal corps—the information Stuart was supposed to provide.[26]

Lee's apprehension, extending almost to physical agony, impressed itself forcibly on Dr. J. L. Suesserott, one of Chambersburg's leading physicians, although the doctor did not understand its cause. He went to Lee on Monday, June 29, to obtain an exemption of his neighbor's blind mare from seizure. While Lee had the paper prepared, the doctor studied the features and movements of the noted commander. He said he had never seen so much emotion depicted on a human countenance as on Lee's. "With his hands at times clutching his hair, and with contracted brow, he would walk with rapid strides for a few rods and then, as if he bethought himself of his actions, he would with a sudden jerk produce an entire change in his features and demeanor and cast an inquiring gaze on me, only to be followed in a moment by the same contortions of face and agitation of person."[27] Even if allowance is made for some exaggeration, it is clear that Lee was deeply disturbed or physically unwell.

Major General Henry Heth, who saw him from time to time, said he discussed the absence of Stuart with every officer who visited him. "Can you tell me where General Stuart is?" he would say, or, "Where on earth is my cavalry?" or "Have you any news of the enemy's movements? What is the enemy going to do?" And again: "If the enemy does not find us, we must try to find him, in the absence of the cavalry, as best we can."

Mrs. Ellen McClellan visited Lee mainly to get his autograph but ostensibly to request help for the town's needy, which Lee supplied. She was impressed with his sadness. He told her war was a cruel thing: all he desired was that "they" would let him go home and eat his bread in peace. Mrs. McClellan particularly noticed that Lee had the headquarters horses carefully picketed so that they could not injure the trees in the grove where he camped.[28]

On one of his last days in Messersmith's woods, a caller was heard to congratulate him on having a mediocre opponent in the new Federal commander. Lee corrected him quickly; Meade, he said, was a soldier of ability and intelligence, conscientious and painstaking. He would make no mistake in front of the Confederate army, as some of his predecessors had done, and if Lee made a mistake, Meade would be certain to take advantage of it.[29]

Quite as much as the cavalry, Lee missed Stuart himself, on whom he had come to rely for inspiration almost as much as for information. As Sorrel pointed out, the cavalry which Stuart had left with Lee amounted to nothing. "It was the great body of that splendid horse under the leader Stuart that Lee wanted. He was the eyes and ears and strong right arm of the commander. . . ."

Stuart's delay possibly cost Lee also the Wrightsville bridge, which the cavalry might have taken and held until Early could bring up his infantry. That would have allowed Early to operate on the north side of the Susquehanna against Lancaster and Harrisburg. The odds were great that both would have fallen.

Lee's concentration toward Cashtown and Gettysburg was in full progress on June 30. Longstreet arrived in the early morning; after a brief discussion Lee broke up his headquarters in Messersmith's woods and the two rode together to Greenwood, a hamlet in the South Mountain pass between Chambersburg and Cashtown.

The concentration had begun in the early morning hours. Sometime after midnight in Chambersburg, Jacob Hoke, who had been sending all important information to Governor Curtin, awakened his wife with news of activity in the Confederate army. The roll of a drum was heard from Pickett's camp. Lights shown for miles along South Mountain and up the valley toward Shippensburg. The Hokes peered through half-closed shutters at the long line of heavily loaded wagons groaning on their axles as they passed through Chambersburg. Some were being driven at a trot. They were coming from the direction of Carlisle, turning at the diamond and heading toward Gettysburg.[30] Next morning Hoke dispatched a messenger to Governor Curtin, telling of Lee's concentration. Apparently the intelligence got through to Washington by telegraph and on to Meade's headquarters in Taneytown that night.[31] Confirmatory information that Lee was falling back from the Susquehanna was sent by Brigadier General Hermann Haupt from Harrisburg at 11:30 P.M., June 30. York and Carlisle had been evacuated and Lee's aim, Haupt suggested, apparently was to move suddenly against Meade. His concentration was expected near Chambersburg instead of at Gettysburg.

5. Meade's Object Is to Fight

Meade's plan, as he drove northward, was to find the enemy and fight him: "My object being, at all hazards, to compel the enemy to loose his hold on the Susquehanna, and meet me in battle at some point." He was not thinking then in terms of a defensive action, of holding Lee, but of expelling him.

When it became clear on June 30 that the Southern army was concentrating, Meade began to study the terrain. He directed Reynolds to proceed to Gettysburg and examine the ground there. He told the accomplished engineer, Brigadier General Andrew A. Humphreys, commanding a division of Sickles' corps, to determine the nature of the positions around Emmitsburg. He ordered his engineers to examine the topography in his immediate section of northern Maryland and draw up a defensive line along which the army could concentrate if Lee crossed South Mountain.

They laid out a line along Pipe Creek, reaching from Manchester, on the right, to Middleburg on the left. The right was on high ground and the left near the confluence of Pipe Creek with the Monocacy River. This line would be of particular value in guarding the approaches to both Baltimore and Washington. It was a strong line, with the meandering stream immediately in its front. The two eminences in its rear,

Paris Ridge and Dug Hill Ridge, would be suitable for the location of reserves and for a secondary defense in case of trouble. It had a good base at Westminster, a road center to which Meade ordered the army trains retired.

Late on June 30 Meade issued his Pipe Creek Circular, assigning to the corps commanders their positions in the Pipe Creek line. The orders were tentative. The line would be adopted if developments did not dictate his fighting elsewhere. Employment of this line would involve a withdrawal, to which some of the Federal generals took exception, but its preparation was a wise precaution even though the chance encounter of the armies elsewhere meant that it was never used.

Meade's instructions to Reynolds at noon on June 30 gave a clear, concise picture of his situation: "We are as concentrated as my present information of the position of the enemy justifies. I have pushed out the cavalry in all directions to feel for them, and as soon as I have made up any positive opinion of their position I will move again. In the meantime, if they advance against me I must concentrate at that point where they show the strongest force."[32]

Those instructions, rather than the Pipe Creek Circular, guided Reynolds as he went to Gettysburg.

On the night of June 30 Lee's infantry was well up, extending from Heidlersburg to Chambersburg, a distance of about twenty-eight miles. The Federal army was extended about the same distance but had greater depth. Hancock at Uniontown was twenty miles south of Gettysburg and Sedgwick at Manchester was thirty-five miles southeast. In a concentration at Gettysburg Lee would have the advantage of bringing his army together near its center, while Meade would have to close on the corps farthest to his left. Meade's concentration consequently would require more time.

Of Lee's army, Ewell's corps had been most dispersed. After Lee had told Trimble to join Ewell and help capture Harrisburg, Trimble began to apply pressure. He reached Ewell in Carlisle on Sunday, June 28, told him the city could be captured easily, emphasized that Lee expected it, and volunteered to take it with one brigade. Ewell fell in with the idea. They arranged their plans on the twenty-ninth and Trimble made ready to march on Harrisburg before daybreak on the thirtieth.

Jenkins had taken his cavalry brigade into Mechanicsburg, eight miles from Harrisburg, on the night of the twenty-eighth and had bivouacked his men two miles nearer the city. His patrols reached almost within sight of the Pennsylvania capital. It is likely Trimble could

have carried the town, defended only by militia, although he might
have required more than a brigade. But on the night of June 29 Ewell
received Lee's concentration orders, notifying him to march to Cashtown or Gettysburg "according to circumstances."

Lee's attitude, leisurely for several days, now called for celerity.
Ewell at once dispatched Captain Elliott Johnston with a copy of the
orders for Early at York, together with oral instructions for Early to
return speedily to the foot of South Mountain. At daylight on June 30
Early's troops were moving toward Heidlersburg and Gettysburg. Ewell
left Carlisle with Rodes and Trimble on the same morning and stopped
at Heidlersburg. Johnson kept his division in the vicinity of Fayetteville
guarding the corps trains that had passed during the night of the twenty-
ninth through Chambersburg.

After dark on June 30 Early, on whom Ewell had come to rely so
heavily as to be almost dominated by him, joined the corps commander
at Heidlersburg, his division having been left in bivouac three miles
east. The four generals—Ewell, Trimble, Early and Rodes—met in conference and studied Lee's dispatch.[33] Ewell was a general devoted to
the letter of his orders. He had received some false information that
the Eleventh Federal Corps was in Gettysburg and was baffled about
how to comply with Lee's wishes. The dispatch from Lee was read and
reread and commented on repeatedly. Early in particular let fly a stream
of oaths about an order written with such ambiguity as to name both
Cashtown and Gettysburg, seven miles apart, as concentration points.
Which one, the generals debated, did Lee prefer? Ewell asked Trimble's opinion. He had been with Lee more recently than the others and
had seen Lee touch the map at Gettysburg. He said he could interpret
the order in only one way, which was that they should advance on
Gettysburg and notify Lee at once of their movement.[34] But talk continued and nothing was determined that night.

Next morning Ewell decided on what was, in effect, a straddle. They
would march toward Middletown, Pennsylvania, the town being about
what its name implied—a midway place from which either Cashtown or
Gettysburg might be reached conveniently. As they began their march
a messenger was sent to Lee for more positive orders. Ewell reached
Middletown at ten o'clock on the morning of July 1. Fifteen minutes
later a message came from A. P. Hill requesting Ewell to come to
Gettysburg with all possible speed.

CHAPTER EIGHT

Pettigrew's Encounter

1. A Rifleman, a Nephew and a Scholar

Heth, commanding Hill's advance division, was at Cashtown on the night of June 29, Pettigrew's brigade holding the forward position. As a precaution Pettigrew sent Company B of the 52nd North Carolina Infantry, under Lieutenant W. E. Kyle, to Millerstown, a village five miles to the south and a short distance north of Fairfield, which was on the main road from Hagerstown to Gettysburg.[1]

Buford's Federal cavalry division, which had been at Middletown, Maryland, had crossed South Mountain into the Cumberland Valley early on the morning of June 29, moved up the western side of the range from Boonsboro, Maryland, to Waynesboro, Pennsylvania, and again crossed the mountain, moving to the east side by way of Monterey Pass.

As Buford left the mountains one of his brigades, under Colonel William Gamble, passed near Fairfield and saw the bivouac fires of Lieutenant Kyle's outpost on Newpilman's farm north of the town. Later in the evening Gamble drew nearer to drive off the Confederates if possible, and some shots were exchanged—a skirmish, both Gamble and Kyle termed it.[2] Gamble did not want to bring down additional Confederates by heavy artillery firing. Buford seemed confused about this force, saying it was two Mississippi regiments which he could have destroyed had he been given timely information and a guide. He declared the inhabitants knew of his arrival and the enemy's whereabouts

93

but appeared to be afraid to tell, saying, "the rebels will destroy our houses if we tell anything."[3]

Buford withdrew southward to Emmitsburg on the morning of the thirtieth and reported the incident to his chief, Pleasanton, who passed on to Reynolds news of Gamble's brush with Southern infantry, the first encountered in the Gettysburg area. Kyle continued his outpost at Millerstown until that night, then rejoined Pettigrew on Marsh Creek, three and a half miles west of Gettysburg.

Heth's division, which was becoming the spearhead as Lee approached Gettysburg, had been the last organized of the Army of Northern Virginia, having been brought together from scattered brigades and regiments to fill out the new corps created for A. P. Hill.

Henry Heth, usually called Harry, had fallen instinctively into a military career, being the grandson of an officer in Washington's army and son of an officer in the War of 1812. He was cousin of George Pickett and had been at West Point at the same time, though he had been appointed from Virginia a year later than Pickett, appointed from Illinois. Like Pickett, he had remained in the regular army until Virginia, their native state, seceded.

Heth had the distinction of being the foremost authority on the rifle in the old army, a recognition he had won by much study, practice and writing as a lieutenant and captain after the Mexican War. When the 9th and 10th Regular Army infantry regiments were organized in 1855, they were designated rifle regiments and given special drill and equipment. For field music they had bugles in place of the customary fife and drum corps. They wore distinctive uniforms with green facings. They held regular rifle practice under the direction of Captain Heth. Heth's book, *A System of Target Practice,* was the official range guide used in the service.

At the age of thirty-seven, when he was given a division in the Confederate army, he was looked on as a capable officer despite his failure to halt the enemy in West Virginia, a theater that had proved unfortunate for Confederates and propitious for Federals in earlier stages of the war. He was an intelligent conversationalist whose company Lee enjoyed, yet he lacked Hood's verve or Early's brusqueness and does not stand out among the sharp, vital personalities of this spirited army. Some of his associates came to regard him as impetuous in decisions and rash in combat, but there was no tendency as yet to distrust him.

Heth's division included two brigades that had served in A. P. Hill's old division, the Virginians now under Colonel John M. Brockenbrough and the Alabama and Tennessee regiments of Brigadier General James

J. Archer. The others were Pettigrew's North Carolinians and a brigade thrown together from the Richmond defenses, consisting of Mississippi and North Carolina troops, commanded by Brigadier General Joseph R. Davis, nephew of the Confederate President.

The President's nephew had been commissioned in the autumn of 1862, a bit of nepotism that provoked grumblings in the Confederate War Department. Favorites were advanced, ran the complaint, while "men of mind, men who wrought up the Southern people . . . are hurled into the background."[4] The promotion was also noted as an event that helped bring on the resignation of George Wythe Randolph, grandson of Thomas Jefferson, as the Confederate Secretary of War, possibly having "operated on him as an emetic."[5] Davis was a pleasant and unpretending man; he would have been more discreet, considering his lack of military experience and his kinship to the President, to take a lower grade.

Of the four brigade commanders in the new division the most arresting was Pettigrew. In the brief term of life that remained for him before a Federal bullet found his vitals, he was to bring on the battle and end the campaign, and command nearly half the troops in the most spectacular assault of that epochal combat.

Brigadier General James Johnston Pettigrew—he dropped the James for most purposes—was regarded in North Carolina as versatile almost to the point of genius. A superior officer judged him capable of assuming the responsibilities even of Lee himself,[6] should events make it necessary, although he had never attended a class in professional military tactics. His early education by private tutors at the spacious family estate of Bonvara, in coastal Tyrrell County, North Carolina, was aimed at a professional, not a military career. But his comprehension was keen and his capacity for acquiring new information apparently inexhaustible. The peaceful homestead where he spent his early years overlooked the blue waters of Lake Scuppernong, and the plantation extended along the Scuppernong River, from which the luscious Southern grapes, with their rare bouquet, take their name.

Pettigrew was a slender, handsome man of quick gestures and prompt decisions, with shining black hair and mustache and a dark complexion denoting the strong Latin strain of his French ancestry. His black eyes were sharp and penetrating. Now a soldier at the age of thirty-five, he had already achieved recognition as author, diplomat, lawyer, linguist, and legislator.

His marks were the highest that had ever been made at the University of North Carolina,[7] which had graduated many eminent scholars and men distinguished in national and state affairs. A graceful, athletic youth, he had led his class at Chapel Hill in fencing, boxing and the singlestick, as well as in mathematics, the classical languages, and all the other liberal arts courses.

Pettigrew had received distinction from the start. When he delivered the valedictory address at the graduation exercises in 1847, the silver-haired President of the United States, James Knox Polk, had by chance returned to visit his alma mater, where he, too, had won high scholastic honors. Polk was accompanied by a fellow alumnus, Secretary of the Navy John Young Mason, and by Captain Matthew F. Maury, the distinguished naval hydrographer and meteorologist, who was then engaged in establishing the National Observatory and Hydrographic Office, and was launching into his career of oceanography and the preparation of his great work, *The Physical Geography of the Sea*. Before the commencement events, these three looked in on the final examinations in mathematics and astronomy, and were so impressed with young Pettigrew's proficiency that they invited him to return with them and become an instructor in the Naval Observatory. There he also worked as a teacher in the Nautical Almanac Office.

The ardor of his devotion to the cause of the Southern people was a revolt, no doubt, from association with his cantankerous uncle, James Louis Petigru, dean of the Charleston, South Carolina, bar. When Johnston Pettigrew decided to take up law, he studied for a time in Baltimore and then entered his uncle's office, where the shingle was confusing because the contentious senior preferred the shorter version of the family's Huguenot surname.

Petigru the elder had been combating public opinion in South Carolina ever since the nullification days of John C. Calhoun, standing always for the Federal Union. By 1863, when he was seventy-one years old, he was looked on as the only man in the state who had not seceded. This distinction he prankishly sought to emphasize in church each Sunday morning by rising from his knees when the rector in his prayer reached the regular request for divine assistance for the President of the Confederate States.[8] Petigru appeared to delight in the consternation his intransigence provoked. The eminent old man left behind the monumental work of the codification of South Carolina laws, for which he is still respected. But long after he is forgotten his trenchant irony will be remembered in a wartime witticism often repeated in periods of inflation that "you take your money to the market in your market basket and bring home your groceries in your pocketbook."[9]

After obtaining his license to practice in South Carolina young Pettigrew departed to study civil law in Germany. He traveled extensively, became proficient in French, German, Italian and Spanish, with a reading knowledge of Hebrew and Arabic, and spent seven years abroad writing and in diplomatic service.

Pettigrew sensed the approach of hostilities between the states. Late in 1859, as a lawyer in Charleston, he entered a rifle company and soon became its colonel. His command of a North Carolina brigade resulted from the fortuitous circumstance that he was recognized on the Raleigh railroad station platform as he traveled to Richmond with South Carolina troops. Delay in mustering his Charleston regiment into the Confederate service caused it to disband, so that the men might enlist with other units. The impatient Pettigrew enlisted as a private in Hampton's Legion, which was heading for the front. Word passed among his North Carolina friends that he had been seen going to battle without even a corporal's stripes. Almost in a twinkling he was elected colonel of the 22nd North Carolina Regiment, then stationed at Camp Ellis near Raleigh.

An officer who tented near him for several months described him: "He was quick in his movements and quick in his perception and in his decision. . . . His habit was to pace restlessly up and down in front of his tent with a cigar in his mouth which he never lighted. . . . As gentle and modest as a woman, there was [about him] an undoubted capacity to command, which obtained for Pettigrew instant obedience." He was "courteous, kindly and chivalric," and "unfailingly a gentlemen."[10]

When he was offered a brigadier generalship he declined it. But both President Davis and General Joseph E. Johnston had noticed Pettigrew and the offer was renewed with more emphasis in the spring of 1862. Pettigrew commanded a brigade in the early part of the campaign at Yorktown. He was left for dead on the Fair Oaks battlefield and his loss was mourned in Richmond and Raleigh. But he recovered consciousness in a Federal prison camp and was exchanged, to find that his brigade had been assigned to his fellow Carolinian, Brigadier General Dorsey Pender. A new brigade was formed for Pettigrew, which he led on the North Carolina coast and at Gettysburg.

2. Pettigrew's Quest for Shoes

In Cashtown on the night of June 29 Heth recalled Jubal Early's report of a quantity of boots and shoes in Gettysburg. The need for shoes in both armies was already refuting the oracular Napoleon's dictum that "an army marches on its stomach"; Heth directed Pettigrew to take his brigade and probe Early's statement.[11]

Pettigrew mustered his brigade for pay at Cashtown in the early morning of June 30, then marched down the Gettysburg road, the 11th North Carolina Regiment in front, preceded by skirmishers.

The 11th was one of the most highly regarded regiments in the service. At the time it was incorporated, the inspector general stated to General Lee that "the Eleventh Regiment of North Carolina troops is the best drilled, the best equipped and the best armed regiment in the Army of Northern Virginia."[12] It contained the survivors of the old 1st North Carolina Volunteers, called the "Bethel Regiment," that at Bethel had fought the first engagement of the war and suffered the first loss of life in battle in the cause of Southern freedom. Its colonel, Collett Leventhorpe, was looked on as "probably the best finished and equipped field officer in the Confederate service."[13]

About two miles from Gettysburg the advance party arrested a well-mounted civilian who said he was a physician making a visit to a patient. Though not suspecting that any enemy was near, Colonel Leventhorpe questioned the doctor closely. To his surprise the man said there were between four and five thousand Federal troops in the vicinity and a much larger Federal force a few miles distant.[14]

Whether the doctor knew or was trying to frighten the Confederate regiment is not clear, but his statement caused Leventhorpe to halt until he could consult Pettigrew, farther back in the column. The doctor's account—whether he spoke from knowledge or guile—and Leventhorpe's halt probably served to prevent a clash between elements of the two armies in Gettysburg until the day following.

Another of Pettigrew's regiments had a delaying encounter. The 47th North Carolina was marching eagerly from Cashtown, supposedly on an expedition for shoes—many of the soldiers were barefoot—when a civilian on a farm horse rode leisurely out of a near-by woods and asked where he could find the commanding officer. Some of the men thought he was a spy, but he was sent to the head of the column. Almost at once the regiment was halted and the men were directed to take cover. A minute later several shots were fired at long range from woods on both sides of the road. The farmer had come not to spy, but to warn. The regiment was quite certain it escaped an ambuscade.[15] He was probably the member of the Knights of the Golden Circle whom Pettigrew's assistant adjutant general, Captain Louis G. Young, said rode out to tell the general that Federal cavalry was close at hand.

While Petttigrew was marching toward Gettysburg, Harrison, Longstreet's spy, rode past into the town. Before the troops approached the outskirts, Harrison rode back and confirmed for Pettigrew the information he already had from two other sources that elements of the Army of the Potomac were not far distant.[16] These warnings made the general still more circumspect. An officer reported he heard a drum roll on the other side of the town. Pettigrew had been told that he would likely encounter home guards but orders to him were "pre-emptory," that if he found any portion of the Army of the Potomac, he was not to attack it.[17]

Pettigrew rode abreast Leventhorpe at the head of the column and halted the brigade near the Willoughby Run crossing a mile outside the town. He went forward with an advance party to the ridge crossed by the Cashtown pike northwest of Gettysburg, from which he could view the surrounding country. Gettysburg with its ten roads, a town of about three thousand people, lay drousing in a peaceful valley, with golden wheat fields stretching north and south and the glory of early summer spread about; beyond the town broken, wooded hills were capped by a jutting promontory at the southern end. Southern eyes swept the country cursorily, their interest fastened on the village, about which hurried numerous civilians gathering at the public square. It was near noon. The appearance of Southern infantry again had caused the town to seethe with excitement.

Observing that Gettysburg was unoccupied by Federal troops, Pettigrew sent skirmishers ahead and was preparing to move the entire brigade forward when his attention was arrested by a movement far to the south. There on the road from Emmitsburg was a long dark column. Through his glasses he was able to identify it as Northern cavalry.

Buford's two brigades had come through Emmitsburg after encountering Pettigrew's picket near Fairfield on the preceding evening. Dashing ahead of Buford's division was a detachment of Company C, 3rd Indiana Cavalry, commanded by Captain Henry B. Sparks. They entered Gettysburg at a gallop and picked up three or four Confederate prisoners.[18] These may have been some of Pettigrew's skirmishers, but in view of the Indianian's account that they "seemed to be straggling through the streets and mingling with the citizens,"[19] more likely they remained from Early's passage four days before.

Gamble, commanding the first of Buford's brigades, took credit for driving Pettigrew out of Gettysburg, but there was no exchange of fire and Pettigrew retired slowly, reluctant to abandon the needed shoes.

Pettigrew's orders were not sufficiently flexible to allow him to hazard his brigade in a chance encounter with a large force that might have infantry support. He halted three and a half miles out on the Cashtown road, just west of the stone bridge over Marsh Creek, where the brigade bivouacked in a beautiful grove south of the roadway.

Guard duty falling on the 26th North Carolina, Lieutenant Colonel John R. Lane established a picket line that included a segment of the roadway. Later two distressed women conducted by a sentry told him they had been cut off from their houses, which were close at hand. Lane promptly reassured them that the regiment did not make war on women, ordered the picket line re-established so that it would embrace their houses, and let them pass.[20]

Pettigrew rode into Cashtown in the late afternoon and was telling Heth of his encounter when A. P. Hill came up and received the report in person.

"The only force at Gettysburg is cavalry, probably a detachment of observation," said Hill. "I am just from General Lee and the information he has from his scouts corroborates what I have received from mine—that is, the enemy are still at Middleburg, and have not yet struck their tents."

"If there is no objection, General," interjected Heth, "I will take my division tomorrow and go to Gettysburg and get those shoes."

"None in the world," Hill replied.[21]

Both Hill and Heth discredited Pettigrew's information. He had served under neither and they appeared more impressed with his civilian background than his extraordinary capacity. As he moved away from Gettysburg Pettigrew had left two mounted staff officers, Captain Young and Lieutenant Walter H. Robertson, to watch Buford. They found the assignment easy because the rolling country offered ridges behind which they could hide.[22]

The Federal troopers came out of Gettysburg and moved northwest on the Cashtown road. Whenever their advance party came within three or four hundred yards, the two Confederates showed themselves atop a ridge and the Federals halted. This process was repeated several times, each side being more intent on observation than on molesting the other.

As Pettigrew talked with Hill and Heth he saw that neither believed that units of the main Federal army were anywhere near Gettysburg. Pettigrew was insistent that where cavalry was clearing the way, infantry would not be far behind. Hill and Heth apparently became a bit impatient. In the words of Captain Young, they "expressed their doubts so positively"[23] that Pettigrew called Young over and asked him to tell the corps commander exactly what he had seen while reconnoitering the force that had followed them out of Gettysburg. Since Young had served under Hill during the Seven Days' Battles around Richmond, Pettigrew thought his words might have weight where those of a brigadier general did not.

Hill asked Young to describe the character of the troops he had seen and Young said their movements were unquestionably those of trained soldiers, not home guards. But it was difficult to dislodge fixed notions. Hill had prejudged the case and would not correct his conclusions. He still did not think any portion of the Army of the Potomac was in their front. Then, in "emphatic words," he asserted that he indeed hoped it was true, as that was exactly the place where he wanted the Army of the Potomac to be.[24] It was clear from his attitude, however, that he did not accept the intelligence at full value even after talking with Young.

"This spirit of unbelief had taken such hold," Young wrote, "that I doubt if any of the commanders of brigades, except General Pettigrew, believed that we were marching to battle, a weakness on their part which rendered them unprepared for what was about to happen."

Pettigrew then sought General Archer, whose brigade by the normal process of rotation would head the march on the next day. Pettigrew described in minute detail the topography between Cashtown and Gettysburg. He called attention to a road leading in at right angles from the south which the enemy might employ to disrupt his line of march. He cautioned about the right flank. He reviewed also the configuration of the ground around Gettysburg and mentioned in particular a ridge west of the town which would be suitable for defensive purposes, and where, he emphasized, Archer "would probably find the enemy."

Captain Young commented: "Archer listened, but believed not [and] marched on unprepared."[25]

Buford's long column of blue-clad hussars quieted and inspired the Gettysburg citizenry. As the column passed out the Cashtown road Buford galloped ahead to the crest of the western hill to witness the retirement of the brigade of hostile infantry. He sent the information to Reynolds at once. Back from Reynolds to Meade, then on to Halleck and Stanton in Washington, went the word that large infantry detachments of Lee's army were emerging east of the South Mountain passes. This gave the most positive notice yet received that Lee was abandoning his efforts against Harrisburg and Philadelphia and was concentrating toward Baltimore and Washington to shake off the Federal army that had followed him across the Potomac.

Buford established pickets west and north of the town. He deduced that the Confederates would return in greater strength in the morning, and wholly on his own responsibility he determined to hold the ground until Reynolds could bring up infantry assistance. He spent the evening inspecting the terrain and outlining his plan to his two brigade commanders, Gamble and Colonel Thomas C. Devin. He gently rebuked Devin when that confident officer assured him he could look after everything in his front for the next twenty-four hours.

Buford selected for his main line the ridge on which stood the McPherson house and farm buildings a scant mile northwest of the Gettysburg town square, overlooking the long sweep of the road toward Cashtown.

Preparations were being made as well in the Confederate camp. On the night of June 30 Hill sent couriers informing Lee of Pettigrew's encounter with Buford and advising Ewell that he intended to advance the next morning. At five o'clock on the morning of July 1 Heth took up his line of march, accompanied by Pegram's battalion of artillery, and Hill ordered Pender to fall in behind with his division and McIntosh's battalion of artillery. The quest for shoes and Federal soldiers would be undertaken in force. At Marsh Creek Heth picked up Pettigrew and in the hot mist of the July morning approached Gettysburg, concealed behind its hills.

CHAPTER NINE

McPherson's Heights

1. Reynolds Decides on a Battlefield

As Heth moved toward Gettysburg with Archer's veteran Alabama brigade in the lead, first place in the march went to the 13th Alabama regiment commanded by Colonel Birkett Davenport Fry.

Fry, a subtle old soldier whom General Braxton Bragg called "a man with a gunpowder reputation,"[1] had been a top lieutenant of the Tennessee adventurer William Walker in the conquest of Nicaragua. He had fought at Rivas, commanded a brigade at Granada, quieted the Metagalpa Indians, and no doubt ultimately would have been noosed with his chief had he not been sent on a recruiting expedition to San Francisco. He obtained the men but not return transportation, and Walker's cause meantime spiraled downward.

A Virginian by birth, a wanderer by instinct, he studied at Washington College, Pennsylvania, at Virginia Military Institute, and at West Point, though he did not graduate; gained distinction under Joseph E. Johnston in the Mexican War; became a Sacramento, California, lawyer, then a Tallassee, Alabama, cotton ginner, and when the war broke, leader of an Alabama infantry regiment.

And thus the Confederate army set out for Gettysburg with a toughened Central American filibusterer heading the front rank, while in the procession of command behind him were Brigadier General Archer, who might be counted on to swagger in without much caution, impulsive Harry Heth, and quick-tempered A. P. Hill. It should have been obvious that the forward elements of Lee's army would find on that humid

103

Wednesday morning some more entertaining employment than seeking shoes.

Half a mile beyond the village of Seven Stars and about three and a half miles from Gettysburg the regiment entered the woods and swamplands of Marsh Creek, where Fry halted to reconnoiter. A light, misty rain began to fall, a threatening carry-over from the intermittent mountain showers of June 30.[2] Fry rode to the rear of the regiment and told the color-bearer to uncase the colors. That, done in the drizzle, was notice to the men that they were about to meet the enemy and would fight.

The Federals soon showed themselves, a dismounted cavalry patrol in a field to the right. They dashed off, three to the rear and a fourth to the bridge where the Cashtown road crossed Marsh Creek. Fry ordered his men to load at will. Archer then came up and directed them to file to the right through an old apple orchard. He had Fry throw out three companies of the 13th and all of the 5th Alabama battalion as skirmishers; when the balance of the brigade was up, he moved it through the orchard on the south side of the turnpike, formed it in battle line, and resumed the advance.[3]

Davis' brigade, the second in Heth's column, took a corresponding position on the north side of the pike. The brigades of Pettigrew and Brockenbrough followed in support. As Archer's skirmish line approached the Marsh Creek bridge a shot rang out, the first of the battle. It was fired by one of the four men who had been in Gamble's forward picket. The other three rushed off to tell Buford that the Confederate infantry was in sight. The first shot of the battle is credited to both Corporal Alpheus Hodges, Company F, 9th New York Cavalry, and Lieutenant Marcellus E. Jones of Du Page County, Illinois, 8th Illinois Cavalry. Probably the distinction belongs to Jones, who seized the carbine of Sergeant Leir S. Shafer and fired.[4]

Moving abreast, Archer and Davis easily drove in the Federal skirmishers until they approached Willoughby Run a mile west of Gettysburg.

Heth's troops had been delighted to see Major William J. Pegram, who had been ill since Chancellorsville, suddenly appear to take command of his artillery battalion. He immediately moved it from the reserve, with Pender, to the front with Heth. A gunner wrote to his father: "Now what was the astonishment that morning when the skirmishing began, to see our 'fighting Major' galloping up to our camp crying out, 'harness and hitch,' which being quickly done, off he took us . . . in advance of the whole army."[5]

Others also were pleased to welcome Pegram. Lee had seen him farther back and told Hill, "I have good news for you. Major Pegram is up."[6] The artilleryman, one of the best in the service, was still feverish when he reported but after hearing of the invasion he would not be left behind. Of his battalion, Captain Mayre's Fredericksburg battery moved first and opened the battle, followed by the Purcell and Crenshaw batteries.

The dominating feature of the terrain toward Gettysburg was a double ridge merging together to the north into a larger, timbered elevation called Oak Hill. Between the two ridges at the place where the Cashtown road crosses is a gentle dip of 400 yards, with a little ripple of a ridge about the center. These can best be identified as McPherson's Ridge to the west; the Ripple; and Seminary Ridge to the east. The first was named after the farmhouse and barn of Edward McPherson south of the pike. McPherson, a former editor of the Pittsburgh *Daily Times,* was a lame-duck Congressman from the Gettysburg district. The district had gone Democratic in November 1862, showing the existence of a strong peace party. He had much later prominence, including that of presiding over the Republican National Convention at which Robert G. Ingersoll delivered his famous "Plumed Knight" oration, but none so noteworthy as having the battle of Gettysburg begin on his farm, though he was not present to witness it. The Ripple has never been so named, but the designation is appropriate.

An apple orchard stood west and north of the McPherson house while to the south was a wood lot of about five acres. Elsewhere the hill was cleared and cultivated. The eastern ridge, which is little more than the eastern face of the small plateau, was known as Seminary Ridge because a Lutheran seminary was situated on it in a grove of great trees 100 yards south of the Cashtown road. The road as it crosses Seminary Ridge is 1,400 yards from the Gettysburg town square.

Unlike McPherson's, Seminary Ridge was little cultivated, but was crowned with timber north toward Oak Hill and south to where it petered off toward the Emmitsburg road.

Soon after dawn Buford learned from his pickets of the stirring among Confederates beyond Marsh Creek and hurried word to General Reynolds, commanding the left wing of Meade's army, that Southern infantry was moving toward Gettysburg. Reynolds had bivouacked on Marsh Creek, downstream from Pettigrew's camp, at a point four and a half miles south of Gettysburg on the Emmitsburg pike. Buford was confident he could rely on Reynolds for speedy relief and told his troopers to hold. He had John Calef's six guns of the regular artillery to assist. The early morning hours wore on without either vigorous pressure from the Confederates in front or the arrival of Northern reinforcements. While waiting for Pender's division, Heth was engaged mainly in what he termed a feeling process, which satisfied him that he faced nothing but dismounted cavalry. Shortly after eight o'clock the Confederate general decided to brush the cavalrymen off McPherson's Heights and move into the town. One of his shells hit Trooper John E. Weaver of the 3rd Indiana Cavalry, the first man killed in the battle.[7]

Heth seems to have retained an aberration that he began the battle on some sort of time schedule. Thirty years later, when he was going over the field in a carriage with Chief Justice Walter Clark of North Carolina, pointing out the position of Confederate troops, he drew a large silver watch from his pocket and said, "By that watch the battle of Gettysburg opened." Clark recorded his statement without explanation.[8] Heth must have been thinking of the moment when he ordered Archer and Davis forward.

At 8:30 A.M. Buford was feeling the new pressure. He made a final survey of his situation, recognizing that he could not sustain a contest long. The sun was burning through the clouds and a hot mist was rising over the countryside, promising a sultry day. Buford retired to the seminary, a three-story brick building crowned with a cupola, and mounted the high ladder to the top.[9] Through the lifting haze, he viewed the long stretch of the pike toward Cashtown, now filled in the distance with the gray of Pender's advancing division.

Buford glanced south toward Emmitsburg. His pulse tingled and his heart jumped, for there on the roadway was a long, dark column. Faintly discernible at the front, alongside the Stars and Stripes, was the First Corps emblem. Reynolds had kept his word. The infantry was coming.

Elated, Buford rushed down the ladder to carry the news to his hard-pressed cavalry. A familiar voice sounded beside him, asking calmly, "What is the matter, John?"

Turning, he looked into the composed face of General Reynolds. "Hell's to pay," he answered quickly.

G. B. Garrison, one of Buford's scouts, who had a feeling for history's details, jotted down the time in his notebook—Reynolds reached the field at twenty-five minutes before nine.[10] The general's aide-de-camp, Captain Stephen M. Weld, Jr., noted, in his diary, the events that followed in rapid succession.

Reynolds had seen the approach of Confederate soldiers. He decided instantly that Gettysburg was the place for a major battle.

To Weld he said: "Ride at once with your utmost speed to General Meade. Tell him the enemy are advancing in strong force, and that I fear they will get to the heights beyond the town before I can. I will fight them inch by inch, and if driven into the town, I will barricade the streets and hold them as long as possible."[11]

Then Reynolds galloped back to the Emmitsburg road to show the approaching column the shortest route to its combat position. Meade had told him he meant to strike at the point where the enemy showed the greatest strength. On the mucky morning of July 1 Reynolds had found it. He sat on the west side of the Emmitsburg pike inspecting the head of the corps as it passed. "We had a fair view of his features," wrote Captain Robert K. Beecham. "The general looked careworn, and we thought, very sad. . . . It was the last time we ever saw him."[12]

2. A Quaker with an Iron Brigade

The 1st Division of the First Corps of the Army of the Potomac reached McPherson's Heights quickly, led across the fields by Reynolds and its commander, Brigadier General James S. Wadsworth, breaking down fences, throwing aside haversacks and blankets, stripping for action.

Wadsworth, the squire of Geneseo, New York, wealthy planter and upstate philanthropist and politician, was as ardently devoted to the cause of the Federal union as any man in Meade's army. To it he gave much of his fortune and eventually his life. His uncle, William Wadsworth, had commanded the New York militia in the unfortunate affair at Queenston Heights in the War of 1812. The general had declined to leave the army to campaign when nominated by the Republicans as candidate for governor of New York in 1862. He had been defeated by Horatio Seymour, apparently much to his satisfaction, because he enjoyed the excitement of service with the troops. At fifty-six he was one of the oldest of Meade's generals.

Cutler's brigade of Wadsworth's division was in the lead, carrying at its head the blue banner of the Empire State. Reynolds directed the brigade to the ground north of the Cashtown pike, the 76th New York on the right, the 56th Pennsylvania in the center and the 147th New York on the left. This last regiment commanded the unfinished railroad grading that ran parallel to and 150 yards north of the Cashtown road and had sharp cuttings through Seminary and McPherson's ridges and the Ripple. The right of way had been prepared but the ties and iron tracks had not been laid.

Colonel John W. Hofmann had just brought the 56th Pennsylvania into line when the Southern infantry showed in his front. A crash resounded over the field as the 56th let loose a volley, the first Northern infantry fire of the battle. Two members of the color guard of the 55th North Carolina dropped. The Confederates replied; their first fire unhorsed General Cutler and two of his staff. The exchange continued for fifteen minutes, while the balance of the Federal division was coming up.

Reynolds, returning from his quest of Wadsworth, rode with Captain James A. Hall of the 2nd Maine Battery, which was composed of six three-inch guns and men from Knox, Lincoln, Cumberland, and other rugged seacoast counties, augmented by infantrymen detailed from the 16th Maine Regiment. Reynolds showed Hall where to put his pieces to sweep the Cashtown road, replacing Calef's horse artillery. He pointed to the locations from which about twenty Confederate cannon were shelling the ground over which Wadsworth's soldiers were deploying and told Hall, "Pay your attention to those guns and draw their fire from our infantry while it is forming."[13]

Wadsworth's other brigade, celebrated in Northern song and story, came up, the men wearing their familiar black sombreros,[14] rolled and looped up on the right side and adorned with a plume and the light-blue infantry ribbon which gave Archer's Alabamians the certain knowledge that they were no longer fighting merely cavalry. This was the 1st Brigade, 1st Division, of the First Army Corps—the "Iron Brigade." Heth's men had suspected that infantry was near when they had heard a band playing the strains of "The Girl I Left Behind Me."

Tradition and romance already clustered about the Iron Brigade's achievements. The tenacity and hardihood of these men from the Northwest had won them their celebrated name—bestowed on them by McClellan. Solomon Meredith, a giant North Carolina Quaker, six feet six, who had moved to Cambridge City, Indiana, and with his three sons cast lots with the Union, led the brigade into action. His love for the Federal cause deepened as succeeding sons fell from Southern bullets. Of peaceful faith, he commanded one of the most audacious of combat units.[15]

Meredith, reared in poverty, had known the hardships of being a

poor white laborer in the South. He was uneducated and without a
trade. He worked at day jobs and at the age of thirty went North and
got work cutting cord wood at six dollars a month. Out of this he
reared his family, saved, paid for schooling, and developed into a man
of commanding presence and great personal force. He was elected
sheriff and appointed United States Marshal for Indiana by President
Tyler. His natural leadership caused the men to elect him colonel of
the 19th Indiana, which regiment became the darling of the tough-
fibered Indiana governor, Oliver P. Morton. Meredith had but one
military defect: his great body made him an easy target. When he went
down it was in a hot corner where his men were going with him.

Reynolds directed the Iron Brigade into line *en échelon,* the 2nd
Wisconsin in front on the right, nearest the Cashtown road, followed
by the 7th Wisconsin, 19th Indiana, and 24th Michigan, while the
closing regiment, the 6th Wisconsin, had been halted and held in reserve
on Seminary Ridge. Mindful that west of Gettysburg his right flank
was exposed to an enemy approaching from the north, he sent orders
to Major General Abner Doubleday, commanding the First Corps division next in line: "I will hold on to this road [Cashtown] and you
hold on to the other [Mummasburg]." This would bring Doubleday's
division into line north of the Cashtown pike and on Wadsworth's right.

The 6th Wisconsin, last in line of the Iron Brigade regiments, was
commanded by Lieutenant Colonel Rufus R. Dawes. It had a lusty-
lunged sergeant, John Ticknor, whose voice could usually be heard on
the march above the scuff of leather and rattle of canteens and scabbards. Ticknor already had been a part of one of the great American
episodes. In late 1861, returning from McClellan's review at Bailey's
Cross Roads, the regiment had been accompanied back to Arlington
by Julia Ward Howe. She heard Sergeant Ticknor's clear tenor lead
the regiment in "We'll Hang Jeff Davis to a Sour Apple Tree," set to
the tune of "John Brown's Body," which in turn was that of the old
spiritual, "Say Brothers, Will You Meet Us, on Canaan's Happy Shore."
The regiment's bayonets glistened in "burnished rows of steel" and
about it spread "the watchfires of a hundred circling camps." All this
had inspired Mrs. Howe that night to write the "Battle Hymn of the
Republic," the treasured song of the Northern armies.[16]

But as the 6th Wisconsin came up the Emmitsburg road Colonel
Dawes told Drum Major R. N. Smith to play, not this hymn, but the
equally stirring notes of "The Campbells Are Coming." The regimental
band struck up the old Scottish battle song just as the firing opened in

front of Cutler's brigade. General Meredith's aide, Lieutenant Gilbert M. Woodward, came dashing up with orders, more stirring than the music: "Colonel, form your line and prepare for action." The men loaded their muskets as they advanced on the run but they were disappointed to learn that for the moment they would have to wait in reserve.

3. Meade Loses His "Noblest and Bravest"

At mid-morning, before McPherson's Heights, two Confederate brigades, Archer's and Davis', faced the two Federal brigades of Meredith and Cutler. The alignment was far from exact. On the Confederate left, Davis overlapped Cutler, while on the Confederate right, Archer was overlapped by Meredith. The result was that in the opening phase of the battle, the right regiments of Archer, the Confederate, and Cutler, the Federal, were pressed back.

As the other Iron Brigade regiments followed the 2nd Wisconsin into McPherson's Woods, the 19th Indiana and 24th Michigan at the left of the Federal line worked down the incline on the edge of the timber and felt for Archer's flank at the very moment when he was embarrassed by having half his command on the west and half on the east bank of Willoughby Run. Near the summit of McPherson's Ridge, Reynolds was directing the two regiments in the enveloping movement. He was mounted on his black horse and wore the major general's shoulder straps. Carelessly exposing himself and obviously an officer of high rank, he at once drew the fire of Archer's skirmishers, who had crossed Willoughby Run and worked their way up the wooded hillside.

Reynolds, expecting support, had turned in the saddle to look toward the crest of the ridge behind him. It was 10:15 A.M. He was struck in the back of the neck by a Minié ball fired by a marksman from a tree on the bank of the stream. The ball passed through his head and came out the other side at the eye.

The Minié ball, used freely in the War between the States, had been invented by Captain C. E. Minié of Vincennes, France, during the Crimean War. It was a long, hollow bullet into which an iron cup was inserted in its base. Upon firing, this cup pushed the bullet into the rifling of the barrel.

Reynolds fell forward without speaking a word. His frightened horse was dashing toward the open fields when his aides caught it. The body dropped lifeless from the saddle. They wrapped him in an army blanket, and a detail from the 76th New York carried him to the seminary and on to the little stone house of George George on the Emmitsburg road. While the fateful battle he had elected to begin still roared west of Gettysburg, his body was put in an ambulance for Baltimore and Lancaster, Pennsylvania. The Confederates learned of his death quickly but thought it resulted from one of Pegram's shells.[17]

Reynolds was perhaps the most universally admired among the generals of the Army of the Potomac. Meade called him the "noblest" and "bravest,"[18] and even his opponent Heth, when informed of his death, said the country "well might mourn, and in doing so honor herself."[19] Reynolds was a handsome man, six feet tall, narrow-waisted, with black hair and a deep tan gained from years of exposure. He was rated almost by concensus the army's best horseman. He was forty-two years old when he fell.

Had Archer entrusted the command of the front line to the wily filibusterer Fry, or had he heeded the warning given him on the previous evening by Pettigrew, all might have gone well for his brigade. Pettigrew had studied the approaches to Gettysburg carefully and had cautioned Archer to guard against his right flank being turned. Pettigrew described McPherson's Ridge and suggested that this would probably be the line the Northern army would defend.

Here it was that Meredith, undeterred by the death of Reynolds, pressed the action against Archer. While the 2nd and 7th Wisconsin engaged him in front, the 19th Indiana and 24th Michigan appeared almost at right angles to his disconcerted line caught halfway across the stream. The 19th Indiana was able to work undetected around the shoulder of the heavily wooded bluff above the creek and confront Archer unexpectedly. This regiment had been on picket duty the night before and the men's guns were already loaded, which gave them a time advantage over the Confederates, cramped up along the two banks.

The color-bearer of the 19th, whose name was Cunningham, was about to uncase the colors for the charge when a staff officer rode up and shouted, "Do not unfurl that flag."[20] Near by was Cunningham's companion, A. J. Buckles. Cunningham, seeing the battle line moving, defied the adjutant and said to Buckles, "Abe, pull the shuck." Off came the casing, and the Stars and Stripes flew in the breeze. It brought a shower of bullets and Flag-Bearer Cunningham fell. Buckles dropped his gun, caught up the flag, and kept it so far in advance of the line that Lieutenant Colonel W. W. Dudley rebuked him for his daring. Before the first day's battle ended eight color-bearers of the 19th Indiana had been shot down.

Dudley, a well-known Indiana political figure—who came to be called "Blocks of Four" Dudley because of his custom of bringing in his henchmen on election day in more than single units—led the firing line. A Confederate ball that day took off his foot.

The quick fire of the Hoosiers sprayed the Confederates who had gained the east bank. On the west bank Colonel Fry with the right regiment fought a gallant battle. The old filibusterer was not to be trapped. Lieutenant Colonel G. H. Stevens of the 2nd Wisconsin was killed. A few minutes later the regiment's colonel, Lucius Fairchild, had his arm shot off. Major John Mansfield took command.

But the impetuous Alabamians found themselves hopelessly outflanked. They faced not the right, but almost the center of the Federal line.[21] The situation was what Pettigrew had feared. Archer had been heedless. Here, where Pettigrew said he would find the Federal army, he had allowed himself to be surprised and outmaneuvered because, as predicted, they were there. "All we could do," wrote Private E. T. Boland, of Brewton, Alabama, "was to wind them around ourselves." The fight was sharp but short. Archer, in the front line, had dismounted to lead his brigade. He and two companies of the 13th Alabama, recruited in Greenville and Camden, tried to put up a resistance in a clump of willows on the west bank of Willoughby Run.[22] But the Wisconsin men came crashing in on them while the Hoosier regiment held them in front. Fry was able to extricate most of them, but Archer and seventy-five others were taken prisoner.

The capture of Archer sent a stir of elation through the Iron Brigade. The details were related with relish. Private Patrick Maloney, an Irishman of Company G, rushed after Archer as he was trying to escape, caught him and marched him to Captain Charles C. Dow, who greeted him courteously. Archer offered to surrender his sword.

"Keep your sword, General, and go to the rear," said Dow. "One sword is all I need on this line."[23]

Archer crossed Willoughby Run and walked toward the Federal rear. He had covered about forty yards when he met Lieutenant D. B. Dailey of Meredith's staff, who demanded his sword. Archer explained that he had retained it by the indulgence of Captain Dow, but the lieutenant, who had taken no part in the capture, insisted on the trophy. Another Iron Brigade captain, Robert K. Beecham, observed that "it is not always that the man on the outmost line receives the reward which is his due."[24] The incident must have nettled Archer and with the humiliation of his capture, left him in ill humor. When General Doubleday, an

Heth's attack on Wadsworth. July 1, 1863, 10:00 to 11:30 A.M.

acquaintance in the old army, rode up with the greeting, "General
Archer, I am glad to meet you," Archer refused his hand.

"I am not glad to meet you, sir," he replied coldly.[25]

The story of the capture came to have embellishments. Pat Maloney
—who was killed later in the day and could have had no part in the
elaborations—was said to have seized the general by the throat, and
commanded: "Roight about face, Gineral. March." At the seminary,
Maloney saluted and said, "Gineral Wadsworth, I make you acquainted
with Gineral Archer."[26] But in truth Archer never got beyond the
lieutenant and that officer was the one who retained Archer's sword.
No other general officer of the Army of Northern Virginia had been
captured since Lee took command. Fry now took over the brigade.

4. Davis Is Tricked by a Railroad Cut

The misfortunes which befell Davis were more severe even than those
encountered by Archer. Triumph was suddenly turned into disaster.

The 11th Mississippi was on detached service and only three of
Davis' regiments were present, the 2nd and 42nd Mississippi, and the
55th North Carolina. The last was distinctly a young man's regiment,
not a member of it having attained the age of thirty.

"Old Graybeard" Cutler's brigade was divided and part of it was isolated as it went into action.[27] Three of the regiments—the 56th Pennsylvania and the 76th and 147th New York—were north of the railroad cut. Two others, the 84th New York (14th Brooklyn) and 95th New York, connected with the Iron Brigade south of the railroad right of way and the Cashtown road. The 7th Indiana was behind the lines, bringing up the division trains. Hall's guns occupied the position between the road and the right of way. Thus a distance of a hundred yards separated Cutler's three right regiments from the balance of the Federal infantry.

Davis advanced against Cutler with the 55th North Carolina on the Confederate left, the 42nd Mississippi in the center and the 2nd Mississippi nearest the Cashtown road and the railroad cut. As the North Carolinians reached Cutler's flank, they wheeled to the right with a rush. Colonel John Kerr Connally seized the battle flag, jumped to the front and aligned the regiment on the colors. The gesture was foolhardy. Instantly he drew Federal fire and fell with his leg wounded and his arm so shattered that it had to be amputated. Major A. H. Belo ran to inquire if he were badly hurt. "Yes," said Connally, "but pay no attention to me. Take the colors and keep ahead of the Mississippians."[28]

Captain J. V. Pierce of the 147th New York heard the cry that ran down the Federal lines, "They are flanking us on the right."[29] He described the movement: the Confederate regiment was "pressing far to our right and rear and came over to the south side of the rail fence, their colors dropped to the front. An officer in front of the center corrected the alignment as if passing in review. It was the finest exhibition of discipline and drill I ever saw before or since on a battlefield."

The flank attack broke Cutler's regiments, which retired at a run across the fields 400 yards to the northern extension of Seminary Ridge. Here they paused briefly, then continued their retrograde movement to the outskirts of Gettysburg. Hall meantime found his battery exposed and its infantry supports vanished. He had opened on the enemy at 10:45 and had been firing for twenty-five minutes when Davis' men showed within sixty yards of his right gun. Hall fired with canister, which broke their advance, but when the infantry fled he had to withdraw the battery hastily by sections, and abandon one gun.

In response to Doubleday's messengers, Lieutenant Colonel Dawes, guided by a staff captain, brought the 6th Wisconsin forward at the double quick. He saw the flight of Cutler's men "in disorder" and the

withdrawal of Hall's battery. A group of officers passed in front of
the regiment carrying something in a blanket, but no one knew it was
the body of General Reynolds. They plunged ahead to the fence
along the Cashtown road, where they faced north. Their volley struck
the flank of the Confederates who were in a headlong pursuit north
of the railroad right of way. The gray line swayed and buckled. Cutler's two regiments south of the road, the 14th Brooklyn and 95th
New York, now faced north on the left of the 6th Wisconsin, and fired
obliquely almost into the rear of the Mississippians.

Then the two Mississippi regiments, surprised by the enfilade attack,
made a fatal mistake. Partly because Davis had allowed them to get
out of hand, and partly because of their instinctive search for cover
under flank fire, they crowded into the railroad cut. The 2nd Mississippi on the right and a part of the 42nd Mississippi in the center
quickly gained the security of the steep bank at the cut in the Ripple,
midway between the two ridges. It was too deep to serve as an en-
trenchment. In it the men lost command of the approaches and to all
effective purposes, they were out of action. Davis ordered their further
retirement and directed the 55th North Carolina to cover it.

But it was too late. Dawes, seeing the Confederates huddled in
the cut, rushed to Major Edward Pye, commanding the 95th New
York, and said, "We must charge." "Charge it is," replied the major,
and together they gave the command, "Forward, charge!"[30]

Across the field from the road to the cut streamed the two regiments,
followed by the 14th Brooklyn under Colonel E. B. Fowler. The Confederate fire proved much more destructive than Dawes could have
anticipated, coming chiefly from the North Carolinians on the other
side of the cut. Of the 420 Wisconsin soldiers who left the roadside
fence, only 240 reached the railroad right of way, but there they were
complete masters of the Mississippians gathered helplessly beneath
them.

In this internecine conflict there were chivalric episodes of courtesy
and indulgence not so often encountered in later-day wars, where the
propaganda machines take over to coarsen the conflict and make all
allies virtuous and all enemies brutes. Here the first instinct of the
Wisconsin soldiers was not to kill, but to save the lives of the men
at their mercy. Lieutenant Colonel Dawes, advancing on foot, heard
his men shouting, "Throw down your muskets! Down with your
muskets!" Forcing his way through the line he reached the edge of
the cut and, as he described it, "found myself face to face with hun-

dreds of rebels." In later years, when he thought of this moment, he
was always thankful for his presence of mind. "Surrender or I fire,"
he shouted. An officer in gray uniform silently handed over his sword.
He was Major John A. Blair, commanding the 2nd Mississippi. At
his word about 250 men threw down their guns.

Said Dawes, in reflecting on the restraint of his soldiers: "The coolness, self-possession, and discipline which held back our men from
pouring in a general volley saved a hundred lives of the enemy, and
as my mind goes back to the fearful excitement of the moment, I
marvel at it."[31]

Dawes took Blair's sword and those of six other officers and turned
them over to Adjutant E. P. Brooks; to Major John F. Hauser he
assigned the task of taking the prisoners—7 officers and 225 enlisted
men, mainly of the 2nd Mississippi—to the provost guard. Other
prisoners were captured by the two New York regiments, which
brought Davis' loss to about half his force. The balance of the brigade
withdrew to the west side of Willoughby Run. The Federals re-established their old line facing west along McPherson's Ridge, and Cutler
again advanced his regiments.

Meredith in a companion realignment brought the victorious Iron
Brigade back to the east side of the run, on the line it had occupied
before Reynolds sent it against Archer. The 19th Indiana changed
places with the 24th Michigan and took the left of the line, while the
7th Wisconsin held the right. Buford meantime had been ordered to
the far left as a flank guard. The five companies of the 3rd Indiana
Cavalry declined to hear the order and remained to fight with the
Iron Brigade.[32]

Heth, too, reorganized his division by moving Archer's remnants
to the right and bringing Pettigrew forward to the center. He pulled
Davis out of the line to allow him to collect his stragglers, judging
him almost useless for the rest of the day. He sent Brockenbrough
to Pettigrew's left. It was 11:30. Two Confederate brigades had
been deplorably led and badly worsted. Instead of taking advantage of his numerical superiority over Wadsworth—a Confederate
division had greater strength than a Federal—Heth had attacked tim-
idly with half his force and had seen it defeated and scattered without
making an effort to support it. That he had expected to encounter
nothing but cavalry was not a sufficient explanation. Pathetically
droll was his report that "the enemy had now been felt, and found

to be in heavy force. . . ." To that some hundreds of dead Confederates might have liked to testify.

On the Federal side, the two remaining First Corps divisions were coming into line. While Doubleday was commanding the corps, his own division was led by Brigadier General Thomas A. Rowley, a West Point graduate from Pennsylvania, who had two small brigades, one his own, mainly Pennsylvanians, now commanded by Colonel Chapman Biddle, and the other consisting of three Pennsylvania mountain regiments commanded by Colonel Roy Stone.

The other First Corps division was that of Brigadier General John C. Robinson, a bushy-whiskered West Point graduate from New York, with two brigades, commanded by West Point graduates, Brigadier Generals Gabriel R. Paul and Henry Baxter. At Reynolds' order they had marched behind Wadsworth. On separate roads they arrived almost simultaneously on the battlefield.

Doubleday used Rowley's men to strengthen the line held by the Iron Brigade. He put the two brigades on the two extremes of McPherson's Woods, Biddle on the left and Stone on the right. Stone's right rested on the Cashtown road. Robinson's division was held in reserve at the Seminary.

5. A Shot Is Fired from the Rear

At the outbreak of the war a young West Point graduate, Lieutenant Colonel Thomas Leiper Kane, began to drill a rifle regiment from the Pennsylvania mountain country. Their distinctive garb was a cap adorned with the tail of a buck deer. The regiment had the successive official names of the 1st Rifles, the 13th Reserves and the 42nd Pennsylvania Infantry, but to the Federal army it was known as the "Bucktails."[33]

Kane, ahead of his time, realized that the rifle had ended the close-order infantry attack and had drilled his men in infiltration tactics, instructing them to scatter under heavy fire, to make full use of whatever cover the ground offered, to press continually forward where the ground gave an advantage, and to fire only when they had a target in their sights. He placed emphasis on the individual soldier's responsibility. He conducted regular target practice among men already skilled as squirrel and deer hunters, and specialized in long-range firing, from 200 to 1,000 yards.

Such was the success of the Bucktails as sharpshooters and skirmishers in the early fighting that the War Department wanted more of them. In July 1862 it detached Major Roy Stone from the 1st Rifles, sent him into the Pennsylvania mountains, and told him to bring out an entire new brigade of riflemen with bucktail caps. The 149th and 150th Regiments were the result. They were assembled from fourteen counties, from Potter, McKean, and Tioga bordering on New York, through Lycoming, Mifflin, Clarion, Clearfield, and Huntingdon, and from Crawford on the Ohio line to a scattering from Philadelphia at the east. Sergeant William R. Ramsey gave their qualifications: ". . . well formed, of hardy habits, skilled in the use of the rifle. . . ." To these two Bucktail regiments was joined the 143rd Pennsylvania Infantry, recruited in the Wyoming Valley.

The original Bucktails were incensed. They claimed the Secretary of War had authorized them to wear the bucktail as a distinctive badge to which green recruits were not entitled. They summed up their attitude: "There was but one Bucktail regiment, viz., the First Rifles, Pennsylvania Reserves." Public opinion rallied to the side of the 1st Rifles. Stone's men were scorned and dubbed contemptuously the "Bogus Bucktails."

But now the Bogus Bucktails were to have an opportunity such as had never come to those mountaineers who had pre-empted the bucktail name. Doubleday came out to meet them on the field east of the seminary, accompanied by Rowley and their staffs. The artillery bombardment had opened in more deadly earnest across Willoughby Run, and, scarcely heard above the exploding shells, Doubleday addressed the three regiments, emphasizing the importance of victory. As Pennsylvanians, he reminded them, they were defending their own soil. Major Thomas Chamberlain of the 150th noted that it was 11:30 when the regiment, aggregating 397 officers and men, took position on the north end of the woods that concealed the Iron Brigade. To the right of the 150th, extending past the McPherson farm buildings to the Cashtown pike, were the 149th and 143rd.

When Stone's men reached this position, littered with the debris of the battle between Cutler and Davis and manifestly the center of the Federal line, the Bogus Bucktails let out a shout, "We have come to stay, boys!"[34] They could not then know how prophetic was their cry.

Colonel Langhorne Wister of the 150th now sent out his Company B as skirmishers, telling them to work ahead until they felt the enemy. They moved down the western slope of McPherson's Ridge to Willoughby Run, where they encountered Heth's skirmishers on the opposite bank. The rivulet along which the fighting had begun was still the dividing line between the armies.

The action lulled. From the ridge Stone's men could look across and see Pender's division in Heth's rear. "The enemy seemed to be formed in continuous double lines of battle," said Major Chamberlain; "as a spectacle it was striking."[35] Although Heth's bombardment continued, the Confederates made no effort to renew the infantry battle.

At noon a fleshy little man, old and peculiar, dragging an antiquated Enfield rifle and wearing a blue swallow-tailed coat with burnished brass buttons—of a style not commonly seen for forty years—a buff vest, and a high silk hat, appeared on the left of the 150th and asked, "Can I fight with your regiment?" He was referred to Colonel Wister, who was coming up. The peculiar intruder was a resident of Gettysburg, John Burns, more than seventy years old.

"Well, old man, what do you want?" the colonel asked bluntly.

"I want a chance to fight with your regiment."

"Can you shoot?"

"Oh, yes," said the old man, a smile stealing over his face. "If you knew you had before you a soldier of the War of 1812, who had fought at Lundy's Lane, you would not ask such a question."

The colonel inquired about his ammunition and Burns slapped his pockets. "Certainly you can fight with us," Wister said. "I wish there were many more like you."[36] But he told him to go into the woods and fight with the Iron Brigade, where he would have better shelter.

The old man obeyed reluctantly. In the woods he encountered the 7th Wisconsin, where Colonel Callis discouraged him: "Old man, you had better go to the rear or you'll get hurt."

Just then a shell burst near by. "Tut! tut! tut! I've heard that sort of thing before," said Burns.[37]

When Callis again ordered him to the rear, he took out an old-fashioned powder horn and a cartridge box of bullets, and said if he could not fight with the regiment, he would have to fight alone. "There are three hundred cowards back in that town," he said, "who ought to come out of their cellars and fight. I will show you that there is one man in Gettysburg who is not afraid."

Someone handed him a better gun, captured from Archer. His condemnation of his home town was scarcely appropriate. Company

K of the 1st Pennsylvania Reserves, 5th Corps, part of McCandless'
brigade, was composed of veteran soldiers from Gettysburg. A company of students from Pennsylvania College and the Theological
Seminary had skirmished with Early's division and then marched off
to Harrisburg under the command of a theological student, Captain
F. Klinefelter. Some in Gettysburg were in hiding, to be sure. But
the Burns "bushwhacker" warfare, celebrated in poetry by Bret Harte
and monumented on the Gettysburg battlefield, was of the exact type
the Federal General John Pope had threatened to suppress in Virginia with retaliatory shootings.

Lee had not been oppressive in Pennsylvania. He made no war on
civilians and there was no just occasion for them to rise in a partisan
outbreak. Lee, in fact, had spared civilians, even when they fired on
his men at Chambersburg. He had merely confiscated their guns.

Fighting with the 7th Wisconsin, Burns dropped a Confederate
officer from a white horse.[38] When the Federal line later was dislodged, he crawled away from his gun and buried his ammunition.
When he was found wounded, he denied to the Confederates that he
had been a combatant and said he was hit while seeking help for his
invalid wife. The truth and heroics had gone out of him. A pitying
Southern officer had his four wounds dressèd by a Confederate surgeon. Then several Confederates loaded him carefully into a wagon,
to be taken home for acclaim and renown as "the hero of Gettysburg,"
a title neither discerning nor deserved.

John Burns had scarcely departed when a shot was heard from the
rear and a shell burst behind the Bogus Bucktails. Colonel Edmund
L. Dana of the 143rd thought it was from a Federal battery. When
a second shell followed he sent word to Colonel Charles S. Wain-
wright, commanding the First Corps artillery, demanding that the
reckless firing be stopped.[39]

Another shell, and the truth broke on Stone's men. Rodes's division, heading Ewell's corps, had pushed down from the north and
seized Oak Hill, the eminence on the flank of the Federal line. The
entire First Corps, facing west and suddenly menaced from the north,
was in a most critical situation.

Fortunately Robinson's division was still in reserve at the seminary.
Doubleday hurriedly formed a new line north of the railroad, prolonging that of the balance of the corps. Stone's brigade was shifted
to secure protection where possible from the enfilade artillery fire.
Stone kept the 150th Pennsylvania facing west and changed front

with the 143rd and 149th regiments. The 143rd faced north along the edge of the Cashtown road, forming a salient where it joined with the 150th.

Anticipating an assault on the salient, Stone advanced his other regiment, the 149th, to the line of the railroad right of way that had proved a trap for the Mississippians. The regiment was in position when Daniel's brigade of Rodes's division—the 32nd North Carolina flying the new Confederate banner—approached across the northern field.

But Doubleday was fortunate. Along with the arrival of Ewell's 1st division under Rodes, Howard's Eleventh Corps of the Federal army was sighted by the seminary lookout, marching up the Emmitsburg road at top speed for Gettysburg.[40]

Oak Hill

1. Schurz Is Greeted with a Salvo

Major General Oliver O. Howard, young, nervous, and a question mark in the army since Chancellorsville, reached Gettysburg about mid-morning, riding ahead of his men and escorted by two companies of the 1st Indiana Cavalry. Reynolds had sent him an urgent message to bring on the Eleventh Corps, which had camped near Emmitsburg and was already on the road when the courier met it.

Howard had been under marching orders for the morning of July 1 and had anticipated the need for speed. Dividing his corps, he had put Brigadier General Francis C. Barlow on the direct road from Emmitsburg to Gettysburg and had shifted his other two divisions, those of Major General Carl Schurz and Brigadier General Adolph von Steinwehr, to the Taneytown Road. Due to obstructions on the main road caused by the passage of the First Corps artillery and wagons, he expected the two detachments to reach Gettysburg at about the same time.

Howard's arrival was timed by witnesses all the way from 9:45 to 11:30 A.M. and he was uncertain about his own watch, but the hour was probably about ten-thirty. He witnessed the retreat of Cutler's regiments under pressure from Davis in the opening phase of the battle. That was the cause of his doleful and premature report to Meade that the First Corps had fled on its initial contact with the enemy.[1] The oral message was the first of his criticisms of the First Corps which disturbed Meade and caused him to send Major Gen-

122

eral John Newton, commander of a division of the Sixth Corps, to
supersede Doubleday, who had been guilty of nothing more than leading one of the best day's fighting in the whole history of the Army of
the Potomac. Newton did not arrive until after the conclusion of the
first day.

Howard was in the cupola of Pennsylvania College[2] at 11:30 A.M.
surveying the country when he received intelligence that Reynolds,
for whom his couriers had been searching, but whom he had not
sought himself, was lying dead at the seminary; thus, by virtue of his
seniority Howard commanded all the left-wing forces present on the
battlefield.

Howard had not seen Buford or Doubleday and knew nothing of
the conditions of the conflict. But he learned quickly from Devin's
cavalrymen that fresh Confederate columns were expected at any
instant along the roads leading into Gettysburg from Carlisle and
Harrisburg. His view of the action west of the town, which had
lapsed into exchanges between the artillery and skirmishers of the
two armies, reassured him that there was no emergency in that quarter.
Gray-coated prisoners, those captured from Archer and Davis, were
being herded into the town and it appeared that Doubleday had turned
an initial defeat into a Federal victory. Howard was forced to post-
pone a visit to the seminary to inspect the lines west of the town, but
he left Doubleday in charge there, while he returned—"slowly" he
said—to the Emmitsburg road. At the foot of Cemetery Hill he met
Schurz, who likewise had ridden ahead of his men. Howard turned
over to Schurz the command of the Eleventh Corps and gave him
directions about posting his own division, now under Brigadier General Alexander Schimmelfennig, and that of Barlow, north of Gettysburg.

Howard directed his remaining division, Steinwehr's, to remain in
reserve on Cemetery Hill south of the town. One of the minor but
prolonged controversies after the battle concerned whether Howard
did this of his own inspiration or in compliance with orders received
from Reynolds. The selection of the position was presumed by most
of Washington officialdom, grown accustomed to defeat, to be the
main reason for Northern victory. Cemetery Ridge provided a strong
rallying point with many tactical advantages, and consequently the
selection of the ground, more than the army or its commander, was
held to be the essential thing, and the most important of all the decisions at Gettysburg. But the ridge was so conspicuous that none

could miss it, and whether Buford, Reynolds, Howard, or—more certainly in the final decision—Hancock selected it, the army was fairly sure to gravitate to it when a rallying point was needed. A general was not called for—any private could have picked it out readily and made his way there without orders.

Howard received the thanks of Congress for selecting the position. Congress is not infallible in such matters, nor was the Congress in question particularly studiously inclined, and certainly all the evidence was not in. At this later day it seems clear that Reynolds fought a delaying action west of Gettysburg for no other purpose than to secure Cemetery Ridge as a concentration point for the other Federal columns coming up. Both direct and circumstantial evidence support this view. Reynolds had told Meade his purpose was to save this high ground: such was the implication of his statement that he feared the enemy "will get to the heights beyond the town before I can." He had said he would fight "inch by inch" through the streets. This could mean only that, in his mind, he was falling back all the while to Cemetery Ridge.

More direct testimony was supplied by Doubleday, who said that one of Howard's aides arrived soon after Reynolds descended from the seminary cupola after an inspection with Buford. The aide requested instructions regarding the Eleventh Corps, and Reynolds "directed that General Howard bring his corps forward at once and *form them on Cemetery Hill* as a reserve."[3]

Lieutenant Joseph G. Rosengarten of Reynolds' staff said this order was given in his presence. Howard held Rosengarten in error.

Even more persuasive is a consideration of the dangerous nature of Reynolds' position on McPherson's Ridge. It was exposed to flank attack by the enterprising enemy known to be approaching. Reynolds' keen military perception would have rejected it for anything more than a holding engagement which he would try to sustain until other Federal corps came up to his relief.

The Eleventh Corps had an unenviable reputation in both armies. It was preponderantly German, made up mainly of immigrants who had fled their mother country during the uprisings of 1848, and who were drawn to the Federal cause by their leaders, notably Blenker, Schurz, and Franz Sigel. Being chiefly artisans, most of them had settled in the North. Their ardor for the cause could not be expected to equal that of soldiers possessing an American heritage. Their inability to speak English caused Confederates to believe they were mercenaries like the Hessians of the Revolutionary War. Antiforeign sentiment was still rampant at the outbreak of the war because the heavy immigration had depressed wages in the 1850s and crowded the slum areas of the Northern cities. The antipathy had its expression in a wave of nativism and, politically, in the Know-Nothing Party, which had made substantial headway for a time in the decade before the war.

Oliver Howard was thirty-two years old, a native of Leeds, Maine, and a graduate of Bowdoin and West Point. He took command of a Maine regiment when war broke out and led a brigade at First Manassas, but at the battle of Fair Oaks he lost his right arm. The question might have been raised with him as with Ewell, whether one maimed in battle retained the same zest for combat. Howard was a man of deeply religious sentiments who prayed in his tent each night. He won respect, but, because of a testiness, little affection. This was his last battle with the Army of the Potomac. Later he served congenially in Sherman's "scorched earth" campaigns in Georgia and the Carolinas.

The positions Howard designated for Schimmelfennig and Barlow were north of Gettysburg, in open, cultivated country, running at a right angle with Doubleday's line west of the town. Howard, since he commanded troops that had shown uncertain qualities at Chancellorsville, might have reflected on the disadvantage of fighting a battle in the clearings. The information he already possessed, forecasting the approach of heavy Confederate columns from the north, might have suggested that he station his corps at the outset on Cemetery and Culp's hills, to which Doubleday could then have retired in orderly fashion, although losses in any withdrawal would have been inevitable.

But time was short and decisions had to be made in haste. Doubtless Howard considered a withdrawal of the entire army to Cemetery Hill premature. Slocum had reached Two Taverns, only five miles distant, with the Twelfth Corps, and might reasonably be counted on for support. Sickles was eleven miles away with the Third Corps at Emmitsburg, and Howard now sent urgent messages for assistance to both Sickles and Slocum.

Sickles received Howard's summons at two o'clock in the afternoon; though he was under orders to maintain his position at Emmitsburg and watch the South Mountain pass, the fighting spirit was strong in his heart. Whatever the orders, a part of the army was in danger. He required only a moment for reflection. Leaving two of his brigades to watch the pass, he put the balance of his corps on the road for rapid marching to Gettysburg.

Slocum, believing that an army could respond to but one commander, declined to budge without direct orders from Meade, maintaining that the commanding general's Pipe Creek Circular—which Sickles considered no obstacle to succoring a force under attack— fixed a battle position farther back. It would be unwise, he thought, to bring on a general engagement elsewhere without Meade's positive instructions. Howard repeated his entreaties to Slocum and finally sent his aide and brother, Major Charles Howard, to request Slocum to come to the field in person, even with no troops. The Twelfth Corps commander declined "to go to the front or take any responsibility."[4]

Slocum's attitude amazed his soldiers, who had been forewarned of the proximity of the enemy when skirmishers were thrown out well to the front and flanks, though they were marching through an open country where visibility was good in all directions. Puzzled that the pace was not increased with an enemy near, they filed leisurely into a field at Two Taverns and went into bivouac, still perplexed, because the firing ahead indicated the battle had grown more intense. Three couriers dashed up to Slocum in rapid succession, their horses lathered and jaded. The men looked on curiously; a knot of officers and orderlies would form around the commanding general with each arrival, then would break up and scatter. Through the grapevine the private soldiers finally heard that Slocum was being summoned by Howard but since he was acting under Meade's orders, he would not join the fighting yet. Late in the day the corps resumed its march toward Gettysburg.[5]

Schimmelfennig's troops, with their blaring German bands, marched into Gettysburg at twelve-thirty. Schimmelfennig was a Prussian officer who had served in the Schleswig-Holstein revolution of 1848-1850, and with the Prussian force that invaded Baden to quell insurgents in 1849. He became colonel of the 74th Pennsylvania Infantry, a Germant regiment recruited largely in Pittsburgh, which he was reputed to have made into "a model regiment in drill and discipline."[6]

After halts and conferences, Schurz directed Schimmelfennig to march out the Mummasburg road and occupy Oak Hill, on the right of Doubleday. The division commander threw out skirmishers and began his advance, but even as he left the town he was arrested by a salvo from Rodes's batteries proclaiming that the Confederates were ahead of him and had occupied the hill.

Instead of falling back to a new position where he might fight in conjunction with Doubleday, Howard chose to defend the line in the fields which Schimmelfennig had reached when he came under fire. Its left ran partly along a small stream that had its source at the base of Oak Hill and flowed eastward into Rock Creek, crossing the Carlisle road less than half a mile north of Gettysburg. Howard and Schurz placed Barlow on the right of Schimmelfennig, his right resting on a wooded hump on the bank of Rock Creek, which came to be known as Barlow's Knoll.

Rock Creek gave some protection on the right and the open fields gave security against surprise attack from any direction, but the position was untenable because the Heidlersburg road, along which Devin had reported the enemy's approach, led directly to Barlow's right rear and allowed the position to be easily turned.[7]

On the opposite flank, Schimmelfennig had halted before he made a juncture with Doubleday's line. A fatal gap of a quarter of a mile remained between the two corps. After the line was formed Howard came out from Gettysburg and approved it, then rode to Doubleday's position and gave orders that if retreat became necessary, the First Corps commander should retire to Cemetery Hill.

At this moment Doles's brigade of Rodes's division moved along the eastern slope of Oak Hill and advanced toward the gap that separated Howard from Doubleday. But Doles's mission for the moment was only to hold the Eleventh Federal Corps in check until Rodes could strike Doubleday's right with his other brigades, mainly those of O'Neal and Iverson.

2. The Slaughter of the Carolinians

Iverson's brigade, which at the June 30 muster numbered 114 officers and 1,356 enlisted men, a total of 1,470 present for duty, had headed the march of Rodes's division and Ewell's corps on the morning of July 1, and was the first to turn south at Hill's summons.

As they approached Gettysburg from the northeast, along the Heidlersburg road, they heard heavy firing. Two miles from the town Rodes marched them by the right flank under cover of the woods toward the Mummasburg road, which runs southeast into Gettysburg. When they reached Oak Hill, the importance of which Rodes intuitively recognized, he had Lieutenant Colonel Thomas H. Carter, commanding the division's artillery, put sixteen guns in position on the promontory and open on the flank of Doubleday to the south. It was 1:30 P.M.

As the first shells exploded amid the gnarled cherry trees of the McPherson farm, Rodes could see the quick movements among the startled Federals and the deployment of fresh troops coming from Gettysburg. These were the first of Robinson's two brigades hurrying into line, Baxter in front, to be followed shortly by Paul. The new line was recessed from Stone's salient, a broken extension of the line of Wadsworth and Rowley. Baxter was on the right but Paul sent two regiments in rear of the extreme right of Doubleday's line, and bent them around to reach toward Howard. Paul placed the rest of his brigade in line, prolonging Baxter's left, reaching toward Cutler on Seminary Ridge north of the railroad. Rodes could see also units of the Eleventh Federal Corps marching rapidly out of Gettysburg.

Rodes formed his division for attack, Iverson on the right, O'Neal in the center, and Doles on the left, while Daniel and Ramseur were held in support. Daniel was to assist Iverson and if not needed was to attack on his right.

Iverson is entitled to attention because he was perhaps the most conspicuous Confederate failure at Gettysburg. His father, Alfred Iverson, Sr., former United States Representative and Senator from Georgia, whom Robert Toombs had defeated for the Confederate Senate, was one of the earliest and most fiery advocates of secession. He was scholarly, a Princeton graduate, an orator of great power, and a close friend of President Davis, with whom he had served in the United States Senate.

Iverson, Jr., was reared in Columbus, Georgia; he was seventeen and a student at the military institute at Tuskegee, Alabama, when war began with Mexico. The father raised and equipped a regiment which the son entered as a soldier. In 1855, when Jefferson Davis was Secretary of War and Iverson, Sr., was a Senator, he was appointed by Davis a first lieutenant in the 1st United States Cavalry. The regular army commission of that grade was a distinction for a young man fresh from civilian life. He served during the Kansas statehood troubles and when the Southern states seceded he resigned to obtain a commission from his old patron, Davis. Stationed with the 20th North Carolina Regiment, he was elected camp commander and in consequence colonel.

Rodes's confused attack from Oak Hill. July 1, 1863, 1:30 to 3:00 P.M.

From the commanding position on Oak Hill, Rodes watched Robinson's men aligning themselves in his front and misunderstood their movements, which were merely to secure the best defensive position available. He judged they were preparing an assault and sought to anticipate them. "Boys," he said to the 12th North Carolina, one of Iverson's regiments, "they are advancing upon us. Go ahead and meet them."[8]

Rodes's division was formed in an obtuse angle, with Doles and O'Neal facing south, Iverson facing southeast, and Daniel and Ramseur facing south in the rear. Iverson was attacking a Federal front that ran directly north and south, and therefore was approaching on an oblique line that put the brunt of the action on his left regiments, which were being supported by O'Neal. Iverson's line, from left to right, was made up of the 5th, 20th, 23rd, and 12th North Carolina regiments. The 12th, on the far right, had its flank in the air, except for the support it might expect from the advance of Daniel, who was much to the rear.

The line which Iverson was preparing to assail ran through the Forney farm, immediately south of Oak Hill. The farmhouse stood south of the Mummasburg road and the fields extended along the road for about a mile, the cultivated land being a quarter of a mile deep. It was bounded on the east by a stone fence which marked the Federal line, extending south about 550 yards from the road to a clump of timber north of the unfinished railroad.

The Federal defending line, from its right to left, or from the Mummasburg road to the stand of timber, consisted of the 90th Pennsylvania—with its right resting on the road—12th Massachusetts, 88th Pennsylvania, 83rd New York, 11th Pennsylvania, and 97th New York. They comprised Brigadier General Harry Baxter's brigade, excepting the 11th Pennsylvania, which was detached from Paul's brigade.

Even before Iverson could move out, O'Neal's brigade on his left had attacked prematurely and had been beaten back, leaving his left flank, which—owing to his oblique position—was the one heading his assault, grievously exposed. Baxter had seen O'Neal's advance and had quickly moved the 90th Pennsylvania and 12th Massachusetts to the right, changed their front to face northwest, stopped the Confederates with a destructive fire, and sent them reeling to the rear. The two Northern regiments then returned to their original position in time to meet Iverson.

Second Lieutenant Walter A. Montgomery of the 12th North Carolina, on Iverson's far right, could look down the line as the brigade went into action. It was two o'clock. The Federal position was half a mile ahead and the ground in front of it was barren of any protective features. Montgomery could not see a single bush or tree. But Iverson ordered his men forward with the words "Give them hell," and seemed to take little further interest in the matter.[9] He did not follow the advance or undertake to correct the brigade's faulty alignment. Nor had he or Rodes effectively reconnoitered what was in his front. The men were ignorant of the nature of the defensive line or the size of the force crouching behind the wall. Not a Federal flag showed above the parapet of rocks. Not a blue-capped soldier raised his head. Iverson, in a disastrous lapse from established practice, had neglected to send skirmishes ahead of his battle line.

"Unarmed, unled as a brigade, we went to our doom," said Captain Vines E. Turner of the 23rd North Carolina in the center of the line. "Deep and long must the desolate homes and orphan children of North Carolina rue the rashness of that hour."[10] One of Ramseur's soldiers, more blunt, charged that Iverson had been drinking and was "off hiding somewhere."[11]

The North Carolina regiments were close to the wall when the Federal line rose up and poured in a deadly fire at point-blank range. The 5th, on the left flank, suffered the greatest shock, but the blast caught also the 20th, the 23rd, and the two left companies of the 12th. Even the Federals were appalled. "We delivered such a deadly volley at very short range, that death's mission was with unerring certainty,"[12] said Lieutenant Colonel A. J. Sellars of Baxter's right regiment. This, the 90th Pennsylvania, aided by the 12th Massachusetts, was able to get in a destructive enfilade fire. Two regiments of Paul's brigade, on Baxter's left—the 16th Maine and 94th New York—also put in a raking fire.

All that Iverson's men could do was to run or hit the ground in the open, and the regiments were not of running material. The men found a shallow dip in the field about 80 yards in front of the stone wall. There, little protected from the Federals behind the wall and openly exposed to the flank fire, they tried to form a firing line. Lieutenant Colonel William S. Davis, commanding the 12th, saw a small bottom in a wheat field and moved his regiment into it, giving them the only worth-while protection along the front. He looked to the right and left and could see huge gaps in the Confederate line in both directions. Daniel's brigade was still far removed to his right rear.

"I was left alone without any orders," he said, "with no communication with the right or left, and with only 175 men confronting several thousand."[13] Owing to the exposure of this flank, Cutler's brigade near the railroad grading changed front and put an enfilade fire into Iverson's right, as had Paul.

The 20th North Carolina in the left center was pinned down and helpless. "I believe every man who stood up was either killed or wounded,"[14] said Lieutenant Oliver Williams, who was himself hit. This regiment had participated in a touching event, well remembered by both armies. At Fredericksburg in late 1862, after the Sharpsburg campaign, it had held a dress parade at which the band played "Dixie." Across the Rappahannock a Northern band heard and played back the song as a bit of camaraderie. The band of the 20th

North Carolina responded by playing "Yankee Doodle." Then both bands, as if by prearrangement, joined in "Home, Sweet Home." The chorus ran along the lines and both armies sang and wept.[15]

Now, many of the men, trapped in the most critical moment of the regiment's history, again were thinking of their North Carolina homes. The survivors never forgot the hour. They would inscribe in the regiment's records: "Initiated at Seven Pines, sacrificed at Gettysburg, and surrendered at Appomattox."[16]

Every commissioned officer of the 23rd North Carolina except one was either killed or wounded. "Unable to advance, unwilling to retreat, the brigade lay down in this hollow . . . and fought the best it could," Captain Turner said.

While the brigade was pinned down, alert General Baxter pushed out the 88th Pennsylvania and the 83rd and 97th New York to a point 80 yards due west of the stone fence and captured about 300 prisoners, including 200 of the 20th North Carolina, and the regiment's flag. The flag and some of the men were recaptured later in the day by Captain A. H. Galloway of the 45th North Carolina, of Daniel's brigade. Using their bayonets and gun butts as clubs, the Federals drove in forty-nine additional prisoners from the 23rd North Carolina and captured that regiment's flag.

Iverson apparently received only garbled accounts of what was happening, for he notified Rodes that one of his regiments had put up a white flag and gone over to the enemy.[17] The preposterous charge he later found to be untrue, although he adhered to an assertion that he had seen white handkerchiefs raised. Even this explanation, which is sometimes accepted, is doubtful. The North Carolina regiments did not record it.

Iverson said he found later that 500 of his men were lying dead and wounded in "a line as straight as a dress parade" and he exonerated the brigade "with one or two disgraceful individual exceptions."[18] But because of his false report, word spread over the army that a North Carolina regiment had surrendered en masse. It reached the 6th North Carolina of Early's division, where such irresolute men were cited as a warning by Lieutenant Colonel Samuel McDowell Tate.[19] No regiments served more gallantly than those so miserably led by Iverson. Rodes agreed that they "fought and died like heroes"; and he, too, reported that the dead and wounded lay on the field in a distinctly marked line of battle.[20]

After the battle rolled on elsewhere, Rodes, riding behind his line, thought he saw a regiment lying down to escape the fire of the Northern muskets. As he drew closer, he perceived they were all corpses.

Current regimental reports of the casualties were lost. Later returns showed 512 killed and wounded and 308 missing. Perhaps a more accurate estimate of the dead and wounded was made by Captain Turner, who placed the figure at 750. This would about check with the estimate of Lieutenant Montgomery of the 12th Regiment, who said between 350 and 400 were on hand when the brigade reassembled, out of 1,470 officers and men engaged.

Captain Turner reported that one of the privates of the 23rd was found dead, still clenching his musket, with five bullets through his head. That told the story of the leaden hail under which the men had lain. Lieutenant George B. Bullock of the 23rd said it was the only battle from Williamsburg to Appomattox where the blood actually ran in a rivulet, and it did just that at the bottom of the depression.[21] The brigade, and apparently with it the spirit of much of Rodes's division, was virtually destroyed. Daniel Harvey Hill, who had commanded the division in days of its greater glory, had never allowed a brigade to be sacrificed so needlessly.

Iverson was in such a distressful and played-out condition that Captain D. P. Halsey, his assistant adjutant general, had to reorganize the shattered regiments.[22] Iverson a little later was relieved from service in the Army of Northern Virginia. The steps are not quite clear. The North Carolinians refused to serve under him any longer. They attributed their catastrophe to the lack of a commander on the field. President Davis, some claimed, shielded Iverson from a court-martial. He was returned to Georgia, where later in the war he commanded a cavalry detachment.

The memory of Iverson's defeat lingered long in North Carolina, as Captain Turner had predicted. It was, perhaps, the North State's darkest hour. That night Lee's pioneers dug some shallow pits at the bottom of the depression behind Iverson's line in which the dead were buried in a few common graves. These came to be known over the Pennsylvania countryside as "Iverson's Pits." The unhappy spirits of the slaughtered North Carolina soldiers were reputed to abide in this section of the battlefield. Lieutenant Montgomery returned in 1898, thirty-five years after the battle, and learned from John S. Forney that a superstitious terror had long hung over the area. Farm laborers would not work there after night began to settle.[23]

Montgomery walked over the fields with Forney, who still owned and lived on the farm, as he had at the time of the battle.[24] They went to the pits, where the grass each year had shown a deeper verdure in springtime, and crops were luxuriant on years when the land was tended. Using the staffs they carried as pointers, they easily traced the edges of the pits by the more exuberant vegetation.[25] Though the bones had been disinterred during the general removal of the Confederate dead from Gettysburg to Richmond, the soil had been enriched with human flesh and blood.

Captain Turner of the 23rd Regiment visited the field that same year and dug into the empty pits. He found them "a veritable mine of war relics"—bullets, grapeshot, and shrapnel fragments released as the bodies of the soldiers had decayed.[26]

Montgomery noticed that Jessup Sheads had built a house on the site which the 97th New York, on Baxter's left, had occupied while it faced the 12th North Carolina. He said Sheads furnished wine to visitors to that part of the battlefield, and the arbors were on ground where the 12th North Carolina had left its dead.[27]

What remained of Iverson's brigade after the Federal descent on its left flank and the capture of the prisoners was saved by the arrival of Ramseur. Rodes had not thought to caution Ramseur against the same fate that befell Iverson's men. Ramseur was moving straight toward the stone wall when two lieutenants ran back and warned him,[28] suggesting that he trail off to the left and strike the right flank of the Federals.

That was the precise maneuver the brilliant young brigadier general made. Robinson saw the menace to his right and tried to change front to meet it, but Ramseur was quick and caught Baxter's men while they were thus engaged and before they could bring their guns into play. He held his fire until he could enfilade the entire line behind the stone wall, then delivered it with devastating effect.

Stephen Dodson Ramseur, Lee's youngest brigadier general—called the Chevalier Bayard of the war by the Richmond press[29]—was a handsome, black-eyed, highly intelligent graduate in the last class out of West Point before the states seceded. He was slim, erect, martial in his bearing, but boyish with his high, rounded brow, thick dark hair and an open, friendly manner that endeared him to his men. None sat with more grace or managed his horse with greater skill. His love was for the artillery and he always seemed a little reluctant that he was pushed ahead so rapidly in infantry commands.

A Lincolnton, North Carolina, youth, he had attended Davidson College when Daniel Harvey Hill was professor of mathematics there, and had applied for a cadetship at West Point with Hill's encouragement. Ramseur was twenty-five years old when given a brigade and had just passed his twenty-sixth birthday when Lee headed north, using him to head the invasion. He had led the charge at Malvern Hill and the advance for Jackson at Chancellorsville, being wounded in both attacks.

On one matter the army appeared to be agreed: that there was no more courageous brigade commander in the service. A memorial sketch apparently written by his old professor and commander, Harvey Hill, emphasized this quality, and stated that he "revelled in the fierce joys of strife," and that "his whole being seemed to kindle and glow amid the excitements of danger."[30]

Ramseur swept down the stone wall of the Forney farm from left to right, dislodged Robinson's division, one of the most stubborn commands of the Federal army, and pushed the two brigades back step by step slowly toward the seminary. Iverson and Ramseur had identical assignments; the one threw his brigade away, the other triumphed skillfully. In this action General Paul, commanding Robinson's First Brigade, was shot and permanently blinded in both eyes.

3. The Stand of the Bogus Bucktails

To the right, Daniel's brigade came into action after Iverson had been all but destroyed. Moving from the western slope of Oak Hill, Daniel had to travel a longer distance and, being the right brigade of Rodes's division, he had to make a contact with Pender's division of A. P. Hill's corps. The brigade had 2,100 men in five regiments and one separate battalion, all from North Carolina. While Iverson was confronting Baxter, Daniel skirted across the front of Cutler's brigade, passed through the hollow to Iverson's right, and moved toward the railroad cut and the Cashtown road, where he at once came under the fire of Stone's Bogus Bucktails, rated among the best marksmen of the Northern army.[31]

Stone's men had been under a constant pounding from Rodes's guns on Oak Hill and from Heth's batteries on Herr Ridge beyond Willoughby Run, and while the position was highly uncomfortable, Major Chamberlin considered the casualties not heavy because of the defective nature of the Southern ammunition. But the ammunition was good enough to force withdrawal of the Federal guns from the edge of the woods in Stone's rear.

Without knowing of the existence of the railroad cut, Daniel approached it and encountered a withering fire from the 149th Pennsylvania on the opposite side, which drove him back. Lieutenant Colonel Walton Dwight ordered the 149th to follow him across the cut. Dwight's men with great difficulty descended the embankment and clambered up the north side, where sliding shale slowed them.

But Dwight was the kind of man for whom the Pennsylvania mountaineers would go up the sheer sides of a precipice if he gave the word. He, too, had a combination of the varieties of courage. When Secretary Stanton closed the army to all visitors and issued a ban on passes, Dwight put in an application for a pass for an old man to visit his dying son. Stanton arbitrarily denied it and must have been stunned when Dwight stormed in with a blistering reproach. He told the domineering Secretary of War exactly what was on his mind: "My name is Dwight, Walton Dwight, Lieutenant Colonel of the One Hundred and Forty-ninth Regiment of Pennsylvania Volunteers. You can dismiss me from the service as soon as you like, but I am going to tell you what I think of you."[32]

Then he lit into Stanton with such vigor that the rebuked Secretary gave Dwight the pass and rescinded the entire order.

Dwight was now out in the open, with a resolute enemy in his front and the railroad cut in his rear. His men and Daniel's blazed away at each other. Doubleday watched the movement and thought it bold. Dwight fired two volleys, then charged with bayonets and pressed Daniel back farther, but the Carolinians returned and soon had the 149th scurrying to the other side. Daniel brought up a gun and stationed two of his companies to enfilade the railroad cut. Stone's men were held thereafter to the southern side. Stone, the gallant commander of the Bogus Bucktails, had come up to take charge of the movement and was heedless of his personal safety. While trying to extricate the regiment, he was hit by two bullets and carried out of the action. He was succeeded by Colonel Langhorne Wister of the 150th Pennsylvania.

Daniel's men now returned to the close-quarter fighting. With the 149th Regiment hard pressed, Wister called on his own regiment, facing west, to change front and face north along the roadway, a difficult maneuver which was nevertheless readily executed just in time for the

150th to pour a fire on Daniel at close range. The advancing Confederates were again driven into the woods. Fresh from the Carolina coast, the brigade was one of the best in the Southern army. Of it a regimental colonel said that "it never refused to advance when ordered and was never known to retire without command."[33]

Colonel Thomas S. Kenan, of the 43rd North Carolina, noted that Daniel handled the brigade "with consummate skill."[34] Now that he perceived Stone's markmanship, he broke up his close formations and sent in clouds of skirmishers close to the cut, where a destructive fire was exchanged with the 149th Pennsylvania, which Wister advanced. In this fighting Colonel Wister was shot through the face, and the Bogus Bucktails lost their second commander. Colonel Edmund L. Dana of the 143rd Pennsylvania took command. In the same fighting Lieutenant Colonel Dwight, of the 149th, and Major Chamberlin and Lieutenant Colonel H. S. Huiedekoper of the 150th were wounded.

Neither the Carolinians nor the Pennsylvanians had been able to gain an advantage after some of the hardest close-range fighting on the field, and the action now settled into a continuous exchange of rifle fire destructive to both commands. It was 2:30 P.M. The Bogus Bucktails had held their salient, but they had not yet felt the full impact of the forces being arrayed against them. Daniel's left meantime had engaged part of Paul and Cutler, indecisively, at longer range.

Rodes had attacked by his brigades in succession rather than in concert and by mid-afternoon three of them had met either with check or disaster. His battle had not opened any more auspiciously than Heth's. The brilliancy he had shown under Jackson at Chancellorsville had been lacking during the unusual opportunity for distinction that had been presented to his division by its timely arrival on Doubleday's flank at Gettysburg. Ewell, who was with him, had not helped. He was already disclosing that he was not aggressively commanding, but was merely accompanying his soldiers.

But new factors had entered the battle northwest of Gettysburg. Heth, who had not yet engaged the brigades of Pettigrew and Brockenbrough, had been restive under the restraint imposed on him by orders from Lee not to bring on a general battle. General Lee was now in the rear, in the neighborhood of Marsh Creek, and Heth rode back to him.

"Rodes is heavily engaged," he told the commanding general. "Had I not better attack?"

"No," he quoted Lee as replying. "I am not prepared to bring on a general engagement today. Longstreet is not up."[35]

Heth returned to his division, where he detected that the Federals were moving troops from his front to support those attacking Rodes. They were apparently Stone's men, on the bald crest of McPherson's Ridge, where they could be seen easily, changing front to fight Daniel. He reported this intelligence to General Lee, this time probably by courier, as he made no reference to a second trip to the rear. On the second request he received permission to resume his attack.[36]

The Battle of the Two Colonels

1. *Zeb Vance Inspires a Regiment*

Heth's assault was now about to precipitate one of the most gripping incidents of the Confederate War—the meeting of the 26th North Carolina Regiment of Pettigrew's brigade, commanded by the "boy colonel" Harry King Burgwyn, and the 24th Michigan of Meredith's Iron Brigade, led by an expatriate Virginian, Colonel Henry A. Morrow.

The episode manifested again that wars are most stubbornly contested between peoples of the same race and cultural heritage. Historically foreign wars have been made by governments, often as an expression of baffling statecraft. They have been a game which, in the words of Cowper, "were their subjects wise, Kings would not play at." Civil wars, on the other hand, are popular uprisings where each side sees the compelling necessity of its own stand. Distrusts between governments set off foreign wars; revolutions arise out of solemn popular convictions. Whipped-up hatreds attend foreign wars; civil strife is marked not so much by aversion as by a sense of righteousness felt deeply enough to tear a nation asunder.

So it was in the War between the States, where each side found a spiritual justification, transcending all emotion, in a belief that it fought in the sacred name of Freedom. Only this could explain the intensity, the firm resolution and the heedless personal sacrifice that distinguished this internecine struggle above all other American wars.

The 26th North Carolina Infantry, a name synonymous with blood,

139

death, and glory, had been Governor Zebulon Vance's regiment, recruited largely in the Piedmont counties, although two companies of
hillmen were among them. Vance was a mountaineer, a native of
Buncombe County, who had begun his career as a hotel clerk at Hot
Springs. His great natural force, with which his regiment came to be
imbued, was rated among the mountain dwellers as powerful as that
of his own French Broad River, which wrested and twisted its way
through the lofty barrier of the Great Smoky Mountains.

War had taken Vance from Congress to the command of a company, Buncombe County's hard-hitting Rough and Ready Guards,
which, in Ramseur's brigade, had been first across the Potomac of
Lee's army. A fall from an apple tree in early boyhood had broken
Vance's left hip and left him with a shortened leg and ambling gait.
This was more than compensated for by his intense ardor, superb
command of language, ready wit, and extraordinary capacity for making solid friendships. Soldier, Governor, United States Senator, Vance
enjoyed as have few other men in the country's history the abiding
affection of the people of his own state. A little later in the war he
would make an inspirational speaking tour of the different commands
of the Army of Northern Virginia. Jeb Stuart, who accompanied him,
declared that, measured by results, "Vance is the greatest orator that
ever lived," and General Lee was quoted as saying his visit to the
army was "worth 50,000 recruits."[1]

Such was the inspiring man who had met the impressionable youths
of the 26th Regiment. After electing Vance colonel the regiment had
gone on to choose Burgwyn, the camp instructor, its lieutenant colonel.
Almost immediately a good many judged that here the regiment had
made an appalling mistake. The young man was all intensity. The
regiment was literally snatched out of bed and shaken to attention.
"At first sight," said Corporal John R. Lane, who would soon rise
to become lieutenant colonel, "I both admired and feared him."[2]
Burgwyn, the son of a wealthy Northampton County planter, had
been educated by tutors and prepared for West Point, but had been
diverted to the University of North Carolina, where, like Pettigrew, he
had led his class, though he was graduated at the early age of eighteen.
His father, hearing the rumblings of the oncoming war, had influenced
him to continue his studies at Virginia Military Institute, where he
caught the attention of the austere T. J. Jackson, professor of artillery
and natural philosophy. Jackson gave him the top recommendation
one might expect from such a stern recluse, saying he would "make

an ornament not only to the artillery, but any branch of the military service."[3]

Vance inspired the regiment with his own tough, unyielding spirit, but he left the drill and military formalities to Burgwyn. The lieutenant colonel, twenty years old, conducted it with all the zeal of a V.M.I. cadet who had gratified "Old Jack." However cherished may have been the rugged independence of these Carolinians who had never recognized the frailest filaments of repression or restraint, war was something real to the diligent lieutenant colonel who meant to have a regiment that would obey him in battle. Something had been imparted to him from the intense light that burned in T. J. Jackson's pale-blue eyes.

Some of the men, looking on the war as a short-term lark that nobody needed to get excited about, grumbled at the martinet officer and swore that he would get the proper kind of attention when they fought their first battle. But they found in their first action that Burgwyn was the very prop they needed. He was in front when they advanced and in their rear when they retreated.

They perceived what it meant to have a coolheaded lieutenant colonel who knew how to conduct an engagement. Thoroughly disliked before the battle, Burgywn came out of it "the regiment's pride and joy."[4] The 26th went on to Virginia and took terrible punishment in the assault on Malvern Hill.

The test for Burgwyn came when Vance was elected Governor of North Carolina. He left the regiment in August 1862. The lieutenant colonel was still not twenty-one. The 26th was under Brigadier General Matt W. Ransom, who declared that he "wanted no boy colonel in his brigade."[5] The regiment decided to show its dander. The men made it known that they would have no other colonel than young Burgwyn, and petitioned to be taken out of Ransom's brigade. Hard-fighting D. H. Hill interceded; by all means Burgwyn should be promoted. Vance employed his influence. He knew the 26th needed Burgwyn. On his departure he had delivered a stirring speech: "It is fight to the end. All you can expect is War! War!! War!!!"[6]

So youthful Harry King Burgwyn was appointed colonel of the 26th by the Confederate War Department, field officers no longer being elected, and the regiment was assigned a little later to Pettigrew. John R. Lane, captain, but lately corporal, was appointed lieutenant colonel. The regiment knew what he would do for the soldiers. When they had charged up Malvern Hill he had carried inside his blouse the company's pay, wrapped in a newspaper. In the blood and excitement of the assault the package disappeared, and such were the demands of the wounded that night that he did not discover the loss until the next morning. Lee's army had been repulsed. Lane, unaware that McClellan also had retired during the night, set out alone to search the ground that had been saturated with Southern blood. Diligently he looked, and finally, half covered by dead and wounded, he found the packet of money, still wrapped and tied.[7] He hurried back and the company rejoiced with him.

One of the soldiers observed that Pettigrew and Burgwyn were "made for each other," being alike in their intensity, courage, zest for battle, martial bearing, and skillful horsemanship. Lieutenant Colonel Lane developed into a good drillmaster and the 26th came to vie with the 11th as "the best drilled regiment in the Confederate service."

2. The Factories Answer with Men

The 24th Michigan, which Burgwyn's regiment faced, had been born out of a Detroit riot. When Lincoln issued a call for 300,000 volunteers in the critical summer of 1862, the sentiments of Detroit, like those of other northern cities, were mixed, and the great mass meeting called together by the city authorities broke up in pandemonium. The Knights of the Golden Circle, augmented by refugee Confederates from the Canadian side of the Detroit River, had mobbed the meeting, drowned out the orations with catcalls, and finally wrecked the platform and driven off the speakers.

Ruffianism controlled the town. Sheriff Mark Flanigan and his deputies restored order to the shocked community. The good citizens determined to redeem their standing and display good faith to the nation by recruiting not only the six regiments called for under President Lincoln's proclamation, but also a seventh, a bonus regiment, which would prove to the world the city's loyalty to the cause.

The city judge, Henry A. Morrow, raised and led the regiment. Morrow had come to Detroit when a lad. Born in Warrenton, Virginia, he had been left an orphan without money or friends, and had made his way to Washington. There, being bright and courteous, he got a job as a Senate page boy, where the old soldier, General Lewis Cass, Senator from Michigan, who had raised himself by his own energies on a turbulent frontier, became attached to the young Virginian. Cass inspired him to read assiduously and encouraged him to move to Detroit and take up law.[8]

After reaching Detroit young Morrow enlisted as a private in a Michigan regiment and served in the Mexican War. Afterward he returned to Detroit, to begin a law practice, became recorder, and when the Recorder's Court was established in 1858, became its first judge.[9] Soon he was a familiar figure in Detroit public affairs, genial and pleasant, an excellent public speaker, an avid reader, and a respected jurist.

He was just the man to conduct a rapid, high-pressure campaign, sparkling with patriotism and publicity, to raise the bonus regiment. With the aid of Sheriff Flanigan, he had a full roster ready for muster into the Federal service in the remarkably short time of thirty days.

While he was making an eloquent appeal at a recruiting mass meeting, some wag in the crowd called out, "Why don't *you* enlist, Judge?"

"I'm going to," Morrow replied quickly.[10]

And he kept his word. When the regiment was organized the governor appointed him colonel. Sheriff Flanigan became lieutenant colonel.

On August 29, 1862, the 24th Regiment was assembled on the Campus Martius for departure to Virginia. The eyes of Michigan were on it and in performance it would have to excel. The ceremonies were elaborate. Local business houses had prepared a costly flag, with quilted stars on the blue field, inscribed with the words "24th Michigan Infantry,"[11] a regimental name destined to become as honored as that of any who ever carried the Stars and Stripes.

Colonel Morrow accepted the colors and the top officers took the swords that the admiring groups of citizens of Detroit presented—the lawyers to Morrow, and the deputy sheriffs to Flanigan.[12] Of the regiment's ten companies, eight were from Detroit, one from Plymouth and one from Livonia. Detroit even then had industrial pretensions and the factories had poured out their men. A public purse was collected to tide over families of the industrial recruits. Receptions and demonstrations occurred en route to the front, but the regiment was on its own when it was finally incorporated into the Army of the Potomac.

Rufus R. Dawes, then a major of the 6th Wisconsin, an Iron Brigade regiment, wrote from camp near Sharpsburg: "A fine new regiment has been added to our brigade . . . a splendid looking body of men . . . they are, as we were, crazy to fight."[13] A month later the brigade was at Warrenton, Virginia, without a single cracker. The veteran regiments, accustomed to scarcity, waited patiently for provisions to come up. The Wolverines were indignant at not being fed in their colonel's home town. They went about all day bellowing loudly, "Bread! Bread!" The balance of the brigade looked on contemptuously, but there was no contempt after the Detroiters had gone through the bloody battle of Fredericksburg. Dawes told the story in his letters home: "No soldiers ever faced fire more bravely. . . . Col. Morrow . . . enterprising, brave, and ambitious . . . stepped into a circle of the best and most experienced regimental commanders of the Army."[14]

3. Pettigrew Carries McPherson's Ridge

At a signal from Heth, Pettigrew advanced his brigade, numbering about 3,000 officers and men, a quarter of a mile across a wheat field, down the incline to Willoughby Run, and into McPherson's Woods, where the obstinate Iron Brigade that had scattered and captured Archer four hours earlier still waited.

Brockenbrough was on Pettigrew's left, moving against the McPherson farmhouse and outbuildings. At that point the Iron Brigade joined Stone's Bogus Bucktails, who held the Cashtown pike. Some remnants of Davis' brigade moved on Brockenbrough's left. Archer's survivors, commanded by Colonel Fry, marched on Pettigrew's right. Heth's line thus consisted, from left to right, of Davis, Brockenbrough, Pettigrew, and Fry. Opposed to them, from the Federal right to left, were Stone, Meredith, and Biddle. Meredith's regiments in the woods were, right to left, the 2nd and 7th Wisconsin, 24th Michigan and 19th Indiana.

Pettigrew appeared on his dapple gray, matching his trim, fresh uniform,[15] and rode forward with the men. "Oh, what a splendid place for artillery!" Colonel Burgwyn exclaimed to Lieutenant Colonel Lane, as the 26th moved out from Herr Ridge. "Why don't they fire on them?"[16]

The Southerners had scarcely gained momentum when Heth was hit. He had ordered the attack but knew nothing more about it until the next day. A Minié ball struck him on the head and rendered him insensible for thirty hours. Undoubtedly he would have been killed had his new hat not been too large. In Cashtown his quartermaster had exchanged Confederate script for Yankee headgear and offered Heth his pick. The one he selected was so big he had put a folded newspaper inside the sweat band. The bullet was slowed by the folds and did not penetrate his skull, although the impact took him out of the rest of the battle. Pettigrew assumed command of the division.

Meredith also went down early. He and his horse were hit by fragments of the same shell, and the horse rolled on him, causing severe
internal injuries. Command of the Iron Brigade passed to Colonel
Morrow, but he paid little attention to the brigade and continued to
fight with his Michigan regiment.

Young Colonel Burgwyn was impatient as he marched his Carolinians in perfect alignment. While waiting in the wheat on the opposite hill, he had been conscious of the frightful loss of time. With a
concerted attack Heth might have walked into Gettysburg. He attributed it to Hill's absence. The men had passed jokes as they waited.
"Religious services were not held, as they should have been, owing
to the absence of our chaplains."[17] In the woods 300 yards away they
could catch glimpses of the tall, bell-crowned black hats of the Federal
infantrymen, showing conspicuously through the green foliage. The
hot sun was on their necks and the sweat ran down their arms and
slickened their gunstocks. Off to the left Rodes's troops could be
seen battling against Robinson. "Never was a grander sight beheld.
The lines extended more than a mile, all distinctly visible to us."

Taking the center of the regiment, Burgwyn sent Lane to the right
and Major John T. Jones to the left. The 26th moved at a quickstep,
marching into action at attention, as on the drill ground. The stand-
ard-bearer, J. B. Mansfield, was four paces in front of the line, with
four color guards on either side of the standard. All kept step and
made a "pretty and perfect line."[18]

It was two o'clock when Pettigrew's soldiers struggled through the
heavy underbrush and blackberry briers that still formed a barrier
along the banks of Willoughby Run, after much threshing about of
skirmishers and Archer's regiments. They came at once under the
fire of Cooper's battery, posted on McPherson's Ridge to their right,
between the Iron Brigade and Biddle. Cooper's guns were soon joined
by those of Stewart's Battery B, of the 4th United States Artillery,
stationed on the ridge behind the juncture of Stone and Meredith.
After the battle this battery would claim that more men fell before
its guns than before any other battery of the Federal army.

On crossing Willoughby Run, Burgwyn's men crowded to the
center. Cooper's battery caused frightful loss from its enfilade position. Along the bank Burgwyn restored the alignment and the regiment moved ahead into the woods. For a moment bullets seemed to
fill the air like hailstones. Then the men came face to face with the
24th Michigan and the two lines fired point-blank at each other. The

smoke billowed in great white waves. The Federals receded and
Burgwyn pressed on. Lane hurried from right to center.

"It is all right in the center and on the left," said Burgwyn. "We
have broken their first line."

"We are in line on the right, Colonel," said Lane.[19]

Now the regiment began to work through the center of McPherson's
Woods, a deceptive piece of ground a third of a mile in depth from
Willoughby Run to the crest of McPherson's Ridge. After the first
steep ascent the regiment passed over a rounded shoulder, then
through a small valley about fifteen feet deep, with a dry bed of a
stream at its bottom. Along this bed stood great oaks and chestnuts.
The shoulder in front of the dry bed provided an excellent line of
defense, while another defensive line ran only a hundred yards in the
rear, where a stream fringed with thickets cut through another valley.
Then the hill, heavily wooded, rose to the summit near which Reynolds
had been killed. All through the woods the fighting raged as the
Federals were forced back. Each stubborn halt was costly to both
sides. By the time the North Carolina regiment reached the main
Federal line at the crest of McPherson's Ridge, eight color guards and
ten bearers of the colors had been shot down.[20]

Here Pettigrew and Burgwyn encountered determined and deadly
resistance. While the two lines were blazing at each other, Captain
W. W. McCreery, Pettigrew's assistant inspector general, rushed forward with a message from Pettigrew to Burgwyn. "Tell him," said
Pettigrew, "his regiment has covered itself with glory."[21] What remained of it had also covered itself with sweat, grime, powder stains,
and blood. McCreery was fired by the high zest of the attackers.
Though he belonged with the staff, he foolishly seized the regimental
flag, waved it back and forth, and rushed out in front of the line. He
was shot instantly through the heart. Lieutenant George Wilcox of
Company H ran forward and pulled the blood-covered flag from under
the body; Wilcox had taken only a step when two bullets struck him.
The Detroit factory hands had become deadly shots.

At this juncture Burgwyn's line hesitated. Stone was resisting
Brockenbrough doggedly on the left, although still pressed by Daniel.
To Burgwyn's right, the 47th North Carolina was locked in a desperate struggle with the 19th Indiana. The sweat on the rifle barrels and
ramrods made it difficult to ram down the cartridges, and the attackers
jammed the rods against stones to force the charges home.[22] The
advancing line thus became undressed and ragged. Colonel George

H. Fairbault of the 47th tried to correct it as they passed through a wheat field to the right of the woods. Forty yards to the front a fresh enemy appeared, and the Carolinians went on with a rush. The regiment almost vanished as it ran ahead. "The earth seemed to open and take in that line," said Captain John A. Thorpe.[23]

The 47th overlapped the 19th Indiana and confronted Biddle, whom Thorpe said "deserved to command a corps." He related how a Federal officer rode rapidly forward carrying a large Federal flag. The Federals "swarmed around him as bees cover their queen." The mass of men was "acres big." Every Confederate gun turned on it and "seemingly shot the whole to pieces." The officer was Biddle. "It was with genuine and openly expressed pleasure our men heard he was not killed."[24]

Still farther on Pettigrew's right, the 52nd North Carolina felt the flank attack of Buford's cavalry, which guarded the extreme Federal left. The regiment formed a square to meet a charge of the horsemen, but Buford drew off and remained satisfied with long-range firing.

But the battle for the possession of McPherson's Heights, which commanded the main road by which Lee would have to reach Gettysburg, had developed into a duel mainly between two colonels, the boy Burgwyn and old Judge Morrow. Neither had any intention of giving way as long as men could stand.

In front of the 26th North Carolina, Colonel Morrow's men had been taking frightful punishment. Morrow's first volley had not checked Burgwyn's advance. The Carolinians "came on with rapid strides, yelling like demons."[25] He watched while the 19th Indiana was overpowered and pushed back, and to guard against a cross fire he swung his left companies back. Before the shift could be completed Burgwyn came storming against his front, and he was forced to another line in the rear.

Here on this last line occurred the final desperate fight between the two regiments. The crisis had been reached. Burgwyn told Lane the laudatory words received from Pettigrew and asked him to inform the men. Seeing the regiment waver, Burgwyn seized the flag as it fell from the hands of Lieutenant Wilcox and shouted, "Dress to the colors." Then he started forward with the flag. Private Frank Honeycutt of Company B ran from the ranks and requested the honor of advancing it. Burgwyn had turned to hand over the flag when a bullet struck his left side, passed through both lungs, spun him around with its force, and dropped him mortally wounded. He carried the colors down with him.[26] Honeycutt seized them, but almost instantly he was shot through the head. Thus for the thirteenth time in the attack the flag of the 26th North Carolina was on the ground. That should have been enough to end the mad vainglory of carrying the colors in battle. But the pride of showing the flag was to continue through this and future battles—and this and future wars—until the futility of the assignment had been adequately demonstrated. Eventually the colors came to be cased during battle.

Lane rushed to his fallen commander, the mere boy who had won the regiment's deep affection. He asked if he were hurt severely. Burgwyn's response was a pressure on Lane's hand. Then he got out a few words, "Tell the general my men never failed me."[27] The regiment was going forward and could not carry him back. That night they buried him, with a gun case for a coffin, beneath a large walnut tree near where he fell. He was twenty-one years old. The martinet drillmaster whom some of the men wanted to finish in the first battle died one of the most loved and admired officers in the Confederate army.

Only two days before the battle he had heard that some of his men had pilfered honey from a Pennsylvania farmer's beehive. He had found the owner and paid him for the honey.

Lane did not wait, but turning to right and left shouted to the remaining officers, "I am going to give them the bayonet. Close your men quickly to the left." At the center he found the colors still on the ground. He was raising them when Lieutenant Blair of Company I rushed out with earnest entreaty: "No man can take those colors and live." Lane shouted at him, "It's my time to take them now. 26th North Carolina, follow me!"[28] The thin line of survivors again let out the Rebel Yell and forged ahead. The last resistance broke. The Iron Brigade was swept from the crest of McPherson Ridge and pushed back to the entrenchments on Seminary Ridge.

Morrow's color-bearers had tossed their lives away as freely. By the time the third had fallen the regiment's ranks were so wasted that scarcely one fourth of it remained. Retreating to successive lines, Morrow had determined finally to stand and slug it out. He told Corporal Andrew Wagner of Company F to plant the flag where he pointed, but Wagner fell before he could obey the order. Morrow grabbed it up but Private William Kelley of Company E snatched it from his hand. "The colonel of the 24th shall never carry the colors while I am alive," said Kelley; almost instantly he too fell dead.[29]

Private Silburn Spaulding of Company K then carried the flag to the last stand in the barricade around the seminary. In all, nine color-bearers fell. At the end Morrow was shot. A Minié ball hit the top of his head and ripped along the skull, covering him with blood. He was left on the ground and the Confederates captured him as they advanced.

The firing had almost died away. Sergeant Charles H. McConnell of the 24th Michigan saw the commanding figure of Lieutenant Colonel Lane carrying the Confederate flag, and waited to take a parting shot. He rested his rifle against a tree only thirty paces away. The bullet crashed through Lane's jaw and mouth, and for the fourteenth time the flag of the 26th North Carolina fell.

Lane survived. Forty-four years later, when the Confederate monument was dedicated at Pittsboro, North Carolina, the last commander of the famous 26th Regiment, which claimed to have lost more men at Gettysburg than any other regiment of either army in any battle of the war, served as chief marshal. The old man rode a spirited horse at the head of the procession, sitting "erect as an Indian."[30]

The battle between the regiments ended more from extermination than exhaustion. Of the 496 officers and men who went in with the 24th Michigan, 399 were killed or wounded, a loss of 80 per cent.

"Our loss was very large," said Morrow, "exceeding perhaps the losses sustained by any regiment of equal size in a single engagement in this or any other war."[31]

The 26th North Carolina encountered not only the Michigan regiment, but at times in its advance the 19th Indiana and the 151st Pennsylvania, the right regiment of Biddle's command. The loss in killed and wounded was recorded in North Carolina annals as 82 per cent. Losses were heaviest in the two center companies, E and F, which marched at the sides of the colors. Company E on the right went in with 82 officers and men and ended the attack with 2 untouched. Company F, deer and bear hunters from the slopes of Grandfather Mountain, commanded by Captain R. M. Tuttle, later a Presbyterian minister, went in with 3 officers and 88 enlisted men. All were killed or wounded. Only Sergeant Hudspeth could report for duty after the fight, and he had been stunned for a time by an exploding shell. This company had three sets of twins and 5 of the 6 were left dead on

McPherson's Ridge. Company A of Ashe County went in with 92 and ended the fight with 15.

Pettigrew's adjutant general, Captain Young, was attracted by what he called "dreadful howls" from some of the wounded in the woods. He did not specify whether they were Federals or Confederates or both, but he approached several and found they were foaming at the mouth, as though mad, and were apparently unaware of their sounds. This was the only time during the war Young saw such a reaction; he attributed it to the shock of "a quick, frightful conflict following several hours of suspense."[32]

He gave his impression of the fighting: "I have taken part in many hotly contested fights, but this I think, was the deadliest of them all, not excepting the third day's charge on Cemetery Ridge; and never have I seen or known of better conduct on the part of any troops, under any circumstances, or at any time."[33]

After the battle Pettigrew wrote to Vance: "Their loss has been heavy, very heavy. . . . Your old command did honor to your association with them and to the State they represent."[34] Pettigrew might have added a line: Not a man of his brigade was taken prisoner.[35]

When Heth got around to aggregating his losses he said he began the action with 7,000 muskets and in twenty-five minutes lost 2,700 men.

The three Federal brigades found scant time behind their seminary entrenchments to collect stragglers and strengthen their lines. When Pettigrew's attack was spent, immediately behind came Pender's fresh division, moving against Doubleday's last stand on Seminary Ridge.

4. The Color Ruse of the Bucktails

When the Iron Brigade was beaten back to the seminary by Pettigrew's vehement attack, carrying Biddle with it, Stone and the remnants of Cutler were left exposed at the McPherson farm buildings and the railroad cut. Brockenbrough had been unable to dislodge them and had himself been momentarily repulsed. Now Daniel again aligned his brigade for a final decision with the Pennsylvanians, who were confronted by Brockenbrough on their left, Daniel on their right and the approach of Pender behind Brockenbrough in their front.

The spectacular stand of the Bogus Bucktails at their salient on the Cashtown road was made possible partly by a ruse perpetrated by Color Sergeant Henry G. Brehm of the 149th Pennsylvania volunteers, at the instigation of Colonels Stone and Dwight. In front of the angle of the brigade were two piles of fence rails formed at right angles, which had been made into a barricade by one of Buford's cavalry pickets on the night of June 30. The pile was fifty yards north of the Cashtown pike and 115 yards south of the railroad cut through McPherson's Ridge. Wheat stood waving in the fields around the barricade, but the rails were easily visible to the north and west.

When Rodes seized Oak Hill and sent his shells crashing through the old cherry trees in Stone's rear, Stone and Dwight pointed out the barricades to Sergeant Brehm and asked him if he could advance the colors to that point. Brehm agreed. Two thirds of the 149th lay along McPherson's farm lane facing west, and a third faced north along the Cashtown pike; the barricade was fully fifty yards from the closest point in the line. Crawling, Brehm led his color guard through the wheat and secured both the national and state flags to the fence rails. Almost immediately the Confederate artillery fire was lifted from the men in the line and directed against the colors. All through the afternoon, while Daniel's and Brockenbrough's men charged the Bogus Bucktails, the colors were held fast in their isolated position, seen easily from both Herr Ridge and Oak Hill, defiantly challenging the Confederate gunners and sharpshooters. Brehm and his color guard crouched in their holes and behind their rails, while the storm raged overhead. They held the position amid the bursting shells and hail of bullets. Even when Daniel's men finally burst in on him Brehm was reluctant to let his colors go.

"This is mine," said a Confederate, seizing a flagstaff.

"No, by God, it isn't," said Brehm, wielding his gun butt. But he and the color guard went down, all killed or wounded. They had drawn enough fire to annihilate the brigade, had it been dropped along the lane and roadway.[36]

The end had finally come for the Bogus Bucktails. One of the graphic contemporary pictures of the battle of the first day showed the thin line of survivors moving back along the Cashtown road at the double quick, with a Confederate brigade running abreast them on either side and another pressing their rear, all pouring a fire into them, to which they were replying as best they could. At the Ripple midway between McPherson's and Seminary Ridge, Stone's men undertook to make another stand but they were isolated and soon had to resume their retreat.

Never again did the army apply the term "Bogus" to Stone's Bucktails. Today the traveler approaching Gettysburg on the Cashtown road sees as almost the first monument the figure of the Pennsylvania mountaineer holding his long deer rifle, stationed at the point where the 149th Regiment bent its line from McPherson's Lane to the Cashtown pike, at the hot corner of the first day's battle. There Stone's men stood for nearly five hours and there, as Doubleday asserted, most of them, true to their first promised shout, remained.

CHAPTER TWELVE

Through the Town

1. Two Georgia Brigades Converge

Henry T. Thomas, writing in later years of his glorious 12th Georgia Regiment, bemoaned the passing of the old order in the deep South. Change had come to the land of honeysuckle and wide verandas, where the mockingbird sang in the mimosa tree, the plover ran the meadow and the whippoorwill called in the moonlight.

One of the ancient customs that had well nigh disappeared was the event of hog killing in the first winter chill, when the lads blew up bladders, neighbors came to cook melts, chitterlings, souse and sausage, and the Negroes hovered about to share in the delightful tastes and odors of fresh pork frying on the hot stones.

Such was the rural society and luxurious times that had given way before "the Yankee, the western farmer and the New South,"[1] he complained, as he went on to tell the story of his intrepid regiment of Doles's brigade, one of the most celebrated bodies of men ever to come out of the red lands, and an aggregation typical of the culture and independent thought of central Georgia.

Although Thomas did not relate it, no man, not even Stonewall himself, could put a rein on the free spirit of the 12th. The regiment had given the Confederate high command "Clubby" Edward Johnson and had served in Johnson's brigade at the battle of McDowell. When Jackson had tried to retire it, the 12th had contemptuously ignored the orders and held to its exposed position on the forward side of

153

the ridge. A lank youth explained for his comrades that "we ain't cum all the way he'ah to Vuginia to run frum Yankees."[2]

The brigade carried a *sang-froid,* a devil-may-care attitude and a sensitiveness about points of honor characteristic of the Georgian plantation society. Life was not so dear it had to be husbanded. Officers brought their slaves as personal retainers, but punctiliously kept them in camp during the fighting, with firm admonitions not to venture near the firing line. In few instances in the army was there a closer affection between the brigade and its commander. George Doles, who would be so fortunate as to survive until Cold Harbor where his brigade met the main impact of Grant's attack, was justly rated "one of the bravest, best loved and most accomplished soldiers Georgia furnished to the Confederate army."[3] After he fell the men tried to express their love for him by adopting his daughter Minnie as the "daughter of the regiment."

Born and reared in the Georgia capital of Milledgeville, Doles became captain of the Baldwin Blues, one of the oldest and best-trained military aggregations of the state. His military proficiency was apparent to the soldiers who were his neighbors along the Oconee River, and when the war came and they were mustered into the Confederate service, they elected him colonel.

Doles, now thirty-three years old, was a handsome man with penetrating eyes under a lofty forehead. Like Pettigrew, he wore a beard but no sideburns and, also like Pettigrew, reflected a quiet self-assurance and a high order of intelligence. He had been wounded leading the charge at Malvern Hill and had been in the front line when Jackson rolled up the Federal flank at Chancellorsville, always showing a competence his superiors admired. Now he was moving again toward Schurz's Germans holding the line north of Gettysburg, the same troops he had confronted two months before at Chancellorsville.

Rodes had intended that Doles, on his left, should merely detain Schurz while Iverson and O'Neal delivered the main attack against Doubleday, but it was Daniel on his extreme right and Doles on his extreme left who carried the major fighting load of the division. The story of Doles's assault on Schimmelfennig was summed up quickly by the scribe of the 12th Georgia: "Our brigade charged with that soul-stirring rebel yell, which once heard on the field of battle can never be forgotten." The Yankees soon broke, and "fled in wild confusion, pursued by our shouting, exultant men."[4]

The attack was not quite so simple. Doles, menacing the gap between the First and Eleventh corps, which Schimmelfennig had been able to close partially with the batteries of Dilger and Wheeler, was confronting the better part of a corps with a single brigade. Moving across the open ground, he was without support on his left and was detached from O'Neal on his right, thus having both flanks open and dangerously exposed. Schimmelfennig advanced Von Amesburg's brigade to explore the gap between Doles and O'Neal, but the Georgian countered quickly by changing front, striking Von Amesburg and rolling him back on Schimmelfennig's second brigade, that of Kryzanowski, whose line ran across the fields between the Mummasburg and Carlisle roads. There the fences gave protection and Kryzanowski held.

Barlow, on Schimmelfennig's right, meanwhile observed that Doles's left flank was in the air and directed Von Gilsa to assail it. The opportunity was inviting. Doles, still confronting two divisions with his single brigade, seemed in danger of being overlapped and taken in reverse.

That was the situation at three o'clock when Early's division appeared along the Heidlersburg road, deployed across the hills on the opposite side of Rock Creek, moving rapidly toward Barlow's flank and rear. On Early's right the first of his brigades to come into contact with the Federals was John B. Gordon's, composed of six Georgia regiments. The Eleventh Corps in its exposed position thus suddenly found its flanks assailed by two converging Georgia brigades.

Early's march from Heidlersburg on the morning of July 1 had not been rapid, nor was there intimation of the battle until the head of his column was three or four miles northeast of the town. Then, after noon, firing was heard; however, because of freak atmospheric conditions the subdued roar sounded more like a cavalry engagement twenty miles distant than an infantry combat close at hand. Just then young Major John Warwick Daniel, Early's chief of staff (who in later life was elected five times to the United States Senate from Virginia), was seen riding at top speed to the front with directions to hurry the march. He described how Hill's corps was desperately engaged at Gettysburg, from which the infantry firing could finally be heard in heavy volume. The men stripped off their blankets, heaped them and other unneeded accouterments in piles to be gathered by the wagon train, and made the last mile toward Gettysburg at double-quick time.[5]

Near at hand they could see the clouds of white powder smoke floating over the town. When the division was formed in battle line Early ordered ten minutes' rest to let the men catch their breath.

Almost simultaneously with the appearance of Early northeast of Gettysburg, Pender's division of A. P. Hill's corps passed through Heth's exhausted troops and assaulted Seminary Ridge, where the remnants of the Federal brigades from McPherson's Heights had gathered behind the stone walls and bastions thrown up by the regiments that had waited there in reserve. Rodes at last pressed his brigades forward in unison, and for the first time during the scattered and intense fighting of July 1 the Confederate army managed to obtain something like concerted action. Lee was riding with his staff from Marsh Creek, still concerned over the prolonged firing ahead, which suggested that the "chance encounter" had turned into a major engagement. But the needed co-operation had now been arrived at between Hill on Herr Ridge and Ewell on Oak Hill.

Ewell could observe the advance of Early through the wheat fields on the opposite side of Rock Creek, Gordon on the right, Hays in the center, and Hoke's brigade, commanded by Avery, on the left, with Extra Billy Smith in reserve. A heavy mist began to fall, cooling the men after their hot march and momentarily obscuring the sun.

Early now re-formed his division after its brief rest, a pause which Jackson would have frowned on while other troops were fighting. Turning to his aide Daniel, he scurried off orders to Gordon, Hays, Avery and Smith to double-quick to the front and open the lines for the artillery to pass. Colonel Hillary P. Jones came thundering down with his four batteries, the horses at a run, and while he was getting his guns into position Gordon's clear voice rang out with its command, "Forward, Georgians!"[6]

The gleaming steel bayonets shone above the yellow wheat—"a silver wave across the cloth of gold," Major Daniel grandiloquently called it[7]—as Gordon moved west against the Federal flank and reached out to clasp hands with Doles's other Georgians attacking Barlow's division directly in front. Announcement of Early's arrival was carried the length of the Confederate line by the Charlottesville, Virginia, artillery opening fire at Early's personal command.

Early's extreme left regiment was the 57th North Carolina of Avery's brigade. "From our position," said Colonel Hamilton C. Jones, "we could see the Confederate and Federal lines arrayed one against the other in open ground, no breakworks, no fortifications, but

Concerted attack of Early, Rodes, Heth, and Pender.
July 1, 1863, 3:00 to 4:00 P.M.

they stood apart in battle array and were in plain view for two miles
except where the line was lost in the depressions of the hills."[8]

That was the striking feature about this phase of the battle of the
first day—the visibility of the entire battle line from both flanks of
each army. Pender, attacking the seminary, could see Early's division
assailing Barlow, and Avery's men on Early's left could look to the
far right and see Pender. The foliage and buildings of 1863 did not
obstruct the view.

What Colonel Jones observed as he stood on the left of the Confederate line sheds important light on the order of events during this
phase of the battle. Far off to the right he could see a Southern brigade
going into action. It must have been Perrin's, of Pender's division.
White smoke billowed out from the Federal line, next there was a
rattle of musketry, scarcely audible at that distance against the under-

tones of the artillery. "Then there came the expected yell, a rush, and the enemy's line broke," Jones said. While he watched, another brigade attacked in echelon, with the same yell, and again the enemy broke. This must have been Ramseur. Closer came the assaults and before each of them the Federal line gave way and the scattered blue-coated soldiers fell back toward the town.

"As the conflict neared our position," said Jones, "the effect was marvelous; the men were wild with excitement, and when their time came they went in with the wildest enthusiasm, for from where they stood they could see two miles of the enemy's line in full retreat. It looked indeed as if the end of the war had come."[9]

Robert Stiles, riding close to Early, noticed that the general's glossy black ostrich plume trembled and shimmered on the wide brim of his felt hat as though it were alive.[10] Major James McDowell Carrington, captain of the Charlottesville, Virginia, artillery, also with Early, found the general silent and absorbed, but uncertain enough about the attack to warn the artilleryman to be prepared to unlimber and provide a rallying point if Gordon should be severely handled. But the Georgian emerged through the great sycamores and willows and fell impetuously on Barlow at the Federal right.

By coincidence Barlow's right brigade was Von Gilsa's, which had been on Hooker's extreme right at Chancellorsville and had been the first to feel the shock of Jackson's flank attack. Perhaps it was this earlier experience that unnerved the Germans, for Gordon sent their line reeling back from its anchor on Barlow's Knoll, across the stream north of Gettysburg, past the almshouse, a group of brick buildings on the Heidlersburg road, where they halted momentarily, and into the outskirts of the town. The open fields northeast of Gettysburg were covered with their dead. Howard tried to save his right by hurrying Coster's brigade of Steinwehr's division down from Cemetery Ridge, but before the Federals could establish a second defensive line they were struck again by the brigades of Hays and Avery on Gordon's left.

Colonel Jones's command, the flank regiment of Early's division, encountered little resistance. Jones said the enemy broke at the first fire of the 57th North Carolina. "In fact, they scarcely waited to receive the fire,"[11] he asserted. The other regiments of Avery's brigade, the 6th and 21st North Carolina, experienced stiffer opposition and fought a bloody combat as they pressed ahead.

On reaching the field Gordon had at once noticed the threat to Doles

by Von Gilsa's flanking movement. With what some have termed
"savage cries,"[12] but what Gordon described as "a ringing yell,"[13] his
men had fallen on Barlow's line, fought it hand to hand for a brief
interval and had broken it. This placed his brigade obliquely in the
rear of the Federal position. "Any troops that were ever marshalled
would, under like conditions, have been as surely and swiftly shattered," said Gordon. "There was no alternative for Howard's men
but to break and fly, or to throw down their arms and surrender."[14]
Most of them chose flight and crowded down the road past the almshouse into Gettysburg. As Major Daniel described it, "The Federal
flank had been shriveled up as a scroll."

Meantime Doles, being relieved from the menace of Von Gilsa by
Gordon's attack, again assailed Von Amesburg and began the collection of prisoners among those unable to scurry back into Gettysburg.

Gordon rode ahead with his troops. The artilleryman Stiles observed the Federal retreat and described it as "pell-mell over the rolling wheat fields, through a grove, across a creek, up a little slope, and
into the town itself."[15] Early's three brigades followed so rapidly
that although Stiles brought his guns into battery several times, he
could not fire because the two armies were so close together.

Stiles thought that Gordon at this moment was "the most glorious
and inspiring thing I ever looked upon." He was riding "a majestic
animal, 'whose neck was clothed with thunder,' " a coal-black stallion
captured from one of Milroy's officers at Winchester. "I never saw a
horse's neck so arched, his eyes so fierce, his nostrils so dilated." The
speed of the Georgians was shown by the fact that Gordon rode at a
trot, with the horse's head "right in among the slanting barrels and
bayonets." He was bareheaded. "In a voice like a trumphet" he
urged his men ahead. That sonorous voice would lead the last charge
at Appomattox, by which time Gordon had risen to the command
of half of Lee's army, and would long sound in the United States
Senate halls, but never was it more inspiring than at this moment at
Gettysburg. Stiles said he would not have risked a dime then against
the independence of the Confederacy. He called to Gordon, "General, where are your dead men?"

"I haven't got any sir," Gordon bellowed back. "The Almighty
has covered my men with His shield and buckler."[16]

Later in Richmond as Stiles aided the wounded, he asked one man
what his outfit was. The man's face lighted up. "I belong to Gordon's
old brigade, Captain," he said. "Did you ever see the gin'ral in battle?

He's the most prettiest thing you ever did see on a field of fight. It 'ud put fight into a whipped chicken just to look at him."[17]

In the Federal debacle an officer who had tried to rally the men was hit by a Minié ball; Gordon discovered him on his back with the afternoon July sun beating down in his face. All about him were Northern dead and he, too, appeared to be dying. Gordon dismounted, lifted his head, gave him water from his own canteen, and asked his name. He was Barlow, the Federal division commander, who did not appear likely to survive many hours. A ball had passed through his body near the spinal cord, paralyzing his legs and arms. Gordon had him carried to the shade, took a packet of letters he wanted destroyed and later, learning that Mrs. Barlow was with the Federal army, sent her a flag of truce for passage through the Southern lines. The Federal general survived, to command a division later in Grant's army.[18]

When Howard's men were scattered most of the Southern soldiers considered the battle won and Southern independence a virtual certainty. Carrington and his artillerists thought the wild yelling denoted victory. Just then Early ordered his guns advanced to the town. Carrington halted in the main street, unlimbered three pieces, and prepared his canister. But Early by that time thought the Federals were out of range.

In this battle, fought by two divisions of the Eleventh Corps mainly against two Georgia brigades, the Confederates were heavily outnumbered, even after Hays and Avery had brought their brigades into the attack. But Howard had placed his troops in a calamitous position, with a road—over which a Confederate division was approaching— leading to their rear. The fault was not so much in the troops as in their leader.

Doubleday, distrustful of the position from the start, had had little opportunity to influence Howard, who confided nothing and fought his own battle. The line, in Doubleday's opinion, was too far removed from the town and would have been more secure if it had been echeloned behind the right flank of the First Corps, with its right resting on the almshouse,[19] which was much easier to defend and much more difficult to turn than Barlow's Knoll. The Cemetery Hill position farther back would, of course, have been even safer.

As Gordon had now exhausted his ammunition and had stopped to refill his cartridge boxes, Early sent a summons to Smith. Impatient when he got no response, he repeated the order.[20] But Extra Billy was lost somewhere amid the white smoke clouds rolling off to the rear. He failed to appear, and it was not until later that Early learned he was off chasing a bugbear.

2. A "Steel Division" Assails the Seminary

West of Gettysburg, where first Buford, then Reynolds, and finally Doubleday had been doggedly holding off A. P. Hill since early morning, the Federal army enjoyed no such numerical superiority as Howard north of town. But the weakness of the First Corps lines had not been fully exploited and Doubleday had profited from the lack of coordination in the Confederate attack. Now, with most of his brigades already shattered, Doubleday was suddenly faced with the fierce onslaught of Pender's fresh division.

Pender's had been A. P. Hill's celebrated light division; its timely arrival on Lee's right had saved the army at Sharpsburg, and on the Peninsula it had been described as "made of steel, rather than flesh and blood."[21] It consisted of the North Carolina brigades of Lane and Scales, the Georgians of Thomas, and the South Carolinians of McGowan, these last being commanded at Gettysburg by Colonel Abner Perrin.

William Dorsey Pender, youngest among Lee's infantry division commanders, was an unusual combination of sweetness and gentleness with whirlwind military aggressiveness. He had the soft brown eyes of a dreamer but hit like a hammer in an attack. His love letters to his wife, written almost daily even during intense campaigning, show a deep religious faith and a compassion and softness altogether out of harmony with the fierce ruthlessness of the battlefield.

Both at Chancellorsville, after A. P. Hill was wounded, and at Gettysburg, Pender commanded a division, and while his term was brief in this enlarged responsibility, he obviously could not have given Lee a more impressive account of himself. Lee was later to bemoan the fact that he did not give Pender a corps. Had Pender rather than Hill led the Third Corps, and commanded it as closely at the scene of the fighting as was his custom, the story of Gettysburg might have been different. Because President Davis adhered so closely to the seniority system, Pender's promotion to major general had been delayed beyond what his friends felt were his deserts. Leadership of a corps was not thought about until after his death.

Medium tall, Pender was described by his brother as "well formed and graceful," but one of his early military feats suggests that he was a more muscular and powerful man than these words imply.[22] While campaigning against the Indians in the far Northwest, as a lieutenant of dragoons, he had ridden alone to bring up reinforcements at the battle of Spokane Plains, when he was suddenly intercepted and attacked by an Indian chief. He had no time to draw his sword and would have been killed had he not grasped his attacker's upraised arm, then his neck, and pinioned him. Holding the powerless Indian, he put spurs to his horse and galloped toward his men. When he reached them he picked up the Indian and hurled him back among the dragoons.

This was no puny young officer, whose voice was low and cultivated and whose words came in a soft Carolina drawl. One of his officers, First Lieutenant Benjamin H. Cathey of the 16th North Carolina, summed him up: "He was one of the coolest, most self-possessed and one of the most absolutely fearless men under fire I ever knew."[23]

He had been a close friend of Jeb Stuart at West Point and after their graduation in 1854 they had visited another classmate, Samuel Turner Shepperd, at the family's country seat, Good Spring, near Salem (now Winston-Salem), North Carolina. The distinguished father, Augustine Henry Shepperd, had represented his district nine terms in the United States Congress. At Good Spring Pender met the eldest daughter, Mary Frances Shepperd. They were married in 1859 and for the four years left to them—two years in the West and two under the Confederacy—their romance was one of pure beauty.

Pender, a regular army officer, had made no commitment until Lincoln called on North Carolina for troops to serve against other Southern states, whereupon he resigned his commission to become a lieutenant colonel and drill instructor at Camp Garysburg, North Carolina. Thereafter his rise, like Ramseur's, was rapid.

Mary Shepperd Pender, the congressman's daughter and general's wife, was a woman of gentle expression but strong convictions, as Pender's letters disclose.[24] Her devoutness made her reluctant to see the Southern army in the role of invader. Pender wrote her on June 24 from Shepherdstown, Virginia, a trifle apologetically: "Tomorrow I do what I know will cause you grief, and that is to cross the Potomac. . . . May the Lord prosper this expedition and bring an early peace out of it."

He had faith in the righteousness of his cause. Earlier he had written: "Take a few examples and see how hard and almost impossible it is to subdue a people determined to be free. The Netherlands whom Philip tried to crush; Spain against Napoleon. This country in '76. . . ."

In his last letter, from Fayetteville, Pennsylvania, where his division was resting after its march of 157 miles from the Rappahannock, he was confident but unsettled: "The people are frightened to death and will do anything we intimate to them. . . . I am tired of invasions for although they have made us suffer all that people can suffer I cannot get my resentment to that point to make me feel indifferent to what goes on here."

He knew enough about pillaging to understand that it ruined discipline. "But for the demoralizing effect plundering would have on our troops, they [the Pennsylvanians] would feel war in all its horrors." He would not be indebted to those he fought. "I have made up my mind to enjoy no hospitality of friendship from any of them," he declared.

"I never saw troops march as ours do. They will go 15 or 20 miles a day without having a straggler and sing (?)[25] and yell on all occasions. Confidence and good spirits seem to possess every one of them. I wish we could meet Hooker and have the matter settled at once." Thus Pender expressed his confidence.

Now Hooker's army was before him—as he had wished—though under a new commander, and Pender's turn had come. Most of the day the division had been waiting in the fields beyond Herr Ridge. On word from Hill at 3:30 P.M. his brigades in battle order crossed Willoughby Run.

Scales was on the left, Perrin in the center and Lane on the right, with Thomas in reserve. Pender's orders to them were to move through Heth's division and engage the enemy closely. In no circumstances were they to stop. "Rout him from his position."[26] Each brigadier was to manage his brigade according to his own judgment.

"Our men," said Perrin, "moved as bravely forward as any men ever did on earth. We charged over Pettigrews brigade; the poor fellows could scarcely rise to cheer us as we passed."[27]

Perrin's brigade had been built around South Carolina's famous Palmetto Regiment, which had been the first to enter Mexico City in the Mexican War, and in which its recently wounded commander, Samuel McGowan, had served as a private. Fighting alongside it in Mexico had been the 12th U.S. Infantry, commanded by the South Carolinian Colonel Milledge Luke Bonham, under whom Perrin served as a captain.

Bonham, McGowan, and Perrin, all from the back country of

western South Carolina, were close friends. Bonham was elected
Governor of South Carolina in 1862 and left the Confederate Army.
These old army comrades exchanged letters on confidential terms, one
of which, from Perrin to Bonham, gives intimate observations on the
battle of Gettysburg.

The Federal line at the seminary consisted of hurriedly constructed
earthen breastworks and bastions of stone walls and rail fences.
South of the seminary a stone wall began at the large brick house, the
home of the Shultz sisters, Maria and Cornelia, and ran southwest-
wardly along the crest of Seminary Ridge. North of the seminary on
the turnpike batteries which all day had exacted a heavy toll from the
Confederates were still strongly posted when Pender began his attack.
Pender's entire division was south of the turnpike, on which Scales
rested the left of his brigade.

Here he struck the remnants of the Iron Brigade, now commanded
by Colonel W. W. Robinson of the 7th Wisconsin, intermixed with
survivors of Stone's Bucktails. Colonel Dawes with the 6th Wisconsin
had reached the seminary by running down the railroad that had
proved a cul-de-sac for his opponent earlier in the day, and waited
for the oncoming assault. He gave a picture of Pender's approach:
"For a mile up and down the open fields in front, the splendid lines
of the veterans of the Army of Northern Virginia swept down upon
us. Their bearing was magnificent. They maintained their alignment
with great precision."[28] But the remnants of the Bucktails and the
Iron Brigade still had fight left in them, and here perhaps they put
in their most glorious performance. Strung out along Seminary Ridge,
the men lay in the woods and kept up an incessant fire on the approaching gray lines.

Scales suffered fearful losses from what was described as a "sheet
of flame"[29] spurting from the Federal riflemen and was arrested in
front of the embankment. He was personally only seventy-five feet
from the Federal guns when he was checked, wounded. His men hit
the low places in the treeless plateau in front of the seminary and
returned the fire without being able to close for a hand-to-hand encounter.[30] All the field officers of Scales's brigade except one were
killed or wounded.

Lane had no better fortune on Pender's right. His brigade extended
from the Fairfield road south to the McMillan house. Here one of
Buford's cavalry brigades again guarded the Federal flank after a
brief relief. The redoubtable Gamble, who had opened the battle

for the Federal army, had gathered his remaining troopers to share in the final contest for Seminary Ridge, and had been given the critical position south of the Fairfield road. Here he seemed to threaten Lane both with an enfilade fire and with a cavalry charge, for which his troopers appeared to be preparing.

Doubleday had ordered a charge—a desperate undertaking against veteran infantry—but Buford did not attempt it. The menace from the cavalry, perhaps not great, was sufficient to disturb the young Confederate brigade leader, Lane. As one of Pettigrew's regiments had done earlier, he faced some of his regiments to the south and formed squares. Then he felt for the main Federal line on Seminary Ridge gingerly, maintaining little more than long-range firing against it and the Federal cavalry.

Although Scales and Lane were arrested, Perrin moved against the Federal center with an impact more characteristic of Pender's assaults. His men had received a whisky ration, unusual in the army, on the night before.[31] The South Carolinians were not to be denied. The hail of fire from the seminary works seemed less to retard than spur them on. In the words of Lieutenant Colonel Joseph N. Brown of the 14th South Carolina, "To stop was destruction. To retreat was disaster. To go forward was 'orders.' "[32] The intrepid Perrin was perhaps the most fortunate officer in the Confederate army. He came dashing through the ranks on his beautiful horse, his sword glinting in the late afternoon sun, and for the last 300 yards he personally led the charge over the open ground against the seminary.[33] Officers and men fell about him but he came through unscathed. Both sides fought with desperate earnestness, recognizing that possession of the seminary meant the command of Seminary Ridge and in turn the town of Gettysburg. The battle west of the town was in its decisive stage.

Biddle's Pennsylvania brigade, which all day had been meeting Heth's fierce onslaughts, was massed closely in the brick buildings and at the stone fence, and here the South Carolinians converged to make their most determined assault.[34]

3. The Palmetto Flag at the Diamond

It was approaching four o'clock. Doubleday's situation was desperate. His reserves were exhausted, and his thin, weak line was being hammered unremittingly; one flank was in immediate danger of being turned by the obstinate Daniel and enterprising Ramseur, and he was protected on the other only by a weak cavalry brigade.

Long ago he had sent his adjutant, Captain Richard F. Halsted, with urgent appeals to Howard, who was supposed to be commanding the entire battlefield. He besought assistance from Steinwehr's idle division on Cemetery Hill. But Howard tended to scoff at Double-day's need, insisted that Halsted had been mistaking rail fences for advancing Confederates,[35] declined to order the First Corps to retire, and refused to send succor from Steinwehr. He did direct Halsted to find Buford, who was in feeble condition to give help; but Buford restored Gamble to the extreme left flank just in time to retard the advance of Lane.

Time had now run out for Doubleday west of Gettysburg. His lines were bent back on either flank by Pender's unabated pressure, leaving the seminary and its near-by buildings a salient. Ramseur, aided by O'Neal, was pressing Baxter and Paul and, with Daniel, coming to the assistance of Scales. And Perrin, at the center of Pender's assault, had now reached the salient at the seminary.

With a rush the South Carolinians carried the stone wall and bar-ricades. The Federal line was broken and pushed back, "at first rap-idly and disorderly, with our men close on them,"[36] said Colonel Brown. Cohesion was lost quickly in some of the First Corps units. In the pandemonium of the rout the Federal artillery limbered up and dashed off toward Cemetery Ridge and the fields south of Gettys-burg, making a remarkable withdrawal with the loss of only two guns. These Perrin captured in his close pursuit, but he bemoaned the fact that Pender's other brigades had not kept pace with him. "If we had any support," he said in his confidential letter to Governor Bonham, "we could have taken every piece of artillery they had and thousands of prisoners."[37]

While Perrin had made the break through in the final assault, the alert Ramseur was not to be outdistanced. The Federals in his front could move neither to the right nor to the left because of the rout of the Eleventh Corps on the one hand and the loss of the seminary on the other; they could reach Gettysburg only along the unfinished railroad or the parallel Cashtown pike. "We had the Yankees like partridges in a nest," said one of Ramseur's men, "and the only way they could get out was up the railroad."[38] The entire brigade saw the situation in a twinkling and began shouting to the general, "Bring us a battery! Bring us a battery!" Ramseur turned to his courier and in a sudden outburst shouted, "Damn it, tell them to send me a bat-tery! I have sent for one a half a dozen times." The words were scarcely out of his mouth before the devout young Presbyterian threw up both arms, looked upward and in the hearing of the entire brigade said, "God Almighty, forgive me that oath!"[39] As an almost immediate answer to one or the other of his entreaties, a battery rushed up and began throwing shells at the Federals retiring down the railroad. He and his brigade went off toward Gettysburg in hot pursuit.

"I could almost hear their bones crunch under the shot and shell," said Colonel Bennett of the 14th North Carolina.[40]

Nearly every regiment had men who performed deeds of great courage. The entire 16th Maine regiment played a heroic role. General Robinson selected it as the rear guard. It held the stone wall on the Mummasburg road, near the scene of Iverson's defeat, until it was engulfed. Said Abner R. Small, the adjutant: "For this little battalion of heroes, hemmed in by thousands of rebels, there was no succor, no hope."

When a Confederate officer was about to seize the flag the men crowded around it, clutched at it, tore it into bits, and secreted the small pieces in their clothing. Years later the flag of the 16th Maine was scattered in treasured fragments over the Pine Tree State. "In albums and frames and breast-pocketbooks" could be found the gold stars and silken shreds, "cherished mementoes of that heroic and awful hour."[41] The "Forlorn Hope" saved much of Robinson's division, then tried to extricate itself. "And so the Sixteenth Maine," said Adjutant Small, "was the last regiment that left the extreme front on the 1st of July—if four officers and thirty-six men can be called a regiment."[42]

The confused masses which had been the brigades of Cutler, Meredith, Stone, Biddle, Baxter, and Paul, straggled back, some into the town, most of them to the south of it and up the inviting slopes of Cemetery Hill. The retreat became so uncontrolled that one of Ramseur's officers grew apprehensive. "I was fearful their running troops would crush our little brigade," he wrote to his mother.[43] He, too, saw that some of the Federals were trapped. "We had them fairly in a pen, with only one gap open—the turnpike that led into Gettysburg—and hither they fled twenty deep, we all the while popping into them as fast as we could load and fire." In the town "we rushed pell-mell after them."[44]

This anonymous officer, whose letter home gave the North Carolina newspapers the first full account of Ramseur's attack, was in the skirmish line and pressed close to the Federals. "They hid by hundreds in houses and barns, and I had the felicity of capturing any number."[45] Ramseur's brigade was credited with capturing more than its own numbers in prisoners.[46] The same claim was made by Hays, and in both instances it was no doubt accurate.[47]

But the honor of being the first Confederates into Gettysburg went not to Ramseur, but to Perrin and the 1st South Carolina—the Palmetto Regiment, which repeated at Gettysburg its performance at Mexico City. Perrin knew that in battle one does not halt before a broken enemy. He did not tarry after capturing the seminary. The 14th South Carolina passed around the building at a rush, Colonel Brown conducting the left wing and Major Edward Croft the right, picked up the two Federal cannon, and marched on. It gave an artillery horse to Captain T. P. Alston of the 1st Regiment so that he might ride while leading the brigade's skirmishers into Gettysburg.

Perrin ordered the 1st and 14th regiments to make the entry and this they did simultaneously, with their flags unfurled.[48] The 1st South Carolina went down the Cashtown road to Chambersburg Street, the main east-west street, and thence to the Diamond, or public square. The 14th marched between North Boundary Street and the railroad embankment, until it reached Carlisle Street, the main north-south thoroughfare. The 14th then turned and marched toward the square.[49] As it moved south it passed a mounted figure under the shade trees. Pender had ridden up to give his compliments to the captors of Gettysburg.[50] The 14th did reach Carlisle Street ahead of any other troops, but at some distance north of the square, while the 1st, commanded by Major C. W. McCreary, got to the center of the town and there planted the Palmetto banner.[51] "The Yankee infantry," said Perrin, "literally swarmed through the streets."[52]

Pender had been momentarily concerned while observing, from Seminary Ridge, the close fighting and Perrin's rapid pursuit, in which his men appeared to mingle with masses of blue-clad soldiers. When Perrin dipped out of sight, Pender hastened ahead, met a lieutenant of the 12th Regiment, and expressed concern that the impetuous brigade might have been captured. "No, it is over the hill yonder," said the lieutenant.[53] Pender then stationed the 12th and 13th South Carolina between the town and the seminary to protect the right flank of the eager South Carolinians, and rode hurriedly into Gettysburg. Within a few minutes Ramseur's men appeared, entering farther to the north. Ramseur was followed a short time later by Hays of Early's division, coming in from the east.[54]

After the entry of Rodes, Pender withdrew the 1st and 14th South Carolina regiments to the position occupied by the balance of Perrin's brigade, between the town and the seminary.[55] Perrin's loss was heavy, about 600 out of 1,100. His largest regiment, the 14th, stormed the seminary with 475 and lost 200 in killed and wounded. The brigade proudly averred that it suffered no loss in prisoners.

Perrin wrote to Governor Bonham: "We captured the town of Gettysburg and hundreds of prisoners, thousands of small arms, two field pieces, . . . and four standards, two of which I intended to send to you to be placed in the State House at Columbia, but they made me turn them in here to be sent to Richmond, I suppose."[56] Among them were the corps standard of the First Army Corps and a beautiful flag presented to the 104th New York, the Wadsworth's Guards, by General Wadsworth.

Federal troops jammed into Gettysburg from north and west. The broad streets were soon congested, the alleys and yards were thronged with refugees, and milling, confused crowds tried to get out of the town as others sought to enter. At no time at Chancellorsville had there been such panic. As Doubleday rode through with his staff, citizens came out offering food and beseeching protection. "Pale and frightened women," he said, ". . . implored us not to abandon them."[57] Stone's Bucktails were among the last to yield their Seminary Ridge position and suffered heavily in prisoners. This was the brigade that had come under Ramseur's fire, and many were intercepted before they could gain the shelter of Gettysburg houses.[58]

Never was the Southern army in greater need of cavalry than at this instant of chaos in the Federal defense. Stuart on the field might have cut off the disorganized units from Cemetery Hill and doubled the number of prisoners taken. In such an instance, cavalry might function against fleeing soldiers, where it could make little impression on the solid ranks against which generals still liked to employ it. But the bag of prisoners captured in Gettysburg was impressive. Ramseur's officer placed the number at 7,300, with no doubt many duplications. The aggregate was perhaps nearer 5,000, the captures being made chiefly by Ramseur, Doles, Perrin and Hays. General Schimmelfennig was caught in the press, could not extricate himself, and had to hide under a woodpile for the next two days.

Of the brilliant actions in the fighting west of Gettysburg, the most sanguinary was the storming of McPherson's Woods by Pettigrew's brigade, and most conspicuous in that assault was the duel between the 26th North Carolina and the 24th Michigan. Second, if not equal, to this was Perrin's violent and triumphant attack on the seminary fortifications. At times it has been contended that Pettigrew did the hard chore and Pender's division only reaped the easy victory. That was far from the case; the casualty lists attest the true story.

Some other points are salient in considering the July 1 fighting. One is that Hill was tacitly, perhaps even covertly, looking for battle as well as for shoes. Ordinarily a full division is not employed for a foray or a reconnaissance, but in this case Hill consented not only to have Heth go to Gettysburg, but had Pender aroused by three o'clock in the morning with orders to follow him and give support. Manifestly something more than shoes was expected. Yet the full intention was not made clear to General Lee. The fact that Heth spent the balance of his life lamenting his role in bringing on the battle suggests that his own conscience was never eased or his conduct fully justified in his own reflections.

The defeat of the First Federal Corps west of Gettysburg could scarcely be attributed to the defeat of the Eleventh Corps north of the town. The First Corps was overpowered by superior numbers. Even had the Eleventh Corps held fast, the First could not likely have maintained its position another five minutes. It was cut in the center, not on the right flank where the Eleventh Corps crumbled. While Doubleday at the last minute did signal his units to fall back, the retirement was anything but voluntary. Some of both Wadsworth's and Robinson's regiments managed to retain a semblance of order, and a few colonels, like Dawes, insisted that their withdrawal was both prearranged and deliberate, and due wholly to the breakup of the Eleventh Corps. Perhaps in the frenzy of close fighting it seemed that way, but Doubleday's departure had few aspects of a calculated withdrawal.

North and west of Gettysburg the Federal army had fought two separate and distinct actions, under different commanders, to all practical effect. That was what Buford had in mind when in his midafternoon report to Pleasanton, who was with Meade at Taneytown, he wrote a pertinent closing sentence, "In my opinion there seems to be no directing person."[59]

Both forces gave way independently and at so nearly the same time that the one had substantially no effect on the other. The First Corps fought a prolonged engagement against heavy odds; the Eleventh disintegrated rapidly after being attacked by an inferior force.

Though entitled to acclaim, Doubleday got little more than demotion out of one of the great fights in American history, and after the battle he passed out of the Army of the Potomac, unwanted by Meade or Grant and unprotected by Halleck or Stanton. About the best tribute he received was from Colonel Dawes, who, prior to Gettysburg, in a letter home called him a "gallant officer" and said, "I saw him at Antietam . . . he was remarkably cool and at the very front of battle."[60] That was where he had been at Gettysburg.

The Southern, like the Northern army, fought the engagement without united leadership. Early's and Pender's divisions were well handled, Heth's and Rodes's poorly. The Confederate fighting was essentially by brigades and here the leadership was in most instances brilliant. Nothing better could have been asked of Gordon, Doles, Ramseur, Daniel, Pettigrew, or Perrin. Iverson, Archer, Davis, and, to a lesser extent, O'Neal were brigade failures. In the Federal army, the entire First Corps resistance was nothing short of heroic, and one brigade could with but difficulty be singled out above the others.

The Confederate victory at this stage was more impressive than that won two months earlier at Chancellorsville. There one Federal corps had been shattered; here two. On the Confederate side seventeen brigades had been brought to the field, four each by Heth, Early and Pender and five by Rodes. Two, those of Thomas and Smith, had not been engaged.

On the Federal side, fourteen brigades, including Buford's two cavalry brigades, were in line, although one of Steinwehr's had remained unemployed on Cemetery Hill. Ordinarily the Confederate brigades were stronger; thus approximately 22,000 Confederates with twenty batteries had fought 16,500 Federals with ten batteries. While the odds strongly favored the Confederates, they did not presage such a complete rout of the Federal army.

Great crowds of fugitives were making their way down the Baltimore road intent on nothing but escape. Some were arrested by the provost guard of the Twelfth Corps. Five thousand prisoners were in Confederate hands, while by a conservative estimate 4,000 were lying on the field or in hastily improvised hospitals. The Army of the Potomac had suffered a shattering blow.

CHAPTER THIRTEEN

High Ground and Golden Minutes

1. Early Shuns the Offerings of Fortune

Jubal Early stirred mixed emotions and remained an enigma both during the war and long after, when he became the manager of the notorious Louisiana Lottery, which probably blighted more Southern homes than were ever wrecked by Sherman's army.[1] He was rated by Sorrel, a competent judge, one of the best strategists in the Confederacy, yet Sorrel conceded that he lacked ability to handle troops effectively, while "his irritable disposition and biting tongue made him anything but popular."[2] He never married. He felt on the defensive when Ewell, after the capture of Milroy's army in Winchester, delegated him to speak to a group of women. "I never have been able to make a speech to one lady, much less to so many," he countered quickly.[3]

Having no family, Early devoted himself to causes and applied himself with unusual gusto to whatever he undertook. For a considerable period he campaigned against secession. He was among the most ardent supporters in Virginia of the old Federal union, though when the state seceded there was no doubt but that his extraordinary enterprise and irascibility would be thrown wholeheartedly into the cause of his native state.

While he was rated by some among the best scholars of the army—and his later writings and speeches were engaging, pungent, and voluminous—his conversation often was rough and ungrammatical and peppered by repeated oaths. At times he was epigrammatic. "The

172

main use I have for a pioneer corps is to bury dead Yankees." Better
examples were apparently unpublishable. Stiles judged him not a
"superb magnetic leader like Gordon" nor could he "deliver quite
as majestic a blow in actual battle as Longstreet," and summed him
up: "Early was in some respects a bundle of inconsistencies and con-
tradictions; of religion and irreligion; of reverence and profanity."[4]
He admired both Lee and Jackson almost to the point of worship, but
was the only officer ever heard to swear in Lee's presence. Lee's mild
reproof, not without affection, was conveyed by treating Early as
"my bad old man."[5] Had Lee been incapacitated so that Longstreet
had to take over the command, Early would have been en route to an
obscure sector the next morning, for Old Pete distrusted and despised
him. After the war these two tough-fibered fighters enjoyed a lifelong
quarrel, each intent on destroying the other, which came to involve
in one manner or another almost all the surviving officers of the Army
of Northern Virginia. It ended only with Early's death, as a recluse,
thirty-one years after Gettysburg.

Early had turned lawyer after graduating from West Point, had
gone back to the army during the Mexican War, then returned to law,
and again resumed his military career when the states seceded. In
Mexico he had contracted a rheumatism—probably arthritis—that for
spells twisted and bent him[6] and made him appear one of the army
ancients, although at Gettysburg he was only forty-six years old. But
the soldiers usually called him "Old Jube" and the other officers
respected his long, untrimmed beard and his years, even if many of
them had little use for his character or personality. The war gave
him several unusual opportunities but perhaps none approaching that
which now fell to him as he sat astride his horse on Barlow's Knoll
and watched the disorganized Federal soldiers streaming back into
Gettysburg.

His division was still fresh. Gordon's losses were inconsequential;
so were those of Hays and Hoke, while Smith had been unengaged.
The artillery was well up. Colonel J. Thompson Brown, commanding
the Second Corps guns, was under the impression the division would
follow the defeated enemy and take the wooded hill (Culp's) on the
left. He sent an officer to move with the division and find a road for
the artillery.

Early rode into Gettysburg, passed the crowds of prisoners being
taken to the rear, with virtually no guard, he noticed, and encountered
Hays, who was forming a line along a street on the east side of the

town. Shells were dropping from Cemetery Hill. Federal sharpshooters still occupied some of the houses near the foot of the hill, and the
bluecoats had a skirmish line along its base. Early found it "very
apparent" that the hill held a force which had not participated in the
fight north of the town.[7] Avery meantime had placed his brigade
behind a low ridge on the Culp farm, where the rolling ground gave
protection from the Federals on Cemetery Hill. Thus Hays and
Avery were within striking distance of the heights in front, and Gordon
was close by.

This was a supreme instant for Early, although of course he could
not appreciate the great consequences of his actions to the cause of
Southern independence. Napoleon had a maxim: "The destiny of
States depend upon a moment."[8] Never did it have more pertinent
application than when Early stood on the outskirts of Gettysburg with
three fresh brigades and a fourth within reach and looked up at the
eminences immediately ahead of him.

Culp's Hill, to the left, was unoccupied. It was much later that
Wadsworth was able to collect there some of the scattered remnants
of his division and form a meager defending force around the nucleus
of the 7th Indiana Regiment, which had not shared in the fighting
west of Gettysburg. Seminary Hill held the distraught Eleventh Corps
refugees, estimated by Hancock after his arrival at 1,000 to 1,200
organized troops "at most." Howard had been distressfully unable to
re-form much of the Eleventh Corps as it passed over Cemetery Hill
and took to the Baltimore roads beyond.

Buford had his cavalry in solid formation on the fields to the right
of Cemetery Hill and gave some protection to that flank, but none in
front or on the Confederate left. Early was under no restraints. He
had at this stage of the battle received no orders to check his pursuit,
and certainly none of any nature applicable to his new situation. Nothing called for the perspicacity of Jackson. Early had routed an enemy,
and any textbook or any corporal would know the next move. The
enemy was making a fresh stand and there were still four and a half
hours of daylight, or time for half a dozen victories.

Napoleon had another dictum: "There is but one step between
triumph and ruin." That step Early now prepared to take, in the
wrong direction. Instead of ordering Hays and Avery to occupy the
high ground in their immediate front—as he was to order twenty hours
later when it bristled with bayonets—he groped about Gettysburg looking for either Ewell or Rodes, or both. He had not seen them that

day, and he wanted "to urge that we should advance at once upon the hill in our front, before the enemy could re-form."[9]

Early found neither general but encountered some of Rodes's soldier's, probably Ramseur's, on the other side of the town. Then he rode out the Cashtown road "to look at the position from that point of view and see if I could find Ewell or Rodes."[10] As Early rode west from Gettysburg, destiny was ticking off one of the great hours of the Confederacy. Jackson had made chance his handmaiden; Early became its servant. It seems in the case of Jackson that chance yielded to the strength of his character. However that may be, Early rode directly out of the arms of the fortune that had sought to embrace him, and cast himself on his irresolute corps commander, Ewell.

On the Cashtown road Early met one of Pender's staff officers and asked him to find A. P. Hill and say that if he would "send forward a division, we could take that hill."[11] Early was in error in contending that at this time none of Hill's troops had advanced beyond Seminary Ridge. Perrin's two regiments had preceded Ramseur. Apparently the South Carolinians had been withdrawn by the time Early reached the square.

Just then Colonel Abner Smead, inspector general of the Second Corps, rode up—Early does not make clear how far he had advanced toward the seminary when Smead appeared—with information from Ewell. Johnson's division was approaching and Ewell wanted Early's opinion where it should be placed.

Ewell meantime had ridden down the slopes of Oak Hill, followed closely by Trimble, who had been observing from the high ground where Oak Hill merges into Seminary Ridge. Everywhere were evidences of a great Confederate victory. The ground was covered with dead and wounded soldiers. Strewn about were rifles, muskets, haversacks, canteens, and large quantities of other equipment. Trimble had witnessed the flight of the Federals through the town and across the fields, and was fired by the sight. Before Ewell reached the square he and Trimble were joined by Gordon, whose eager spirit also had been fully aroused. Gordon was anxious for the chase, on which he could see that the fortunes of the day depended. As they rode into Gettysburg, Gordon was startled by the thud of a bullet hitting the corps commander, but Ewell jokingly remarked, "You see how much better fixed for a fight I am than you are. It didn't hurt a bit to be shot in the wooden leg."

Captain James Power Smith, Ewell's aide, placed Ewell's arrival at

the town square at about five o'clock. He remained in the saddle beneath a shade tree, "chatted amiably with his men," and "pleasantly
declined" a bottle of wine one of his young officers had brought up
from a cellar.[12] Manifestly there was nothing pressing in the attitude
or actions of the corps commander, and Captain Smith, who watched
it all closely, agreed the events assumed a more critical importance
in later reflection than at the time. "But even then, some of us who
had served on Jackson's staff, sat in a group in our saddles, and one
said sadly, 'Jackson is not here.'" Ewell was "simply waiting for
orders" when every moment "could not be balanced with gold."[13]

2. *Trimble Throws His Sword Away!*

After dallying in Gettysburg, Ewell rode northeast to temporary headquarters at a farm near the almshouse. While in town he had received
intelligence that Johnson's division was approaching and had dispatched Colonel Smead to find Early.

Lee's concentration had been impeded because the bulk of his army
had to move through the single South Mountain pass and along the
clogged Chambersburg-Gettysburg road. Johnson's division, which
had reached Green Village on the night of June 30, was given the
right of way over Longstreet, and on Wednesday July 1 moved through
Fayetteville and over the gap to Cashtown. As they crossed the
mountain the men heard the sound of distant artillery firing. Midway
between Cashtown and Gettysburg Johnson sent Major Harry Kyd
Douglas ahead with notice to Ewell that the division was "in prime
condition" and ready to enter the line on its arrival.[14] When Douglas
delivered the message he tried to convey something of Johnson's
earnestness.

Gordon who was still with Ewell said he could join with Johnson
in the assault, but Ewell demurred. Douglas quoted him: "General
Lee told me to come to Gettysburg and gave me no orders to go
further. I do not feel like advancing and making an attack without
orders from him, and he is back at Cashtown."[15]

Gordon said nothing more. Ewell gave notice that Johnson should
halt when he was well up and wait for further directions. As Douglas
departed, Ewell's chief of staff said to him, in an aside:

"Oh, for the presence and inspiration of Old Jack for just one
hour!"[16]

Trimble took note that the firing had now ceased, but he thought
Ewell was moving about uneasily, "a good deal excited," and "seemed

to me to be undecided what to do next."[17] Trimble decided this was a good moment to give advice: "Well, General," he said, "we have had a grand success. Are you not going to follow it up and push our advantage?"

Again Ewell referred to the lack of new orders from Lee. With the awful evidences of battle about him, he was going back to the instructions he had received early in the morning, which might or might not be applicable, according to a corps commander's views, to an altogether fresh set of conditions brought about by the expulsion of the enemy from Gettysburg.

Trimble was quick to see a discrepancy. "That hardly applies to the present state of things," he said, "as we have fought a hard battle already and should secure the advantage gained."

Ewell made no reply. Trimble judged him "far from composed." He was putting the brakes on the army when he should have been accelerating its movements. Trimble, recognizing this as "a critical moment," rode off for a closer view of Culp's and Cemetery hills. Quickly he returned and pointed to Culp's Hill.

"General," he said, "there is an eminence of commanding position and not now occupied, as it ought to be by us or the enemy soon. I advise you to send a brigade to hold it if we are to remain here."

"Are you sure it commands the town?" asked Ewell.

"Certainly it does, as you can see, and it ought to be held by us at once," Trimble asserted.

He did not record Ewell's response other than to say it was impatient.

Trimble's anger at this stage erupted. He had grasped in an instant what writers and historians have been speculating about for nearly a century, namely that the corps commander had grown timid.[18]

"Give me a division," he said, "and I will take that hill."

Ewell declined. His precise words were not given by Lieutenant McKim, the faithful recorder of many of the details of Gettysburg.

"Give me a brigade and I will do it," Trimble continued. When Ewell still declined, the despairing Trimble implored: "Give me a good regiment and I will engage to take that hill."

That too being denied, Trimble threw down his sword and stalked out of Ewell's headquarters in a huff, asserting that he would no longer serve under such an officer. He could do this, McKim explained, because he was merely acting as a volunteer aide to Ewell and had no established command. The Confederacy might have fared better with "old man Trimble" in command of the corps, or of Early's division. That would have been more practical than to yearn for the dead Jackson.

In the Confederate army, where private soldiers did not hesitate to express opinions, the general received some prompting. Major Daniel noted that when the men saw the delay and the hills ahead they shouted, "Let's go on!" Colonel Jones of Avery's brigade reflected a common viewpoint: "There was not an officer, not even a man, that did not expect that the war would be closed upon that hill that evening, for there was still two hours of daylight when the final charge was made, yet for reasons that have never been explained nor ever will be . . . some one made a blunder that lost the battle of Gettysburg, and, humanly speaking, the Confederate cause."[19]

Gordon was not a professional soldier and had merely risen from the command of the "Raccoon Roughs" of the northern Georgia hills, but he had better military intuition than some of the veteran officers of the old army and he understood the critical nature of the moment. A short time earlier he had looked down the lines and as far as he could see the enemy was retreating. Large numbers were throwing down their arms. Those farther away had fight in them still, but they, too, could be taken in flank. "In less than half an hour," he said, "my troops would have swept up and over those hills, the possession of which was of such momentous consequence."[20]

Gordon had, in fact, paid no attention to the first orders to halt. "Not until the third or fourth order of the most peremptory character reached me did I obey," he said. In later reflection he doubted that he would have obeyed even then except for the explanation that General Lee, who was several miles removed from the field, did not want to fight at Gettysburg.

While Early was talking with Colonel Smead on the Cashtown road, an aide from Extra Billy Smith arrived greatly excited, bringing word that Federal infantry and artillery were advancing along the York road, which would place them on the flank and rear of Early's division. Smith, according to Early's account of it,[21] said he would be unable to hold off this force; this was the reason he had not advanced when Early had sent for him during the attack on the Eleventh Corps. Early doubted Smith's accuracy but felt the troops would be disturbed by the report of an enemy on their flank, even if it proved untrue, so he sent a staff officer to Gordon directing him to take his brigade to the York road, and, in Early's words, stop the "stampeding." That ended the possibility of using Gordon against Culp's or Cemetery Hill.

Up to this time Early had not seen Ewell. He had just pointed out Culp's Hill to Colonel Smead as the place Johnson should occupy when another courier arrived, saying Ewell wanted to see Early in town. Ewell merely wanted to ask orally where Johnson should be placed and Early again pointed to Culp's Hill as the proper position. Then, according to Early's account, he urged that they should push ahead and occupy Cemetery Hill. This he had not done earlier, when the opportunity was most inviting. But Ewell suggested that they ride together toward the hill and reconnoiter it, which they did until they encountered the fire of Federal sharpshooters who still held the southern fringe of the town. Ewell then concluded that it would be best not to advance until Johnson arrived.

There is abundant information on this critical moment in the history of the Confederacy because Early in later years, smarting under the suggestion that perhaps he, and not Longstreet, was responsible for the Southern defeat, went to great length to build up a record, which, in the end, left a number of inconsistencies. While he urged Ewell to attack an hour or so after the Federals had broken, he explained in the record that he did not have a sufficient force for it; that the job could be done more readily from A. P. Hill's position; and that the Federal army was in such strength that an attack would have been doomed to failure, after all. He thought Smith was in a self-engendered panic, yet he emphasized in his account that an approach of the enemy on the York road was not improbable because Stuart had fought near Hanover the day before and Colonel White, his own cavalry leader, had reported an enemy infantry force on the Hanover road.[22]

Rodes now joined them, and while they awaited Johnson the three generals, Ewell, Rodes and Early, rode together out the York pike to probe into the nature of Smith's alleged encounter with the enemy. They could look down the road for two miles and on their arrival it was clear of troops. Early reaffirmed his first statement that he "placed no confidence in the rumor."[23] Rodes tended to believe it, and Ewell "seemed at a great loss as to what opinion to form." The reports of the enemy's presence on the road had come mainly from cavalry stragglers who Early thought were "waifs from the battlefield of Hanover."[24]

But while they looked and talked, far out to the right of the York road a line of skirmishers appeared, moving apparently in their direc-

tion. "There they come now!"[25] exclaimed Rodes. Blue and gray
soldiers looked alike at that distance. Early answered in "somewhat
emphatic language," which for him would mean a stronger than usual
oath, that they must not be enemy skirmishers because Gordon, who
was situated in that area, would fire on an enemy. Lieutenants T. T.
Turner of Ewell's staff and Robert D. Early of Early's were sent out to
investigate; they returned with the information that the skirmish line
was Smith's, which Gordon was realigning. They found that Culp's
Hill was unoccupied. Both armies were still being very casual.

Sunset was now at hand. Ewell departed and Early returned to
the brigades of Hays and Avery on the eastern outskirts of Gettysburg. It was about 7:45 P.M. when he was again summoned by Ewell,
for a conference with Lee.

3. Lee Wants the High Ground Taken

Daniel's brigade was resting with its left on the railroad cut at 4:00
P.M., after going through some of the toughest fighting and suffering
some of the heaviest casualties of the battle. The men were much too
exhausted to be sent after the fleeing Federals. Confederate guns on
Seminary Ridge were testing the range to Cemetery Hill without committing themselves to a sustained bombardment, and were being answered by Steinwehr.

During this sporadic exchange Daniel's men saw a party of officers
riding up the road from Cashtown. The horsemen drew up on Seminary Ridge where the pike reaches the summit, and their leader took
up his glasses and looked down on the town of Gettysburg, then across
at the range of hills.

Daniel's soldiers pulled themselves to their feet and took off their
hats. There was no cheering—the Carolinians were too fagged out to
manage anything except a salute, delivered more with their hearts
than their hands. Colonel Thomas S. Kenan merely called his regiment to attention.[26] But all along the Confederate line passed a thrill
of expectancy and elation, for General Lee had reached the field.

The commanding general had been progressing toward the firing
line since early morning, halting from time to time to receive dispatches and maintain a headquarters where he might be reached by
couriers.

The correspondent of the Savannah *Republican* was sitting on the
wet ground west of Cashtown on the morning of July 1, his back
against a tree, writing a story, when Lee passed. "He seemed to sniff

battle in the breeze," the correspondent noted in his dispatch.[27] Longstreet had ridden with him for a time and found him cheerful.

At Cashtown he established temporary headquarters in an old house on the turnpike. On an inside door someone had nailed up a map of Adams County, Pennsylvania, of which Gettysburg is the seat. With his penknife Lee cut out the map, put it in his pocket, and carried it to Gettysburg. The incident has perhaps been unrecorded and there is no information about whether the map was of value or whether he paid anyone for it; if he did not, this was probably the only petty depredation he committed during the campaign.[28] When he set up headquarters around the Thompson House on Seminary Ridge later in the day he had a door taken off the hinges and laid across two braces, or chairs in a tent across the road; he used it for his map table during the battle.

Captain James Power Smith, Ewell's aide, made two trips in the late afternoon from Gettysburg to the seminary, and on the first he witnessed the arrival of the commanding general. Smith studied Lee carefully and reflected on his "superb physique," his quiet bearing, and his carefully cut gray uniform.[29] His felt hat had a medium brim, his boots fitted neatly, and everything about him was trim and military. "An unruffled calm upon his countenance" showed his concentration and control. He had stopped in the grass field to the north of the seminary, where, mounted on Traveler, he looked down the long slope toward the heights beyond Gettysburg. Federal soldiers were still streaming across the fields and climbing the heights.

The ubiquitous McKim was there, too. "I saw him sweep the horizon with his glasses, and noted he scanned that elevation [Little Round Top] with great attention."[30]

The whole panorama of the subsiding battle lay before him, the positions north of the town that had been carried by Early's arrival on the Federal flank; Oak Hill, which had been seized by Rodes; and the ground on which he stood, which had been the scene of the most stubborn fighting. He was quick to see the advantages of the high ground south of Gettysburg. He immediately directed Colonel Walter H. Taylor to inform Ewell that from the position he, Lee, occupied, he could see the Federals retreating over the hills in great confusion and without organization, and that it "was only necessary to press 'those people' in order to secure possession of the heights."[31] He wanted Ewell, if possible, to do this.

Taylor went immediately to Ewell and delivered the message, noticing that Ewell offered no objection to the orders conveyed, nor mentioned any obstacle to their execution. He received from Ewell information about the number of prisoners captured and returned to Lee to report that his message had been delivered. Taylor left several accounts of this transaction, all in substantially the same language. He returned to Lee with the impression that Ewell would carry out the orders. Lee would have been better served had Taylor waited and fretted Ewell until that general began the execution of the order. He could then have reported to Lee that the order had been complied with, not merely delivered.

Captain Smith had returned earlier and Ewell now sent him again to Lee. Possibly he passed Colonel Taylor en route, or possibly the message he carried was in the nature of an afterthought. He was directed to inform Lee that Early and Rodes thought they could go forward if supported by Hill on their right. South of the cemetery was a position which they felt should be taken at once because it commanded the cemetery. Whether this was the Round Tops or the extension of Cemetery Ridge is not clear, but Smith judged Ewell was thinking of the high ground immediately beyond the cemetery, and not of the more remote Round Tops.

On this trip he found Lee in a field some distance to the south. It was now five o'clock. Longstreet had ridden ahead of his troops and Lee and Longstreet had dismounted for a careful scrutiny of the terrain, especially the position south of the cemetery. Smith delivered his message and Lee wanted to know what position Ewell meant by "the ground to the south." He handed his glasses to Smith so that the captain might designate it. According to the captain, Lee said "the elevated position in front was, he supposed, the commanding position of which Early and Rodes spoke."[32] Then he added that some of "those people" were already there.

Smith thought they were cavalry scouts. But Lee continued that he did not have a force available to take this position. He asked Longstreet about the locations of the First Corps divisions, and was informed that the leading division, McLaws' was still six miles from the field. Lee then gave Smith his reply to Ewell: "He regretted that his people were not up to support him on the right; but wished him to take the Cemetery Hill if it were possible; and that he would ride over to see him very soon."[33]

As Colonel Taylor described Lee's message and as Captain Smith quoted his later instructions, Ewell was not cautioned against bringing on a general engagement prior to the arrival of Longstreet's troops. The only qualification carried by Taylor was "if possible," a condition that gave Ewell some discretion to weigh the chance of success before committing himself. The same qualification, "if it were possible," occurred in Lee's orders sent through Captain Smith. Any caution against bringing on a general engagement was clearly that imposed earlier in the day, as Taylor pointed out.

Lee's decision against an attack on the right with the troops already at hand, as well as his view that the position behind the cemetery was already occupied, resulted partly from the reconnaissance just made by his military secretary, Colonel Long. Long reported that Cemetery Hill was occupied in strength, part of the force being posted behind a stone fence near the crest of the hill, and the rest on the reverse slope. As he summed it up later, "In my opinion an attack at this time, with the troops then at hand, would have been hazardous and very doubtful of success."[34] That must have been an hour after Lee's arrival and almost two hours after Perrin had carried Seminary Ridge and after Early had halted in front of Culp's Hill and Cemetery Ridge.[35]

Anderson's division was close at hand, and there was restiveness among some of Pender's officers and men, as well as Early's, over the failure to take the ground on which the Federals had rallied. Major David Gregg McIntosh, commanding a battalion of Third Corps artillery, thought the army relaxed once it had captured the town, when it should have redoubled its efforts and made the assaults that proved so costly on the second and third days. His description of the situation is persuasive:

The Union troops driven into the town from different directions were wedged and jammed in the streets, and soon became a disorganized mass. Artillery and ambulances struggling to get through the tangled crowd added to the confusion. Had the fugitives been allowed no pause, and had the Confederates followed close on their heels, the very momentum of the flight, to say nothing of the contagion of panic, would have swept aside every support, and the pursuers could easily have rushed the Cemetery and surrounding heights.[36]

His main point was that concentrated Confederate artillery fire on Cemetery Hill would have been disastrous to the Federals and might have caused them to abandon the heights. Ample artillery was at hand. The two Third Corps battalions which had been at the front all day had suffered severely in casualties but still retained their fighting efficiency, each with a complement of 16 guns. Half these guns were rifled and Cemetery Hill was well in range. Garnett's battalion had just arrived fresh, and McIntosh estimated that between 30 and 40 guns could have been employed on Seminary Hill as they were in the great bombardment of July 3 before the Pickett-Pettigrew assault.

The decision was left to Brigadier General William Nelson Pendleton, chief of the army artillery, who had reconnoitered the woods to the right and along the ridge to the Fairfield road, his object being to find a position for Garnett's guns, which he had already ordered to the right. Cemetery Hill was in range from the Fairfield road position. Ramseur at that time came out of Gettysburg, now occupied by his troops, met Pendleton on Seminary Ridge at the Fairfield road crossing, and told him that if the batteries opened, they would draw a concentrated fire on his men, who were much exposed from Cemetery Hill. Only one side of this conversation is available, and Ramseur did try to press on that same evening. But Pendleton decided that unless his bombardment should be a part of a combined attack on Cemetery Hill "it would be worse than useless to open fire there."[37] That probably was a sound conclusion, although the onus of the decision should not have been placed on a single brigade general. Despite McIntosh's confidence in his guns, they would not likely have dislodged the Federal army unless followed by a strong infantry assault.

Pendleton may have been confused about Ramseur's request, which probably was not that he should refrain from drawing the enemy's fire, but that he should be careful about where he aimed his own. Doles's Georgians had just come under the fire of two Confederate brass pieces on Oak Hill and some had been killed, others wounded.[38] Three of Rodes's brigades were prepared to storm Cemetery Hill, and Ramseur no doubt was anxious to alert the Confederate artillery about the prospective attack. Doles registered a vigorous protest against the "indifference and neglect" of the battery commander who was careless with his shells.

The three brigades ready for the attack were those of O'Neal, Ramseur, and Doles. O'Neal, recovered to an extent after his repulse earlier, had ordered up artillery and formed in line with Doles, who had passed to the southern part of the town. O'Neal was preparing to begin the assault when he was recalled and directed to form his brigade north of the railroad.

A. P. Hill's report on the final phase of the first day's battle was almost an apology. The substance of it was that he—fighter though he

Armies at end of first day.

185

was known to be—was satisfied with half a loaf of victory at supper that night. It is true, as stated, that here the want of cavalry was seriously felt. But impressed with the belief that the enemy was "entirely routed," and with the exhaustion of his two divisions after six hours of hard fighting, "prudence led me to be content with what had been gained, and not push forward troops exhausted and necessarily disordered, probably to encounter fresh troops of the enemy."[39] He credited his corps with the capture of 2,300 prisoners and "the almost total annihilation of the First Corps of the enemy."

Ensign J. A. Stikeleather of the 4th North Carolina was on Ramseur's skirmish line. His letter to his mother, which reached the North Carolina press, said the Cemetery Hill position could have been carried readily with the loss of less than five hundred; that "Washington would have been evacuated, Baltimore freed, Maryland unfettered, the enemy discomfitted, and our victorious banners flaunting defiantly before the panic-stricken North." He told the attitude of the troops: "The simplest soldier in the ranks felt it. . . . But, timidity in the commander that stepped into the shoes of the fearless Jackson, prompted delay, and all night long the busy axes from tens of thousands of busy hands on that crest, rang out clearly on the night air, and bespoke the preparation the enemy were making for the morrow." This letter by a junior officer immediately after the battle contained perhaps the first attack on Ewell for the disastrous inaction of that evening.[40]

Longstreet meanwhile was surveying the country, especially the Federal position on the long ridge connecting the formidable hills at either end; chance, he noted, had provided the enemy with an exceptionally strong rallying place. Apprehensive that Lee might want to attack it, he returned to Lee and offered a counterproposal. The entire Confederate army, he suggested, could be moved by the right flank and put in position south of Round Top, where it would threaten to interpose itself between Meade and Washington. Meade would therefore be dislodged by strategy instead of assault.

Longstreet's account of this meeting is no doubt correct in general purport, but contains phrases that must have injected themselves into his thinking in later years.[41] After he had looked over the ground for five or ten minutes, he turned to Lee.

If we could have chosen a point to meet our plans of operation, [he said] I do not think we could have found a better one. . . . All we have to do is to throw our army around to their left, and we shall interpose between the Federal army and Washington. We can get a strong position and wait, and if they fail to attack us we shall have everything in condition to move back tomorrow night in the direction of Washington, selecting a good position into which we can place our troops to receive battle next day. Finding our objective is Washington or that army, the Federals will be sure to attack us. When they attack, we shall beat them, as we proposed to do before we left Fredericksburg, and the probabilities are that the fruits of our success will be great.[42]

Lee's reply was prompt: "No, the enemy is there, and I am going to attack him there."

Longstreet's account was written well after Lee's death; his phrase, "as we proposed to do before we left Fredericksburg," would have perplexed Lee had it been uttered on Seminary Ridge. Irrespective of what Longstreet may have proposed at Fredericksburg, Lee never committed himself arbitrarily to any plan, or felt bound by anything except the conditions immediately before him. So much he made clear, himself.

Longstreet was not a dissembler, and while he might maneuver a corps, the only approach he knew in conversation was frontal. He argued boldly, a trifle impudently, with Lee, contending that his proposal would give Lee command of the Washington roads.

"No," Lee answered again with finality, "they are in position and I am going to whip them or they are going to whip me."

Longstreet desisted but did not consider himself defeated. He would wait. As it developed, Lee did not brush Longstreet's project aside contemptuously. Later that evening he analyzed it more closely and apparently toyed with the notion of putting some modification of it into effect. Military comment has been well divided over the near-century since the battle about the feasibility of the turning movement. The difficulties would have been major. Lee still had no cavalry and did not know where the enemy was or would be. He could not undertake a prolongation of his right beyond Round Top so long as Ewell was gripped like a shepherd's crook around Culp's and Cemetery hills. He might have considered the plan more earnestly had he been able to shift Ewell to the far right, but Early always had so many impressive reasons against it.

What would have been the history of the Confederacy if he had made this turning movement? Perhaps it was possible for Lee to win

the campaign either by the battle plan he adopted or by the strategy
Longstreet proposed. Rarely in military matters is there but a single
road to success. The execution is all-important. Victory in the end
depends on the degree of skill and the force of character, and always
a modicum of luck, behind any plan. A capable general considers all
eventualities. When he has weighed the different factors he must
select one plan, and only one, and then refrain from mulling over
what might have happened had he chosen another.

Lee made his final choice on the basis of numerous cogent reasons.
There are no means of comparing the battle of Gettysburg—the battle
of history which he fought—with the might-have-been battle under
Longstreet's flanking movement. That battle could have been lost, too.

None in the army understood the opportunities of the moment better
nor grieved more bitterly than Gordon, who all through the late afternoon wanted only to be unleashed. That night he was unable to
sleep. He mounted at 2:00 A.M. and with two staff officers rode to
the red barn which Ewell and Early were using as a headquarters.
Through the night he had heard the Federal soldiers with picks and
shovels digging trenches on the hills, and the rumbling wheels of guns
being put in position. He forecast to Ewell and Early that at daylight
they would be able to see heavy works, guns, and infantry ranks
frowning down on them, and he declared that he, even at that hour
of two in the morning, could carry those works by a vigorous assault.
After daylight, he said, it would cost 10,000 men.

Gordon seemed to detect an inclination on the part of the two
superior officers to yield to his entreaty, but in the end his request was
denied. "Those works were never carried," he said, "but the cost of
the assault upon them, the appalling carnage resulting from the efforts
to take them, far exceeded that which I ventured to predict."[43]

Johnson reached Gettysburg with his men "very much jaded from
hard marching,"[44] in the words of Lieutenant McKim, who noted that
it was still daylight as he entered the town. He was able to read a
letter handed to him by Colonel Douglas.[45] And there was enough daylight to win a battle, although conditions had been altered vastly in
the Federal army. Douglas thought Johnson was "spoiling for a
fight"[46] because of the rapidity of his marching and he did expect to
go immediately into action. He had covered twenty-five miles that
day. Leaving the Cashtown road, the division followed the railroad cut
and halted at the Pennsylvania College grounds while Johnson went
to find Ewell. Some of the brigades passed straight on through to the

position designated for them on Early's left. Johnson, never reluctant to fight even at a late hour, put his division in battle line. For what he referred to in later years as "some unexplained reason," he received orders from Ewell to halt.[47] He was not allowed the opportunity to assault Culp's Hill in the fading daylight of July 1.

Ewell, being an intelligent soldier, could not have been too happy with his management of affairs. After the war when a prisoner at Fort Warren, he told his fellow prisoner, Eppa Hunton, that "it took a dozen blunders to lose Gettysburg, and he had committed a good many of them."[48] Nobody has ever been in a strong position to dispute him. But Ewell's greatest deficiency, of course, was lack of foresight. He might have replied to his critics in the words of General Lee to an officer who was analyzing some of the mistakes of Gettysburg.

"Young man," said Lee, "why did you not tell me that before the battle? Even as stupid a man as I am can see it all now."[49]

CHAPTER FOURTEEN

Moonlight and Marching Columns

1. *"The Damned Dutchmen . . . Ran Like Sheep"*

L. L. Crounse, chief correspondent of the New York *Times* with the Army of the Potomac, brought the first objective account of the clash at Gettysburg to Taneytown and Meade's headquarters. Crounse galloped up in the midafternoon while the Cincinnati correspondent, Whitelaw Reid, was talking with the Federal commander in his tent.[1]

Meade had been getting sketchy reports all morning, but here finally was a more comprehensive, eyewitness version. Crounse said he had just ridden from the small town, ten to fifteen miles distant, where a battle of uncertain magnitude was still in progress. Reynolds had been killed and the air was heavy with Northern misfortune. He had hurried back to get access to a telegraph wire and file a preliminary dispatch. The other correspondents who had been moving close to headquarters must have obtained fill-ins, for all began writing stories on a Taneytown tavern porch. These dispatches were sent by messenger to Frederick, where communication with Washington and the North had been restored after it had been cut by Stuart. Then the newsmen galloped off toward Gettysburg.

En route they rode into the backwash of a great battle, into refugees with new rumors, distraught men and women with fresh eyewitness accounts. One was that "the damned Dutchmen of the Eleventh Corps broke and ran like sheep, just as they did at Chancellorsville." Another: "Wadsworth's division was cut to pieces . . . half of its officers killed." Still another: "We were driven pell-mell through

Gettysburg and things look black enough, I tell you."[2] The area of
Two Taverns was filled with skulkers from the front. Frightened
women were questioning the fleeing men about the battle. Prospects
of Federal victory on Pennsylvania soil were anything but promising.

Through the early morning the Second Corps, Hancock's, had been
marching up from Uniontown, where it had rested since the night of
June 29. When it reached Taneytown at eleven o'clock, the men
were allowed a coffee rest, which became extended as Meade awaited
messengers from the front and pondered whether the battle ought to
be fought at Gettysburg or along his more favored Pipe Creek. Buford's early-morning cavalry fight had indicated little, but shortly
before one o'clock Meade had begun to comprehend the major nature
of the engagement west of Gettysburg. He had heard of Reynolds'
death and of the heavy pressure on the First Corps from the assembling Confederate army.

Meade might have gone himself to Gettysburg but he elected to
send Hancock. The decision disclosed that he had not yet abandoned
his intention of fighting along Pipe Creek and thought it more likely
that the three corps which formed the left wing—the First, Eleventh
and Third—would have to be brought back by the routes he had
already specified, than that the rest of the army would go forward.
But the severe nature of the fighting suggested that it might now be
too late to withdraw. The final decision would have to be made on
the basis of just what was happening at Gettysburg, and on whether
the terrain offered defensive advantages for the army as inviting as
those along Pipe Creek appeared to be.

Certainly if Meade judged his duty was at headquarters in the rear
instead of on the fighting line, he could not have made a better choice
of a substitute than Hancock. The fact that Hancock was junior to
both the Eleventh and Third Corps commanders, Howard and Sickles,
did not matter to Meade. His and the army's trust in Hancock was
strong and he had full authorization to disregard rank in an emergency.

Meade kept Hancock at headquarters an hour, explaining his intentions and reviewing the orders already issued. He gave Hancock wide
latitude at the front, to order the removal of the three corps and their
trains to the rear for alignment behind Pipe Creek, or to establish a
battle line at Gettysburg if he judged that expedient. These powers
were fully as comprehensive as those of the commander in chief.

Hancock turned over command of the Second Corps to John Gibbon, the artilleryman who before the war had instructed the West

Point cadets in the use of the guns and had become McDowell's chief of artillery, then Meredith's predecessor as commander of the Iron Brigade. Although a Pennsylvanian by birth, he had been reared in Charlotte, North Carolina, and had three brothers fighting in the armies of the South, one of them, Dr. Robert Gibbon, being the surgeon of Lane's brigade. At two o'clock Hancock rode with his staff for Gettysburg, thirteen miles away. The time he required to cover this distance, almost two hours, is explained by the fact that he rode part of the way in an ambulance, so that he might study his maps. He sent his aide, Major William G. Mitchell, ahead to notify Howard of his coming.

Both Hancock and Mitchell placed the time of his arrival at three thirty; others thought the hour later. Doubleday said it was after Lee's arrival on the opposite hill,[3] which was at four o'clock. Lee and Hancock appear to have reached the field almost simultaneously, about four.

Rarely in warfare has the arrival of a single officer on a battlefield been more timely and consequential than Hancock's at Gettysburg. One of his subordinates gave the picture: before he came, "wreck, disaster, disorder, almost the panic that precedes disorganization, defeat and retreat were everywhere." After he appeared on Cemetery Hill, "soldiers retreating stopped, skulkers appeared from under their cover, lines were re-formed": in place of a rabble seeking Cemetery Hill as a sanctuary, an army with a purpose—under a leader who could lift it to extraordinary efforts—confronted the Confederates.

There was something dominating and inspiring about Hancock. The men of his corps were essentially the same as those of any other, but at the end of the war they could say that the Second had captured more enemy guns and more enemy colors than all the rest of the army combined. After Grant had taken command and had gone through the Wilderness, Hancock could tell him proudly that the corps had never lost a color or a gun, though oftener and more desperately engaged than any other. The Galena tanner was to use the corps cruelly at Cold Harbor, but it nevertheless finished the war, and with a record of a larger number of engagements and an aggregate of more killed and wounded than any other corps in the Northern armies.[4]

Hancock, one of twin brothers born in Montgomery County, Pennsylvania, owed his military eminence as much to his great industry as to his intelligence and striking appearance. He devoted the eleven years between 1850 and 1861 to assiduous preparation for the responsibilities of high command if it should ever come to him. He was so thorough that army detail work, which provoked some and baffled others, neither irritated nor bogged him down. He undoubtedly was one of the great soldiers of American history, though he never had the opportunity to command his own army, mainly because no commander of the Army of the Potomac from the Peninsula to Appomattox could dispense with him for an instant.[5]

McClellan had used the term "superb" in connection with his name, and the adjective was so fitting that the army adopted it and knew him thereafter as "Hancock the Superb," a difficult cognomen for any officer, but one he was able to handle with seemliness. The word "beautiful" is not ordinarily applicable to the male form, but it seemed to fit Hancock as it did Gordon. His mien and carriage were like those of a race horse at the starting line, and called for a stronger descriptive word than handsome.

Altogether, Hancock's aspect, poise, and common sense gave him an abundance of the quality of leadership, and officers and men turned to him instinctively. "One felt safe to be near him," said a junior. Young Frank Aretas Haskell gave a dramatic, though highly partisan, account of the Federal officers at Gettysburg. It contains some vivid word pictures, but he brought out his choice terms for Hancock, "the tallest and most shapely" of them all. Haskell was impressed with his innate ability to lead: "I think that if he were in citizens' clothes, and should give commands in the army to those who did not know him, he would be likely to be obeyed at once."[6]

That was not precisely the case, even though he was in uniform, when he arrived on Cemetery Hill to take over the duties that had proved such a heavy burden for Howard's shoulders. The senior officer demurred. As with most of these Gettysburg controversies, the versions of what happened vary widely, but Howard's attitude on the appearance both of Hancock and of Meade later that night seemed so intensely personal that he appeared to be thinking of his own rather than the army's standing.

Doubleday, who was near, said "quite a scene occurred" when he confronted Hancock. "Why, Hancock, you cannot give orders here!" Howard exclaimed. "I am in command and I rank you!"[7]

Hancock told of his orders from Meade, although his aide had already advised Howard of their scope. But, according to Doubleday, Howard still declined to recognize Hancock's authority.

Howard's own account shows a disposition to act either independently or as the officer who was directing. "All right, Hancock," he quoted himself as saying, "you take the left of the Baltimore Pike and I will take the right, and we will put these troops in line." He said his remarks were friendly, and Hancock "did as I suggested."[8]

Words almost identical with Doubleday's were attributed to Howard by Major Halstead, the First Corps adjutant general, who heard Howard exclaim: "No, I do not doubt your word, General Hancock, but you can give no orders here while I am here."[9]

Hancock explained that Meade had told him to select a field for battle; he thought the place where he stood was the strongest natural position he had ever seen. If Howard felt likewise, he would select it. Howard consented and Hancock said, "Very well, sir, I select this as the battle-field."[10]

Howard of course could not have truly commanded an army with Hancock present. Things did not work out that way in days when generals exercised immediate instead of remote control over troops and remained in their presence under the stress of battle. Expecting men to look to Howard would be like expecting them to go to Henry Dearborn for guidance with Andrew Jackson or Oliver Hazard Perry at hand. Men turned to Hancock's sureness where they would have recognized only Howard's insignia. In a supreme trial they would have sought strength and not rank.

The Maine artilleryman, Lieutenant Edward N. Whittier, went to Hancock for orders, found him unruffled by the confusion all around, and felt "his very atmosphere strong and invigorating." Whittier noticed that even after his long ride his linen was still clean and white. His sleeve was rolled back from his "firm, finely moulded hand." Everything about him imparted fresh courage to others.[11]

After his exchange with Howard, Hancock found Doubleday more co-operative. "General Doubleday," he said, "I command this field and I wish you to send a regiment over to that hill."[12]

Hancock had seen at once that Culp's Hill must be garrisoned or the Federal army would have to abandon Cemetery Hill. Like Trimble, he grasped instantly the paramount importance of the companion eminence on the right of Howard's position.

"My corps has been fighting, General, since ten o'clock," Doubleday entreated, "and they have been all cut to pieces."

"I know that, sir," said Hancock, "but this is a great emergency and everyone must do all he can." Hancock moved away, but taking no chances, he soon returned to find out whether his order had been followed. It had. Doubleday's regiments had been reduced to the size of companies, so he sent the remnants of the division under General Wadsworth.[13]

Wadsworth fortunately had a fresh regiment, the 7th Indiana of Cutler's brigade, which had been working its way up the Emmitsburg road after a day of guarding cattle and commissary trains. Although the regiment was fairly close on the south, the stratum of sultry air had deadened the sound of the firing. The first day's battle could be heard as far west as Pittsburgh, 180 miles away, but it passed unnoticed a dozen miles to the south and southeast. The day was mostly clear and in some localities the sun had dried the roads enough that marching columns stirred up dust. But the 7th Indiana was being drenched by a mountain shower when a messenger arrived with news of the battle.[14]

Marching rapidly to Cemetery Ridge, the regiment came alongside its division commander, General Wadsworth, sitting forlornly on a stone fence by the roadside. "His head bowed in grief, [he was] the most dejected woebegone person one would be likely to find on a world-around voyage," said Private Thomson of Company G.

Wadsworth said to the regiment, "I am glad you were not with us this afternoon."

Surprised, an officer declared that had the 7th Indiana been present they could have held their position.

"Yes," Wadsworth countered, "and all would now be dead or prisoners."[15] Just as after the first battle at Manassas, where he served on McDowell's staff, Wadsworth was as much overwhelmed by the humiliation of defeat as by the enormity of the losses.

The Hoosiers from the Ohio River towns found Culp's Hill much like the knobs and bluffs of southeastern Indiana, heavily timbered and strewn with rocks varying in size "from a chicken coop to a pioneer's cabin."[16] They went to work immediately felling trees and digging ditches while Major Ira G. Grover, their commander, personally conducted a patrol down the eastern slope.

Here he encountered an unsuspecting squad of scouts from the 42nd Virginia and brought in some prisoners.[17] Of far greater significance to the battle, however, his men gave notice to Johnson's newly arrived Confederate division that Culp's Hill was now in Northern hands, and corrected any impression the enemy may have held that the hill was open for the taking. Old Trimble had been correct hours earlier when he said it could be had with a regiment, but now it was held by an entrenched division. Also William's division of the Twelfth Federal Corps had come up to Rock Creek, close enough to give assistance.

Major Grover always believed that his bumping into the Virginia patrol was the decisive moment at Gettysburg, because it saved Culp's Hill for the Federals. Very likely Johnson, a more thorough man than Early, would have seized the hill had his patrols been able to work undetected to the summit. Although Ewell had restrained Johnson, he could scarcely have censured him for occupying high ground in his immediate front without becoming involved in a skirmish. But Grover showed him it was now occupied, and Johnson held off.

During the night an alarm was sounded on Culp's Hill, but it was found to be no more than the nightmare of a private of Company K, 7th Indiana, who let out wild yells that aroused several regiments to the left. They, half awake, thought the enemy was attacking and grabbed their guns. Some leaped over the breastworks and charged down the hill firing, while a few were seen "charging as vigorously to the rear."[18]

Stevens' 5th Maine Battery, which had blazed away all day against Heth, Rodes and Pender, was in position on the left of Culp's Hill, commanding the valley between it and Cemetery Hill. Hancock had seen it near the gate of the cemetery, called to Captain Stevens, pointed to the hill, and told him to "stop the enemy from coming up that ravine." "Fifth Battery, forward," said Stevens instantly, and the guns and caissons rolled across the plateau, east on the Baltimore pike until they found a lane that led to a house near Culp's Hill, and on to the summit.[19] They began dropping shells on Hays's Louisiana brigade even before the 7th Indiana arrived to give them infantry support.

Hancock stationed other batteries to command the Baltimore pike and the approaches from Gettysburg and Seminary Ridge. In half an hour he had a defense which he felt could hold the position, at least until darkness, although he conceded that had Howard been pursued vigorously he would have been driven beyond Cemetery Hill. Steinwehr had been on Cemetery Hill most of the day. He had neither put a protective patrol on near-by Culp's Hill nor been energetic in constructing fortifications.

Hancock later emphatically denied that Steinwehr threw up a lunette around each gun and built high, solid works around smooth, level gun platforms. All Hancock could find in the way of "works" were "some holes (not deep) dug to sink the wheels and trails of the pieces."[20] When he issued his orders to the artillery Hancock required his aide to listen carefully, then said: "I am of the opinion that the enemy will mass in town and make an effort to take this position, but I want you to remain until you are relieved by me or by my written order and take orders from no one." He was taking no chances of having the guns moved.

When his work was completed Hancock had a presentable line running from Culp's Hill on the right to the Round Tops. Williams' division was in the rear of Wadsworth. The other Twelfth Corps division, Geary's, had now arrived, and Hancock moved it to the left to occupy the ground toward Round Top and prevent a turning movement to his left. What remained of the First Corps beyond Wadsworth's division was used temporarily to strengthen Howard on Cemetery Hill. From time to time Hancock had sent back word to Meade: an oral message at 4:30 P.M., describing the position and informing the commanding general that it could be readily defended with good troops, followed by a message of the same purport in writing at 5:25 P.M.[21]

Major General Henry W. Slocum, commanding the Twelfth Corps, had finally reached the field; since he was Howard's senior there was no question about who would give orders after Hancock's departure. It was seven o'clock. Hancock transferred the command to Slocum and rode back to Taneytown to report to Meade. He soon met his own corps approaching under Gibbon, and halted it to serve as a rear guard; Hays's division went on to replace the battle-frayed Robinson on the left of the Eleventh Corps. Before morning the two other divisions were aligned to the left of Hays.

2. Meade Comes to Gettysburg at Last

Sickles' Third Corps, marching since it had been summoned by Howard, began to come up at seven o'clock, to be greeted by an appreciative Howard, who, as the New York *Herald* correspondent got it, said to the old Tammanyite: "Here you are—always reliable, always first."[22] The brigade of the Frenchman, Colonel Philip R. de Trobriand, plus the New Jersey brigade of Colonel George C. Burling, had been left behind to comply nominally with Meade's instructions for the Third Corps to watch the South Mountain pass near Emmitsburg.

For the balance of the corps the march was like a triumphal procession partly because the distinguished—even notorious—politician, Major General Daniel E. Sickles, always brought out the crowds, and partly because everyone in the countryside knew a battle was shaping up on which the course of the war would likely be determined. From Emmitsburg to Gettysburg the community centers and crossroads were filled with farm folk gathered to watch the soldiers pass. They cheered, waved hats and handkerchiefs. Flags were flown, and as evening came on lighted lanterns were hung hospitably at farmhouse gateways[23] while inside farmwives stood all day baking hot bread.

Ward's brigade of Birney's division, Third Corps, arrived at ten o'clock and bivouacked near the big red barn of the Codori farmhouse on the Emmitsburg road. The atmosphere was vaporous and smoky clouds scurried across the night sky, often obscuring the full moon. Colonel Elijah Walker of the 4th Maine laid out a bed of grass and leaves in a little clump of trees which two days later would be made famous for all time by the amount of blood shed there.[24] He was not yet asleep when orders came to establish a picket line connecting the Third with the First Corps pickets on the right and the Second Corps on the left. They went out to a rail fence two hundred yards west of the Emmitsburg road and heard the enemy pickets on the watch two hundred yards farther on. The division commander, Major General David B. Birney, saw the men assembling and whispered to a lieutenant, "I wish I were already dead."[25]

Carr's brigade of the Third Corps, coming up in the darkness, with the 26th Pennsylvania leading, marched by the wrong road and suddenly found itself inside the Confederate lines at Black Horse Tavern. Luckily it saw the error before the enemy could sound the alarm. It captured the picket into which it had blundered, about-faced quietly, groped until it found the proper road, and reached the Federal lines at midnight.[26]

Last to arrive before sunup was the Fifth Corps, which had already completed its day's march to Hanover, Pennsylvania, from Union Mills, Maryland, and had pitched its tents when at six o'clock orders arrived to continue to Gettysburg. The distance was thirteen miles and Major General George Sykes, who commanded, did not know the road, but a resident, a "country gentleman," volunteered to guide them. The corps trudged along until one o'clock and halted, feeling near enough to the battle zone to be available. At 4:00 A.M., without breakfast or coffee, it pushed on the remaining three miles to Gettysburg.[27]

The rapidity of some of these marches suggests that the Federal soldiers were traveling lighter than formerly. In the Chancellorsville campaign they had been laughed at by the Southerners as "too well fed, too well clothed, and have far too much to carry." What they carried was eight days' rations, sixty rounds of ammunition, a musket or rifle, woolen blanket, rubber blanket, overcoat, extra shirt, drawers, socks, and shelter tent, amounting to sixty pounds, an unconscionably heavy load for troops from whom upward of twenty-five miles in a single day might be expected. Thus while the roads behind the Confederates were littered with old shoes those behind the Federals as they advanced toward Gettysburg were strewn with brand-new overcoats, blankets, shelter halves, and anything else not useful in fighting.

Having fully determined to concentrate at Gettysburg, Meade ordered up the Third Corps brigades of De Trobriand and Burling that had been held at Emmitsburg; they arrived about 10:00 A.M., July 2. The Federal concentration was now complete except for the big Sixth Corps under Sedgwick.

The moon at the full[28] had proved a boon to the columns of the Federal army which was completing by night what Lee had accomplished largely during the day. By morning the Federals would overcome the numerical advantages which the Southerners had possessed on July 1. The task of concentrating in an advanced position had meant grueling marches, aching backs, and much confusion and disorganization, but had proved incalculably easier than a retrograde concentration behind Pipe Creek would have been in darkness. Meade at 6:30 P.M., when he had had time to reflect on the messages from Hancock, had decided to fight at Gettysburg. Any other course, he could see, would be a stunning blow to the Federal cause. A withdrawal on the night of July 1, even if sound strategically, would magnify the importance of that day's engagement and be of immense psychological advantage to the South. The Confederate victory of July 1 would quite justifiably assume proportions greater than those at Manassas and Chancellorsville. Lee might then detach Ewell to march on Harrisburg or Philadelphia.

These matters must certainly have passed through Meade's mind as he reflected on the inauspicious beginning of his term in the same uncomfortable shoes that had been worn by the dreary line of McDowell, Burnside, Hooker, others. So he determined, manifestly with reluctance, to abandon his Pipe Creek plans and fight on the field which chance had selected. He had surveyed the Pipe Creek line carefully and understood it, whereas, although he was a Pennsylvanian by family ties and had resided much in that state, he had never visited the Gettysburg area, could not visualize the terrain, and could only rely on Hancock's description of it.

The moon, described by some of the soldiers as pallid, was showing intermittently behind the racing clouds, giving a wan light through the towering sycamore trees that lined the Pennsylvania roadways, when sometime after 1:00 A.M. Meade's party of horsemen set out from Taneytown for Gettysburg. Why Meade delayed his departure so long is one of the curiosities of the battle, but probably one reason was that he imperatively needed some sleep. Earlier in the evening he had completed his marching orders for those elements of the army not already on the move: the Third Corps rear guard at Emmitsburg, the Fifth Corps at Hanover, and the Sixth Corps at distant Manchester.[29]

Meade reached the arched brick gateway into the cemetery between two and three o'clock in the morning, ahead of his escort. Howard, who was there, gave the time as "about 3 A.M.," but all he judged by was that it seemed so brief a time before daylight.[30] Howard was disturbed over the events of July 1. He met Meade just inside the gateway and was comforted by his chief's first kindly words. "I believed I had done my work well the preceding day," Howard explained later: "I desired his approval and so I frankly stated my earnest wish. Meade at once assured me that he imputed no blame."[31] He must have wondered at concern over a reputation when so many had died in the cause.

Sickles and Slocum joined Meade and Howard and spoke favorably, as Howard had, of the army's position. "I am glad to hear you say so, gentlemen," Meade responded, "for it is too late to leave it."[32]

The moon had now brightened. Meade decided he would not wait for daylight before inspecting the lines along which the battle would likely be joined. He was engaged in his tour when dawn came. Howard rode with him. As the sun rose Meade took the highest point in the cemetery and with his glasses looked across the dew-soaked fields to the lines of the Confederate army just beginning to stir on Seminary Ridge. This section was what Howard referred to as the army's left. Meade did not pursue his inspection to the region of the Round Tops.

When he completed it he made his preliminary decision, that the Federal army would attack with its right as soon as Sedgwick arrived with the Sixth Corps.[33] Meade had hurried off a messenger to the

Sixth around seven o'clock the evening before, and the corps would long since have been on the way.

3. Sedgwick Frolics and Waits

On the evening of July 1 Major General John Sedgwick sat at his headquarters under the towering trees near Manchester, Maryland. About the village and through the groves that extended down the valley lolled the members of the big Sixth Corps of the Army of the Potomac, enjoying a faint touch of breeze after a sweltering day.

Some were writing letters that would go to homes scattered from the Penobscot to the Wisconsin, for the corps that had lost heavily during Hooker's recent fiasco knew it was due for another battle. Some pitched mule shoes along the banks of the little streams where Sedgwick camped. But most of the men were merely lounging and resting.

Stocky General Sedgwick—"Uncle John" to the troops—labored over army papers in the dulling July twilight. Present for duty were about 15,000 officers and men. Lieutenant Colonel Martin T. McMahon, more of a companion to Sedgwick than a chief of staff, sat near by and helped with the calculations. Lee's army was in Pennsylvania to be sure, but that had no bearing on the paper work.

The corps had completed on the previous evening its rapid march from Virginia, via Poolesville and Westminster, Maryland, to its present camp site. The trains and baggage, except for ambulances and ammunition carts, had been left in Westminster. Now Sedgwick was learning that the situation of his corps in Manchester, consigned to a day of idleness while the balance of the Federal army plunged ahead to find Lee, was scarcely conducive to concentration on payroll vouchers.

Sedgwick had made his headquarters in the little brick Fort Hill school that had stood since 1803 on what had once been the old Indian trail from the Potomac to the Susquehanna River.[34] Manchester, partly on a ridge, is the high point between Harrisburg and Baltimore. Sedgwick could view from a summit near the school a great expanse of Maryland and southern Pennsylvania and see far away the soft mountain ridges between Gettysburg and Chambersburg over which Lee's army had that day been passing. But the road to Gettysburg was by way of Westminster,[35] thence northwest through Littlestown, a total distance of 35 miles. The position was almost isolated from the rest of the army. Meade could have sent his largest corps

there only because Lee's advance had reached York, and Manchester
was directly between York and Baltimore.

Sedgwick and McMahon inspected the camp, which lay along what
in recent times has been known as the John Green farm, with its two
springs and abundant timber. The corps commander observed with
satisfaction that the men were rested and in good spirits. July 1 had
been an extraordinary day. Nobody remembered anything more serene
in the whole experience of this march-mad army. Most of the regiments had reached Manchester at the close of a hot June and had
assumed that the corps would be on the move again at July daybreak.

But reveille sounded, the corps breakfasted, and to the surprise of
the men, no orderlies shouted the familiar call to ranks with full packs.
Details were assembled for fatigue and picket duty, and the balance
of the troops fell out, nominally under regimental confines. The soldiers, anxious to use every minute of the unexpected leisure, mingled
with the gathering crowds of the most appreciative population they
had encountered since they had begun, fifteen months before, the
march with McClellan on Richmond.

News spread rapidly over the Maryland hills that a sizable portion
of the Federal army had halted at Manchester. On foot and horseback, in buggies, buckboards and wagons, more and more of the
curious thronged in. Near-by houses discharged their residents. Farm
wives began baking bread feverishly. Hawkers appeared, and soon
the village took on the appearance and gaiety of a carnival or county
fair.

Through the dimming years of succeeding decades the memory of
those soldiers carried pictures of the gathering: girls in bright calico
gaily swinging their bonnets from long ribbons; housewives bringing
fruit and jelly; small boys begging permission to draw a bayonet, touch
a gun, or test their teeth on a piece of army hardtack; peddlers dron-
ing their refrains through the crowds; wagoners selling jugs of apple
and peach brandy. The young men of the district were gone, which
prompted inquiries as to the location of different Union regiments.
About these the Sixth Corps members had nothing more than guesses.
The soldiers wrote their names and regimental units on their white
paper collars and gave them to the girls as souvenirs, hoping for letters
in return. They read old newspapers from near-by households; they
lavished their pay so enthusiastically on tobacco and brandy that the
supplies were soon short even in this Maryland section. They played
poker and old sledge, cleaned equipment and tossed baseballs, but

most of them simply sat chatting under the shade of the great oaks.[36]

Uncle John Sedgwick presided over the impromptu carnival with a mild indifference. His main concern was about the rye whisky and the brandy, distilled in abundance in the neighborhood. He issued orders for the arrest of anyone bringing liquor into camp. The men, he felt, were entitled to a good rest so long as Meade did not need them elsewhere. The Pipe Creek Circular showed the Sixth Corps already in position. The balance of the army, after it located Lee, would align itself on the Sixth and await a Confederate attack.[37] But any plan was likely to be changed; confirmation was long overdue from the army commander.

Sedgwick's attachment to the enlisted men was well understood in the Sixth Corps, even though it was never manifested by laxity or sentimentality. Uncle John had no family except his soldiers; he was one of the few bachelors among the senior officers. His affection for his men was hidden by a stern aloofness, although occasionally his genial spirit broke through and the soldiers and the general had a laugh together. In his own quarters Sedgwick was a jester and tease. Many in the army thought he might have had the high command succeeding Burnside if he had made any effort to line up friends in Washington. With Secretary Chase backing Hooker, opponents of the Chase faction had looked appraisingly at Sedgwick. But Uncle John seemed satisfied with the leadership of a division. He was a frank admirer of McClellan and could do nothing suggesting disloyalty to his memory,[38] which always hung broodingly over the army. He was contemptuous of officers who had politicians pleading their cases at the White House and in Congress. He was a soldier. He would stand on his record as a soldier, just as his grandfather had done under General Washington at Brandywine and Valley Forge.

His big frame, his military carriage, his wide, large-featured face, but more than these his solid self-assurance, gave him an instant power in an emergency. His leadership asserted itself naturally on the firing line, where he usually stripped off his epaulets and wore a private's blouse. He was an overflowing reservoir of confidence and strength. His shrewd Yankee wit was sufficiently penetrating to give its owner distinction among the officers of the high command. Yet Sedgwick at heart was placid and unpretentious. Secretly he longed for relief from the pounding of war and for peaceful retirement in the home he had left, when scarcely more than a boy, in a quiet Connecticut valley.

A peaceful man in an era of passion and turbulence! Few battles

had been fought in three decades of empire building and empire saving without the presence of this sturdy officer in the press of action.
Vera Cruz, Cerro Gordo, Churubusco, Chapultepec. His bravery had
given him three promotions in Mexico. Seminoles, Cherokees, Chey-
ennes; Utah, Solomon Fork, Grand Saline: he rarely missed Indian
or border skirmish. Usually he was in the front of the fight showing
his men how to be contemptuous of bullets.

Sedgwick had been born while the echo of Oliver Perry's guns
sounded from Lake Erie. His soul would pass as cannon roared at
Spottsylvania. And the thunder would rumble across the Connecticut
mountains as his neighbors lowered him into his final resting place,
peaceful at last, near the old family home in Cornwall Hollow.[39]

Thus, with Sedgwick looking on, the largest corps of the Union
army loitered in the Manchester grove, while less than thirty miles
away, as the crow flies, two other Union corps were being severely
handled in the first day of the battle beyond Gettysburg. The sound
of the battle was deadened; the men at Manchester knew nothing of it.

As daylight faded the crowds that had come to see the troops scattered again. The flag that had floated before headquarters was furled.
Campfires over which numerous chickens had lately sizzled were in
embers, and about the grove settled the stillness of a summer night.
The men along the company streets awaited the drumbeat that would
signal them to silence. The night of July 1, 1863, promised to be
peaceful for the big Sixth Corps, resting in bivouac. And at headquarters Sedgwick sat, shuffling papers with McMahon.

Faintly through the night came the distant rhythm of galloping
hoofs. The nearer clash of steel shoes sounded on gravel highway. The
picket challenged. Saddle leather groaned as the rider dismounted.
A dust-covered courier stood in Sedgwick's doorway. It was Trooper
Oliver of the army headquarters staff who had ridden down his second
horse to reach Sixth Corps headquarters with dispatches from General Meade.[40]

Sedgwick read and listened. The story of the first day's action at
Gettysburg was unfolded.

John Reynolds was dead. Even in the midst of momentous events,
how deeply does the personal touch one! The life of one man was as
nothing compared with the greater, endless purpose of the Union. Yet
Reynolds! Sedgwick's dear friend, who but yesterday was the ideal
soldier of the army; the fine equestrian who had excelled in the old

garrisons of the West, who sat his mount so handsomely, and could pluck a dime from the ground while riding at a gallop![41]

Reynolds was dead and the left wing of the Union army was shat-~red. The First and Eleventh corps had been broken and forced back. ᵗ town of Gettysburg had been captured. The balance of the ᵤnion army was concentrating to resume the battle in the morning. How soon, Meade asked, could the Sixth Corps be at Gettysburg?

Sedgwick looked at his watch. He calculated from his map the indirect road of thirty-five miles between him and the main army. He turned to the courier, Oliver: "Say to General Meade that my corps will be at Gettysburg at four o'clock tomorrow."[42]

As Oliver left the general's headquarters, he muttered to some near-by soldier, who was to embody his words in the Sixth Corps tradition, that such a march might just be possible, but he doubted that a corps— even the old Sixth—could do it.

Here was, indeed, a test for Sedgwick. The modest big-shouldered man may have felt that he had accomplished very little in thirty years of soldiering to disprove the early opinion of his former neighbors that the barefoot boy who had taught the Cornwall Hollow school could never become a real army officer. Senator Jabez Huntington had reflected that doubt when, with but a slight ring of conviction to the West Point examining board, he had guardedly predicted that young Sedgwick would "become of some service to the country."[43]

4. Sedgwick Encounters the Army Trains

Mellow and clear through the Maryland night sounded the head-quarters bugle, followed by the crashing drum roll. Not tattoo, as the soldiers expected, but the sharp notes of assembly.

A few seconds of silence followed, then out from beneath the tow-ering trees came the clank of rifles, bayonets and scabbards, the hissing of water on campfires, the drone of voices as the men unfastened their shelter halves, the shouldering of haversacks, the dull tramping of countless feet across the lumpy sod, and the heavy shouts of the sergeants bellowing, "Fall in! Fall in!"

The regiments were formed. The officers moved front and center to the brigadiers for instructions. Then out to the open pike moved the head of the big Sixth Corps, bound on a mission that none could guess.

Now despite the fact that, as an army ordinarily moved, he was two days' distant from Gettysburg, Sedgwick had made his calculations carefully; he knew his corps better than the courier Oliver. He had allowed ample time for these men of hardened legs and durable backs to reach the main army. Nevertheless, there were no moments to be wasted. To move a corps rapidly from camp to roadway involved a deal of logistics and was more difficult in darkness. The Sixth was, in fact, an army. It was organized and officered for action apart from the main body, such as it had fought at Marye's Heights and Salem Church in the Chancellorsville campaign. It had 36 infantry regiments, 8 batteries of artillery, and a cavalry complement, aggregating at full strength 18,000 officers and men. It was a blue monster whose rifles and cannon could belch a ton of lead at one breath. Its infantry units, without their trains, stretched ten miles on the roadway, and required three hours of marching time to pass a given point.[44] Its three divisions were commanded by Wright, Howe, and Wheaton. John Newton, who usually headed the third, had been rushed off by the dispatch from Meade to take command of the First Corps, superseding Doubleday.

But Sedgwick had based his promise on no more than the information he possessed when he quickly arranged his march. His head of column was already moving on the road to Taneytown when a later messenger specified the Baltimore pike direct to Gettysburg. It was a disconcerting command. A halt was ordered while Sedgwick and his staff hurriedly restudied their maps. Regiments were shunted across the fields; delays occurred in the darkness. Finally the column was readjusted.

But when the 98th Pennsylvania Regiment moved off again in the lead, the advance party encountered a much more serious obstacle. General Meade had ordered his huge supply trains back on Westminster, and now they sprawled along the turnpike, fifteen miles of slow-moving mules and wagons.[45] Sedgwick roared commands; messengers scattered through the night. Officers hurled oaths at teamsters and teamsters cursed at mules. Team were shunted into side roads. Nothing was more irksome to soldiers than the strain of the hobbled marching behind the teams. Some of the regiments still waited in the camp at Manchester, packs on, accouterments ready. Not until four o'clock on the morning of July 2 did the corps finally clear the town. At daybreak the regiments had covered an average distance of only six miles. Disaster loomed for the Northern army, for Sedgwick's word to Meade was surely broken.

A white sun rose over the eastern hills, promising another scorching day, but after such a night daylight of any nature was welcome to the Sixth Corps. There was a final delay which some of them sought to utilize for cooking breakfast. But the corps was now clear of its blockade and Sedgwick had no intention of giving his troops food when the fate of the Union depended on their marching. An officer rudely kicked over some of the coffeepots that were beginning to boil.[46]

Jauntily the 98th Pennsylvania stepped out at the head of the long column. Despite its Company A, the "Irish Wing,"[47] this regiment wore the name of the "German Regulars," so called because it had made a tenacious stand at Williamsburg. The corps artillery moved under Colonel Charles H. Tompkins, the 1st Massachusetts in the lead, followed by the 1st New York. (Captain Andrew Cowan, your words will live in granite at the high-water mark on Cemetery Ridge![48]) After the 3rd New York moved two batteries of the 1st Rhode Island and two batteries of the 2nd and one of the 5th United States Artillery. Infantry regiments were there with records that remain among the most resplendent in American military history. The Green Mountain Brigade, a heritage of the Revolution; Alexander Shaler's brigade (Lincoln with his own hand had fastened the brigadier's star on Shaler's shoulder). Young Emory Upton marched at the head of his regiment. Although only twenty-three years old, he was already known as the model colonel of the army.

The Sixth Corps was a trained, seasoned, formidable army, which Sheridan came to admire in later fighting in Virginia. (Seven years after Gettysburg Sheridan was an observer with the German staff when the French surrendered Metz. He told Prince Frederick Charles that if he had had one division of the Sixth Corps in Metz, he could have cut his way through the German iron ring.[49])

Thus was Sedgwick off to Gettysburg. At the head of the column, flying in the morning breeze alongside the Stars and Stripes, was the banner of the Greek Cross, the Sixth Corps emblem. The sunshine glinted off polished steel. Blue masses stood out on the white macadam roadway. Sedgwick's round, straw hat was pulled down over his dust-rimmed eyes. His jaw was set, his face as hard as the jutting rocks of his own Litchfield mountains.

Because of the absence of the farm boys, the harvest of 1863 was late. The wheat stood ripened, giving a golden hue to the rolling hills of what in any season is a section of unusual beauty. White clouds

rose up and filled the men's ears and nostrils, invaded the cartridge
boxes and settled in drifts around their shoulders. They had relief
from the crushed stone and gravel road at times where dirt side trails—
"summer roads"—had been worn over the level stretches by farmers'
buggies. The blazing sun sent ahead a shimmering haze on the white
pike. Uniforms dripped, men plodded ahead, sometimes silent, sometimes chanting the corps refrains:

> "The foremost in the conflict,
> The last to say, 'tis o'er.
> Who know not what it is to yield.
> You'll find the old Sixth Corps."[50]

Quick step and no rations. "It's hell, boys," shouted a barrel-
chested Philadelphia volunteer, "but if Lee's in Pennsylvania I'd walk
there on stumps." Mingled with the comments was the constant command of the junior officers to step lively and close up.

At length a stir passed along the winding column. Carried back
by "scuttle-butt," "latrine rumor," or in 1863 the "grapevine telegraph," the news went to the dozen Pennsylvania regiments. The
corps had reached the Mason-Dixon line.

Meade's orders for all commanders to address their men on the
crisis of the Southern invasion had been complied with in the Sixth
Corps units. The 93rd Pennsylvania had heard a speech from Colonel
James M. McCarter, a chaplain during the three months' service in
1861, who had become a line officer and the regiment's gallant commander at Fair Oaks, where he was wounded. Although almost an
invalid, he stayed in the saddle during the Gettysburg campaign. He
spoke unsupported from his horse and told the men with fiery elo-
quence of the stupendous issues that faced the Army of the Potomac
on Pennsylvania soil.

No cheer followed his remarks and there was no shouting now as
the men of the 93rd saw the green hills of their own state. The sentiments of the regiment had been stirred. The regimental colors were
unfurled. The drums beat the quickstep. The companies moved at
parade order. No reviewing officer could have desired a finer sight or
more even array of rifles at the "carry." To the time of their sharply
falling footsteps, the soldiers struck up the old, familiar song, and
passed into Pennsylvania singing, "Home, Sweet Home."[51]

Sedgwick was at the head of the column, a massive figure that seemed to bespeak the indissoluble Union. Mounted on his horse Cornwall, he paused at the side of the road to observe the corps as it passed him. An occasional bit of banter was tossed at the general from the ranks. "Get a fresh horse, Uncle John, and try to catch us," shouted a company wit. The general smiled and lifted his hat.

So it was, less than a year later, as he jested to steady a frightened soldier, Sedgwick was hit by a Southern marksman. The familiar smile was on his face as he lay dead in the Wilderness. There the men built a bower for his body out of pine-tree boughs. They covered all but his face with a flag and as they went into action they filed by as though passing in review, in their final reverence.[52]

As the march continued the men learned that their goal was Gettysburg, but the details of the first day's action were still unreported. The need for haste was obvious. Here and there men dropped limply. The column veered until they could be lifted into the shade along the roadside. Ambulances in the rear picked up as many of the stricken as possible. Wet uniforms weighed heavy, and backs ached with the dull hurt of exhaustion. Grime gathered on perspiring necks and the dust and mud made the blue regiments look much like the gray-and-butternut detachments Lee had led across the Potomac. Obviously there could be no halt for dinner and no chance to snatch food by straggling. Uncle John Sedgwick was in white-hot earnest.

Finally along the roadway began to appear traces of yesterday's engagement. Ambulances were rearward-bound. One of the muleteers hauling wounded thought he should have right of way on the road, and was dissuaded by a saber point at his throat. Another driver demanding the road with bread for the army saw it dumped into the ditches. Men going forward had first right; then ammunition. Food and wounded had to wait. At Littlestown, where they crossed the railroad, wounded gathered on the streets and in improvised hospitals. Gettysburg was ten miles away. Far to the west the undulating hills rose toward the tender outline of South Mountain. The men, silent now, moved grimly along. The sun beat in their faces. Two knobs at length stood out before them, one rising above the other. Still there was no sound of firing. The quiet was broken only by the heavy infantry tread and the groans of the lumbering caissons.

While the Sixth Corps marched, a tense nation awaited reports from Gettysburg. Throngs hovered about the telegraph and newspaper offices in Philadelphia and New York, discussing the drama of the invasion. In Washington Halleck clung to his telegraph wire, rushing

Stanton each message from Meade. Lincoln went to his room at the White House, got down on his knees, and burying his head in his arms, said to the Lord, "You know I have done all I can." Then he cried out, "Oh, God, give us a victory."[53] Strength seemed to reach him. Arising, he went to his office with a conviction that the invasion would be repelled and the Union saved.

And while the Sixth Corps marched, the balance of the Federal army remained in position on Culp's and Cemetery hills. The battle had not yet been resumed. Most of the officers were puzzled by Lee's inaction. They recalled the long quiet that had preceded Jackson's surprise attack just two months earlier at Chancellorsville. They remembered that Lee rarely struck where he was expected.

From the elevation of Little Round Top, scanning the roads, a signal officer saw far down the southeastern pike a haze and then distinctly a moving column. Officers seized their glasses and watched intently. "Cavalry," someone muttered. The remark caused consternation.[54] Was this Stuart in the Federal rear? Then some keen-eyed officer saw sunlight flashing from bayonets, and shouted that it was not gray calvary, but blue infantry. There was the flag and beside it the Greek Cross. "It is the Sixth Corps!" "The Sixth Corps has come!"

At two o'clock on the afternoon of July 2 Major General John Sedgwick reported to Meade at army headquarters, and the 98th Pennsylvania Infantry sucked the water of Rock Creek behind the Round Tops. Great cheers rolled down the Union line as word passed from division to division that the Sixth Corps had reached the field. They swept across the valley to Seminary Ridge, where the astute Lee, still having no information from his cavalry, mused and wondered.

At 4:00 P.M. the corps was well up and by five it was concentrated on the left flank of Meade's army, a reserve that made a battle feasible. Shortly before four while the men of the advance regiments were bathing their feet, the Southern bombardment suddenly erupted. The carnage of battle was to be continued; the future of America was to be determined. By one of the magnificent marches of warfare, the big Sixth Corps had reached the field of Gettysburg on time.

CHAPTER FIFTEEN

Lee's Attack Plans

1. Early Answers for the Second Corps

Why the long lull? On the evening of July 1, in the fading daylight, Lee rode through Gettysburg and out the Heidlersburg road to Ewell's headquarters at the Blocher farm northwest of Barlow's Knoll.

There he met Ewell, Early, and Rodes. Unfortunately, Johnson, perhaps the strongest of Ewell's division commanders and certainly neither so designing as Early nor as inhibited as Rodes, was posting troops and had no part in the consultations. Although the sun had set, the generals sat in the coolness of an arbor in the rear, where they enjoyed a relaxed conversation after a day of much anxiety, excitement, and physical exertion. There was common but unspoken assent that the battle of July 1 was now over; the talk should concern the next day.

Lee wanted information on three main points: the condition of the troops, the enemy's position, and the measures now to be deemed advisable. Early, a facile talker and skillful lawyer who knew how to present his case, took over as the Second Corps spokesman, with Ewell's tacit consent. Ewell merely affirmed what Early offered. Early became the only historian of the meeting,[1] and included Rodes as also in agreement with his propositions. The correspondent of the Petersburg *Express* who observed these two men at Orange Court House two months later might just as readily have obtained his thumbnail sketches from this earlier conference, for Early "seemed as one who could not be brooked in any thing he wished" while "General

211

Rodes is the most pleasant looking man I have seen in many a day."[2]
Rodes was certainly pleasant and harmonious at this conference, and
Early obdurate.

Lee made it evident at the outset that he had in mind a further
offensive against the Federal army. Nobody dwelt on defensive plans.
After he had heard a report on the condition and situation of the
troops, he asked the three generals conjointly, rather than the corps
commander in particular, one question: "Can you, with your corps,
attack on this flank at daylight tomorrow?"[3]

Early's answer was negative. Though he claimed to have been
pressing Ewell through the late afternoon to attack, he now shifted his
position. He said that he had reconnoitered in and about Gettysburg
both that day and when he had passed through en route to York on
June 26, and had observed: that the ground was steep and rough;
that the enemy was fortifying and concentrating in his front; and that
the houses and streets of the town would impede formation of a battle
line designed to move against the heights. It would be necessary to
attack from the left of the town, close up to the hills. The result would
be doubtful and success, if attained, would be attended by great loss.

Early clearly had a point when he said that the hills were being fortified and that the Federal army was moving to its own right in strength.
He had been unable earlier in the evening to have Hill's corps make
the attack on Cemetery Ridge and now he again called attention to
what he described as the more inviting aspect of the ground on the
other side of the town. The party must have moved to a vantage place,
for he pointed to the Round Tops, still discernible in the dusk, and
identified them as keys to the Federal position. He mentioned the
"more practicable nature of the ascents" on that side; an attack from
the Southern right flank, he said, would have better chances.

After Ewell and Rodes had concurred and Lee had seemed to agree
on the inadvisability of attacking with his left, Lee asked a disconcerting question: "Then perhaps I had better draw you around toward my
right, as the line will be very long and thin if you remain here, and the
enemy may come down and break through it?"[4]

The suggestion was critical in its bearing on the fortunes of the
army. Early did not reflect but "spoke at once in reply."[5] His main
objection was the loss of morale and equipment that would be en-
tailed. His men were elated with their success and should not be
compelled to give up the ground they had won. Some wounded were
not in a condition to be moved. The Gettysburg streets held stacks
of captured muskets that should not be abandoned.

Quite clearly Early wanted to stay where he was. Seeking to allay Lee's apprehension that the Federals might break the line, he declared the corps could repulse any force sent against it. He said it was more difficult for the enemy to come down than for the Confederates to go up to attack, although he did not elucidate. Again Ewell and Rodes concurred with Early's reasoning.

There is a hint, even as the story is related by Early, that Lee felt vaguely he was being pushed around a bit. He still was contemplative in his next remark: "Well, if I attack from my right, Longstreet will have to make the attack."

Then he paused and according to Early "held his head down in deep thought." When he looked up again, he added, "Longstreet is a very good fighter when he gets in position and gets everything ready, but he is *so slow*." The italics were Early's, and he explained, "The emphasis was just as I have given it, and the words seemed to come from General Lee with pain."[6]

The inconsistency of the remark with Eggleston's statement, quoted earlier, that Lee thought Longstreet speedier than Jackson is unimportant, because opinions will vary. But it is significant in that it showed Lee was forewarned and therefore might have found the means of forearming when he decided that Longstreet should begin the attack. Lee understood Longstreet better than some of the others could because he was, himself, more thorough than impulsive. Jackson had described Lee as "not slow" but "cautious." Lee must have known better than anyone else in the army that Longstreet would always be deliberate, and this was probably why the commanding general usually relied on him for the knockout punch rather than the first blow.[7]

Lee was far from satisfied when he departed from this anything but heartening conference. It showed him how fully Ewell had come under the dominance of the more sprightly minded Early. It is clear from the comment of Colonel Taylor that Lee had been intent on following up the success already gained; with the arrival of Johnson, Lee thought Ewell could go forward at dawn on the next day. What he obtained at the conference was a solid front of opinion that they should wait for Longstreet, who would then be employed against the enemy's "weak left."

One must wonder if more important to Early than the terrain was not the fact that Longstreet's corps had been resting at Suffolk while the balance of the army fought at Chancellorsville, and had not yet been engaged at Gettysburg. Certainly by the rule of rotation it was time for Longstreet to carry the major load of a battle. Early hinted

broadly at this.[8] He had not reconnoitered the ground south of Gettysburg, was not familiar with the approaches to the Round Tops and
could not have stressed the ease of making an attack there on the
basis of any firsthand knowledge. He had reached Gettysburg late on
June 26 and was too hurried then to have inspected the country
south of the town with any care. Now he did not welcome the opportunity, which a soldier like Gordon probably would have leaped at,
of moving to the far right himself and conducting the attack over the
allegedly soft ground.

As it developed, Early's contentions left Lee with the necessity of
planning the next day's operations with troops that had not yet
reached the field, whose leader was known to be very methodical, if
not, indeed, aggravatingly slow. Early's guile and reluctance had a
profound bearing on the battle developments. Lee's active mind was
comprehending all the possibilities. A few hours earlier on Seminary
Ridge Longstreet had stubbornly reiterated his proposal for a flanking movement around the Federal left, by which Lee might interpose
or threaten to interpose his army between Meade and Washington.
The possibility of such a move, Lee later disclosed, was in his mind
during his consultation with Ewell. Still, the move would be con-
tingent on the shifting of Ewell and the willing co-operation of his
subordinates, and that was not forthcoming.[9]

Early himself has provided perhaps the best analysis of Lee's
method of command, which serves to explain not only his yielding in
this July 1 conference, but also his transactions on the next day.
According to Early, Lee "did not regard his officers as mere machines
to execute his will," but as rational beings capable of reasoning and
giving suggestions.

He had likewise a profound knowledge of human nature, and it
was his custom to talk freely to officers about movements they were
to make, get their views about the proper mode of making them, in
order to ascertain whether they could be relied upon for the work in
hand, adopt any judicious views they might suggest, and leave them
under the impression that they were carrying out plans in the formation of which they had some part. . . .[10]

Lee knew that one of the first elements of success is "a confidence
on the part of an officer entrusted with a movement in its feasibility."
Early, it later developed, would apply this line of thought to himself
but sparingly when dealing with the relations between Lee and Long-

street. The extreme of Lee's method can be found in his instructions in late April 1863, when he was informed that Hooker had crossed the Rappahannock: "Say to General Jackson that he knows just as well what to do with the enemy as I do."[11]

Manifestly, then, no plan for the attack on the morning of July 2 had been made when in darkness Lee rode back from Ewell's headquarters to his own on Seminary Hill. Longstreet meantime had returned to his camp beyond Marsh Creek with a distinct understanding that his corps should be brought up as quickly as possible in the morning, but without any orders for a sunrise attack.

Lee was purposely employing almost altogether verbal orders. His distrust of written directions in the presence of the enemy sprang from the well-near fatal loss of the orders in the Sharpsburg campaign, which revealed to McClellan how he had divided his army. Orders by word of mouth meant greater safety for the army, but greater confusion for historians who for nearly a century have had to feel their way hesitatingly and often with contrary judgment through a great mass of conflicting testimony about Lee's battle plans.[12]

2. A Headquarters Staff in a Cottage

Lee had his headquarters tents pitched in a field of grass just south of the Cashtown road on the reverse slope of Seminary Ridge. He conducted part of his work in the stone dwelling across the road, which even then was an old house, dating from 1779.

About the grounds were apple, plum, and cherry trees, while grapes grew over an arbor on the south side, screening the windows from the Cashtown road. The house was owned by Thaddeus Stevens, who rented it to the widow Maria Thompson, a slight, elderly woman, perhaps in her sixties, who volunteered to cook some of the meals for the Confederate officers. She had been indifferent when shells dropped near by, but the water in her cellar caused by the heavy rains of late June had finally persuaded her to seek better quarters in the town. Lee had offered to pay her rental but she declined it.

How he and his officers ate is a wonder. The little pine table on which Mrs. Thompson supposedly served them was only forty-one by forty-eight inches, and according to tradition not only Lee and his staff, but Longstreet, Ewell, Hood, Early, and others had their meals there at one time or another. Some of course must have eaten standing. Lee had scant time for sleep in his tent but he got some naps in a rocking chair.

Long after the battle some argued insistently that Lee did not use the Thompson house in Gettysburg; that he was seen much of the time elsewhere and observed riding over Seminary Hill as though coming from a headquarters farther behind the lines. The matter is of passing interest because of Lee's previous aversion to houses. But there is abundant testimony that he occupied the Thompson house for conferences and meals. Kyd Douglas, who tented with Colonel Taylor across the road, referred to it, as did couriers. The interior of the house was burned in the 1890s but was reconstructed, as the stone walls were left intact.

One room Lee used as an office and another as a reception room. The inadequacy of his staff is in no manner more clearly seen than from its ability to cramp itself into one or two tents and this simple stone house, measuring thirty by thirty-three feet. Lee tended to simplify the management of the army much as the private Confederate soldier simplified the load he carried on his back. He had no Berthier or Gneisenau, nor even a Rawlins to operate his headquarters or act in his absence. One of the amazing and, from a Confederate standpoint, distressing things about the battle was the amount of detail work Lee was compelled to carry personally in the midst of such a supreme trial of strength, and all this business was transacted in the cramped quarters of Mrs. Thompson's stone cottage. Needless to say, Lee had won some splendid victories with his meager staff, but the paucity of his headquarters assistance became more evident under the stress of Gettysburg.

After eating Mrs. Thompson's supper on July 1 Lee decided to do whatever he could to end Stuart's waywardness—the matter that had been causing him the greatest impatience and concern of the campaign. Having heard nothing, he was fearful, according to Longstreet, that his cavalry had been destroyed.[13] As Stuart did not seem able to find him, he would have to find Stuart. Lee asked the dashing raider, Harry Gilmore, who had accompanied Johnson, to send a good detail to headquarters and soon a Marylander, James D. Watters, was at hand with a squad of about eight men. All were mounted, as Lee had directed, on good horses.

Each man was given a copy of sealed orders to General Stuart. They were to scatter over the country and find Stuart as soon as possible. If they ran into danger of capture they were to destroy the orders but were to reach Stuart at all hazards and tell him to join Lee at Gettysburg with the least possible delay.[14] Watters happened to be the courier who found Stuart and brought him to headquarters, riding ahead of his men. Long afterward he told the story of the episode.

3. The Question of the "Sunrise Attack"

Lee must have thought he had been sold a peculiar bill of goods by Early and Ewell, because back in his headquarters that night he soon reversed his decision about letting his left remain idle. He sent Colonel Marshall with a message reopening the question of an attack on the heights, and summoning Ewell to headquarters. Johnson's division meantime was in position and its commander was optimistic about his ability to carry Culp's Hill, which he had found occupied soon after his arrival. Ewell, due to Johnson's opinion, reversed his own position and said he would attack. Though no time was set, this again dissuaded Lee from shifting Ewell to the far right. Ewell left Lee's headquarters about midnight. All that had really been decided was that Lee would continue the offensive in the morning after Longstreet's troops arrived.

No definite orders were issued for any corps. Yet one of the fixed popular misconceptions of American history is the belief that Lee at this night meeting ordered Longstreet to attack at daybreak on the morning of July 2. Early made it the crux of his case against Longstreet.

This writer on a recent visit to Gettysburg, where the battle is still continually analyzed and discussed, made it a point to inquire among residents in restaurants, stores, etc., why, in their opinion, Lee lost the battle. A majority answered that Lee lost because Longstreet failed to carry out orders for an attack at daybreak on the morning of July 2. Perhaps the most persistent controversy ever waged about the battle was that of the 1870s concerning this "sunrise attack." Lee, according to some of his officers, notably Early and Pendleton, ordered Longstreet to make it and lost the battle because Longstreet failed to comply. This has come to be almost the settled verdict of popular history.

Part of the uncertainty about the orders to Longstreet undoubtedly has resulted from a misunderstanding of Longstreet's actions on the night of July 1. The assumption has been that Longstreet was with Lee that night, and that Lee made his decision and imparted it to Longstreet. Longstreet himself contributed to this misunderstanding by saying in one of his accounts that he left Lee "quite late on the night of the 1st."[15]

The errors that crept into Longstreet's documents are no doubt attributable in part to his use of ghost writers, the most famous of whom was the Atlanta editor, Henry W. Grady. Grady likely contributed some of the striking passages in Longstreet's accounts. But the general used other writers too, because of his crippled right arm, and he apparently was not careful or experienced in editing and let errors creep through.

Longstreet may have meant merely that he left late in the evening of July 1. In another account he placed the time at seven o'clock. In still another he quite clearly suggests that he had no contact with Lee between the time he saw him on Seminary Hill in the evening, sometime between five and seven, and their meeting on the morning of July 2. Colonel Long told of Lee's addressing Longstreet and Hill on the "evening" of July 1 but specified no time. "Evening" is an indefinite word in the South.

But there is external evidence bearing on Longstreet's actions that is conclusive. He left Seminary Ridge and rode to his camp beyond Marsh Creek. He had progressed half a mile when he encountered Dr. J. S. D. Cullen, the Third Corps medical director, who said it was "about dark."[16] That, on July 1, would mean after eight, but in any case after seven-thirty. He traveled four miles or more to his headquarters and was moody. Fremantle rode back with him and left an account of it. The British correspondent Ross was traveling with Barksdale, near whom Longstreet camped. He said it was "pitch dark" when the fires were lighted for supper. Some doctors joined them, and Longstreet and his staff "presently came up" and confirmed news about the first day's fighting. This would place Longstreet's return from Gettysburg at around 9:30 P.M. More time would have been consumed at dinner. McLaws said he met Longstreet coming from Gettysburg that night about ten o'clock, which is more definite.

According to Longstreet's testimony, he was up the next morning while the stars were still shining. "It was still dusk," said Ross, when he went to the general's tent for breakfast.[17] Longstreet must have arisen sometime between three and three-thirty. The earlier time is usually used.

Considering that half an hour to forty-five minutes would have been required for normal night riding between Longstreet's and Lee's headquarters, it does not fit in that Longstreet could reasonably have attended any night conference with Lee. It would have involved a round trip in the middle of the night with no apparent purpose.

Had he felt that other business was necessary he would scarcely have returned to his camp in the early evening; had he been with Lee in a conference that did not end until around midnight, why would he have ridden five miles to get two hours' sleep and return by daybreak, when by remaining on Seminary Hill he might have got three or four? It does not appear that Lee called him. Lee's courier, F. S. Gore, left a letter saying he was sent that night to summon Ewell.[18] There is no reference to anyone's summoning Longstreet from Marsh Creek, and Lee did not mention his presence. Manifestly he was not there.

When, then, did Lee issue his orders for Longstreet to attack early on July 2, if at all? On this point Longstreet said that at the time of his departure from Lee on the night of July 1, "I believed that he had made up his mind to attack, but was confident that he had not yet determined as to when the attack was to be made."[19] Certainly if Longstreet had been ordered to attack, he or someone else would have known of it that evening. Here Longstreet's memories are well confirmed and to be trusted fully.[20] Not only was Lee uncertain that night about *when* the attack was to be made, but also *where,* as his later movements attest clearly.

When Longstreet met McLaws he said nothing about his division attacking in the morning, as he surely would have if Lee had ordered it at "sunrise."

As Lee went to sleep his last words to his secretary, Long, showed that indecision still existed.

"Colonel Long," he said, "do you think we had better attack without the cavalry? If we do, we will not, if successful, be able to reap the fruits of victory."[21]

Long thought it would be best to go ahead. The time when Stuart might come was uncertain.

4. *An Anxious General Roams the Lines*

How thoroughly unsettled Lee was is evident by his dispatch of Colonel Venable at sunrise with a further message to Ewell, inquiring again what Ewell thought of an attack from his position. Daylight permitted a better reconnaissance and Ewell might have new thoughts. That Ewell's reply was negative is suggested by Venable's statement that the corps commander "made me ride with him from point to point of his lines, so as to see with him the exact position of things."

Ewell was not likely to assent to an attack in Early's absence! Venable did make it clear that the purpose of Lee's message—Lee was explicit about this—was to determine whether he should move Ewell's troops around to the right. The old question was thus reopened. Lee's prudence still emphasized that Ewell's concave lines, largely isolated from the rest of the army, were unsound and invited attack, which, incidentally, Meade was at that instant considering. Venable did not think when he went to Ewell that Lee was contemplating any "sunrise attack." Manifestly his plans were still being formed.

Not satisfied with sending Venable, Lee soon followed. His first concern was with his exposed left and with Culp's and Cemetery hills. To carry those eminences would win the battle.

Ewell was engaged in his reconnaissance with Colonel Venable when Lee reached the corps headquarters. Trimble, unemployed since stalking away from Ewell on the previous evening, met the commanding general there. Lee wished to survey the country from an elevation and get a view of the enemy's position.

The cupola on the almshouse was not so commanding as the cupolas on the Lutheran Seminary or Pennsylvania College but it was the best point in their vicinity. Lee and Trimble climbed to the top. They had a good view of Culp's Hill and Cemetery Ridge and in the distance could see the Round Tops.

Lee turned to Trimble: "The enemy have the advantage of us in a shorter and inside line and we are too much extended," he said. "We did not or we could not pursue our advantage of yesterday and now the enemy are in a good position."[22]

Those words—"we did not or we could not pursue our advantage of yesterday"—were, for Lee, a rebuke, indicative of his deep displeasure with the closing events of July 1. Anyone might see that Ewell "could" have continued his attack, and therefore Lee considered it a matter of neglect. In any event, he repeated the words several times that morning, as he met Early, Rodes, and others.[23] Trimble said their significance was impressed on him especially in view of Lee's statement at Hagerstown that he would fall on the enemy as he came up and crush him in detail. That plan was not working out so readily as he had a right to expect.

The precise hours at which Lee made his trips about the battlefield that morning are difficult to determine and if they were known would not be especially significant since they did not contribute either to the development of plans or the progress of the battle. For the better part of the morning Lee was groping for a means to launch a co-ordinated

offensive that would have the wholehearted support of his corps commanders; failing in this, he finally was compelled to make an arbitrary
decision and order Longstreet to attack the Federal left forthwith. The
hour at which the positive orders were issued was probably about
eleven o'clock—it could scarcely have been earlier.[24] Too, that is the
hour given by Colonel Taylor.

Lee's eagerness to have Longstreet's men on the field began to express itself soon after daybreak. Needless to say, no offensive could
be undertaken anywhere until these fresh divisions were present. During the morning Lee made two visits to Ewell's lines on the left, passed
along A. P. Hill's front, and was now and again in consultation with
Longstreet, Hill, and others on Seminary Ridge. His anxiety to get
the battle under way expressed itself not in any severity of tone or
language, but in a restless wandering.

Lee was not in good physical condition on July 2. His difficulty
may have been induced or aggravated by his mental distress. Several
noticed his agitation, which was not dissimilar to that observed by
Dr. Suesserott in Messersmith's woods near Chambersburg three days
before.

Major Justus Scheibert of the Prussian Royal Engineers—who was
on Seminary Ridge as an observer, as he had been at Chancellorsville,
and whose admiration of Lee was almost boundless—made a revealing
comparison of the commanding general's attitude in the two battles.[25]
At Chancellorsville Lee was "full of calm, quiet, self-possession, feeling that he had done his duty to the utmost."

This calmness was wanting at Gettysburg, where:

Lee was not at his ease, but was riding to and fro, frequently changing his position, making anxious inquiries here and there, and looking
care-worn. . . . This uneasiness . . . was contagious to the army, as
will appear from the reports of Longstreet, Hood, Heth and others,
and as appeared also to me from the peep I had of the battlefield.[26]

Lee's manner has sometimes been attributed to the wounding and
capture of his son Rooney.[27] Rooney had received a leg wound at
Fleetwood and had been taken to Hickory Hill, the home of W. F.
Wickham near Richmond, to recuperate. The house was raided by
Federal cavalry and Rooney was captured. But General Lee does not
appear to have heard of the capture until he was at Williamsport after
the battle of Gettysburg,[28] although he knew his son had been

wounded. In no case could it have been the cause of such evident agitation. Lee as a soldier had steeled himself to loss. Moreover, the uneasiness was temporary. Scheibert emphasized that the general after the battle "resumed his accustomed calmness."

Longstreet treated the difficulty as emotional: "He seemed under a subdued excitement, which occasionally took possession of him when 'the hunt was up,' and threatened his superb equipoise." A Texan's view was that temperamentally Lee was a "game cock" when challenged by the enemy.[29] This was not far from the opinion of Heth, who looked on the commanding general as the most aggressive man of the army, "not even excepting Jackson."

Still, his agitation at Gettysburg was above any normal combativeness. Lieutenant Colonel Blackford offered what is perhaps the most plausible explanation, that Lee was suffering severely from diarrhea. That could explain also the unusual actions observed in Messersmith's woods by the Chambersburg physician. Blackford, after the army had been located for Stuart, rode ahead of the cavalry and was sent to report to Lee on some brushes that day with the Federals. A staff officer told him he could not see Lee, whom he had usually found accessible for such reports. So he made his report to either Venable or Taylor—he could not recall which—and then sat at headquarters half an hour relating some of the events of Stuart's long ride.

In that period Lee came out of his tent several times hurriedly and went to the rear, walking as though weakened and in pain. Blackford inquired and was informed that the general was suffering from diarrhea. This, he thought, could explain why some things were not pushed with their accustomed vigor on that day.[30]

The difficulty of diarrhea or flux was so common in the armies that it was often termed the "'old soldier's disease." Particularly was it present in the early fruit season, and the Confederate army, as we have seen, had been partaking freely all along the route. Early apples grown on Seminary Ridge were just ripening. They were being eaten heartily and it is not unlikely that Lee had been enjoying these and cherries, too. As we saw earlier, he had relished fresh raspberries in Maryland.[31]

The British correspondent Ross rode with Longstreet in the faint dawn to Gettysburg. Daylight had come when they mounted Seminary Ridge, where they met Lee. They "lay about for some time looking through glasses at the Yankees,"[32] who were so close that each individual figure could be distinguished.

Ross saw at once that it would be "a long time" before Longstreet's corps could be put into position, so he rode into Gettysburg with two doctors of Barksdale's brigade. They found the battlefield of July 1 well policed. Both Confederate and Federal dead had been buried and the wounded had been removed to hastily set-up hospitals. They met Ewell, "a gruff-looking man." They took note that the town had not been sacked, or even disturbed, and returned to find the generals still conversing on the ridge, having been joined by A. P. Hill and Heth.[33] Heth, wearing a bandage about his head, was not yet fit for action.

The Gettysburg district was finding the sudden descent of more than 150,000 men a severe strain on its water supply, and the wells were failing by the morning of July 2.[34] On Seminary Ridge Hill asked for a drink and one of the men brought him "some dirty stuff in a pail," with apologies; if he could wait, good water could be brought up from about a mile.

"Oh no, that will do very well," said the sickly general. It caused the correspondent Ross to understand that he was on a battlefield.[35]

Longstreet soon after his arrival again broached to Lee his plan for a flanking movement and found Lee no more receptive than on the previous afternoon. A hard loser, Longstreet urged as much as he thought a fairly tense situation would stand, then desisted. Lee had given it the most careful thought and decided against it. The two armies were face to face and a battle was the only solution for either of them.

Longstreet's corps, in its own view of things, was the main army. As one of Kershaw's brigade put it:

There was a kind of intuition, an apparent settled fact . . . that after all the other troops had made their long marches, tugged at the flanks of the enemy, threatened his rear, and all the display of strategy and generalship had been exhausted in the dislodgement of the foe, and all these failed, then when the hard, stubborn, decisive blow was to be struck, the troops of the First Corps were called on to strike it.[36]

Old Pete put it differently in addressing Lee: "My corps is as solid as a rock—a great rock."[37]

Mrs. Chesnut saw the troops two months after Gettysburg as they were going to Chickamauga: "Not one man was intoxicated; not one rude word did I hear." She felt a thrill of sympathy when "a knot of boyish, laughing young creatures" passed her.[38]

But these carefree youths had an *esprit de corps* and a confidence in their commander unsurpassed in the Confederate service. According to D. August Dickert, the brigade's scribe:

No battle was ever considered decisive until Longstreet, with his cool, steady head, his heart of steel and troops who acknowledged no superior, or scarcely equal, in ancient or modern times, in endurance and courage, had measured strength with the enemy. This I give not as a personal view, but as the feelings and confidence and pardonable pride of the troops of the First Corps.[39]

Now they were coming down out of the mountains to deliver the *coup de grâce* on a field where the other corps had fought brilliantly but without the power to put in the finishing blow.

Much of the day of July 1 they had waited idly at Greenwood while Johnson's division and then his long train—miles of caissons and wagons, including those of Rodes's division as well as his own, that had awakened Jacob Hoke as they rumbled through Chambersburg—had the right of way on the road to Gettysburg. The wagons broke and rutted the soft road and made it more difficult for infantry. Here was a signal example of Lee's inadequate staff work. Men should have been given preference. The fifteen miles of creeping vehicles kept McLaws' and Hood's divisions waiting by the roadside four to six hours and then slowed their progress when they were finally in column. Johnson, in turn, had been forced to wait until Anderson cleared the road ahead of him. The single pike was woefully inadequate for the great demands suddenly put on it, and it was employed in almost a haphazard fashion while Lee was figuratively wringing his hands for troops at Gettysburg.

George Pickett with his three Virginia brigades remained at Chambersburg. The task of guarding the rear and the army trains would normally have been Stuart's. Since he was missing, a division had to be sacrificed until Imboden could come over the mountains from Cumberland and McConnellsburg and relieve it. Here was an unfortunate, possibly a disastrous consequence of Stuart's absence. A whole division was kept away from Gettysburg at a time when it was most urgently needed.

McLaws' troops had not camped or marched compactly and some of them had not halted until 3:00 A.M. If a "dawn attack" had been ordered they could not have been present. Kershaw's brigade pulled up at what the general called midnight and some of the others

3:00 A.M., and from the eminence beyond Marsh Creek surveyed the sleeping Confederate army strung out toward Gettysburg, "a great sea of white tents, silent and still."[40] Kershaw's South Carolinians "learned with delight" that the Palmetto Regiment had planted the first flag in Gettysburg. A man coming up asked the scribe Dickert if he would have a drink. "You may have heard angel's voices," he recalled. "I was so tired, sleepy and worn . . . I said 'Yes, Yes!' " There was enough in the jug for Color Captain John W. Watts too.[41]

Longstreet gave Hood first place in the early morning march of July 2, and the Texan was in the lead as the First Corps began to reach Gettysburg.

5. Hood's Men Stack Arms and Rest

Hood's division had left Chambersburg at two o'clock on the afternoon of July 1, about the time Early and Pender were preparing their assaults. He lost only about four hours at Greenwood while Johnson's trains passed. But there were further delays. After moving only a hundred yards the command was halted and this irritating halting was repeated time after time, a process more tiring than straight marching.

Broken marching continued until 2:00 A.M. when Hood reached Cashtown. The men stretched out on the bare ground and almost immediately were asleep. Two hours later came the drum roll and in ten minutes the division was on the way to Gettysburg. It arrived at Lee's headquarters soon after sunrise.

Both Hood and his men clearly understood the urgency. Soon after daybreak Hood rode with his staff into the field where Lee was in consultation and reported to the commanding general. In a field a short distance back the troops were ordered to stack arms and rest until further notice.

Through the early morning Hood, Longstreet, and A. P. Hill were with Lee on the heights inspecting the Federal lines on the opposite ridge. Although it was a sultry July morning Lee had his coat buttoned to the throat.[42] He was walking back and forth under some towering trees and seemed to Hood to be both hopeful and "buried in deep thought." At one of his pauses he remarked to Hood: "The enemy is here, and if we do not whip him, he will whip us."[43]

That was a simple conclusion but one which some of his subordinates had not grasped yet. Their thought was not whether the army could gain a victory, but the method by which that victory could most readily be obtained. Defeat was not dreamed of. Longstreet heard

Lee's remark as he came up. When he had a chance he took Hood aside. They sat on the ground, leaning against a tree trunk, and Longstreet explained: "The general is a little nervous this morning; he wishes me to attack; I do not wish to do so without Pickett. I never like to go into battle with one boot off."[44]

Thus, as Hood observed, the morning of July 2 wore away.

Neither Lee nor Longstreet, who were together, seemed to be ready for Hood's troops after all the haste to get them there. They waited an hour and a half in the field, and when they were moved it was not into line for an attack. They were marched about a mile south to a valley where they could get water and fuel. The Texas brigade was ready for the skillet wagon to unload, fires were being built and the men were awaiting their issue of flour, when a small incident occurred that threw light on the status of Lee's attack plans at this hour, which was perhaps eight to nine o'clock.

A Confederate soldier, Private Ferdinand Hahn of the 4th Texas, wandered to the crest of the rising ground and saw a group of Confederate generals conversing. As a clerk in the Menger Hotel in San Antonio, he had become acquainted with many of the officers of the old army who were often at that famous hostelry during their tours of service in the Southwest. He moved up as close as he dared and identified Generals Lee, Longstreet and Hood, all of whom had stopped at the Menger. Sacrificing his breakfast, he stayed in hearing range for half an hour, then returned to his company loaded with information. Some of the men were still heating their skillet lids, on which to cook biscuits.

"You might as well quit bothering with those skillet lids, boys," said Hahn. "It'll not be twenty minutes before we are on the move again."

Several shot at him the same question: "What have you heard, Hahn?"

"Only this. I got up pretty close to General Lee and old Longstreet and Hood awhile ago, and while I stood there an officer rode up and, addressing General Lee, reported that the Yankees were moving troops to Round Top. General Lee at once turned his glasses in that direction and, after looking through them a minute or two, said: 'Ah, well, that was to be expected. But General Meade might as well have saved himself the trouble, for we'll have it in our possession before night.' That means, of course, that we'll have to take it, and to do it, we'll have to move from here as soon as Hood can send orders."[45]

True to his forecast, the brigade was called to attention within ten minutes, and for the next six hours Hood's division was on its devious journey, with many long waits, to a position from which it could launch its attack on the Round Tops.[46]

Longstreet's reserve artillery under Colonel E. P. Alexander was in camp at Greenwood and for some unaccountable reason had heard nothing about the battle being fought at Gettysburg sixteen miles away. Darkness brought the news, along with an order for the artillery to move at 2:00 A.M., and Alexander had his own battalion of 26 guns and the Washington Artillery of 10 guns, which together composed the artillery reserve, on the road punctually.

The moon was bright, the infantry was out of the way, and the marching was easy, and at an hour given vaguely as "about 8 or 9 A.M.,"—certainly much too late for an attack at sunrise—the guns were hauled into a woods in the vicinity of the battlefield.[47]

Alexander reported at once to Lee and Longstreet, who were together, showing no sign of haste, on a hill behind the Confederate position. He was informed that the enemy's left flank would be attacked; that he should take command of Cabell's and Henry's battalions, each having 18 guns, and his own, making a total of 62 guns; that the Washington Artillery should be placed in reserve and that he should reconnoiter the ground and co-operate with the infantry. He was cautioned against exposing the guns to the view of the signal station on Little Round Top.

Alexander did not get the impression that General Lee felt things were being delayed unnecessarily.[48] He made his reconnaissance, which consumed three hours.[49] The time must have been between ten and eleven o'clock when he went back for his battalion, and probably it was nearly noon before he had it at the schoolhouse near the Herr Tavern west of Willoughby Run.

6. The Armies Are Finally Face to Face

One reason for Lee's delay in ordering an attack on the Federal left was that he wanted a report on a reconnaissance on which he had sent one of Longstreet's engineers, Major J. J. Clarke, and Captain S. R. Johnston of his own headquarters. They left early, and while they were absent McLaws arrived, about eight o'clock, riding ahead of his men, who had given way to Hood on the road.

Lee showed him, both on the map and by pointing, the objective of the pending attack. The Confederates would move up the Emmitsburg road and take Cemetery Hill in reverse. Lee thought the Federal army faced mainly to the north, with lines running east and west across Cemetery and Culp's hills, but recessed on the left flank an indeterminate distance. The attack would sweep up the east side of the Emmitsburg road, with the Confederate left flank on the roadway.

When Lee asked McLaws if he could carry this line the Georgian replied noncommittally that he knew of nothing to prevent it but that he would like to take some skirmishers and reconnoiter the position. Lee told him a reconnaissance already was in progress and he volunteered to join it. Longstreet here stepped in and declared forcibly that he did not want McLaws to leave his division.

The corps commander seemed disturbed about the whole proposition. Nobody knows whether he was perturbed because the frontal attack he opposed was becoming more and more inevitable, or was merely piqued because Lee was issuing orders over his head to McLaws directly. That was what had caused A. P. Hill to explode against Jackson, and it may have been a source of Longstreet's irritation here. The compassionate Lee made no issue of the matter and Longstreet prevailed. McLaws was not allowed to make his reconnaissance.

In one other matter there was danger of sparks flying between Lee and Longstreet. The corps commander touched the map and told McLaws where he should place his division when it came up.

"No, General, I wish it placed just opposite," Lee corrected him.[50]

Where either of them meant for McLaws to fall in cannot now be determined, but soon Clarke and Johnston returned from their reconnaissance and the time had arrived for the attack. About all the information they had was that, sure enough, the Federal army occupied the opposite ridge. They could not be so positive about Little Round Top. They clambered up a shoulder—perhaps Vincent's Spur or Devil's Den—and could see no Federals on Little Round Top.

With respect to that eminence, Lee had already recognized what many later-day students of the battle have ignored, that its occupation by the Federal army was to be expected momentarily. The situation here was different from Culp's Hill, where Confederates were at the base. To reach Little Round Top they had to operate at a distance, and Federal troops were always nearer, first Geary, then Sickles, Sykes, and Sedgwick. Any Confederate advance against it was fairly certain to be detected. Round Top, the larger and more heavily wooded eminence, might be approached under better cover.

Even though the Federals had left the summit of Little Round Top unoccupied they probably could beat an enemy force to it. The first baseman's foot is not on the bag but he can ordinarily get there in advance of the runner. Lee must have had that in mind when through his glasses he saw Federal troops moving in the direction of Little Round Top. Probably this was Sickles trying to find a good position around the base.

But the report of Major Clarke and Captain Johnston was of high significance in that it cleared the way for Longstreet to step off. Still, there was one more obstacle. Law's Alabama brigade, an essential part of Hood's division, was marching at top speed for the battlefield. Because Longstreet had not been allowed to "get his other boot on" by awaiting Pickett's arrival, he set down what he might have considered his bare foot about moving before he had Law. The Alabamians had left New Guilford at 3:00 A.M. and marched through without a break. They got to Gettysburg, according to Law, "shortly before noon," which meant they had marched twenty-four miles in less than nine hours. That Lee had become reconciled to the need for preparations could be seen from the permission he gave Longstreet to await Law's arrival. Longstreet called this the best marching in either army, and it did exceed anything except Sedgwick's march from Manchester. Sedgwick's was eleven miles farther and any soldier would say that the last eleven miles are the hardest.

Law found the balance of Hood's brigade in the Willoughby Run valley—they had not made much progress since Private Hahn brought back his news—and thus Longstreet had two full divisions at hand.

After Lee issued his orders he left to see Ewell again and explain his plan for the army to attack by brigades *en echelon*. Beginning on the army's far right, the attack would progress in sequence through Longstreet's corps, then A. P. Hill's. Ewell would not wait until Hill's nearest brigade attacked, but would get his signal from the sound of Longstreet's guns. As the observant E. P. Alexander pointed out, it was getting rather late in the day for an echelon attack. Such a method is good on some mornings. If it is begun in the afternoon, darkness may come before the last brigades can attack. Perhaps it would have been better for the entire army to attack in unison.

At noon, with Law coming in, Longstreet began his movement and the rest of the army awaited its turn. Lee and Meade faced each other with about the same degree of concentration. Lee was minus Stuart's cavalry and Pickett's Virginians. Meade still was waiting for the Sixth Corps. He had left French's 10,000 men back at Frederick, a rear guard that would have posed a problem for Lee in any flanking movement. After an inspection by Slocum, who recommended against it, Meade had abandoned any thought of taking the offensive against Lee's left.

Meade's peak campaign strength was 105,750 and Lee's 88,754, but as they faced each other on the field, with allowance for absenteeism from many causes, Meade's infantry and artillery aggregated probably 82,000 and Lee's 68,000. Infantry and cavalry, Meade probably brought to the battle area about 92,000 and Lee about 79,000 men. The Federal army had 354, the Confederate 272 guns.[51]

The high hope of the South for freedom, the firm determination of the North to preserve the Union intact—issues long argued in the legislative halls—were about to be resolved at last on the battlefield.

CHAPTER SIXTEEN

The Story of the Missing Canteens

1. The Guide Doesn't Know Where He's Going

Longstreet's two divisions now set out on as strange a march as was
ever made on an American battlefield. They had been lying all morning in the depressions behind McPherson's and Herr's ridges. When
the order came they were hurried back, some for the better part of
three miles toward Cashtown, along the road they had traveled earlier
that day in their hasty march to Gettysburg.

McLaws' division was in the lead, accompanied by Alexander's
reserve artillery, while Kershaw, already well advanced, had first place
among the brigades. Lee sent Captain Johnston, who had made the
morning reconnaissance, as a guide. The artillery was dragged along.
That it was to be a factor in preparing for the assault was inconsistent
with the element of surprise if anything like Chancellorsville was to
be duplicated. Yet stealth was, to Longstreet, a much more vital consideration than speed. Of time he appeared to have an abundance
when he selected his long, devious route for reaching Meade's flank.
But while he did not rush, neither were his actions so deliberately slow
as to warrant a charge of sulking.

The march can be reconstructed with difficulty, because no two
units covered the same distance and different routes must have been
employed. In the beginning Longstreet's two divisions were spread
over the country west of Gettysburg, with Law resting in the neighborhood of the McPherson farm—he said he was a mile from the town—
and Kershaw, the forward element of McLaw's division, already was

near Black Horse Tavern, where he had been most of the morning.

Approaching Seven Stars, the main body struck south along a little-used road following the course of Marsh Creek and leading to Black Horse Tavern, where the 26th Pennsylvania Regiment had stumbled into a Confederate picket on the previous evening. Johnston rode part of the time with Longstreet and part with McLaws, but he did not turn out to be a well-informed guide for either. Lee accompanied Longstreet for a time, having returned from visiting Ewell.

Johnston himself was appalled when he learned the others were relying on him for directions. He said later that he "had no idea that I had the confidence of the great General Lee to such an extent that he would entrust me with the conduct of an army corps moving within two miles of the enemy lines while the lieutenant general was riding in the rear of the column."[1]

Lee had asked Johnston to make a sketch of the country he had covered on his reconnaissance and on the basis of this map had appointed him to escort Longstreet. What he had covered in his reconnaissance, however, was the terrain east of Willoughby Run and the approaches to the Round Tops. Now he was traveling roads and byways apparently as unfamiliar to him as if they were in Africa or Massachusetts. Longstreet had a guide, to be sure, but a guide who had to feel his way, Indian-fashion, through the woods and valleys and hope for the best.

Johnston told Fitzhugh Lee that he did not even know where General Longstreet was going.[2] He thought he was there only to provide the benefit of the reconnaissance he had made earlier in the morning. He was not conducting the column, merely going with it.

From his position near Black Horse Tavern, Kershaw could look across the fields about two miles to the Emmitsburg road in the region of the Kerns house, southwest of the Round Tops. There, during the morning, he had witnessed the passage of a large Federal body, protected by flankers to the left, moving to join Meade's army.[3] This obviously was De Trobriand's brigade hurrying up from Emmitsburg—it arrived at 10:00 A.M. At noon or one o'clock—the hour was indefinite to Kershaw—he got the order to take the road leading along Marsh Creek, and to advance but remain concealed from the enemy.

Kershaw passed the Black Horse Tavern and "followed the road leading from that point toward the Emmitsburg Pike,"[4] which runs past the Plank farm to Willoughby Run, turns south, follows the west bank of the run, crosses it, and reaches the Pitzer schoolhouse about

Longstreet's flank march. July 2, 1863, 12:30 to 3:45 P.M.

midway between the Sachs and Flaharty farmhouses. Kershaw went
only a fifth of a mile, moving southeast, to the crest of the hill, where
the road forked. If he had passed over the crest beyond this fork, he
could have been seen from Little Round Top.

Longstreet had come to the front, and Captain Johnston explained to him the danger of being detected at the crest. Longstreet and Mc-Laws went cautiously up the hill and, sure enough, the wooded summit of Round Top and the craggy slopes of Little Round Top were clearly visible. When they returned both "manifested considerable irritation."[5] But Johnston was using good judgment for a guide who did not know where he was going. By passing around the shoulder of the hill and through a field, he told Longstreet, the column would still be hidden from the enemy, if the enemy should, indeed, be looking out from the Round Tops toward Black Horse Tavern.

Johnston said that when Longstreet went to the top of the hill his march was discovered, but there is no other evidence of it,[6] and the report from Little Round Top is to the contrary. If they were seen, it benefited no one, for Longstreet was disgusted and peremptorily called off the entire movement. He wanted another route. He ordered an about-face and a return toward the Cashtown road. This meant that Hood, who was in the rear of McLaws, now headed the column, and owing to the readjustment McLaws had to wait an hour before he could move at all. Alexander passed through the meadows with his artillery by a route he did not describe very clearly, and wondered why the infantry did not follow. He estimated that two to three hours were lost by the countermarch.[7]

On reaching the region of the Cashtown road again, Longstreet marched toward Gettysburg until he found another little-traveled road leading south and following generally Herr Ridge and the bank of Willoughby Run. He moved partly down this and partly along the bank until he came at last to the Pitzer school; he had been near this point at Black Horse Tavern. Thence he cut across country through Pitzer's and Biesecker's woods toward the Emmitsburg road.

A check of the distances involved in Longstreet's flank march shows that the route covered about thirteen miles. This does not mean all the troops marched that far, nor, indeed, that very many of them marched the full distance. But if the tail of the column on Willoughby Run had followed the route all the way to Black Horse Tavern, then retracted its steps to and along the Cashtown pike, and eventually reached the region of Round Top, it would have traveled thirteen miles or more, while those who assailed the Wheat Field would have gone almost thirteen miles.

Considering that McLaws lost an hour at the tavern while the tail

of the column was being turned about and moved far enough ahead
to release the front elements, and that broken terrain was traversed,
Longstreet's men did some respectable marching that afternoon. It
is reasonable to assume that the average soldier covered eight miles
to reach his stepping-off place. That would mean a minimum of two
and a half, and perhaps three hours. Where some mileage may have
been saved by not using the roads, time probably was sacrificed by
the slower pace in the rough woods and fields.

It is quite clear that Law's brigade could not have made this entire
march and performed as nobly as it did during the remainder of the
day. But what it did was not pleasant. "We moved very slowly," Law
said, "with frequent halts and deflections from the direct course."[8]
In the fields the two divisions doubled and moved abreast each
other and at length Hood passed across the front of McLaws. This
put Law's brigade on the extreme right of Lee's army.

From Kershaw's statement that Willoughby Run was dry,[9] it may
be conjectured that the Confederates had to rely on the map Johnston
had drafted hurriedly for Lee. The run had had plenty of water
farther upstream because of the heavy June rains. Kershaw must not
have been oriented on his map, or else was forgetful when he wrote in
later years.

Kershaw's men were toiling along when Longstreet passed them
"his eyes cast to the ground, as if in deep study, his mind disturbed."
He had "more the look of gloom" than had ever been noticed before.[10]
Obviously disconsolate, he was none the less submissive.

Did Longstreet unnecessarily delay the attack that should have been
delivered in the morning? There are these points: Lee consented to
await the arrival of Law's brigade before attacking.[11] Law came at
noon.[12] The time of the delay is thus reduced to three and a half
hours, from 12:00 until 3:30 P.M., when Hood was in position to
begin his bombardment.[13] These hours are well accounted for by
Longstreet's march behind the battlefield, as he groped for a good
route by which to reach Meade's flank undetected. The afternoon may
have been filled with mistakes, but not with stalling. Some have accounted the lost hours precious, but none can ever know.

The original fault unquestionably goes back to Stuart. Had he
been playing his accustomed role he would have explored the roads
and known the routes Longstreet should follow to gain the enemy
flank. That was the purpose of cavalry. Also Lee did not have a

large enough staff to make the necessary reconnaissance in a strange country, where he could draw but little on the civilian population either for guides or reliable information.

But with conditions as they were—without Stuart and without adequate knowledge—the fault in the main undoubtedly was Longstreet's. He should have investigated the routes in the wasted morning hours while Law was hastening to join him. He should have checked just how much Johnston knew before the column reached Black Horse Tavern and was about to be exposed.

Longstreet's ardor mounted as he went forward. He wanted to fall suddenly and unexpectedly on the Federal left and roll it up, as Jackson had done at Chancellorsville. All that was lacking was a touch of Jackson's ingenuity and intuition. In the end, nobody in the army was more impatient to begin than Longstreet,[14] and when he finally launched his divisions, nobody could have attacked more furiously.

Did Longstreet's march and countermarch impair Lee's chances of victory and damage the Southern cause? Careful critics are compelled to wonder, because there were events also on the Federal side of the valley, some of them errors of alignment that unquestionably assisted Longstreet's assault.

2. Sickles Finds Butternuts in the Woods

Cemetery Ridge, extending south from Cemetery Hill, loses elevation just as Seminary Ridge recedes immediately opposite it.

One of those large lumps of ground that seem to complicate battle-fields rises at this point about midway between the two ridges. Colonel Long had observed the ground, had reconnoitered it as a position for Confederate artillery and was apprehensive the Federals would get there before Longstreet.[15] Some felt the Confederate line should rest here and continue along the Emmitsburg road instead of in the woods to the west along the lower Seminary Ridge.

At the summit of the hump, where the Emmitsburg road crosses it, a byroad leads back to the Taneytown road. At the southwest corner of the intersection was a peach orchard, opposite which was the Wentz farmhouse. This high ground, constituting a short ridge that commanded the depression between Cemetery Ridge and Little Round Top, might be used to advantage by either Confederate or Federal artillery; under certain conditions it might become the key to the battlefield, as the similar rise of Hazel Grove was at Chancellorsville.

Having little cover except the thin foliage of peach trees, it could be hammered by the artillery of either army and turned into a charnel house. It was not so much a place to be on as a place not to let the enemy hold. It could serve the Confederates better than the Federals because just west was Pitzer's woods, where supports would have cover, while on the eastern side were cultivated fields that afforded little protection to infantry. Should the main Federal battle line run through the Peach Orchard, a salient would be created, with neither face of the salient possessing any natural strength.

Meade's orders to Sickles contained some of the ambiguities that at times ruin battles or empires. He told Sickles to fall in on the left of the Second Corps, in the position that had been occupied by the Twelfth Corps during the night. Geary's division of the Twelfth Corps, by Hancock's instructions, had camped at the base and sent two regiments to the summit of Little Round Top, which gave security to the Federal left. Now Meade—and here was an uncertainty—told Sickles to extend his corps to the left to Little Round Top, "provided it was practicable to occupy it."[16] When Sickles extended his lines, he found he was not on high ground, but rather in a depression between Cemetery Ridge and Little Round Top, with fields made mushy here and there by the recent heavy rains. In front of this low land a creek, Plum Run, emerged to flow down a narrow valley into Rock Creek south of the battlefield.

Early in the morning Meade sent his son and aide, Captain George Meade, to Sickles to inform the corps commander where army headquarters would be located, and to ascertain if the Third Corps was in its proper position. Having been up most of the night, Sickles was taking a nap in his tent, so Meade, Jr., talked with Captain George E. Randolph, commander of the Third Corps artillery. Randolph went into Sickles' tent and came out with word that the corps was not in position and that Sickles had some doubt about where he should place it. The time was about 6:00 A.M.[17]

At 7:00 A.M. young Meade returned with more positive instructions for Sickles—to take over the position vacated by Geary. Geary had left at 5:00 A.M. to join the rest of the Twelfth Corps near Culp's Hill, but he had been so concerned about Little Round Top that he had sent a staff officer to describe it and request that, if troops were not to occupy it at once, Sickles should send a staff officer to see the ground. Sickles answered noncommittally that he would attend to the matter. Neither troops nor staff officer came, and Geary finally pulled out and left Little Round Top untenanted.

Birney, commanding one of Sickles' divisions, came up at 7:00 A.M. and extended his line to cover Little Round Top; all again appeared to be well. Still Sickles was dissatisfied, feeling that it would be harder to defend the valley if pounded by artillery than the elevation along the Emmitsburg road. He requested Meade to inspect the ground in person. When Meade did not come, Sickles about the middle of the morning rode to headquarters. Meade told him again that he was to occupy the position Geary had held on the previous evening. Sickles informed Meade, according to Meade's explanation of the conversation, that Geary had had no position so far as he could see, though in the neighborhood of his corps was good ground for artillery. He desired Meade to send a staff officer to see if it would not serve that purpose. This high ground was the Peach Orchard ridge.

When Sickles asked Meade if he were not authorized to align his corps in the manner he judged most suitable, Meade, by his own account of the conversation, replied, "Certainly, within the limits of the general instructions I have given you; any ground within those limits you choose to occupy I leave to you."

Meade then directed his chief of artillery, Brigadier General Henry J. Hunt, to look over the ground in question.

The New York *Herald* correspondent on the field, who claimed to have made the closest possible investigation of the meeting between Meade and Sickles and other phases of this episode, did not credit the commanding general with words so gentle. To Sickles' complaint that his front was exposed, Meade was quoted as replying: "Oh, generals are apt to look for the attack to be made where they are."

Meade was capable of sharpness and may have so worded it. Sickles did not take time to determine whether it was a jest or a jibe, but implored Meade to look over the ground himself. Meade, still concerned about his right, declined.

But Hunt went, looked over the situation, and tended to agree with Sickles that the high ground in front was superior to what he occupied in a direct line between Cemetery Ridge and Little Round Top.[18] Still, Hunt saw disadvantages and declined to issue any orders, until he could consult with Meade; orders would no doubt be forthcoming.

Careful and intelligent as Meade's course had been to that time, it is difficult to understand his stubborn reluctance personally to investigate his left flank. Perhaps he believed with Lee that the battle lines were running mainly east and west, and that the armies faced north and south. The Round Tops then would be too far in the rear to require more than garrisoning. Whatever was in his mind, Meade ignored Sickles' pleadings.

Meade was justifiably concerned about his right. He could not understand why Johnson would be coiled around him there unless the plan was to attack the soft underside of the Federal army along the Baltimore pike, a lifeline as essential to Meade as the Cashtown road was to Lee. But his left was worth a glance at least.

The afternoon rolled along and no orders came to Sickles. He learned that Buford's cavalry, which had been protecting the Federal left in the region of Round Top, had been ordered back to Westminster to recuperate. Thus the left flank of the army was exposed, and Ward's brigade of Birney's division became the left element of the army. Sickles remonstrated to Meade that Buford's withdrawal had left his flank naked, and Meade replied that he had not so intended and would have Buford recalled. But the cavalryman was well on his way toward Westminster and did not return to the theater; all the other cavalry, except a few corps details, was on the army's right.

Having no cavalry protection and with woods in his front that might hide a lurking enemy, Sickles sent out some of Berdan's regular army sharpshooters and a good Maine regiment, the 3rd, which all afternoon had been puzzled by what it considered the "unaccountable sluggishness"[19] of the Confederate army, the aggressiveness of which it knew from many other fields. Under Colonel Moses B. Lakeman the Maine men crossed the Emmitsburg road, moved west beyond the Sherfy house and entered the deep Pitzer woods, where on the previous evening the pickets of the 4th Maine Regiment had heard the soft drawling words of men obviously not Yankees. It was now twelve o'clock.

They had advanced less than a hundred yards into the heavy timber when ahead of them they detected skirmishers of what proved to be the 8th, 10th, and 11th Alabama infantry regiments of Wilcox's brigade, Anderson's division, Hill's corps.

Working with Berdan's sharpshooters, the Maine infantry drove these skirmishers back and soon unveiled three long enemy infantry lines, waiting 300 yards away. The Maine men claimed that the regular sharpshooters had taken all the trees and they had only the open spaces, but they looked on themselves as "one of the hardest fighting regiments in the Army of the Potomac." They declined to give way until they had battled Anderson's division for twenty-five minutes. Then they went back through the woods, across three quarters of a

mile of open farmland, reached Sickles' lines in the depression, and
reported to the corps commander that the main Confederate army
was not facing Culp's and Cemetery hills, or menacing Meade's right,
but was ready to step off from the woods directly in his front.[20]

3. Sickles Takes the High Ground

That was enough for the burly old politico-warrior who commanded
two of the army's most distinguished divisions. He had asked Meade
for help and had been treated cavalierly, at the very least. Now the
only things left to him were the drums and bugles. The Army of the
Potomac was about to witness one of the great sights of its spotted
and often spectacular career. It was three o'clock.

Across the open ground, three quarters of a mile in depth, moved
the two veteran divisions in battle order, drums beating the quick
step, flags waving, artillery rolling, heavily laden caissons growling on
their axles, cavalry patrols on the flanks, a cloud of skirmishers in
front. Old Dan Sickles was going to the war.

The right division, once Hooker's, was now commanded by Brigadier General Andrew A. Humphreys, commonly recognized as one of
the most capable general officers in the Federal Army. Meade had
wanted him for his chief of staff but did not judge it prudent to drop
Butterfield in the middle of a campaign. His grandfather had designed
and built the frigate *Constitution,* which had figured in great moments
of American history. Humphreys, a Pennsylvanian, had become an
engineer after being graduated from West Point, but he could not be
spared from infantry commands, where he was repeatedly cited for
gallant and meritorious service.

Sickles' other division was led by the Alabama-born David B.
Birney. It had been commanded earlier by one of the most gallant
of Americans, Major General Philip Kearny, who had been killed at
Chantilly. The tradition and spirit of this soldier of fortune, who had
fought on three continents, still hung over the division; long after the
war the legend persisted that he might be seen at night riding a white
horse through the sky or across the Jersey meadows, calling his men
to follow him in quest of glory.

One of his old regiments, the 20th Indiana raised at Lafayette,
became known as the "Fighting Three Hundred." They were mostly
farmers' sons, clerks, and Lafayette high-school boys, and they liked
to say that they were all Western-born except Patrick Maloney, who,
when he enrolled and was asked about his birthplace, replied, "I was
born in Ireland, sir, but I think Indiana is me native state."[21]

The Hoosiers were observers on the Peninsula when Kearny, punctilious in his military requirements, saw several officers of another command loafing by the roadside. Thinking they were of his division, he admonished them for straggling—he had a stinging tongue. They listened to him courteously, then one saluted and said with quiet dignity that the general was mistaken and they did not belong to his command.

"Pardon me, gentlemen," Kearney said apologetically. "I will take steps to know how to recognize my men hereafter."

On returning to headquarters he devised a diamond-shaped piece of red cloth for all of his division to wear on their caps. The soldiers called it the "Kearny Patch." The division wore it and eventually the corps adopted it.[22] The idea spread and when Hooker took command he assigned to each corps its identifying insignia. The custom has prevailed in the American army to the present day, though the patches are now worn on the sleeve.

From no point along the line was the advance of Sickles' ten thousand soldiers a more spectacular sight than at Hancock's position on Cemetery Ridge. Hancock had just ridden up and dismounted, and was talking with Brigadier General John C. Caldwell, commanding his 1st division, Colonel Patrick Kelly, commanding the 88th New York, and Colonel Richard Byrnes of the 28th Massachusetts. A few minutes after three o'clock, many of the soldiers were playing euchre while others were toasting hardtack and frying bacon. The day was warm and now clear; open fields stretched away to the Emmitsburg road. Suddenly the Second Corps men detected a commotion on their left. They dropped their cards and hardtack and crowded to where they could witness the simultaneous and orderly movement of this great body of men. "How splendidly they march!" "It looks like a dress parade, a review."[23]

Hancock leaned on his sword and rested one knee on the ground. He watched with surprise, even with some amusement. The placement of the Third Corps half to three quarters of a mile in advance of the main line left a great gap between it and his left. Grave as this was, it was almost ludicrous. Turning to the other officers, he smiled and said, "Wait a moment, you will see them tumbling back."[24]

But it was more than a moment. An hour passed before he called quietly, "Caldwell, get your division ready."[25]

The period of grace allowed the Third Corps at its Peach Orchard salient was due to Lee's plan of attacking *en echelon*. The storm had not yet broken on the far Federal left. Sickles would be given enough time to align his men, post his artillery, and make ready for the enemy. He leveled fences to facilitate the movements of his troops and to provide a field of fire. Birney's division was on the left, stretched thin from the orchard to the great hump of rocks in front of Little Round Top called the Devil's Den. He could not reach back as far as Little Round Top, and so it was left uncovered. The line ran along the front of a wheat field and faced southwest.

Humphrey joined Birney north of the Wentz farmhouse and ran along the Emmitsburg road, facing northwest. This left a sharp angle, or salient, at the Wentz house and the Peach Orchard. The advance of the corps had invited Confederate fire, and now the shells crashed through the Peach Orchard and apple trees farther up the road. The men hugged the ground, knowing it was a prelude to an infantry attack. The 3rd Maine had not been permitted to rejoin its brigade, Ward's, which was on Birney's left at the Devil's Den, but had been retained with Graham after it had come back from Pitzer's woods. It faced along the Emmitsburg road behind the orchard fence. It was 3:45 P.M.

Colonel Lakeman could look out to the south across the country beyond the Emmitsburg road, and there he saw the gray ranks and glistening bayonets of heavy masses of Confederate infantry moving far on the left. Hood's division was marching toward the Round Tops. Lakeman hurried off word to Captain Randolph, the artillery chief of the Third Corps, who threw some shells at the distant gray columns. Thus the battle of July 2 was opened.[26]

Meade, meantime, had called a council of his corps commanders at his headquarters cottage just behind the lines on the Taneytown road. There appears to be little basis for the contention that he intended at this stage to retreat to his Pipe Creek line, though he did not seem warmly attached to the position. Nothing had happened to make his situation worse, and much to improve it, since he had reached the field. The Sixth Corps was coming up and formidable works had been constructed on Cemetery and Culp's hills, where artillery had been skillfully placed to enfilade the approaches. The arrival of the Sixth Corps allowed him to shift his reserves. The bulk of the corps was placed on his right, where the Fifth Corps had been in support. He moved the Fifth to the left and the units were marching or resting behind the Round Tops while the council was in progress.

Sickles was not prompt to answer Meade. He was busy arranging his new lines. But at a final peremptory summons he left the work to Birney and Humphreys and rode more than a mile to the rear.

At the door of the headquarters he was met by Meade, who had heard the voice of Longstreet's guns opening far down the line to his left. "General, I will not ask you to dismount," Meade said to Sickles. "The enemy are engaging your fronts. The council is over."[27]

Under the pressure of Longstreet's guns Meade at last rode with Sickles to inspect the lines along the wheat fields and at the Peach Orchard salient. With him rode Brigadier General Gouverneur K. Warren, chief engineer of the Army of the Potomac, whom he hurried off to Little Round Top to make certain it was garrisoned. The conversation with Sickles has been variously reported. Meade is alleged to have berated Sickles. But the New York *Herald* correspondent talked with "several officers" who heard him; their version was probably more accurate than the account after the wording had been polished up for the official reports or for exhibits in the Meade-Sickles controversy that followed.[28]

"Are you not too much extended, General?" Meade inquired. "Can you hold this front?"

"Yes," replied Sickles, "until more troops are brought up. The enemy are attacking in force and I shall need support."

Meade again indicated his uncertainty about the amount of front covered by the corps, which was stretched thin indeed.

Sickles said, rather defensively, "General, I have received no orders. I have made these dispositions to the best of my judgment. Of course I shall be happy to modify them according to your views."

"No," said Meade, "I will send you the Fifth Corps and you may send for support from the Second Corps."

"I shall need more artillery," said Sickles.

"Send for all you want to the artillery reserve," Meade told him. "I shall direct General Hunt to send you all you ask for."[29]

Such was the situation at the time Longstreet's blow was delivered against the Federal left.

Had Longstreet's delay been disastrous, or had his attack been delayed until the happy hour when the Third Corps would be caught isolated and exposed? A short time before, Longstreet could not have attacked up the Emmitsburg road because it was merely a no-man's-land between the two armies. There would have been nothing to attack. A short time before, Birney's troops covered Little Round Top and, even moderately defended, it would be impregnable. The Federal line ran straight along Cemetery Ridge. Longstreet would have had to change front and deliver his blow across three quarters of a mile of open land to reach the Third Corps line.

Longstreet's slowness did indeed seem fortunate. If he could launch a strong assault and Lee could follow it with timely companion assaults by Hill and Ewell, the battle might be won between four o'clock and darkness. This much is clear: that if Sickles erred in marching to the Peach Orchard, Longstreet was lucky in having delayed his attack.

Sickles has been called a Bully Boy,[30] and the name is apt if it implied guts and gusto. While Gettysburg ended the war for many, it merely began it for Sickles. Always there was divided sentiment about the prudence of his move. The intolerant Frank Aretas Haskell, Gibbon's aide, attacked him because "he was neither born nor bred a soldier," which might have been said about many of the regular officers, and as "a politician and some other things"—"a man after show and notoriety, and newspaper fame, and the adulation of the mob!"[31] These comments occurred in a private letter which was published during Sickles' lifetime. Two months before Gettysburg Sickles had seen Chancellorsville lost because he was pulled back unnecessarily from Hazel Grove. He was taking no chances. Spunk was a good thing to infuse in the Army of the Potomac, which from the beginning had woefully needed some fighting souls among the officers, whether they carried the union cards of the regular army or not.

In a survey of 56 generals who participated, Colonel John B. Batchelder, the official governmental historian of Gettysburg in the generation after the battle, found the opinion respecting Sickles' advance about equally divided. But Meade condemned him both in his official report and later, and the army tended to side with Meade, which gave the Bully Boy a lifelong issue. In the end, fighting all the way, he won handily because he outlived his detractors and went down swinging at the age of ninety-five. He got fifty years of argument, political appointment, and glory out of one afternoon of fighting, but never a monument—like the other corps commanders—on the battlefield.

In all that time the only man to reduce the controversy to its proper proportions was Lincoln. The President had to pass on Sickles' request for a court of inquiry to determine the fairness of Meade's charges that he brought on the battle before the Federal commander was prepared and thereby endangered the whole army and cause. Lincoln met him thus:

Sickles, they say you pushed out your men too near the enemy, and began the fight just as that council was about to meet, at three

o'clock in the afternoon of the battle. I am afraid that what they say
is true, and God bless you for it. Don't ask us to order an inquest to
relieve you from bringing on the battle of Gettysburg. History will set
you all right and give everybody his just place, and there is glory
enough to go all around.

Sickles' advance was unsound, though none can be certain how he
would have fared in his old position. The one at the Peach Orchard
meant a ragged battle line. With all his importuning for guidance from
headquarters, the blame is scarcely assessable against the corps commander alone. The old veterans, in their stories of the affair, usually
said he "stuck out like a sore thumb." He offered Longstreet a pretty
target and distressed his fellow corps commanders, but he did succeed
in getting the two armies locked in a combat from which they could
not emerge until they were reeling and spent, and until the future
courses of the two governments were fairly determined. That much
Sickles contributed, and it is rarely judged an outrage of grave proportions when a general whose commanding officer is preoccupied, be-
lieves his purpose on a battlefield is to go forward and fight.

4. Hood Discovers an Exposed Flank

As soon as he received notice from Longstreet that he would attack
the enemy's left, General Hood sent Lieutenant John McPherson
Pinckney, of Hempstead, Texas, with a detail of five others from the
4th Texas Infantry, Robertson's brigade, to determine the Federal
army's position and locate its flank.

They crossed the Emmitsburg road, scouted through the woods,
climbed to the summit of Round Top, looked down on the Federal
army with its trains and artillery reserve that had been parked with a
scant guard in the rear of the Round Tops, and discovered that its
flank was in front of these eminences. Thousands of Federal soldiers
could be seen along lines extending to the north but none were on the
summits.

Pinckney sent two of his scouts in haste to Hood with a message that
the left flank of the Army of the Potomac was in the air and that behind it were trains and artillery parks which might be made an easy
prize by a prompt movement to the south and to the rear of Round
Top. He urged that the high points, Round Top and Little Round
Top, be occupied by the largest force possible.[32]

Pinckney's scouts reached Hood just as Longstreet had finally got his and McLaws' divisions into line for the assault. It was approaching four o'clock. Hood saw at once the importance of the intelligence and hurried to the corps commander a request that the impending assault, instead of being directed up the Emmitsburg road and toward the Federal concentration already detected at the Peach Orchard, should envelop the enemy left, pass around Round Top, and take the trains in the rear.

No more difficult question could have been presented to Longstreet at this moment. The turning movement recommended by Hood, though more limited, was of the nature he had been urging on Lee ever since he reached the field, and in his bluff and uncompromising manner he had insisted to a point where their relations were becoming strained.

Longstreet has been severely censured by some writers for not at once revising his entire attack plan; at least, he should have halted Hood until he could again consult with Lee. It may be easily imagined that Lee, having waited what seemed almost interminably for the sound of Longstreet's guns, and finding the day slipping away from him, would have been provoked in the extreme had the attack again been checked to submit a modified version of the proposal that he had rejected again and again in the last two days. Such a last-minute delay would have seemed a mere pretext, and would have given him ample grounds for relieving Longstreet of his command.

These considerations must have passed through Longstreet's mind, for he flatly rejected Hood's recommendation. Accounts vary, but the story as told by Hood has become the accepted version. Hood said that after receiving the intelligence from his scouts he opened with some of his guns and developed the Federal line, which had its left resting on or near Round Top and ran concavely to the Emmitsburg road, with a considerable force on high ground near a peach orchard.[33]

All the difficulties of an attack across a country strewn with great boulders and broken by sharp ravines, which would disorganize and scatter an attacking force, now impressed themselves on Hood; he perceived also that an assault on the Peach Orchard and up the Emmitsburg road would expose his force to an enfilade fire from the main Federal line running from Cemetery Hill to the region of the Round Tops. He consequently judged it his duty to report even at this late hour that an attack up the Emmitsburg road was unwise, and to suggest the envelopment of the enemy's flank and rear.

Longstreet's reply was prompt and blunt: "General Lee's orders are to attack up the Emmitsburg Road."

Hood was not satisfied, having by now developed a strong conviction against the direct assault. He sent a second aide to Longstreet, only to receive the same unyielding and unelaborated answer: "General Lee's orders are to attack up the Emmitsburg Road."[34]

Clearly Longstreet judged that his province of discretionary action had been so sharply circumscribed that all he could do was to obey Lee's words implicitly. Hood meantime continued to explore with his batteries. If, as he thought, the enemy now occupied Round Top, it would be impregnable. It could be defended, he believed, without gunfire. The enemy would merely have to roll the huge boulders down the mountain side as his men started up. So he sent his adjutant general, Colonel Harry Sellars, whom he judged an officer of great ability, to explain the hazards and request Longstreet to come and inspect the ground himself.

Sellars returned with the same monotonous answer. Major John W. Fairfax of Longstreet's staff followed with equally emphatic notice that General Lee's orders would have to be obeyed.

Hood's disappointment was keen. "After this urgent protest against entering the battle of Gettysburg, according to instructions—which protest is the first and only one I ever made during my entire military career—I ordered my line to advance and make the assault."

As he moved out, Longstreet rode up. Hood again voiced regret that he was not being allowed to take Round Top in flank. He quoted Longstreet as replying: "We must obey the orders of General Lee."[35]

The evidence from Hood is not one of a sulking Longstreet. Though Longstreet had now discovered that his own views were strongly and independently supported by a division commander regarded as one of the best strategists and fighters in the army, he expressed neither personal satisfaction nor bitterness over Lee's rejection of them. The picture obtained from Hood is one of co-operation, not pique. Hood's reports were enlightening, yet they contained nothing that might not have been assumed by Longstreet when he made his initial recommendations. Longstreet would have moved the entire army whereas Hood would begin with a division, perhaps even a brigade. But Lee's plan was bolder and more aggressive. He would strike where the enemy was, not where he was not.

Another interesting account is available. William Youngblood, of

Birmingham, Alabama, a courier, said that Lee was present at the final meeting of Longstreet and Hood just before Hood's division went into action. He said that Lee shook hands with both generals and said "God bless you" as they departed. He heard Hood beg Lee to be allowed to send a brigade around the right of Round Top, through a pass or ravine which his scouts had described to him, that would lead to the enemy's rear, apparently the depression between Round Top and Little Round Top. Hood insisted that he could flank the Federal army and attack Round Top from two sides. But Lee had personally decided against Hood.

Youngblood quoted Lee's words: "I cannot take the risk of losing a brigade. We must do the best we can. When the signals are given you, General Hood, advance your men and do the best you can."[36]

The statement of a scout, made voluntarily when the incident was under discussion, cannot be disregarded. Also even a general may be forgetful about the details of how his proposal came to be rejected. Youngblood's account is persuasive, for one reason, because it places General Lee at the point where he might be expected when the main attack was launched. The commanding general would not normally be five or six miles away when Hood was about to make the decisive movement of the day at the opposite end of the line. Nobody was riding behind Lee with a notebook on July 2 and his movements cannot be reconstructed, but he saw Longstreet repeatedly and must have been near by at the time of the assault. Possibly Hood received a first report while Lee was there and had more complete information later that caused him to repeat his pleas to Longstreet.

One thing is certain: there was ample notice to Hood and, in turn, to his subordinates, that the flanking movement around Round Top was not favored by the commanding general.

Hood launched his attack with his right brigade, Law's, from the neighborhood of the Bushman farm, between the Emmitsburg road and Round Top. The Round Tops are two craggy mountains, the smaller a spur of the larger, and they are about 1,000 yards apart on a line from summit to summit. Little Round Top is more accessible mainly because it is 120 feet lower, but the ascent of both is steep and rugged except on the eastern side of the larger, where the drop is sheer. Superficially Little Round Top came to be rated as having greater military value, partly because artillery could be drawn up its sides more readily, but mainly because the Weikert brothers, Charles and John, had taken off the timber in the fall of 1862 to help meet the war's ravenous demands for lumber. Round Top was heavily wooded; Little Round Top was a bald crag. Visibility was difficult through the trees from Round Top; it was open and easy from Little Round Top.

That accounted for the placing of a Federal signal station on Little Round Top instead of Round Top, which commanded more of the surrounding country. The trees on Round Top also seemed to make it unsuitable for posting guns.

5. Colonel Oates Looks from Round Top

Brigadier General Evander McIver Law, a professor of history and belles-lettres, was twenty-six years old at the time of Gettysburg. A South Carolinian, he had a heritage of in-the-woods fighting. His grandfather and two great-grandfathers had been soldiers under Francis Marion and one had lost his life while serving in the "Swamp Fox's" little band. General Law had taught at Kings Mountain Military Institute, then had established a military school at Tuskegee, Alabama, of which he was principal when the war came. From his captaincy of the Alabama Zouaves to his command of the Alabama brigade of Hood's division, his service had been brilliant and his promotion rapid. Now, after Hood, he was the senior officer in what would probably have been rated, by public opinion in the South, Lee's outstanding combat division.

Law had opportunity to rest his brigade only a few minutes after its march of twenty-four miles to the battlefield. Then he fell in with Hood, marched and countermarched, and eventually reached the far right of Lee's army in the woods in front of Round Top.

Law's brigade was formed with the 44th and 48th Alabama on the right, the 47th and 4th on the left and the 15th Regiment, commanded by Colonel William C. Oates, in the center. Robertson's Texas brigade was next in line to the left, then "Tige" Anderson's Georgians. "Rock" Benning with another Georgia brigade was in the rear of the center as a division reserve.

Irrespective of the long delay that had attended Longstreet's preparations, the attack signal came a few minutes too soon for Oates's 15th Alabama. The line had been formed at 3:30 P.M.[37] and shortly thereafter Hood drew fire from Federal batteries in the Devil's Den region in front of Little Round Top. During this bombardment which destroyed any remaining element of surprise, and while the regiment was awaiting the attack signal, the canteens were found low on water.

Colonel Oates detailed two men from each of his eleven companies to take the canteens to a well about 100 yards in the rear—probably that of the Snyder or Bushman farm—to supply the regiment with fresh water before it went into battle against the formidable-appearing hills ahead. The twenty-two water carriers would have returned in another five minutes, but, as Oates pointed out, it was never the custom to ask the colonels if they were ready. When it was time to attack, then attack it was, without question. He wanted to await the water detail, but "the order was given and away we went."[38]

When the detail discovered that the regiment had gone on, it tried to follow, but it went in the wrong direction, inclining to the left. The twenty-two men entered a woods and shortly found themselves inside the Federal lines, prisoners, carrying virtually every canteen of the regiment.[39] The day was hot, cloudless, sticky, and in such an assault water was as essential as cartridges.

Oates moved the regiment along but found that Law had recessed his two right regiments, the 44th and 48th, then had sent the 44th to participate in the attack on the Devil's Den and had dropped the 48th back as a reserve. This put the 15th on Lee's far right flank— under Lee's plan of attack, the step-off regiment of the army. Oates noted that the Texans and Benning were moving *en echelon*. He compared the Confederate line to the rim of a half-opened fan. When Law struck the base of the Round Tops, which were treated as a single mountain in much of the Confederate comment, each brigade would hit the enemy a flank or quartering blow. That plan, however, was deranged somewhat by Sickles' advance and now the brigades were compelled to assail Sickles' line in front and not obliquely.

Oates complained that Law's skirmishers, five companies from two regiments, were commanded by two captains instead of one field officer. They did not work in harmony, but finally bore to the right, passed around Round Top, and reached the eastern side. Both captains, A. O. Dickson, of Brooksville, and J. Q. Burton, of Opelika, Alabama, confirmed this.[40] Oates complained that had these companies continued entirely around the mountain and joined him he could have captured the Federal ordnance trains behind Round Top.

As Hood's and Law's other regiments pressed ahead, they made a half left wheel in order to assault Birney's line, but the skirmishers ahead of Oates continued straight ahead against Round Top. Oates thought that an informed field officer would not have allowed this to happen, but the regimental commanders did not know the objective

Attack on Federal left. July 2, 1863, 4:00 P.M

251

of the attack until they were on the march. Oates followed the skirmishers.

Law finally rode alongside Oates, to tell him that his regiment was
the right of the army, that he should go up the valley between the
two Round Tops, feel for the Federal left flank, and do it all the
damage possible. He said also that the 47th Alabama on his immediate left had been ordered to guide on the 15th and act under Oates's
orders.[41]

Oates emerged from the woods, crossed Plum Run without stopping for water, and entered the heavy woods in front of Round Top,
where he found himself confronted by the 2nd United States Sharpshooters under Major Homer S. Stoughton, part of Sickles' command,
posted behind a stone wall close by the southern face of Round Top.

Oates continued despite the fire but noticed that he was being deprived of aid from the 48th Regiment, which was marching off in the
rear to support Robertson's brigade, already warmly engaged at Devil's
Den. A second round from the sharpshooters brought down Lieutenant Colonel I. B. Feagin and some of the men, and Oates concluded that he would have to oust these marksmen before going any
farther, which he did by swinging to the right with the 15th and part
of the 47th, and moving against the front of the sharpshooters with
the balance of his command.[42] This took him farther south and farther
from the gap between the Round Tops.

Then followed what must have been one of the most onerous
labors of the war, the advance of the two Alabama regiments up the
south side of the Round Top Mountain in the face of an annoying and
often effective fire from the retreating sharpshooters.

Here the mountain is steep and treacherous. Oates said his men
caught hold of the ledges and bushes and clambered over the giant
boulders in the face of the enemy bullets, while the sharpshooters
took cover and fired from crags and rocks "thicker than gravestones
in a cemetery."[43] Most were vastly larger than gravestones, and behind them whole squads might hide and fire in volleys.

Only young men as lightly equipped as these Southern regiments
could have made the ascent even if freed from harassment by expert
riflemen. But they were fortunate in that here the sharpshooters belied
their name and usually shot over the heads of the oncoming Confederates. Halfway up the mountain they abandoned the battle, divided,
passed around the waist of Round Top, and disappeared, apparently
issuing into the heavily wooded trough between the two Round Tops.

Colonel Oates was now alone on Round Top with two regiments, one having no water. He moved Company A to protect his right and continued the toiling journey up the southern face of the mountain, which is more difficult of ascent than the western. Hanging onto the bushes and clutching the edges of stones, the two regiments made their way finally to the summit.

During this tortuous struggle the 15th had ceased to think of blue-coated enemies, of rocks, bushes, the great oak trees that rose above them, or anything except one vital element—water and their missing canteens. Many fainted on the final lap, succumbing to heat and thirst. Oates halted them at the rocky peak, his right resting where the observatory now stands. The ascent is such that this point cannot be reached even today by motorcar, but only by a winding pathway, which meanders up the western face. One who climbs to the summit can appreciate the difficulties of the Alabamians, opposed halfway by sharpshooters and afflicted by an increasing intense craving for fresh water.

As Colonel Oates looked out through the trees, he saw below him Devil's Den, which Robertson's Texans were beginning to assault. The smoke of battle billowed away slowly, to hang like a cloud in the heavy upper strata of air. He saw the long battle line of Sickles' corps running like a thin ribbon from Devil's Den to the Peach Orchard, then bending and following the Emmitsburg road to the northeast. Farther away he could see the town of Gettysburg sprawling on the plain between Oak and Cemetery hills, while the flat land stretched away to the north as far as eye could reach.

Immediately beneath him, as though he could throw a stone to its summit, was Little Round Top. North of it, but within artillery range, was Cemetery Ridge, dense with Federal troops, and behind it the busy little white house, with its adjutants and couriers, where Meade had his headquarters.

As the commander of the 15th Alabama gasped at the view, he saw something else even more clearly. Guns planted on Round Top would make Little Round Top untenable. He could visualize their explosive shells falling into Birney's line and the abundant Federal artillery from Devil's Den to the Peach Orchard. In fancy he could see the Federal army dislodged from Cemetery Ridge, and the long gray column on the road again, marching on Washington. He could picture his Alabamians on Pennsylvania Avenue; the new red flag with its blue cross and eleven white stars floating above the Capitol; South-

ern independence ratified at the cannon's mouth; the war ended and
the boys going back to the loamy plantations of the Alabama black
soil belt, free and independent at last.

Let Law give him cannon on Round Top and the battle of Gettysburg was won!

Law's brigade had marched twenty-four miles and Oates's regiments had ascended without water the steep sides of a rugged mountain, carrying their muskets, ammunition, and haversacks. Few men,
according to Oates, would have been able to climb it even without
accouterments. "Greater heroes never shouldered muskets than these
Alabamians," he said. It was, indeed, a superb accomplishment. Now
they required rest.[44]

The two regiments had been halted five minutes when Captain
L. R. Terrell, Law's assistant adjutant general, appeared on horseback, having picked his way through the boulders on the southeast
side of the mountain, which is close to the sheer face, an extraordinary
feat of horsemanship. Terrell had been the author of a report charging
the 55th North Carolina with the loss of a gun at Suffolk, which
caused Colonel John Carr Connally to demand satisfaction. Terrell,
to give it, had specified double-barreled shotguns loaded with buckshot. But the matter had been adjusted. Now Connally had fallen
maimed near the railroad cut in the very first fighting at Gettysburg,
and Terrell had entered into a leading role at a high point of the battle,
where he might be able to give greater purpose to Connally's sacrifice.

His first inquiry was why Oates had halted his men. The answer
was before him: they were exhausted. Terrell brought information
that Hood had been wounded, that Law now commanded the division,
and that Law wanted Oates to press ahead immediately, turning the
Federal left and capturing Little Round Top. Oates explained his
present position. He pointed out the near-precipice on the northern
and eastern sides, and the difficult nature of the ascent over the stones
and through the timber on the west. The enemy, he declared, could
reach the summit only by the long wooded slope on the northwestern
side, where the pathway now winds to the observatory, which approach, he insisted, could in half an hour be converted into a Gibraltar
that he could hold against ten times his numbers. It should be occupied with artillery without delay; being higher than Little Round Top,
it commanded the entire battlefield.[45]

The question of whether or not artillery could have been drawn to
the summit of Round Top has often been answered in the negative.

But artillery, in the course of war, has been taken up difficult ascents. Wolfe in his quest for glory dragged two fieldpieces up the cliff at Anse du Foulon and fired grape on the Heights of Abraham.[46] Napoleon pulled his artillery over the Alps.

The Confederate army happened to have an engineer officer on the field who was an expert in such matters. He had served as guide for the advance of Twigg's division of Winfield Scott's army at Cerro Gordo, over what young Lieutenant Ulysses S. Grant would later call "chasms so steep that men could barely climb them" and "animals could not."[47] They broke down the guns and drew them up the opposite slopes piece by piece, by ropes slung from the tops of the cliffs. The engineer who picked out the route and supervised the operation could easily have shown how guns might be taken to the summit of Round Top.[48] He was probably not more than a mile away and his name was Robert E. Lee.

Oates urged that Round Top be held; though Terrell agreed it no doubt would be the best thing to do, he had no authority to change old or initiate new orders. Oates understood. Had the adjutant sanctioned it, he would have remained on what he regarded as the key to the battlefield until he could consult General Law.[49] But Law was on the left of the division, where Hood's other brigades were beginning to close with Birney, and Terrell's own mission was to urge Oates to hurry on and drive everything in front of him.

Here again may be seen how the inadequacy of Lee's and, in turn, Longstreet's staff hampered these generals in the conduct of the battle. The high command had no representative on the far right. No liaison was maintained. From the times Oates went into action against the sharpshooters on Round Top, until the morning of July 3, when on his part of the field the battle was over, he did not have contact with a single general or any staff officer except Captain Terrell, who merely brought a reiteration of his orders.[50]

If the Confederate soldiers who were lost a few minutes later in the assault on Little Round Top could have been concentrated to hold Round Top, and had Law devoted his main effort to dragging a battery to or near the summit, the story of the battle on the Confederate right surely would have had a different ending. More trees than the Weikert brothers had felled on Little Round Top in an autumn could have been cut by 500 Alabama axmen before sundown. Who could doubt that had Meade looked out on a well-supported battery on Round Top before going into his council of corps commanders that night, he would have reflected even more earnestly on the advantages of his Pipe Creek line and the prudence of withdrawing the badly hammered Federal army?

Oates, in compliance with his orders, moved his command down the northwest side of the mountain, meeting not a single squad of Federal soldiers. Perhaps it was with the descent of these Alabama regiments from Round Top, step by step, that the cause of Southern independence languished. The Confederates passed to the rear of what has become known as Vincent's Spur, a toss-up of earth and rocks between the Round Tops. Less than 300 yards away was the great park of Federal trains, the supply and ordnance wagons of the army that had been concealed behind these hills at the time the main battle line was presumed to be farther north at the town. Oates thought them an easy prize, so he detached Company A of the 15th Alabama, Captain Shaaf, to pick them up.[51] A single regiment from Early's division, which Lee had wanted to shift to the right but which Ewell and Early had held tenaciously on the left, would have proved convenient for the Confederate cause on the right at this juncture.

With all but this one company, Oates moved toward Little Round Top. At a ledge of rocks forming a natural bastion he came up against four regiments—the 16th Michigan, 44th New York, 83rd Pennsylvania, and 20th Maine—composing the brigade of Colonel Strong Vincent, of Barnes's division, Fifth Federal Corps.

They had, according to Oates's calculations, been in position ten minutes—the ten minutes he had lost resting his men on the summit of Round Top because the 15th Alabama had been compelled to step off without its canteens.[52] Longstreet's assault may have been sorrowfully delayed on the afternoon of July 2, because of thoroughness, sluggishness, recalcitrance, coincidence or other cause, but finally it had been launched five minutes too soon for Oates to recover his canteens and get his Alabamians on top of Little Round Top.

The Prize of Little Round Top

1. A Decision on the Far Flank

Although Little Round Top had defenders hurrying to it from front
and rear, the man who first reached the menaced peak was Colonel
Strong Vincent, whose quick energy prevented Law from turning the
left of the imperiled Northern army.

Vincent was on the Taneytown road in the rear of Round Top,
awaiting orders near the home of John Weikert, when a messenger
sped up from Sykes looking for Brigadier General James Barnes, who
commanded the division of the Fifth Corps that included Vincent's
brigade. Barnes was hard to find that day and, according to Oliver
Wilcox Norton, Vincent's bugler and flag-bearer, had not been seen
since morning, was not at the head of the column, and "if he gave
an order during the battle to any brigade commander I fail to find a
record of it in any account I have read."[1]

So Vincent intercepted the orders from Sykes to Barnes to send a
brigade to Little Round Top, and declared he would take the responsibility of getting one there.

Vincent, who was not long out of Harvard, had been warmly admired by most other officers because he had made his regiment, the
83rd Pennsylvania, so precise and splendid in drill that McClellan
had rated it first in Porter's division. That was an achievement for
one who had prepared himself in the liberal arts and his father's iron
foundry at Erie, Pennsylvania, instead of at military school. But

Strong Vincent's personality was like his first name and would have marked him for advancement in any citizen army.

His young wife, a skilled equestrienne, had visited him on the Rappahannock and their long horseback rides, their gaiety, and their striking good looks made them familiar figures to the army, greatly admired for their ideal love. Vincent had passed his twenty-sixth birthday on the march north toward Gettysburg. All the while he knew the desperate nature of the impending battle. Near Hanover, on the evening of July 1, as he watched the flag of his beloved 83rd Pennsylvania unfurled at headquarters after the long march, he took off his hat and said prophetically to a staff officer, "What death more glorious can any man desire than to die on the soil of old Pennsylvania fighting for that flag."[2]

After telling Colonel James M. Rice of the 44th New York to bring up the brigade, Vincent dashed ahead to find a position, which he selected with an eye on the slope instead of the summit. It would require his men, if they had to fall back, to go toward rather than from the peak, and would allow reinforcements coming up on the other side of the mountain to form a line above him. That is precisely what happened. General Warren had been seeking other help. When he reached Little Round Top after leaving Meade, he caused a rifled battery at the base to send a shell into the woods east of the Emmitsburg road, which he suspected of concealing the enemy. He caught the gleam on the gun barrels and bayonets of Hood's men as the shell whined overhead, and learned, as Sickles had earlier, how the Confederates were massed on Meade's left, when they were supposed to be clustered around Gettysburg. Warren rushed off word to Meade, who ordered Sykes to secure the hill with the Fifth Corps.

The results came rapidly. Before Warren descended, First Lieutenant Charles E. Hazlett brought up a battery of rifled cannon and planted two of them—all he could find room for—on the summit, with Warren's help. The horses were lashed ahead but the straining men supplied most of the motive power, pulling and pushing at the spokes of the gun-carriage wheels and tugging them around the boulders and jutting ledges. Warren and Third Corps stragglers lifted one to the top.

When the guns were up, Warren, not knowing that Vincent was already beneath him in the woods to the left, descended the forward slopes of Little Round Top and almost at once caught the rear of Weed's brigade of Ayer's division, Fifth Corps, moving west on the

Defense of Little Round Top and Devil's Den. July 2, 1863.

Peach Orchard road to support Sickles. Warren's old regiment, the 140th New York, was last in the column, under command of the scholarly Colonel Patrick H. O'Rorke.

Warren, "apparently greatly excited," spoke to O'Rorke in his "usually impulsive style."[3] The colonel replied that he was expected by his brigade commander.

"Never mind that," said Warren; "bring your regiment up here and I will take the responsibility."[4]

That was all the young colonel required. He had distinguished himself in the Rochester, New York, schools and had been first in the class of 1861 at West Point, in which the cavalryman, George A. Custer, now one of Pleasanton's brigadier generals, stood last. O'Rorke's perception was quick; he saw Warren's need and responded. When Weed learned the cause of O'Rorke's about-face, he took his entire brigade to Little Round Top. Much as Vincent had anticipated, the reinforcements came in above him and soon his line of battle, drawn around the waist of Little Round Top, was being supported by

Hazlett's battery, then by O'Rorke above him, and finally by Weed's entire brigade, which fell in on his right.

Vincent had tossed the bridle rein of "Old Jim" to Norton, had reconnoitered the mountainside on foot for a few minutes, and had selected a line of strength before his regiments arrived.[5] The most critical post went to the 20th Maine, commanded by Colonel Joshua Chamberlain, a former Bowdoin professor, for whose stanchness during the next hour and a half Congress would vote him the Medal of Honor.

Oates with his two Alabama regiments that had passed over Round Top now assailed the right of Vincent's brigade, and were joined on their left by Law's other Alabamians from beyond Devil's Den and the 4th and 5th Texas of Robertson's brigade. The Confederates attacked Vincent's rocky citadel with desperate drive, seeking both to break the Federal line and turn it. Oates said the first greeting from the Federals was the most destructive fire he ever encountered; it shook but did not shatter his regiments. He drove in the Maine skirmishers, who could be seen through the smoke dodging from tree to tree, then advanced his right and overlapped the left of the 20th Maine Regiment, which constituted the extreme left flank of the Federal army.

Oates hoped, prayed, and cried out for support. Here was what chance does not often award a regimental officer, a second opportunity to win a great battle. Before him was the Federal flank he had been ordered to find and strike with all his power. Where now were some good Confederate regiments to help hit and destroy it? Where merely one regiment which might prove sufficient? This was what Oates believed: "If I had had one more regiment we could have completely turned the flank and have won Little Round Top, which would have forced Meade's entire left wing to retire."[6]

Even the five companies of skirmishers that had gone around the mountain to the east side and then disappeared would have helped. But there was not enough power to make the flanking movement effective. Chamberlain promptly refused his left companies and the Maine regiment held, though it was badly mauled and its front was subjected to a destructive enfilade fire. "The edge of the fight swayed backward and forward like a wave,"[7] Chamberlain said. Captain Howard L. Prince of the 20th used similar words: "Again and again was this mad rush repeated, each time to be beaten off by the ever-thinning line that desperately clung to its ledge of rock."[8] The regiment consisted of lumberjacks and fishermen from the rocky coast.

Strong Vincent exposed himself recklessly and fell early. His last words were typical: "Don't yield an inch." That night Meade sent a telegram to President Lincoln, who issued his brigadier general's commission, dated from the field. President Charles W. Eliot of Harvard recalled Vincent's student days: "He was one of the manliest and most attractive persons that I ever saw." Longstreet later acknowledged him as the man who saved Little Round Top and the Federal army.[9]

Oates was now in the front rank, fighting over the blood-stained rocks on which his two regiments were being wasted away by the burning yellow spurts from the Federal muskets. Often the lines surged so close together that neither side had time to load. They battled with bayonets, gun butts, and stones. Small parties broke through both lines and fought until beaten down. For a moment the Alabama colors floated over the Federal defenses. The Maine colors seemed certain to be lost, but when the next cloud of black smoke lifted, the flag was aloft, attended by no more than a single color sergeant, Andrew J. Tozier. He was holding his little sector alone.

Chamberlain had prepared for the fight by calling up the pioneers and provost guard, releasing the company prisoners, putting every spare man on the firing line. The sick list responded, dropping their pills and taking up their muskets.[10] Still the line looked knife-thin in many places.

Farther to the Confederate left the fight raged with equal fury. Gallant, gray-haired Lieutenant Colonel M. J. Bulger, commanding the 47th Alabama, was shot through the lungs. The old squire knew little of drill and nothing of discipline but had more than ample courage to compensate for those wants; although fifty-eight years old, he was unchallenged in the leadership of his regiment. As an Alabama delegate he had voted against secession; none now supported the Southern cause more ardently. He sat with his back against a tree, stranded when his line was driven back.

A captain of the 44th New York demanded his surrender and threatened to shoot him if he did not immediately hand over his sword.

"You may kill and be damned," said the lieutenant colonel, who had seen enough years not to worry about a few more when his men were dying about him.

He declined to yield except to an officer of equal rank. Colonel

Rice was brought forward to gratify the old colonel's whim in what were regarded his last moments. But he astonished his captors by living, and living lustily. The next year he was exchanged and was promoted to full colonel; after the war he graced heartily the town of Dadeville, Alabama, until 1900, when he expired at the age of ninety-five.[11]

2. The Lone Star Over Devil's Den

While Law's brigade assailed the brigades of Vincent and Weed, an equally desperate battle was being fought along the banks of Plum Run, on ground that came to be known as the "Valley of Death," and about Devil's Den, a citadel as rugged as but lower than Little Round Top. When Robertson attacked it was held by Ward's brigade, Sickles' corps, consisting of New York, Pennsylvania, Maine and Indiana regiments.

Two of Robertson's regiments, the 4th and 5th Texas, were helping Law on Little Round Top, while his other two regiments, the 1st Texas and 3rd Arkansas, threw themselves against Devil's Den, where a little later they were joined by Benning's Georgians. Robertson directed the Devil's Den attack personally,[12] while on the front slope of Little Round Top his other regiments, like the Alabamians farther around the mountain, fought on their own, without a brigadier general.

Devil's Den is no more than a sharp fissure, though the name is usually applied to the great mass of rocks that rise into a hill about it, and which are separated from Little Round Top by the narrow valley of Plum Run. In all directions were boulders, ranging in size, by a Texan's comparison, from that of a hogshead to a small house.

The Federals had managed to get Captain James E. Smith's 4th New York Battery in position at Devil's Den, on the extreme left of Sickles' line, with the 4th Maine and 124th New York in support. Four guns were on the crest and two were 75 yards in the rear. The battery opened with destructive fire, one shell killing or wounding 15 men.

Private James O. Bradfield, Company E, 1st Texas, described the Devil's Den fighting as "one of the wildest, fiercest struggles of the war,"[13] and none who was there disputed him.

The Texas brigade had a kind of symbol of its spirit in a jolly youth under twenty, Will Barbee, who served as a courier for Hood, and whom Private Bradfield described as "a reckless daredevil" utterly without fear. When a battle was joined he managed to get to the firing line and the soldiers had learned to watch for him. Now, as the fight grew desperate, someone called, "Here comes Barbee!"

The men saw the high-spirited lad dash up on a little sorrel, waving his hat. His horse fell but he "hit the ground running," grabbed a gun, jumped on top of a high rock behind which there were already many wounded, stood erect, exposed and fearless, and began firing. Below him the wounded loaded and passed up their guns, and he blazed away at any exposed bluecoat. Bradfield, a few paces away, knew that no man could live in the leaden hail where the lad stood.

Finally Barbee was knocked off with a wound in the leg. But he crawled back. Then he was hit in the other leg; again he got to his exposed perch. At length he was wounded so severely that he could not climb back unaided. He was last seen "crying and cursing" because the boys would not restore him to his place of danger.[14]

In front of Little Round Top and on its forward slopes the reckless charges continued. Colonel Van H. Manning, commanding the brigade's Arkansas regiment, was wounded, and Colonel R. M. Powell of the 5th Texas was riddled. Major Rogers took command of the 5th.

John Haggerty, a courier for Law, rode up the slope. He said: "General Law presents his compliments and says hold the place at all hazards."

"Compliments hell!" roared Rogers. "Who wants compliments in such a damned place as this? Go back and ask General Law if he expects me to hold the world in check with the Fifth Texas Regiment."[15]

When the fighting was at its hottest the men noticed a pint-sized private of the 3rd Arkansas behind a stump, biting the cartridges, aiming, and firing as rapidly as he could, all the while, between bites and shots, singing lustily:

> "Now let the world wag as it will,
> I'll be gay and happy still."[16]

Private Joe Smith of the 4th Texas was feeling the heat when he went in. He soaked a white handkerchief in Plum Run, tied it around his head, and started. When they buried him, they counted eleven holes through the neat white target.

Private Bradford complimented the Federals on their bravery at Devil's Den. But the Southern fire was too hot. Benning's Georgia brigade came up—"Old Rock, that peerless hero," the Texan called him.[17] It was 5:30 P.M. Benning walked back and forth along the front of his line issuing only one order: "Give them hell, boys—give them hell."[18] As the near-by private Bradford observed, the boys were following instructions. Within twenty-five minutes after the Georgians struck the 20th Indiana, it lost its Colonel John Wheeler, shot through the temple in the first fire, and 146 of its 268 men.

The Federal line bent in the Plum Run valley, then broke on Devil's Den. As Bradford put it: "The Lone Star flag crowned the hill and Texas was there to stay."[19] It was six o'clock.

Meade threw in two fresh Fifth Corps brigades, and the advance up Plum Run Valley was checked, but the Texans and Georgians held grimly to Devil's Den until the last gun was fired at Gettysburg. Benning captured about 300 prisoners and three of the six guns of Smith's battery, one having been disabled. His loss was heavy, among the dead being two of his regimental commanders.

3. The Retreat Is Made up the Mountain

From the eastern to the southern and western slopes of Little Round Top the battle rolled, with the same resolute vigor being displayed on both sides. On the western face the Texans and Law's other Alabamians battled Weed's brigade. The Texans and O'Rorke met head-on and in the first blast O'Rorke and 27 of his officers and men were killed. Warren had greatly admired the youthful colonel who answered his summons. "He was glorious," Warren said in simple tribute.

The battle lines wavered up and down the hill, like ribbons fluttering in the wind. The Federal commander, Brigadier General Stephen Hinsdale Weed, twenty-nine years old, a native of New York City and an artillery specialist at and after West Point, was on the bald summit of Little Round Top, exposed to the Confederate sharpshooters now concealed among the rocks of Devil's Den. He was hit and killed almost instantly. Captain Hazlett was standing beside him and stooped to catch any words he might utter. In an instant Hazlett, too, was shot dead. He did not speak, but Lieutenant Colonel David T. Jenkins, of the 146th New York, who stood near by, thought he heard Weed say, "My sister."

While the fighting surged up and down the slopes and among the giant boulders of Little Round Top, marked by charge and counter-charge and frightful carnage all along the line, the final decision was to be reached on the flank where Oates battled Chamberlain.

On another advance, Oates found the fire so destructive that his line inclined forward as it moved—he compared it to a man trying to walk against a heavy wind. Oates saw his brother, Lieutenant John A. Oates, fall mortally wounded close by. The loss of officers was appalling. But the gallant regiment with a shout made its final charge against the ledge of rock where it had already spilled so much blood. Oates used his pistol "within musket length," but the Maine soldiers would not be dislodged. "Five times they rallied and charged us," he said. As he looked back on this fighting, he thought the outcome of the battle was decided in this deadly struggle amid the rocks on the far left of Meade's army.[20]

The Confederate position was rapidly becoming desperate. It was 6:30 P.M. Stoughton's sharpshooters appeared from nowhere and threatened the Alabama rear. Oates said, "The blood stood in puddles in some places on the rocks." Still hoping for reinforcements, he told his captains: "Return to your companies; we will sell out as dearly as possible."[21] But soon with better judgment he ordered a retreat. Chamberlain saw the fagging of the Southern pressure and called for the bayonet. Oates claimed the retirement was by his order, but this spirited bayonet charge was persuasive also. Oates described his retirement: "When the signal was given we ran like a herd of wild cattle."

Dismounted Federal cavalrymen in the rear near Stoughton's sharpshooters were nearly crushed by the Confederates as they passed over and through them. Some of the troopers were grabbed by the collars and carried off prisoners. Alongside Oates was an Alabama private whose windpipe had been severed by a bullet; his breath screeched through his open throat as he ran. Captain D. B. Waddell, regimental adjutant, had been on the extreme Confederate right. He escaped but some of his men were cut off and captured. Oates thought he lost 40 or 50; Chamberlain thought he captured 400 or 500. The Federals probably picked up the companies of skirmishers that disappeared on the back side of Round Top. They vanished from sight and from the accounts.

Captain Shaaf rejoined the 15th Alabama with Company A that had been looking hungrily at the Federal trains without having quite the dash to move against them or the judgment to rejoin the regiment during the emergency on the slopes of Little Round Top. Shaaf had seen guards in the woods, some of the sharpshooters perhaps, and one Maine company, and had hesitated.

On Round Top Oates stopped Chamberlain with a determined stand and formed a line for a time along the lower northwestern slope. Then, in one of the amazing episodes of the battle, he retired to the very summit of Round Top. His men toiled a second time up the rugged slopes as though they had not marched twenty-four miles to the field, marched and countermarched for four or more miles getting into position, lost their canteens, and fought one of the most desperate battles of American history, all in a single day.

On the crest of Round Top Oates made an effort to re-form his survivors. But the men were scattered and the heat was still intense; numerous details were helping the wounded. Finally the gallant commander whose spirit had been the dominating factor of the attack on Little Round Top went down, overcome by exertion and heat. When he was revived by his physician, he ordered the regiment to form a line at the foot of the mountain. Darkness was coming on. The extreme right regiment of Lee's army rested at the base of Round Top on the night of July 2.

That night the Texans on Devil's Den could hear the bluecoats talking and working on Little Round Top. According to Private Val C. Giles, 4th Texas, the Yankee officers on top of the ridge were "cursing men by platoons," and in reply the men were telling the officers to "go to a country not very far from them." Something approaching hell could be found anywhere near by. The lines in some places were fifty yards apart. Giles thought there was not much good spirit on this sector that night. "Both sides were whipped and all were mad about it."[22]

Robertson's brigade (formerly Hood's) had helped win Devil's Den, but its regiments had been stopped on the slopes of the higher hill on the Federal left. The battle here was summed up succinctly, from the Texas viewpoint, in one of the postwar orations: "At the first roll of the war drum, Texas sent forth her noblest and best. She gave the Army of Northern Virginia Hood's matchless brigade—a band of heroes who bore their country's flag to victory on every field, until God stopped them at Little Round Top."[23]

There were other versions of why the Confederates failed to take the hill. Colonel Elijah Walker of the 4th Maine, fighting in the Plum Run valley, thought that if Benning had gone to Law's rather than Robertson's support the Confederates would have carried Little Round Top as they did Devil's Den. Hood had placed Benning in the rear to serve as Law's support, but in the advance through the woods and smoke the front-line units could not be readily identified. Emerging, Benning followed what he thought was Law's brigade. It proved to be Robertson's, and when Robertson called for help he responded. It was a natural but probably a costly error.

Longstreet, far off to the left, never knew until after the battle—years later, according to Oates—that two of his regiments had passed over the summit of Round Top. Oates took into action what he regarded "the finest and strongest regiment in Hood's division," numbering 500 officers and men, and came out with 223, a loss of more than 50 per cent.

Colonel William Calvin Oates, of Abbeville, Alabama, was twenty-seven years old when he became the main factor in the Confederate attack on Little Round Top. He was wounded six times in the war and lost his right arm at Petersburg, but being a man of capacity as well as courage, went on to serve his southern Alabama district seven terms in Congress, was governor of his state, and commanded a brigade at Camp Meade, Pennsylvania, in the Spanish-American War. With his left hand he wrote a gripping account of the desperate battle for the Round Tops. He omitted only one thing: He never did tell when his Alabamians finally got some water.

That evening the Federal army awoke to the importance of big Round Top. Colonels Rice and Chamberlain met Colonel Joseph Fisher, commanding a Pennsylvania brigade of Crawford's division, Fifth Corps, and they concluded that if the enemy should fortify it, Little Round Top would have to be abandoned. The decisions in both armies on this far flank were being made that day by junior officers.

Rice ordered Chamberlain to take the 20th Maine up the mountain. At 9:00 P.M. Chamberlain began the slow ascent, guided by the moonlight streaming through the foliage. At the summit his men captured 25 prisoners, then labored to construct a defensive line. The stone wall they built still shows that the New Englanders knew their rock work even by moonlight. Later they were joined by the 83rd Pennsylvania and 44th New York, and the extreme left of Meade's army was at last secure.

CHAPTER EIGHTEEN

Crushing the Orchard Salient

1. McLaws' Belated Attack

John Clark Ridpath, biographer and historian in the generation fol-
lowing the Confederate War, in writing his *Life and Work of James
A. Garfield,* described the incessant volume of orders transmitted
from headquarters during the battle of Chickamauga, where the future
President served as chief of staff to the Federal army commander,
Rosecrans.

He contrasted this with Gettysburg, where few orders were issued,
and said Meade "had little to do with the battle." The country around
Gettysburg being open, the division commanders merely stationed
troops where they would do the most good.[1]

This was a pertinent observation, but the striking fact often lost
sight of is that it applied to Lee's army even more than to Meade's,
and still more pointedly to Lee's corps. After the fighting was begun,
at few points did the corps commanders exercise more control over
the action than the greenest corporal. About all they could govern
was the time at which the different divisions or brigades might be sent
in; once a command was embattled the soldiers took over and the
top generals became simply onlookers. Eager observer Fremantle
noted that throughout the battle of the afternoon of July 2, Lee sent
only one message.[2]

Longstreet, in the decades after the battle, was made the object of
some just and many trumped-up criticisms—"jaundiced and malicious
charges,"[3] one of his men called them—but his main error was largely

268

overlooked. It was that of withholding McLaws for an hour and a half, under the unfortunate echelon plan of attack, while Hood fought unaided, with almost unprecedented fury, against the two Federal corps of Sickles and Sykes, and ultimately some of Hancock and Sedgwick as well.

Here, at a point where he had full control, Longstreet let his temperamental slowness hold sway. Instead of allowing McLaws to follow Hood in a matter of minutes, he restrained the Georgian and in turn his impatient brigadiers. The sharp edge of Hood's attack was dulled to butter before the lieutenant general gave the signal that sent in McLaws, and this tardiness slowed the rest of the army.

Hood had been wounded severely in the arm twenty minutes after the action commenced. Knocked from his horse, he was compelled to leave the field. The wound was a calamity to the Confederacy on more than one count. It deprived Lee's right wing of the supervision of a combat leader of great courage, experience, and mental agility, and left it under the professor of belles-lettres, McIver Law, an excellent young general, but lacking in Hood's inspirational and rugged combat qualities and experience in divisional command.[4]

The wounding of Hood also had a more far-reaching effect, for it sent him to his first recuperation in Richmond, to be followed by a second after he lost his leg at Chickamauga. There he established a circle of ardent friends; his winning personality even warmed chill President Davis. His conversation around the capital—with his critical analysis of the conduct of the Gettysburg campaign—stamped him in the civilian mind as a man who knew how to lead an army and win a battle. The result was his appointment later in the war to replace Joseph E. Johnston commanding the army confronting Sherman. Here again one of Lee's capable division leaders showed that although he possessed a full measure of courage and dash, he lacked the moderating qualities of caution and discernment required for high, independent command; thus, in more ways than one, was the Confederate War lost on the field of Gettysburg.

McLaws was more phlegmatic than Hood. He possessed a Grant-like stolidity but had strong compensating points, such as reliability and some of Grant's doggedness, which made his division as hard to dislodge as any in the army. His complexion was swarthy, his hair was very black, and his eyes were "coal black," according to the good reporter, Robert Stiles. He was short and compact, with big, square shoulders, deep chest, and large, muscular arms, and Stiles thought

that "of his type, he is a handsome man." But in dealing with him
one thought more of his tenacity than his grace, for impassiveness
and unflinching fortitude seemed to show all over him. Stiles compared him to the Roman centurion who stood at his post in Hercu-
laneum until the lava flowed over and engulfed him.[5]

Born and reared in Savannah, McLaws had been a student at the
University of Virginia when he received an appointment to West
Point. After his mature traits began to assert themselves, he was
found to have the same deliberate tendencies as his West Point classmate and present commander, Longstreet, though, unlike Longstreet,
who rarely showed a tender side and shunned paper work, he was
fond of detail and innately sentimental. On the Rappahannock he
and Barksdale would go to the river-bank at night and listen wistfully
to the Federal bands playing the familiar old army songs.[6] Stiles told
of riding with him through camp. He made "quite a notable figure on
his small white horse,"[7] but his men went on with their work, cleaning
equipment and guns, and paid no attention to him unless questioned.
They were respectful but not enthusiastic. He was not the most brilliant of Lee's division commanders. Because of his persistence he was
perhaps the superior of Early or Richard H. Anderson or Heth,
though not equal to Hood, Johnson, or Pender. And he was an officer
who could probably get more out of a situation than either Ewell or
A. P. Hill.

Hood went in at four o'clock, McLaws at five-thirty. McIver Law
contended that he halted the advance of Hood's division because of
lack of support on his left. He went to Kershaw, who commanded
McLaws' right brigade, found he had received no attack orders, urged
him to move forward, and thus initiated the attack of McLaws' entire
division.[8] Kershaw, however, said he stepped off at a signal from
Cabell's artillery, which opened about four o'clock.[9] The brigade
leaped over a stone wall, and Kershaw thought they moved with
"great steadiness and precision." Longstreet walked on foot with
Kershaw at the head of the South Carolinians until they reached the
Emmitsburg road. They could hear on their left Barksdale's drums
beating the assembly to take up the echelon attack in due season.
They marched east, then wheeled to face Birney's line and the Federal
battery east of the Peach Orchard.

McLaws was moving in the form of a right angle against the Peach
Orchard salient. Kershaw, supported by Semmes, faced north to attack past the Rose house to the Wheat Field. Barksdale, with Wofford

in his rear, faced east and attacked the Peach Orchard and Wentz farm. Kershaw came into line on the left of Hood's left brigade, commanded by Brigadier General George Thomas Anderson,[10] who had been assailing the right of Ward's brigade west of Devil's Den while Robertson and Benning were pressing back its center and left. Kershaw attacked at 5:30 P.M.[11]

Kershaw's cultured sensibilities may have influenced the South to call that first major battle of the war Manassas instead of Bull Run. According to a Richmond report, he had asked Beauregard to change the name of the stream because "Bull's Run was so unrefined." Beauregard countered with: "Let's try to make it as great a name as your South Carolina Cowpens."[12]

Manassas prevailed, though probably for other reasons. Kershaw had written up his independent account of the battle and made it public without reference to Beauregard, who was astonished, but Mrs. Chesnut, often the final arbiter of such matters, explained, "He meant no harm. He is not yet used to the fine arts of war."

Now, two years later, Kershaw had learned that the "fine arts of war" usually simmered down to spirited rushes and rapid volleys, matters in which his South Carolinians had become expert. He began against De Trobriand, who was worthy of the best South Carolina could offer. The emotional Frenchman, heedless of his own danger, rode up and down in front of his line, unaccompanied even by an orderly, exhorting his men to hold. The division commander, Birney, was in De Trobriand's rear, while Bully Boy Sickles roamed the lines insensible to the devastating fire from the Southern cannon.[13]

The battle of the Wheat Field and Peach Orchard was rendered complex by the converging of numerous brigades from both armies over a period of three hours. For an hour Anderson and Kershaw assaulted De Trobriand with great vigor and scant success. The Wheat Field was a triangular parcel of land about 400 yards on each of the three sides, defended in front by the 17th Maine, 5th Michigan, 110th Pennsylvania, and, at the Peach Orchard, by the 3rd Michigan and 3rd Maine, linking De Trobriand with Graham. The 17th Maine had the advantage of a stone wall at the southern edge of the field, where it had already met the successive attacks of Robertson and Anderson of Hood's division before Kershaw assailed the right of De Trobriand's line.

The two brigades of Barnes's division remaining after Vincent had rushed to the defense of Little Round Top—those of Sweitzer and

Tilton—were sent by Sykes to the aid of Birney and fell in on De Trobriand's right. Kershaw and Anderson attacked in concert and at six o'clock they were supported by the resolute advance of Paul Semmes's Georgia Brigade of McLaws' division, which came in on Kershaw's right. The Confederate pressure asserted itself. Semmes, whose brother, Raphael Semmes, was commanding the Confederate cruiser *Alabama* at that hour making for the South African coast, fell mortally wounded at the first fire. But Barnes's brigades were pushed back and De Trobriand's flank was threatened.

The miserable showing made by Barnes at this juncture was the source of complaint, denial, and recrimination. Certainly the brigades which later fought with great resolution under a new commander, failed to stand in the Wheat Field under Barnes. The New York *Herald* correspondent on the scene wrote that after Barnes gave way he refused to go back into line, while De Trobriand asserted that he fell back even before being engaged. Birney stated that when he saw Barnes withdraw without firing a shot he remonstrated, but without effect.[14] Barnes's retirement enabled Kershaw to advance through the woods on the west side of the Wheat Field and threatened De Trobriand's exposed flank and rear, at the very moment when McLaws' other brigades became menacing.

The Frenchman found great difficulty in disengaging his troops from their fierce struggle in front. "Third Michigan," he cried, "change front to right! I give ze order three or four times. Change quick, or you will be gobbled up. Don't you see you are flanked? Ze whole rebel army is in your rear."[15]

Birney, fearful that his entire line was about to collapse, ordered a charge by the 17th Maine, which was momentarily effective and gave the 17th and the 5th Michigan a position halfway across the wheat. Barnes's two brigades remained from 100 to 300 yards in their rear.

Sickles was watching the action near the Trostle house behind the Peach Orchard-Little Round Top road when he was hit by a cannon ball that shattered his leg. Captain M. J. Foote of the 70th New York, Sickles' old regiment, fearful that the men might be affected on the Third Corps line, formed a detail of a sergeant and six soldiers, who quickly covered the corps commander with a blanket and carried him into the Trostle farmhouse. His leg was amputated above the knee that night and he passed out of the Army of the Potomac. When Meade heard he had fallen he rode hurriedly to Hancock and placed him in command of the Third Corps as well as his own.

On the Confederate side, Robertson and "Tige" Anderson were wounded. Colonels in both armies were taking over the brigades.

Meade had already directed his cavalry commander, Pleasanton, at about 5:00 P.M., to get together what cavalry and artillery he could find, take a position in the rear, and be prepared to cover a retreat of the army from Gettysburg.[16] It was a wise precaution, because the battle was not developing satisfactorily for the Federal commander and it was good judgment to be prepared for the worst.

Birney meantime had called desperately on Hancock for help and now at 6:40 P.M. Caldwell's division, consisting of the brigades of Cross, Zook, Kelly, and Brooke, reached the region of the Wheat Field.

Colonel Patrick Kelly commanded the famous Irish Brigade, formerly led by Brigadier General Thomas Francis Meagher, that flew the green flag with golden harp alongside the Stars and Stripes from Manassas to Gettysburg and on to Appomattox. Possessing a preponderance of Catholics among its members, the brigade chaplain was a Catholic priest, the Reverend William Corby.

On every side was evidence of the desperate fury of the battle. As the Irish Brigade prepared to enter, the men were drawn up in column of regiments, with arms "at order" so that Father Corby might give absolution. Major St. Clair A. Mulholland, commander of the 116th Pennsylvania, which was attached to the brigade, described the striking ceremony.[17] Hancock stood close by, surrounded by his staff and high officers from other commands. Father Corby, mounted on a large rock, explained that absolution could be obtained if each individual made an act of sincere contrition and resolved to confess his sins at the first opportunity. He declared that the Catholic Church would refuse Christian burial to the soldier who turned his back on the enemy and deserted his flag. The men dropped to their knees, the chaplain stretched out his right hand, and spoke the words of general absolution. For many it was their last prayer. Said Mulholland, "It was awe-inspiring."[18]

Across to their left the battle roared around Little Round Top and the Peach Orchard. Caldwell moved his eager division toward the Wheat Field in the center of the distressed Federal lines.

Hancock looked on fondly as Caldwell went in. As Colonel Edward E. Cross, commander of the 1st Brigade, who had led the 5th New Hampshire in earlier battles, passed with his four trim regiments, Hancock called out to him, "Cross, this is the last time you'll fight without a star."

The laconic colonel did not even halt. "Too late, general. This is my last battle." Ten minutes later he was dead.[19]

Zook was in the lead. As they approached the Wheat Field, his way was blocked by the disorganized troops of Barnes's division. "If you can't get out of the way," stormed Zook, "lie down and we will march over you."

Birney, who was close at hand, also gave blunt orders for Barnes's troops to lie down, and Zook's brigade passed over their prostrate bodies as they went into line on De Trobriand's left. Zook began an advance through the Wheat Field and was driving the enemy when he was shot dead. Samuel Kosciusko Zook, of New York City, was a native of Chester County, Pennsylvania, who as a young man had won notice by his discoveries and inventions in electricity and had got into the army by prewar service in the New York State Militia.

Caldwell's division had marched south from Cemetery Ridge and had deployed in front of Little Round Top, then swept up to the Wheat Field, with each brigade joining the action as it arrived. After Cross and Zook, Kelly went in on their right and was soon at close quarters with Kershaw. Mulholland said his regiment, armed with smooth-bore muskets, was firing "buck and ball," consisting of one large ball and three buckshot, with which "a blind man could not have missed his mark."[20] Brooke made a spectacular charge through the wheat. After fifteen minutes the fresh Federal division prevailed, and the brigades of Kershaw and Semmes were driven back. The old Third Corps line was maintained and in some places advanced.

De Trobriand's wearied regiments passed to the rear through Caldwell's line. The 5th Michigan and 17th Maine had stood as sacrifices during some of the fiercest fighting of the battle. One soldier of the 3rd Maine was picked up with 48 wounds.[21]

That night when De Trobriand was making his inspection he came to the bivouac of the 5th Michigan and saw the pitiful little group of survivors. He inquired about others and was told, "These only are left." Quickly his eyes filled with tears, and he exclaimed with all his Gallic fervor, "Oh! My little Fifth! My little Fifth! I would rather command you than to command a division."[22]

2. Barksdale's "Most Magnificent Charge of the War"

But the battle of the Peach Orchard and the Wheat Field was about to take a new turn. Under the *en echelon* plan, the attack passed to Longstreet's only Mississippi brigade, commanded by William Barksdale.

The big Mississippian possessed a national but not everywhere an enviable reputation. This was not so much because of his ardent championship of the Southern cause in Congress, but because he was reputed to have walked to the Senate chamber with his fellow veteran of the Mexican War, Representative Preston S. Brooks, and looked as though he might hold off interference at the time Brooks rained the vengeful blows of his gutta-percha cane on the head of Massachusetts Senator Charles Sumner. Identities may have been mistaken.[23] A friend who accompanied Barksdale in Mexico commented, "What a noble, generous heart beat in that broad bosom!" Although a quartermaster with the Mississippians in Mexico he could be seen coatless, with a big sword, at the very front when fighting was promised.[24]

The Virginia artilleryman Stiles said Barksdale's was the brigade "I knew and loved best of all in Lee's army";[25] he felt safe when it supported his guns. The Mississippians were described as "irrepressible" by a Southern observer,[26] and the careful scribe Jacob Hoke, who tried to detect the distinguishing characteristics of soldiers from the different states as they passed through Chambersburg, decided "those from Mississippi and Texas were more vicious and defiant. . . ."[27]

As he waited for an opportunity to attack, Barksdale was nettled by Longstreet's delay and irritated by the battery that Graham had put up at the Peach Orchard, which kept his men pinned down only a quarter of a mile away. Longstreet passed along the lines.

"I wish you would let me go in, General," said Barksdale. "I would take that battery in five minutes."

"Wait a little," Longstreet replied. "We are all going in presently."[28]

"Presently" was not good enough for Barksdale, but he bore the orders. Longstreet objected when the men began tearing down a fence, saying it would draw the enemy fire, but when he rode off they leveled everything in front of them. Some, contemptuous of the Federal artillery, roamed about getting water and cherries. They began to hope when Alexander brought up twenty or more guns to their immediate rear. The guns were unlimbered behind the hill and the infantrymen rolled them up by hand. The delightful roar and stomach-shaking concussion were suddenly experienced as the guns were unloosed on the Peach Orchard, where Graham's bluecoats were scooping the earth with their bayonets and fingernails and hiding behind fences. After an hour or so the Mississippians heard an order for the guns to cease firing, and they knew their moment at Gettysburg had come.[29]

Barksdale rode along the line hatless. The great shock of sandy hair that had tossed in the halls of Congress was now white, a beacon for his brigade. When he rode he leaned forward as if trying to push his horse faster. "He had a thirst for battle glory," said one of his men. It was generally noticed that the fury of conflict kindled in him an incandescence that warmed all near by. His brigade was in line, with Colonel Benjamin Grubb Humphreys, planter, lawyer, and legislator, commanding the 21st Mississippi on the right. Humphreys had been dismissed from West Point after the great Christmas Eve riot of 1826, when the army authorities demonstrated that letting off steam was reserved for the liberal-arts colleges. A man of marked leadership, he was the first governor of his state after Appomattox.

The roar of Law's battle sounded on the far right, and nearer at hand Kershaw and Caldwell were locked in a deadly, unyielding struggle. It was six o'clock. Barksdale had about 1,500 avid soldiers who thought the war might be ended here.

The clearest, most ringing voice was Humphreys', and as he called his regiment to attention it brought the men up "like an electric shock."[30] Barksdale moved out in front of his old regiment, the 13th, and took his place before the flag. The men cast off their scanty packs —a blanket and a change of underwear—and each regiment heaped them and assigned a single guard to them. The field and staff officers dismounted. Orders were that none below the rank of brigadier general might ride because, as the brigade chronicler naïvely observed, "the government had a great deal of difficulty replacing the horses."[31] Then the drum rolled and Barksdale started, his shock of white hair waving in the evening breeze. The men let out the savage rebel yell, took the double-quick and, as they emerged from the timber, rushed the two rail fences lining the Emmitsburg road. The fences seemed to disappear as if by sorcery.

George Clark, of Wilcox's Alabama brigade, immediately on Barksdale's left, observed the unbroken line at the salient and called it "the most magnificent charge I witnessed during the war," and so it came to be termed in Mississippi annals.[32] Clark, later a Waco, Texas, judge, declared Barksdale seemed to be fifty yards in front of his men. John S. Henry of the 17th Mississippi quoted a Northern colonel as saying, "It was the grandest charge that was ever made by mortal man."

Captain G. B. Lamar, Jr., aide of McLaws, who carried the step-off orders to the brigade, said Barksdale's face "was radiant with joy." The general's long white hair reminded Lamar of the white plume of Henry of Navarre.[33] The enraptured captain watched him as far as his eye could follow, still out in front. "I have witnessed many charges marked in every way by unflinching gallantry . . . but I never saw anything to equal the dash and heroism of the Mississippians," Lamar said.

The British correspondent Ross who had been trailing Longstreet up and down the lines, was on hand to witness Barksdale's attack:

It was a glorious sight. The men who had been lying down sprang to their feet and went in with a will. There was no lagging behind, no spraining of ankles on the uneven ground, no stopping to help a wounded comrade. Not one fell out of line unless he was really hurt. . . . The guns in the Peach Orchard were pounced upon, and half of them taken in a thrice, whilst the others limbered up and made off. Hundreds of prisoners were captured, and everything was going so satisfactorily for a time we hardly doubted the enemy would be driven from his very strong position on the hills in front.[34]

Graham's brigade had plenty of spunk. It, too, had been pinned down, not for an hour, as Barksdale's men estimated the length of the bombardment, but for two hours according to Captain E. C. Strouss of the 57th Pennsylvania. When the enemy line was seen emerging from the woods, Graham's men did not wait. The 57th and the 114th Pennsylvania ran forward across the Emmitsburg road to meet them. The 57th jumped into the Sherfy house and outbuildings. About them the battle raged furiously for a time, and then the Mississippians swept on, having captured many trapped in the house and barn.

When the 114th Pennsylvania retired from the Sherfy buildings in front of the 18th Mississippi, the only avenue of retreat was up the Emmitsburg road. Captain A. W. Given, who had taken command when the higher officers fell, conducted the regiment, closely pressed by the enemy. Soon the road was filled with dead and wounded. One of the wounded officers of the 114th, prostrate on the road, witnessed a Confederate battery dash up with its guns. When the officer in charge saw the dead and wounded, he stopped the horses, had his men lift the dead to the side and carry the wounded into a cellar, probably that of the Klingle or Rogers house. He left them with a supply of water and said he would return after he had "caught the rest of the Yankees."[35] Who he was they never knew. He was off again quickly with his guns.

Break-through of Barksdale and Wofford at the Peach Orchard.
July 2, 1863.

The 141st Pennsylvania, stationed immediately behind the Wentz house, went in with 9 officers and 200 men. In "several minutes" it lost 6 officers and 145 men. After the regiment retreated a battery dashed up and unlimbered in the Wentz yard. The young gunner in charge dismounted and looked over the familiar surroundings. Sergeant Henry Wentz had come home from the South, wearing a gray uniform.[36]

The 68th Pennsylvania was at the angle. Here General Graham, personally directing the firing line, was wounded and he was carried to the rear. He insisted on returning and this time he was pitched to the ground when his horse fell; being stunned, and weak from loss of blood, he could only grope about when he rose. The attack of the 21st Mississippi passed over him and he was captured.

A native of New York City, Charles Kinnaird Graham had already built a career in the Navy when war came. He had served in the Gulf in the Mexican War, then had become a civil engineer at the Brooklyn Navy Yard. When he volunteered for the army, 400 coworkers followed him and he organized the 74th New York Regiment of Sickles' Excelsior Brigade.

As about 1,000 prisoners were being taken back by Major Fairfax, of Longstreet's staff, Graham among them, the Southern Artillerist William M. Owen talked with him. Fairfax had ordered a courier to dismount in order that the wounded Federal general might ride. Graham asked the name of the officer who had led the charge against his brigade. "Our generals do not do that sort of thing," Owen quoted him as saying.[37]

"It was a terrible afternoon in that orchard," said Private Alfred J. Craighead of the 68th Pennsylvania, which faced south at the corner.[38] In the orchard 12 of the regiment's officers were killed or wounded, leaving but 4 to extricate the regiment in the retreat. Colonel A. H. Tippin of the 68th took command of the brigade when Graham was captured. The 105th Pennsylvania, called the "Wildcat Regiment," left half its men along the Emmitsburg road.

Graham's men fought gallantly and retired slowly, pressed step by step by the relentless Barksdale, who stayed in front, all the time calling, "Forward, men, forward!" Eventually the Federal retirement became a rout. Barksdale drove straight ahead, indifferent to his flanks.

As Longstreet had escorted Kershaw, so he accompanied Wofford's brigade that followed Barksdale. It attacked the flank of Birney and Caldwell, left exposed by the rout of Graham. The courier William Youngblood, who accompanied Longstreet, said the general's attention was so occupied trying to see what Hood's troops were doing farther to the right that he did not notice how far he had advanced in front of Wofford's line. Youngblood had to warn him to save him from capture, and they checked their horses to let the infantry pass.

Wofford, a native of Habersham County, Georgia, had become a prosperous plantation owner and lawyer in Cassville, Georgia, before the war. He published the weekly newspaper and opposed secession to the very end. He had been a captain under Scott in Mexico.

Kelly's Irish Brigade was battling Kershaw and Semmes when Major Mulholland noticed a column passing from the Peach Orchard toward his rear. It looked like Confederates. Uneasy, he reported it to Kelly, who sent him to inform one of Zook's regiments a short distance behind in support. This regiment moved fifty yards and discovered that the column was indeed Confederate. It was Wofford's brigade coming in on Barksdale's right and threatening to cut off Birney and Caldwell.

Sickles' old line had now been penetrated in two places—at Devil's Den by Robertson and Benning and at the Peach Orchard by Barksdale followed by Wofford. Between these two points Graham's fragments and the remnants of Birney still faced Anderson, Kershaw, and Semmes. Being all but surrounded, the entire Federal line suddenly collapsed. Some units managed a fairly orderly withdrawal to the east side of Plum Run; others broke into a rout. "We were in a trap," said Mulholland. "A line of the enemy was advancing on the Wheat Field from the South, and Wofford's brigade . . . was closing in from the North."[39] He told his men of the 116th Pennsylvania to look to their own safety in the region of Little Round Top, furled the regimental colors, and moved down the corridor between the two lines of Confederates. Cross and Brooke were extended beyond Wofford's advance and were not critically exposed, but Kelly and Zook "were completely surrounded, and the only way out of the trap was to pass down between the two lines of the enemy."[40] Caldwell's division managed to extricate itself at frightful loss. The disorganized units found security behind Ayres's fresh division of the Fifth Corps, consisting largely of Regular Army troops.

Barksdale advanced about three quarters of a mile and came to Plum Run, behind which was a slight ridge. The Federal chief of artillery, Hunt, who in going about the field had been attracted by defensive positions much as a bootblack is by a pair of dirty shoes, had noted this ridge and labeled it the Plum Run line, keeping it in mind as a possible substitute for the Peach Orchard in its front or Cemetery Ridge in its rear. Here Barksdale hit something solid. Only the redoubtable West Point rioter, Colonel Humphreys, got his Mississippi regiment across Plum Run, where it ran smack into three fourths of the Federal army being rushed forward by Meade.

In the new line were elements of Burling's New Jersey brigade of General Humphreys' division, called back from the Emmitsburg road, but mainly some of Hancock's fresh troops. Burling had seen Barksdale in front of his men and assigned a company to pick him off. The new Federal line came out of the elderbushes along the creek and poured a withering fire into Barksdale's front, which was ragged and disorganized by the long advance over rough, broken ground. Barksdale fell; the Mississippians recoiled, then retreated.

Private J. C. Lloyd of the 13th Mississippi, who was close to Barksdale, was hit by a Minié ball; as the retreat passed over him a comrade stopped long enough to make a sling for his arm. Left between the lines, he heard a weak voice speaking on his right, and, turning, saw Barksdale on the ground. He crawled over and held his canteen to the general's mouth, but there was no water. The canteen had been pierced by a ball. He ran back for litter bearers, wandered into the Northern lines, escaped in the thick smoke, made a wide circuit, and got back to a field hospital the Confederates had set up in a barn. Meanwhile the Federal line had advanced and the general could not be reached.[41] That night Barksdale was found in front of a Vermont regiment. On the next morning he died.[42]

Meade continued to rush reinforcements to his imperiled left wing, stripping his center and right heedlessly in the supreme emergency. Soon most of the Federal army was marching rapidly toward the Round Tops. Ayers was brought up from the Baltimore pike half a mile west of Rock Creek to the defensive line established behind Devil's Den. Part of Gibbon's division marched from Ziegler's Grove on Cemetery Ridge to Hunt's Plum Run line. Newton, commanding the First Corps, sent in the weakened divisions of Doubleday and Robinson. Finally Meade ordered the Twelfth Corps, posted behind the walls and trenches it had been constructing on Culp's Hill, to hurry to the left, and it moved quickly, leaving a single brigade behind. Two Sixth Corps brigades were rushed to the left.

Longstreet was not much in error in saying Hood and McLaws faced upward of 50,000 soldiers. Said Longstreet with pride: "History records no parallel to the fight made by these two divisions on the 2nd of July at Gettysburg."

CHAPTER NINETEEN

Cemetery and Culp's Hills

1. Humphreys Extracts His Division

Humphreys, commanding the remaining division of Sickles' corps after the defeat of Birney, was left strung out along the Emmitsburg road destitute of support on either side. Graham's survivors, who had guarded the Peach Orchard on his left, were streaming back beyond Plum Run, their leader captured, their organization destroyed, their effectiveness ended. His right, far out in front of the main Federal line, was suspended, resting on no more than a fence corner where a lane ran south of the great red barn of the Codori farm. The lower part of this barn, a center of the fighting on July 2 and 3, was of stone and provided good shelter; the upper was wood, painted red, after the Pennsylvania Dutch custom established in Colonial times. It served as a landmark readily seen from almost every part of the battlefield.

Humphreys' position clearly was untenable. He stood alone, far out in front of the army. Before he had much opportunity to appraise it or attempt a withdrawal, he was hit by two brigades of A. P. Hill's corps—Wilcox' and Lang's—who were prompt to attack after Barksdale went in on their right.

Meade and Hancock, well aware of the danger, took measures to save Humphreys, who began a withdrawal which he hoped to keep systematic and unhurried, but which in time became chaotic. Hunt had combed the field for guns and now brought up 40, chiefly from the artillery reserve, and opened on the advancing Confederates to give

Humphreys time. Hancock detached Willard's brigade from Hays's division and then reinforced it with three regiments from Harrow's brigade, Gibbon's division—the 106th Pennsylvania, 15th Massachusetts, and 1st Minnesota—to help fill the yawning gap between Humphreys and his own Second Corps, the unemployed portions of which were still back on the main line—almost theoretical at this stage—that ran from Cemetery Hill across the low ground to Little Round Top. Meade, seeing the approach of Lockwood's brigade, a newly-attached New York and Maryland unit, placed himself at its head and led it into position.

The troops assailing Humphreys, who threatened to overlap his right and sever him from Hancock, were the fresh division of Major General Richard S. Anderson, who had reached the field too late on July 1 to take part in the battle. For most of the day Anderson's men had been lying in the woods west of the Emmitsburg road, waiting for the attack order to reach them as it moved through the succession of brigades. Of Hill's three divisions, Anderson was on the right, Pender on the left connected with Rodes of Ewell's corps in the town, and Heth, commanded by Pettigrew, was in reserve behind them on Seminary Ridge. As Anderson attacked, the order of his brigade from right to left was Wilcox, Perry, Wright, Posey, and Mahone. Perry was suffering from typhoid fever, and his small Florida brigade was commanded by Colonel David Lang, of the 8th Florida.

Anderson, whose influence on the progress of the battle promised to be of the first significance, was an officer who, as Sorrel pointed out, was loved so warmly by all who knew him that they hesitated to criticize him; yet he was, in fact, indolent. Longstreet had been able to get good service out of him when he commanded a brigade and he had performed well with a division in a defensive role at Chancellorsville. But Gettysburg was his first battle under Hill, who lacked Longstreet's blunt firmness and was likely at times to be so temperamental or erratic as to leave a slothful subordinate indisposed where Longstreet would have enforced action. Sorrel rated Anderson's capacity and intelligence as excellent: "but it was hard to get him to use them."

At about 6:15 P.M. on July 2, he arrived at the greatest opportunity of his career, when the question of his capacity was to receive its clearest test. Meade had been weakening his center, along with his right, by the dispatch of troops to succor his hard-pressed left, and somewhere there must be soft spots. Hancock, who manned the Federal line here, could expect no further service that day from Caldwell, and thus one third of his corps was gone. He had been using elements of his other two divisions piecemeal to bolster the endangered line, and while Gibbon's division was fairly intact, it had been left with a long front between Howard—who was still licking his wounds on Cemetery Hill—and the mass of the army that had been concentrated on the Plum Run line. If Anderson should hit with all his power, he was likely to discover something worth exploiting somewhere along his front.

Perhaps one of the tragedies of the battle, from the Confederate standpoint, was that in the alignment of the divisions, in which the order of their arrival was highly influential, Pender was not on Hill's right in place of Anderson, where he would have followed McLaws. But Pender remained on the ground he had won, and Anderson, coming later, was stationed on his right and ahead of him in the progress of the battle from Lee's right to left.

Anderson's brigades were to attack "individually and successively," and in that manner they began. Wilcox, an officer from the old Regular Army, was a bit on the shelf as a brigade commander alongside the zestful young men who in their twenties were giving Lee such outstanding performance, and he was disquieted at being passed over for divisional command. He always turned in a creditable, rarely a brilliant performance. His Alabama troops were as good as could be found in the army but things seemed not to work out for the best for their commander.

Wilcox, followed by Lang on his left, drove Humphreys ahead of them as they advanced to the base of Cemetery Ridge, all the time meeting a devastating artillery fire from guns on the crest of the ridge and musketry from behind the stone walls. Wilcox passed the Emmitsburg road about 300 yards south of the Codori house, while Lang brushed the farm buildings with his left flank as he advanced, passing over ground that would be traveled a day later by Kemper of Pickett's division.

Even the most adept of generals may lose their discretion in a supreme emergency. Humphreys, laboring desperately to extricate his division, had ordered the brigade of Colonel William R. Brewster, formerly Sickles' "Excelsior Brigade," to change front to the rear, an army method of saying things were getting too hot and the men had better get out, presumably in an orderly way at a double-quick, but in usual practice at a run. Hancock had sent reinforcements, and the 19th Maine of Harrow's brigade was lying in the grass in the rear of the Excelsiors, who, when they received the "change front to the rear" order, seemed about to break into a rout. Humphreys hurried back to Colonel Francis E. Heath of the 19th Maine, 150 paces in the rear, and asked him to have his regiment stand up and stop the Excelsiors with their bayonets.

Heath apparently thought that was not what his boys had come down from the Maine woods to do and declined to obey Humphreys—although the reason given later was that he did not want his own men disorganized by the broken troops. Humphreys then rode down the Maine line and ordered the men, over their colonel's head, to give his fleeing men the bayonet. Heath immediately countermanded the order; it is not difficult to know which officer the men obeyed.

Humphreys, enraged, ordered Colonel Heath to the rear, but the colonel, who had been stationed by Hancock, said firmly, though still respectfully, "I was placed here by an officer of higher rank [than you] for a purpose," he said, "and I do not intend to go to the rear. Let your troops form in the rear and we will take care of the enemy in front."[1]

The Excelsior men were now passing; some in good spirits shouted to the Maine regiment, "Hang on, boys! We will form in your rear."

They did that, but when Hancock tried to put Humphreys' division into the hole that had been left by the departure of Caldwell, the division had virtually been dissipated. Said Hancock, "I directed General Humphreys to form his command on the ground from which General Caldwell had moved . . . which was promptly done. The number of his troops collected was, however, very small, scarcely equal to an ordinary battalion, but . . . composed of the fragments of many shattered regiments."

Wilcox and Lang were not fortunate enough to strike a soft spot, but they moved ahead, firing and advancing until about 7:00 P.M. Colonel Lang claimed his command routed everything in its front until it reached a small stand of timber in front of the main Federal line. Here he called a halt to allow his wearied men to rest briefly. Wilcox's attack had fallen principally on Brewster's Excelsiors, while Lang attacked the brigade of Joseph B. Carr, a mixed command composed of Massachusetts, New Hampshire, New Jersey, and Pennsylvania regiments. The battle waged by these two brigades, which had comprised Humphreys' forward line along the Emmitsburg road, was more destructive to the Federals than the assailants, and Lang, who was applying a pressure on Carr's front and flank, declared that at no time in the war had he seen so many dead Federal soldiers on the ground over which he passed.[2]

2. *The Georgians Perch on Cemetery Ridge*

Anderson's next brigade was commanded by Brigadier General Ambrose R. Wright, who had enlisted in the 3rd Georgia regiment as a private at the beginning of the war. A poor boy from Jefferson County, Georgia, he had literally reared himself by his hoe handle, working a small patch of land while he studied at night by the light of a pine knot. He became an Augusta lawyer and a man of great force in Georgia public affairs, who did not wait for a commission when the sudden call to arms was heard. He was president of the state senate for a period in 1863 and presided while on furlough, but returned to the army after the session. At Sharpsburg he had been wounded critically in the breast and at Chancellorsville had been hit in the knee with a piece of shrapnel, but he was in his full vigor at Gettysburg, commanding his four Georgia regiments with all the fervor of a natural-born leader fighting in the cause of independence.

Wright took up the march at about six-forty-five across the long stretch of open ground between the woods west of the Emmitsburg road and the ridge where the center of the Federal army now rested. He crossed the road north of the Codori house; there the ground is undulating but exposed to artillery and infantry fire from Cemetery Ridge, and men were soon dropping from his ranks. His brigade front was about 400 yards, and his attack was directed at a battery which opened on him from Gibbon's position between the small clump of trees and Ziegler's grove on the crest of the ridge to the north. His brigade would just fit the distance between the clump and the grove.

The excitable Frank Aretas Haskell, Gibbon's aide-de-camp, described the advance: "The whole slope in our front is full of them; and in various formation, in line, in column, and in masses which are neither, with yells and thick volleys they are rushing toward our crest."

"On they came like the fury of a whirlwind," said Captain John E. Reilly of the 69th Pennsylvania, Webb's brigade of Hancock's corps.[3] The guns at which Wright aimed his charge were Lieutenant T. Fred Brown's 1st Rhode Island Battery, behind which was the 69th Pennsylvania, while the remainder of Webb's brigade was over the crest in the vicinity of Meade's headquarters.

Wright swept up the hill, captured the Rhode Island guns, and stood with his brigade on the crest of Cemetery Ridge, at almost the exact spot that would be the focal point of Lee's attack on the Federal center on the following day. While Wright's lodgement is often called a penetration of the Federal center, that was not precisely the case, because Webb's brigade of Gibbon's division, which manned the line at this point, was largely behind instead of on the crest, and had to be reckoned with before Wright might claim an actual piercing of the Federal army. But he was inspired by a sight of the Baltimore pike, loaded with refugees leaving the battlefield.

The instant was one of the critical moments of the battle for General Lee, and a continuation of the attack by brigades *en echelon* would have held a distinct promise of breaking the weakened Federal center. But Wright was alone and unaided on the ridge. On his right Wilcox and Lang faltered. While Lang was in the small woods re-forming his command, he saw what he described as a heavy column thrown against Wilcox that forced him back.[4] This was a portion of Harrow's brigade. Hancock personally directed the 1st Minnesota, a small regiment which made one of the gallant sacrifice charges of the battle and lost close to 75 per cent of its numbers.[5] Wilcox's retreat was followed by that of Lang, who held to his trees until he saw the Federals 100 yards in his rear. Unable to find a defensible line in the open fields over which he had passed, he was compelled to retreat to the woods west of the Emmitsburg road.

Lang lost some men as prisoners in his withdrawal. One of them was a big Floridian named Lewis Thornton Powell, alias Lewis T. Paine, who was sent to Baltimore wounded. He escaped, deserted, got into civilian clothes, and became so captivated by John Wilkes Booth that he offered himself as Booth's devoted follower; eventually he was a principal in the plot to assassinate Lincoln, his own role being the knifing of Secretary of State Seward.

Wright's spectacular assault was doomed to failure. His was a single brigade a mile in advance of Lee's main army. His thrust could not be regarded a heavy blow from the shoulder, with the weight of the body behind it, but more a hard cuff from the wrist, which annoyed but did not rock Meade severely. But it was enough of a shock that a supporting, straight-from-the-shoulder follow-up blow could have knocked the Federal army off Cemetery Ridge.[6]

Webb's brigade made certain it was the Confederates, not the Federals, to be knocked off the ridge. While the 69th Pennsylvania assailed Wright in front, the 106th Pennsylvania moved against his right, exposed by Lang's retirement. Lieutenant Colonel W. L. Curry had the 106th Pennsylvania put three effective volleys into Wright's flank, then ordered a bayonet charge.

Hancock was hurrying up other troops, and Wright's brilliant exploit now seemed likely to be turned into a disaster for the courageous Georgians. Soon they were all but surrounded, but before Curry's attack reached them, they abandoned their captured guns and fairly cut their way out of the circle. They halted at a fence at the bottom of the hill, delivered a volley, and continued their retreat, only to be caught by the shells as the bombardment reopened on them from Cemetery Ridge. A second time they faced about, re-formed and battled off their pursuers.

Wright was followed closely by units of Doubleday's division and by the 106th Pennsylvania, which before reaching the Emmitsburg road captured Colonel William Gibson, and a number of his 48th Georgia Regiment. Colonel Curry halted his Pennsylvanians along the road, threw out skirmishers, and sent back to Webb for orders. The brigade commander recalled the regiment. It was about seven-thirty.

If any small-unit action controlled the outcome of the battle, it was perhaps the affair in no man's land brought about when Curry left behind two companies, to be deployed as skirmishers, connecting with the skirmishers of the 1st Delaware Regiment at the Bliss house and barn in the field west of the Emmitsburg road.

Posey advanced his Mississippians belatedly, after Wright had been beaten off, and was arrested by the 1st Delaware skirmishers, whom he finally ousted from the Bliss buildings. His fire drove back one of the Pennsylvania companies which it took in flank, but the second company came up to relieve its comrades. Brigadier General Alexander Hays, seeing this fighting far out in front of the army about midway between the two lines, sent five companies of the 12th New Jersey, which, with the help of the spirited Pennsylvania company, assailed and recaptured the Bliss farm buildings. That was enough for Posey. Though his brigade had not been hurt much—he lost 92 prisoners in the barn—he did not attempt a further movement. Longstreet had escorted his brigades in, but neither Hill nor Anderson, who were not far removed, gave Posey orders or encouragement.

So the Confederate advance was stopped at the Bliss farm.[7] Here Lee's echelon plan broke down completely. The small action proved one of the most consequential of the battle. When Posey tarried,

Mahone on his left withheld his attack and would heed no entreaties from the troops engaged. Pender's division still farther to the left was governed by the advance of Mahone. Both Anderson and Hill appeared lacking in the necessary enterprise at the moment when a resolute attack by Posey and Mahone, acting together, would have had an excellent chance to penetrate the enemy line. Anderson, of course, should have used his brigades in some sort of concert. The *en echelon* plan ordinarily would be more effective if brigade followed brigade in prompt succession, but would be foredoomed to failure under lackadaisical management, by which it might become a series of individual attacks by isolated brigades, each being repulsed in turn by the whole enemy army.

Another important aspect of the Bliss farm fight was that by discouraging Posey, it left Hancock free to watch the right of the Federal army; he possessed enough unengaged troops to send assistance if needed. The 106th Pennsylvania had not been back in its old position many minutes before a call came for it to join Carroll's brigade and go to Howard's assistance on East Cemetery Hill. Certainly Carroll could not have been spared had Posey and Mahone attacked. Wilcox insisted that had Posey and Mahone been sent in at the time he dispatched his adjutant to Anderson for help, the Federal line could have been broken. The opportunity was even more promising when Wright captured the battery and held the crest of the ridge.

At least one southern correspondent with the army saw that here a great opportunity to win the battle was cast away. An analysis of the action in the center, made five days after the battle and published by the Richmond *Enquirer,* is as clear an explanation of the failure of Hill's corps as any that has yet been written. It embodies the essential facts.[8]

Pender, anxious to participate and sensing that Anderson's left brigades were not entering the action, rode to the right of his division to ascertain the cause. Perrin was certain that Pender did not mean to be held back by the faltering Mahone. But he was hit in the leg by a shell fragment just at the moment of decision. While the wound was severe, it was not of a fatal type. Pender was carried back, placed in an ambulance and started next day on the journey to his North Carolina home. At Staunton, Virginia, there was a hemorrhage of the wound. His brother came and he appeared to improve, but a second hemorrhage necessitated amputation of the leg. He died within a few hours after the surgery.[9]

General Lee, believing that Pender was about to go in with his division at the time he was wounded, attributed the loss of the battle to his fall: "I shall ever believe if General Pender had remained on his horse half an hour longer we would have carried the enemy's position."[10]

Major Joseph A. Englehard, Pender's adjutant general, spoke for the division when he said, "Seldom has the service suffered more in the loss of one man."[11] The misfortune was indeed akin to the loss of Jackson and in view of the critical moment at which Pender fell, probably fully as significant to the Southern cause.

Ewell's corps on Pender's left was not included in the plan to attack *en echelon,* but was to be governed by the sound of Longstreet's guns. The guns had been sounding since four o'clock—and now they were subsiding—but Ewell had not moved.

As the battle was dying on the far left of the Federal army, the brigade of Colonel William McCandless, of Brigadier General S. Wiley Crawford's division, Fifth Corps, which included the original "Bucktails," advanced across Plum Run and applied enough pressure on Longstreet to cause him to realign his right division. That night he retained the ground from which he had ousted Sickles, but lay close to the Federals only where his far right held Devil's Den and rested on the base of Round Top.

When Longstreet rode back from the lines in the early night, he was still trailed by the British correspondent Ross, to whom he declared, "We have not been as successful as we wished."[12] Then he attributed the lack of success to the wounding of Hood and the death of Barksdale.[13] Ross and Longstreet tied their horses to a fence, used their saddles as pillows, and that night slept on the meadow.

3. Hays and Avery Attack at Sundown

The flaming sun of July 2, 1863, that had looked down on some of the most sanguinary fighting of modern warfare, gradually sank into a red sky after a torrid day. Twilight was creeping across the battlefield. Far off to the right the angry booms could still be heard from Longstreet's guns. Bursts of infantry fire told that the attack on Meade's center had subsided but was not yet spent.

It was seven-thirty. The Carolinians in the hollow of the Culp spring were thinking of home. The candles and pine knots would soon be lighted on far-off farms. The delicate pink afterglow would be crowning the bold summits of the Blue Ridge. Corn must be tossing with full tassel in the Piedmont bottoms. The hungry Yadkin still ate the yellow hills. Families would be lingering at the supper tables watching the day die out of the sky. In countless North Carolina homes the mother was reserving an empty chair, as something of a devotion or fetish or symbol of her hope, against the day when her boy would be returning from Lee's army. Now that Lee had carried the war into the unscathed regions beyond the Potomac, word of his movements was awaited with taut expectancy. North Carolina listened, anxious, uncertain.

On East Cemetery Hill the heavily manned Federal line rose above the town of Gettysburg. The batteries of Weidrich, Ricketts, and Reynolds swept the green approaches across the undulating acres of the Culp farm. The regiments of Von Gilsa's brigade, the German immigrants to New York, who had been flanked by Early on the afternoon of July 1, manned the stone works and trenches which followed roughly the crest of Cemetery Hill. From their elevated position these Federal troops could look down on the valley of Rock Creek, through which the evening dusk was stealing, and on the red homestead and outbuildings of the farm of the Pennsylvania Dutchman, William Culp, one of whose sons, by a play of chance, was fighting across the fields in the army of the South, while another was fighting in the army of the North.

There, in the wheat field near the Culp house, on the outskirts of Gettysburg, the Northern soldiers could observe in the twilight the forming of a Southern assault column.[14] It was composed of the three infantry regiments of Hoke's North Carolina brigade and Hays's five demi-regiments from Louisiana, all of Early's division. The intrepid Hoke, whose soldiers, by their tenacity, were later to give to North Carolinians the name of "Tar Heels,"[15] was absent. He had been wounded at Salem Church, and his brigade was commanded by the senior colonel, Isaac E. Avery, of the 6th North Carolina.

This regiment, which had been a part of Bee's brigade at the first battle of Manassas, had been partly an outgrowth of the North Carolina Military Institute at Charlotte. There many of its members had come under the inspiration of the devout soldier, author, mathematician, and hard fighter, Major General Daniel Harvey Hill, who had presided over this institution in the days before the war.

Hoke's, or Avery's, brigade consisted at Gettysburg of the 6th, 21st and 57th North Carolina Infantry regiments. It was weakened by the detachment of the 54th Regiment, which had been sent back to Staunton, Virginia, as the escort for the prisoners of Milroy's army captured by Lee at Winchester.

Forming on the right of Avery was the brigade of Brigadier General Harry T. Hays, known as the Louisiana Tigers, and composed in heavy measure of French-speaking Creoles. They had been commanded formerly by Dick Taylor, and with him had won glory under Stonewall Jackson in the Valley. A gay, dashing, guitar-playing aggregation, they could march and fight all day, then sing and dance around the campfires the greater part of the night.

All during the day of July 2 these two brigades had been lying near the Culp spring, in a treeless hollow, or in the open wheat under a sweltering sun.[16] Major James F. Beall of the 21st North Carolina Regiment witnessed the delight with which the men hailed the attack order when it finally ended the almost insufferable suspense. Ewell had at last acknowledged Longstreet's guns and in the approach of darkness was bestirring himself.

The clear notes of the bugle called across the fields. The North Carolinians moved out in sharp alignment, marching toward the valley that divides Culp's and Cemetery hills. Colonel Hamilton C. Jones of the 57th North Carolina, the center regiment, noted the striking manner in which the men kept their order, guiding right on the Louisianians. Years later he applied to the advance the single descriptive word—"beautiful."[17]

The federal artillery greeted the movement with sudden blasts from both Culp's and Cemetery hills. "Really," said Major Beall, "the enemy's artillery, reopening at the going down of the sun, fell like music on our ears."[18] It heralded the moment of decision. The Maine artillery lieutenant, Edward N. Whittier, using a French ordnance glass, had taken the range during the afternoon on all of the positions in front of Culp's Hill and now he blazed away with case shot. The six guns of his battery fired simultaneously, startling the Massachusetts regiment at the base of Culp's Hill, which could not yet detect the Confederate approach over the broken ground.

Whittier then ordered the guns to fire at will. Although the range was measured and the firing unusually rapid, the attacking line moved firmly ahead. It crossed fences and stone walls and worked over the rising ground behind the Culp homestead. Loading and firing as they advanced, and slowed at times by the 6 guns looking directly down on them from Culp's Hill and the 16 others of the three batteries on Cemetery Hill, the Confederate force required almost an hour to pass the 700 yards of rocky and uneven ground between the Culp house and the wall and trenches at the base of East Cemetery Hill.[19] Here, with a dash and shout, they crashed through the first Federal line.

The first assault proved costly. The brigade commander, Colonel Avery, had bravely but imprudently ridden his horse. He was the only mounted man in the column and was among the first to fall.[20] Just as his men reached the Federal line at the base of the hill, he was hit by a musket ball that passed through his neck and shoulders and knocked him from his mount. The attack swept on without him and it was some time before the brigade knew he had fallen. Prostrate and alone, he perceived that his wound was mortal. His shoulder and right arm were shattered. But he took a lead pencil and paper from his pocket and scribbled a note to his fellow officer, Lieutenant Colonel Samuel McDowell Tate, who had succeeded to the command of the 6th Regiment when Avery took the brigade. The faltering handwriting showed life was ebbing. The message merely said, "Tell my father I fell with my face to the enemy."[21] Nothing needed to be added. The place where he fell was marked by his men, but more enduring than their marker, which long ago was lost or obliterated, were the words of the note which spoke so truly the spirit of the Southern army.

The 57th North Carolina restored its alignment that had been broken by the rough terrain. The brigade wheeled to the right and looked up the hill toward the main Federal wall and breastworks. The commander of the 57th, Colonel Archibald Campbell Godwin, was now the senior officer and assumed command of Hoke's brigade. A native of Nansemond County, Virginia, he had heard the call of gold when the precious metal was discovered in California and, at the age of nineteen, had trudged across the continent on foot. He had been among the few able to turn the lure into abundant yellow washings and had amassed wealth. But when Virginia seceded he hastened eastward, leaving most of his tangible assets behind. Colonel Hamilton C. Jones, writing in later years, bestowed on him the ultimate accolade: "A Virginian in command of a North Carolina regiment and afterwards a North Carolina brigade, he was as much beloved and admired by those under him as if he had been a North Carolinian, or they Virginians."[22] He fell a year later, at Winchester.

It was now 8:20 P.M. Darkness came on rapidly after eight-fifteen. Hays, by virtue of his seniority, commanded the two brigades. Creoles from the Louisiana bayous, together with descendants of the British,

Scottish, and German pioneers who had pushed down the mountain valleys or westward across the North Carolina plains and Piedmont, now began together their ascent of East Cemetery Hill. Hays thought his command was saved from annihilation by the gathering darkness and the smoke which billowed down the hillside from the three batteries on the summit and the infantry brigades firing rapidly from three directions. The heavy locust trees afforded some protection. But speed had bearing on the success. The charge up the steep incline was impetuous. Breaking through a second Federal line halfway up the hill, the storming party appeared to gather strength as it pressed forward. With a confident shout the men at length reached the crest.

Von Gilsa's German New Yorkers broke.[23] They had not expected such internecine fury in New World fighting. The Federal Corps commander, Howard, was standing on East Cemetery Hill with Major General Schurz. "Almost before I could tell where the assault was made," said Howard, "our men and the Confederates came tumbling back together."[24] The North Carolina and Louisiana troops poured over the Federal entrenchments. Daniel Harvey Hill could have asked no better from his old cadets. Godwin, the prospector, was finding the gold of victory in these Pennsylvania hills.

The situation on the Federal front was rendered critical by the flight of Von Gilsa's brigade. Colonel Andrew L. Harris, commanding another of Howard's brigades, ordered the 17th Connecticut Regiment to fill the hole left by the disappearance of Von Gilsa. The movement of the 17th Connecticut in turn left an opening in Ames's front and through this gap rushed the 6th North Carolina and 9th Louisiana. They pushed out on the plateau occupied by the Federal artillery. Here they struck another of Ames's regiments, the 75th Ohio, and rolled back the right companies, causing the balance of the regiment to change front and face to the right. The other North Carolina and Louisiana regiments continued the battle in their front at the summit.

The Federal artillery, deprived of infantry support, fought desperately but ineffectually. Some of the cannoneers seized abandoned infantry muskets and jabbed and rammed at their assailants with the butts, while others fought with handspikes, clubs, and stones. The swabbers wielded their sponge staffs and swung them in wide arcs. Storming past the guns of Weidrich's New York battery, the North Carolinians unloosed a volley point-blank into Ricketts' light Pennsylvania artillery. "Over the wall and into the midst of the guns they came," said the Federal Colonel J. P. S. Gobin, "and around these raged the conflict with whatever was in reach to fight with."[25] Two of the batteries were overrun and the guns captured. Some of Ricketts' pieces were spiked. Howard was fearful that the Confederates would carry off all this precious artillery and scurried about for reinforcements. Hays hoped to turn it on its owners, given a little assistance and time.[26]

Suddenly the shouting stopped. Hays noticed that the uproar of the guns died away. There were moments of quiet and suspense on the crest of Cemetery Hill. "At that time," said Hays, "every piece of artillery that had been firing at us was silenced."[27]

It was an instant of which the people of the South who had been eagerly awaiting reports from Pennsylvania might well take note. Here was a high point, possibly *the* high point, of Lee's invasion of the Free States.

"We had full possession," said Captain Ray, "of East Cemetery Hill, the key to General Meade's position."[28]

But there was a Federal general of quick perception and action only a quarter of a mile from the point of the Confederate break-through. Hancock, who had just saved the Federal center following the defeat of Sickles, now, more by intuition than direct information—"a happy inspiration," a Federal officer called it[29]—sensed the menace on his right. Although Howard had not asked him for assistance, Hancock ordered Colonel Samuel S. Carroll, commanding a brigade of Ohio, Indiana, and West Virginia troops, augmented by the 106th Pennsylvania that had just returned from beating off Wright, to hasten to East Cemetery Hill. Then he added the 71st Pennsylvania as insurance.[30]

Carroll was a young officer of great verve and dash, a West Point graduate born in the District of Columbia, whose war service was marked by a succession of promotions for gallantry on nearly every major field of battle. His brigade was in instant motion. Night had now fallen. Although a moon had risen and lighted the fields at intervals, the East Cemetery plateau, wooded, was in darkness. Carroll had no guide, but he led his men directly toward the flashes from the Confederate infantry fire across the plateau.

The moment of final decision had arrived. Howard was collecting remnants of the First and Eleventh corps. Nearest at hand was Colonel Kryzanowski's brigade of 800 men, who went in at the double-quick. Newton began to extend the line of the First Corps to enable Howard to shorten his front.

The 6th North Carolina had formed behind the stone wall that had earlier marked the Federal line. Twice the Federal advance was driven back by infantry volleys. Anxiously the Carolinians looked for reinforcements. None came.

Hays heard the approach of Carroll's brigade through the darkness but held his fire. He had been warned that he possibly would encounter other Confederate units in his front. Longstreet had attacked on the far right and might come crashing through the Federal lines. Johnson was assailing Culp's Hill on the left. Rodes presumably would be giving support close at hand, to be followed by Lane with Pender's division. This mass of infantry advancing through the darkness might be the forward elements of Longstreet's or Rodes's triumphant line. The memory of how Jackson had been shot by his own men hung heavily over the army.

Hays waited hesitatingly until Carroll had fired his third volley. Even then he would not have replied, perhaps, except that Carroll's men were now so close that the flash of their muskets revealed their blue uniforms. Then Hays ordered his men to return the volleys.

But the brigades of Hays and Godwin had been wasted and exhausted. The feeble fire which the men could offer checked the oncoming Federals only momentarily. Hays found the enemy overlapping him and moving toward his rear. The rear of the North Carolinians was likewise threatened. Reluctantly he ordered a retreat. Godwin called back his regiments in concert, forced to abandon a greater fortune in fame than he had ever left in gold in California. The survivors of the two brigades retired 75 yards to another fence, then dropped back to their original position near the Culp farm buildings. Hays brought back 4 Federal flags and 100 prisoners.

Here Gordon had held his supporting brigade, awaiting word from Early before following the assault up the hillside, but Early had not cared to risk his sole available reserve. His only other brigade, Smith's, had been sent to the far left to watch for the approach of Stuart. Said Captain Neill W. Ray of the 6th North Carolina: "By not supporting Hoke's brigade of North Carolina and Hays' brigade of Louisiana in the storming and capturing of Cemetery Hill, the battle of Gettysburg was lost. I do not know whose fault it was, but I feel assured in saying it was not the fault of the assaulting column."[31] In writing to Governor Vance about the 6th Regiment, Lieutenant Colonel Tate declared: "Such a fight as they made in front of the fortifications has never been equalled." Then with pride he said, "This regiment has had a reputation, you know."[32]

That was the story. Half a mile in front of the main Confederate lines, two brigades again had fought hand to hand unaided, until almost surrounded by reinforcements rushed up from three Federal corps.

Very likely they would have effected a permanent lodgment on East Cemetery Hill had Rodes provided the expected assistance on the right. Through the afternoon before the advance the negotiations went back and forth to establish concert of action between Early and Rodes. Late in the day Rodes did make ready. His division occupied the town of Gettysburg, and he found it impossible to advance in battle order through the streets. He, too, was concerned about his right, and about the co-operation of Lane, of Hill's corps, who had taken command of Pender's division.

Rodes finally disentangled himself from the streets and notified Lane that he would attack at nightfall. Ramseur and Doles advanced their brigades toward Cemetery Hill at about the time Hays and Avery left the Culp farm but had much farther to travel. That Ramseur's men were in high spirits was suggested by their countersign: "North Carolina to the rescue."[33]

Word passed through the ranks that the attack would be made just as the moon rose. Pocketbooks and last messages were given to the surgeons. "We marched boldly forward, sweeping through the tall wheat," said a lieutenant. They reached the base of the hill with the graveyard above them, facing the opposite slope of the same broad elevation Early's brigades were assailing from the other side. At the base a low command passed along the two brigades for the men to lie down. Ramseur was crawling ahead personally to inspect the position his troops were to assail. The brigades waited in suspense. The moon went behind a cloud. Someone said, "Boys, if I come out of this battle alive, I'm coming out with a Yankee canteen."[34] A Confederate canteen "leaked like a sifter," being two simple tin plates often fastened insecurely.

Finally Ramseur returned. He had reconnoitered, then conferred with Doles; together they had concluded that the fortifications on the front of the hill, with numerous batteries ready to pour in a direct and enfilade fire, made an assault impractical. The order ran along the line: "Fall back without noise." Again, with nobody of higher rank at hand, the important decisions were being made by brigadier generals. But scarcely were two brigadier generals better qualified to pass judgment on the full capabilities of their troops.

"Our general saw the foolhardiness and madness of the attempt," said an officer writing home. "For that act there are many Carolina mothers . . . who should pray blessings on his head."[35]

The best Rodes could do that late hour was to consolidate a line along an abandoned road bed facing the hill and await the coming of morning.

Responsibility for the failure rested first with Ewell and then with Early. Ewell had not established with Rodes the imperative need for Rodes and Early to attack simultaneously nor had he co-ordinated their movements. He does not appear to have given any personal, on-the-spot supervision. Early had sent his brigades into a most desperate undertaking without certainty that they would be assisted, and then had withheld Gordon while the impetus of the assault was being wasted on the plateau and among the stone fences at the summit. With Gordon's help, the army might have obtained a lodgment on Cemetery Hill for the night, subject to exploitation at dawn by Rodes or by Pickett's fresh division.

Either the attack should not have been made or it should have been supported. Lack of careful preparation and lack of follow-through— the second a fault that would plague Early and ultimately lead to his dismissal from the command of an army—explained the repulse of Hays and Godwin. Two small brigades could not do more. Early had failed to seize the heights on the previous afternoon when the opportunity was most inviting. Now he had compounded that error by wasting some of the South's best soldiers against them.

The penciled note Tate wrote Governor Vance at the first opportunity after the assault was in compliance with his promise to the 6th North Carolina: "to acquaint you with the truth, that history may speak truly of them." He distrusted Early and said that since Avery had been killed "we have no friends" who would tell of their action. The official report Early was yet to write was already suspect. Tate explained that he knew it had not been written, but he still felt free to attack it as a "monstrous injustice." An irascible general does not inspire confidence. "I know the disposition so well that I look for no special mention of our regiment," he said. Then he summed up the account of how the regiment and the 9th Louisiana had planted their colors on the heights: "The enemy stood with a tenacity never before displayed by them, but with bayonet, clubbed musket, sword and pistol, and rocks from the wall, we cleared the heights and silenced the guns. In vain did I send to the rear for support. . . ."[36]

The day would come when North Carolina regiments would chant of their dislikes:

"Old Jimboden's gone up the spout,
And old Jube Early's about played out."[37]

But in July 1863 Jube was making some peculiar decisions for Lee's left wing at Gettysburg.

4. Old Man Greene Holds the Trenches

Lieutenant Randolph H. McKim, aide and spiritual counselor to the devout Brigadier General George H. Steuart, stood on the far left of Lee's army, east of Benner's Hill, on the afternoon of July 2 and held his watch in hand. It was approaching four o'clock.

He was counting the artillery discharges after Longstreet opened his bombardment on the other flank of the army, and he found that Longstreet was firing at a rate of 180 guns a minute. Considering that Alexander had put only 46 guns into batteries on the Confederate right, and that each gun had to be swabbed, loaded, and rammed between discharges, either some astoundingly rapid firing was in progress or some woefully poor arithmetic was involved in the gentle McKim's calculations.[38]

But the point was that Ewell, who has often been excused for delaying his attack on the score that he could not hear Longstreet's bombardment, could not have escaped it with a feather bed over his head. He must have been at that time in his Hanover road headquarters north of the Culp buildings, between Gettysburg and Rock Creek, where he had moved from the almshouse to be closer to his troops. But wherever he was along his lines, the bombardment, so easily heard by McKim and by the Federals across the Rock Creek Valley on Culp's Hill, was surely audible to him and to his staff, who should have been on the alert for it.

This bombardment, under Lee's orders, was the signal for Ewell to launch an assault on Meade's right, sustaining Longstreet's assault on the Federal left. Ewell's attack was an imperative part of Lee's battle plan. After the commanding general had reluctantly assented to the entreaties of Ewell and Early that their corps be retained in its extended position on the army's left, encircling Meade's right even to overlapping part of his rear, he had assigned to Ewell a role of easy execution but of profound bearing on the Southern army's prospects

of victory. Ewell's duty was simple and clear: when Longstreet attacked on the right, Ewell would attack sharply on the left to prevent
Meade from shifting troops to bolster his left after Longstreet assailed
it. The advantage Meade would have in moving fresh units to points
of danger had been clear to Lee when he looked out with Trimble
from the almshouse cupola. He had taken every precaution to neutral-
ize that advantage when he finally developed his plan, the main feature of which was the simultaneous attack on the two flanks, followed
by the attack *en echelon* by brigades moving from the right to the
center of the army.

The record of Ewell's personal activities at this stage of the battle
remains hazy: apparently his movements were not sufficiently emphatic for anyone to take especial notice of them. For more than
twenty hours Johnson's division lay in attack formation east of Rock
Creek, mainly north of the Hanover road, Nichols on the right, Jones
in the center, and Steuart on the left, with Walker, commanding the
Stonewall Brigade, drawn up perpendicularly behind Steuart. He
faced east in the woods just beyond a little stream that meanders
southward and joins Rock Creek directly east of Culp's Hill. Steuart's
brigade was thus on Lee's left flank, with the Stonewall Brigade in
support. Steuart at his closest point was a mile from the eastern face
of Culp's Hill, which under Johnson's attack plan—when it was finally
put into effect—he was to assail; he was six miles, following Lee's long
front, from Longstreet's right, but only about two miles away as the
crow flies.[39]

While Johnson's division idled through the hours, McKim held
religious services. The men, awaiting attack orders, seemed thankful
for this divine worship. For many it was their last.[40] Not until after
6:00 P.M., when Meade was stripping his right of troops to support
his left and center, did Ewell order Johnson's division into motion.
Not until about seven-forty-five—at best three hours late—had the regiments worked their way to the eastern face of Culp's Hill. Most of the
intervening period had been devoted to Ewell's artillery preparation,
which was being wasted against the vacant hillside and empty trenches
that in the afternoon had housed the Twelfth Corps divisions of
John W. Geary and Alpheus S. Williams, now off to their left giving
Meade the margin of security he needed against Hood, McLaws, and
Anderson. They had moved out about six-thirty, and their old lines
were vacant by seven.

Johnson's artillery was commanded by youthful Major Joseph W.

Latimer, who rimmed the crest of Benner's Hill with guns. The Federals replied and the exchange gave the illusion of activity on Lee's left, but the six batteries Ewell had put into position on Benner's Hill were stark targets on the open crest, being shielded by nothing resembling embankments or lunettes, or any natural protective ridges, or the stone fences so common in this Pennsylvania section, and having not even a covering of timber for the gun crews. The Federal artillery across the sharp valley of Rock Creek had the security not only of the heavy woods and numerous natural citadels, but also of stone and log fortifications on which Wadsworth's and Slocum's men had been laboring incessantly, part of them for more than twenty-four hours.

The result of the exchange was unfortunate for Ewell's guns. Instead of making a quick assault—which would have complied with Lee's orders and held the Federal infantry in place—he undertook a sustained bombardment, allowed the Federal infantry to avoid him, and ended with most of his artillery silenced and his gun crews crippled. Among the mortally wounded was the competent young commander, Major Latimer, who had been a sophomore at the Virginia Military Institute when war broke and was not yet twenty-one when he fell. He was hit while withdrawing the guns. By Ewell's orders, one battery was left in its exposed position to cover Johnson's infantry advance.

Meade, in his anxiety to save his left from Longstreet's crushing blows, had denuded his right recklessly. Culp's Hill had been garrisoned strongly after the arrival of Slocum's corps. Wadsworth's division of the First Corps already was on the summit when Slocum took his position in the early morning of July 2. Wadsworth held the left of the crest, looking north and west toward Cemetery Hill and Gettysburg. Slocum, whose corps included only two divisions, extended Wadsworth's line on the right. Geary's division was on Wadsworth's right, curving around with the convex crest of the hill and facing east, and Williams' division was to the right of Geary. Williams' reached along the broken, wooded shoulder of Culp's Hill, passing in front of a spring in a grove near the Henry Spangler homestead, but continuing along Rock Creek through the woods to McAllister's Mill. The length of the Twelfth Corps line from its juncture with Wadsworth to its termination in a marshland near the mill was slightly less than a mile.

Largely on the insistence of Brigadier General George S. Greene,

Geary's division had devoted the morning and early afternoon to building entrenchments, which, when completed, were formidable barricades of logs, fence rails, cord wood, and rocks. Greene's brigade of
upstate New Yorkers was on Geary's left, joining Wadsworth, which
proved to be a fortunate coincidence for the Federal army because of
Greene's dogged character. Slocum objected strenuously to Meade's
order stripping his right wing and baring the entire east face of Culp's
Hill to an enemy known to be lurking in heavy force in the woods
on the other side of Rock Creek, and was able to wring permission
from Meade to leave a single brigade.[41] The order to move the entire
Twelfth Corps has commonly been characterized with one word—
"suicidal." Having Geary's division on the march toward him no
doubt gave Meade comfort while Longstreet was hammering on his
left, but the division remained unemployed and actually was not
needed. Two brigades, Candy's and Kane's, became confused,
strolled down the Baltimore pike, moving farther and farther from
the battlefield, and accomplished nothing except to get lost.[42] Williams' division gave Meade valuable help in his repulse of Anderson,
and Lee's army would have been well served had he been kept engaged on Culp's Hill by Ewell.

Greene's brigade, being on Geary's left and next to Wadsworth,
naturally was selected to remain behind. For three hours that night
the fate of the battle and possibly the destiny of the Federal cause
hung on the stanch shoulders of "Old Pop" Greene, whose sturdiness
had much to do with saving the hill for the Federals when its loss
would have been calamitous.

Pop Greene was in his sixty-third year, probably the oldest Northern fighter on the field after the guerilla John Burns had been hauled
off to his place of safety. His New York youths, mostly under
twenty-one, looked on him as an ancient out of the Revolution or the
War of 1812, though he had not graduated from West Point until
1823 and was a hardy man who spent most of his time in the saddle.
He outlived many of these soldiers who had thought a bullet would
hurry to get him before his normal time ran out; he died in his ninety-
eighth year and retained the West Point longevity record until early in
1958.[43]

Greene was a native of Warwick, Rhode Island. He stood second
in his class at West Point, where he instructed for a time; after years
of dull garrison duty in the West, he resigned to build railroads and
other works, among them the reservoir in Central Park, New York,

and the enlarged High Bridge over the Harlem River. On the outbreak of war, he became colonel of the 60th New York, recruited along the St. Lawrence River.

Greene's five New York regiments on Culp's Hill aggregated 1,310, of whom 70 were officers. To have stretched them over the Twelfth Corps's old front would have meant a musket every four feet, or a line as thin as skirmishers. Greene did extend his front more than a fourth of the distance, into the rifle pits that had been dug by Kane's brigade; then he set his men to digging a traverse at the end of his line, turning back to his right and facing south. When the thin line was manned Greene had a single rank, with no reserve, with only about one foot between elbows. The Federals could hear in their rear the attack being made on Cemetery Hill by Hays and Avery; finally in the rapidly approaching darkness Johnson's four brigades, Jones and Steuart in front, followed by Nichols and Walker, were seen descending the opposite slope and entering the waters of Rock Creek. It was 7:45 P.M.

The creek was waist-deep, but the Confederates held their lines and began in the twilight to work their way up the rough, eastern slope of Culp's Hill, which though not so precipitous, resembled Little Round Top and had the same importance to Meade's right as the other eminence had to his left. Culp's Hill rises above Cemetery Hill which is due west and looks down to the southwest on Cemetery Ridge, behind which was Meade's headquarters. Scattered around were the reserve artillery and ammunition trains. More important still, the hill commanded the Baltimore pike, Meade's avenue to Baltimore and Washington, which many of his less stalwart soldiers were already employing. Possession of Culp's Hill was essential to Meade's safety. He might lose other positions and still hold his lines, but not Culp's Hill.

Steuart, on the Confederate left, kept the 1st North Carolina in reserve as a flank guard, then worked up the hill until he struck Greene's line in Kane's old rifle pits. Darkness was coming on rapidly, but the engagement soon grew heated. Because of the dim light the lines drew close, and Steuart's losses became so heavy that he sent Lieutenant McKim to bring up his reserve regiment. McKim, using the flash of the muskets as a guide, led the Carolinians up the incline until he encountered a line of troops 100 yards ahead. They were discernible through the thick foliage and fading light only by their gun flashes, which seemed to be directed downhill. He had the regiment open fire, only to learn an instant later that he was firing on the 3rd

North Carolina, Steuart's right flank regiment.[44] This anguishing mistake delayed but did not unnerve Steuart.

On Steuart's right Brigadier General John M. Jones led his Virginia brigade, supported by Nicholls' Louisianans, commanded by Colonel J. M. Williams in Nicholls' absence, against Greene's left. Here for more than two hours the battle raged in the dusk, then the darkness, with intense fury. Pop Greene would not be pushed aside. He retained his mount, riding back and forth behind his lines through the trees and boulders. Four times Jones charged the entrenchments, but each time the thin line held, and Jones was forced back to the foot of the hill, only to re-form his lines for another assault.

Greene meantime called for help. One of the closest regiments was the 6th Wisconsin, which Wadsworth sent. All day the First Corps officers in groups on Culp's Hill had watched Longstreet's distant assault, and gained the bitter impression that Meade was being defeated on his left. About dark they heard the Rebel yell sound suddenly on their right. The desperate nature of the battle there was speedily apparent. A staff officer directed Colonel Dawes to take his regiment and find Greene. When approached, Old Pop, who in his fighting clothes looked more like a farmer than a general, wrote his name and brigade on a card in the darkness and handed it to Dawes to identify himself. The incident suggests the intensity of the firing. But he managed an audible order that put the Wisconsin men behind some breastworks which, by a quick descent, they recovered from Confederates already entering them. Dawes was followed by the 14th Brooklyn, and Greene's left began to take on strength.

On his right he was less successful. Steuart's flank skirmishers overran the empty trenches reaching toward McAllister's Mill, then the Marylander again worked his way up the hill to Greene's immediate front. He found Greene's entrenchments to be five feet thick, made of earth and heavy logs and protected by abatis. Old Greene had built railroads, bridges, canals, and was a specialist on entrenching, as his works showed. Steuart's men had been fighting in front of them for two hours when, at nine-thirty, by a sudden assault, the 1st North Carolina and 1st Maryland regiments burst into the works. As Lieutenant Green Martin, Company B, 1st North Carolina, led in the storming party, he received a mortal wound.[45]

Johnson now had a lodgment on Culp's Hill and easy access to the soft underside of the Federal army. He had part of Greene's trenches, but the traverse protected the Federal flank and prevented it from being turned. In the darkness, or fitful moonlight, neither Steuart nor Johnson knew at first of the full prize that was open to their taking. Two hundred yards beneath them, in easy musket shot, was the Baltimore pike, the jugular vein of Meade's army. Hancock and the entire Cemetery Ridge position could be taken in reverse. Surely the ridge could be carried from the rear with any kind of co-operation from Hill's corps in its front. One factor, and only one, nullified the importance of Steuart's achievement—it came at 9:30 P.M. Even in the darkness Johnson might have set off a panic by driving into Meade's reserve ammunition trains and thus notifying the Federal army that he was operating in its rear. His troops were ample for the purpose. The Stonewall Brigade had scarcely been scratched, Jeb Stuart had finally reached the battlefield, and Extra Billy Smith, who had diligently completed the restful duty of watching for him on the York pike, was now available for battle service.

Skirmishers from the 1st North Carolina managed to locate the Baltimore pike and sent back word to Johnson that it was within musket shot.[46] Johnson tried to get Smith's brigade in motion but Smith lacked orientation. Darkness paralyzed him and he stopped.

The two armies settled down to await the coming of daylight. Spangler's Spring gave water to both blue and gray soldiers. Water details of both armies exchanged banter as if they were all on a school picnic. Nobody wanted to deny anyone water, even if he had to be disemboweled with a bayonet the next morning.

Confederate McKim became quite worked up over the assertion that the trenches his chief, Steuart, occupied were those from which the Federal troops had been withdrawn. The withdrawal orders, he asserted, *"came from the men of Steuart's Brigade, and they were delivered at the point of the bayonet."*[47] The Confederate dead in front of the captured works told the correct story.

Late at night the Twelfth Corps brigades began moving back to the right and to their amazement found Confederates in their old entrenchments. Kane and Candy came back first from their goose chase down the Baltimore pike, and eventually Williams. All they could do was lie in the fields north of Power's Hill, reach up to Greene's right and wait. Ewell was aware that the hard part of the battle was still ahead of him. He had lent Extra Billy Smith's brigade of Early's division to Johnson, and followed it now with the brigades of O'Neal and Daniel from Rodes's division. Clearly something would erupt on Culp's Hill on the morning of July 3.

Through the early part of the night Johnson's soldiers trying to sleep on the hill heard the rumbling of artillery on the Baltimore pike, the sound receding instead of advancing. They reported it to Ewell, and the corps commander for a time expected to wake up the next morning and find the Federal army gone. The noise stopped soon after midnight.[48] Could it have been the beginning of a Federal withdrawal? Some of the officers of both armies went to their graves believing so. It was, in any event, an unexplained mystery that seemed to be a part of one of the dramatic episodes of the battle, enacted by the Federal officers while the soldiers slept.

CHAPTER TWENTY

The Council and the Captain

1. The Corps Commanders Vote on a Plan

Sometime about 11:00 P.M. Meade called a council of corps commanders to review the fortunes of the army and recommend the course for the next day.

That he called the council was evidence of his uncertainty. It had become almost axiomatic to behind-the-lines observers that councils were vacillating, pusillanimous, and pretty certain to come up with the wrong decision.

Lincoln was not impressed with them; neither Lee nor Jackson had held them. But in the Army of the Potomac they had become something of a fixture and they were not wholly unrelated to the checkered nature of that army's career. Meade's council, it developed, had positive opinions about what should be done, whereas the commanding general seemed uncertain. It made bold, concise recommendations which Meade accepted. It reversed the old proverb that "councils never fight."

There is much to suggest that Meade wanted to withdraw to his Pipe Creek line on the night of July 2, and the evidence is sufficiently cumulative not to be brushed aside lightly. Certainly it is not conclusive, but the contention of some of his own officers that he preferred withdrawal is a valid part of the Gettysburg story. He did not retreat and he did not at any time issue an order to retreat; consequently, he is entitled to full credit for staying on the field and slugging it out with Lee on the third and decisive day of the battle. But quite

307

naturally he was uncertain about the wisdom of this course, and surely there was reason for him to be uncertain.

The Army of the Potomac had, indeed, been severely handled. The First, Eleventh and Third corps had been broken up, and while the survivors had been reassembled to an extent, troops that had been so thoroughly routed and disorganized are rarely fully serviceable in the same battle. The loss of field and company officers had been staggering. The Second and Fifth corps had fought hard battles, and they too had suffered heavily in loss of men and officers. Meade's casualties for that day alone were around 8,000 killed and wounded, plus an indeterminate number of missing. The First and Eleventh corps losses on the first day aggregated nearly 9,000 in killed and wounded, and thus the army had lost 17,000 plus the missing, which would include upward of 5,000 prisoners. That night Meade estimated his combat strength at 58,000, based on the reports of his corps commanders.[1] The figure seems approximately correct. It shows how his great army was being hacked away.

Two corps were fresh, the Sixth and Twelfth. The Sixth, with the exception of Shaler's brigade, was concentrated, that night, on the left, about the Round Tops, and gave ample protection to that flank. The Twelfth was on Meade's right, poised to undertake the recovery of its old Culp's Hill position on the coming of daylight.

Butterfield, Meade's chief of staff, testified before the Committee on the Conduct of the War that Meade had ordered him on the morning of July 2 to draw up a retreat order and had taken pains to see that he was uninterrupted in an upstairs chamber until he could complete the work. But the conference at which this was to be considered was the one rudely broken up by Longstreet's attack on Sickles. Prior to Meade's hasty departure to the front at the time Longstreet struck, Butterfield had completed the withdrawal order and handed it to Meade. There was no doubt about this order. John Gibbon read it, and checked on the map the towns it mentioned.[2] But here again, as in Meade's instructions to Pleasanton—to be prepared to cover a retreat—the commanding general was merely taking precautions, as any conservative general might under similar circumstances. The only thing peculiar about this order was that it was later discovered that all the copies had been destroyed. According to Assistant Adjutant General Seth Williams, none could be found among his records, and: "it must have been destroyed within a day or two after it was prepared."[3] The destruction of this order—by whom none ever knew—

was one of the weak points in the long insistence by Meade's close followers that he never had the remotest thought of retiring from Gettysburg.[4]

Some of Meade's partisans came to believe that there had never been such an order; that Butterfield conjured up the whole notion. Of course, Meade did not intend to use the order except in an emergency. Even while it was being drafted, he sent Halleck a dispatch at 3:00 P.M., ending: "If not attacked, and I can get any positive information of the position of the enemy which will justify me in so doing, I shall attack."[5] That did not look as if he were considering a withdrawal. But Lincoln in his blessing to Sickles clearly believed that a withdrawal that afternoon was under consideration.

Meade sent another dispatch to Halleck at 8:00 P.M.—while the fighting on his right was at its height but before he had lost the Culp's Hill trenches: "I shall remain in my present position tomorrow, but am not prepared to say, until better advised on the condition of the army, whether my operations will be of an offensive or defensive character."[6]

Why did Meade, after sending these two messages to Halleck, then call a meeting of his corps commanders to pass judgment on the very question of whether he should or should not remain at Gettysburg and continue the battle? Meade had been around long enough, of course, to know that consistency and achievement do not always work together under the same yoke. Did he change his mind abruptly after he lost the Culp's Hill trenches? His actions that evening do not give a clear picture of his impulses. One thing was elucidated by Birney: that when Meade began the council, he stated that he would be governed by the verdict of his corps commanders.[7] That in itself was a surprising acknowledgment for a commanding general locked in a desperate engagement about which he, at headquarters, would be presumed to know more than anyone else on the field.

The main room in the quaint little headquarters house was ten feet by twelve, and into this crowded Meade, Butterfield, the wounded Warren, Newton (First Corps); Hancock and Gibbon (Second); Birney (Third); Sykes (Fifth); Sedgwick (Sixth); Howard (Eleventh); and Slocum and Williams (Twelfth). Adjutants and couriers hovered outside. Meade seemed to look on Williams as an uninvited guest at a wedding, and the men of "Pap" Williams' division learned of this and described it as "droll,"[8] apparently believing Williams capable of advising God himself in a pinch; but Slocum thought he was still commanding the right wing and brought along Williams as commander of the Twelfth Corps, though Meade had not understood it that way and thought Slocum's wing assignment had ended. Pleasanton was not there, being engaged, as he explained, in making arrangements for the army's withdrawal, a task that held him until midnight.[9]

A rickety bed stood in one corner and a cheap pine table in the center, and thus, with candles providing the only light, the council began talking. The generals leaned against the walls, some lolled on the shaky bed, some sat on the floor, and all were composed. They were "as modest and unpretentious as their surroundings," and "as calm, mild-mannered and as free from flurry or excitement as a board of commissioners met to discuss a street improvement," according to the report Williams carried back.[10] There was a wide range in the capacity of these officers of fairly equal rank, as would be the case in any army, but Meade must have known that the opinions of Hancock, Sedgwick, Slocum, and Newton would have a broader base and be more closely reasoned than those of Sykes, or Howard, or some of the others.

Unfortunately, no actual minutes were kept. Butterfield recorded the votes on a yellow slip which years later was found among Meade's personal papers, and by this tally sheet it is known that every corps commander voted in favor of remaining on the field.[11] The votes were taken in writing and the most succinct statement was that of Slocum: "Stay and fight it out." Prior to the vote, much talk dwelt on the possibility of Lee's undertaking a flank movement to Meade's left—the plan Longstreet had proposed. Newton, who was looked on by many as the best engineer and one of the best infantry commanders in the army, anticipated the flank movement and also saw faults in the details of the line which ought to be corrected; but he voted against withdrawal. Gibbon quoted him as saying, "This is no place to fight a battle in."[12]

All the time Meade expressed no opinions and made few comments of any nature.[13] Warren was asleep in a corner, said nothing, and apparently heard nothing. Hancock's views coincided with Slocum's. In the discussion, he said the Army of the Potomac already had retreated too much.

When Meade announced his decision after the voting, different generals heard him say different things. Gibbon heard him say, "Such then is the decision." Slocum, whose integrity none could doubt, heard him say: "Well, gentlemen, the question is settled; we will remain here, but I wish to say I consider this no place to fight a battle."[14]

Doubleday was not present but was so close to Butterfield that the source of his information is not to be doubted, and he was positive in his assertion: "There can be no question that, at the council referred to, General Meade did desire to retreat."[15] Doubleday presented some attractive reasons why this would not have been bad judgment; he felt that the enemy was weak on ammunition, was too far from base, and was too exhausted to pursue; that the Army of the Potomac could be refitted where Lee could not; and that it would be the safer course not to risk a complete defeat by remaining on the field, when withdrawal might win the campaign even if it lost the battle.

Birney, as he rode back from the council, told his adjutant, Major J. B. Fassitt, that Meade had said Gettysburg was no place to fight in.[16] Unhappily, one of the methods followed in this and the Sickles controversy was to impeach the character of some of those who questioned the full measure of Meade's discernment. The whole matter might have been kept minor except that such a controversy makes good newspaper copy. When the question of whether Meade did or did not want to leave Gettysburg got into the press, Meade's son and aide circulated among the generals who had been at the council and found that most of them had not heard Meade express dissatisfaction with the battlefield. The wording of the younger Meade's question was either not penetrating enough or too penetrating: he said the commanding general (Meade) desired a short statement "giving your recollection of what transpired at the council," and mentioning "whether he at any time insisted on a withdrawal of the army from before Gettysburg."[17] The word "insisted" was of course out of place. Nobody ever contended that Meade "insisted" on a withdrawal. Had he done so, the army most certainly would have been withdrawn, for he commanded.

Hancock refused to make any statement to such a query. He had appeared before the Committee on the Conduct of the War, and although he had said nothing there about the withdrawal issue, he declined to elaborate on his testimony. He held himself aloof from all these petty controversies. No answer was received from Slocum. Those who thought Meade had wanted to withdraw, or had been toying with the notion, included Slocum, Birney, Pleasanton, Butterfield, Doubleday, and, respecting the afternoon conference, Sickles. So many high-ranking officers manifestly would not have been engaged in a cabal against Meade's reputation. Those who had not heard him express dissatisfaction included Sedgwick, Newton, Sykes, Williams, Gibbon, and Howard.

The issue had some bearing on how close the Federal army was to retreating on the night of July 2; irrespective of Doubleday's argument, retreat would have lost the battle and possibly the war. There are, however, other interesting aspects. Meade decided to stay, but was it altogether, or even mainly, because of the vote of his corps commanders?

The controversy, the lack of minutes of the council, and the uncertainty about what was said, even by the commanding general, left open to question the exact nature of what went on behind Meade's lines during the middle hours of the night of July 2, when Ewell's scouts heard the receding rumble of artillery wheels and Pleasanton was so busy making withdrawal arrangements that he could not attend the council. The suggestion believed by many in the South that Meade was actually beginning a withdrawal has been a subject of interesting speculation. According to this belief, or deduction, it was not the council of war that kept him on the field, but a minor incident which had occurred that afternoon on the other side of the mountains.

2. *Lee's Letters Are Found in the Mailbag*

Captain Ulric Dahlgren had a roving Federal cavalry squadron, which on July 2 he took across South Mountain at the Monterey Pass, led through Waynesboro, and halted at Greencastle, where he was greeted much as if he were a conqueror, to the gratification of his pride and vanity.

He had just reached the age of twenty. His father, Admiral John Adolf Dahlgren, after whom the big, bottle-shaped, smooth-bore naval guns were named, was one of Lincoln's close confidants, whom the President, with his tinkering and inventive instincts, delighted to visit. Ulric was well acquainted with all the great figures of Washington whom the President brought to Admiral Dahlgren's house, stopping on visits to the Navy Yard, and probably could have had any type of military career he desired. But he had entered the dashing cavalry arm and was serving as a foot-loose patrol of Kilpatrick's division around Gettysburg.

Young Dahlgren was about to engage in an exploit that would fascinate the army and the capital, enliven the newspaper columns, win him a jump promotion over two grades, from captain to colonel, and ultimately lead to his death in circumstances that left him one of the figures in the Federal Army most odious to the South.

The sight of Dahlgren's blue column, in the rear of Lee's army, aroused the citizens who had watched so long the passing of the Southern host. The entire Greencastle population was brought to the streets. Dahlgren, accepting their cheers for a time, ordered them back into their houses and restored the town to a normal appearance. Then he hid his troopers around the corners of the public square, making ready to intercept any communications on that afternoon between Lee's army and the Confederate capital, for he was on the main route. With the trap set, he climbed to the belfry of the Dutch Reformed Church and surveyed the surrounding country with his glasses.

Sure enough, a Confederate cavalry company was approaching from the south. It was not well led and came into town blindly, without even outriders or an advance party. Jeb Stuart had contributed so much already to Lee's discomfiture that it seems superfluous to mention other instances. But if Stuart had been on hand properly discharging his duties, one of which was to protect the army's communications, Lee's rear would not have been exposed to the molestation of such small Federal bodies as Dahlgren's. Robertson, Jones, and Imboden were supposed to be watching, but their forces were limited and Stuart's vigorous leadership was lacking.

As the Confederate troop came into the square, Dahlgren's men dashed out suddenly with a shrill yell, fired their pistols, and, more by the impetuosity of their assault than by their numbers, threw the Southern column into disorder and flight.[18] The prisoners included 3 officers and 14 men.

Then Dahlgren discovered what a treasure of intelligence he had captured. The detachment was bringing up the official Richmond mail addressed to General Lee, and even a cursory examination disclosed to the Federal cavalry captain its significance. Dahlgren set out at once for Meade's headquarters, about thirty-five miles away. So concerned was he lest he encounter another body of Confederates and have his packet wrested from him, on leaving Waynesboro, he split his command and had part of the men form a barricade on the eastern hill by piling wagons and farm equipment across the roadway. He crossed again over Monterey Pass, moved by Emmitsburg, and finally handed the Confederate mailbag to Meade's chief of staff, General Butterfield. Butterfield read the letters and went at once to

Meade. The hour is uncertain, but it must have been near midnight.

The correspondence showed that Lee's force on Seminary Hill was the full load of the invasion.

Lee would not receive the reinforcements of Corse's, Jenkins', or Cooke's brigades. He would have to detach men from his own army to keep his communications open. Beauregard would not establish a second front in Virginia threatening Washington. This highly important phase of Lee's planning—the assembly of an actual army, or "an army in effigy," at Culpeper, to menace the Federal capital from the south while Lee was on its flank in Pennsylvania—had collapsed.

All this was clear from the correspondence. Meade need not worry about any sudden foray on Washington, or the arrival of reinforcements for Lee, or operations against his own rear, or anything except the embattled Confederate army in his immediate front. The reading of these dispatches bolstered Meade's confidence; if, as some have felt, it had been as limp as a wisp of smoke, it quickly came as stiff as a gun barrel.

Lee's recommendation had been given rather cavalier treatment in Richmond. The captured correspondence, soon published in the Northern press, showed that Jefferson Davis had not been diligent to create an army at Culpeper. Though Lee had proposed it in his letter of June 23, Davis had never heard of the idea when Adjutant General Cooper went to discuss it with him on the night of June 28. The government was behind with its correspondence. Instead of threatening Washington, Davis was fearful about Richmond with Lee away.

All that the Richmond authorities would have had to do was pull together the brigades and regiments scattered through Virginia and the Carolinas. But they did not recognize what Lee had emphasized: that every man who could be spared had to be thrown into this great invasion effort. A New York *Herald* story dated July 3 told that a member of Longstreet's staff had been captured heading south, on his way, he said, to Culpeper, "to ascertain what had become of Beauregard's army." It merely had never been born.

Colonel Edward A. Palfrey, of New Orleans, claimed to have obtained, second-hand of course, Dahlgren's own account of what had happened respecting the dispatches. In summary: when Dahlgren saw their importance, he rode to Meade's headquarters, arriving shortly after midnight, and found Meade consulting with his corps commanders. Meade, according to this verson, had already resolved to withdraw to Pipe Creek, but a perusal of the captured dispatches caused him to change his plans abruptly. The artillery was ordered back into position. Palfrey found his own conclusions verified to some extent, or to his own satisfaction, by the unusual preferment given young Dahlgren by Lincoln and Stanton.[19] It appeared they thought he had performed an unusual service indeed. It is a fair speculation—but only a speculation—that young Dahlgren told Lincoln and Stanton how he delivered the captured dispatches just in time to hold Meade on the battlefield; and that Lincoln's response, as in the instance of Sickles, was an impulsive "God-bless-you-for-it" attitude. The only solid fact is that Captain Dahlgren became Colonel Dahlgren almost on the spot.

The bounty of fortune and glare of fame were strong stimulants for the young man, whose story should be completed. In the following March Colonel Dahlgren, still not twenty-one, led part of a cavalry attack on Richmond. Next morning William Littlepage, thirteen, saw a "dead Yankee" in the ditch and searched for a watch, but all he found was a cigar case and memorandum box. In the box was enough to show it was Dahlgren's body, together with orders by Dahlgren for his men to release the Belle Island prisoners, cross the James River to Richmond and "destroy and burn the hateful city, and not allow the Rebel leader Davis and his traitorous crew to escape." Another admonition was: "The men must keep together and well in hand, and once in the city it must be destroyed, and Jeff Davis and Cabinet killed."[20] The orders were a burst of individual braggadocio, of course, but they united the South, stiffened the resistance, and probably contributed to many Northern casualties.

About the rumbling of the guns there could be little doubt. Pickets in the midst of a deadly battle do not manufacture information and then have it verified by other attentive scouts. Steuart's men reported it; Ewell had the account to him verified; Nicholl's Louisiana brigade must have heard it also, because the story was current in New Orleans after the war and Palfrey declared there were men in that city who would testify to its correctness.[21]

Is it possible they heard Candy trying to get back to Culp's Hill? This wandering brigade that had marched down the Baltimore pike never knew where it was going or where it had been. Said Captain Joseph A. Moore of the 147th Pennsylvania:

It seemed to be a night of bewilderment to all, for I have failed to discover any two members of the 147th whose views coincided on the route traversed.[22] It was a night of slow, tiresome, roundabout maneuvering, through fields, over fences, now on the pike; then a whispered halt! a rest for a few minutes; the men asleep! Wake up! a forward march. . . .

But all the while Candy's men were coming closer to Culp's Hill and the rumbling artillery was moving farther and farther away.[23] Were they Federal guns or phantom guns? Was it the apparition of unconquered Stonewall rolling his specter caissons over the Pennsylvania hills on a long flank march behind the Federal lines? Many great battles have had their mysteries. Gettysburg has "The Strange Case of the Retiring Artillery."

3. The Wandering Cavalryman Returns

Lee's headquarters cottage that night was crowded with officers, some seeking orders, some greeting friends from other commands, some responding to the summons of the commanding general; adjutants coming and going; altogether a pack that made passage inside the little house difficult. Outside, crowds of soldiers hovered in the neighborhood, those who liked to gossip about what the army's next move might be, drawn to the headquarters like yokels to a magician's tent.

At ten o'clock soldiers were cooking supper along the streets of the town, obviously in top spirits as a result of the battle progress that day. An unidentified officer summoned to headquarters found it crowded with staff officers who had assembled from all parts of the battlefield. At eleven o'clock a stir of muffled excitement and suspense passed over the crowd as two muddy, fatigued generals, with staffs, dismounted on the Cashtown pike, walked through the short yard and entered the headquarters building. The long-missing J. E. B. Stuart, followed by Fitzhugh Lee and Major Henry B. McClellan, Stuart's adjutant, was reporting his arrival to the commanding general.

Only one account is known to exist of the meeting between Lee and Stuart and it is far from satisfactory. It was set down fifty-two years after the battle by Brigadier General Thomas T. Munford, who was not present but who had the information from Major McClellan. Munford, one of Stuart's colonels in the Gettysburg campaign, wrote from Roanoke, Virginia, July 24, 1915, to Mrs. Charles H. Hyde, of Lookout Mountain, Tennessee, that McClellan had told him the meeting was "painful beyond description."[24]

Lee had raised his arm—there was no suggestion that he intended to strike Stuart, but more likely, it seemed, in a gesture—and said, "General Stuart, *where have you been?* Not one word from your command has been received by me! Where have you been?"

Stuart, according to McClellan, "wilted." He told Lee the course he had followed and, in what would appear an appeal for mitigation, added, "I have brought you 150 wagons and their mule teams."

"Yes, general, but they are an impediment to me now! Let me ask your help. We will not discuss the matter longer."

Lee then gave Stuart directions for his part in the battle of the next day, and Stuart left. On the same page of this letter, but in a different hand, was a memorandum note that Munford said McClellan had quoted one more of Lee's remarks: "I have not heard a word from you for days, and you the eyes and ears of my army."

Lee at first reflected wrath, then great tenderness, the notation added.

The account does not fit conveniently into one's conception of Lee's character, in which self-control was the dominant note. Considering the lapse of more than half a century before it was written down, the wording cannot be looked on as in any respect exact. Stuart surely could not have attached great importance to 150 wagons (the correct number was 125) when the army had thousands. Nor would Lee have called them an impediment now, however much they may have slowed the cavalry earlier.

Remembering how George Cary Eggleston had observed that Lee spoke in crisp, compact, even epigrammatic sentences, one is more inclined to accept the conventional story of the meeting, in which Lee, when the cavalry commander presented himself, looked at him and said, "Well, General Stuart, you are here at last."[25]

For those who knew Lee, there could scarcely have been stronger censure.

Stuart had reached Gettysburg without difficulty after Lee's scout had found him. Colonel R. L. T. Beale, of the 9th Virginia Cavalry, who attended Dickinson College at Carlisle and knew the territory brought down the wagons, the pitiful little exhibit of achievement Stuart had to offer. There was not a modicum of what he loved most—glory.

After Stuart had left, Powell Hill reached the headquarters, where he went about shaking hands with friends he had not seen since leaving Virginia. Apparently he was in the best of spirits and showed no trace of his illness of the last few days. Battle always exhilarated him.

It is not clear, but apparently Hill (of all people!) was receiving congratulations on the day's work. Lee was busy in his office room, but Hill's voice carried to him over the hubbub. The affection of the commanding general for his singular subordinate was warm and genuine, almost fatherly. He attached no blame to Hill for stopping the army's attack when it reached the middle of his corps.

Lee made his way through the crowd of other officers and clasped Hill by the hand. "It is all well, General," he said. "Everything is well."[26]

Then he and Hill walked away from the others—they must have gone into the little back room Lee was using for an office—and talked together for a quarter of an hour. This was about the nearest Lee came to holding a "council of war" that night. Longstreet was sleeping on his saddle; Ewell was preparing for the bloody battle the next morning on Culp's Hill.

The unidentified officer whom Lee had summoned commented that the general looked well, which may have meant that he was recovering from the diarrhea Blackford had found disturbing him earlier in the day. The line of people waiting to see Lee must have looked like the patients in the office of a popular country doctor on a Saturday morning. General Lee was busy with a plan for evacuating the wounded, work a competent staff should have discharged smoothly without ever bringing it to the commanding general's notice.[27] But he dropped everything when Colonel Marshall announced this caller. He thought that this man and a Captain Brockenborough were well acquainted with the upper Potomac fords and he wanted them to go with General Imboden, who was expected to arrive in the morning with his cavalry brigade from Chambersburg, and start a convoy of wounded for Virginia. Lee's staff had been remiss even in the most ordinary of secretarial duties, because Lee had been misinformed and was wasting his time with officers who were intimately acquainted with the fords of the Rappahannock, not the Potomac. An adjutant might have learned this by one or two questions, before showing them in; in fact, a competent adjutant would have acquainted himself with the purposes of most of Lee's callers.

When the mistake was discovered, Lee was advised that the expert on Potomac fords was a man named Logan, from Winchester, Virginia, serving in Rodes's division. He turned at once to Marshall or Taylor—both staff members were with him—and said, "Hunt up Mr. Logan and send him to me at once."[28] It was then 1:00 A.M.

With all this detail, how much attention was Lee actually allowed to give to the renewal of the battle on the morrow? He has been pictured as morose on the night of July 2, believing he was about to be defeated.[29] That obviously was not the case. He was mired down in office work.

"He was full of business," said his caller, "and his strong mind and intellectual energies were taxed to their utmost." This man went on to describe the surrounding scene: "The fences all around the head-quarters were lined with soldiers who had participated in the struggle of the day, relating their experiences. The writer remained with these until the morning sun appeared on Friday, July 3."[30]

That would be the way in such a gregarious, high-spirited army. Men about to continue on the next day one of the hardest fights of human history would prepare themselves by staying up all night talking about it.

4. The Sleepy Armies Fight to Exhaustion on Culp's Hill

Had Ewell possessed prescience, time, and ample men—had Pickett's, a fresh division, been thrown around to Lee's left, augmented by Stuart's newly arrived cavalry—Ewell might have exploited the breech made by Steuart's brigade in the Federal defenses on Culp's Hill, driven past the Baltimore pike and the Taneytown road, and hit the center of the Federal army in its rear.

The soldiers might pray for an hour of Jackson, who would have supplied all the intuitive judgment needed, but even Stonewall would have needed some good brigades. As it developed, Ewell's attack did not go past the flank to the mushy Federal rear—which must have been sensitive and yielding—but directly against the entrenched line, which was as firm as the great boulders amid which it was anchored.

Ewell possessed none of these prerequisites of prescience, men, and time, least of all time. Before he was astir on the morning of July 3, Slocum was ahead of him.

If, on this far flank of the armies, the Southerners were led hesitantly by Ewell, they possessed in Johnson one of their most stubborn fighters. They were opposed by one of the toughest of the Federals—Major General Henry W. Slocum, who would never fight until he had to, and then, as the saying went about army favorites, he confused himself with a wildcat.

He had been a colonel at First Manassas and ended the war heading two corps as commander of the Army of Georgia, and all the time the

men serving under him never lost a stand of colors or a gun. Some
liked to say it was because Slocum preferred maneuvering to battling—even maneuvering to keep out of sight when hard assignments
were in prospect. The instance of his coolly refusing to answer Howard's call to come to Gettysburg without orders on July 1 was an
example. The aggregate of the record, however, was different.

Slocum, an upstate New Yorker and West Point graduate (he
roomed with five-year-man Sheridan and yet was an honor student),
went into the artillery, but while serving at Fort Moultrie he kept his
active mind occupied by reading law in the office of the eminent
South Carolina judge, B. C. Presley. In 1857 he left the army and
hung out his shingle in Syracuse, New York, where he became county
treasurer and then a state legislator. There was something independent, even perverse, about him. He wore only a mustache in an army
that decreed whiskers. Being an ardent Republican before the war,
he became after the war, at a time when almost anybody could be
elected under the Republican label, a Democrat, because, though he
had been second in command of Sherman's "Bummers," he did not
like the "scorched-earth policy" the radicals of Congress were applying to the defeated South. A hard fighter, he was a magnanimous
winner; he resigned from the army with the coming of peace, became
a Brooklyn lawyer, amassed a tidy fortune, and left a more enviable
record than those generals who, like Grant, were ambitious above
their talents.

In arranging his battle plans for July 3, Lee had told Ewell to
attack on the Federal right as a cover for an assault he was planning
against the center, but here was where Ewell lacked time.

Slocum had been up all night making arrangements. Powerful batteries already had been ranged along Power's and McAllister's hills,
commanding the valley of Rock Creek and the south and east face
of Culp's Hill. The Confederate guns, on the other hand, had been
left far behind. They could not be drawn over the rugged ground, and
with no cannon Johnson faced the prospect of an uneven battle.

The summer dawn was showing faintly when Brigadier General John
W. Geary drew his service pistol and fired a single shot into the air.[31]
It was 3:45 A.M. At once an inferno of artillery fire was turned loose
on the Confederates rousing themselves in the old Federal trenches
or lying in groups at the east base of Culp's Hill. Then the infantry
brigades of Candy and Kane let out a rapid rifle fire, which McDougall,
Colgrove, and the Eastern Shore Marylanders under Lockwood, in-

Battle of Culp's Hill. July 3, 1863.

cluding the Federal 1st Maryland, quickly joined. Virtually none of
Slocum's men had had sleep since reaching Gettysburg, and many of
them, lying prone on the firing line at this early hour, fell asleep with

the battle roaring about them. Company officers had to move along
the line and prod them.

"We can see no Rebs to fire at," complained a private of the 147th
Pennsylvania. He was told that orders were to keep firing "continually
and without intermission"[32] through the trees in their front, across a
little field and into the woods beyond. There Johnson's Confederates
had been planning to do some attacking themselves, but the initiative
had been stolen from them.

Pap Williams, whose division was commanded by Brigadier General Thomas H. Ruger, a West Point graduate who had come up
through the command of a Wisconsin regiment, was on Geary's right
and quickly shared in this pre-daylight fighting.

John W. Geary, a huge man, built solidly, whose size did not prevent him from carrying himself like a soldier, was a Pennsylvanian
who had already been postmaster of San Francisco, governor of Kansas, and a colonel in the Mexican War. After the war he would serve
two terms of governor of Pennsylvania. At times he was given a wide
berth by many in the army because of his violent temper, which was
an antisocial characteristic in a man nearly six feet, six inches tall.

Since Slocum had returned to Culp's Hill by way of the Baltimore
pike, he was inside the arc that had been thrown around Culp's Hill
by Johnson. Geary had taken position on Greene's right, and Ruger
continued the line to Spangler's Spring. They faced the old Federal
trenches still held at the coming of daylight by the Southerners. Kane's
little brigade numbered about 650. Brigadier General Thomas L.
Kane had been absent on sick leave for several weeks, but when action
was promised, he appeared in an ambulance and tried to command
from his bed. His strength was not sufficient and Colonel George A.
Cobham, 111th Pennsylvania, who later fell before Atlanta leading
his regiment at Peach Tree Creek, took the command.

As a prelude to their infantry attack, the Federal artillery blasted
the trenches along the southeast shoulder of Culp's Hill, then Geary
advanced on Johnson's right and center while Ruger undertook a
flanking movement across the marshy ground and small stream that
flowed from Spangler's Spring. Scarcely had this attack been beaten
off when Johnson, in desperate fury because he could not answer the
destructive Federal artillery fire, responded with an infantry assault
along his front. The Confederates came on in three close lines.

"The enemy advanced steadily," said Captain Moore of the 147th
Pennsylvania, "and in splendid order, and was certainly under the im-

pression that Lee's hopes depended upon their success." When their columns were less than 100 yards from the Federal position, Geary's long line poured a "deliberate and most deadly fire" into them. Moore said it was with "well-aimed precision, such as old veterans alone could do."[33] The assaulting column was well-nigh destroyed.

McKim wrote in his diary:

The men were mowed down with fearful rapidity. . . . It was the most fearful fire I ever encountered, and my heart was sickened with the sight of so many gallant men sacrificed. The greatest confusion ensued—regiments were reduced to companies and everything mixed up. It came very near being a rout."[34]

McKim made another and a revealing entry in his diary: "The storm of shot and shell was terrible, yet I went to sleep in the midst of it several times."[35]

On this assault Johnson's men obtained a clear view by daylight of the Baltimore pike, littered with the behind-the-lines debris, loaded with wagons and refugees, enlivened by squadrons of cavalry dashing about to check stragglers continually trying to escape from the battlefield. The sight inspired Johnson to redoubled efforts.

Captain Joseph Matchett of the 46th Pennsylvania, McDougall's brigade of Ruger's division, maintained that Johnson had actually reached the pike the night before but, fearing a trap, hesitated and pulled back. He attributed the apprehension to the intervention of providence. "They were made afraid when there was nothing to fear."[36]

Now Ruger's men in turn assaulted the line of Steuart and Walker. Colgrove's brigade made a bloody, impassioned charge. This attack showed how the desperate nature of the fighting caused the soldiers of both armies to forget all else, including any sense of time. The 27th Indiana had begun firing at 3:50 A.M. It helped make the assault on the Confederate works and was beaten off with heavy loss. Later when officers and men tried to establish the time of the assault, some thought it was as early as five and some as late as ten o'clock in the morning.[37] In the attack the 27th moved with the 2nd Massachusetts.

"It cannot be done. It cannot be done," said the Hoosier Colonel Silas Colgrove, commanding the brigade, muttering to himself, when he got the attack order. "But if it can be done," he added, "the 2nd Massachusetts and 27th Indiana can do it." He questioned sharply the adjutant who brought the order, and when assured it was genuine, he declared, "It is murder, but it is an order. Up men, over the works! Forward, double-quick!"[38]

Near the Confederate line the three right companies of the 27th seemed to be knocked over together, and a withering volley hit the rest of the line. "The air was alive with singing, hissing and zipping bullets." They pressed on, but fell short of their objective and the survivors of the two broken regiments had to be recalled. That was much the story with regiments of both armies all along the line.

For seven hours the battle of Culp's Hill rolled up and down the rocky slope, with neither side content to remain on the defensive, and both insisting on carrying their attack to the heart of the enemy's position. Now and again, as the battle would lull momentarily, Johnson would try vainly to catch the sound of Longstreet's battle, which he presumed was raging far off to his right.

Random bullets flew high through the air, passed over Culp's Hill and sang, almost spent, through Hancock's ranks on Cemetery Ridge about a mile away. On Cemetery Hill the men followed Slocum's fight by the sound of the firing and "almost held their breath in anxiety." But Longstreet remained silent in front of them.

Big Geary charged back and forth along the lines like a bull trying to find a gap in a tight fence, while on the opposite side "Clubby" Johnson limped about cursing, admonishing, praying. Back in Richmond, War Clerk Jones had written: "Instead of a sword he goes into battle with a stout cane in his hand, with which he belabors any skulking miscreant found dodging in the hour of danger."[39] But Johnson's tongue must have been sufficient, though some of the men began to call him "Fence Rail" Johnson, which suggested he used his big stick as a bar.

When the battle opened in the morning, the Confederate brigades that had been engaged until ten o'clock on the evening before found themselves short of ammunition. The 3rd North Carolina had but two rounds, and the men hunted about among the dead and wounded and temporarily replenished their supply. Steuart sent a staff officer and a detail across Rock Creek to the reserve ammunition wagons, which were parked a mile and a quarter away, near where Johnson had launched his attack. They emptied boxes of cartridges into a blanket, swung the blanket on a fence rail, and carried the load over the rocks and through the bushes to the front.[40]

The sun came up, burned off a thin morning mist, and beat down with a heat more intense than that given off by the thousands of gun blasts and the hot Federal cannon. Nobody on the firing line got a minute's relief in seven hours of intense fury. The battle here was without any general movement or form, other than that each side fought with the desperate determination to exterminate the other or drive him from the slopes of the hill.

Major Henry Kyd Douglas, concerned that Extra Billy Smith might not get his brigade up in the proper place, had galloped back at 5:00 A.M. and helped the old politician. Smith was "cool and deliberate—too much so, just then,"[41] but he put his men into line. Ewell, in compliance with Lee's orders, although without effort to co-ordinate his movement with any Longstreet might be making, ordered a final attack all along Johnson's line. Daniel brought his shredded brigade up from Rodes's line to support Steuart and both he and Steuart, looking at the forbidding hill in front of them, deplored the attack order. The line Steuart would have to assail was that of the traverse trench running almost at right angles to his own line. Behind this was a sort of ravelin giving the Federals two parallel entrenched lines, each heavily manned. Steuart remonstrated, but when the time came he jumped from the trenches with his men, formed a line of battle on the other side, ordered bayonets fixed, and, drawing his sword, charged up the hill at the head of his brigade. The brigade was checked on a flank but reached to within twenty or thirty paces of the Federal entrenchments before being beaten back. By this time Culp's Hill was being called by the Confederates the "Hill of Death."

"That last charge on the third day was a cruel thing for the Third," said Colonel S. D. Thurston, of the 3rd North Carolina.[42] At the end of the fight it had 77 muskets out of 300, a loss of almost 75 per cent.

When time came for a withdrawal, Johnson's men were not pursued. The firing seemed to stop by mutual agreement. Both armies were exhausted. It was 11:00 A.M. Johnson retired slowly to the foot of the hill, then formed a new line along the west bank of Rock Creek, which he held for the remainder of the day. Slocum did not undertake to dislodge him.

When the results were reviewed, it was recognized that Culp's Hill had been the scene of some of the most determined, sanguinary fighting of the war. Geary always thought that the main battle of Gettysburg was won by Meade's army on Culp's Hill.

Kane's brigade found 500 dead Confederates in its front. Somewhere among them was a squat little man, Wesley Culp, a private in Company B, 2nd Virginia, of the Stonewall Brigade. He was twenty-four and because he was only five feet tall, Colonel Douglas had had a special gun made for him.[43] Where he fell he could look at the house where he was born. Like Henry Wentz, he had gone to Virginia to sell Gettysburg carriages and Southern eyes made him stay.

CHAPTER TWENTY-ONE

Pickett, Pettigrew, and Trimble

1. Arrival of the Virginians

At two o'clock on the morning of July 2 the long roll sounding in the Chambersburg streets aroused Pickett's men, and well before dawn they were on the road—dusty that morning—marching toward the battlefield with which their name will forever be associated.

The division was the smallest in Lee's army because the two veteran brigades of "tough old bull-terrier" Montgomery D. Corse and "ardent" Micah Jenkins[1] had been left to defend Richmond—temporarily, by Lee's intentions. Had Pickett received his missing brigades, his division would have numbered about 8,000, instead of less than 4,800 at Gettysburg,[2] and the difference might have been decisive.

Pickett had been busy in Chambersburg while awaiting the coming of Imboden's cavalry to relieve him as the rear guard for Lee's army. All liquor had been kept under lock in the courthouse.[3] He had destroyed the railroad and railroad shops, depots, and all public machinery, though he had reluctantly followed Lee's orders respecting private property. Now that most things made of iron had been twisted, rolling stock flattened, turntables burned, the last cattle rounded up, and the country cleaned of provisions, he regarded his duty done and his rear-guard service ended. He was happy, as he passed the ruins of Thaddeus Stevens' Caledonia Iron Works, to see that Early had made a delay there unnecessary.

Pickett's division, after the detachment of Jenkins' Georgia Brigade, was all-Virginian. As it took up the march, Garnett headed the column. Brigadier General Richard Brooke Garnett, forty-four years old, was a somewhat pathetic figure for whom keen sympathy existed in Lee's army. A West Point graduate who had remained in the old Federal service, he was, under the Confederacy, an officer about whom one of Jackson's most embittered personal battles had centered; the unforgiving Stonewall had pursued it almost to the point of persecution.

Garnett was an able soldier, the son of an Essex County plantation owner, whose devoted twin brother had given his life in nursing sufferers in the yellow-fever epidemic in Norfolk in 1855.[4] Richard was of the same selfless and courageous mold, but too easy in his attitude to suit his zealous commander. Garnett had first incurred Jackson's displeasure in the mid-winter Romney campaign of early 1862, on which Jackson pressed his poorly clad men so mercilessly through the snow that the discipline of Loring's division broke down, a storm of public criticism was aroused, and in the charges and recriminations, Jackson submitted his resignation, which he withdrew only after the intercession of Governor Letcher. Garnett commanded the Stonewall Brigade in the campaign and had his brush with Jackson when he rested his cold and hungry men as they toiled over the mountains. Jackson rode up, demanded the reason for the delay, and reprimanded him curtly.[5]

This should have been warning to Garnett that Jackson would expect the ultimate with scant thought of the men as long as they had an ounce of strength left to give for the cause. At the battle of Kernstown, where Jackson had not imparted his plans to his subordinates, Garnett fought with great bravery and ordered a retreat only when the line was broken elsewhere by a superior Federal force. His officers thought the withdrawal justified, but Stonewall was enraged and believed it lost the field for him. He was unsparing thereafter in his efforts to keep Garnett out of any command in the Confederate service. He relieved the brigadier general and preferred charges. The case dragged on for months, much to Garnett's distress, because Jackson never was in one place long enough for a court-martial to convene.[6] Finally Lee, short of trained officers as usual, assigned Garnett to Pickett's brigade for the Sharpsburg campaign, after Pickett had been wounded at Gaines' Mill, and the charges against him were pigeonholed in the light of his unfailing diligence.

But his spirit had been crushed by the reproaches of his severe commander and stirred by a deep sense of injustice, and he believed

Jackson guilty of deliberate falsehoods. When Pickett became a major general in September 1862, Garnett retained the brigade permanently as a part of Pickett's division.

Garnett's charitable nature was disclosed when he grieved over Jackson's death and marched as a sincere mourner in the procession of generals who followed the great leader to his grave, but Pickett's widow and biographer felt that "the sensitive mind of the brave general . . . never recovered from what he regarded as a stigma upon his military career."[7] That was the reason, she felt, and probably Pickett had the same belief, why Garnett insisted on leading the brigade at Gettysburg at a time when he was scarcely strong enough, after a debilitating illness, to sit on his horse. Nothing in his animated conduct suggested his physical weakness. He gave his orders with vigor and rode the lines with apparent enthusiasm. The only hint was that he wore his heavy blue overcoat[8] on the hot summer day.

Walter Harrison, inspector general of Pickett's division, thought that Garnett's whole purpose was to expose himself, even unnecessarily, "to wipe out effectively, by some great distinction in action, what he felt was an unmerited slur on his military reputation."[9] Eppa Hunton said of him simply, "He was one of the noblest and bravest men I ever knew."[10]

Armistead's brigade followed Garnett. Probably no officer in the army was more spirited and none possessed a more martial family background than Brigadier General Lewis A. Armistead. Like Wilcox, who was a career soldier of comparable rank out of the old army, he was somewhat above the average age of Lee's brigadier generals. But this, as in Wilcox's case, appeared due to chance instead of any reluctance by superiors to trust him. In this army of extraordinarily able brigade commanders, Armistead, by his courage, experience, and good judgment, would have stood in nearly everyone's top group.

Armistead's family had left its name on some of the peaks of American history. His uncle, Major George Armistead, had commanded Fort McHenry and kept the flag flying in Baltimore harbor during the attack by the British fleet September 13-14, 1814, which inspired Francis Scott Key to write "The Star-Spangled Banner." His grandfather had served under Washington. His father, Captain Walter Keith Armistead, an army engineer who had graduated in the second class at West Point, had laid out the defenses of Norfolk, Virginia, in the War of 1812. The gallant defense of Norfolk and the American victory in beating off a formidable British expedition headed by Major

General Sir Sidney Beckwith, June 1, 1813, had heartened the country at one of the most depressed moments of its history.

The Armistead family was from New Market, Virginia. Though Lewis was born in New Bern, North Carolina, he entered West Point from Virginia, and would have been graduated in 1838 had he not been expelled in his junior year because he wielded a plate effectively against Jubal Early's head. Early's scalp was merely cracked and there would be no basis for any supposition that this might have permanently affected Early's military judgment; nor did it retard Armistead's career, for, despite his ejection, he went in the service with a commission. His father had become the army's chief engineer and a brevet brigadier general, and was closely associated in the Florida wars with blunt old Zachary Taylor under whom Lewis became a second lieutenant in the 6th Infantry in 1839.

Young Armistead showed unusual bravery in the Mexican War and won repeated citations and brevets. He was on garrison duty with his good friend Hancock at Los Angeles when war came in 1861, but when the decision had to be made, he crossed the continent with Albert Sidney Johnston and cast his fortunes with Virginia.

Third in the column was the brigade of handsome James Lawson Kemper, thirty-nine years old. His only military experience had been as a volunteer captain in Mexico, though he reached Taylor's army too late for the battle of Buena Vista. He had graduated from Washington College (now Washington and Lee) at Lexington, Virginia, and studied law in Charleston; had turned to a legislative and legal career, served ten years in the Virginia House of Delegates, and for a term was Speaker. He volunteered on the outbreak of the war, commanded the 7th Virginia at First Manassas, served in turn under Early, Longstreet, and A. P. Hill, and finally was assigned under Pickett.[11]

Some of Pickett's men had been stationed beyond Chambersburg and a march of about thirty miles was ahead of them, but they left the town with loud shouts and with "more spirit and élan" than their leader had ever before observed in them.[12] The hot July sun burned their faces as they marched over the mountain. At Cashtown they heard the "sullen booming" and learned, in the staccato language of a behind-the-lines quartermaster, that the army had: ". . . been fighting for two days—driving the Yankees all the time—got 6,000 prisoners already—hurrah for Lee! . . ."[13] Soon they passed "acres of bluecoat prisoners" in a field and came upon a beautiful, "splendidly caparisoned black charger" which had been General Reynolds' mount. Within four miles of the battlefield in the late afternoon the division bivouacked, and the men "fell asleep to the lullaby of deep reverberations from the battle front."[14]

Pickett had ridden ahead to report to Longstreet. Being punctilious about the formalities, he did not go to Lee, but sent Harrison, his inspector general, to advise the commanding general of his presence and the proximity of his troops. Harrison reached Lee on Seminary Ridge while he was watching Anderson's brigades going into action. It was probably about 7:00 P.M. He told Lee that Pickett had marched twenty miles that day but with two hours' rest would be ready for use on any part of the field. Lee apparently was sanguine about the progress of the battle. At about that time Longstreet had signaled to him: "We are doing well."[15]

"Tell General Pickett," he said, "I shall not want him this evening; to let his men rest, and I will send him word when I want them."[16]

2. Lincoln's Protégé is Longstreet's Favorite

The drum roll sounded at 3:00 A.M. on the morning of July 3, and in the predawn blackness Pickett held a conference with his three brigadier generals—a "heart to heart powwow," he called it.[17] Pickett had not been apprised of the battle plans and the "powwow" turned out to be more frolicsome than somber. "Old Man Armistead," who was all of forty-six, and a widower like Pickett, though not a suitor, took a ring from his little finger, handed it to the love-smitten division commander, and said, "Give this little token, George, please, to her of the sunset eyes." In writing about it to his sweetheart, Pickett gushed with sentiment: "Dear old Lewis—dear old 'Lo' as Magruder always called him, being short for Lothario."

Whiskered, thoroughly military, ripened in middle age, Lewis was anything but a blade. Pickett, however, was in the clouds with thoughts of "My Sallie," the beautiful young LaSalle Corbell, whom he would marry after the Gettysburg campaign, and he must have looked on all the world as lovers. Longstreet, in after years, in his life long diligence to protect Pickett, told of his subordinate's devotion to the military profession, "tolerating no rival near the throne," except for the "beautiful, charming and talented lady"[18] he was courting.

Sorrel was not certain but that the lady held the scepter and military duty sat on the footstool, remembering how Pickett, while at

Suffolk, would steal off to see her without leave, asking him to cover up with Old Peter in case of difficulty. Sorrel was fearful an emergency, or movement of the corps, might occur while the general was A.W.O.L., but Pickett's need to go was desperate.

Typically Sorrel would say, when Pickett came to him, "No, you must go to the Lieutenant General."

"But he is tired of it and will refuse; and I must go, I must see her. I swear, Sorrel, I'll be back before anything can happen in the morning."[19]

Sorrell would not allow himself to be persuaded, but Pickett went nevertheless.

"Nothing could hold him back from that pursuit," according to Sorrel, who added, "I don't think his division benefited by such carpet-knight doings in the field."[20]

Pickett said he would take Armistead's ring to John Tyler, the Richmond jeweler, and have it made into a breastpin, "set around with rubies and diamonds and emeralds," with Sallie as the pearl. As they parted, Pickett grasped Armistead's hand. "Good luck, old man," he said warmly, as he rode off through the dawn to find Longstreet.[21]

For a time rain threatened northwest of Gettysburg. Clouds and mist hung low over the countryside. The order of march to the field was Kemper in the lead, followed by Garnett and Armistead, a normal rotation for the day which accounted for the assault order that placed Kemper and Garnett in the line and Armistead in support. At 7:00 A.M., the division was strung out behind Seminary Ridge, part of it in a field of rye. In front of the men was a long line of artillery, silent after the heavy duty of the day before; on the far left the roar of Slocum's artillery and the incessant rattle of musketry were the only indications that a battle was in progress.

The sun burned through the mist and soon the day was hot and humid. "Few believed they would be killed," said David Johnston of the 7th Virginia, but an exception was the colonel of that regiment, W. Tazwell Patton, known everywhere as one of the courageous, tough fighters of the army. He always had a presentiment that he would be hit, and he usually was, and his men knew that some day the bullet would be final.[22] His great-nephew, Lieutenant General George S. Patton, Jr., would be outstanding in the Second World War.

Marching with Armistead was the adjutant of the 9th Virginia, James Frank Crocker, of Isle of Wight County, Virginia, through whom a nostalgic pathos must have stirred, for he was returning after thirteen years to the scene of his scholastic triumphs at Pennsylvania College in Gettysburg. Now he could look out from Seminary Hill on the little town with its tree-lined streets, and see the college tower and long building ahead of him. Perhaps some of his old professors were in its halls. Crocker looked across at the Federal heights and told a group of the officers that it would be "another Malvern Hill."

Lee's attack plan was simple—to use Pickett's fresh division as the shock troops in an effort to break the Federal center. The Confederate commander had to continue the battle. He could not withdraw after two days of successful fighting. His attacks on Little Round Top and Culp's Hill had caused the Federal army to concentrate on its flanks; hence, its weakest point must be its center. The many advantages gained on July 2 convinced him that victory was possible on the third. He was no more inclined to favor Longstreet's enveloping movement around the Federal left than on the first day. The battle was joined and he would fight it to a decision on this ground.

Pickett and Pettigrew would advance on the same line. Pettigrew now commanded Heth's division. Two brigades would be added from Pender and two from Anderson. Stuart would be sent to Meade's rear to aggravate and pursue the Federals in case Pickett and Pettigrew achieved a break-through.

At 8:00 A.M. Pickett was summoned by Longstreet to the crest of Seminary Ridge, where he found the corps commander in a conversation, only one degree removed from heated, with General Lee. Pickett quoted Longstreet's words overheard as he came up:

Great God! Look, General Lee, at the insurmountable difficulty between our line and that of the Yankees—the steep hills—the tiers of artillery—the fences—the heavy skirmish line. And then we'll have to fight their infantry against their batteries. Look at the ground we'll have to charge over, nearly a mile of that open ground there, under the rain of their canister and shrapnel.[23]

Lee answered in what Pickett described as "his firm, quiet, determined voice, "The enemy is there, General Longstreet, and I am going to strike him."[24]

Longstreet's approach was rough, but that could not have impaired Lee's judgment. There is wonder that he could have been won to a hazardous alignment of his army by Early's persuasiveness, but rejected Longstreet's cautioning peremptorily. The reason undoubtedly was that being locked in battle, he would accept no less than a final decision.

Lee, Longstreet and Pickett rode along the line of Pickett's infantry. The men had been ordered to lie prone so as not to attract the attention of the enemy signal station clearly seen on Little Round Top, and had been told not to cheer. They merely lifted their caps as Lee and the others passed. Pickett, at his first opportunity, went off to write another letter or add a paragraph to his sweetheart:

Well, my darling, their fate and that of our beloved Southland will be settled ere your glorious brown eyes rest on these scraps of penciled paper—your soldier's last letter, perhaps.[25]

With Lee, Longstreet, Pickett and Armistead in close proximity on Seminary Ridge, about to launch an attack, it would have been natural for all of them to think back sixteen years to the storming of a citadel even more forbidding than the slopes of Cemetery Ridge.

Engineer officer Lee had provided the plan by which Scott had reached Mexico City. As Scott's army faced the towering fortress of Chapultepec, which seemed impregnable, Lieutenant Armistead was at the head of the 6th Infantry storming party. He was first to jump into the formidable ditch surrounding the castle and among the first to fall wounded. Near by was Lieutenant Hancock of the 6th, and a few paces behind, carrying the American flag, was Lieutenant Longstreet, who fell grievously wounded. As the colors dropped they were snatched up by Lieutenant George E. Pickett—newly from the academy—and carried forward.[26] In the words of Longstreet, Pickett "was first to scale the parapets" and "was the brave American who unfurled our flag over the castle."[27] For raising the Stars and Stripes and also the regimental flag of Longstreet's and his own 8th Infantry over the heights that gave the Americans Mexico City, Pickett, a low-ranking lieutenant, was brevetted captain.

Pickett maintained a fairly even level of mediocrity as a general, but when he rose it was to unusual heights. "A singular figure indeed!" exclaimed Sorrel, who retained through his life the memory of the day when the erect, well-built man of medium height, with a neatly fitted uniform and an elegant riding whip, reported to Longstreet to command a brigade in his division. His appearance, according to Sorrel, was "distinguished and striking." But what amazed the chief of staff was his extraordinary hair. "Long ringlets flowed loosely over his shoulders, trimmed and highly perfumed." That was not the most of it. His beard, likewise curly, was fragrant in the extreme, giving out, as Sorrel put it, the "scents of Araby."[28] In an army so stingy of time that Jackson would not let Garnett feed his men, where sleep was rationed scantily, and every moment had to be employed in the cause of independence, Pickett found ample leisure for arranging his coiffure and primping, as well as for writing his lengthy love letters. Still—apparently to Sorrel's surprise—he made in many respects a good brigadier general.

Pickett had been born in Richmond, Virginia, but owed his army career to a foxy Springfield, Illinois, lawyer, Abraham Lincoln, who procured his appointment to West Point from Illinois by interceding with Representative John Todd Stuart, of the Third Illinois District. Lincoln had served with Stuart in the Black Hawk War and had joined him as a law partner when, a melancholy, near-destitute young politician of twenty-eight years, he had first gone to Springfield. Stuart was a first cousin of Mary Todd.

Another of Lincoln's close friends was Andrew Johnston, a Springfield lawyer, who later returned to practice in Richmond, Virginia. The attachment between Lincoln and Johnston was based on the aspiration of both to write poetry. They exchanged their compositions, among them being Lincoln's famous poem of twenty-two verses on "A Bear Hunt," written when he was thirty-seven.[29]

Johnston's nephew, George Edward Pickett, came to Springfield to study law under his uncle, and Lincoln took a fancy to the frank, sensible young man. Pickett, not desiring to excite his uncle's choler, made Lincoln his confidant when he developed an aversion to lawbooks. His cousins, Harry Heth, Basil Duke and John Hunt Morgan, all of whom became Confederate generals, were talking of West Point, and when Pickett imparted to Lincoln his secret ambition to go there, the shrewd lawyer soon came up with the appointment from Congressman Stuart.

Thereafter, even in the grip of a deadly war, Pickett always spoke reverently of Lincoln,[30] and Lincoln used no harsher term about Pickett than "the rascal."[31]

Longstreet had met Pickett first at West Point,[32] and had been with the 8th Infantry when Pickett joined it as a second lieutenant in 1846.

"In memory I can see him," wrote Old Peter affectionately thirty-five years after Gettysburg, "of medium height, of graceful build, dark, glossy hair, worn almost to his shoulders in curly waves, of wonderous pulchritude and magnetic presence. . . ." His temperament was "open, frank and genial," and never did he by one word blame or censure his superior officers.[33]

When Sorrel took orders in an emergency, he could see how the corps commander always looked after Pickett "and made us give him things very fully; indeed, sometimes stay with him to make sure he did not get astray." That and the perfume caused Sorrel to summarize: "Such was the man whose name called up the most famous and heroic charge, perhaps, in the annals of war."[34]

But there were pinnacles, as at Chapultepec. His humanitarian service was extraordinary among the Northwest Indians, where he learned the language and dialects of the tribes, taught them, translated for them the Lord's Prayer and some of the American hymns and airs, and became known to the Nootkams and Chinooks as the "Great Chief," all of which indicated that the garrison years—which wore down many regular officers and sent some of them to the bottle— were not wasted by Pickett.

In the dispute with Great Britain over San Juan Island in Puget Sound, he refused to be budged with his sixty-eight men when threatened by a British naval force with a thousand, and said to his men calmly, "We will make a Bunker Hill of it."[35] War was averted and Pickett remained on San Juan until he resigned his commission to go with the Confederacy.

Yet despite Chapultepec and other Mexican engagements, in all of which he showed his mettle, and his resolution at San Juan, there was in the minds of some a question about Pickett's personal courage. Eppa Hunton rode along the lines at Suffolk with Pickett and his staff, past a position exposed to enemy fire, and noticed that Pickett, and his staff after him, lay flat against the necks of their horses, which amazed the colonel, who considered it showed a very bad example for the troops. Hunton, though he knew it was imprudent, rode "bolt upright in my saddle," and wondered about his general.[36]

3. Alexander Brings up the Guns

With staff and orderlies riding the lines, Lee's party was large enough to command the attention of enemy sharpshooters, and occasionally the Federal artillery threw a shell at them. Scattered about were the dead, wounded, and wreckage of the July 2 battle. The pleading eyes of a Federal Zouave, mortally wounded, seemed to beseech Lee's aid and compassion, but he was beyond the help of either the commanding general or physicians working over the field.[37] Although the dead were being buried, the number was so large that not much progress had been made in the early morning.

West of the Wheat Field Lee and Longstreet encountered General Wofford. The morning had advanced considerably, because Wofford placed the meeting as "before the artillery opened fire." He would scarcely have done so if it had been some hours before the bombardment, which opened at one. As they looked over the terrain Wofford told Lee he had nearly reached the crest of Cemetery Ridge on July 2. Lee asked him if he could go there again.

"No, General, I think not," Wofford replied.

"Why not?" asked Lee.

"Because, General, the enemy have had all night to entrench and reinforce. I had been pursuing a broken enemy and the situation is now very different."

Lee rode on without contradicting Wofford; still, he was not dissuaded. His confidence in the striking power of his army was strong. He seemed to have special trust in Pickett's Virginia division. When it had passed through Richmond for Drewry's Bluff in February, War Clerk Jones noted in his diary: "General Lee writes that this division can beat the army corps of Hooker, supposed to be sent to the Peninsula. It has 12,000—an army corps 40,000."[38] Jones may have been a little askew with his figures, but probably not about Lee's reliance on Pickett's men.

Meantime Lieutenant Colonel E. Porter Alexander had received orders before daylight to post the artillery to cover an assault, and he was busy assembling guns. Dearing's battalion of artillery had come up with Pickett, giving the corps a welcome addition. Longstreet had placed Alexander in charge of the First Corps artillery without notifying Colonel J. B. Walton, commander of the Washington Artillery and the ranking artillery officer of the corps. Friction was averted until the brooding years after the battle. Now Alexander, as Longstreet's personal representative, labored diligently all morning to arrange an impressive artillery line in front of the infantry. He was an officer given to action, and he stirred the artillerists to unusual efforts. He put 75 pieces along the First Corps front, the right of the line resting on the high ground at the Peach Orchard that had been wrested from Sickles, and the left joining the artillery of Hill's corps, which would take part in the bombardment of the Federal center.

Despite the potentially explosive situation with Colonel Walton, the

Washington Artillery was brought up from reserve near the Cashtown road and put in the middle of the line. Alexander had all the artillery animals that had been taken to the rear for pasture and forage returned to the front to move the guns into position and give mobility in the impending action. Caissons that had gone to the reserve trains for fresh ammunition supplies were brought forward. Guns were drawn over from Devil's Den.[39] He borrowed from General Pendleton, chief of the army's artillery, seven 12-pounders of Richardson's Battalion of the Third Corps artillery. He looked over the ground behind the lines carefully, found a safe spot for these guns, and put them by as a reserve so they would be available to accompany Pickett's troops on the advance. If the other batteries should be disabled or depleted of ammunition, here at least would be seven pieces with fresh horses and full ammunition chests, ready to support the infantry at the critical moment of the battle.[40]

Aware that an army operating so far from its base is never flush with ammunition, Alexander restrained the First Corps artillery from firing that morning while he looked as best he could into the reserve situation. Apparently the ammunition was a matter to which Chief of Artillery Pendleton had given little attention, for no inventory had been kept as the battle progressed, and Lee unknowingly was just about to begin his supreme effort with no certainty that his infantry could expect sustained artillery support.

According to Alexander, each piece carried in its limber and caisson between 130 and 150 rounds, including canister, which would be useful only to a limited extent in bombarding lines nearly a mile away. Artillery at the time of Gettysburg was firing a wide range of ammunition, including solid shot, explosive shells and shrapnel of different types, rifled projectiles, canister, case shot, grape. The rounds carried with each piece would be enough for rapid firing for no more than an hour and a half. The question that remained was what was in the reserve ordnance trains. Alexander calculated that the maximum reserve taken into Pennsylvania was 100 rounds per gun but he doubted that the amount exceeded 60 rounds, the practice in the Richmond area having been to carry only 50 rounds in reserve per gun.[41] Pendleton gave neither Lee nor Longstreet, on whom Lee imposed the over-all command of the assault, information on the condition of the ordnance reserve and such information was vitally important considering that the army had been fighting for two days and must have expended a considerable part of its supplies. Lee's staff must share in the blame for this appalling oversight, but the responsibility would seem to be more directly chargeable to the chief of artillery.

Alexander's horror can be imagined when at about eleven o'clock all of Hill's 63 guns began sportive firing at the Bliss barn in their front, where skirmishers of both armies had been carrying on desultory fighting.[42] The barn had little tactical value, but when the Federal artillery joined in the battle between the skirmishers, Colonel Lindsay Walker, commanding Hill's artillery, replied capriciously, with Hill interposing no objection. The artillery combat lasted half an hour, the barn was blown to bits, the skirmishers retained pretty much their respective positions, and it should have been obvious that the Confederate Third Corps management was thinking more about letting off steam than conserving powder in order to win a battle. By about eleven-thirty this firing died away. The Culp's Hill engagement had ended at eleven, and an expectant silence settled over the two long ridges crowded with the hostile armies.

Pender's two brigades assigned to participate with Pickett and Pettigrew were those of Lane and Scales, both composed entirely of North Carolina troops. Scales had been wounded on the first day and the command had passed to Colonel William L. J. Lowrance, of the 38th North Carolina.

Brigadier General James Henry Lane, twenty-nine years old, filled competently the highly difficult role of a Virginian leading North Carolina troops. The antipathy between the two states, which was usually expressed mildly but seethed on occasions, was a heritage of colonial times, when North Carolina planters, possessing no adequate seaport north of Wilmington, had been forced to use Norfolk, an irritating expedient from which the Carolinians felt they suffered at the hands of astute Virginia traders. Though the hostility, ordinarily latent, had been largely laid aside in the war, it was being fanned into flame at the time of the Gettysburg campaign because of the politically inept appointment by President Davis of a Virginian to be Confederate tax collector in North Carolina.

Lee's march into Pennsylvania commanded little more attention in the North Carolina press than this gaucherie of the Richmond government. In Raleigh the appointee, the "chief Tithingman," was referred to in no more deferential fashion than "a person by the name of Bradford,"[43] and when it was made known that a wounded North Carolina officer had been rejected, a demand was set up that "foreign mercenaries must be withdrawn from the state."[44] Resolutions were adopted, the people were informed that South Carolina or Georgia would not submit to such an indignity, and the storm subsided only when the appointment was withdrawn. It set the stage for the later exchanges between individuals in the two states over phases of the third day at Gettysburg.

But Virginian Lane held the strong affections of a North State brigade that was being chaffed by the rest of the army because the fire of one of its regiments, the 18th North Carolina, had brought down Stonewall Jackson at Chancellorsville.

The 18th North Carolina carried a heavy burden of sadness for its role in this tragedy and grieved in common with all the Confederate cause. The regiment made no effort to shift the blame; the only explanation was that they had been told to fire at anyone coming down the road and did so.

The temper of the men with whom Lane had to deal could be seen from their reaction to a rebuke by A. P. Hill when, half an hour after Jackson was wounded, he reproved them for firing at a noise and, incidentally, hitting him in the calf of the leg.

A backwoodsman in Company B, 18th North Carolina, talked back to Hill. "Everybody knows," he said, "that the Yankee army can't run the Light Division and one little general needn't try it."[45]

Hill merely limped down the road.

Stonewall Jackson had given the brigade its greatest tribute after the battle at Cedar Run, August 9, 1862, where it had plugged the gap when the Stonewall Brigade had fallen back. Jackson had not used words. He had ridden to the brigade, then Branch's, and silently removed his cap and dropped it on the ground in front of the men.[46]

The brigade, known as "the flower of the Cape Fear section," had petitioned after Sharpsburg—where its early commander, Lawrence O'Brien Branch, was killed—to have Lane, then colonel of the 28th North Carolina, promoted to brigadier general. He was born on a Virginia plantation, educated by tutors, and stood second in his class at V.M.I.; then studied science three years at the University of Virginia and returned to V.M.I. to become assistant professor in the departments of mathematics and tactics. He went on to the North Carolina Military Institute, where he held the chair of natural philosophy and military tactics at the outbreak of the war. He became major of the 1st North Carolina, of which Daniel Harvey Hill was colonel. On reaching Virginia in 1861, Lane conducted the scouting party which encountered the enemy and brought on the battle of Bethel, the first of the war. He served thereafter in all the major engagements and surrendered with Lee, and thus, possibly alone of all Lee's officers, represented the story of the Confederate army from Bethel to Appomattox.[47]

Lane was the senior brigadier general of Pender's division, and took command when Pender fell, but Lee, having a surplus major general in Trimble, assigned him to command the brigades of Lane and Lowrance (formerly, Scales's).

The selection of brigades appears to have been made at random, and Lee obviously did not have prudent guidance either from Hill or any of his subordinates closely acquainted with the condition of the corps. Lane's brigade was a proper choice. Being on Pender's right flank in the July 1 attack on the Seminary, it had been occupied casually by Buford's cavalry, and had suffered only minor losses. Scales, on the other hand, had lost heavily. Not only was the brigade commander out of the action, but every field officer except one had been wounded. Captains were commanding regiments and sergeants companies.

Mahone's brigade of Anderson's division, and Thomas' of Pender's division had scarcely been under fire. Posey's brigade of Anderson's division was comparatively fresh. These brigades might have been used to provide the initial impetus to Hill's attack, along with Lane, thus leaving Pettigrew's division (Heth's) in support. Rodes, who had lent O'Neal and Daniel to Ewell, could help but little. He had two brigades in good condition in Ramseur and Doles. But they were holding Gettysburg and the line to the right of the town and were the reliance against a Federal offensive from Cemetery Hill that might threaten to break Lee's army and isolate Johnson and Early. If they were to be used with Pickett, it would be necessary to replace them with other troops.

Longstreet's two divisions other than Pickett's, those of Hood and McLaws, had carried most of the fighting load of July 2, and were reduced to not much more than 50 per cent of their striking power. They had lost heavily in officers and were manning thinly the long line from the base of Round Top to the Peach Orchard. Any brigade that might be withdrawn for concentration with Pickett would leave a gap that might be inviting to the Federals whose skirmishers were in close contact with the Confederate front. Longstreet's line extended over relatively flat ground quite different from the Federal

position on the Round Tops and Cemetery Ridge. It possessed few
strong defensive features, and if it was to be maintained during the
thrust at the Federal center, the troops of Law (Hood) and McLaws
were no more than adequate for the task. Lee seemed to recognize
this tacitly during his conversation with Wofford, whose brigade remained in as good condition as any in the two divisions. When he
left Wofford without giving him any indication that he was expected
to attack following Pickett, it was obvious that Lee did not expect a
forward movement by his entire right wing, as has often been contended. No such movement was ordered and apparently none was
considered, unless, of course, the center of the Federal army should
be broken, when such a success would become a signal for a general
advance all along the line. Longstreet did ride over and tell Law to
be prepared to follow Pickett, but a threat by the Federal cavalry
made it imperative that he hold his lines.

Merritt's and Farnsworth's brigades of Kilpatrick's Federal cavalry
division appeared in the rear of Law's Division, Farnsworth having
passed in full view between Plum Run and the Round Tops at about
eleven o'clock, and taken position in the open country beyond Round
Top. Law was compelled to detach Robertson's brigade to protect
his exposed flank. It was apparent that a weakening of the Confederate right would be exploited promptly by a vigilant enemy cavalry.

Thus it may be seen that Lee had no abundance of unemployed
troops from which to make selections for his column of assault, but
Anderson's two fresh brigades, Mahone and Posey, plus Thomas,
would have seemed a more logical choice than Pettigrew's depleted
division, which two days before had taken merciless punishment when
it ousted the Iron Brigade from McPherson's Heights.

No troops in the army were of stancher material than Pickett's,
but the bulk of the commands of Pettigrew and Trimble were inured
in more recent fighting. Pickett's division had been on duty around
Richmond, Petersburg, and in North Carolina—"picnic grounds," the
others called these theaters—and had not been engaged at Chancellorsville.

Part of Pettigrew's own brigade likewise was from the "picnic
grounds," and had never been with the Army of Northern Virginia;
part had served in the Peninsular campaign and all had been tested
and found steadfast on July 1. Pettigrew's other brigades were
Archer's, which had been long with the army and had distinguished

itself at Chancellorsville; Brockenborough's, formerly C. W. Field's, a veteran brigade that had served in A. P. Hill's division; and Davis', which included veteran regiments. The brigades under Trimble—those of Lane and Lowrance—were composed of veterans long a part of the Army of Northern Virginia.

The selection of Pettigrew's division to deliver the shock of the attack alongside Pickett's fresh troops disturbed Colonel Venable, who said "they were terribly mistaken . . . in this planning."[48] "They" could have referred only to Lee, the nearest the staff officer could come to personal criticism of his chief. Continuing, he said the division had suffered more than was reported on the first day and had not recuperated. As proof that Davis had gone almost into Gettysburg, he said "Rodes found dead Mississippians on the wooded hill just above the town."[49] The division had been sadly battered but it did no complaining. Hill might have been expected to protect it, but he is not known to have put in any protest. What was needed was not a division of different character, but one fresher and with larger numbers.

Colonel Taylor, who was with Lee during the morning discussion with Longstreet, said the plan as he understood it was for two divisions to make the assault while the remaining divisions moved forward to support them.[50] This does not answer the vital question of whether the supporting divisions were to move forward before or after Pickett, Pettigrew, and Trimble had broken the enemy's line. If before, then Lee intended a forward movement of his entire army. At no time did he order such an advance. What he ordered was an attack by Pickett reinforced by "two divisions of the Third Corps."

Taylor did not give the wording of the order he thought Lee intended, but merely said it was the result of the conference "as understood by me." That neither Hill, who was in Lee's company during the assault, nor Longstreet made an effort to advance anything except the designated units—Pickett, Pettigrew, and Trimble—is fairly good evidence that they did not understand that Lee contemplated a broad movement of the entire army ahead of the break-through.

4. Lee Designates the Troops and Objective

Responsibility for the timing of the attack of July 3 had to be shared jointly by Lee and Longstreet because the two were together much of the morning. Lee had seen neither Longstreet nor Pickett on the night before, and he had not settled on the attack until he made his reconnaissance, though he had stated his general purpose at the time Pickett joined him and Longstreet on Seminary Ridge.

As the hour approached eleven, timing became less consequential than careful preparation, for Johnson's attack and defense on Culp's Hill had petered out and unless Lee initiated a fresh supporting movement—which he did not contemplate and for which he scarcely had the troops—the full responsibility of engaging the Federals would be left to the column of Pickett, Pettigrew, and Trimble. So long as the attack was not to be co-ordinated with other movements, the hour was not of the first significance. Johnson on the far left had been unable to await the arrival of Pickett, because the Culp's Hill battle of July 3 was begun not by him, but by Slocum.

Now that Lee and Longstreet had ridden the lines, they returned to a point in front of Pickett's troops. It was clear that Lee had not altered his desire to undertake a massed infantry offensive against Meade's center and he was prepared to issue his attack orders. He formally designated the objective and selected the troops that were to participate. The objective has always been known as the "clump of trees," though in July 1863 the clump consisted mainly of an umbrella-shaped tree, with a few scrub oaks about it and bushes running along a stone wall. Two trees, apparently maples not much larger than saplings, stood north of the clump; elsewhere the hill was bald.

Pickett would have the forward role, with Pettigrew, followed by Trimble, advancing abreast him on his left, and Wilcox and Perry *en echelon* on his right. Longstreet was still blunt in his objections to a frontal assault. He told Lee he had examined the ground on his right—his nerve must have been unbounded to have alluded to this subject again—and thought the best plan would be to move to the Federal left in a wide flanking movement. The record of conversation that ensued is Longstreet's.

"No," said General Lee, "I am going to take them where they are on Cemetery Hill. I want you to take Pickett's division and make the attack. I will reinforce you by two divisions [Heth's under Pettigrew and Pender's under Trimble] of the Third Corps."

"That will give me fifteen thousand men," Longstreet responded. "I have been a soldier, I may say, from the ranks up to the position I now hold. I have been in pretty much all kinds of skirmishes, from those of two or three soldiers up to those of an army corps, and I

Launching the assault of July 3, 1863.

think I can safely say there never was a body of fifteen thousand men who could make that attack successfully."[51]

Lee was disturbed, if not angered. As Longstreet described it, he "seemed a little impatient at my remarks, so I said nothing more."[52] That was the last contact, before the attack, between the commanding general and his ranking subordinate. Nothing suggests that Lee ever thought of entrusting the attack to other supervision than Longstreet's, though many in later years have wondered why he did not. It would have been just as easy for Lee to lend Pickett to Hill as it was to lend Pettigrew and Trimble to Longstreet. That he did not evidenced how fully he retained confidence in Longstreet's pre-eminent ability to handle a large-scale assault.

Those capabilities the First Corps commander had demonstrated fully on the afternoon of July 2. On the basis of what had transpired since the army had reached Gettysburg, could Lee have committed the main attack to Hill or Ewell, or Early or Rodes? He needed Jackson, of course, but it is as well to say he could have used Napoleon, Soult, or Ney, or any other military figure out of the past. He had to work with the tools at hand. Unquestionably Longstreet, partial as he had been from the beginning to the flanking movement, had conducted on the afternoon of the second the hardest fighting on the field and possibly the hardest of the war, and had been partially successful against vastly superior numbers. There was no reason why Lee should doubt his effectiveness, even though it had been necessary to overrule him in ordering the frontal assault. The situation on the third was not different from what it had been on the second, when Longstreet had fought well an action with which he was not sympathetic. After the battle was joined, his strong competitive instinct— the will to win—as well as his devotion to the cause always asserted themselves.

As Lee left Longstreet and Pickett he was heard to say, largely to himself, "The attack must succeed."[53] He knew he was staking almost everything on it. He rode to an elevated position about the center of the Confederate line where he could witness the assault. Correspondent Ross noted that the entire morning had been devoted to reconnaissance and consultation by the top generals.

Longstreet assumed command over the brigades assigned to him from Hill's corps, though the transaction was little more than nominal. Pettigrew reported to him, then aligned his troops on Pickett's left.

Longstreet next told Alexander to find a position from which he could readily observe the effect of the Confederate artillery fire on the center of the enemy's line. The signal for the opening of the bombardment which Longstreet would order personally, would be two shots from fieldpieces of the Washington Artillery fired in quick succession, upon which the guns would open all along the line and converge their fire on the Federal lines running approximately a quarter of a mile along Cemetery Ridge from Ziegler's Grove to the umbrella-shaped oak beyond the Codori farm buildings. When Alexander saw that the Federal batteries were silenced or crippled, he would advise Pickett, who on this notice would launch his assault. Longstreet showed Pickett where his troops should rest during the bombardment, then rode to the crest of the ridge with him and pointed to the objective Lee had designated.

"He seemed to appreciate the severity of the contest . . ." said Longstreet, "but was quite hopeful of success."[54]

Pickett in fact was elated. Alexander went to him just before the bombardment and found Pickett "entirely sanguine" about the success of the attack and "congratulating himself on the opportunity."[55] He had had no recent chance at distinction.

For a lieutenant general Longstreet was singularly reluctant to assume the responsibility for an attack he knew to be inevitable. Scarcely to his credit was his effort to impose it on a young subordinate. Alexander, who had found a good place for observation at the left of his artillery line, where a point of woods stood out toward the Federal position, was talking with General Wright when he received a note from Longstreet. The corps commander said that if the fire did not drive off the enemy "or greatly demoralize him so as to make our efforts pretty certain," he would prefer that Pickett not be advised to make the assault. Longstreet added that he would rely a great deal on Alexander's judgment.[56]

The lieutenant colonel of artillery had the spunk to repel Longstreet's effort to charge him with the final accountability for the major movement of the entire battle. Alexander discussed the situation with Wright, then wrote Longstreet saying he would be able to judge the effect of his fire only by the return fire of the enemy, because the Federal infantry was but little exposed and smoke would cloud the field. Then he passed the responsibility back to his chief: "If, as I infer from your note, there is any alternative to this attack, it should be carefully considered before opening our fire, for it will take all the artillery ammunition we have to test this one thoroughly, and, if the result is unfavorable, we will have none left for another effort."

Alexander then gratuitously, and, as some commanders might have judged, almost impertinently, affixed his own opinion about the assault: "And even if this is entirely successful it can only be so at a very bloody cost."[57]

Longstreet replied at once, but still left the decision to Alexander. The intention, he asserted, was to advance the infantry if the artillery drove the enemy off, or had "other effect such as to warrant us in making the attack," a contingency which he did not explain. Then he said that when that moment arrived Alexander should advise Pickett "and of course advance such artillery as you can use in aiding the attack."[58]

The alert Alexander perceived that Longstreet had again put the load of the decision on his shoulders. It was noon or later. "I felt it very deeply," said Alexander, "for the day was rapidly advancing . . ." and whatever he was to do had to be done promptly.[59] His only consolation was General Wright, who on the previous evening had stood on the very ground Pickett had as his objective. Wright told Alexander that the difficulty was not so much in reaching and taking Cemetery Ridge, but in holding it, because the entire Federal army was massed in the shape of a horseshoe and could shift troops and reinforce points rapidly, which a long attacking line could not. Alexander felt partly reassured, because he had heard, from some source he did not name, that Lee intended to employ his entire army in the assault, and that would mean ample support for the attacking column.

But before replying to Longstreet's last note, Alexander rode back to see Pickett, who was in good spirits and eager to go ahead. When Alexander returned, his mind was fully made up that *"if the artillery opened Pickett must charge."*[60] It was one chance or nothing. He wrote Longstreet a final note showing the full scope of his own responsibility, which was no assurance, such as Longstreet seemed to demand, that the bombardment would guarantee the success of the infantry:

"General: When our artillery fire is doing its best I shall advise General Pickett to advance."[61]

CHAPTER TWENTY-TWO

At Fearful Price

1. *"Times When a . . . Life Does Not Count"*

The day that had begun with heavy mists in the valleys had retained
a vaporous, almost steaming hotness, uncomfortable both to the
long lines of expectant Confederates lying in the woods and rye and of
Federals beneath the violent sun in the open fields and pastures.
Though the temperature was recorded at only 87 degrees in the shady
town, the humidity made it seem like 100 on the rolling meadows.

White, billowy clouds lay lethargic on the western and northern
horizons, but the sun beat down with such fury that Meade's men here
and there put up their shelter tents for shade. Some thought that
the battle was over and Lee would withdraw behind the mountains;
others that he would renew and perhaps intensify his desperate efforts
to pierce the Federal army. On the Confederate side, where the men
were cooking bean broth and salt pork, to which they had been forced
when the battle ended foraging, the conviction was still strong that
the fight would be pressed relentlessly until they carried the opposite
heights.

It was one o'clock. The midday bell would just be ringing on the
Mississippi plantation, calling in the field hands from laying by the
cotton. The sweet fragrance of the clematis hung over Tennessee
verandas. Scant patches of Carolina tobacco were ready for the harvest. Dull, heavy summer lay across the South, where the Alabama
cattle ruminated beneath the water oaks and the hot mists rose from
the Georgia swamps.

At one o'clock Longstreet, in final capitulation to Lee's orders, sent notice to Colonel Walton to fire the signal guns and at 1:07—timed exactly by those who like to record the precise hour of great events— a field piece from the Washington Artillery spoke. It seemed to silence the hosts scattered about the battlefield, and to give notice that something momentous was impending. There were sixty seconds more of suspense,[1] another gun, and then all in both armies knew it was the hour of final decision, for the earth shook and a holocaust of flame and shell sprang from the Confederate woods.

If anyone on the Federal side was surprised about the point along the lines where, it was at once apparent, Lee was concentrating his fire, it was Meade himself. Meade had told Gibbon after his council of war on the night of July 2 that the enemy would attack again on July 3 and would strike him at the Federal center.[2] But he had not held long to that conviction. He was overheard to tell Hancock and others, at about 9:00 A.M. on July 3, that he did not think the center was the danger spot. The reasons he gave were that the artillery had an unobstructed field of fire in his front; that the Confederates were not partial to attacks in the center; and that he could reinforce his center very rapidly from his wings.[3]

Meade anticipated another attack on his left, where he held heavy masses of the Fifth and Sixth corps and remnants of the Third.

On the Federal side, at one o'clock, the generals had just seated themselves at Gibbon's field headquarters for a mess of stewed chicken garnished with cucumber pickle.[4] The top rank of the army was there: Hancock, Meade, Newton, Pleasanton, and others. The generals had procured cracker boxes and blankets; the staff officers sat on the ground. Though it is not related in the graphic accounts written about this luncheon, probably the staff ate the backs and wings and more pickle than chicken. Then the generals and aides who had finished lighted cigars and began to rehash the events of the day before. Meade reiterated his view that if the enemy attacked it would be the left, and Hancock ventured that it would be the center.

The answer was not long delayed. A gun spoke from across the wide, shallow valley, then another, and suddenly the air above them erupted with countless explosions, spreading panic among the lolling crowd, sending the generals scurrying to their commands, frightening the servants who had spread the meal, and filling the whole region with the din of roars, moans, and shrieks—"the voice of the rebel-

lion," young Haskell termed it.[5] An orderly who had been serving
the butter was cut in two. The Federal guns—80 along this immediate
line, perhaps 200 in all from the Cemetery to Little Round Top—
answered, and almost before anyone was certain of what had happened, the greatest cannonade in the annals of the North American
continent was upon them.

Only to the artilleryman Alexander did the volcanic prelude to the
assault carry a sweet refrain, which provoked a simile: "As suddenly
as an organ strikes up in church, the grand roar followed from all
the guns. . . ."

Correspondent Samuel Wilkeson of the New York *Times,* who
continued his dispatches though his son had been killed in the July 1
fighting under Barlow, was at Meade's headquarters, where the Confederate shells burst and screamed "as many as six a second, con-
stantly two a second," and "made a very hell of fire that amazed the
oldest officers." Horses of the aides and orderlies hitched near by
plunged about in pitiful panic.[6]

After the firing, Wilkeson found sixteen horses dead at the headquarters, still fastened by their halters, and giving the appearance of
being "wickedly tied up to die painfully." An ambulance careened
by at top speed, drawn faithfully although one horse had a hind leg
shot off at the hock. As the cannonade continued, the army seemed
to disappear. "Not an orderly, not an ambulance, not a straggler was
to be seen upon the field swept by this tempest of orchestral death,
thirty minutes after it commenced." Camp followers and skulkers
were disappearing down the Baltimore pike; the soldiers had dug in
until the violence passed.

The shells that hit in the region of Meade's little white house were
in large measure wasted, for they had cleared the ridge and passed
over the heads of the soldiers. The commanding general was forced to
evacuate his headquarters and find space with Slocum on Power's
Hill. But these high explosives that struck the rear of the army blew
up caissons, dismantled guns, and disrupted the army's supply lines.

Here and there on the ridge men and horses were blown into bits,
to become a part of the flesh and blood that before nightfall would
saturate acres of this sod. In direct hits the slaughter was frightful;
General Webb said a Federal battery lost twenty-seven of its thirty-six
horses in ten minutes.

A gruff colonel who never showed weakness was told he would be hit if he persisted in standing in the open. A shell fragment tore his cheek and knocked out two teeth. Someone asked solicitously if he were wounded.

"No, sir," he barked; "just had a tooth pulled."[7]

He fought till the battle ended.

Each side employed a greater concentration of artillery than Napoleon ever achieved. This artillery bombardment seemed to fall on both Northern and Southern armies like brimstone showers descending in an inferno. The air was rent with sickening blasts. Bursting shells tore and seared the flesh and threatened to destroy life as completely as a wave of fiery lava creeping down a mountainside.

While the cannonade was at its height, the Federal soldiers were witness to a breath-taking incident. The men were hugging the unsteady earth, digging with bayonets and fingernails, crowding in behind the stone walls, when a horseman followed by a small staff appeared at the north end of the Second Corps line where the Taneytown road crossed Cemetery Ridge, and began moving deliberately down the crest. When the men could look up, they saw it was Hancock riding the lines, to inspire confidence for the attack. Shells burst above and around him and solid shot struck and rolled with its ominous thud. Beside him the Second Corps flag, the clover leaf, was carried by Private James Wells of the 6th New York Cavalry. Hancock did not stop until he had reached the far left of his line, a distance of perhaps three quarters of a mile.[8]

One of his brigade commanders said, "General, the corps commander ought not to risk his life that way."

"There are times," replied Hancock, "when a corps commander's life does not count."[9]

Across the valley where the Confederate army waited, some of the 7th Virginia noticed that the sun, brilliant when the cannonading was begun, soon was clouded and almost darkened by the enveloping smoke issuing from the numerous guns.[10] Company D of this regiment claimed something of a distinction, in that it believed its abortive efforts early in the war to shout in unison at the drillmaster's demand—efforts that turned into a raucous discord—gave birth to the "Rebel yell," which was often considered an imitation of the Indian war whoop. The company had been organized in Pearisburg and drilled by the town doctor, W. W. McComas, a captain in the Mexican War. They had first emitted their blood-curdling whoop before the banquet where the town of Pearisburg assembled to see them off, never dreaming that in its chilling effect on the enemy, this spine-tingling shout would come to have more worth than a round of bullets.

The eager school lad David E. Johnston had run all the way home and back, two and a half miles in the country, to get his uncle's consent, fearful that the rolls would be filled without him. Now a seasoned soldier, he was lying in a rye field, suffering from lack of water, and filing away the picture of his surroundings in his memory: "Turn your eyes whithersoever you would, there was to be seen . . . guns, swords, haversacks, human flesh and bones, flying and dangling in the air or bouncing above the earth, which now trembled beneath as if shaken by an earthquake."[11]

Dr. Joseph Hold of the 11th Mississippi, Davis' brigade, anticipated that the afternoon would be busy and set up his dressing station early in a shelter behind Seminary Ridge about a mile from Gettysburg. When the cannonade opened and the Federals' guns replied, stretcher bearers, crouching low, began bringing in the wounded. Among the first was an athletic young man with reddish golden hair, "a princely fellow," the doctor called him, with a calm manner and delightful smile, one of that gay, turbulent company that had left with the University Greys of Oxford to form Company A of the 11th Mississippi.

The physician examined the left arm, torn off at the elbow, and offered encouragement.

"Why, doctor, that isn't where I am hurt." The boy pulled back a blanket and showed where a shell had ripped deep across his abdomen, carrying away much that was vital. "I am in great agony," he said, still smiling. "Let me die easy, dear doctor."

But before the lad drank the cup containing the concentrated solution of opium, the doctor held up his right arm so he could write: "My dear mother. . . . Remember that I am true to my country and my regret at dying is that she is not free . . . you must not regret that my body cannot be obtained. It is a mere matter of form anyhow. . . . Send my dying release to Miss Mary. . . ." He signed, JERE S. GAGE, Co. A, 11 Miss. By that time the letter was covered with blood.

Then he raised his cup to a group of soldiers. "I do not invite you to drink with me," he remarked wryly; then with fervor, "but I drink a toast to you, to the Southern Confederacy and to victory."[12]

His was a code to die by, as well as live by.

But men adjust themselves even to the stunning concussions of a great bombardment. The prolongation of the cannonade finally

brought an easy contempt of it. The 16th Vermont was not only at
the point of the concentrated Southern fire, but was lying almost
beneath the muzzles of the Federal guns. Colonel W. G. Veazey said
that many of them, "I think the majority, *fell asleep,*" and it was all
he could do to stay awake himself.[13]

A Southern soldier, waiting for the command to advance, rested a
careless foot in the fork of a small tree and dozed. A shell hit and
so mangled his ankle that he knew it would have to be amputated.
He looked at the mutilated leg and drawled: "Boys, I'll be damned
if that ain't a thirty-day furlough!"[14]

Despite the havoc from the shells, the main body of the infantry
on both sides survived, and was not materially impaired in fighting
ability. Consuming though the cannonading seemed to be, and charred
and pitted as the land was, the infantrymen of both armies crawled
from their holes, shell craters, heaps of fence rails, and stone walls,
and up, it seemed, out of the bowels of the earth, singed, shaken,
bruised, but with lines intact. And the soldiers in the ranks of both
undoubtedly said to one another that after all the blowing and puffing
of long-range battle, the decision would only be reached when the
infantrymen came face to face.

2. "If Old Peter's Nod Means Death . . ."

While the Confederate soldiers had been awaiting the lifting of the
bombardment, Pickett had been scribbling prose poems of his love.
In them he told about the signal guns, the unloosing of the fearful
volcano of shot and shell, the low-spoken orders, and of how his
Virginians were to lead the assault. "Oh, God, in mercy help me as
He never helped before!"[15]

How Pickett found time to write these lines is one of the astonishing
things of the battle, but he gave a concise running account of his
actions:

I have ridden to Old Peter. I shall give him this letter to mail to
you and a package to give to you if—Oh, my darling, do you feel the
love of my heart, the prayer, as I write that fatal word "if"?

Old Peter laid his hand over mine and said: "I know, George, I
know—but I can't do it, boy. Alexander has my instructions. He will
give you the order." There was a silence, and his hand still rested
on mine, when a courier rode up and handed me a note from Alexander.

Now, I go; but remember always that I love you. . . . I will keep up a brave heart for Virginia and for you, my darling."[16]

All this was presumably inscribed just before the step-off. That Pickett was able to fit it into so portentous a moment reveals an abnormal sense of high personal drama and emotionalism. At such a time his full thoughts might have rested on firing the elation and looking to the preparedness of his men. One cannot remotely picture Oliver Hazard Perry writing anything like these transports of passion as he prepared his fleet down to the duties of the last cabin boy to fight the British on Lake Erie.

The lines composed before the attack were supplemented by additional details written on the following day. Pickett told of riding up to Longstreet: "I found him like a great lion at bay. I have never seen him so grave and troubled. For several minutes after I had saluted him he looked at me without speaking."[17]

Alexander had estimated that the average distance was 1,400 yards. His first intention had been to wait until his guns and Hill's got the range, which he calculated would take ten to fifteen minutes, then signal Pickett to advance, but the Federal return fire proved so heavy that he felt the infantry would be unable to face it over such a long distance in the open under a hot sun; so he sustained the bombardment in the hope it would develop a more inviting situation. More time went by with no abatement of the intense firing on either side. Correspondent Wilkeson timed the cannonade at one hour and forty minutes.

Alexander calculated that the critical moment had come, and would soon pass. He wrote Pickett the note received in Longstreet's presence, saying: "If you are coming at all you must come immediately or I cannot give you proper support; but the enemy's fire has not slackened materially, and at least eighteen guns are still firing from the Cemetery itself."[18]

Just then the Federal batteries in the cemetery limbered up and drew off—to replenish their ammunition, it developed—and within five minutes after Alexander had written Pickett the Northern fire slackened all along the line. He was not sure yet what it meant, whether a withdrawal or only a change of position, but he judged the Federals had suffered and he was encouraged.

Varying reasons are ascribed for the slackening of the Northern artillery, but the most logical appears to have been that Warren from his customary point of observation on Little Round Top saw that it was only molesting and not damaging the Confederates greatly, while it was filling the level ground with smoke. Under the cover of this cloud they might reach close to the Federal lines undetected. He advised Meade, who told Chief of Artillery Hunt. Hunt also wanted to reload his caissons and lure the Southerners into attack in the belief that the Northern artillery was largely silenced.

Alexander waited five minutes longer, then hurried a courier to Pickett with an urgent note: "For God's sake come quick; the eighteen guns are gone."[19]

Pickett was still with Longstreet. He showed the note to his commander and asked if he should obey.

"He looked at me for a moment, then held out his hand. Presently, clasping his other over mine without speaking, he lowered his head upon his breast. I shall never forget the look in his face nor the clasp of his hand when I said: 'General, I shall lead my division on.' "[20]

Pickett had started away when he remembered his letter to LaSalle Corbell. He wrote across the corner of the envelope: "If Old Peter's nod means death then good by and God bless you, little one." Handing over the missive, he asked Longstreet to mail it, and saw the tears shining on the old soldier's cheek and beard. Said Pickett: "The stern old War Horse, God bless him, was weeping for his men. . . ."[21]

"I could not speak," said Longstreet on a visit to Gettysburg years later. "I merely gave a nod of assent, and then the tears rushed to my eyes as I saw those brave fellows rush to certain death."[22]

Now that Pickett was ready, Alexander sent for Richardson's seven 12-pounders to come up from their haven, prepared to move out with the infantry and carry on the indispensable function of shelling the Federal lines at the last minute before the Southern infantry struck. To his consternation the guns were gone. Pendleton, who had contributed so little to the preparation, now had interposed his authority, innocently perhaps but blunderingly, in a manner almost certain to foredoom the attack to failure. Without informing Alexander, the chief of artillery had removed Richardson's pieces. He had sent four of them to some other section of the field and the other three had disappeared at the same time.[23] Alexander could not find them. It was too late to replace them effectively with other guns because of the low ammunition supplies in the caissons.

As Pickett left Longstreet, Cadmus Wilcox came up to him, drew a flask, and offered liquor. "Pickett," he said, "take a drink with me. In an hour you'll be in hell or glory."[24]

Pickett said he had promised the young lady back in Virginia that he would not touch spirits.

He went back to his division and rode down the line. Randolph A. Shotwell of the 8th Virginia, Garnett's brigade, thought he looked cool, "rather dandyish in his ruffles and curls," well mounted, and "ready to ride to death if need be."[25]

Garnett was drawing at a cigar to show his unconcern.[26] "Have you any further instructions?" he asked.

"No, Dick," said Pickett. "I don't recollect anything, unless it is to tell you to make the best kind of time in crossing the valley. It's a hell of an ugly-looking place over yonder."[27]

Then Pickett stood in front of his division and gave the final word: "Charge the enemy, and remember old Virginia." His voice was clear and strong as he spoke the order: "Forward! Guide center! March!"[28]

After Pickett had left him, Longstreet rode to Alexander's observation post, and the artilleryman explained the situation: his ammunition was low and he feared he could not give Pickett the required assistance, especially since Richardson's 12-pounders had disappeared.

Longstreet, deeply agitated, spoke sharply. "Go and stop Pickett right where he is and replenish your ammunition."[29]

Alexander said the ordnance wagons were nearly empty, with not 20 rounds remaining per gun, too scant an amount for much to be expected of it; meantime, the enemy would recover from the shelling already delivered.

"I don't want to make this charge," Longstreet declared emphatically. "I don't believe it can succeed. I would stop Pickett now, but that General Lee has ordered it and expects it."[30]

Further remarks showed he wanted some excuse for calling off the whole attack.

But Longstreet and Alexander had lost control. As they talked the turf trembled about them and the long line of gray infantry broke from the woods. First came Garnett's Virginians, the general in front, his old blue overcoat buttoned tightly around his neck. Abreast was Kemper's trim line marching majestically into the open fields, the fifes piping "Dixie," the ranks in nearly perfect alignment. Far off to the left could be heard the drum rolls of the Carolina regiments— Pettigrew and Trimble were in motion. The hour of the generals had passed. The infantrymen from the Richmond offices and Pearisburg farmlands, the "greys" from the halls of "Old Miss" and the "flower of the Cape Fear section," had taken the Confederate cause into their hands.

3. The Shells Go "Whicker, Whicker"

Pickett's men were cheered by the begrimed cannoneers as they passed through the artillery and took up the tramp down the long slope and up the companion ridge toward the hostile army, barricaded and waiting.[31] As they left the woods, the "hell of an ugly place" ahead seemed much more than a mile, although the average distance was about three fourths that. Along Pettigrew's line the artillerymen had been cutting fuses for a mile and a quarter, and Pickett would have to regulate his advance until these more distant troops could fall in beside him and give the assaulting party an unbroken front.

Said Crocker:

As the lines cleared the woods that skirted the brow of the ridge and passed through our batteries, with their flags proudly held aloft, waving in the air, with polished muskets and swords gleaming and flashing in the sunlight, they presented an inexpressibly grand and inspiring sight.[32]

The vast body of men was now in the gentle, open valley midway between the lines, and for an instant the two armies on the ridges seemed enthralled, spellbound. Then the Federal artillery opened, firing first solid shot, next explosives and finally, as the column drew nearer the works, canister.

Though Lee was more an inspirational than a book general, the model for the massed infantry assault of Pickett, Pettigrew, and Trimble, following a thorough artillery preparation, was supposed to have been Macdonald's frontal attack at Wagram, where Napoleon had concentrated his artillery stealthily, delivered a concentrated cannonade, and had then broken the center of the enemy line by the weight of Macdonald's numbers. But Napoleon was not assailing troops of the same character and stability possessed by these Northern soldiers.

The gray-coated marchers learned abruptly that the Federal cannon had by no means been silenced. The massing of flags along the heights —scores of them fifty paces apart—told of the presence of hostile infantry in heavy numbers, and the sudden resumption of the full-scale cannonading gave notice that the artillery was ample for a stout defense.

Harassing to Pickett's entire force and especially destructive and impeding to Kemper on the right was the battery on Little Round Top, which with its excellent view of the field, kept the range and threw its shells and canister with devastating effect.

Far down the lines Oscar McMillan, whose handsome house on Seminary Ridge had been taken over by the Confederates, viewed the awesome panorama from the summit of Little Round Top. He had seen the approach of the battle and calculated that denuded Little Round Top, shorn of its timber, would be the best point of observation, and there he passed the first three days of July, observing the struggle with the anxiety of a violent Unionist, feeling that the arm of the Lord was slow to action. Now as Pickett's men filled the fields he was on his knees, with arms stretched toward Heaven, and the delighted Federal gunners heard between their firings his shouted exhortations and recommendations to Jehovah!

One of Pickett's soldiers described an oncoming shell—first the boom of the Yankee cannon, then a shriek in the air that sounded like a frightened horse neighing, "a kind of a whicker, whicker, whicker."[33]

Crocker saw a shell explode in the left company of his regiment; he said, "Men fell like ten-pins in a ten-strike." But the survivors did not even break step. In a surge of emotion he described it: "My God! it was magnificent—this march of our men."[34]

He asked himself what inspired them to such courage, and answered: "It was the fervor of patriotism—the high sense of individual duty."

When Robert W. Morgan was hit on the right instep by a Minié ball, he stopped to examine the wound and another ball tore his other foot from toe to heel. He made crutches of his own musket and an abandoned one and hobbled to where his Negro servant, Horace, could carry him on his back to a wagon that would take them home to Virginia.[35]

Dabney Tweedy was carried back on a stretcher, his blood spurting, and all the while he sang an anthem.[36] Charlie Jones, a private who had been ahead of the officers at the step-off, saying "Come on, boys, let's drive away those Yankees,"[37] was killed early.

While in Chambersburg, David E. Johnston of the 7th Virginia had had a dream in which he saw himself bleeding on a battlefield, his left side mangled by an exploding shell. Now he lay bleeding on the field, but it would be three days before consciousness returned for him to know an exploding shell had shattered his left side.[38]

The assaulting column consisted of 41 regiments and one battalion, excepting the supporting brigades of Wilcox, Lang, Thomas and Perrin, who did not reach Cemetery Ridge. Nineteen of the regiments were from Virginia, 15 from North Carolina, 3 each from Tennessee and Mississippi, and one regiment and one battalion were from Alabama.

The Codori house and its outbuildings were the only obstructions apart from the Emmitsburg pike, which seemed a sunken roadway, perhaps a trap, as the men approached. The skirmishers in front of them pulled down part of the fence, piled the rails into a breastwork, and in the long grass began firing at the Federal line as they awaited the advance of their own main body.[39]

Looking back, they could see Pickett riding over the crest of Seminary Ridge and coming into the open. Noticing that his skirmishers had stopped, he sent his brother, Charles Pickett, to tell them to keep 120 yards ahead of the attacking column.[40]

Garnett, with a big voice issuing from his frail body, rode ahead of his line regulating the pace, admonishing his men not to move too rapidly. From the skirmish line Captain Shotwell obtained one of the rare views of the Confederate advance: the "glittering forest of bright bayonets," the column coming down the slope "in superb alignment," the "murmur and jingle" and "rustle of thousands of feet amid the stubble" which stirred up a cloud of dust "like the dash of spray at the prow of a vessel."[41]

In front of Pickett flew the blue banner of the Old Dominion with its motto, *"Sic Semper Tyrannis,"* and the Stars and Bars of the Confederacy (the red battle flag with its blue cross not yet being in general use). The regimental flags flapped. A soft warm wind was blowing from the land they loved.

4. A Green Vermonter Reassures Hancock

While infantrymen might scorn the artillery when under cover, such was not the case when they were advancing in the open field. There the long lines were exposed targets, especially sensitive to unanswered artillery fire on their flanks. When Pickett started, Alexander hurriedly tried to scrape together an artillery support for him, but what he could get was low on ammunition and promised little.

The Federal center on Cemetery Ridge was held by two of Hancock's divisions, those of Gibbon and Hays, and, ranging south, by Doubleday's division of the First Corps, which had been joined by Stannard's Vermont brigade that had not participated in the First Corps battle of July 1. Beyond Doubleday's left were remnants of Hancock's other division, Caldwell's, and then the Third, Fifth, and Sixth corps.

The Federal line at the clump of trees was commanded by Brigadier General Alexander S. Webb, twenty-eight years old, an honor graduate of West Point in the class of 1855, who had fought at First Manassas and all battles of the Army of the Potomac. As chief of staff of the Fifth Corps in the Sharpsburg and Chancellorsville campaigns, he had been so conspicuous that he was promoted to general and assigned to command the Philadelphia Brigade, of Gibbon's division, Hancock's corps. Webb's grandfather, Samuel B. Webb, had been one of the little band of minutemen who stood with Captain Jonas Parker on Lexington Common, April 19, 1775; his father had been a regular army officer, a diplomat, then a newspaper editor in New York City, where Alexander was born.[42]

Pickett's most sensitive point was his right, where Kemper advanced with his flank in the air, riddled by the Federal guns on Little Round Top. Pickett, seeing this ghastly exposure, sent repeated messages to Wilcox and Lang to come up, but as they had not possessed quite the impetus to go up abreast Wright on the afternoon of the second, so they now became lost in the smoke and drifted farther and farther to their right, leaving a gap between themselves and Kemper wide enough for Meade to throw in a division had he been near by and so minded.

What happened was that an alert Vermonter, with a relatively green brigade, detected the great opportunity of the day and seized it promptly. Brigadier General George J. Stannard, whose men had performed brilliantly on the afternoon before, recapturing a battery under the eyes and at the personal request of Hancock, was in Doubleday's line on the left of Gibbon. Before July 2, the brigade had never come under fire and since it had enlisted for only nine months and the term was almost expiring, Newton, the uncertain First Corps commander, had put two veteran lines of battle behind it. Kemper had been making directly for Stannard, but as he crossed the Emmitsburg road he suddenly changed front and moved off to his left, both to close a gap that had developed between him and Garnett and to converge on the clump of trees. This took him directly across the front of the 14th Vermont, of Stannard's brigade, which poured a withering fire into his flank. After moving about 300 yards to his left, Kemper changed front to the right, again faced the main line of the Federal army, and advanced on the clump of trees. Here Kemper's men broke out with the wild Rebel yell and started up the incline to the Federal works.

Stannard now executed a bold maneuver, which he was enabled to do because Wilcox and Lang were offering Kemper no protection. He threw his Vermont brigade forward and changed front, so part faced north, perpendicular to the main Federal line facing west, and immediately on Kemper's flank. In this new position, his left was more than 300 yards in front of the Federal position.

Hancock, close by, observed this individualistic movement by the Vermonters and was apprehensive that it would leave a hole through which an enterprising enemy lurking behind the smoke might pass. But Stannard vouched that he could get back in time to meet any troops on Pickett's right. From this position the brigade threw a deadly fire into Kemper's flank, which no troops in the world could have withstood.[43]

Kemper meantime had seen the critical situation on his right and had ridden back to Armistead. "General, hurry up," he said. "My men can stand no more."[44]

Armistead turned to his 1st Regiment and ordered, "Colonel, double-quick." From a fast step the men broke into a run, then a fast charge.

But Kemper was no longer a participant. He was knocked from his horse critically wounded, and the report went through the army that he had been killed.[45]

Meanwhile, Garnett had pushed straight ahead, maintaining an even pace. He continually called, "Faster, men! Faster, but don't double-quick." At the Emmitsburg road he struck the Federal skirmish line, which, in the words of an observer, he swept away "like trash before the broom." His men began a scattering fire but he galloped along the line ordering, "Cease firing," and the remarkable discipline of the brigade caused it to shoulder arms again and move ahead.[46]

Garnett was across the road climbing the slope toward the stone wall when he saw far on his right a long blue column—apparently Stannard's—coming up on Kemper's unguarded flank. If the works ahead of him were to be carried it would have to be done quickly,

Assault by Pickett, Pettigrew, and Trimble.
July 3, 1863, 3:00 to 3:30 P.M.

before these flankers hit Kemper's right, exposed by the inertia of Wilcox.

As they neared the Federal works, Garnett's men could see the flags above them but no bluecoats to fire at. But when Garnett was halfway up the slope the Federal line rose. Their polished muskets shone for a moment in the sunlight, then a great, devastating blast spurted from the crest, a cloud of smoke rolled out, and much of the Confederate column seemed to sink into the ground.[47]

Garnett was not close enough yet for the charge. He rode the line steadying the men: "Don't double-quick. Save your wind and ammunition for the final charge." The words were scarcely spoken when his men noticed that he was covered with blood. Still he rode, but his head began to drop toward his horse's neck. Then horse and rider fell together. Garnett had been hit in several places—how many none ever knew—and did not rise, but the horse struggled back to his feet and galloped down the hill.[48]

James W. Clay of the 18th Virginia was hit by a shell a hundred yards below the clump of trees and stumbled blindly into some rocks, from where he could see Garnett on his black horse ahead of his brigade as it approached the stone wall. The general was waving his black felt hat with its silver cord, cheering on his men, his sword still sheathed at his side, when he collapsed and fell.[49] Captain Archer Campbell, 18th Virginia, had been hit with a ball that broke his arm and was lying beside Clay when Garnett's horse, a jagged hole in his shoulder, came dashing down the hill in frenzied flight.

Clay was puzzled that his general's body was never found, for Garnett's new uniform beneath his old overcoat was adorned with the Confederate wreath and general's star, and he wore officer's boots and spurs. He judged it "inexplicable that his remains were not identified."[50] But one wonders about the blue overcoat, probably a heritage from his days with the Regular Army before the war. Because of it, could this gallant officer who gave his life at the supreme moment of the Confederacy sleep in an unmarked Federal grave?

5. A General Falls Inside the Works

But Armistead was coming up. Garnett's men could hear the thud of their feet on the sod just behind them, while above them the canister and grape sounded, as Captain H. T. Owen described it, like the whirring of a flock of quail rising in sudden flight.

The blue flanking column on the right meantime had well-nigh destroyed Kemper and now poured its fire into Garnett's and Armistead's men. These two brigades, tangled and confused, rushed the stone wall, clubbing muskets and jabbing with bayonets. None had time to load. At the front was Armistead. The Federal artillery fired its last round, the guns shotted to the muzzle, when the Virginia soldiers were but a few feet from them.

As strong runners seeing the goal ahead draw together their reserve powers for a burst of supreme effort and speed more swiftly across the finish line than at any point on the back course, so these daring soldiers, their objective just before them, impelled themselves to efforts which a few minutes earlier they would have judged beyond their powers, and pushed, clambered, jumped, and fell across the wall.

Armistead was in front of them. Just before they had begun this final dash he had walked along the line with final words of cheer. He had met on his left a mounted man, probably Garnett, who leaned from his horse that they might have a final word before making the rush together. Then "Old Lo" Armistead had plunged ahead, and Garnett had fallen. He put his black hat on his sword point and held it aloft for the whole brigade to see.[51] When he was over the wall, about 150 of his men rushed pell-mell behind him.

Here, face to face, the general could see whom he was fighting. He called back, "It's the Philadelphia Brigade. Give them the cold steel, boys."

That was his last order. He put his hand possessively on the Federal cannon into which his men had charged, as though his thought was to turn it about, but at that instant, with his hat on his sword and his hand on a gun, he fell mortally wounded, fairly riddled with bullets. Some of them came from revolvers fired at arm's length.

An unidentified Federal colonel, who admired Armistead's courage and saw his peril, was at that very instant trying to ride into him and knock him down, to save him from the hail of bullets.[52] The story that he pitifully sent word to Hancock that he had chosen the wrong side appears to be apochryphal.[53] When Armistead fell the command of his brigade passed to Colonel William R. Aylett, grandson of Patrick Henry. Half of those who crossed the wall with Armistead were killed.

As Armistead was being carried back, Captain Harry Bingham of Hancock's staff met the bearers and asked if he could be of help. Armistead requested that Hancock send his spurs and watch to his relatives. This Hancock did. Old Lo's sword had been taken where he fell.[54]

All along the line the Confederate regiments were approaching the wall, their ranks thinning at every step. The whirring canister and sheets of rifle and musket fire withered their line away. As Armistead's men poured over the barrier, Webb's Pennsylvanians—a thin front line for such a critical sector—were driven back, but the triumph for the small party inside the Federal works was short-lived.

What Pickett needed mainly was support coming up behind him. Had another division—the brigades of Mahone, Thomas, and Posey—been close in his rear, it is not unlikely he would have carried the heights. But while Armistead was having his flash of triumph inside the Federal lines, help was being rushed to Webb from all directions. Hall's brigade of Gibbon's division came up at a run. Hancock transferred a part of Harrow's brigade at double-quick. Doubleday swung into action. Part of the Third Corps hastened. Webb formed his men into a second line, and the threat of a more serious break-through at this point rapidly vanished.

When Webb's regiments gave way before the impact of Garnett and Armistead, the onrush of new Federal defenders to the threatened salient was so impetuous that most of Harrow's and Hall's regiments lost all form and became masses of individuals seeking only to repel their desperate assailants. The nearest of Harrow's regiments, the 19th Maine, charged "wildly," its scribe recorded, "with little regard for ranks or files." The men fired as they ran and in their anxiety "thrust their rifles over the shoulders, under the arms and between the legs, of those in the front ranks of the melee." As Hancock explained it, "the men of all the brigades had in some measure lost their regimental organization, but individually they were firm." Harrow's men moved past the south end of the little copse to the wall in front, still held by the Confederates, where "by sheer strength," the enemy was pushed beyond the wall.

The defense, quite as much as the attack, was sublime in its heroism. Young Lieutenant A. H. Cushing, commanding Battery A of the 4th U. S. Artillery, was at his guns when hit in the abdomen by a bursting shell. All of his pieces had been disabled except one. Holding his intestines back with one hand, he helped run his remaining gun down to the stone wall, and shouted to his general, "Webb, I will give them one more shot."

After the gun spoke he called again: "Good-by." Then he fell dead across his last cannon.

Before Cushing fell or his battery was disabled, Cowan dashed up

near by with his 1st New York Battery that had moved with the
Sixth Corps from Manchester, and issued his orders to give them
"double canister at ten yards," the words which were chiseled on the
battery's monument on Cemetery Hill. Double canister meant ninety-
eight iron balls, each about an inch in diameter. In a single charge,
canister was packed in seven layers of seven balls each. A double
charge—the balls would spread like shot from a shotgun—was certain
to make havoc of anything in its front.

Hancock was with Stannard, looking down on the masses of Confederate infantry—Pettigrew's and Trimble's men, who were pressing
up the hill some distance to his right—when he was hit in his right
thigh. The bullet passed through the pommel of his saddle and carried
wood fragments and a nail into the deep wound. He reeled and would
have fallen had not Stannard's aides caught him and laid him on the
ground, where he bled so profusely that his life seemed endangered.
Stannard jumped from his horse and made a tourniquet with his
handkerchief and pistol barrel. With the flow of blood checked, Hancock remained where he was, refusing to allow the men to move him
to the rear until he could determine the outcome of the assault.[55]

Meantime Harrow's brigade had come to the assistance of Stannard
and joined in the attack on Kemper's survivors. With their leader
down and virtually all their field officers gone, this remnant of a splendid brigade was sent flying to the bottom of the hill.

When Wilcox and Lang made their closest approach to the Federal
lines and began a desultory firing against Caldwell's division on Doubleday's left, Stannard's Vermont brigade repeated the maneuver it
had employed against Kemper, and poured a fire of musketry into their
flank while the canister and Caldwell's men were tearing up their front.
Caught in this crossfire, they retired rapidly, leaving many prisoners
with Stannard. Stannard himself was wounded in the upper leg soon
after Hancock and, like Hancock, refused to leave the field.

6. Planting the Tennessee Flag on the Wall

The Pickett-Pettigrew-Trimble assault of July 3 had some of the aspects of Longstreet's attack *en echelon* of July 2, in that while the
brigades of the Confederate line approached the Federal works in a
well-dressed line, the critical fighting moved from the Confederate
right to the left and was without essential concert.

Pickett's battle was waning as Pettigrew's began, and Pettigrew in
turn had shot his bolt when Trimble put in his greatest effort. Yet the

impression often conveyed that only Armistead's soldiers stormed the wall and penetrated the Northern works does not spring from the events of the battle. The "high-water mark" is more symbolic than actual, because the conformation of the Federal line caused three of Pettigrew's and both of Trimble's brigades to strike the Northerners farther in advance than Pickett and nearer the summit of the ridge.

The Pettigrew-Trimble march across the open fields was as stirring and magnificent as the inspiring advance of Pickett's Virginians. One of the group of Confederate officers observing on Seminary Ridge said Pettigrew's front as it burst from the woods appeared to cover twice that of Pickett's. These officers, thrilled by the sight, thought from the way the column filled the plain that it must be Hill's entire corps. They shouted, "Here they come! Here they are! Hurrah!"[56]

The words, except the last, were almost exactly those that were running along the Federal line as this splendid force, coming into line with Pickett and giving the assaulting column a front of three quarters of a mile, appeared through the smoke.

When Captain Randolph A. Shotwell on the skirmish line first saw Pettigrew's column, it was nearly half a mile to the left and rear of Pickett. It met the storm of shell which "fairly melted away the two left brigades," those of Mayo and Davis. "Pettigrew's old brigade . . . and the remnants of Archer came on with springing steps,"[57] not far behind the left of Pickett's line.

Pettigrew's column had to travel a longer distance than Pickett's and move diagonally across the field in order to converge on the umbrella-shaped tree.[58] The ground was less undulating than that traversed by Pickett, and though in Pickett's case the protection was scant, in Pettigrew's there was none at all. This terrain was particularly exposed to the batteries in the cemetery and Ziegler's Woods, which sent in an oblique fire.[59] Colonel W. H. Swallow observed that the first Federal fire shook them as if they had been "struck by some unseen power, some great physical body." The column reeled and halted momentarily. When the smoke cleared they were moving steadily ahead again though the ground behind was covered with the fallen. Reaching the Emmitsburg road, they had no dead space and came directly under the fire of the blue line behind the stone wall on the crest.

The tough old filibusterer, Colonel Birkett Davenport Fry, who had led Heth's advance to Gettysburg on July 1, commanded Pettigrew's right brigade, Archer's Alabama and Tennessee survivors of the first day's battle. Though there had been apprehension because of the distance between Pettigrew's and Pickett's divisions at the beginning, the gap was skillfully closed by Fry and Pettigrew. The timing proved exact, for according to some of the Confederate observers, Fry's right met Garnett's left precisely at the Emmitsburg road and they moved up the slope abreast, both suffering staggering losses as they advanced.

Federal observers thought the juncture was not so neatly done— there was considerable crowding of Pickett into Pettigrew, resulting in confusion for Pickett and a slackening of the assault.

Pettigrew's own brigade, led by Colonel James K. Marshall of the 52nd North Carolina, was on Fry's left, then came Davis and Brockenborough. This last brigade was commanded by Colonel Robert M. Mayo of the 47th Virginia. The time required to climb the front of Cemetery Ridge seemed interminable, but as Fry and Marshall neared the crest the men let out a shout and ran forward toward the wall. Trimble was close behind them, in the rear of the right of Pettigrew's division. As Fry and the left of Garnett struck the wall together, a Virginia lieutenant and a Tennessee captain shook hands. "Virginia and Tennessee will stand together on these works," the Virginian said.

Where these brigades met, the wall formed an angle, and turned back to the east for a distance of about 80 yards. Then it turned again to the north. Thus the section of the wall hit by Kemper, Armistead, and Fry was 80 yards closer than the section hit by Marshall and Davis. As Fry's Tennesseans clambered over the wall following the mixed commands of Kemper and Armistead, Marshall and Davis rushed past them and struck the wall ahead. Here they menaced the flank of Webb, facing Fry and the Virginians. But they were in turn critically exposed on their right and encountered a destructive fire from Webb and Hancock's oncoming supports.

The 14th Tennessee had marched from Clarksville, its point of concentration in northwest Tennessee in 1861, with 960 men. It had moved across virtually all of the battlefields of Virginia and counted 365 bayonets when it went into the first day's fight at Gettysburg. The battle on McPherson's Heights had reduced it to only 60 men, commanded by a captain, L. B. Phillips. Here where the wall turned, at what came to be known as the "bloody angle" of Gettysburg, all but three of these remaining 60 fell.

The requiem was indeed affecting:

Thus the band that once was the pride of Clarksville has fallen. . . . A gloom rests over the city; the hopes and affections of the people were wrapped in the regiment. . . . Ah! what a terrible responsibility rests upon those who inaugurated this unholy war.[60]

In front of the wall Colonel Marshall, leading Pettigrew's men, was shot and fell dead from his horse. Pettigrew's hand was shattered by a ball but he paid no attention. Along the wall nearly all of the Virginia colonels were killed. Though Armistead had broken through and some of Garnett's men had swarmed in, the only colors planted on the Federal works were those of the gallant Fry, who took in the 1st and 7th Tennessee and the 13th Alabama, then fell, wounded and remained a prisoner when his men were killed or forced back.[61]

But the Confederate attack was not yet spent. Old Man Trimble, who, Kyd Douglas said, had enough fight in him "to satisfy a herd of tigers,"[62] was coming up behind Pettigrew.

7. *"All Hell Can't Take It"*

Trimble was at disadvantage, commanding at this high point a demi-division he had scarcely seen before, replacing the wounded General Pender. He had time before the firing of the signal guns to ride down the line and talk to the different regiments, saying he would lead them against Cemetery Hill at three o'clock. His timing was accurate, and from his position the advance of the long line of Confederate soldiers with their fluttering banners was steady and inspiring. Soon Trimble, who had marched in rear of Archer and Marshall, obliqued to the left to the rear of Mayo, whose brigade, destitute of flank protection, was suffering from the enfilade fire and, like Kemper on the other flank, was beginning to disintegrate.

Major J. A. Weston, 33rd North Carolina, of Lane's brigade, thought the attack would have succeeded if artillery had been pushed forward with the infantry. As he saw it, Pickett's men struck the Federal line ahead of Pettigrew or Trimble, owing to the terrain and fences, and for a time held the ground they had taken, but finally fell back under the tempest of fire.

As Trimble's men came up to Pettigrew's, someone cried, "Three cheers for the old North State," and both of his brigades let out a shout.[63] Turning to his aide, Trimble declared, "I believe those first fellows are going into the enemy's line!"[64] Trimble, his command merging with Pettigrew's, then struck the wall, with Lane and Lowrance battling on after Pettigrew had been slaughtered and forced back following Pickett. These two brigades—Lane and Lowrance—

went to the wall with a rush, but were met by volleys from the second Federal line.

Trimble was wounded near the fence, while encouraging his men to storm it, and fell into enemy hands, but he remained an observer of the assault.

With Trimble down, Lane was now fighting the battle virtually unaided. On his left the enfilade fire had become so destructive that he directed Colonel Clark M. Avery, commanding the 33rd North Carolina, to change front and face the new enemy.

Avery nearly exploded. "My God, General," he shouted, "do you intend pushing your troops into such a place unsupported, when the whole right has given way?"[65]

Lane looked to his right and saw that Pickett's line of battle was gone. No Confederate troops were visible there. Avery meantime was at the stone wall, his men firing and cheering, but Lane called them back.

Said the general: "My brigade, I know, was the last to leave the field, and it did so by my order."[66]

Professor James H. Lane, mathematician and scientist, devoted his life to teaching in Virginia, North Carolina, and Missouri, except for the four years he was a colonel and general in the Confederate army. No doubt the educational years were the more constructive, but his most intense moment was about 3:30 P.M. on July 3 when his brigade closed on the Federals on Cemetery Ridge. Captain John H. Thorpe, of the 47th North Carolina, Pettigrew's old brigade, saw him on horseback at the wall, urging his men forward with his hand, as though trying to push them over. Blood spurted from his horse and they went down together.[67] Smoke obscured the picture for Thorpe, but Lane was up again quickly to try again and then to take the skeleton of his brigade slowly back across the long valley over which it had moved with high ardor only half an hour before. He was unscathed.

Lowrance had a story similar to Lane's of the sustained attack by Trimble, and declared that at this stage all others had apparently forsaken his men and Lane's. "The two brigades, now reduced to mere squads, not numbering in all 800 men, were the only lines to be seen upon that vast field, and with no support in view, the brigade retreated."[68]

Lane and Lowrance retired in fair formation. Major Weston was emphatic that there was no disorder. In Trimble's words they fell back "sullenly and slowly, in almost as good order as they had advanced."[69] Trimble summed it up: "If the troops I had the honor to command today couldn't take that position, all hell can't take it."

Then he described the clash: "At the fence the exposure was dreadful. The incessant discharge of canister, shell and musketry was more than any troops could endure. The brigades of Pender, yielding ground, began to move back slowly and in good order, not even breaking ranks."[70]

Looking across, Trimble saw from where he lay wounded that the battle had ended in front of Pickett. Of his own men he said, corroborating Lane: "I know these brigades were the last troops to leave the field." He cited an axiom: "No single line of infantry without artillery can carry a line, protected by rifle pits, knapsacks and other cover, and a numerous artillery, if the assaulted party bravely avails itself of all its advantages."[71]

All along the lines the Federals had captured numerous prisoners and sheafs of regimental flags. Lowrance's 38th North Carolina reversed the normal process by capturing 30 Federal prisoners beside the works and shooting many, but the regiment's own loss was staggering. Company A had two survivors; the entire regiment only 40, commanded by a lieutenant. Two months earlier the regiment had been a factor in Jackson's flank march at Chancellorsville. Now it was virtually gone.

When the cleanup was begun in front of the Federal position, some of the wounded Confederates were found to be still angry. One, mortally wounded, declined defiantly to allow the 69th Pennsylvania relief workers to take him to a hospital. He said he wanted to die where he fell.[72] Said Major St. Clair A. Mullholland: "In front of the Second Corps the dead lay in great heaps. . . . Out on the field where Longstreet's Corps had passed, thousands of wounded were lying."[73] As there were no means of reaching them, many lay between the lines until the second day, when Lee's army had gone.

8. The General Was with His Men

One baffling question for later years was: Where was Pickett? Colonel Eppa Hunton, commanding the 8th Virginia, said, "No man who was in that charge has ever been found, within my knowledge, who saw Pickett during the charge."[74] Hunton was not observant or well advised, for Pickett was not missing. One account said he was behind a "ledge of rocks" about 100 yards in the rear of "where the division was just prior to the charge." One of Hunton's men said he carried

water to Pickett and his staff, but the location described was so vague
that it might have been either near Seminary Ridge or where the brigades re-formed after crossing the Emmitsburg road. Hunton was
told by General L. L. Lomax, the Confederate representative on the
Gettysburg Commission, that although there had been frequent references to this ledge, no such ledge had ever been located.[75] Nothing
that answers the exact description is to be found on the ground over
which Pickett's division attacked.

In analyzing the question of Pickett's whereabouts Hunton made
a strong point that neither Pickett nor any of his staff, all mounted,
was killed or wounded, nor were any of the horses injured, whereas,
he asserted, "every man who was known to have gone into the charge
on horseback, was killed or wounded or had his horse killed."[76] Garnett and Kemper were good examples. Hunton himself was wounded
near the red Codori barn. He conceded that several of Pickett's staff
said Pickett accompanied the men, but Hunton could not learn
how far.

The question was booted about in later years and the impression
was strong that Pickett went at least as far as the Codori barn, which
is certainly as close to the front line as the division commander ought
to go.[77] Near the barn is some dead space, protected from Cemetery
Ridge, and whether Pickett was there, in the field, or behind the stone
foundation of the barn probably depended on when a courier or
orderly happened to reach him. The rock foundation of the barn may
have been what Hunton's soldier meant as a "ledge of rocks" to
which he carried water.

Captain W. Stuart Symington, one of Pickett's aides, said that
Pickett ordered Armistead to move up to the left as he advanced and
the left became exposed; that would have been after the division was
near the Federal wall. Pickett was therefore following the action
closely. Captain R. A. Bright, also of Pickett's staff, gave more exact
information. Pickett and four of his staff rode on the right of Armistead's brigade until they reached the Emmitsburg road, which at
the Codori farm was about 400 yards from the copse of trees that
marked the objective of the assault. Here Pickett sent Bright back
to Longstreet to tell him he could carry the heights but could not hold
them without reinforcements. When Bright returned he found Pickett
"between the Emmitsburg Road and Cemetery Heights." That would
mean closer than the Codori barn. Pickett then sent Bright, Symington, and Captain E. R. Baird, also of his staff, to urge Wilcox to come

up; Bright on his return from that unsuccessful mission, found him "near the descent of the last hill, facing the Federal works." This was close indeed to the enemy line—closer than a major general would ordinarily venture in an attack in the open fields.

About 100 yards beyond the Codori barn the ground sinks to an old stream bed. In this depression, up which Kemper had moved across the front of Stannard's brigade, troops were not visible to watchers on Seminary Ridge, where Lee and Longstreet were anxiously trying to observe. Between the depression and the Federal wall, about 300 yards, the gentle incline is broken by an outcropping of rocks, scarcely a ledge, though rough and protruding. The land here is untillable and unsuited even for pasture and is covered with low hemlock, scrub oak, and wild cherry.

This is most likely, though not certainly, the point to which Pickett advanced personally, and in such case he is entitled to the full honor of leading his desperate charge. From here the enemy lines were just 100 yards distant. This may have been what the water carrier had in mind as the ledge, and it might readily be termed "the last valley in front of Cemetery Ridge," where Bright said he found his commander. Lomax must have been looking for his ledge too far in the rear.

Another mission on which Pickett sent his aide, Bright, was to Dearing's battalion, to ask it to open and protect the left flank of the assaulting column. He brought back word that Dearing had only three rounds but had opened with them at once.

When the attack was finally reviewed after the battle it was found that each of the three commands—Pickett, Pettigrew, and Trimble—had entered the enemy line at some point.

Dead and wounded of both Pettigrew's and Trimble's divisions were found in the orchard beyond the stone wall. The well-known justice of the North Carolina Supreme Court in later years, then Captain J. J. Davis of the 47th North Carolina, Pettigrew's brigade, was captured inside the wall.[78] The fact that Pettigrew and Trimble attacked the stone barrier where it was 80 yards recessed from the wall assailed by Pickett took those two commands closer to the heart of the enemy position. A review of the claims of the different units shows that the troops which probably advanced the farthest were Captain E. Fletcher Slatterfield's company of the 55th North Carolina Regiment. The regiment was commanded by Captain George Gilreath. At this point, where the high tide of the Confederacy surged and receded, Slatterfield fell.[79]

Members of Davis' brigade, this company was part of the regiment that pursued Cutler's men north of the railroad cutting on the first day of the battle. The point of farthest advance was established—at least to the content of North Carolinians, and to the apparent satisfaction of the Gettysburg battlefield authorities of that day—when Lieutenant T. D. Falls, of Fallstown, Cleveland County, North Carolina, and Sergeant Augustus Whitley, of Everitts, in Martin County, visited the terrain, made affidavits about the point they had reached, and had it marked by the Gettysburg Commission.[80] This testimony, according to Adjutant Charles M. Cooke, of the 55th, had other corroboration.

Taken with the advance of Lane and D. H. Hill in the pre-Manassas affair on the Peninsula, and the fact that Cox's brigade fired the final round of the Army of Northern Virginia, this bold feat of the 55th Regiment went to establish North Carolina's most cherished tradition of its part in the Confederate War: "First at Bethel, farthest at Gettysburg and last at Appomattox."

Unhappily for the North Carolinians, the principal press accounts of the battle were from the Richmond correspondents. In one of the first conspicuous dispatches to the *Enquirer,* Pettigrew's command, containing some of the stanchest veteran regiments of the army, was termed "raw troops," and Pickett's defeat was attributed to Pettigrew's "faltering." North Carolina has not yet recovered.[81]

This impression worked its way into early Southern history and no doubt influenced the writing of some of the official army reports prepared within a few months after the battle. Longstreet's tended to exonerate Pickett and blame Hill's troops,[82] and Pickett's was so bitter that Lee declined to receive it and requested that it be rewritten.[83] The assault, much to the annoyance of North Carolina participants and the state's postwar writers, came to be known as "Pickett's charge" without ever a reference to Pettigrew or Trimble. That name is probably a historical fixture, though Pickett commanded little more than a third of the attacking column and performance was equally courageous all along the line.

Going into the attack with both flanks in the air foredoomed the movement to failure, and the troops naturally faltered first at the two extremes of the line. This was no reflection of the right under Kemper

nor the left under Mayo. No troops could have withstood the enfilade
fire while assailed by artillery and musketry in their immediate front.
It was not the character of the units but their positions which caused
the disintegration that eventually affected the entire assaulting force.

Many factors contributed to the repulse apart from the terrain and
inadequate numbers: improper organization of the movement, inadequate staffwork, the faltering of Wilcox and Lang, the failure of Hill
to move Thomas and Perrin into close support of the left flank of the
column, and, by no means last, Pendleton's inexcusable blunder of
depriving the assaulting column of well-stocked artillery that could
have helped keep the Federal flankers in check.

9. "The Task Was Too Great for You"

As Shotwell of the 8th Virginia was dragging himself up Seminary
Ridge after the heartbreaking experience in the valley, he saw a horseman observing alone, and as he approached, was surprised to find it
was the commanding general. Shotwell gave a brief picture of Lee at
this moment. "His bridle rein was carelessly upon his horse's neck,
and in the whole attitude of the trim, soldierly figure was an air of sadness, weariness, regretfulness, akin to depression, such as I had never
known in him before."

Shotwell saluted Lee and was about to pass on when the general
stopped him. "Are you wounded?" Lee asked.

"No, General," he replied, "only a little fatigued; but I am afraid
there are but few so lucky as myself."

"Ah! yes," said Lee. "I am very sorry—the task was too great for
you. But we mustn't despond. Another time we shall succeed. Are
you one of Pickett's men?"

"Yes, sir."

"Well, you had better go back and rest yourself. Captain Linthicum
will tell you the rendezvous for your brigade."

An officer came up at a gallop and told Lee a division—Shotwell was
so filled with emotion that he did not get the name, but it was more
likely Wright's brigade than a division—was coming into line behind
the ridge, and Lee gathered up his reins. "It is well," he said. "Those
people over yonder seem to be advancing, and I am becoming a little
anxious."[84]

The advance Lee detected was only heavy waves of skirmishers,
but they might have heralded a more general movement of Meade's
army.

Shotwell had one other touching experience. When he found Linthicum, "our soldier-parson," the captain was standing with his head resting on the neck of a horse, weeping for the man whose blood covered the saddle—his dear friend General Richard S. Garnett.[85] Dick Garnett now was with Stonewall Jackson, and if the stern old genius had been looking down at the assault on Cemetery Ridge it is likely he had already wiped the slate clean for Garnett's retreat at Kernstown.

Lee was at his greatest in this moment of adversity. He made no effort to shift the least part of the blame. "It was all my fault," he repeated again and again as officers came to him. Then he urged them to "do the best we can toward saving what is left us."[86] Already he was looking toward other battles and offering his soldiers resolution instead of remorse.

The Confederate army was indeed in peril when the troops of Pickett, Pettigrew, and Trimble came streaming back, but Longstreet allowed no moments to escape him. He anticipated that the Federals would pursue quickly, Meade at their head. But neither Longstreet nor Lincoln a little later seemed to understand that Meade—who had been selected because he was a safe, cautious general, temperamentally the opposite of Hooker—would go on being cautious and safe to the end.

Longstreet rode the line of his batteries to inspire a resolute defense, determined that his last gun would be sacrificed if necessary in repelling a counterattack. He was not so sparing of ammunition but that he opened on the dense waves of skirmishers and they were soon driven back. That night Law and McLaws were withdrawn from the base of Round Top to Seminary Ridge, and Johnson was retired from Benner's Hill to Seminary Ridge and Oak Hill to make the defensive line more compact.

Lee remained at the line of guns on the fringe of the woods where he awaited the soldiers returning from the assault and spoke to them cheeringly. Meade at that time left his Power's Hill headquarters and rode to Little Round Top, greeted by swelling cheers all along the line. Lee heard them and told a lieutenant to ascertain their meaning, but nothing gave evidence of the counterattack he feared.[87] The Federal army clung to its ridge as though it, too, was spent, and all Meade attempted was a gingerly reconnaissance by a brigade of the Fifth Corps. Could Meade at this moment have attacked successfully? Who knows? If so, his losses would have been terrific, for he in turn would have had to cross the open ground and charge up the slope. The Confederacy, at fearful price, had made its great thrust for freedom, and Meade's army had repulsed it; both sides seemed to recognize that enough blood had been poured already across these Pennsylvania hills.

Of Pickett's fifteen regiments only one field officer escaped injury. He was Lieutenant Colonel Joseph C. Cabell, who survived to fall near Richmond. Seven colonels were dead in front of their men and an eighth was mortally wounded; all the others were casualties. The loss in company officers and noncommissioned officers, while unrecorded, was undoubtedly as severe. True to his presumption, Colonel Patton fell at the wall.

One of the pathetic pictures of the Confederate War was that of Pickett back on Seminary Ridge, dismounted, holding his reins, his hat off, reporting to Longstreet, "General, my noble division is swept away."

That was substantially the case, for the retreat of the survivors, virtually without officers, degenerated into a rout.

Though some of the attacking column, maddened by the repulse, pleaded to be taken back again[88] and Lane heartily invited a Federal counterattack so his men might return some of the favors handed to them along the wall,[89] most of the soldiers knew that for them the battle was over. They stumbled across the fields distraught, winded, assailed from the rear by rapid Federal fire. What destroyed their morale utterly was this return journey across nearly a mile of open country covered with the bodies of their comrades, while shells still exploded overhead and men were dropping about them.[90] Facing the firing guns had been easier than having them at their backs.

Even with a Malvern Hill in its record, the Army of Northern Virginia had experienced no such sanguinary repulse. Efforts to stop the refugees on Seminary Ridge were abortive. Regimental and company formations had been lost; there was no longer a division, or brigades, or regiments. There were merely groups of battle-shocked men seeking shelter from the ghastly carnage. Several hundred yards beyond Seminary Ridge the remnants came to a country road running down a valley, which would lead eventually to a juncture with the Fairfield road. Because of a bluff on one side and a swamp on the other, the fleeing men had to converge and pass through a defile. Here, in the blind frenzy that overtakes men in flight, they threw away much of their equipment—blankets, haversacks, and guns. Efforts by the handful of officers to halt them were as unsuccessful as they had been on Seminary Ridge. Finally some of the privates themselves saw the unreasoning nature of their retreat. Standing firm, they soon brought others into their group until they formed a guard of about thirty men across the road and checked the rout. Sorrel called it "a sight never before witnessed—part of the Army of Northern Virginia in full, breathless flight."[90]

Pickett was weeping without restraint. A man of his high emotions could not control the tears even in front of his soldiers. Riding after his men, he came to the volunteer guard barring the roadway and said, "Don't stop any of my men. Tell them to come to the camp we occupied last night." Then, a pitiful and solitary figure, unaccompanied by aides or orderlies, he rode back toward his old camp on Marsh Creek.

Charles Marshall of Lee's staff came along after Pickett departed, set up a patrol several hundred yards to the rear along a small stream, and kept it there until sunset. By that time the frenzy of the defeat had subsided, and Marshall marched the assembled group back to Seminary Ridge, where Lee spoke kindly to them.

Pickett next morning on Marsh Creek mustered 800 men in place of the approximately 4,800 who had followed him into battle. The division, now calmed, was put in charge of about 4,000 Federal prisoners and started for Virginia.[91] The last to reach the battlefield was the first to depart.

But while the survivors marched away, their name lingered. Pickett's division had been denied the aura of victory, but it had been chosen by fame to identify eternally what is probably the most renowned infantry assault of Anglo-Saxon history—an assault that was "the high-water mark of the Rebellion" and of a type of warfare more akin to chivalry than to the fighting of our present day.

10. The Cavalry Charges Around

Stuart's part in the effort to break the Federal center on July 3 was entirely negative. He took his troopers to the far Confederate left, between the York and Hanover roads, and fought inconclusively at the Rummel farm with Gregg's Federal cavalry, augmented by Custer's brigade of Kilpatrick's division.

The action, begun by dismounted pickets, gradually drew in the heavier columns until Stuart had about 6,000 and Gregg about 4,000 on the field. After a series of charges and countercharges, compared by one of the contestants to "the crash of ocean waves breaking on a rock-bound coast,"[92] the tide receded and there was not an unusual amount of driftage left on the shore. Stuart pulled off when it was obvious that he could not reach the rear of Meade's army and that it had not been broken. He saw unengaged Federal horsemen massing on his flank and knew a bitter and prolonged fight was promised.

Like all the other elements of the Gettysburg campaign for Stuart, this battle in the Federal right rear was barren of glory. It was all he did at Gettysburg and it was worth no more than his pitiful exhibit of 125 wagons, the fruit of his long ride around the Federal army. Wade Hampton was severely but not critically wounded. Stuart retired in the late afternoon and fell in on Ewell's flank.

More spectacular but altogether vain was the attack by the Federal Brigadier General Elon J. Farnsworth, who had worn his star only four days, against some of Law's regiments on the far right of the Confederate army. Farnsworth had passed to the Confederate flank with Kilpatrick, and Law had added Tige Anderson's Georgia brigade as a flank protection. Robertson's 1st Texas Regiment was close by and Benning's Georgians were in supporting distance. Skirmishers of the 1st Texas were so close they overheard the Federal cavalry planning the charge, then an angry voice exclaiming, "If you are afraid to attack, by God, I will lead the charge myself."

Law said he learned later that Kilpatrick was the speaker and that Farnsworth, who knew the harebrained nature of the movement, would not have made it on his own judgment.

Captain H. C. Parsons of the 1st Vermont Cavalry was close when Kilpatrick gave the order and noticed Farnsworth's emotion as he replied, "General, do you mean it? Shall I throw my handful of men over rough ground, through timber, against a brigade of infantry? The 1st Vermont has already been fought half to pieces; these men are too good to kill."[93]

Parsons quoted Kilpatrick's reply in words similar to those overheard by the Texans: "Do you refuse to obey my orders? If you are afraid to lead this charge, I will lead it."

"Take that back," cried Farnsworth in high passion, rising in his stirrups and facing his superior boldly.

Kilpatrick was apparently the one who lacked personal courage in such an encounter—though he was intrepid enough in action—and sidled away from his affronted subordinate. "I did not mean it; forget it," he said.

The ability of the cavalry to break infantry began to pass with the introduction of gunpowder, but Kilpatrick did not seem to realize this; according to one of his officers he thought the cavalry could "fight anywhere except at sea." The ground here was anything but suited to cavalry, being covered with great rocks, lined with stone walls and spotted with clumps of timber.

Farnsworth took two of his regiments, the depleted 1st Vermont and the 1st West Virginia, out of the woods near the base of Round Top and threw them against what a near-by Federal cavalry colonel judged was the best-guarded spot along the entire Confederate line.[94] Anderson's brigade was astride the Emmitsburg road watching Merritt's cavalry brigade which had come up from Emmitsburg and driven in his skirmishers. Farnsworth dashed pell-mell against the front of the 1st Texas, in line between the road and Round Top, and was repulsed, but his front extended beyond that of the enemy; the 1st Vermont, overlapping the Texans, rode on until it found itself between the Confederate artillery and their main line, Farnsworth riding with it.

Law had already ordered the 9th Georgia, Anderson's brigade, from the Emmitsburg road, and it came at a run. He told an aide to find the first available regiment and throw it across Farnsworth's path and the aide brought up the 4th Alabama. Law then ordered Colonel Oates of the 15th Alabama to close the gap on the flank of the 1st Texas where Farnsworth had entered.

The gallant Federal cavalryman was now enclosed, and what his charge consisted of was riding in large circles around the fields, dashing himself here and there against the infantry, seeking an escape. Riding north up the valley he struck the 4th Alabama first, recoiled, moved against the Confederate batteries with their infantry supports, which tore his little command apart at close range, and then circled again in an effort to emerge at his point of entry. Here he struck the Alabamians, bounced back once more, and gained temporary security in the woods, from where about six of his troopers worked their way out past the flank of the 1st Texas.[95]

Most of Law's division, including its commander and General Benning, watched the frantic efforts of the Federal cavalry leader, who could be distinguished by a linen havelock worn over his military cap. Benning said it was as if enacted in an amphitheater. When Farnsworth reached the woods he rode dauntlessly with a handful of men to the 15th Alabama. Flourishing his pistol, he called on the lieutenant commanding the firing line to surrender. He received a volley that emptied most of his saddles, killed his horse, and wounded him in several places. As the lieutenant approached him and demanded his surrender, Farnsworth put his pistol to his head and blew out his brains. His reason can only be surmised. Possibly he believed that all that remained for him was the scorn of his superior, Kilpatrick. That part of the command which had not entered behind the Confederate lines retired in good order.

Colonel Frederick C. Newhall of the 6th Pennsylvania Cavalry, Merritt's advance regiment, which was near by, said later that if Kilpatrick really dared Farnsworth to charge, "it was a crime."[96] About this there could be little doubt, because part of a good cavalry brigade was tossed away capriciously, against the attacking officer's advice, and it seemed largely to embellish a general's swashbuckling. Newhall appeared to believe the story, which was adequately attested, but hoped it was not true that this brave general "rode to his death with that contemptible taunt goading him."

Some of the Confederates who interviewed the prisoners told Benning the attackers "were all drunk."[97] That probably was not the case, but the conclusion is understandable because of the senseless nature of the attack. Nothing was better managed, according to observer Benning, than the manner in which Farnsworth was hemmed in and repulsed. His attack was the final episode of the battle.

That night it rained.

CHAPTER TWENTY-THREE

Retreat to Virginia

1. "I Cain't Find No Rear"

The rain fell in such torrents that, as War Clerk Jones observed, it "washed the blood from the grass all night,"[1] while the historian of the Army of the Potomac, J. H. Stine, thought the heavy cannonading of the three days had so agitated the elements as to unleash the violent storms.[2]

The gods of the thunder, challenged by the blasts of the guns, shot giant bolts with rumbles and reverberations across the hills, deluged the valleys and, except when the eerie flashes lighted the ghostly fields, covered the country with "a darkness like that of Egypt."[3] Canvas gave scant protection, and the Confederate army lay in gloomy silence, drenched, with the rain beating in their faces and depressing any remaining battle ardor for the moment.

The rain finally slackened, reserving some of its torrents for the succeeding days, and although the mud mired down the artillery, Lee was able to withdraw his two wings so that his line ran straight along Seminary Ridge.

Johnson extricated himself skillfully from his remote and always hazardous position hooked around Meade's right, where an enterprising antagonist possessing interior lines might have concentrated an overwhelming force against him. He began his withdrawal at 1:30 A.M., July 4, and conducted it so quietly that it was undetected by Federal pickets only fifty yards away.[4] The noise of the rain must have helped him in his stealth, but it was not likely Slocum would have tried to interfere in the darkness.

Early followed him, then Rodes. When day broke, the Federals on Culp's and East Cemetery hills looked out on the empty Confederate lines, which they could not yet know for certain presaged the death of the Southern cause. But the Federal soldiers had notions.

Where the skirmish lines were still close enough for conversation a Northern soldier called across to a Southern picket, "Hello, Johnnie, have you got any butter?"

"No," the Confederate answered. "Why?"

"Because," the Yank went on, "you'll need it to slide back into the Union on."[5]

Victory and defeat are not always matters of men and bayonets, but often conditions of the mind. All through the night of July 3 the Confederate soldiers thought they would continue the fight in the morning. So did Meade. Few in the ranks were defeated or, in any event, prepared to recognize it. But as the day of July 4 wore on and Lee's intentions became apparent, the Southern army came to understand that the campaign in Pennsylvania had failed, and Meade to know that he had won a great victory.

On the night of July 3 Lee summoned Imboden to headquarters. The cavalry officer arrived about eleven only to learn that Lee was at Hill's headquarters. There Imboden found him and Hill seated on camp stools examining the Adams County map by the light of a single candle, talking earnestly, carefully preparing for the withdrawal of the army, which Hill's corps would commence. Lee directed Imboden to return and await him at army headquarters, which the commanding general reached about one o'clock. The skies had cleared temporarily, for Imboden said Lee could be seen approaching slowly by the moonlight, but he was so exhausted he could scarcely alight. After the cavalryman had assisted him he rested himself against his horse, his arm across the saddle, and stood for a time looking at the ground as though too fatigued to go further.

Sympathetically Imboden broke the silence with a word of understanding. "General, this has been a hard day for you."

"Yes, it has been a sad, sad day for us," Lee responded, his thoughts as always on the army. He gave Imboden clear instructions for the conduct of the wounded to Virginia, specifying the route via Chambersburg and Williamsport to the Potomac.[6]

The rain resumed soon after noon on July 4 and, according to Imboden, "the meadows became small lakes; raging streams ran across the road . . . the storm increased in fury every minute." At 4:00 P.M.

Imboden moved by the Cashtown pike with the long train carrying the thousands of wounded soldiers—seventeen miles of them, a slow-moving convoy that required thirty-four hours to pass a given point.

Lee's spirits were restored after the painful task of evacuating the wounded. Hill's artilleryman, McIntosh, thought the greatness of his character was never more clearly revealed than at this time when his plans had crashed: "He never appeared more serene than on the days succeeding the battle."[7]

All day July 4 the two armies faced each other, sickened by their appalling losses, bogged down in mud and water, each watching for the other to disclose its intention. Ewell entrenched along the ridge northwest of Gettysburg and awaited the Northern army, and though Lee's artillery was short of ammunition, the infantry had plenty for another engagement.

But Meade had decided with finality against attacking Lee on Seminary Ridge. Hancock had written him from his stretcher just after Pickett was repulsed, urging a counterattack. The Federal cavalry chief, Pleasanton, had ridden up to Meade, congratulated him, then badgered him.

"General," Pleasanton said, "I will give you half an hour to show yourself a great general. Order the army to advance, while I will take the cavalry, get in Lee's rear, and we will finish the campaign in a week."

Meade's reply was typical. "How do you know Lee will not attack me again? We have done well enough."[8]

On the gloomy night of July 4 Hill's drenched corps marched, followed by Longstreet, then Ewell. All moved by the Fairfield road toward Hagerstown, which gave protection to the trains going by the Cashtown route. Meade could not shift toward Lee's left and unblock Washington. Just as on Lee's approach to Gettysburg, too many men had to move along a single road, and it was not until ten o'clock on the morning of July 5 that Ewell was on the way from Seminary Ridge. Gordon's brigade, the rear guard, left Gettysburg at noon, unmolested.

Dickert, of Kershaw's brigade, described the retreat: ". . . down mountain sides, through gorges and over hills, the army slowly made its way. No haste, no confusion. . . . The rain fell in torrents, night and day. The roads were soon greatly cut up, which in a measure was to Lee's advantage, preventing the enemy from following him too closely."[9]

Lee, according to his custom, fell in with Longstreet and when the correspondent Ross observed them at Bream's Tavern on the Fairfield road, they were standing apart, talking earnestly, while the staff officers huddled around the fire that was a protection from the chill rain, or, exhausted, slept with the rain beating into their faces, using logs or fence rails for pillows.[10]

Lee said later that he considered countermanding his retreat order because of the rain. He declared he would not have left his position if he had anticipated such dreadfully bad weather."[11] But the wagon trains would be endangered if the army did not follow. Quite obviously he still had unbounded confidence in his men and accepted defeat with deep reluctance.

Ross talked with him and Longstreet at Hagerstown, where the commanding general expressed opinions of interest because they were his first recorded after the battle. He said he would not have attacked had he known that Meade had been able to concentrate his entire army, and he complimented Meade on this achievement. He had not intended, in fact, to bring on any full-scale battle, but, "led away, partly by the success of the first day, believing that Meade had only a portion of his army . . . and seeing the enthusiasm of his own troops, he had thought that a successful battle would cut the knot so easily and satisfactorily that he had determined to risk it."

He attributed his lack of knowledge about Meade to Stuart's absence. The fact that he had been forced to wait three days at Chambersburg had deprived him of the advantage he had secured at the beginning of the invasion. As Ross interpreted his views, Lee felt that if he had not been compelled to wait—and the absence of the cavalry was what slowed him—he could have taken the entire army into the Susquehanna valley, following Ewell, threatened Philadelphia, and severed the Army of the Potomac from the north except by sea. Meade could not have menaced his communications seriously without exposing Baltimore and Washington. "He might have taken a position where it would have been very difficult for Meade to attack him; and without further fighting, by merely maintaining his army near Harrisburg or some other central point, incalculable results might have been secured."[12] That was essentially Longstreet's "defensive tactics" proposal made at the beginning of the campaign.

Lee reached the Potomac on July 7 and found the river in flood and his pontoons destroyed by raiders operating against his rear from French's force at Frederick. He constructed works extending from

Conococheague Creek near Hagerstown, to the Potomac, then awaited either attack by Meade or a recession of the river.

Meade straggled up on July 12, reconnoitered Lee's strong lines, and, against Lincoln's specific injunction to "call no council of war," called a meeting of the corps commanders on the night of July 12. All but two—Howard and Wadsworth, the temporary First Corps commander—opposed an attack, a judgment to which Meade for the time yielded. But after another reconnaissance on July 13, with the rain still pouring, he decided to attack on the fourteenth. When he moved out on the morning of the fourteenth, Lee had gone.

Lack of flour more than lack of ammunition impelled Lee to cross.[13] Adequate supplies for his artillery had been brought up from Winchester on July 9. Meade, too, recognized that Lee's caissons were now loaded. His information, though he regarded it as scanty, was that ammunition trains had been ferried to Williamsport.[14] Why Lee's staff and chief of artillery had not brought up ammunition from Winchester and made it available to him at Gettysburg is an unanswered question. There must have been time while Lee waited at Chambersburg before the battle.

Lincoln was deeply disappointed that Lee was allowed to "escape," and Halleck's telegram reflecting the President's view was so severe that Meade tendered his resignation, which was declined.

The question of whether an attack by Meade might have succeeded will, of course, never be answered. Lee had a larger force than that with which he withstood McClellan at Sharpsburg. He was entrenched in a superior position and his men were eager to retaliate for Gettysburg. It seems unlikely Meade could have done much better than Burnside did at Fredericksburg. That the spirit of the army was by no means crushed could be seen by the attitude of the officer interviewed by Ross: "We will fight them, sir, till hell freezes over, and then, sir, we'll fight them on the ice."[15]

Even when across the river some still thought Lee had really won. Surgeon Welch wrote to his South Carolina wife from Bunker Hill:

We drove the Yankees three miles from the battlefield to a long range of high hills, from which it was impossible to dislodge them. General Lee had to fall back to keep them from getting the advantage."[16]

How the in-the-ranks Federals regarded it could be seen from the letter from Josiah Williams of Putnamville, Indiana, about how he found things when he rejoined his regiment, the 27th Indiana, from the hospital.

Gettysburg was an awful fight the boys saying it was more terrific than anything they ever saw, which is emphatically some. Men laying in piles, our Regiment losing 100 in about 3 minutes in a charge made upon the Breast-works. . . .[17]

Though Meade did not attack before the crossing, his artillery was annoying while the Confederate army had its back to the river. McKim told a story of a servant who came too close to the lines, where his master admonished him.

"Caesar, what are you doing here?" asked the Confederate officer. "Have I not ordered you always to keep in the rear when the fighting is going on?"

"Yes, Marster," the Negro answered, "I know you is told me dat. But I declar' fo' God, I'se look ebery whar on dis here battle field dis day, and I cain't find no rear."[18]

Heth, restored to duty, covered Lee's crossing. His depleted division was north of the river on the morning of July 14, while Pender's, closer to the stream, was preparing to cross. Heth's men had marched all night and were asleep. Heth put out no pickets, although Pettigrew set up a guard for his own brigade.

While his exhausted men napped, Pettigrew examined the lines. His aide, Captain Louis G. Young, met him on foot in the rear center of his command. While they talked, Heth rode by and told him his brigade would be the rear guard. Pettigrew expressed regret that he had been given no artillery but told Young to arouse the men, which the captain did.

. Just then Pettigrew and Young noticed a body of cavalry on rising ground a mile distant and inquired of Heth about its identity. The general said that if it should be an enemy party it could be driven off easily. While Heth and Pettigrew were watching, another small cavalry squadron rode out of the woods only 500 yards distant, flying the United States flag. Heth, for some reason, thought they could not be the enemy but were displaying a captured flag in a spirit of braggadocio. Said Young: "It was difficult to believe sane men would attack as this small body of cavalry did."[19]

The bold Federal squadron rode close to Pettigrew's soldiers, who were only awaiting orders to fire, demanded their surrender, and dashed about firing their revolvers. Pettigrew was tossed from his startled horse. One of his arms was still weak from a wound received at Seven Pines and the other was in a sling from the hand injury suffered at Gettysburg.

His troops meantime formed a line along a fence. When he arose he directed them calmly and the Federal cavalrymen began to fall. One of them took a position on the flank where he fired so effectively that Pettigrew ordered his men to get him. They apparently did not hear, so he started at the man with his own pistol and, heedless of his danger, tried to get so close he could not miss. Before he could fire the Federal trooper shot him in the abdomen. His wound was mortal and he died three days later at Bunker Hill, Virginia, probably the last casualty of the Southern army in the campaign. All North Carolina mourned him.[20]

The small attacking party was annihilated by the Confederate fire. Correspondent Ross called them "forty tipsy cavalrymen,"[21] and others claimed they were drunk, though it is hard to see how that could be determined with all of them dead. It is probable they were only foolhardy.

2. Some Reasons for Victory and Defeat

Meade approached many of his decisions gropingly, owing probably to his brief tenure in command. In the end, his decisions seemed to be unfailingly correct.

He gave battle at Gettysburg instead of along his more favored Pipe Creek line; the Gettysburg position with its interior lines was a major element in his success. He remained on the defensive at every stage, which proved good judgment. When he won he prudently conserved his victory. Unlike many past generals initially successful in dealing with a resourceful adversary, he did not chance spoiling success by an ill-conceived and hastily arranged counterattack or, a little later, by an assault on strongly fortified lines.

In the conduct of the battle, Hancock was as vital a factor as Meade himself—and it was to Meade's credit that he knew how to employ so capable a subordinate; he knew when not to yield to his views, as on the afternoon of July 3 when Hancock, being a more daring warrior, counseled a counteroffensive. As the battle progressed, Hancock's quick decisions and prompt actions meant on more than one occasion the difference between defeat and victory.

It is true that Meade might have won more decisively by taking the offensive. He wisely decided, at an hour when defeat would have meant disaster to the Federal cause, that a victory in hand, even though it did not destroy his adversary, was preferable to risking his own badly battered army further, when there was nothing in the history of Lee's generalship or that of the Army of Northern Virginia which gave much promise that by a frontal attack that army could be captured or destroyed.

Probably the preservation of the union depended a great deal at this hour on Meade's conservatism. He had the sense to recognize that after three days of fighting, he possessed, not striking power, but position.

Lee offered no apologies for his failure at Gettysburg, and needed none; it was a part of his greatness that after the war he refrained from the temptation that besets generals to write accounts of justification and explanation. His words were not required to tell why the Confederacy lost the war and why he did not win it.

But Lee did fail to dislodge his opponent in the decisive battle of the war, and it is pertinent to examine the reasons. Perhaps no battle has been subjected to such searching analysis, yet even at this late date it seems that part of the blame has been misassessed and that some of the areas—such as Lee's selection of his subordinates and the composition of his own staff—have been looked on as sacrosanct by many Southern writers and have been ignored by many Northern.

Of the factors which contributed to Lee's defeat, this writer has listed some which appear outstanding. They are:

Inadequate staff work. This was at the heart of Lee's battle problems and accounted for most of his earlier difficulties. It was evident at the outset in the loose wording of the orders given to Stuart, which deprived Lee of his cavalry. The inadequacy of his staff was present at every hour at Gettysburg, in the inability of the commander to enforce his will on his subordinates and dominate the action as a victorious general must do. Lee needed as chief of staff a soldier of the stature of Hood, Johnson, Gordon, or Benning, with appropriate rank and a sufficient number of subordinates to make certain that (1) the commanding general was informed of all developments on the field (like the value of garrisoning Round Top), and (2) that the commanding general's main purposes were not flouted because of minor developments (like the stoppage of the *en echelon* attack by the Bliss farm skirmish). As it was, after giving his orders to his corps commanders, Lee lost all control of the battle action. This chief of staff should not only have taken over the detail work, but should have maintained close contact with the War Department in Richmond, keeping it informed of the army's condition, causing it to respond to Lee's suggestion for an "army in effigy," and insisting on the forwarding of Pickett's missing brigades.

Failure of Ewell and Early to follow their advantage of July 1. This appears to have been the major tactical error of the battle, for quick pursuit of a broken enemy almost certainly would have deprived Meade of his Cemetery Ridge position, necessitated his concentration behind Pipe Creek, and given Lee a significant psychological victory on July 1, instead of merely a preliminary advantage that was a prelude to defeat. Lee himself might have ridden more speedily to Gettysburg and assumed a more vigorous control of the action on his arrival. He did not need to await Longstreet when a broken, fleeing enemy was before him.

Absence of the cavalry. This led to the battle in circumstances that were not of Lee's choosing, deprived him of intelligence about Meade's concentration, and severely handicapped him at every turn both in the campaign and on the battlefield. A typical instance of the latter was Longstreet's groping flank march of July 2 without cavalry guide and over terrain no cavalry had reconnoitered.

Failure to transfer Ewell's corps to the army's right. After Ewell and Early had missed the opportunity to take Culp's and Cemetery hills at the close of the first day's fighting, Johnson was allowed to beat his division and three additional brigades to pieces against the Culp's Hill citadel without maintaining any concert with the balance of the army. Lee had recognized from the almshouse cupola on the evening of July 1 the weakness of his strung-out, concave line and had urgently desired a more compact, straight line of battle along Seminary Ridge. But he had allowed himself to be induced by the glib, persuasive lawyer, Jubal Early, to maintain his faulty position. With Ewell on his right he might have rolled up Meade's army on July 2, and he could always have imposed more of a threat of a flanking movement around Meade's left, about which the Federal commander seemed sensitive.

Pender's fall on July 2. The loss at a critical moment of this intrepid officer, who had demonstrated on July 1 how ably he could conduct an attack, was a cause of defeat which Lee himself mentioned, although inadvertently or through error in reporting, he placed Pender's fall on the wrong day. Lee's thought was clear enough.

Had Pender not been mortally wounded, it is fairly certain the attack of July 2 would not have petered out in the center of the army, even if the brigade on Pender's immediate right (Mahone's) had remained unemployed. The success of Wright showed that if Pender had hit the Federal center with his customary impact, the Federal line there, weakened by the transfer of troops to the Wheat Field, very likely would have yielded. Hancock would not have been able to send Carroll's brigade to the succor of Howard when East Cemetery Hill was assailed by the brigades of Avery (Hoke) and Hays. Surely the fall of Pender came at an unhappy moment for Lee's fortunes.

Ewell's failure to attack in concert with Longstreet on July 2. Had he done so, the Federal left could not have been reinforced by the Twelfth Corps, and the center might have been further weakened, with a resultant greater opportunity for the brigades of Wright, Wilcox, and Lang.

The capture of Lee's correspondence. This was undoubtedly a strong factor in holding Meade on the battlefield on the night of July 2, when there were valid inducements in his mind to suggest retirement to Pipe Creek. Merely by maintaining his position—by standing firm—he was able to win a great victory.

Longstreet's attack on July 2. While the delay in this attack is generally advanced as a reason—often as *the* reason—for Lee's defeat, two factors are ignored. The first is the historical misconception that Lee ordered a sunrise attack by Longstreet or that Longstreet could have had his troops in hand had Lee so ordered. The second is that the Federal army would not have been unprepared.

Meade had achieved as good a concentration as Lee on the morning of July 2. He had garrisoned Little Round Top, first with Geary, then with Birney. It was vacated on the afternoon of July 2, when Longstreet attacked. The Federals were always closer and could reach it first if it were threatened.

In many respects it seems that Longstreet's attack was delivered, fortuitously more than by intent, at exactly the right moment, because it was at the only time he was likely to catch Sickles' Third Corps so grievously exposed. Earlier than three o'clock Longstreet would have been compelled to attack a more compact Federal line, over a long stretch of open fields, in the same unfavorable circumstances that attended Pickett, Pettigrew, and Trimble a day later.

By attacking when he did, Longstreet disrupted Meade's entire army, shattered some of its best divisions, and brought it so close to defeat that if Ewell had supplied the co-operation which Lee expected, and if Hill had not faltered when less than half his forces were engaged, it is highly likely that the Federal army, already brought to the verge of defeat, would have been dislodged.

The long and vindictive campaign against Longstreet carried on for a generation was initiated by Pendleton and Early on the false premise that Lee had issued a "sunrise attack order." Longstreet was able to refute this easily from the records and Lee's own staff. But the ground continually shifted in the criticism, and Early, a vindictive assailant, finally goaded Longstreet, who was for a long period indifferent, into indiscretions that aligned much sentiment against him. His political defection had already alienated many. His loss of prestige had its inception not so much in what he did or failed to do at Gettysburg, but in defending his course at Gettysburg. His fame among his contemporaries would have been greater had his pen been more discreet.

A review of Early's extensive writing on this subject in the *Southern Historical Society Papers,* and of Pendleton's original attack, leaves a disinterested reader wondering if the case against Longstreet was not built out of an acute need by these two generals for self-justification of their own conduct during the battle, and perhaps it was an unconscious acknowledgment that they themselves had played no small role in causing Lee's defeat. Certainly Lee never attached blame to Longstreet, nor was the affection he maintained for this peculiar, blunt, domineering subordinate ever moderated, even to the very end.

Finally, the mass assault of July 3. Lee could not know until he tested it how hard it would be to break the Federal center on July 3. After it was over, it was easy to see that too much had been expected from the troops. Before, the assault seemed feasible to him, even if not to Longstreet. The cost was staggering and the failure as complete as Grant's comparable mass attack at Cold Harbor in 1864. These assaults, with others in the War between the States, were part of the costly exactions warfare demands to demonstrate how its established methods become obsolete before many are aware of it. The massed infantry attack over open ground against veteran adversaries was ended, as might have been clear from Andrew Jackson's tremendous victory at New Orleans, but the fact had not been manifested repeatedly and conclusively.

Nevertheless, Pickett and Pettigrew had an outside chance. It was not the case that a mere handful under Armistead reached the enemy lines. Large numbers of assailants surged up to the wall. Had the flanks been protected and an artillery complement been supplied to help keep back the flanking parties, it is not unreasonable to believe that the assaulting column might have gained a lodgment on the crest. What would have happened then, if they could have held or been ejected, would have depended on Longstreet's readiness to send in more troops. Still, in the light of what happened, the attack was a ghastly failure that had better never have been made, and Lee was the first to concede this.[22]

Whether from lack of experience in high command or lack of innate ability, the shortcomings of Ewell and A. P. Hill were critical; compared with them, the deficiencies of Longstreet were indeed venial. Neither Ewell nor Hill at this stage of the war—and it was the decisive stage—knew how to conduct a large-scale attack, and in this Longstreet, with his pugnaciousness, tenacity, and above everything else his supreme desire to win, was superb.

The question occurs, with all the opportunities of hindsight, whether Lee would not have found greater advantage in not attacking on July 2, but in holding his position on Seminary Ridge after bringing Ewell around and forming a straight line with its left flank on Oak Hill. Public opinion and fretting from Washington would have compelled Meade to assail him. There is some misunderstanding that Lee was compelled to attack—that he, being the invader, was committed to the offensive. Many great campaigns have been won by invading armies that fought on the defensive as at Crécy, Agincourt, Senlac and Marengo. Lee had plenty of food and enough powder and could wait. His herds were large—he lost 12,000 head of cattle, and 8,000 head of sheep on his retreat—and when the cavalry arrived it could have rounded up more.[23]

Lee saw the possibility of ending the campaign in a few quick strokes, and quite boldly he responded to that invitation. His troops performed to the full measure of his expectations. Had he achieved a victory, everything he did would have seemed correct. Still great generals do not make victories as often as victories seem to make great generals. As it was, he came so close to success that at several points an additional brigade, like that of Corse or Jenkins, might have changed the outcome of the battle.

That was his own view. When he next saw Micah Jenkins in Virginia, he said, "Jenkins, if I had had your brigade at Gettysburg I would have won."[24]

Probably the best summary of why he lost was his own, contained in a letter written in 1868 to an author contemplating a school history, in which, after referring him to the official accounts of the battle, Lee said:

Its loss was occasioned by a combination of circumstances. It was commenced in the absence of correct intelligence. It was continued in the effort to overcome the difficulties by which we were surrounded, and it would have been gained could one determined and united blow have been delivered by our whole line. As it was, victory trembled in the balance for three days, and the battle resulted in the infliction of as great an amount of injury as was received and in frustrating the Federal campaign for the season.[25]

Charles Francis Adams, a competent Northern authority, thought that in view of the chances always present in warfare: "The Gettysburg campaign was . . . timely, admirably designed, energetically executed, and brought to a close with consummate military skill."

Adams brought out likewise that no hostile force ever invaded an enemy country and retreated "leaving behind less cause for hate and bitterness than did the Army of Northern Virginia in that memorable campaign."[26]

Thousands of battle deaths and nearly twenty-two months of desperate fighting remained before the results of the battle of Gettysburg were confirmed. Victory was not always thereafter a stranger to Lee's army. But the attrition of the South set in and the war rolled on through the Wilderness toward Appomattox. When the fighting had ended it was clear that the Confederate cause was at high tide when it surged against the stone walls and Federal trenches on the crest of Cemetery Hill.

Notes

Chapter One: SUBSTITUTES FOR GENIUS

1 James P. Crocker, "My Personal Experiences in Taking up Arms," *Southern Historical Society Papers,* XXXIII, 113.

2 *Ibid.*

3 Mary Boykin Chesnut, *A Diary from Dixie,* 258.

4 George Cary Eggleston, *A Rebel's Recollections,* 150.

5 G. Moxley Sorrel, *Recollections of a Confederate Staff Officer,* 23.

6 *Southern Historical Society Papers,* V, 176. (Hereinafter *S.H.S.P.*)

7 *Ibid.*

8 Eggleston, 153. The italics are his.

9 William M. Owen, *In Camp and Battle with the Washington Artillery of New Orleans,* 176.

10 Sorrel, 113.

11 *Ibid.*

12 Eggleston, 150.

13 Sorrel, 37.

14 *Ibid.*

15 *Ibid.,* 38.

16 Henry Heth, *S.H.S.P.,* IV, 151, quotes Lee as saying to him, ". . . you, and all my officers know that I am always ready and anxious to have their suggestions."

17 Richard Taylor, *Library of Southern Literature,* XII, 5205. (Hereinafter *L.S.L.*)

18 *Ibid.*

19 *Official Records of the Union and Confederate Armies,* XII, Part III, 9. (Hereinafter *O.R.*)

20 Taylor, *L.S.L.,* XII, 5205.

21 June 19, 1863.

22 Randolph H. McKim, *A Soldier's Recollections,* 134.

23 John B. Gordon, *Reminiscences of the Civil War,* 157.

24 McKim, 134.

25 Washington *Post* interview, June 11, 1893.

26 *Ibid.*

27 Heros von Borcke, *Memoirs of the Confederate War for Independence,* II, 262.

28 Glenn Tucker, *Poltroons and Patriots,* II, 652.

29 Richmond *Examiner,* July 31, 1862, uses the phrase.

30 James C. Birdsong, *Brief Sketches of North Carolina Troops . . . ,* 54. A major asked Hill if he knew Burnside. "Ought to," said Hill. "He owes me $8,000." J. B. Jones placed the amount at $10,000.

31 Richmond *Examiner,* June 28, 1862.

32 Richmond *Whig,* July 11, 1862.

33 Sorrel, 89.

34 Sorrel thought Longstreet largely forgot and became reconciled with Hill, but his later statements, as in the Washington *Post* interview, June 11, 1893, show a lack of warmth.

35 Charleston *Mercury,* September 25, 1862; cited by Douglas Southall Freeman, *Lee's Lieutenants,* II, 148n.

36 Henry Kyd Douglas, *I Rode with Stonewall,* 146f, relates the incident and thinks Jackson "was thoroughly justified."

37 *O.R.,* XIX, Part II, 643.

38 *The Annals of the War, by Leading Participants North and South,* 703. (Hereinafter *Annals.*)

39 Washington *Post,* July 11, 1893.

40 *Ibid.*

41 *Battles and Leaders of the Civil War,* III, 245n. (Hereinafter *B. and L.*)

42 Sorrel, 135.

43 Although born in South Carolina, Longstreet spent much of his early and late life in Georgia and is properly accredited to that state. He was appointed to West Point from Alabama. Hood, born in Kentucky, became a Texan during his army service there.

44 Walter Clark, ed., *Histories of the Several Regiments and Battalions from North Carolina in the Great War, 1861-65,* I, 293ff. (Hereinafter *N.C. Regts.*)

45 Longstreet, *B. and L.,* III, 245n. Longstreet said D. H. Hill was the superior of A. P. Hill "in rank, skill, judgment, and distinguished services." The record supports him strongly.

Chapter Two: THE GRAY HOST UNLEASHED

1 J. B. Jones, *A Rebel War Clerk's Diary,* I, 272.

2 *Ibid.,* 274.

3 The riot details are from J. B. Jones, I, 284-285, or Josiah Gorgas, *War Diary,* 29.

4 Gorgas, 29.

5 J. B. Jones, 286.

6 *Ibid.,* 293, 328. Jones, who saw President Davis often, wrote: "I think he has been ill every day for several years, but this (May 19, 1863) is his most serious illness." Gorgas, 47, said July 2 that the President's physician was seriously alarmed.

7 J. B. Jones, I, 380.

8 *Ibid.,* 314-315.

9 *Ibid.,* 314.

10 *Ibid.,* 325.

11 *S.H.S.P.,* IV, 120.

[12] *Ibid.*, 153.

[13] Gorgas, 26.

[14] Colonel G. F. R. Henderson, "Review of General Longstreet's Book . . . " *S.H.S.P.*, XXXIX, 105.

[15] *Annals*, 415-416; James Longstreet, *From Manassas to Appomattox*, 332.

[16] *Annals*, 416

[17] Gordon, 139.

[18] *S.H.S.P.*, IV, 52.

[19] Charles Marshall, *Papers*, 10.

[20] McKim, 133.

[21] *Ibid.*, 134.

[22] *Ibid.*

[23] *N.C. Regts.*, I, 717.

[24] McKim, 137.

[25] J. B. Jones, I, 315.

[26] *S.H.S.P.*, IV, 152.

[27] June 19, 1863.

[28] John West, *A Texan in Search of a Fight*, 74-75.

[29] *Ibid.*, 75.

[30] *Ibid.*, 76.

[31] *Ibid.*

[32] Spencer Glasgow Welch, *A Confederate Surgeon's Letters to His Wife*, 53.

[33] *S.H.S.P.*, XIX, 314.

[34] Isaac R. Trimble, "The Campaign and Battle of Gettysburg," *Confederate Veteran*, XXV, 209.

[35] *Ibid.*, 209-210.

[36] *Ibid.*, 210. Lee issued his orders against plundering while at Berryville, Va., June 21, but they were not printed until the army reached Chambersburg, Pa.

[37] *O.R.*, XXVII, Part III, 882.

[38] *Ibid.*, 881-882.

[39] Albert J. Beveridge, *Abraham Lincoln*, I, 433. Myrta L. Avary, *Recollections of Alexander H. Stephens*, 21. Lincoln and Stephens were among the seven Whig Congressmen who organized the "Young Indians," a group to advance the candidacy of Zachary Taylor for the presidential nomination.

Chapter Three: THE ARMY CROSSES

[1] *N.C. Regts.*, I, 718.

[2] *Ibid.* This was the company raised by Governor Zebulon Vance of North Carolina at the outbreak of the war, which he headed as captain.

[3] Jacob Hoke, *The Great Invasion*, 97ff. Halleck to Hooker, June 18, 1863, *O.R.*, XXVII, Part I, 50.

[4] Richmond *Examiner*, July 3, 1863.

[5] *Ibid.*

[6] Hoke, 96.

[7] *Ibid.*, 95ff. Hoke quotes notes prepared by Dr. Philip Schaff saying the passage in St. Matthew 24:6, "and ye shall hear of wars and rumors of wars" was arranged in climatic order, since the rumor often was worse than war itself.

[8] Brigadier General Albert Gallatin Jenkins knew many Northerners, having been graduated from Jefferson College, at Canonsburg, Pennsylvania, in 1848, and Harvard Law School in 1850. Although but thirty-two at the time of the Gettysburg campaign, he had served two terms in Congress, representing his

western Virginia district, then had been a delegate to the provisional Confederate Congress in 1861. Commissioned brigadier general August 1, 1862, he would survive until the battle of Cloyds Mountain, in May 1864. One of the Chambersburg newspapers said of him: "He graduated from Jefferson college in this state, and gave promise of future usefulness and greatness. His downward career commenced some five years ago, when in an evil hour he became a member of Congress from Western Virginia, and from thence may be dated his decline and fall." Quoted by LaSalle Corbell Pickett, *Pickett and His Men,* 263, the paper being unidentified.

[9] During McCausland's raid on Chambersburg in 1864, the house was burned and the farm devastated. McClure did not nurse his loss. As the editor years later in the Philadelphia *Times,* he published without bias the stories of participants on both sides. The series is one of the outstanding collections of source material on the war. Many of the articles were collected later in the well-known volume, *The Annals of the War.*

[10] Hoke, 110.

[11] Robert Stiles, *Four Years Under Marse Robert,* 199.

[12] *O.R.,* XXVII, Part II, 297-298.

[13] Richmond *Examiner,* July 3, 1863.

[14] Hoke, 112.

[15] *Ibid.,* 135.

[16] *Ibid.,* 136.

[17] *Ibid.,* 138.

[18] Information from Dr. Jacqueline Bull, Archivist, Margaret I. King Memorial Library, University of Kentucky, based on William H. Townsend, *Lincoln and the Bluegrass* and Thomas M. Green, *Historic Families of Kentucky.*

[19] Marshall, 199.

[20] Reprinted in Richmond *Examiner,* July 7, 1863.

[21] *O.R.,* XXVII, Part III, 914. Marshall, 200.

[22] Marshall, 201.

[23] W. W. Blackford, *War Years with Jeb Stuart,* 222.

[24] Marshall, 202.

[25] *Ibid.,* O.R., XXVII, Part III, 913.

[26] Marshall, 204.

[27] *Ibid.,* 206. *O.R.,* XXVII, Part III, 915.

[28] Marshall, 208.

[29] *Ibid. O.R.,* XXVII, Part III, 923.

[30] Blackford, 222.

[31] H. B. McClellan, *The Life and Campaigns of Major General J. E. B. Stuart,* 316-318.

[32] Blackford, 223-224.

[33] *Ibid.,* 223.

[34] *O.R.,* XXVII, Part III, 931.

[35] *Ibid.* Lee thought the plan would be the best protection against marauding parties.

[36] *Ibid.,* XXVII, Part III, 946.

[37] Eppa Hunton, *Autobiography,* 87.

[38] Katharine M. Jones, *Heroines of Dixie,* 173.

[39] Owen, 234.

[40] J. F. J. Caldwell, *History of a Brigade . . . ,* 97.

[41] *Ibid.*

[42] Welch, *Letters,* 57.

[43] Fitzgerald Ross, *A Visit to Cities and Camps of the Confederacy,* 31.

44 *Ibid.*

45 *Ibid.*, 33. He said, "I do not recollect ever to have seen a drunken private soldier in the South. . . ." Only once or twice had he seen an officer a little "tight."

Chapter Four: FEASTING ON NORTHERN PLENTY

1 The stories of "Darling Nellie Gray" and "Dixie" are taken from Emilius O. Randall, "High Lights of Ohio Literature," *Ohio Archeological and Historical Society Publications,* XXXVIII, 269 (hereinafter *O.A. and H.S.P.*), and C. B. Galbreath, "Song Writers of Ohio," *O.A. and H.S.P.,* XIV, 180-192. For his account of the introduction of "Dixie" in New Orleans, Galbreath cited the article by Dr. G. A. Kane in the New York *World* in 1893, which told of Patti's zouave march and how the Washington Artillery had the tune set to a quickstep by Romeo Meniri. Emmett in 1895 made a triumphal tour through the South as the author of "Dixie."

2 Sorrel, 57-58, noticed that early in the war the soldiers at Centerville sang mainly "Lorena," "Maryland," and "Dixie." There was back-home feeling that "Dixie" did not have the proper dignity and that the South should have a national anthem. "I Puritana" was discussed. But the soldiers adopted "Dixie," made it their favorite, and decided the question.

3 John B. Hood, *Advance and Retreat,* 54. Although the "Yellow Rose of Texas" was set to the tune of the "Song of the Texas Rangers" (W. L. Fagan, *Southern War Songs*), Hood did not mention it at the crossing, nor has reference to it been found elsewhere during the Gettysburg campaign.

4 William C. Oates, *The War Between the Union and the Confederacy . . . ,* 198.

5 *Ibid.*

6 *Ibid.*

7 West.

8 Joseph B. Polley, *Hood's Texas Brigade . . . ,* 147.

9 *Ibid.,* 148.

10 *Ibid.*

11 Sorrel, 177.

12 *Ibid.,* 178.

13 *Ibid.,* 179.

14 Randolph A. Shotwell, *Our Living and Dead,* IV, 81. (Hereinafter *O.L. and D.*)

15 D. Augustus Dickert, *History of Kershaw's Brigade,* 288.

16 *Ibid.,* 230.

17 Ross, 35.

18 *Ibid.,* 35-36.

19 *Ibid.,* 37.

20 George Pickett, *Soldier of the South,* 41. (Hereinafter *Soldier of the South.*)

21 *Ibid.,* 43.

22 *Ibid.*

23 *Ibid.* In *Blue and Gray . . . ,* 107, Colonel William R. Aylett, with whose Virginia regiment Pickett was moving, said, "Struck by her courage and loyalty, Pickett with hat off, gave her a military salute, my regiment presented arms, and we cheered her with a good old-fashioned rebel yell. . . ."

24 *Soldier of the South,* 48.

25 *Ibid.*

26 *O.R.,* XXVII, Part I, 65.

27 Owen, 241.

28 Gordon, 146.

29 Douglas, 245.

30 Stiles, 199.

31 Ross, 40. See the claim of the Virginia company in Chapter 22.

32 Trimble left the story of these transactions in the Ms. later published in *Confederate Veteran,* XV, 210ff.

33 Hoke, 161.

34 *Ibid.,* 164

35 *Ibid.,* 197-198. A request for the needy was made by Mrs. Ellen McClellan, who gained easy access to Lee. She wrote an account of the visit, giving a colloquy with the general, from whom, on departing, she asked an autograph. "He replied: 'Do you want the autograph of a rebel?' I said, 'General Lee, I am a true Union woman, and yet I ask for bread and your autograph.' The General replied, 'It is to your interest to be for the Union, and I hope you may be as firm in your principles as I am in mine.' He assured me that his autograph would be a dangerous thing to possess, but at length he gave it to me. Changing the topic of conversation, he assured me the war was a cruel thing, and that he only desired that they would let him go home and eat his bread there in peace. All this time I was impressed with the strength and sadness of the man."

36 Sorrel, 178.

37 Hood, 55.

38 Sorrel, 73.

39 Eggleston, 141.

40 W. H. Stewart, *A Pair of Blankets,* 94.

41 Eggleston, 142.

42 Sorrel, 74.

43 Chesnut, 264.

44 Eggleston, 142-143.

45 Arthur J. L. Fremantle, *Three Months in the Southern States,* 242ff.

46 A. L. Long, *Memoirs of Robert E. Lee,* 29.

47 Benjamin Harvey Hill, Confederate Senator from Georgia, related his conversation with Lee, speaking before the Southern Historical Society in Atlanta, February 18, 1874. The address is published in *L.S.L.,* VI, 2397.

48 Hill said in thought after the conversation, "Surely Washington is no longer the only exception." *Ibid.*

49 Hood, 17.

50 Long, 31.

51 *Ibid.*

52 J. William Jones, *Life and Letters of Robert E. Lee* . . . , 27.

53 Marshall, XXIV.

54 *Ibid.,* XXV.

55 *Ibid.*

56 *Ibid.,* XX. Lee was able to poke a bit at the press. He told Senator Hill that a mistake had been made at the start of the war. "What mistake is that, General?" the Senator asked. "Why, sir," said Lee, "at the beginning we appointed all our worst generals to command the armies and all our best generals to edit the newspapers." *L.S.L.,* VI, 2397.

A Northern estimate was published in the *Sunday School Herald,* of Dayton, Ohio, XIV, 466 (1906), which told that Lee participated in the camp prayer meetings. Under the heading of "Anecdotes of the Great," it said: "Lee never spoke a scurrilous word of the Federal army. . . . He was a man of clean lips. One has said: 'A soldier would as soon have thought of kissing the lips of a raging volcano as of telling a coarse jest in his presence.' "

57 Ada C. Lightsly, *The Veteran's Story*, 5.

Chapter Five: A MISSIVE AMONG THE ROSES

1 Hoke, 170.

2 *O.R.*, XXVII, Part II, 465.

3 *Ibid.*

4 York was the capital from September 30, 1777, until June 27, 1788. There the Articles of Confederation were adopted.

5 Early in his official report, *O.R.*, XXVII, Part II, 466, said the town authorities came out on the night of June 27 and surrendered to Gordon. But Smith's brigade entered first. Stiles, the chronicler of the event, was at the head of the column.

6 Stiles, 202.

7 *Ibid.*

8 *Ibid.*, 203. The same author pictures Smith as he appeared on the march. He carried a blue cotton umbrella under his arm. He sat his horse by the roadside, smiling and "actually bowing to the artillerymen" who were passing, giving them the hearty greeting "which had, for more than a generation, proved irresistible on the hustings of the Old Dominion." *Ibid.*, 194.

9 *Ibid.*, 202-204, gives the account of Smith's entry and speech.

10 *Ibid.*, 206, tells the familiar story of the Lutheran delegation in Carlisle that asked Ewell if their pastor might pray according to his practice for the President of the United States. "Certainly, pray for him," replied Ewell. "I don't know of anybody that stands more in need of prayer."

11 Gordon, 141.

12 *N.C. Regts.*, III, 412.

13 The Confederates spent liberally in York as elsewhere. York had had experience in an earlier generation with depreciated currency, for there $10,-000,000 of "Continentals" were printed in the Revolutionary War.

14 *N.C. Regts.*, III, 412.

15 Gordon, 142.

16 *Ibid.*, 142-143.

17 *O.R.*, XXVII, Part II, 467.

18 Tucker, II, 592.

19 Gordon, 143-144.

20 *O.R.*, XXVII, Part II, 466.

21 Gordon, 147.

22 *O.R.*, XXVII, Part II, 466.

23 J. D. Hufham, Jr., "Gettysburg . . . ," Wake Forest *Student* (April 1897), 451.

24 *Ibid.*, 454.

25 *N.C. Regts.*, II, 233.

26 *Ibid.*

27 Hufham, 454.

28 Stephen D. Ramseur, Ms. letters, Southern Historical Collection, University of North Carolina Library, Chapel Hill, N.C.

29 Henry W. Thomas, *History of the Doles-Cook Brigade*, 7.

30 *Ibid.*

31 This came to be known as the "battle flag" and is the one commonly recognized and displayed throughout the South. Though the flag over Jackson's

casket was of the new design, it was largely white. Most flags at Gettysburg
were either the Stars and Bars or the state flags, which the Southern regiments
cherished dearly. Henry A. London, historian of the 32nd North Carolina,
N.C. Regts., II, 524, said the flag was made from the design adopted condition-
ally by the Confederate Congress a few weeks earlier. It is at times challenged
that the Confederacy ever adopted an "official" flag, but the battle standard had
full recognition.

32 This account of the ceremony follows London in *N.C. Regts.*, II, 525ff. The
flag of the new design was flown over Castle Thunder in Richmond, June 22,
1863. Richmond *Examiner*, June 23, 1863.

33 McKim, 163.

34 John O. Casler, *Four Years in the Stonewall Brigade*, 240.

35 *Ibid.*

36 McKim, 163.

37 *Ibid.*, 166.

38 This account of the New York *Herald* correspondent's trip through Lee's
army was republished in full, without comment, in the Richmond *Examiner*,
July 18, 1863.

Chapter Six: HOOKER AND MEADE PURSUE

1 *O.R.*, XXVII, Part I, 31.

2 *Ibid.*, 34.

3 *Ibid.*, 35.

4 *Ibid.*

5 Charles F. Benjamin, War Department official, in his paper, "Hooker's Appointment and Removal," *B and L.*, III, 239ff., says, 240, that Stanton "knew"
there were two Hookers in the same man, one "an excellent officer, mentally
strong, clever and tireless, and charming (almost magnetic) in address. It was
the other Hooker on whom he wished to take no chances."

6 Meade, who commanded the rear guard on the retreat from Chancellorsville,
sent an emergency request for additional orders. His adjutant found that
Hooker was sleeping and could not be disturbed, and the adjutant had to take
a mere repetition of old orders from Hooker's chief of staff, Butterfield. Couch,
second in command, retired also. Reynolds said, when applied to, "Tell General Meade that someone should be waked up to take command of this army."
Isaac R. Pennypacker, *Life of George Gordon Meade*, 125.

7 His dispatch was published June 23, 1863.

8 *O.R.*, XXVII, Part I, 55.

9 Hooker's correspondence with Halleck on Harpers Ferry is assembled in
Stine, 443-444.

10 *Ibid.*, 444.

11 General Hardie's delay in reaching Meade's headquarters was due to the
disorganized state of affairs in Frederick. Benjamin, *B and L.*, III, 242n., says
no provost marshall had been appointed and streets and roads were "thronged
with boisterous soldiers, more or less filled with Maryland whisky, and many of
them ripe for rudeness or mischief."

12 Colonel Henry S. Huidekoper in *Pennsylvania at Gettysburg*, II, 1097.
Hancock in a letter to John William Wallace, president of the Historical Society
of Pennsylvania, March 4, 1880, thought it was well established historically that
Reynolds had been offered the place. *Reynolds Memorial*, 94. Benjamin, *B. and
L.*, III, 240, thought Halleck sounded him.

13 *Pennsylvania at Gettysburg,* II, 1097.

14 George B. McClellan, *McClellan's Own Story,* 140.

15 Benjamin, *B. and L.,* III, 241, says Lincoln, Stanton, and Halleck in a conference after Chancellorsville concluded that "both the check at Chancellorsville and the retreat were inexcusable, and that Hooker must not be intrusted with the conduct of another battle." That Lincoln entered into such a compact is to be strongly doubted because his later course was so sharply inconsistent with such a decision. Not only did he urge on Hooker an aggressive pursuit of Lee, which would have involved fighting, but also it would have been clear to him that a successor to Hooker ought to have the advantage of familiarizing himself with the duties of high command as much as possible in advance of a battle. If Lincoln had positively decided within a few days after Chancellorsville that Hooker could not fight again, he would have removed Hooker promptly, or else taken the responsibility before history of retaining a feared general for his own protection, so that the mistake of the selection would not be emphasized. It appears that Hooker's lackadaisical handling of the army after leaving the Rappahannock was the deciding factor in bringing Lincoln over to the view of Stanton and Halleck.

16 George Gordon Meade, *Life and Letters,* II, 3.

17 *Ibid.,* I, 373.

18 *Ibid.,* 365.

19 *Ibid.,* 364.

20 *Ibid.*

21 *Ibid.,* 367.

22 *Ibid.,* 366.

23 The Meade sketch follows Meade, I, 1-11, and Pennypacker, 11-17.

24 Meade, I, 264.

25 Carl Sandburg, *Abraham Lincoln. The War Years,* II, 335.

26 Barton H. Wise, *The Life of Henry A. Wise . . . ,* 367.

27 Meade, I, 367.

28 Joseph W. Keifer, *Slavery and Four Years of War,* II, 25.

29 George B. McClellan, 137.

30 This was a mine case in California; Stanton claimed in a conversation with General H. W. Hitchcock that it was his partner who had a personal controversy with Halleck. George B. McClellan, 137n.

31 *Ibid.,* 137.

32 Frank Moore, ed., *The Rebellion Record,* 86. (Hereinafter *Rebellion Record.*)

33 *Ibid.,* 86-87.

34 *Ibid.*

35 *Ibid.*

36 *B. and L.,* III, 242.

37 Oliver O. Howard, *Autobiography,* I, 395.

38 Abner Doubleday, *Chancellorsville and Gettysburg,* 114-115. Butterfield told him a review would mean the loss of Harrisburg and Philadelphia.

Chapter Seven: CONCENTRATION

1 Sorrel, 164.

2 *Ibid.,* 156-157.

3 *Ibid.,* 161. *B. and L.,* III, 249.

4 Sorrel, 164.

[5] *Ibid.*

[6] Marshall made it clear that Lee thought Hooker was still in Virginia. The commander was becoming anxious that Hooker might move in strength on Richmond. "I heard General Lee express this apprehension more than once while we lay at Chambersburg." Marshall, 217-218.

[7] *Ibid.*, 218.

[8] *Ibid.*, 219.

[9] There is a possibility of confusion in towns. Middletown is eight miles west of Frederick. Middleburg, near the juncture of Pipe Creek with the Monocacy River, is northeast of Frederick. Meade was actually moving toward Middleburg, not Middletown.

[10] *Annals*, 439.

[11] This writer many years ago talked with an older resident of the Great Falls neighborhood who remembered Stuart's horsemen riding along the canal tow-path twelve miles from Washington and was struck by the zest and fine appearance of the men despite their hard riding. Blackford, 224, tells of the crossing.

[12] Blackford, 225.

[13] *Ibid.*, 224.

[14] *Ibid.*, 225.

[15] *Ibid.*

[16] *Rebellion Record*, 85.

[17] *Ibid.*

[18] Blackford, 225.

[19] Randolph H. McKim, "Gen. J. E. B. Stuart in the Gettysburg Campaign," *S.H.S.P.*, XXXVII, 210, says it would have been natural for Stuart to go to Gettysburg since he had been instructed that one column of Lee's army would move by that point. McKim thought Stuart's proper course was by Littlestown to Gettysburg, which he could have reached by 11:00 A.M., June 30, to take his position in front of Lee's army.

[20] Blackford, 225. *Pennsylvania at Gettysburg*, II, 887. The 2nd North Carolina Regiment struck the 18th Pennsylvania Cavalry, which, in its first engagement, suddenly found itself in hand-to-hand combat. After giving way, it rallied and with the 5th New York drove the Carolinians back on their reserves.

[21] *Pennsylvania at Gettysburg*, II, 888.

[22] Colonel W. H. Swallow, *Southern Bivouac*, November 1885, thinks the juncture could have been made around East Berlin, four miles north of the York pike. Hoke, 253-254, who cites Swallow, makes the point that Early had not been alerted on Stuart's ride around the Federal army and was not expecting him, but heard Stuart's guns at Hanover. As Stuart crossed Early's trail, not an inhabitant informed him that Confederate infantry had passed a short time before.

[23] Blackford, 228.

[24] Colonel David Gregg McIntosh, of Hill's artillery, told the story of Marshall's declaration that Stuart should have been shot. Marshall, some years after the war, attended a small dinner party of Confederate officers, who were startled when Lee's chief of staff said he had tried to have Stuart court-martialed. "'Who?' everyone exclaimed, 'not Jeb Stuart,' 'Yes, Jeb Stuart,' he said."

Then he made a statement which McIntosh put down in writing the next day. It told of his great difficulty in getting a report from Stuart on the Gettysburg campaign, for which Lee was pressing him. It was necessary to have all the reports from subordinates before Lee could complete his own report. Finally Stuart's was received and Marshall could go ahead. McIntosh's memorandum continued to quote Marshall: "'I then concluded my report to General Lee. In doing so I dealt with Stuart in the plainest language; in fact, I had told him before I thought he ought to be shot.

" 'General Lee was unwilling, however, to adopt my draft. I had explicitly charged him with disobedience of orders, and laid the full responsibility at his door.' "

Marshall then reviewed the orders Stuart had received and proceeded: ".... in declining to adopt his report General Lee did not question its accuracy, but said he could not adopt my conclusions and charge him with the facts as I had stated them unless they should be established by a court martial." David Gregg McIntosh, *Review of the Gettysburg Campaign,* 27ff.

[25] Marshall, 217.

[26] Marshall, 229, says the Southern army could have reached Gettysburg June 29. Although a good road center, it was not of high value then, for Lee's objective was not to take Gettysburg but to defeat the Federal army.

[27] Suesserott letter, Hoke, 205.

[28] Mrs. McClellan's letter, Hoke, 197-198.

[29] Stiles, 227-228.

[30] Hoke, 217.

[31] *Ibid.,* 226.

[32] *O.R.,* XXVII, Part III, 420.

[33] Trimble, *Confederate Veteran,* XV, 211.

[34] *Ibid.*

Chapter Eight: PETTIGREW'S ENCOUNTER

[1] *N.C. Regts.,* III, 236.

[2] *Ibid.*

[3] W. N. Pickerill, *History of the Third Indiana Cavalry,* 81. Buford report, *O.R.,* XXVII, Part I, 926.

[4] J. B. Jones, I, 209.

[5] *Ibid.*

[6] Major General Matthew F. Maury, quoted by Kemp P. Battle, *History of the University of North Carolina,* I, 507.

[7] Battle, I, 504, 729.

[8] Chesnut, 63-64.

[9] *Ibid.,* 284, 24n.

[10] Walter Clark, *General James Johnston Pettigrew, C.S.A.,* 5.

[11] *S.H.S.P.,* IV, 157.

[12] *N.C. Regts.,* I, 506.

[13] *Ibid.,* 587. Leventhorpe rose to Major General in the Confederate service.

[14] *O. L. and D.,* IV, 82.

[15] *N.C. Regts.,* III, 88.

[16] *Ibid.,* V, 115.

[17] *Ibid.*

[18] This Federal regiment, which thus had the first contact with Confederates in Gettysburg and in the next day suffered the first casualty and first loss of life in the battle, was recruited in southeastern Indiana, mainly from Dearborn, Switzerland, Harrison, Jefferson, Fayette, Rush, Shelby, and Marion counties. Watlington Mss. Indiana State Library.

[19] *Indiana at the Fiftieth Anniversary of Gettysburg* (Report of State Commission), 42.

20 *N.C. Regts.*, II, 342.
21 *S.H.S.P.*, IV, 157.
22 *N.C. Regts.*, V, 116.
23 *Ibid.*
24 *Ibid.*, 117.
25 *Ibid.*

Chapter Nine: McPHERSON'S HEIGHTS

1 Bragg on assigning Fry in 1864. *Dictionary of Alabama Biography*, 619.

2 The weather on the first day was variable and governed by local conditions. The Iron Brigade historian says there were puddles on the road but no thick mud. The lack of mud is further attested by the rapidity of the marching in both armies. Mist is mentioned locally in both morning and afternoon, though some of the men spoke of the clear, hot, sunshiny day. The 20th Indiana, coming up from Emmitsburg, was drenched by a mountain shower. But over most of the area from Manchester to Chambersburg the day was cloudy, hot, and sticky and in some areas the roads were dusty. Such is the best possible interpretation of the many seemingly inconsistent references to the weather of July 1 in regimental and brigade accounts.

Dr. Michael Jacobs made observations in Gettysburg and recorded that from June 15 to July 22, 1863, there was not an entirely clear day. The 2:00 P.M. temperatures were: July 1, 76; July 2, 82; July 3, 87. These were probably shade temperatures. Frequent references by soldiers to the intense heat, "broiling sun," in *Pennsylvania at Gettysburg* I, 317, and the road "aglow with fiery rage," *ibid.*, II, 653, suggest higher temperatures and humidity in roads and fields. During July 1 the sky at Gettysburg was covered with stratus clouds; the afternoons of the second and third were largely clear. From scrapbook of clippings, Gettysburg National Military Park library.

3 *Confederate Veteran*, XIV, 308.

4 The best account of Archer's march noticed is that of Private E. T. Boland, 13th Alabama, of Brewton, Alabama, in *Confederate Veteran*, XIV, 308f.

5 Richmond *Enquirer*, July 15, 1863.

6 *S.H.S.P.*, XIV, 6.

7 A. C. Weaver, *Third Indiana Cavalry* . . . , 4-5.

8 Clark, *Pickett's Charge a Misnomer*, 3.

9 The writer, on a day when the visibility was probably about like that of July 1, 1863, found that the seminary cupola affords an excellent view of the roads reaching Gettysburg from the north, west, and south, along which the armies were converging. As an observation point it is in many respects superior to Little Round Top on which the Federal army relied during the last two days of the battle.

10 Rosengarten in *Reynolds Memorial*, 29.

11 *Ibid.*, 29-30. Captain James A. Hall, commanding the Maine light artillery battery, said he heard Reynolds dictate a message to Meade: "Buford just now reports that he finds a small force of the enemy's infantry in a point of woods near Gettysburg, which he is unable to dislodge, and while I am aware that it is not your desire to force an engagement at that point, still I feel at liberty to advance and develop the strength of the enemy."

12 Robert K. Beecham, *Gettysburg, the Pivotal Battle of the Civil War*, 62.

[13] *Maine at Gettysburg,* 16.

[14] Beecham, 64.

[15] Lincoln was attached to Meredith, one of the few Indiana generals. When the President reviewed the army before Hooker's spring campaign, the Cincinnati *Gazette* correspondent gave the story. As Meredith passed, his men at that time comprising the 4th Brigade of the 1st Division, First Corps, they showed their excellent discipline and condition. Hooker proudly pointed them out to Lincoln: "This is the famous Fourth Brigade," he said.

"Yes," Lincoln replied, "it is commanded by the only Quaker General I have in the army." Rufus R. Dawes, *Service with the Sixth Wisconsin Volunteers,* 131n.

[16] *Ibid.,* 29. Julia Ward Howe in Henry Steele Commager, *The Blue and the Gray,* 571-572.

[17] McIntosh, 44.

[18] Meade address to Pennsylvania Reserves, *Reynolds Memorial,* 57. *Annals,* 210.

[19] *Ibid.,* 32. Heth in an address at Bunker Hill, Virginia.

[20] "The 19th Indiana at Gettysburg," Ms. Indiana State Library.

[21] *Confederate Veteran,* XIV, 308.

[22] *Ibid.*

[23] Beecham, 66.

[24] *Ibid.,* 67.

[25] Stine, 460. Halstead in *B and L.,* III, 285, gives substantially the same language.

[26] *Indiana at Antietam,* 119.

[27] "Old Graybeard" was not a man to be intimidated. In Washington recovering from the wound he received at Gainesville, he bought a new uniform and went to Secretary Stanton's office to pay his respects. After a long wait he got in, but before he could speak, Stanton roared, "What in the hell are you doing in Washington? Why don't you go to your regiment, where you are needed?"

"If I had not been shot and a fool," Cutler replied, taken aback, "I would never have come here. Good day, Mr. Secretary." Dawes, 177.

[28] *N.C. Regts.,* III, 297.

[29] *New York at Gettysburg,* III, 992. Pierce said the orderlies informed them as they came up that "the Rebels are thicker than blackberries beyond the hill."

[30] Dawes, 167-168.

[31] *Ibid.,* 169.

[32] *Reynolds Memorial,* 32.

[33] This account of the formation of the Bucktail Brigade is largely from a paper by Sergeant William R. Ramsey, *Pennsylvania at Gettysburg,* II, 757.

[34] Charles King, *The Iron Brigade,* 311. *Pennsylvania at Gettysburg,* II, 738.

[35] *Pennsylvania at Gettysburg,* II, 746.

[36] *Ibid.,* 746-747.

[37] *Ibid.,* 936.

[38] *Ibid.*

[39] *Ibid.,* 739.

[40] Major General Abner Doubleday, left in command on the field after the death of Reynolds, had led the First Corps after Reynolds took command of the left wing. But no event in the war won him the attention he received for pulling the lanyard that fired the first shot in the defense of Fort Sumter. And that was minor compared with his recognition as "the father of baseball," from having stepped off at Cooperstown, New York, according to the accepted version of the

origin of the game, the baseball diamond, of such well-calculated dimensions that it has never been changed. He helped in the introduction of baseball among the soldiers and thereby did much to establish it as a national sport.

Chapter Ten: OAK HILL

1 Doubleday, 135, called it "baleful intelligence," in which Howard magnified a forced retreat of two regiments "into the flight of an entire corps, two-thirds of which had not yet reached the field."

2 Biddle says Howard was atop the Fahnestock Building, which is still Gettysburg's skyscraper. It gave about as good a view as the college cupola, which he visited also. The view today is obscured by the larger amount of building and apparently a larger growth of timber in some areas.

3 Doubleday, 126.

4 Horace Greeley, *American Conflict,* II, 373.

5 Edmund R. Brown, *27th Indiana Volunteer Infantry . . . ,* 365. Slocum reached Gettysburg at 7:00 P.M., *O.R., XXVII,* Part I, 115. This was the hour of Sickles' arrival, but Sickles marched farther after hearing from Howard.

6 *Pennsylvania at Gettysburg,* I, 428.

7 Pennypacker, Meade's sympathetic biographer, says, 156, "Howard had just come through a bitter experience at Chancellorsville that should have been sufficiently impressive of the catastrophes that might be looked for along roads leading to army flanks."

8 *N.C. Regts.,* I, 634.

9 *Ibid.,* II, 239.

10 *Ibid.,* II, 235.

11 Wake Forest *Student,* April 1897, 451.

12 *Pennsylvania at Gettysburg,* I, 488.

13 *N.C. Regts.,* I, 637.

14 *Ibid.,* II, 119.

15 J. B. Jones, I, 290-291. *N.C. Regts.,* II, 113.

16 *N.C. Regts.,* II, 111.

17 Lieutenant Walter A. Montgomery, historian of the 12th North Carolina, said Iverson "did not at any time go on the fighting field." *N.C. Regts.,* I, 637.

18 *O.R., XXVII,* Part II, 579.

19 *Ibid.,* 486.

20 *N.C. Regts.,* II, 237.

21 *Ibid.,* 238.

22 *O.R., XXVII,* Part II, 554.

23 *N.C. Regts.,* I, 637.

24 Forney had gone on the gold rush in 1849, returned to Pennsylvania in 1859, and bought 150 acres. His house no longer stands, but this writer noticed in 1957 the iris persisting around its site on the Mummasburg Road.

25 An examination of the territory made by the writer in 1957 failed to disclose the location of the pits, and no one was found in Gettysburg who knew of them. At one point a possible trace seemed to remain in a slight depression, but this may have resulted from some later working of the land.

26 *N.C. Regts.,* II, 238.

27 *Ibid.,* I, 634.

28 They were Lieutenants Crowder and Dugger, *N.C. Regts.,* II, 237.

29 Cited in Daniel Harvey Hill, editor, *Land We Love,* V, 2.

[30] *Ibid.*, 1.

[31] Stone's fire was described by one opponent as the most destructive ever witnessed, *N.C. Regts.*, I, 42.

[32] Doubleday, 144n. The statement is judged to have been made orally. No correspondence by Dwight to Stanton can be located in the National Archives or the Pennsylvania State Library.

[33] *N.C. Regts.*, III, 255.

[34] *Ibid.*, 5.

[35] *S.H.S.P.*, IV, 158.

[36] *Ibid.*

Chapter Eleven: THE BATTLE OF THE TWO COLONELS

[1] William S. Burgwyn, "Zebulon Baird Vance," *H.S.L.*, XII, 5555.

[2] *N.C. Regts.*, II, 306.

[3] Unidentified Raleigh, N.C., news story in *N.C. Regts.*, II, 405.

[4] *Ibid.*, 329.

[5] *Ibid.*, 334.

[6] *Ibid.*

[7] *Ibid.*, 333.

[8] The Christian Clemens *Papers,* Detroit Public Library, contain a clipping apparently from a Niles, Mich., newspaper of February 1891, telling of Morrow's death at Hot Springs, Ark. This is the only biographical sketch found giving facts of his early life, and it is the source of this account.

[9] Detroit *Free Press,* January 5, 1908.

[10] *Ibid.*

[11] Robertson, *Michigan in the War,* 439. This flag was carried until lost at Gettysburg.

[12] *Ibid.*, 438-439.

[13] Dawes, 101.

[14] *Ibid.*, 112.

[15] *N.C. Regts.*, II, 343.

[16] *Ibid.*, 369.

[17] *Ibid.*, 350.

[18] *Ibid.*, 351.

[19] *Ibid.*

[20] *Ibid.*, 352

[21] *Ibid.*

[22] *Ibid.*, III, 89.

[23] *Ibid.*

[24] *Ibid.*, 90.

[25] *Michigan in the War,* 441.

[26] *N.C. Regts.*, II, 353.

[27] *Ibid.*

[28] *Ibid.*, 375.

[29] *Michigan in the War,* 441-442.

[30] *Confederate Veteran,* XV, 504.

[31] *Michigan in the War,* 442.

[32] *N.C. Regts.*, V, 119.

[33] *Ibid.*, 120.

[34] *Ibid.*, II, 356.

35 Heth, *O.R.*, XXVII, Part 2, 638, said Pettigrew's brigade "Fought as well, and displayed as heroic courage as it was ever my fortune to witness on a battle-field."

36 J. H. Bassler, "The Color Episode . . . ," *S.H.S.P.*, XXXVII, 266ff.

Chapter Twelve: THROUGH THE TOWN

1 Thomas, 608.

2 R. L. Dabney, *Life and Campaigns of Lt. Gen. Thomas J. Jackson*, II, 73; cited in G. F. R. Henderson, *Stonewall Jackson and the American Civil War*, I, 299. The quotation has been given a colloquial form.

3 Thomas, 47.

4 *Ibid.*, 9.

5 *N.C. Regts.*, III, 413.

6 Address by Major John W. Daniel in J. William Jones, compiler, *Army of Northern Virginia, Memorial Volume*, 102-103.

7 *Ibid.*

8 *N.C. Regts.*, III, 413-414.

9 *Ibid.*, 414.

10 Stiles, 210.

11 *N.C. Regts.*, III, 414.

12 The term the Count of Paris employs to describe the rebel yell.

13 Gordon, 151.

14 *Ibid.*

15 Stiles, 210.

16 *Ibid.*, 211.

17 *Ibid.*, 212.

18 Barlow, a native of Brooklyn, had been first in his class at Harvard, gradu-ating in 1855. He was a reporter on the New York *Tribune*, a lawyer, then a private at First Manassas. After that battle he returned to New York to hang out his shingle, not for clients, but for recruits. They came to a regimental level and he became colonel, then brigadier general. Thus the private at First Manassas was a division commander at Gettysburg. His wife contracted a fever working in army hospitals and died in 1864. *New York at Gettysburg*, III, 1353-1355.

19 Doubleday, 141.

20 *S.H.S.P.*, IV, 254.

21 William P. Snow, *Southern Generals, Their Lives and Campaigns*, 378.

22 Most of the material for this sketch is from the biography of Pender by Hugh B. Johnson, Jr., of Wilson, N.C., published in the *Wilson Daily Times*. It is in the Southern Historical Collection, University of North Carolina Library, Chapel Hill, N.C.

23 *N.C. Regts.*, I, 764-765.

24 Pender's letters here quoted are from the original Ms. in the Southern Historical Collection, University of North Carolina Library, Chapel Hill, N.C.

25 The word is not clearly distinguishable.

26 Varina D. Brown, *A Colonel at Gettysburg and Spotsylvania*, 78.

27 Perrin letter, July 29, 1863, in M. L. Bonham, *A Little More Light on Gettysburg*, 522. University of South Carolina Library, Columbia, S.C.

28 Dawes, 175.

29 Varina D. Brown, 79.

[30] Scales visited the field with Dawes in 1882 and said the fire of one of the batteries was the most destructive he had encountered in the war, Dawes, 175n.

[31] Caldwell, 98.

[32] Varina D. Brown, 80.

[33] *Ibid.*

[34] After Biddle was wounded, the brigade was commanded by Colonel Theodore B. Gates of the 20th New York.

[35] Doubleday, 146.

[36] Varina D. Brown, 81.

[37] Bonham, 522. Perrin, in Bonham, 523, placed the blame for the loss of the battle on Anderson. "His failure to us was the cause of the failure of the campaign," said Perrin, who did not know whether it was Anderson's or Hill's fault. But he was angered to observe that the enemy he drove from the seminary went into action without molestation on Cemetery Hill. "The very batteries which we had run off and which we saw them take off through Gettysburg, were the first to fire a shot from the new position," he said. "The first shell fired by them from that position was aimed at my brigade." Not only Perrin, but others complained of Anderson's slowness. The Richmond *Enquirer* account filed from near Hagerstown July 8 said that Anderson's division halted unnecessarily more than three hours at Cashtown, although it could hear the firing ahead. If Anderson had pushed on, the enemy could probably have been captured and certainly the army would have been able to "get possession of the mountain range" on which the Federals were located. "Fatal blunder!!" The scribe said he learned that all brigade commanders were anxious to advance but that Anderson would not consent.

[38] Wake Forest *Student,* April 1897, 451f.

[39] *Ibid.*

[40] *N.C. Regts.,* I, 719. Many of Ramseur's men were overcome by the heat in this pursuit.

[41] *Maine at Gettysburg,* 47.

[42] *Ibid.*

[43] Raleigh, N.C., *Semi-Weekly Standard,* August 4, 1863. The writer was described as "a gallant young officer of the 2nd North Carolina, Ramseur's Brigade."

[44] *Ibid.*

[45] *Ibid.*

[46] J. Bryan Grimes, "Gettysburg," *Papers,* 3.

[47] *O.R.,* XXVII, Part II, 479.

[48] Varina D. Brown, 82.

[49] Colonel Joseph N. Brown, 3, affirmed it of his personal knowledge that the 1st and 14th South Carolina regiments were first in the town, and gave the details of their entry.

[50] Varina D. Brown, 82.

[51] Adding to much other testimony, B. G. Benson, of Augusta, Ga., wrote to his brother from near Hagerstown July 7, saying a dispute had arisen as to what troops entered Gettysburg first, and said there was no room for doubt, as the 1st South Carolina was already in the middle of the town when he saw the next troops coming up a side street. *Reminiscences,* 173.

[52] Bonham, 522.

[53] Varina D. Brown, 82.

[54] This was the only brigade of Early's division to enter Gettysburg. *S.H.S.P.,* IV, 254.

[55] Colonel Joseph N. Brown, 3, said when they withdrew they observed troops

coming up on the left and Perrin inquired who they were. A staff officer told
him it was Rodes's division. According to Brown, Perrin "showed displeasure on
account of their going in and taking the place captured by us."

[56] Bonham, 522.

[57] Doubleday, 149.

[58] *Pennsylvania at Gettysburg,* II, 753.

[59] *O.R.,* XXVII, Part I, 925.

[60] Dawes, 115. At the dedication of the 143rd Pennsylvania monument at
Gettysburg, Doubleday was referred to as "a soldier of fine military attainments
and personal courage." *Pennsylvania at Gettysburg,* II, 695.

Chapter Thirteen: HIGH GROUND AND GOLDEN MINUTES

[1] How the offer to head the Louisiana lottery affected another outstanding general of the Confederacy was altogether different. Major General Dabney
Herndon Maury was offered $25,000 a year to become president of the lottery.
"The temptation was a terrible one," he said. "I was almost penniless, and there
was no prospect of my being otherwise. Twenty-five thousand dollars a year
was wealth which to me seemed fabulous." He told no one, tossed all night
without sleep, and at dawn decided to reject the offer. "I had never done anything which was not honest, and I determined it was too late to begin in my old
age. Sleep was easy to me then. . . ." He wrote a letter of refusal and never
regretted it. Richmond *Dispatch,* January 14, 1900. *S.H.S.P.,* XXVII, 335ff.

[2] Sorrel, 55.

[3] Freeman, *Lee's Lieutenants,* III, 27, cites Hotchkiss Ms. *Diary,* 213.

[4] Stiles, 189.

[5] *Ibid.*

[6] Sorrel, 55.

[7] *S.H.S.P.,* IV, 254.

[8] The Wilmington, N.C., *Daily Journal* with keen penetration saw the significance of the lack of celerity at Gettysburg and in its July 18, 1863, issue
quoted this and the Napoleonic maxim which follows.

[9] *S.H.S.P.,* IV, 254.

[10] *Ibid.,* 255.

[11] *Ibid.*

[12] *S.H.S.P.,* XXXIII, 144.

[13] *Ibid.*

[14] Douglas, 247.

[15] *Ibid.* Lee was at Cashtown when Johnson's division marched through and
had not ridden past them on the roadway, so Douglas was satisfied he had not
arrived.

[16] *Ibid.*

[17] Trimble, *Confederate Veteran,* XXV, 211. The conversation is as he
reported it in his manuscript.

[18] Trimble's account ended here, but the story was carried on by McKim,
S.H.S.P., XL, 273.

[19] *N.C. Regts.,* III, 414.

[20] Gordon, 154.

[21] *S.H.S.P.,* IV, 255.

[22] *Ibid.,* 256.

[23] *Ibid.*

[24] *Ibid.*

25 *Ibid.*

26 *N.C. Regts.*, III, 5-6.

27 Reprinted in Raleigh *Semi-Weekly Standard,* August 4, 1863.

28 Related to the writer by a resident who had purchased this property and learned from earlier owners the incident of Lee's occupancy. The fact that Lee took it suggests it may have been a map made in 1857, which gives details down to individual houses and their occupants.

29 *S.H.S.P.,* XXXIII, 140-141.

30 McKim, 176.

31 *S.H.S.P.,* IV, 127. Walter H. Taylor, *Four Years with General Lee,* 95. *O.R.,* XXVII, Part II, 318.

32 *S.H.S.P.,* XXXIII, 145.

33 *Ibid.* The wording and subsequent events cause wonder if Ewell did not see in Lee's promised arrival an excuse for withholding the attack until Lee could take charge. When Lee arrived, it was too late.

34 *S.H.S.P.,* IV, 66.

35 Colonel Joseph N. Brown had just withdrawn the 14th South Carolina from Gettysburg when General Lee arrived. Lee congratulated Perrin on "his splendid achievement" and Brown observed that "it was not too late then to have followed the retreating Federals." Later he asked himself the perplexing questions about Lee: "Might he not once in his illustrious life, with the great responsibilities resting on him, viewing the almost impregnable heights in an enemy's country far from his base, with such fearful odds against him, have hesitated who never hesitated before? It was his first battle without Stonewall Jackson and might he not have felt as never before the want of that rushing torrent which always carried everything before it when that celebrated hero was at the helm? Others felt it." Joseph N. Brown, *The Battle of Gettysburg,* 3.

36 McIntosh, 52.

37 *O.R.,* XXVII, Part II, 349.

38 *Ibid.,* 583.

39 *S.H.S.P.,* II, 225.

40 Raleigh *Semi-Weekly Standard,* August 4, 1863.

41 There appears little material difference in Longstreet's various accounts, the purport of all being that he strongly favored a flanking movement.

42 *B. and L.,* III, 339. Other statements of the same nature are in Longstreet, *From Manassas to Appomattox,* 358f., and *Annals,* 421-422.

43 Gordon, 155-157.

44 *S.H.S.P.,* V, 291.

45 McKim, 193.

46 Douglas, 247.

47 *Annals,* 308-309.

48 Hunton, 98.

49 *S.H.S.P.,* V, 175.

Chapter Fourteen: MOONLIGHT AND MARCHING COLUMNS

1 *Rebellion Record,* 87-89.

2 *Ibid.*

3 Doubleday, 143.

4 *Pennsylvania at Gettysburg,* II, 1075-1076.

5 "Hancock received a brigade early in the formation of the Army of the Potomac. He was a man of the most chivalrous courage, and of a superb pres-

ence, especially in action; he had a wonderfully quick and correct eye for ground and for handling troops; his judgment was good, and it would be difficult to find a better corps commander." George B. McClellan, 140.

6 Frank A. Haskell, *The Battle of Gettysburg*, 381-382.

7 *B. and L.,* III, 285. Doubleday, 151.

8 Howard, I, 418.

9 *B. and L.,* III, 285.

10 *Ibid.*

11 Edward N. Whittier, *The Left Attack (Ewell's) at Gettysburg*, 316.

12 Doubleday, 151.

13 Hancock on his arrival found only 1,000 to 1,200 organized troops "at most" on Cemetery Hill. Hancock to Fitz Lee, *S.H.S.P.,* V, 169.

14 Thomson, *Seventh Indiana Infantry . . .* , 162.

15 *Ibid.*

16 *Ibid.,* 163.

17 *Ibid.*

18 *Ibid.,* 165.

19 *Maine at Gettysburg,* 88-89.

20 Hancock to Fitz Lee, *S.H.S.P.,* V, 172.

21 *O.R.,* XXVII, Part I, 366.

22 New York *Herald,* March 12, 1864.

23 Francis A. Osbourn, *"Fighting Three Hundred," the Twentieth Indiana Infantry,* 13.

24 *Maine at Gettysburg,* 159, 179-180.

25 Whittier, 340.

26 *Pennsylvania at Gettysburg,* I, 196. General Humphreys, *O.R.,* XXVII, Part 1, 531, contended that the route via Black Horse Tavern was intentional.

27 William H. Powell, *The Fifth Army Corps,* 509-510.

28 The phase of the moon has sometimes been questioned. The moon was at the full on the night of July 1, 1863. Letter to author from U.S. Naval Observatory, January 6, 1958.

29 *O.R.,* XXVII, Part I, 115. Meade gave different times from those of some observers. He said he broke headquarters at 10:00 P.M. and arrived at 1:00 A.M. July 2.

30 Howard, I, 423.

31 *Ibid.*

32 *Ibid.,* 424.

33 According to Pleasanton, Meade was "strongly impressed" that his right was weakest. *Annals,* 454.

34 The old schoolhouse was used as a tractor barn when the writer visited the site in November 1957. At Manchester the writer talked with Miss Cecelia Shower, 93 years old, whose father had often told of Sedgwick's halt there, and who, with her sister-in-law, gave information about Sedgwick's camp and headquarters site. An indication of how the countryside assisted Sedgwick was seen in the statement of Mrs. John Green that her grandmother cooked bread and had it taken 5 miles to Sedgwick's camp.

35 One of the reasons assigned for Meade's delay at Taneytown was that he wanted to wait until the Sixth Corps came up and therefore gave Sedgwick orders to move by Taneytown. Later, deciding to leave for Gettysburg, he ordered Sedgwick to take the Baltimore pike, the more direct road from Westminster to Gettysburg. Pennypacker, 151. That necessitated a readjustment of the head of the column, which had not moved far from Westminster. It cut across the fields from the Taneytown road to the Baltimore-Gettysburg pike. Meade directed Sedgwick to shunt all the trains out of the road and make a

forced march. *Ibid.* Sedgwick calculated the distance as 35 miles, *Annals,* 211, but some units, countermarching, probably covered 37 miles, as some regimental accounts attest.

[36] Lieutenant Colonel James W. Latta, 119th Pennsylvania Infantry, said, "The day at Manchester was a novel one; we had no such experience before or after." He described it as a carnival and said the friendly population had never seen so many soldiers. "Men and maidens, matrons and children, afoot and in wheeled vehicles, gathered from far and near for the opportunity to witness the sudden increase of male population. No thought was abroad that scarce forty miles away mortal strife was waging hotly." *Pennsylvania at Gettysburg,* II, 652.

[37] Brevet Major General Alexander Shaler, *ibid.,* I, 187.

[38] *B. and L.,* III, 239. When Henry Breckenridge, assistant secretary of war in the Woodrow Wilson administration, accepted the Sedgwick equestrian statue at Gettysburg, he emphasized Sedgwick's modesty and pointed out that "when it seemed that Sedgwick could have had command of the Army of the Potomac by simply stretching forth his hand, he would not make the move" *Proceedings at Dedication of Statue at Gettysburg* (Hartford, Conn.), 69. (Hereinafter *Conn. Proc.*)

[39] *Ibid.,* 52, says: "As the coffin was being lowered to its last resting place, a distinct peal of thunder like the roll of distant artillery reverberated along the hills a most solemn requiem to the buried soldier."

[40] Latta in *Pennsylvania at Gettysburg,* II, 652. The time of the messenger's arrival is placed at nine o'clock in several accounts, slightly earlier in others.

[41] Colonel Henry S. Huidekoper, 115th Pennsylvania Infantry, said, "He (Reynolds) was a superb horseman, and was so much at ease in the saddle as to be able to pick up from the ground, at full speed, a silver ten-cent piece, and to dismount by vaulting, his hands on the pommel." *Pennsylvania at Gettysburg,* II, 1097.

[42] Latta, *ibid.,* II, 652.

[43] Letter from Senator Huntington, 1833; *Conn. Proc.,* 31.

[44] The description of the corps is from Sergeant A. T. Brewer, 61st Pennsylvania. *Pennsylvania at Gettysburg,* I, 378.

[45] *Ibid.,* 377.

[46] *Maine at Gettysburg,* 366. The 5th Maine got no halt for breakfast or dinner. An officer of the 93rd Pennsylvania kicked over the coffee pots. *Pennsylvania at Gettysburg,* I, 506.

[47] Sergeant F. J. Loeble, 98th Pennsylvania Infantry. *Ibid.,* I, 528.

[48] The 1st New York Battery under Captain Cowan was stationed close by the High Water Mark and helped repulse Pickett's assault on July 3. The inscription on the monument includes the words used by Cowan.

[49] *Pennsylvania at Gettysburg,* I, 373.

[50] *Ibid.,* II, 677.

[51] Chaplain J. S. Lane, *ibid.,* I, 506.

[52] *Conn. Proc.,* 48-50.

[53] Address of Maj. Gen. O. O. Howard at National Republican Club, New York. In *Lincoln Day Addresses, 1887-1909,* 280-281, Lincoln related the incident to General Sickles, who told it to Howard.

[54] Charles C. Coffin, cited in *Pennsylvania at Gettysburg,* I, 378.

Chapter Fifteen: LEE'S ATTACK PLANS

[1] This account of the conference is almost wholly from Early's long report, *S.H.S.P.,* IV, 271ff.

[2] *Grayjackets,* 230. Rodes, though born in Lynchburg, Virginia, came into the army with Alabama troops. A graduate of V. M. I., he became a civil engineer and just before the war moved to Tuscaloosa, Alabama, from where he was elected colonel of the 5th Alabama Regiment. That unit became a part of Ewell's brigade. He was a man of soldierly appearance but, according to Stiles (45), had a habit of chewing or holding the ends of his long mustache in his lips.

[3] *S.H.S.P.,* IV, 271.

[4] *Ibid.,* 272.

[5] *Ibid.*

[6] *Ibid.,* 273-274.

[7] Fitz Lee quotes General Lee, *S.H.S.P.,* V, 192, as saying to the Reverend Mr. Jones that "General Longstreet, when once in a fight, was a most brilliant soldier; but he was the hardest man to move I had in my army."

[8] Early said, *S.H.S.P.,* IV, 293: "It was very natural that Longstreet's corps should be selected to assume the initiative on the second day at Gettysburg. Neither of his divisions had been at the recent battles of Chancellorsville and Fredericksburg, except McLaws, and that division, with the exception of Barksdale's brigade, had not been as heavily engaged there as the other corps."

[9] Marshall, 252.

[10] *S.H.S.P.,* IV, 275.

[11] Robert E. Lee, *Recollections and Letters,* 95.

[12] At Chambersburg, Marshall mentioned to British correspondent Ross the calamity of the lost order at Antietam, which he looked on as a greater misfortune to the South than the fall of New Orleans. He said it was lost through the carelessness of a general of division (D. H. Hill, who denied responsibility) who "singularly enough" had lost an order of equal importance just before the Seven Days' Battles around Richmond. In the second instance the order had been found on a prisoner captured at Gaines' Mill, who, not understanding its importance, had not sent it to headquarters. Marshall did not mention Hill by name. Ross, 46.

[13] *Annals,* 435.

[14] McIntosh, 28, obtained the story from Watters when Watters was judge of the Third Judicial District of Maryland.

[15] *Annals,* 422.

[16] *Ibid.,* 439.

[17] Ross, 49.

[18] In Lee's Headquarters Museum on Cashtown pike (Lincoln Highway).

[19] *Annals,* 422.

[20] Because of the long-standing and popularly accepted belief that Lee ordered this "sunrise attack," some statements of headquarters officers, or others in a position to have informed opinions, to Longstreet may be cited to help establish the facts. While taken from context, the meaning is not distorted.

Charles Marshall: "I have no personal recollection of the order. . . . It certainly was not conveyed by me, nor is there anything in General Lee's official report to show the attack of the 2nd was expected by him to begin earlier, except that he notices that there was no proper concert of action on that day." *Annals,* 437. *A. S. Long:* "I do not recollect of hearing of an order to attack at sunrise, or at any other designated hour. . . ." *Ibid.,* 438. *Charles S. Venable:* "I do not know of any order for an attack on the enemy at sunrise on the 2nd, nor can I believe that any such order was issued by General Lee." *Ibid.,* 438. *Walter H. Taylor:* "I never heard of the 'sunrise attack'. . . . If such an order was given you I never knew of it, or it has strangely escaped my memory.

I think it more than probable that if General Lee had had your troops available the evening previous . . . he would have ordered an early attack; but this does not touch the point at issue." *Ibid.*, 437. *Alexander:* "No orders whatever were given to Longstreet that night."

Fully as conclusive as all this is the statement by McLaws that when he saw Longstreet returning from Gettysburg on the night of July 1, he made no reference to any attack orders. Had Lee directed him to attack at daybreak, certainly he would have told the general who would have to do it.

Colonel Taylor in another statement gave a résumé that was as sensible as any on this situation: "I cannot say he (Longstreet) was notified on the night of the first, of the attack proposed to be made on the morning of the second, and the part his corps was to take therein. Neither do I think it just to charge that he was alone responsible for the delay in attacking that ensued after his arrival on the field. I well remember how General Lee was chafed by the non-appearance of the troops, until he finally became restless and rode back to meet General Longstreet, and urge him forward; but, then, there was considerable delay in putting the troops to work after they reached the field and much time was spent in discussing what was to be done, which, perhaps, could not be avoided. At any rate, it would be unreasonable to hold General Longstreet accountable for this. Indeed, great injustice has been done him in the charge that he had orders from the Commanding General to attack the enemy at sunrise on the second of July, and that he disobeyed these orders." *S.H.S.P.*, IV, 130-131.

[21] Burke Davis, *Gray Fox*, 229.

[22] *Confederate Veteran*, 209f.

[23] *Ibid.*

[24] E. P. Alexander, *Military Memories of a Confederate*, 391, says the orders were issued "about 11 A.M." The attack order was issued after Lee's return from his second visit to Ewell, where he had been rebuffed continually in his desire to attack or pull Ewell's corps around to his right.

[25] *S.H.S.P.*, V, 90.

[26] *Ibid.*, V, 92.

[27] Doubleday, 111, says Lee's son was serving as a hostage, because President Davis had determined to hang a Federal captain, but feared Rooney Lee would be hung in retaliation.

[28] That was implied in his letter to his wife, R. E. Lee, 101.

[29] Polley, 153.

[30] W. W. Blackford, 231.

[31] Sanger, in D. B. Sanger and Thomas R. Hays, *James Longstreet*, 163, says that Lee was sick and asked if he was too ill and exhausted to command his army.

[32] Ross, 50.

[33] *Ibid.*, 51-52.

[34] *Ibid.*, 52.

[35] *Ibid.*, 52-53.

[36] Dickert, 234.

[37] *Ibid.*

[38] Chesnut, 241.

[39] Dickert, 234.

[40] *Ibid.*, 230, 232.

[41] *Ibid.*, 230.

[42] Hood, *Advance and Retreat*, 57. This again suggests an indisposition, for it was hot in the early morning.

[43] *Ibid.*

[44] *Ibid.*

[45] Polley, 155.

[46] The common soldier's viewpoint may have been reflected by Polley, 155, when he said Lee had not yet decided where Longstreet's men should advance, and "If at this hour he betrayed anger and disappointment, it was not at the failure of Longstreet's command to be up sooner (how could they!)" nor at the deliberation of Longstreet's movements, but at Ewell's failure to seize Culp's Hill and the delay of the officers he had sent on a reconnaissance. "Not until they reported to him, which was close on to mid-day, did he announce his plan to Longstreet."

[47] E. P. Alexander, "Causes of Southern Defeat at Gettysburg," *S.H.S.P.,* IV, 101.

[48] *Ibid.*

[49] *B. and L.,* III, 359.

[50] *S.H.S.P.,* XXVII, 57. McLaws told of the incident in an address in Savannah, Ga., April 27, 1896.

[51] Comte de Paris, *History of the Civil War,* 240-242, made a careful estimate of numbers as does *B. and L.,* III, 440. These estimates are made from these sources.

Chapter Sixteen: THE STORY OF THE MISSING CANTEENS

[1] *S.H.S.P.,* V, 183-184.

[2] *Ibid.*

[3] *B. and L.,* III, 331.

[4] *Ibid.*

[5] *Ibid.,* 321.

[6] The Little Round Top signal station reported to Meade at 4:00 P.M. that the only enemy infantry visible was on the extreme Federal left moving toward Emmitsburg. This could scarcely have been Longstreet's column, but more likely was one of Hill's regiments being sent as a flank picket to the Kerns house. *B. and L.,* III, 320.

[7] *S.H.S.P.,* IV, 99-102; *B. and L.,* III, 359.

[8] *B. and L.,* III, 320.

[9] *Ibid.,* 332.

[10] Dickert, 235.

[11] *Annals,* 422. Freeman, who is most critical of Longstreet's actions on July 2, concedes, *Lee's Lieutenants,* III, 115, that Lee consented to Longstreet's awaiting the arrival of Law.

[12] *B. and L.,* III, 319.

[13] Oates, 206.

[14] *Annals,* 423.

[15] *S.H.S.P.,* IV, 68.

[16] Hoke, 574, in his appendix, "Did General Sickles Disregard an Order from General Meade on July 2nd, 1863?"

[17] Powell, 517.

[18] *B. and L.,* III, 301.

[19] *Maine at Gettysburg,* 130.

[20] *Ibid.,* 129.

[21] Osbourn, 1.

[22] *Ibid.,* 13. *Pennsylvania at Gettysburg,* I, 349.

[23] *Pennsylvania at Gettysburg,* II, 622.

[24] *Ibid.,* 623.

25 *Ibid.*

26 *Maine at Gettysburg,* 130-131.

27 Historicus in New York *Herald,* March 12, 1864.

28 *Ibid.*

29 *Ibid.*

30 *Time* Magazine, May 7, 1956, 118.

31 Haskell, 367.

32 Pinckney, who headed this scouting venture, was a descendant of Charles Cotesworth Pinckney, author of the statement, "Millions for defense but not one cent for tribute." (Oration in House of Representatives, April 29, 1906, by Robert Lee Henry, Representative from Texas and great-great-great-grandson of Patrick Henry.) He was eulogized also by Representatives John Nance Garner and Alexander White Gregg of Texas. Gregg gave the story of his scouting venture, from which this account is drawn. Pinckney was serving in Congress at the time of his death.

General Law, *B. and L.,* 321, tells of sending a scouting detail to the summit of Round Top, which raises the question of whether two such parties went out or whether Law intercepted Pinckney and received his report on his return. Law had not been on the field during the morning, as had Hood, and while he dwells in detail on the scouts from his brigade, it seems impossible that he could have made an extensive reconnaissance during the short time he was in front of Round Top prior to the assault. He may have been forgetful, or was speaking as the division commander, which he soon became when Hood was wounded.

33 Hood, *Advance and Retreat,* 57-58.

34 *Ibid.,* 58.

35 *Ibid.,* 58-59.

36 Longstreet Papers, Southern Historical Collection, University of North Carolina Library, Chapel Hill, N.C.

37 Oates, 206.

38 *Ibid.,* 212.

39 *Ibid.*

40 *Ibid.,* 207-208n.

41 *Ibid.,* 210.

42 *Maine at Gettysburg,* 255. Oates gave as another reason for ascending Round Top that he was pushed to the right by the 47th Alabama on his left. *O.R.,* XXVII, part II, 392.

43 Oates, 211.

44 *Ibid.*

45 *Ibid.,* 212.

46 Francis Parkman, II, 287-307.

47 U. S. Grant, *Personal Memoirs . . . ,* I, 132-133.

48 Snow, 25. Robert Selph Henry, *The Story of the Mexican War,* 284.

49 Oates, 212. In late years, vehicles of the Gettysburg National Military Park have been driven to the summit of Round Top.

50 *Ibid.,* 213.

51 *Ibid.,* 214.

52 *Ibid.*

Chapter Seventeen: THE PRIZE OF LITTLE ROUND TOP

1 *Pennsylvania at Gettysburg,* I, 461.

2 *Ibid.,* 462. Oliver W. Norton, *The Attack and Defense of Little Round Top,* 285.

3 Powell, 523.

4 *Ibid.*, 524.

5 *Pennsylvania at Gettysburg*, I, 461-462.

6 Oates, 215.

7 *Maine at Gettysburg*, 256.

8 Norton, 90.

9 *Ibid.*, 283, 287-288.

10 *Maine at Gettysburg*, 254n.

11 Oates, 217.

12 Jerome Bonaparte Robertson, commander of the Texas Brigade, was one of the most humane men in Lee's army, who, except for occasional excursions into warfare, was a beloved country doctor in Washington County, Texas. He was 48 years old at the time of Gettysburg. Born in Kentucky, he was apprenticed as a hatter, went to St. Louis, bought his release, and though virtually unschooled, won the favor of a St. Louis physician who taught him, and, upon removal to Owensboro, Ky., made him an office assistant. This tutoring enabled him to enter Transylvania University. After graduation in medicine, he was practicing in Owensboro when the Texas revolution against Mexico excited his compassion and caused him to raise a Kentucky company for Sam Houston's army. He remained in Texas to practice medicine thirty-four years. He took time out for fighting Indians, raised a company for the 5th Texas on the outbreak of war with the North and rose from captain to general. When the war ended he returned to medicine in his home town of Independence, Tex., and later moved to Waco.

13 Polley, 169.

14 *Ibid.*, 171-172.

15 *Ibid.*, 174.

16 *Ibid.*, 175.

17 Henry Lewis Benning, one of the able men of the Confederacy, probably would have been offered a place in President Davis' cabinet had he not organized a regiment in Columbus, Ga., his home, and become colonel at the first clash of arms. Lawyer, legislator, judge of the Georgia Supreme Court, he was industrious and capable and a citizen of the highest integrity, who has been compared in character to Calhoun. He worked diligently for secession, a cause for which he retained hope to the very end. He lost his only son in the war, but was survived by 5 daughters. Fort Benning, 9 miles south of Columbus, Ga.—of 220,000 acres—perhaps the largest U.S. army post in area and number of troops in the country, is named in his honor.

18 Polley, 168.

19 *Ibid.*

20 Oates, 219. At Appomattox, Chamberlain commanded the brigade, including the 20th Maine, which received the surrender of Lee's army. *Maine at Gettysburg*, 286.

21 Oates, 219.

22 Polley, 175-176. The confidence of Robertson's men was unshaken. Private West wrote later, ". . . I do not believe the combined Yankee army can subjugate the Texas brigade. . . ." West, 99.

23 Polley, 172. The orator and occasion are not identified.

Chapter Eighteen: CRUSHING THE ORCHARD SALIENT

1 John C. Ridpath, *Life and Times of James A. Garfield*, 145.

2 Moore, *Civil War in Song and Story*, 320.

[3] J. S. McNeilly, "Barksdale's Mississippi Brigade," *Publications of the Mississippi Historical Society,* XIX, 231.

[4] John Bell Hood—his classmates called him Sam Hood at West Point, though the inquisitive Mrs. Chesnut could not learn why—had "the face of an old Crusader," whose "whole appearance [was] that of awkward strength." Chesnut, 299. Venable, of Lee's staff, had been on many fields and said he had often heard of the "light of battle shining in a man's eyes," but had seen it only once, when he carried Lee's orders to Hood in a hot corner. "The man was transfigured. The fierce light in Hood's eyes I can never forget." That was when the battle was joined. But Blackford, 210, told how he was unwilling to shell the Federals by surprise. He was tall, blond, and blue-eyed, and reserved almost to the point of shyness. In his pocket he always carried a Bible his mother had given him. He was 32 years old at Gettysburg.

His brigade, a long way from Texas, did not have the clothing replacements enjoyed by some of the other commands. Mrs. Chesnut described it as it passed through Richmond: "Such rags and tags. . . . Nothing was like anything else. Most garments and arms were such as had been taken from the enemy. Such shoes as they had on. . . .

"They did not seem to mind their shabby condition. They laughed, shouted and cheered as they marched by. . . ." Chesnut, 231. These were the men now about to assail the Devil's Den and Little Round Top.

[5] Stiles, 223.

[6] J. B. Jones, I, 290-291.

[7] Stiles, 223.

[8] *B. and L.,* III, 325.

[9] *Ibid.,* 334. Though Cabell opened at four, he signaled Kershaw much later.

[10] "Tige" Anderson's brigade had been Bartow's at First Manassas and included the 8th Georgia, the first regiment incorporated into the Confederate service after the government was organized at Montgomery, Ala. Bartow, then chairman of the House Military Affairs Committee in the first Confederate Congress, arranged the induction with President Davis. It included his Savannah company, the Oglethorpe Light Infantry, named in honor of General James Oglethorpe. Bartow was killed at First Manassas. "Tige" Anderson served long as chief of police of Atlanta after the war.

[11] Kershaw was from Camden, S.C., a town that gave the Confederate army 5 generals. There young men grew up under the inspiration of Baron DeKalb, who fell with 11 wounds in the Revolutionary War battle at Camden. Kershaw had entered Mexico City with the Palmetto Regiment and had fought in Virginia beginning at First Manassas.

[12] Chesnut, 63.

[13] DeTrobriand, duelist, poet, novelist, soldier, was born in Tours, France, came to the United States on a dare, married a New York heiress, and after life abroad, returned to New York and became one of the city's literary group of the 1850s. In 1861, elected colonel of the "Gardes Lafayette," he became naturalized, and soon proved he was even more adept at arms than letters. The Federal army did not contain a more romantic or perhaps a more stubborn soldier.

[14] Historicus, in New York *Herald,* March 12, 1864, made the charges and said Barnes's disorganized troops impeded Zook's advance. Barnes answered sharply March 21, 1864. Historicus said April 4, 1864, that he had redoubled his research and "found his picture not only correct, but in nearly every detail and incident exact," and added statements by Birney and deTrobriand. The articles are in Meade, II, 324ff.

[15] *Michigan at Gettysburg,* 76.

[16] Pleasanton in Washington *Post*, February 8, 1883. Meade, II, 397.

[17] *Pennsylvania at Gettysburg*, II, 623.

[18] *Ibid.*

[19] *Ibid.*, 624.

[20] *Ibid.*, 625.

[21] L. W. Minnigh, *Gettysburg, What They Did Here*, 151.

[22] *Michigan at Gettysburg*, 102.

[23] This is stated in the official *Biographical Directory of the American Congress*, 815, and since each House is the judge of the conduct of its own members, the findings in such a publication might be judged conclusive! But the Congressman who stood closest by Brooks was Representative Laurence M. Keitt of South Carolina, with whom Barksdale may have been confused. Barksdale's name does not appear in the detailed account of the incident the writer has examined, but the matter is left open even in such a standard biography as *D.A.B.*

[24] Reuben Davis, *Recollections of Mississippi and Mississippians*, 237.

[25] Stiles, 185.

[26] *Ibid.*, 223.

[27] Hoke, 209.

[28] Owen, 245.

[29] McNeilly, 235-236.

[30] *Ibid.*, 236.

[31] *Ibid.*, 238.

[32] *Ibid.*, 241.

[33] *Ibid.*

[34] Ross, 55-56.

[35] *Pennsylvania at Gettysburg*, II, 612-613.

[36] Hoke, 337. W. C. Storrick, *The Battle of Gettysburg . . .*, 52-53.

[37] Owen, 246.

[38] *Pennsylvania at Gettysburg*, I, 394.

[39] *Ibid.*, II, 627.

[40] *Ibid.*

[41] Meridian, Miss., *Dispatch*, August 3, 1914, in McNeilly, *Publ. M.H.S.*, XIX, 238-239.

[42] Col. William T. Nichols of the 14th Vermont learned from a prisoner that Barksdale was mortally wounded in front of the line, sent a detail and took him to a temporary hospital. G. G. Benedict, *Vermont at Gettysburg*, 9. A ball had pierced his breast and both legs were bloody with wounds.

Chapter Nineteen: CEMETERY AND CULP'S HILLS

[1] *Maine at Gettysburg*, 292 and note.

[2] *S.H.S.P.*, XXVII, 195.

[3] *Pennsylvania at Gettysburg*, I, 404. Haskell, 373.

[4] *S.H.S.P.*, XXVII, 194.

[5] The losses of this regiment, frequently stated as the heaviest in relation to the number of engaged, are scarcely comparable with those of larger regiments, but more readily with some of the company losses. The 24th Michigan and 26th North Carolina, larger regiments, lost more heavily, as did the 14th Tennessee, which, with 3 left out of 365, undoubtedly suffered the highest percentage of casualties of the battle. The divisional adjutant, Haskell, placed the loss of the 1st Minnesota at "more than two-thirds."

[6] Wright returned to the Georgia legislature in the autumn of 1863, quite apparently because of the dislike he developed for Anderson after that general's

failure to support him at a critical moment of the battle. After the session he returned to different rolls in the armies.

7 This writer camped on the Bliss farm in 1922 as a newspaper correspondent covering the re-enactment by General Smedley Butler with the Marine Corps of the assault of Pickett's division, with President Warren G. Harding and other officials as spectators.

8 The July 8 dispatch from Hagerstown to the Richmond *Enquirer* (published July 23) was severe: "But although orders were preemptory that all of Anderson's Division move into action simultaneously, Brig. Gen. Posey commanding a Mississippi brigade and Brig. Gen. Mahone commanding a Virginia brigade failed to advance. The failure of these two to advance is assigned, as I learn upon inquiry, as the reason why Pender's Division of Hill's Corps did not advance—the order being that the advance was to commence on the right and be taken up all along the line. Pender's failure to advance caused the division on his left, Heth's, to remain inactive.

"Here we have two whole divisions, and two brigades of another, standing idle spectators of one of the most desperate and important assaults that has ever been made on this continent—fifteen or twenty thousand armed men resting on their arms, in plain view of a terrible battle, witnessing the mighty efforts of two little brigades (Wright's and Wilcox's, for Perry had fallen back overpowered) contending with the heavy masses of Yankee infantry, and subjected to a most deadly fire from the enemy's heavy artillery, without a single effort to aid them in the assault, or to assist them when the heights were carried. . . . It was now apparent that the day was lost—lost after it was *won*—lost, not because our army fought badly, but because a large portion *did not fight at all*."

9 Perrin, a good soldier, saw the full measure of his commander's ability: "In my humble judgment he was the best general officer in the army." Perrin to Bonham, 522.

10 *S.H.S.P.*, IV, 154. The date of Pender's fall is confused in Lee's statement, being placed on July 3. But his meaning was clear, and applicable to the second, the proper date. The error could have been typographical, or Lee's, or Heth's, who recorded the conversation.

11 *O.R.*, XXVII, Part II, 658.

12 Ross, 56.

13 That view was shared by Private West, who had ideas on the disastrous nature of Hood's loss: "I believe the wounding of General Hood was the greatest misfortune of the day. . . . If a considerable force had been thrown around the mountain to our right, the enemy would have been routed in half an hour. Baltimore would have been ours and the New York riots would have been as famous as the battle of Bunker Hill." West, 96.

14 Edward N. Whittier, commanding a Federal battery on Culp's Hill, gives the picture of the opening of the assault from which this account has been drawn. He times it at between 7:30 and 7:45 P.M. and said the sun had dropped behind the Cumberland mountains. Whittier, 329.

15 Applied to Hoke's division in 1864. Wasler, North Carolina *Folklore*, July 1957, p. 9.

16 *N.C. Regts.*, II, 136.

17 *Ibid.*, III, 415.

18 *Ibid.*, II, 136.

19 Whittier, 330. The twilight was a delaying factor.

20 Colonel Avery, 35 years old, was the youngest of 4 brothers from Morganton, N.C., in the Confederate armies. His grandfather, Waighstill Avery, the first attorney general of the state, was a signer of the Mecklenburg Declaration of Independence.

[21] Oration at Kingston, N.C., February 20, 1864, at Masonic Demonstration in honor of Colonel Avery.

[22] *N.C. Regts.*, III, 421.

[23] Whittier, 332, said they "disappeared at the first approach of the enemy and left their front open." Also *N.C. Regts.*, I, 355.

[24] Howard, I, 429.

[25] *Pennsylvania at Gettysburg,* II, 919.

[26] *O.R.,* XXVII, Part II, 480. Hays in his report said: "Arriving at the summit by a simultaneous rush of my whole line, I captured several pieces of artillery, four stand of colors, and a number of prisoners."

[27] *Ibid.*

[28] *N.C. Regts.*, I, 313.

[29] Hunt in *B. and L.,* III, 313. Birney in Meade, II, 414, said it was sent "at the sound of the firing."

[30] *Pennsylvania at Gettysburg,* I, 551. Howard, who had seen the 106th Pennsylvania in a stand at Sharpsburg, said to his artillery officer, "Major, your batteries can be withdrawn when that regiment runs away."

[31] *N.C. Regts.*, I, 314.

[32] *O.R.,* XXVII, Part II, 486.

[33] Raleigh, N.C., *Semi-Weekly Standard,* August 4, 1863.

[34] Wake Forest *Student,* XVI, 451.

[35] Raleigh, N.C., *Semi-Weekly Standard,* August 4, 1863.

[36] *O.R.,* XXVII, Part II, 485-486.

[37] *N.C. Regts.*, II, 258.

[38] McKim, 184.

[39] The air distance from Benner's Hill to the Wheat Field is slightly more than 2 miles.

[40] McKim, 184.

[41] *New York at Gettysburg,* III, 1335.

[42] Kane's brigade was commanded at that time by Colonel George A. Cobham, Jr., of the 111th Pennsylvania.

[43] On January 10, 1958, Maj. Gen. Henry Clay Hodges, Jr., became 97 years, 6 months, and 23 days old, and on that day passed Greene's and set a new longevity record for a West Point graduate.

[44] McKim, 196.

[45] *N.C. Regts.*, I, 148.

[46] *Ibid.*

[47] McKim, 196. The italics are his.

[48] Colonel Ed A. Palfrey, "Some of the Secret History of Gettysburg," *S.H.S.P.,* VIII, 522f.

Chapter Twenty: THE COUNCIL AND THE CAPTAIN

[1] Other factors were Stuart's arrival and the coming of Pickett's division, which equalized conditions or threw the scale a bit in Lee's favor in the matter of fresh troops, taken with his brigades that had not been heavily engaged. But Meade's over-all strength was much greater than Lee's, though he considered himself to be outnumbered. He testified (*Life and Letters,* II, 365) that he had in all arms about 95,000 men and that Lee had 95,000 infantry, 4 or 5,000 artillery and 10,000 cavalry. This would mean a total of about 110,000. The estimate of 58,000 is from the minutes of the meeting. *O.R.,* XXVII, Part I, 73-74. *B. and L.,* III, 314.

[2] *B. and L.,* III, 411.

[3] *Ibid.*

[4] *Ibid.* Hunt, writing to Webb, January 12, 1888, said Meade "did tell me, July 2d, that he feared we were in no condition to fight at Gettysburg, but in this matter he did give me his reason, so far as it concerned me—'lack of ammunition (artillery).' " Hunt told him there was none to throw away, but enough, and that seemed to satisfy him. Hunt did not say if there were reasons pertinent to others, as Meade's words might imply, but he declined to accept the charge that Meade wanted to withdraw. *Journal of the Military Service Institution of the U. S., XLV,* 54.

[5] The withdrawal order was never issued, and that must have salved Meade's conscience when he testified before the Committee on the Conduct of the War that "he had no recollection of ever having directed such an order to be issued, or ever having contemplated the issuing of such an order." *B. and L.,* III, 410-411. On the second occasion he denied ever having intended or thought to withdraw the army unless future developments might make it necessary.

[6] *O.R.,* XXVII, Part I, 72.

[7] After Chancellorsville, Meade wrote: "Who would have believed a few days ago that Hooker would withdraw his army, in opposition to the opinion of a majority of his corps commanders? Yet such is absolutely and actually the case." Meade, I, 372.

[8] Edmund R. Brown, 377.

[9] Writing the Committee of Congress, October 16, 1865, Pleasanton said Meade "had so little assurance of his own ability to maintain himself, or on the strength of his position," that he gave the order for Pleasanton to prepare to cover a retreat. Meade, II, 403-404.

[10] Edmund R. Brown, 376.

[11] *O.R.,* XXVII, Part I, 73-74.

[12] *B. and L.,* III, 313. With so many in a room, confusion was inevitable, and none would likely catch all remarks.

[13] *Ibid.*

[14] Slocum to Doubleday, February 19, 1883. Meade, II, 398.

[15] Doubleday, 185n.

[16] Meade, II, 398.

[17] *Ibid.,* 413. Some of the replies are in II, 399ff.

[18] Hoke, 180-183. Oates, 194. *O.R.,* XXVII, Part I, 75.

[19] *S.H.S.P.,* VIII, 522.

[20] *Ibid.,* XXXVII, 351. The circumstances under which they were found by a lad looking for a watch on the body of a dead cavalryman, did not lend credence to the charge that the papers were forgeries, though they were by no means orders from responsible authorities.

[21] *Ibid.,* VIII, 522.

[22] *Pennsylvania at Gettysburg,* II, 717.

[23] Captain J. M. Robertson brought up a Federal artillery brigade and moved it back 2 miles on the Baltimore pike to camp for the night. Meade, II, 406, *O.R.,* XXVII, Part I, 1021. But this, the only large movement known in the area except Kane's and Candy's, was much earlier in the evening.

[24] Gen. Thomas T. Munford, Ms. letter to Mrs. Charles F. Hyde, Southern Historical Collection, University of North Carolina, Chapel Hill, N.C.

[25] Thomason, 440.

[26] Hoke, 355.

[27] The comparison is appropriate with a great British general, Henry V, of whom a contemporary said, "He transacts all his affairs himself." John Richard Green, *History of England,* I, 549.

[28] Hoke, 356.

[29] H. J. Eckenrode and Bryan Conrad, *James Longstreet, Lee's War Horse*, 200-201.

[30] Hoke, 356.

[31] Haskell, p. 385, claims to have heard Meade express displeasure over Geary's attack as "not ordered and not necessary" because Geary's position was already good and the works he assailed were valueless. He said he had heard Meade say he sent an order to have the fighting stopped, but it was not delivered until the Confederates had been beaten back. Haskell either must have been mistaken or the remark was a reflection of Meade's generalship, for Culp's Hill was essential to the Federal army.

[32] *Pennsylvania at Gettysburg*, II, 717.

[33] *Ibid.*, 718.

[34] McKim, 188.

[35] *Ibid.*

[36] *Pennsylvania at Gettysburg*, I, 308.

[37] Edmund R. Brown, 379.

[38] *Ibid.*, 380.

[39] J. B. Jones, I, 100.

[40] McKim, 201.

[41] Douglas, 249.

[42] *N.C. Regts.*, V, 195.

[43] Douglas, 250.

Chapter Twenty-one: PICKETT, PETTIGREW, AND TRIMBLE

[1] Walter Harrison, *Pickett's Men* . . . , 98.

[2] *O.R.*, XXVII, Part III, 910. Pickett reported from Berryville on June 24 that his three brigades aggregated 4,795 men.

[3] Charles T. Loehr, *War History of the Old First Virginia Infantry Regiment* . . . , 35.

[4] Harrison, 18.

[5] G. F. R. Henderson, *Stonewall Jackson and the American Civil War*, I, 190.

[6] *Ibid.*, 244, 253. Freeman, *Lee's Lieutenants*, I, 318.

[7] LaSalle Corbell Pickett, 212.

[8] Alexander, *S.H.S.P.*, IV, 108. The overcoat must have been a relic of Garnett's U.S. Army days.

[9] Harrison, 20.

[10] Hunton, 84.

[11] Biographical material on Pickett's three brigadier generals is largely from Harrison and LaSalle Corbell Pickett.

[12] Randolph A. Shotwell, "Virginia and North Carolina in the Battle of Gettysburg," *O. L. and D.*, IV, 87.

[13] *Ibid.*, 86.

[14] *Ibid.*

[15] Snow, 103.

[16] Harrison, 86.

[17] The ensuing conversation is from *Soldier of the South*, 54-55.

[18] LaSalle Corbell Pickett, XI.

[19] Sorrel, 155-156.

[20] *Ibid.*, 156.

[21] *Soldier of the South*, 55.

[22] David E. Johnston, *Four Years a Soldier*, 250.

23 *Soldier of the South,* 55-56.

24 *Ibid.* Pickett said Lee spoke in "his firm, quiet, determined voice."

25 *Ibid.,* 56.

26 Henry, *Story of the Mexican War,* 361.

27 LaSalle Corbell Pickett, XI.

28 Sorrel, 54.

29 Beveridge, I, 385.

30 LaSalle Corbell Pickett, 128.

31 *Ibid.*

32 *Ibid.,* XI.

33 *Ibid.,* XI-XII.

34 Sorrel, 54.

35 LaSalle Corbell Pickett, 112.

36 Hunton, 85.

37 Snow, 103.

38 J. B. Jones, I, 261.

39 Two batteries were taken from Law, *Pennsylvania at Gettysburg,* II, 844.

40 Alexander, *S.H.S.P.,* IV, 103.

41 *Ibid.*

42 *B. and L.,* III, 362.

43 Raleigh, N.C., *Semi-Weekly Standard,* July 3, 1863. The first article was headed "Gross Injustice to North Carolina."

44 *Ibid.*

45 *N.C. Regts.,* II, 38.

46 *Ibid.,* 71.

47 Lane, mentioned but slightly in the histories of Lee's army, was entitled to the comment of Captain Octavius A. Wiggins of the 37th North Carolina: "General James H. Lane . . . was all that a true soldier could be upon a battlefield. Nothing could excite him and when he put his troops in battle he always went with them. Always enjoying good health and miraculously escaping a mortal wound, he kept close to his brigade and passed through as many battles as any person in the Confederate army, dearly beloved by his entire brigade."

48 Taylor, *Four Years,* 103.

49 *Ibid.*

50 *Ibid.,* 104.

51 *B. and L.,* III, 342-343.

52 *Ibid.*

53 *Southern Bivouac,* February 1886; Hoke, 336.

54 *Ibid.,* 343.

55 *S.H.S.P.,* IV, 105.

56 *Ibid.,* 104.

57 *Ibid.,* 104-105.

58 *Ibid.,* 105.

59 *Ibid.*

60 *Ibid.,* 106. Alexander used the italics.

61 *Ibid.*

Chapter Twenty-two: AT FEARFUL PRICE

1 The signal was to be shorter but a friction primer failed, causing delay with the second gun. *B. and L.,* III, 362n.

2 *Ibid.,* 314.

3 Haskell, 390, 387.

4 *Pennsylvania at Gettysburg*, II, 629. Haskell, 391f.

5 *Ibid.*, 395.

6 Wilkeson's dispatch, a near classic, is quoted in *Civil War in Song and Story*, 333, and Hoke, 364.

7 Osbourn, 16.

8 *Pennsylvania at Gettysburg*, II, 629-630.

9 Rhodes, 238.

10 Johnston, 252.

11 *Ibid.*

12 Maud Morrow Brown, *The University Greys . . .* , 38-41.

13 *Vermont at Gettysburg*, 14. Dickert, 200, says most of Kershaw's South Carolinians slept during the cannonade.

14 Dickert, 201.

15 *Soldier of the South*, 57.

16 *Ibid.*

17 *Ibid.*, 60.

18 *S.H.S.P.*, IV, 107.

19 *Ibid.*, 108.

20 *Soldier of the South*, 60. The words vary slightly in different accounts.

21 *Ibid.*, 60-61.

22 Philadelphia *Times* interview in Minnigh, 149.

23 *S.H.S.P.*, IV, 106. Alexander made no complaint in his account, saying the guns might have been lost, but "I always feel like apologizing for their absence." He thought it a "brilliant opportunity" for this artillery escort.

24 LaSalle Corbell Pickett, 302.

25 Shotwell, *O.L. and D.*, IV, 90.

26 Harrison, 98, says Garnett was "in no physical condition to be on the field."

27 Shotwell, *O.L. and D.*, IV, 90.

28 *Ibid.*, 91.

29 *S.H.S.P.*, IV, 108.

30 *Ibid.*

31 Shotwell, *O.L. and D.*, 90. The cannoneers crawled on top of their guns to witness the march and assault.

32 *S.H.S.P.*, XXXIII, 129.

33 William H. Morgan, *Personal Reminiscences of the War*, 53.

34 Crocker, *S.H.S.P.*, XXXIII, 129.

35 Morgan, 167.

36 *Ibid.*, 166.

37 *Ibid.*

38 Johnston, 196.

39 *O.L. and D.*, IV, 91.

40 *Ibid.*

41 *Ibid.*

42 *New York at Gettysburg*, III, 1365.

43 J. H. Stine, *History of the Army of the Potomac*, 527-528.

44 *S.H.S.P.*, XXXIX, 186.

45 Kemper was left partially paralyzed on the field; though permanently disabled, he served a useful later career and became governor of Virginia. Kemper wrote to Colonel W. H. Swallow: "I was nearly up to the Federal line, so near I could easily see the faces and the expression on the countenances of the Union men, and I thought I could identify the individual soldier that shot me." Quoted in letter from Swallow, Hoke, 372n.

[46] Captain H. T. Owen in Philadelphia *Times,* cited in Hoke, 386-387.

[47] *O.L. and D., IV,* 93.

[48] *Confederate Veteran, XIV,* 81.

[49] *Ibid.*

[50] *Ibid.*

[51] *S.H.S.P., XXXIX,* 186-187.

[52] *Pennsylvania at Gettysburg, I,* 410.

[53] The account that Armistead, while lying on the ground wounded, made the call of the widow's son, a fraternal appeal for help, and then sent to his old army friend such words as "Tell Hancock I wronged him and wronged my country" (Stine, 531) is so far out of character and inconsistent with what he was telling his men a few minutes earlier, that it would be questioned and probably discarded as apocryphal even if the circumstances under which the story originated were less doubtful.

Armistead fell in the midst of a group of five Federal soldiers, only one of whom, Private Wildemore of the 71st Pennsylvania, claimed to have caught words spoken in a whisper by Armistead, asking help and saying, as Wildemore repeated the words to his comrades, that "he is the son of a widow." Wildemore was wounded almost at once and the others, understanding the fraternal implications of the call, carried Armistead back, where he died. The story frequently given, that he met death penitently and apologetically, implying that he performed a mental flipflop in favor of those who had just filled his body with lead, and pitifully called for help, is difficult to accept on the available evidence of whispered words heard by only one of five men. Armisteads do not die that way.

[54] Sergeant Michael Specht, 72nd Pennsylvania, got the general's sword and kept it until he was commissioned lieutenant, wore it until the end of the war, and in 1906, at a reunion in Gettysburg, returned it to the veterans of Pickett's division.

[55] Stine, 528-529.

[56] Swallow, *Southern Bivouac,* February 1886. Hoke, 396.

[57] *O.L. and D., IV,* 92.

[58] Pickett had moved forward from the reverse slope and waited at a point in the woods nearer than Pettigrew.

[59] This was evident to the writer from walking over the ground traversed by both commands.

[60] *Civil War in Song and Story,* 220.

[61] Shotwell of the 8th Virginia, after Garnett's repulse, looked over and thought the North Carolinians had gained a lodgment on the crest. He seized a musket and hurried over but before he could join them they were beaten back. *O.L. and D., IV,* 94.

[62] Douglas, 212.

[63] *S.H.S.P., IX,* 29.

[64] *O.L. and D., IV,* 57.

[65] *Ibid.,* III, 462. *N.C. Regts., II,* 564.

[66] *N.C. Regts., II,* 566.

[67] *Ibid.,* III, 91.

[68] *Ibid.,* II, 566.

[69] *Ibid.,* 563.

[70] *Confederate Veteran, XXV,* 213.

[71] *O.L. and D., IV,* 57.

[72] *Pennsylvania at Gettysburg, II,* 631.

[73] *Ibid.*

[74] Hunton, 98.

[75] *Ibid.*

76 *Ibid.,* 98-99. Hunton dictated his memoirs in his eighty-second year, then published them privately, but they show how he retained strong recollections of the battle. He appears forgetful in one point particularly, as Pickett, *Soldier of the South,* 70, said, or strongly implied that he dismounted. Pickett's words were: "Poor Dick Garnett did not dismount, as did the others of us. . . ."

77 When this writer witnessed the re-enactment of the charge by the Marine Corps in 1922, Pickett was represented as going to the Codori barn.

78 Walter A. Clarke's pamphlet, "Pickett's Charge a Misnomer," 7.

79 *N.C. Regts.,* III, 299.

80 *Ibid.*

81 Joseph A. Englehart, adjutant of Pender's division, said the troops with him struck the wall at the point farthest to the front. "I leaned an elbow upon one of the guns of the enemy to rest, while I watched with painful anxiety the flight of Pickett's right." Grimes, Papers, Southern Historical Collection, University of North Carolina Library, Chapel Hill, N.C.

82 Longstreet felt it necessary to defend himself from N.C. strictures resulting from his report, as in *B. and L.,* III, 353.

83 *Soldier of the South,* 62, said the report originally stated "without reserve" the reasons why he believed the charge proved disastrous. The same or similar material was contained in one of Pickett's letters, but it was omitted from those Mrs. Pickett published. J. Bryan Grimes said that by having the division commander alter his report, Lee "saved Pickett from being torn to pieces by his critics." Papers. Pickett did not file an amended report.

84 *O.L. and D.,* IV, 95.

85 *Ibid.*

86 Lee must have made this remark a number of times. Fremantle, the British observer, thought his face was "placid and cheerful" and showed no disappointment. He assured the soldiers: "All this will come right in the end, we'll talk it over afterwards; but in the meantime all good men must rally." Fremantle, 315. Sorrel, 173, mentioned Lee's "extreme agitation" on witnessing the repulse, and quoted him: "It's all my fault. I take it all—get together men, we shall yet beat them." Sorrel added: "I saw no man fail him." Loehr of the 1st Virginia heard him say to Pickett: "General, your men have done all that men can do. The fault is entirely my own." Loehr, 38. Neither then nor at any later time did Lee blame any of his subordinates for the failure of the assault.

87 Fremantle, evidently a free-handed reporter given to quick, superficial impressions, as in congratulating Longstreet on Pickett's success, when Longstreet was already fully aware of the failure, told of Lee reproving an artillery officer who put spurs to his horse when it was frightened by an exploding shell. Alexander gave an account of the incident. The officer, Lieutenant F. M. Colston, was directed by Lee when he heard the cheering, to ascertain if the enemy showed indications of advancing. The lieutenant's horse, used to accompanying Alexander's horse, and as bound by habit as army horses often became, did not want to leave alone. The lieutenant, anxious to be off, did spur him and Lee did object to it. *S.H.S.P.,* IV, 110. He must have been deeply perturbed beneath his calm exterior. But the officer obviously was more zealous than cruel.

88 Behind the lines, when Pickett rode among his survivors, some were thoroughly defeated, some were angry. "General, let's go it again," shouted Charlie Belcher of the 24th Virginia. Loehr, 38.

89 *S.H.S.P.,* IX, 29.

90 Sorrel, 172. The nature of Pickett's rout was soon known in Richmond. Gorgas recorded, 50, on July 17, that the division was wholly scattered and could not be rallied until far in the rear.

[91] *O.L. and D.*, IV, 95.

[92] Stine, 548.

[93] *B. and L.*, III, 394. The conversation follows.

[94] *Pennsylvania at Gettysburg*, II, 845.

[95] This account is summarized mainly from General Benning in *S.H.S.P.*, IV, 176f and Col. F. C. Newhall, *Pennsylvania at Gettysburg*, II, 835f.

[96] *Pennsylvania at Gettysburg*, II, 846.

[97] *S.H.S.P.*, IV, 177. H. L. Parsons of the 1st Vermont Cavalry said Farnsworth fell dead with "five mortal wounds." This differs from the general version.

Chapter Twenty-three: RETREAT TO VIRGINIA

[1] J. B. Jones, I, 373.

[2] Stine, 555. According to the notes of Professor Michael Jacobs there was a thundershower beginning at 6:00 P.M. July 3, another at 6:00 A.M. July 4, and others in the afternoon of July 4.

[3] *Ibid.*

[4] McKim, 189.

[5] Lightsly, 5.

[6] *B. and L.*, III, 420-421.

[7] McIntosh, 79.

[8] *Annals*, 455.

[9] Dickert, 256.

[10] Ross, 69f.

[11] *Ibid.*, 73.

[12] *Ibid.*, 80-83.

[13] Ross, 87, says many were disappointed at the decision to return to Virginia. Their view had been that Lee was merely awaiting supplies to resume the offensive. But Ross thought news of the surrender of Vicksburg may have decided Lee to cross. The losses in both armies were staggering and about equal. Colonel William Allen, *S.H.S.P.*, IV, 34, aggregated Lee's loss at 22,928, made up of Longstreet, 7,659; Ewell, 6,087; Hill, 8,982; and cavalry, 200. From his study he placed Meade's loss at 23,186. The official returns of killed, wounded, and missing give Lee's loss as 20,448 and Meade's as 22,990. Paris, 313 and 298. The final figures of the official records vary little from these totals.

[14] Meade, II, 365.

[15] Ross, 89.

[16] Welch, 59.

[17] Ms. letter, Indiana State Library.

[18] McKim, 190.

[19] *O.L. and D.*, I, 30.

[20] *Ibid.*, 29-31.

[21] Ross, 87.

[22] Alexander, "Causes of Southern Defeat . . ." *S.H.S.P.*, IV, 99, who was one of the best Southern analysts of the cause of the repulse, thought Lee could have taken a position covering Fairfield and maneuvered to force Meade to attack. He added: "They had never driven us from the field since the war began."

[23] Captured by the Sixth Corps, *Sedgwick Memorial*, 38.

[24] Frank M. Mixon, *Reminiscences of a Private*, 41.

[25] R. E. Lee, 102.

[26] Charles Francis Adams, *Lee's Centennial*, 23.

Bibliography

ADAMS, CHARLES FRANCIS. *Lee's Centennial*. Address at Lexington, Va., January 19, 1907. Boston, 1907.

ADAMS, JOHN G. B. *Reminiscences of the 19th Massachusetts Regiment*. Boston, 1899.

ALDERMAN, EDWIN ANDERSON, and JOEL CHANDLER HARRIS, editors-in-chief. *Library of Southern Literature*. 16 vols. Atlanta, 1907-1909.

ALEXANDER, E. P. "Causes of Southern Defeat at Gettysburg," *Southern Historical Society Papers*, IV, 97.

――――. *Military Memories of a Confederate*. New York, 1907.

ALLAN, WILLIAM. "General Lee's Strength and Losses at Gettysburg," *Southern Historical Society Papers*, IV, 34.

――――. *The Strategy of the Gettysburg Campaign*. Military History Society of Massachusetts. Boston, 1903.

――――. "Gettysburg," *Southern Historical Society Papers*, IV, 76ff.

The Annals of the War, by Leading Participants North and South. Philadelphia, 1879.

ASHE, SAMUEL A. *History of North Carolina*. Raleigh, 1925.

――――. *The Charge at Gettysburg*. Raleigh, no date.

――――, editor-in-chief. *Biographical Dictionary of North Carolina from Colonial Times to the Present*. Greensboro, 1907.

AVARY, MYRTA LOCKETT, editor. *Recollections of Alexander H. Stephens*. New York, 1910.

AVERY, ISAAC WHEELER. *History of the State of Georgia from 1850 to 1881*. New York, 1881.

BACHELDER, JOHN B. *Repulse of Longstreet's Assault*. New York, 1870.

――――. "Letter on Gettysburg," *Southern Historical Society Papers*, V, 173.

BALCH, WILLIAM RALSTON. *The Battle of Gettysburg*. Harrisburg, 1885.

434

BANES, CHARLES H. *History of the Philadelphia Brigade.* Philadelphia, 1876.

BARTLETT, NAPIER. *A Soldier's Story of the War, Including the Marches and Battles of the Battalion of Washington Artillery.* New Orleans, 1874.

BASSLER, J. H. "The Color Episode of the 149th Regiment, Pennsylvania Volunteers in the First Day's Fight at Gettysburg," *Southern Historical Society Papers,* XXXVII, 266.

BATES, SAMUEL P. *The Battle of Gettysburg.* Philadelphia, 1875.

BATTINE, CECIL. *The Crisis of the Confederacy.* London, 1905.

BATTLE, KEMP P. *History of the University of North Carolina.* 2 vols. Raleigh, 1907.

Battles and Leaders of the Civil War. 4 vols. New York, 1884.

BEECHAM, ROBERT K. *Gettysburg, The Pivotal Battle of the Civil War.* Chicago, 1911.

BELLAMY, F. J. *War Diary of Co. A, 3rd Indiana Cavalry.* Ms. Indiana State Library.

BENEDICT, G. G. *Vermont at Gettysburg.* Burlington, 1870.

BENNING, HENRY L. "Notes on the Battle of Gettysburg," *Southern Historical Society Papers,* IV, 176.

BENSON, BERRY GREENWOOD. *Reminiscences.* Ms. Augusta, Ga., 1863.

BEVERIDGE, ALBERT J. *Abraham Lincoln.* 2 vols. Boston, 1928.

BIDDLE, CHAPMAN. *The First Day of the Battle of Gettysburg.* Philadelphia, 1880.

BILL, ALFRED HOYT. *The Beleaguered City.* New York, 1946.

BILLINGS, JOHN D. *Hard Tack and Coffee or the Unwritten Story of Army Life.* Boston, 1887.

BIRDSONG, JAMES C. *Brief Sketches of North Carolina Troops in the War Between the States.* Raleigh, 1894.

BLACKFORD, W. W. *War Years with Jeb Stuart.* New York, 1945.

Blue and Gray—Reunion of Philadelphia Brigade and Pickett's Division. Philadelphia, 1906.

BOND, W. R. *Pickett or Pettigrew.* Weldon, N.C., 1888.

BONHAM, M. L. *A Little More Light on Gettysburg.* Pamphlet at University of South Carolina Library, apparently extract from article in Mississippi Valley Historical Review. No date or place.

BORCKE, HEROS VON. *Memoirs of the Confederate War for Independence.* 1886. Republished, New York, 1938.

BOWEN, J. J. *The Strategy of Robert E. Lee.* New York, 1914.

BRADFORD, GAMALIEL. *Confederate Portraits.* Boston, 1917.

BRATTON, JOHN. "Tribute to General Dick Anderson," *Southern Historical Society Papers,* XIII, 419.

BROCK, R. A. *Robert E. Lee: Soldier, Citizen, Christian Patriot.* Richmond, 1897.

BROOKS, U. R. *Stories of the Confederacy.* Columbia, S.C., 1912.

BROWN, EDMUND R. *The 27th Indiana Volunteer Infantry in the War of the Rebellion.* No place, 1899.

BROWN, JOSEPH N. *The Battle of Gettysburg.* Anderson, S.C., 1901.

BROWN, MAUD MORROW. *The University Greys (Co. A, 11th Mississippi Infantry Regiment).* Richmond, 1940.

BROWN, VARINA D. *A Colonel at Gettysburg and Spotsylvania.* Columbia, S.C., 1931.

BURGWYN, WILLIAM S. "Unparalleled Loss of Company E, 26th North Carolina, Pettigrew's Brigade, at Gettysburg," *Southern Historical Society Papers,* XXVIII, 199ff.

————. "Zebulon Baird Vance," *Library of Southern Literature,* XII, 5555.

CALDWELL, J. F. J. *History of a Brigade of South Carolinians Known First as Gregg's and Subsequently as McGowan's Brigade.* Philadelphia, 1866.

CANDLER, ALLEN D., and CLEMENT A. EVANS. *Georgia: Comprising Sketches of Counties, Towns, Events, Institutions, and Persons.* 3 vols. Atlanta, 1906.

CARRINGTON, JAMES McDOWELL. "First Day on the Left at Gettysburg," *Southern Historical Society Papers,* XXXVII, 326-337.

CASLER, JOHN O. *Four Years in the Stonewall Brigade.* Guthrie, Okla., 1893.

CATTON, BRUCE. *Glory Road.* Garden City, N.Y., 1952.

CHESNUT, MARY BOYKIN. *A Diary from Dixie.* New York, 1905.

CLARK, CHIEF JUSTICE WALTER. Memorial address, Bunker Hill, W. Va. *General James Johnston Pettigrew, C.S.A.* Address at the unveiling of the memorial marble pillar and tablet to General Pettigrew near Bunker Hill, Sept. 17, 1920. Pamphlet, no other date or place.

————. *Pickett's Charge a Misnomer.* Address before North Carolina Confederate Veterans Association, Durham, N.C., August 24, 1921. Pamphlet, no other date or place.

————, editor. *Histories of the Several Regiments and Battalions from North Carolina in the Great War, 1861-65.* 5 vols. Raleigh, 1901.

COMMAGER, HENRY STEELE. *The Blue and the Gray.* Indianapolis, 1950.

CONFEDERATE, A. *The Grayjackets: and How They Lived, Fought and Died for Dixie.* Richmond, 1867.

Confederate Veteran. 40 vols. (1893-1932). Nashville, Tenn.

COX, WILLIAM E. *Life and Character of General Stephen D. Ramseur.* Raleigh, 1891.

COX, JUDGE WILLIAM RUFFIN. *Life and Services of General James H. Lane.* Richmond, 1908.

CROCKER, JAMES P. "My Personal Experiences in Taking up Arms" (an address before Stonewall Camp, Confederate Veterans, Portsmouth, Va., Feb. 6, 1889), *Southern Historical Society Papers,* XXXIII, 111ff.

————. "Gettysburg—Pickett's Charge" (an address, same camp, Nov. 7, 1894), *Southern Historical Society Papers,* XXXIII, 111ff.

CURTIS, GEORGE W. Address at dedication of statue of Major General John Sedgwick at West Point, Oct. 21, 1868. New York, 1869.

CURTIS, O. B. *History of the 24th Michigan of the Iron Brigade.* Detroit, 1891.

DALBIAC, COLONEL P. H. *American War of Secession: Chancellorsville and Gettysburg*. London and New York, 1911.

DANIEL, FREDERICK S. *Richmond Howitzers in the War*. Richmond, 1891.

DANIEL, LIZZIE CARY. *Confederate Scrap Book*. Richmond, 1893.

DAVIS, BURKE. *Gray Fox*. New York, 1956.

DAVIS, JEFFERSON. *A Short History of the Confederate States of America*. New York, 1890.

DAVIS, REUBEN. *Recollections of Mississippi and Mississippians*. Boston and New York, 1889.

DAWES, RUFUS R. *Service with the Sixth Wisconsin Volunteers*. Marietta, Ohio, 1890.

DETROBRIAND, REGIS. *Four Years with the Army of the Potomac*. Translated by George C. Dauchy. Boston, 1889.

DICKERT, D. AUGUSTUS. *History of Kershaw's Brigade*. Newberry, S.C., 1899.

DOUBLEDAY, ABNER. *Chancellorsville and Gettysburg*. New York, 1882.

DOUGLAS, HENRY KYD. *I Rode With Stonewall*. Chapel Hill, N.C., 1940.

DOWD, CLEMENT. *Life of Zebulon B. Vance*. Charlotte, N.C., 1899.

DRIVER, WILLIAM R. *Pickett's Charge at Gettysburg*. Boston, 1903.

EARLY, JUBAL A. "A Review by General Early," *Southern Historical Society Papers*, IV, 241.

———. "Causes of the Defeat of General Lee's Army at the Battle of Gettysburg," *Southern Historical Society Papers*, IV, 49-87.

———. "Supplement to General Early's Reply," *Southern Historical Society Papers*, IV, 282ff.

———. "Reply to Count of Paris," *Southern Historical Society Papers*, VI, 12-22.

ECKENRODE, H. J., and BRYAN CONRAD. *James Longstreet, Lee's War Horse*. Chapel Hill, N.C., 1936.

EGGLESTON, GEORGE CARY. *A Rebel's Recollections*. New York, 1875.

EVANS, CLEMENT A. *Confederate Military History*. 12 vols. Atlanta, 1899.

FAGAN, W. L. *Southern War Songs*. New York, 1890.

FARLEY, JOSEPH PEARSON. *West Point in the Early Sixties, with Incidents of the War*. Troy, N.Y., 1902.

FLEMING, FRANCIS P. "Florida Brigade at Gettysburg," *Southern Historical Society Papers*, XXVII, 192ff.

FREEMAN, DOUGLAS SOUTHALL. *Robert E. Lee: A Biography*. 2 vols. New York, 1935.

———. *Lee's Lieutenants*. 3 vols. New York, 1942.

FREMANTLE, ARTHUR J. L. *Three Months in the Southern States*. New York, 1864.

GALBREATH, C. B. "Song Writers of Ohio." *Ohio Archeological and Historical Society Publications*, Vols. XIII and XIV. Columbus, 1904 and 1905.

GALBREATH, E. C. Ms. Notes for Family. Indiana State Library.

GETTYSBURG BATTLEFIELD COMMISSION. Ms. entries entitled *A Record of the Position of Troops on the Battlefield*. At Gettysburg National Park.

GETTYSBURG NATIONAL MILITARY PARK. Scrapbook of newspaper clippings.

GORDON, JOHN B. *Reminiscences of the Civil War*. New York, 1903.

GORGAS, JOSIAH. *The Civil War Diary of General Josiah Gorgas*. Edited by Frank E. Vandiver. University of Alabama Press, 1947.

GRANT, ULYSSES S. *Personal Memoirs of U. S. Grant*. 2 vols. New York, 1885.

GREELEY, HORACE. *American Conflict*. 2 vols. Hartford, Conn., 1867-1869.

GREEN, JOHN RICHARD. *History of England*. 4 vols. World's Best Histories Series. New York and London, no date.

GRIMES, J. BRYAN. "Gettysburg," Ms., *Papers,* Southern Historical Collection, Chapel Hill, N.C., 1911.

————. "The Truth is Let Out as to Gettysburg," Raleigh *News and Observer,* August 6, 1911.

GRIFFIN, CLARENCE W. *History of Old Tryon and Rutherford Counties, North Carolina 1730-1936*. Asheville, N.C., 1937.

HAMLIN, PERCY GATLING. *Old Bald Head (Ewell): The Portrait of a Soldier*. Strasburg, Va., 1940.

HANCOCK, MRS. WINFIELD SCOTT. *Reminiscences of Winfield Scott Hancock*. New York, 1887.

HARRISON, WALTER. *Pickett's Men, A Fragment of War History*. New York, 1870.

HASKELL, FRANK ARETAS. *The Battle of Gettysburg*. From vol. 43, The Harvard Classics. New York, 1910.

HAYS, LOUISE FREDERICK. *History of Macon County, Georgia*. Atlanta, 1933.

HENDERSON, G. F. R. of British Army. "Review of General Longstreet's Book, *From Manassas to Appomattox,*" *Southern Historical Society Papers,* CIV, 117.

————. *Stonewall Jackson and the American Civil War*. 2 vols. London, 1911.

HENRY, ROBERT SELPH. *The Story of the Mexican War*. Indianapolis, 1950.

————. *The Story of the Confederacy*. Indianapolis, 1931.

HETH, HARRY. "Gettysburg" (An account of the opening of the engagement), *Southern Historical Society Papers,* IV, 151.

HILL, BENJAMIN HARVEY. *Tribute to Lee and Davis. Library of Southern Literature*. Vol. VI, Atlanta, 1907. From address delivered before Southern Historical Society, Atlanta, Feb. 18, 1874.

HILL, DANIEL HARVEY, editor. *The Land We Love*. Charlotte, N.C. (A monthly magazine, May 1866-March 1869.)

HILLSBORO *Recorder,* a newspaper. Hillsboro, N.C., 1863.

HOKE, JACOB. *The Great Invasion.* Dayton, O., 1887.

HOOD, JOHN B. *Advance and Retreat.* New Orleans, 1880.

———. "Gettysburg," *Southern Historical Society Papers,* IV, 145.

HOWARD, OLIVER O. *Autobiography.* New York, 1907.

HUFHAM, J. D., JR. "Gettysburg (Being an Account of the Experiences of a Veteran, Told by Himself)," Wake Forest (N.C.) *Student,* April 1897.

HUIDEKOPER, H. S. *A Short Story of the First Day's Fight at Gettysburg.* Philadelphia, 1906.

HUNTON, EPPA. *Autobiography.* Richmond, 1933.

HURST, M. B. *History of the Fourteenth Alabama Volunteers.* Richmond, 1863.

HYDE, THOMAS W. *Following the Creek Cross.* Boston, 1894.

Indiana at Antietam. Indiana Monument Commission report. Indianapolis, 1911.

Indiana at the Fiftieth Anniversary of the Battle of Gettysburg. Indianapolis, no date (1913?).

IRBY, RICHARD. *Historical Sketch of the Nottoway Grays, Afterwards Co. G, Eighteenth Virginia Infantry.* Richmond, 1878.

IREDELL *Express,* a newspaper. Statesville, N.C. 1863 file.

The Iron Brigade at Gettysburg. Cincinnati, 1879.

JACOBS, MICHAEL. *Notes on the Rebel Invasion of Maryland and Pennsylvania and the Battle of Gettysburg.* Philadelphia, 1864.

JOHNSTON, DAVID E. *Four Years a Soldier.* Princeton, W. Va., 1887.

———. *The Story of a Confederate Boy in the Civil War.* Portland, Ore., 1914.

JONES, CHARLES E. *Georgia and the War.* (Brief biographies of Georgia officers.) Atlanta, 1909.

JONES, J. B. *A Rebel War Clerk's Diary.* 2 vols. Philadelphia, 1866. New edition, Howard Swigget, editor. 2 vols. New York, 1935.

JONES, J. WILLIAM, secretary of the Southern Historical Society. *Life and Letters of Robert E. Lee: Soldier and Man.* New York and Washington, 1906.

———. *Personal Reminiscences, Anecdotes, and Letters of General Robert E. Lee.* New York, 1875.

———, compiler. *Army of Northern Virginia, Memorial Volume.* Richmond, 1880.

JONES, KATHARINE M. *Heroines of Dixie.* Indianapolis, 1955.

KEIFER, JOSEPH WARREN. *Slavery and Four Years of War.* 2 vols. New York and London, 1900.

KING, CHARLES. *The Iron Brigade.* New York, 1902.

KINGSBURY, T. B. "North Carolina at Gettysburg," *Our Living and Dead,* I, 193. Raleigh, 1874.

KIRKLAND, FRAZER. *The Picture Book of Anecdotes of the Rebellion.* Hillsdale, Mich., 1887.

KNIGHT, LUCIAN LAMAR. *Georgia Landmarks, Memorials and Legends.* 2 vols. Atlanta, 1913.

LANE, JAMES H. "History of Lane's North Carolina Brigade," *Southern Historical Society Papers,* Vols. VII-X.
———. "Letter to J. William Jones on Gettysburg," *Southern Historical Society Papers,* V, 38.
LEE, FITZHUGH. *General Lee.* New York, 1894.
———. "A Review of the First Two Days' Operations at Gettysburg and a Reply to General Longstreet," *Southern Historical Society Papers,* V, 168ff.
LEE, ROBERT E. (son of General Lee). *Recollections and Letters of General Robert E. Lee.* New York, 1904.
LIGHTSLY, ADA CHRISTINE. *The Veteran's Story.* Meridian, Miss., 1899.
Lincoln Day Addresses, 1887-1909. The National Republican Club, 2nd ed., Copy No. 278, New York.
LOEHR, CHARLES T. *War History of the Old First Virginia Infantry Regiment, Army of Northern Virginia.* Richmond, 1884.
LONG, A. L. *Memoirs of Robert E. Lee.* London, 1886.
LONGSTREET, HELEN DORTSCH. *Lee and Longstreet at High Tide.* Gainesville, Ga., 1905.
LONGSTREET, JAMES. *From Manassas to Appomattox.* Philadelphia, 1896.
LONGSTREET PAPERS. Southern Historical Collection, University of North Carolina Library. Chapel Hill, N.C.
LOSSING, BENSON J. *Pictorial History of the Civil War.* 3 vols. Hartford, Conn., 1874.

Maine at Gettysburg. Portland, Me., 1898.
MARSHALL, CHARLES. *Papers.* Edited by Major General Sir Frederick Maurice. Boston, 1927.
MARTIN, DR. R. W. "Armistead at the Battle of Gettysburg. Extracts from letters to Rev. James Poindexter," *Southern Historical Society Papers,* XXXIX, 186-187.
Maryland at Gettysburg. Baltimore, Md., 1891.
MAURICE, SIR FREDERICK. *Robert E. Lee, the Soldier.* Boston, 1925.
MCCABE, JAMES D., JR. *Life and Campaigns of General Robert E. Lee.* New York, 1866.
MCCLELLAN, GEORGE B. *McClellan's Own Story.* New York, 1887.
MCCLELLAN, H. B. *The Life and Campaigns of Major General J. E. B. Stuart.* Boston and New York, 1885.
MCDANIEL, J. J. *Diary of the Battles, and Incidents of the Seventh South Carolina Regiment.* No date or place.
MCINTOSH, DAVID GREGG. *Review of the Gettysburg Campaign.* No date or place. University of South Carolina Library. (Similar or same article in *Southern Historical Society Papers,* XXXVII, 74ff.)
MCKIM, RANDOLPH H. "The Gettysburg Campaign," *Southern Historical Society Papers,* XL, 253-295.

————. "Steuart's Brigade in the Battle of Gettysburg," *Southern Historical Society Papers,* V, 291.

————. *A Soldier's Recollections.* New York, 1910.

————. "Gen. J. E. B. Stuart in the Gettysburg Campaign," *Southern Historical Society Papers,* XXXVII, 210ff. (A Reply to Col. John S. Mosby.)

McNEILLY, J. S. "Barksdale's Mississippi Brigade at Gettysburg: The Most Magnificent Charge of the War," *Publications of the Mississippi Historical Society,* XIX, 231-265.

MEADE, GEORGE GORDON. Life and Letters of George Gordon Meade. 2 vols. New York, 1913.

MEREDITH, SOLOMON. Defense of General Sol Meredith against the False and Infamous Slanders of George W. Julian. Indianapolis, 1866.

Michigan at Gettysburg. Report of Monuments Commission. Detroit, 1889.

MINNIGH, L. W. *Gettysburg: What They Did Here.* Gettysburg, 1954.

MIXON, FRANK M. *Reminiscences of a Private.* Columbia, S.C., 1910.

MONTGOMERY, WALTER A. *Life and Character of Major General W. D. Pender.* Memorial address, May 10, 1894. Raleigh, 1894.

MOORE, FRANK, editor. *The Rebellion Record.* Vol. VII. New York, 1864.

————, collector and arranger. *The Civil War in Song and Story.* New York, 1889.

————. *Women of the War.* Hartford, Conn., 1866.

MORGAN, WILLIAM HENRY. *Personal Reminiscences of the War, 1861-65.* Lynchburg, Va., 1911.

MOSBY, J. S. *Stuart's Cavalry in the Gettysburg Campaign.* New York, 1908.

MUNFORD, GEN. THOMAS T. Ms. letter to Mrs. Charles F. Hyde. Southern Historical Collection. University of North Carolina Library, Chapel Hill, N.C.

NEW JERSEY STATE PUBLICATION. *Report of Gettysburg Battlefield Commission.* Trenton, 1891.

New York at Gettysburg. 3 vols. Albany, 1900.

NEW YORK STATE PUBLICATION. *Major General James S. Wadsworth at Gettysburg and Other Fields.* Albany, 1916.

NEW YORK *Herald.* Files for 1862-1863.

NEW YORK *Tribune.* Files for 1862-1863.

NICHOLS, G. W. *A Soldier's Story of His Regiment (61st Georgia).* No place, 1898.

"The 19th Indiana at Gettysburg. The Thrilling Story of a Great Regiment in a Great Battle." Typed Ms. Indiana State Library.

NORTON, OLIVER WILLCOX. *The Attack and Defense of Little Round Top.* New York, 1913.

————. *Strong Vincent and His Brigade at Gettysburg.* Chicago, 1909.

OATES, WILLIAM C. "The Battle on the Right," *Southern Historical Society Papers*, VI, 172.

————. *The War Between the Union and the Confederacy and Its Lost Opportunities, with a History of the 15th Alabama Regiment and the Forty-eight Battles in which It Was Engaged.* New York, 1905.

Official Records of the Union and Confederate Armies. Washington, 1882-1900.

Ohio Archeological and Historical Society Publications. Scattered issues. Columbus.

OSBOURN, FRANCIS A. *"Fighting Three Hundred," the Twentieth Indiana Infantry.* No place or date.

Our Living and Dead, a magazine. New Bern and Raleigh, 1873-1876.

OWEN, WILLIAM M. *In Camp and Battle with the Washington Artillery of New Orleans.* Boston, 1885.

PALFREY, COL. ED A. "Some of the Secret History of Gettysburg," *Southern Historical Society Papers*, VIII, 521.

PARIS, COMTE DE. "Battle of Gettysburg," from *History of the Civil War in America.* Philadelphia, 1886-1912.

————. "Gettysburg," *Southern Historical Society Papers*, V, 87.

PARK, CHARLES B. "Notes, Gettysburg Battlefield, June 21, 1913. Compiled from Established Data under Direction of Judge Walter A. Montgomery, member North Carolina Historical Commission." Ms. 1913. University of North Carolina Library, Chapel Hill, N.C.

PARK, R. E. *Sketch of the Twelfth Alabama Infantry.* Richmond, 1906.

PARKMAN, FRANCIS. *Montcalm and Wolfe. (France and England in North America,* vol. II.) Boston, 1899.

PECK, RUFUS H. *Reminiscences of a Confederate Soldier.* Fincastle, Va., no date.

PENDER, WILLIAM DORSEY. Ms. Letters and papers. Southern Historical Collection. University of North Carolina Library, Chapel Hill, N.C.

Pennsylvania at Gettysburg. 2 vols. Harrisburg, 1904.

PENNYPACKER, ISAAC R. *Life of George Gordon Meade.* New York, 1901.

PHILADELPHIA BRIGADE ASSOCIATION. *Reply of the Philadelphia Brigade Association to the Foolish and Absurd Narrative of Lieutenant Frank A. Haskell.* Philadelphia, 1910.

PICKERILL, W. N. *History of the Third Indiana Cavalry.* Indianapolis, 1906.

PICKETT, GEORGE. *Soldier of the South.* Letters. Arthur Crew Inman, editor. Boston, 1928.

PICKETT, LASALLE CORBELL. *Pickett and His Men.* Atlanta, 1899.

PINCHON, EDGCUMB. *Dan Sickles, Hero of Gettysburg and "Yankee King of Spain."* New York, 1945.

PINCKNEY, JOHN MCPHERSON. *Proceedings in the House of Representatives in Memory of Representative John M. Pinckney, December 5, 1905.* Washington, 1907.

POLLARD, E. A. *Southern History of the War.* 2 vols. in one. New York, 1866.

————. *The Early Life, Campaigns, and Public Services of Robert E. Lee, etc.* New York, 1870.

POLLEY, JOSEPH BENJAMIN. *Hood's Texas Brigade. Its Marches, Its Battles, Its Achievements.* New York, 1910.

POWELL, WILLIAM HENRY. *The Fifth Army Corps.* New York, 1896.

PULLEN, JOHN J. *The Twentieth Maine.* Philadelphia, 1957.

RALEIGH *Semi-Weekly Standard.* Raleigh, N.C. Files for 1863.

RAMSEUR, STEPHEN DODSON. Ms. Letters. Southern Historical Collection. University of North Carolina Library, Chapel Hill, N.C.

RANDALL, EMILIUS O. "High Lights of Ohio Literature," *Ohio Archeological and Historical Society Publications,* XXVIII. Columbus, Ohio, 1919.

"REGULARS AT GETTYSBURG," series by different officers, *Journal of the Military Service Institution of the United States,* XLIV and XLV. Governor's Island, 1909.

REID, WHITELAW. *Ohio in the War. Her Statesmen, Generals and Soldiers.* Columbus, 1893.

Reynolds Memorial—Addresses Before the Historical Society of Pennsylvania. Philadelphia, 1880.

RHODES, JAMES FORD. *History of the Civil War.* New York, 1917.

RICHMOND *Examiner.* Files for 1863.

RICHMOND *Inquirer.* Files for 1862-1863.

RICHMOND *Whig and Public Advertiser.* Files for 1863.

RIDPATH, JOHN CLARK. *Life and Times of James A. Garfield.* Cincinnati, 1881.

ROBBINS, W. M. "Longstreet's Assault at Gettysburg," *Histories of the Several Regiments and Battalions from North Carolina in the Great War, 1861-65,* V, 101.

ROBERTSON, JOHN, compiler. *Michigan in the War.* Lansing, 1882.

ROCKWELL, W. S. *The Oglethorpe Light Infantry of Savannah in Peace and in War.* Savannah, 1894.

ROSS, FITZGERALD. *A Visit to Cities and Camps of the Confederacy.* Edinburg and London, 1865.

SANDBURG, CARL. *Abraham Lincoln. The War Years.* Vol. II. New York, 1939.

SANGER, D. B., and THOMAS R. HAY. *James Longstreet.* Baton Rouge, 1952.

SCHEIBERT, JUSTUS (of Prussian Royal Engineers). Letter to J. William Jones, Secretary of Southern Historical Society, *Southern Historical Society Papers,* V, 90.

SCHOULER, JAMES. *The History of the Civil War.* New York, 1899.

SCRIBNER, THEODORE T. *Indiana's Roll of Honor.* Indianapolis, 1866.

SEDGWICK, MAJ. GEN. JOHN. *Proceedings at Dedication of Statue at Gettysburg.* Hartford, Conn., 1913.

SHIELDS, DAVID. "Story of Longstreet's Assault," from Prof. Nixon papers, Southern Historical Collection, Chapel Hill, N.C.

SHOTWELL, RANDOLPH A. "Virginia and North Carolina in the Battle of Gettysburg," *Our Living and Dead*, IV, 80ff.

SMITH, JAMES POWER. "General Lee at Gettysburg," *Southern Historical Society Papers*, XXXIII, 135ff.

SNOW, WILLIAM PARKER. *Southern Generals, Their Lives and Campaigns.* New York, 1866.

SORREL, G. MOXLEY. *Recollections of a Confederate Staff Officer.* New York, 1905. Reprinted, Jackson, Tenn., 1958.

Southern Historical Society Papers. 49 vols., chiefly Vols. 4 and 5. Richmond, 1876——.

STACKPOLE, EDWARD J. *They Met at Gettysburg.* Harrisburg, 1956.

STEELE, MATTHEW FORNEY. *American Campaigns.* 2 vols. Washington, 1909.

STEVENS, GEORGE T. *Three Years in the Sixth Corps.* New York, 1870.

STEWART, W. H. *A Pair of Blankets.* New York, 1911.

STIKELEATHER, J. A. Ms. Recollections of the Civil War in the United States. Among J. Bryan Grimes papers, Southern Historical Collection. Chapel Hill, N.C. Olive, N.C., 1909.

STILES, ROBERT. *Four Years Under Marse Robert.* New York, 1903.

STINE, J. H. *History of the Army of the Potomac.* Washington, 1893.

STORRICK, W. C. *The Battle of Gettysburg, The Country, The Contestants, The Results.* Harrisburg, 1947.

STROUDER, A. C. *Roster and History of 19th Ind. Reg. of Inf.* Muncie, 1907.

SYPHER, JOSIAH R. *History of the Pennsylvania Reserve Corps.* Lancaster, 1865.

T. K. B. (No name). "North Carolina Generals," *Our Living and Dead*, III.

——. "Another Witness: Gettysburg," *Our Living and Dead*, III, 45.

TALCOTT, T. M. R. "Review of Stuart's Cavalry in the Gettysburg Campaign, by Colonel John S. Mosby," *Southern Historical Society Papers*, XXXVII, 21.

TAYLOR, RICHARD. "Reminiscences of Secession, War and Reconstruction" advance sheets, *Southern Historical Society Papers*, V, 136ff.

——. *Destruction and Reconstruction.* New York, 1879.

TAYLOR, WALTER H. *Four Years with General Lee.* New York, 1877.

——. General Lee, His Campaigns in Virginia. Norfolk, 1906.

——. "Gettysburg," letter to J. William Jones, *Southern Historical Society Papers*, IV, 124.

THOMAS, HENRY W. *History of the Doles-Cook Brigade.* Atlanta, 1903.

THOMASON, JOHN W., JR. *Jeb Stuart.* New York, 1930.

THOMSON (of Co. G). *Seventh Indiana Infantry in the War for the Union.* Indiana State Library.

THURSTON, EDWARD N. "Memoir of Richard H. Anderson, C.S.A.," *Southern Historical Society Papers*, XXXIX, 152.

TOOMBS, SAMUEL. *New Jersey Troops in the Gettysburg Campaign.* Orange, N.J., 1888.

TRESCOT, WILLIAM HENRY. *Memorial of the Life of J. Johnston Pettigrew, Brigadier General of the Confederacy.* Charleston, 1870.

TRIMBLE, MAJOR GEN. ISAAC R. "The Campaign and Battle of Gettysburg" (from an original Ms. in possession of his grandson), *Confederate Veteran,* XXV, 209ff.

———. "North Carolinians at Gettysburg, IV, *Our Living and Dead,* 53ff.

TUCKER, GLENN. *Poltroons and Patriots.* 2 vols. Indianapolis, 1954.

TURNER, GEORGE EDGAR. *Victory Rode the Rails.* Indianapolis, 1953.

VEIL, CHARLES H. Letter to General Reynolds' orderly. Mimeograph copy in material of Jacob M. Sheads at Gettysburg.

WALKER, C. IRVINE. *Life of Lieutenant General Richard Heron Anderson of the Confederate States Army.* Charleston, 1917.

WALTON, J. B. "Longstreet's artillery at Gettysburg," *Southern Historical Society Papers,* V, 47.

WARD, DR. B. F. Co. K, 11th Mississippi Regiment Papers. Southern Historical Collection, Chapel Hill, N.C.

WASHINGTON *Post.* Scattered issues, 1893–1934.

WASLER, RICHARD. "That Word 'Tar Heel' Again" in North Carolina *Folklore,* a magazine. Chapel Hill, July 1957.

WATLINGTON, WILLIAM. Typed Ms. "The Third Indiana Cavalry." Madison, Ind., 1915.

WEAVER, A. C. *Third Indiana Cavalry, a Brief Account of the Actions in which They Took Part as Seen by Comrade A. C. Weaver, late Saddler and Brevet Commissary Sergeant of Company A.* Greenwood, Ind., 1919.

WELCH, SPENCER GLASGOW. *A Confederate Surgeon's Letters to His Wife.* New edition with additional illustrations and letters. Marietta, Ga., 1954.

WEST, JOHN C. *A Texan in Search of a Fight.* Waco, 1901.

WHITE, HENRY A. "Gettysburg Battle, Some Literary Facts Connected Therewith," *Southern Historical Society Papers,* XXVII, 52.

———. *Robert E. Lee of the Southern Confederacy.* New York, 1897.

WHITTIER, EDWARD N. *The Left Attack (Ewell's) at Gettysburg.* Military Historical Society of Massachusetts. Boston, 1903.

WILCOX, C. M. "Letter on Gettysburg," *Southern Historical Society Papers,* IV, 111.

WILEY, BELL IRVIN. *The Life of Johnny Reb.* Indianapolis, 1943.

WILMINGTON *Daily Journal.* Wilmington, N.C. Files for 1862–1863.

WISE, BARTON H. *The Life of Henry A. Wise of Virginia 1806-1876* (by his grandson). New York, 1899.

WISE, JENNINGS CROPPER. *The Long Arm of Lee.* Lynchburg, Va., 1915.

YOUNG, LOUIS G. "Pettigrew's Brigade at Gettysburg," *Our Living and Dead,* I.

———. "The Death of Brigadier General J. Johnston Pettigrew of North Carolina," *Our Living and Dead,* I.

Acknowledgments

The author is indebted to many for generous help given during the research and writing of *High Tide at Gettysburg,* especially to gracious staff members at the following libraries where I conducted research: University of North Carolina Library, Chapel Hill; North Carolina Department of Archives and History, Raleigh; University of South Carolina Library, Columbia; South Carolina State Archives, Columbia; Emory University Library, Emory University, Georgia; Alderman Library, University of Virginia, Charlottesville; Virginia State Library, Richmond; Library of Congress, Washington; New York Public Library, New York; Indiana State Library, Indianapolis; Sondley Reference Library, Asheville; Gettysburg National Military Park Library, Gettysburg.

Additional help in response to inquiries was received from the Alabama Department of Archives and History, Montgomery; University of Kentucky Library, Lexington; State of Mississippi, Department of Archives and History, Jackson; Burton Historical Collection, Detroit Public Library, Detroit; National Archives, Washington; Department of the Army, Washington; Pennsylvania State Library, Harrisburg; State Historical Society of Wisconsin, Madison.

Thanks are expressed also to the North Carolina Department of Archives and History for permission to use textually portions of papers on Pettigrew's and Hoke's brigades I read before meetings of the North Carolina Literary and Historical Association at Cullowhee and Raleigh, N.C., and published partially in the April 1958 issue of the *North Carolina Historical Review,* entitled "Some Aspects of North Carolina's Participation in the Gettysburg Campaign."

The *American Heritage* magazine for permission to use textually an article purchased by that magazine entitled "The Sixth Corps Goes to Gettysburg."

Major General John DeF. Barker, U.S. Air Force, retired, a student of military history, for reading the original draft and making valuable suggestions, though he is in no manner accountable for conclusions or factual matter.

Dr. Frederick Tilberg, historian, and Dr. Harry Pfanz, assistant historian, of the Gettysburg National Military Park, for suggestions and material. Dr. Pfanz read and criticized proofs, and made pertinent recommendations out of his store of detailed information about both battle and battlefield, but he is responsible for neither textual matter used nor conclusions reached.

Jacob M. Sheads, history professor at Gettysburg High School, an enthusiastic student of the battle, accredited guide, and authority on Adams County, Pennsylvania, history, who was helpful in conversations and visits about the battlefield.

It is to the Virginia Historical Society, Richmond, that I owe thanks for permission to use material from the Southern Historical Society Papers.

Emory University librarian G. R. Lyle and his staff and Dr. Bell I. Wiley, Emory University professor and historian, who made suggestions of material while I was at Emory University Library, where I engaged in two fairly extended periods of research and covered files of the Southern Historical Society Papers.

For similar help I desire to thank Miss Mary Thornton, North Carolina Collection, and Dr. James W. Patton and his staff, Southern Historical Collection, University of North Carolina Library, Chapel Hill.

My thanks for permission to use excerpts are also due to A. C. McClurg & Co., for *Gettysburg, the Pivotal Battle of the Civil War* by Robert K. Beecham; Continental Book Company, Inc., for *A Confederate Surgeon's Letters to His Wife* by Spencer Glasgow Welch (reprinted with additions, 1954); Appleton-Century-Crofts, Inc., for *A Diary from Dixie* by Mary Boykin Chesnut (1905); Longmans, Green & Co., Inc., for *A Soldier's Recollections* by Randolph H. McKim; The State-Record Company, successor to the State Company, for *A Colonel at Gettysburg and Spotsylvania* by Varina D. Brown; the University of Alabama Press, for *The Civil War Diary of General Josiah Gorgas* edited by Frank E. Vandiver; McCowat-Mercer Press, Inc., for *Recollections of a Confederate Staff Officer* by G. Moxley Sorrel; Maud Morrow Brown, author of *University Greys;* Charles Scribner's Sons, for *Memories of a Confederate* by E. P. Alexander, for *Life and Letters* by G. G. Meade, and for *War Years with Jeb Stuart* by W. W. Blackford; The University of North Carolina Press, for *I Rode with Stonewall* by Henry Kyd Douglas; Houghton Mifflin Company, for *Soldier of the South* by George Pickett; Neale Publishing Company and John L. Gammel, for *Hood's Texas Brigade* by Joseph Benjamin Polley; State Historical Society of Wisconsin for *The Battle of Gettysburg* by Frederick Aretas Haskell; Eppa Hunton IV for *Autobiography* by Eppa Hunton.

Dorothy Thomas Tucker, my wife, accompanied me on numerous trips to Gettysburg. From the long-ago accounts by her grandfather, Henry C. Wheeler, of Dillsboro, Indiana, 7th Indiana Infantry, she was able to locate the stone on which he sat after he was wounded on Culp's Hill. She drew the maps in this volume, executing them as we outlined them together, giving due deference to the John B. Bachelder maps, but examining numerous others, and in instances of more limited engagements using our own sketches and the measurements we made on the field.

I am indebted to many with whom I discussed phases of this battle, who gave impressions or lent books and pamphlets. Writing on a remote North Carolina farm is quite different from writing next door to a well-stocked library and the loan of material has been greatly appreciated, the lenders numerous.

Among those of whom I should make especial mention are Mrs. George Ditchburn, Miss Margaret McMillan and Mrs. Emma Sheffer, all of Gettysburg; Colonel James Ripley Jacobs, retired, author of historical works on the regular army, of Easley, S.C.; Colonel Paul Rockwell, writer and military student, of Asheville, N.C.; Frank L. FitzSimons, historian and banker, Hendersonville, N.C.; the late Clarence W. Griffin, Forest City, N.C., historian; Stanley P. Barnett, retired Cleveland, O., newspaper editor, of Tyron, N.C., for the loan of his set of *Official Records;* Miss Mary L. Davis, Hendersonville, N.C., for pamphlets collected by her father, a Union army veteran; and David Schenck, Greensboro, N.C., for permission to quote from the personal letters of his great-uncle, General Stephen Dodson Ramseur.

Index

Rank indicated is the highest held during the Gettysburg Campaign. All abbreviations are standard, except for the following: c., captured; k., killed; m.w., mortally wounded; w., wounded. A particular military unit—company, regiment, brigade, division or corps—will be found at the appropriate level under either Army of Northern Virginia or Army of the Potomac.